THEOLOGICAL DICTIONARY
OF THE
OLD TESTAMENT

THEOLOGICAL DICTIONARY

OF THE

OLD TESTAMENT

EDITED BY

G. JOHANNES BOTTERWECK

AND

HELMER RINGGREN

Translators

JOHN T. WILLIS and

GEOFFREY W. BROMILEY
(pp. 1-358)

DAVID E. GREENE
(pp. 359-463)

Volume III

הָרַס – גִּלּוּלִים

gillûlîm – hāras

WILLIAM B. EERDMANS PUBLISHING COMPANY
GRAND RAPIDS, MICHIGAN

THEOLOGICAL DICTIONARY OF THE OLD TESTAMENT

Translated from
THEOLOGISCHES WÖRTERBUCH ZUM ALTEN TESTAMENT
Band II, Lieferungen 1-4
Published 1974, 1975 by
VERLAG W. KOHLHAMMER GMBH STUTTGART, W. GERMANY

Library of Congress Cataloging in Publication Data

Botterweck, G   Johannes.
  Theological dictionary of the Old Testament.

  Includes bibliographical references.
  Translation of Theologisches Wörterbuch zum
Alten Testament.
    1. Bible.   O. T.—Dictionaries—Hebrew.
  2. Hebrew language—Dictionaries—English.
  I. Ringgren, Helmer, 1917–   joint author.
  II. Title.

BS440.B5713   221.3   73-76170
ISBN 0–8028–2338-6 (set)
Volume III 0–8028–2327–0

Printed in the Netherlands
by De Walburg Pers Zutphen

CONTRIBUTORS

A. Baumann, Wolfsburg
J. Bergman, Uppsala
K.-H. Bernhardt, Berlin, East Germany
G. J. Botterweck, Bonn (Editor)
A. Caquot, Paris
A. Carlson, Uppsala
H. Cazelles, Paris
S. Erlandsson, Uppsala
H.-J. Fabry, Bonn
D. N. Freedman, Ann Arbor
H. F. Fuhs, Cologne
A. Haldar, Uppsala
V. Hamp, Munich
F. J. Helfmeyer, Cologne
R. Hentschke, Berlin
B. Jacobs-Hornig, Münster
B. Kedar-Kopfstein, Haifa
K. Koch, Hamburg
E. Kutsch, Erlangen
J. Lundbom, Berkeley
H. Lutzmann, Münster
G. Mayer, Mainz
H.-P. Müller, Münster
G. Münderlein, Helmbrechts
A. Negoită, Bucharest
R. North, Rome
M. Ottosson, Uppsala
H. D. Preuss, Neuendettelsau
H. Ringgren, Uppsala (Editor)
J. Sanmartin-Ascaso, Münster
W. H. Schmidt, Kiel
K. Seybold, Kiel
S. Talmon, Jerusalem
S. Wagner, Leipzig
G. Wallis, Halle
G. Warmuth, Kiel
H.-J. Zobel, Greifswald

CONTENTS

Page

ABBREVIATIONS

AANLR	*Atti dell'Accademia Nazionale dei Lincei, Rendiconti*
AASOR	*Annual of the American Schools of Oriental Research*
AB	*The Anchor Bible*
ABAW	*Abhandlungen der Akademie der Wissenschaften,* Berlin
ABL	R. F. Harper, *Assyrian and Babylonian Letters,* 1-14, Chicago, 1892-1914
ABR	*Australian Biblical Review,* Melbourne
abs.	absolute
acc.	accusative
AcOr	*Acta Orientalia*
act.	active
adj.	adjective
adv.	adverb
AfK	*Archiv für Kulturgeschichte*
AFNW	*Arbeitsgemeinschaft für Forschung des Landes Nordrhein-Westfalen*
AfO	*Archiv für Orientforschung*
ÄgAbh	*Ägyptologische Abhandlungen*
AH	*Analecta Hymnica,* ed. G. Dreves and C. Blume, Leipzig, 1886-1922
AHAW	*Abhandlungen der Heidelberger Akademie der Wissenschaften*
AHDO	*Archives d'Histoire du Droit Oriental*
AHw	W. von Soden, *Akkadisches Handwörterbuch*
AJSL	*The American Journal of Semitic Languages and Literatures*
Akk.	Akkadian
AKM	*Abhandlungen zur Kunde des Morgenlandes* (Leipzig), Wiesbaden
AMT	R. C. Thompson, *Assyrian Medical Texts,* 1923
AN	J. J. Stamm, *Die akkadische Namengebung. MVÄG,* 44 (1939)
AnAcScFen	*Annales Academiae Scientiarum Fennicae*
AnBibl	*Analecta Biblica,* Rome
AncIsr	R. de Vaux, *Ancient Israel: Its Life and Institutions,* trans. 1961
ANEP	*The Ancient Near East in Pictures,* ed. J. B. Pritchard, Princeton, 1954, ²1969
ANET	*Ancient Near Eastern Texts Relating to the Old Testament,* ed. J. B. Pritchard, ²1955, ³1969
AnOr	*Analecta Orientalia*
ANVAO	*Avhandlinger utgitt av det Norske Videnskaps-Akademi i Oslo*
AO	*Der Alte Orient,* Leipzig
AOAT	*Alter Orient und Altes Testament,* Neukirchen-Vluyn
AOB	*Altorientalische Bilder zum Alten Testament,* ed. H. Gressmann, ²1927
AOT	*Altorientalische Texte zum Alten Testament,* ed. H. Gressmann, ²1926
AP	A. E. Cowley, *Aramaic Papyri of the Fifth Century B.C.,* Oxford, 1923
APNM	H. B. Huffmon, *Amorite Personal Names in the Mari Texts,* Baltimore, 1965
Arab.	Arabic
Aram.	Aramaic
ArbT	*Arbeiten zur Theologie,* Stuttgart
ARM	*Archives Royales de Mari,* Paris
ArOr	*Archiv Orientální,* Prague
ARW	*Archiv für Religionswissenschaft,* Leipzig, Berlin
ASAW	*Abhandlungen der Sächsischen Akademie der Wissenschaften in Leipzig*
Assyr.	Assyrian
ASTI	*Annual of the Swedish Theological Institute in Jerusalem,* Leiden
AT	Alte Testament
ATD	*Das Alte Testament Deutsch*
AThANT	*Abhandlungen zur Theologie des Alten und Neuen Testaments,* Zurich
AuS	G. Dalman, *Arbeit und Sitte in Palästina,* 1928-1942
BA	*The Biblical Archaeologist,* New Haven
Bab.	Babylonian
BAfO	*Beihefte zur Archiv für Orientforschung*
BASOR	*Bulletin of the American Schools of Oriental Research*

BBB	*Bonner Biblische Beiträge*
BDB	Brown-Driver-Briggs, *A Hebrew and English Lexicon of the Old Testament*
BE	Babylonian Expedition of the University of Pennsylvania, Philadelphia
BeO	*Bibbia e Oriente*
BethM	*Beth Mikra*
BFChTh	*Beiträge zur Förderung Christlicher Theologie,* Gütersloh
BHHW	*Biblisch-Historisches Handwörterbuch,* ed. L. Rost and B. Reicke, 1962ff.
BHK	*Biblia Hebraica,* ed. R. Kittel
BHS	*Biblia Hebraica Stuttgartensia,* ed. K. Elliger and W. Rudolph, 1968ff.
BHTh	*Beiträge zur Historischen Theologie,* Tübingen
Bibl	*Biblica,* Rome
BietOr	*Biblica et Orientalia*
BiLe	*Bibel und Leben*
BIN	*Babylonian Inscriptions in the Collection of James B. Nies,* New Haven
BiOr	*Bibliotheca Orientalis,* Leiden
BJRL	*Bulletin of the John Rylands Library,* Manchester
BK	*Biblischer Kommentar zum Alten Testament,* ed. M. Noth and H. W. Wolff
BL	*Bibel-Lexikon,* ed. H. Haag
BLA	H. Bauer-P. Leander, *Grammatik des Biblisch-Aramäischen,* 1927
Blachère-Chouémi	R. Blachère-M. Chouémi-C. Denizeau, *Dictionnaire Arabe-Français-Anglais*
BLe	H. Bauer-P. Leander, *Historische Grammatik der hebräischen Sprache,* 1922
BM	*Hieroglyphic Texts from Egyptian Stelae &c. in the British Museum*
BMAP	E. G. Kraeling, *The Brooklyn Museum Aramaic Papyri,* 1953
BRA	*Beiträge zur Religionsgeschichte des Altertums*
BRL	K. Galling, *Biblisches Reallexikon,* 1937
BSAW	*Berichte über die Verhandlungen der Sächsischen Akademie der Wissenschaften zu Leipzig*
BSt	*Biblische Studien,* Neukirchen
BT	*The Bible Translator,* London
BuA	B. Meissner, *Babylonien und Assyrien,* I 1920, II 1925
BVC	*Bible et Vie Chrétienne*
BWA(N)T	*Beiträge zur Wissenschaft vom Alten (und Neuen) Testament,* Stuttgart
BWL	W. G. Lambert, *Babylonian Wisdom Literature,* Oxford, 1960
BZ	*Biblische Zeitschrift,* Paderborn
BZAW	*Beihefte zur Zeitschrift für die Alttestamentliche Wissenschaft,* Berlin
BZfr	*Biblische Zeitfragen*
CAD	*The Assyrian Dictionary of the Oriental Institute of the University of Chicago,* 1956ff.
CahRB	*Cahiers de la Revue Biblique*
CBQ	*Catholic Biblical Quarterly*
CBSC	*The Cambridge Bible for Schools and Colleges*
CChr	*Corpus Christianorum,* Turnhout
CD A, B	Damascus Document, Manuscript A, B
CH	Codex Hammurabi
ChrÉg	*Chronique d'Égypte*
CIS	*Corpus Inscriptionum Semiticarum,* 1881ff.
CML	G. R. Driver, *Canaanite Myths and Legends,* Edinburgh, 1956
CollBG	*Collationes Brugenses et Gandavenses,* Gent
comm.	commentary
conj.	conjecture
const.	construct
ContiRossini	K. Conti Rossini, *Chrestomathia Arabica meridionalis epigraphica,* 1931
Copt.	Coptic
COT	*Commentaar op het Oude Testament,* ed. G. C. Aalders, Kampen
CRRA	*Compte Rendu de ... Recontre Assyriologique Internationale*

CT	Cuneiform Texts from Babylonian Tablets, etc. in the British Museum, London, 1896ff.
CT	*The Egyptian Coffin Texts,* ed. A. de Buck and A. H. Gardiner, 1935ff.
CTA	A. Herdner, *Corpus des Tablettes en Cunéiformes Alphabétiques Découvertes à Ras Shamra-Ugarit* I/II, Paris, 1963
CTM	*Concordia Theological Monthly,* St. Louis
CW	*Die Christliche Welt*
DB	*Dictionnaire de la Bible*
DBS	*Dictionnaire de la Bible, Supplément,* ed. L. Pirot, A. Robert, H. Cazelles, and A. Feuillet, 1928ff.
DISO	Ch. F. Jean-J. Hoftijzer, *Dictionnaire des Inscriptions Sémitiques de l'Ouest,* Leiden, 1965
diss.	dissertation
DissAbs(Int)	*Dissertation Abstracts (International* beginning vol. 30, July 1969)
DJD	*Discoveries in the Judaean Desert,* 1955ff.
DLZ	*Deutsche Literaturzeitung*
DN	name of a deity
EA	Tell el-Amarna Tablets
EB	*Die Heilige Schrift in deutscher Übersetzung. Echter-Bibel,* Würzburg
Egyp.	Egyptian
EHAT	*Exegetisches Handbuch zum Alten Testament,* Münster
Einl.	Einleitung
EKL	*Evangelisches Kirchenlexikon,* Göttingen, I 1956, II 1958
EMiqr	*Entsiqlopēdiā Miqrā'it–Encyclopaedia Biblica,* Jerusalem
EnEl	Enuma Elish
Eng.	English
ErfThSt	*Erfurter Theologische Studien*
ErJb	*Eranos-Jahrbuch*
Ethiop.	Ethiopic
ETL	*Ephemerides Theologicae Lovanienses*
EvQ	*The Evangelical Quarterly*
EvTh	*Evangelische Theologie,* Munich
ExpT	*The Expository Times,* London
FreibThSt	*Freiburger Theologische Studien*
FRLANT	*Forschungen zur Religion und Literatur des Alten und Neuen Testaments,* Göttingen
FuF	*Forschungen und Fortschritte*
FzB	*Forschung zur Bibel*
gen.	genitive
GesB	W. Gesenius-F. Buhl, *Hebräisches und aramäisches Handwörterbuch,* [17]1921
GHK	*Hand-Kommentar zum Alten Testament,* ed. W. Nowack, Göttingen
Gilg.	Gilgamesh Epic
GK	W. Gesenius-E. Kautzsch, *Hebräische Grammatik,* [28]1909 (=Kautzsch-Cowley, *Gesenius' Hebrew Grammar,* [2]1910)
Gk.	Greek
GLECS	*Comptes Rendus du Groupe Linguistique d'Études Chamito-Sémitiques,* Paris
Greg	*Gregorianum*
GSAT	*Gesammelte Studien zum Alten Testament*
Ḥaḍr.	Ḥaḍrami
HAT	*Handbuch zum Alten Testament,* ed. O. Eissfeldt, 1st series
Ḥatt.	Ḥattic
HAW	*Handbuch der Altertumswissenschaft,* ed. W. Otto, Munich, 1929ff.
Heb.	Hebrew
Hitt.	Hittite
HSAT	*Die Heilige Schrift des Alten Testaments,* ed. E. Kautsch-A. Bertholet, [4]1922/23

HThR	*Harvard Theological Review*
HUCA	*Hebrew Union College Annual*, Cincinnati
IB	*The Interpreter's Bible*, ed. G. A. Buttrick, 1951-57
ICC	*The International Critical Commentary*
IDB	*The Interpreter's Dictionary of the Bible*, ed. G. A. Buttrick, I-IV, 1962
IEJ	*Israel Exploration Journal*, Jerusalem
ILC	J. Pedersen, *Israel. Its Life and Culture*, 1926, ³1953, 4 vols. in 2
impf.	imperfect
impv.	imperative
In	*Interpretation*
inf.	infinitive
in loc.	on this passage
Introd.	Introduction (to)
IPN	M. Noth, *Die israelitischen Personennamen. BWANT*, 3/10, 1928
JA	*Journal Asiatique*, Paris
Ja	Enumeration according to A. Jamme (Old South Arabic)
JANES	*Journal of the Ancient Near Eastern Society of Columbia University*
JAOS	*Journal of the American Oriental Society*
JBL	*Journal of Biblical Literature*
JCS	*Journal of Cuneiform Studies*, New Haven
JEA	*Journal of Egyptian Archaeology*, London
JEOL	*Jaarbericht ... Ex Oriente Lux*, Leiden
JES	*Journal of Ecumenical Studies*
JNES	*Journal of Near Eastern Studies*, Chicago
JNWSL	*Journal of Northwest Semitic Languages*
JPOS	*Journal of the Palestine Oriental Society*, Jerusalem
JR	*Journal of Religion*, Chicago
JRAS	*Journal of the Royal Asiatic Society of Great Britain and Ireland*, London
JSOR	*Journal of the Society of Oriental Research*, Toronto
JSS	*Journal of Semitic Studies*, Manchester
JTS	*Journal of Theological Studies*, Oxford
Jud	*Judaica*
KAI	H. Donner-W. Röllig, *Kanaanäische und aramäische Inschriften*, I ²1966, II ²1968, III ²1969
KAR	E. Ebeling, *Keilschrifttexte aus Assur religiösen Inhalts*, 1915-19
KAT	*Kommentar zum Alten Testament*, ed. E. Sellin, continued by J. Herrmann
KB	*Keilinschriftliche Bibliothek*, ed. E. Schrader
KBL	L. Koehler-W. Baumgartner, *Hebräisches und aramäisches Lexikon zum Alten Testament*, ²1958, ³1967ff.
KBo	*Keilschrifttexte aus Boghazköy*
KHC	*Kurzer Handcommentar zum Alten Testament*, ed. K. Marti
KlSchr	*Kleine Schriften* (A. Alt, 1953-59; O. Eissfeldt, 1962ff.)
KuD	*Kerygma und Dogma*, Göttingen
Lane	E. W. Lane, *An Arabic-English Lexicon*, London, 1863-1893
Lat.	Latin
LD	*Lectio Divina*
Leslau, *Contributions*	W. Leslau, *Ethiopic and South Arabic Contributions to the Hebrew Lexicon* (1958)
Levy, *TW*	J. Levy, *Chaldäisches Wörterbuch über die Targumim*, 1867f., 1881
LexÄg	W. Helck-E. Otto, *Lexikon der Ägyptologie*, 1972ff.
Levy, *WTM*	J. Levy, *Wörterbuch über die Talmudim und Midraschim*, ²1924 = 1963
LexSyr	C. Brockelmann, *Lexicon Syriacum*, ²1968
LidzEph	M. Lidzbarski, *Ephemeris für semitische Epigraphik*, 1900-1915
lit.	literally
LRSt	*Leipziger Rechtswissenschaftliche Studien*
LThK	*Lexikon für Theologie und Kirche*, 1930-38, ²1957ff.

LUÅ	*Lunds Universitets Årsskrift*
LXX	Septuagint
MAOG	*Mitteilungen der Altorientalischen Gesellschaft*, Leipzig
MBPAR	*Münchener Beiträge zur Papyrusforschung und Antiken Rechtsgeschichte*
MdD	E. S. Drower-R. Macuch, *Mandaic Dictionary*, Oxford, 1963
MDOG	*Mitteilungen der Deutschen Orient-Gesellschaft*, Berlin
MDP	*Mémoires de la Délégation française en Perse*, Paris, 1900
MeyerK	*Kritisch-exegetischer Kommentar über das Neue Testament*, initiated by H. A. W. Meyer, Göttingen
MIFAO	*Mémoires publiés par les membres de l'Institut Français d'Archéologie Orientale au Caire*, Cairo
MIO	*Mitteilungen des Instituts für Orientforschung*, Berlin
MKAW	*Mededelingen der Kon. Nederlandse Akademie van Wetenschappen*, Amsterdam
ms.	manuscript
MT	Massoretic Text
MThS	*Münchener Theologische Studien*
Mus	*Le Muséon, Revue d'Études Orientales*
MUSJ	*Mélanges de l'Université St. Joseph*, Beirut
MVÄG	*Mitteilungen der Vorderasiatisch-Ägyptischen Gesellschaft* (Berlin), Leipzig
n.d.	no date
NedThT	*Nederlands Theologisch Tijdschrift*, Wageningen
NRTh	*Nouvelle Revue Théologique*, Paris
NTS	*New Testament Studies*, Cambridge
NTT	*Norsk Teologisk Tidsskrift*, Oslo
obj.	object
OIP	*Oriental Institute Publications*, Chicago, 1924ff.
OLZ	*Orientalistische Literaturzeitung* (Leipzig), Berlin
Or	*Orientalia. Commentarii periodici Pontificii Instituti Biblici*, Rome
OrAnt	*Oriens Antiquus*
OTL	*The Old Testament Library*
OTS	*Oudtestamentische Studiën*, Leiden
par.	parallel/and parallel passages
pass.	passive
PEQ	*Palestine Exploration Quarterly*, London
perf.	perfect
Phoen.	Phoenician
PJ	*Palästinajahrbuch*, Berlin
PN	name of a person
PN	H. Ranke, *Die ägyptischen Personennamen*, 1935-1952
PNU	F. Gröndahl, *Personennamen der Texte aus Ugarit*, Rome, 1967
prep.	preposition
PRU	*Le Palais Royal d'Ugarit*, ed. Cl. Schaeffer, Paris
PSBA	*Proceedings of the Society of Biblical Archaeology*, Bloomsbury (London)
ptcp.	participle
Pun.	Punic
PV	*Parole di Vita*
PW	A. Pauly-G. Wissowa, *Real-Encyclopädie der classischen Altertums-wissenschaft*, 1894ff.
Pyr.	Pyramid Texts, ed. K. Sethe
QuaestDisp	*Quaestiones Disputatae*, ed. K. Rahner and H. Schlier, 1959ff.
R	H. C. Rawlinson, *The Cuneiform Inscriptions of Western Asia*, London, 1861-1909
RA	*Revue d'Assyriologie et d'Archéologie Orientale*, Paris
RAC	*Reallexikon für Antike und Christentum*, ed. Th. Klauser, 1941ff.
RÄR	H. Bonnet, *Reallexikon der ägyptischen Religionsgeschichte*

RB	*Revue Biblique,* Paris
RdM	*Die Religionen der Menschheit,* ed. C. M. Schröder
repr.	reprint, reprinted
RES	*Revue des Études Sémitiques,* Paris
RES (with number)	*Répertoire d'Épigraphie Sémitique*
RevQ	*Revue de Qumrân,* Paris
RevRéf	*La Revue Réformée*
RGG	*Die Religion in Geschichte und Gegenwart,* ³1957-1965
RHA	*Revue Hittite et Asianique,* Paris
RHPR	*Revue d'Histoire et de Philosophie Religieuses,* Strasbourg, Paris
RHR	*Revue de l'Histoire des Religions,* Paris
RLA	*Reallexikon der Assyriologie,* ed. G. Ebeling and B. Meissner, Berlin, I 1932, II 1938, III 1, 2 1957/59
RLV	*Reallexikon der Vorgeschichte,* ed. Max Ebert, Berlin, 1924-1932
RoB	*Religion och Bibel. Nathan Söderblom-Sällskapets Årsbok*
RS	Ras Shamra
RScR	*Revue des Sciences Religieuses*
RSO	*Rivista degli Studi Orientali,* Rome
RT	*Recueil de Travaux relatifs à la philologie et à l'archéologie égyptiennes et assyriennes*
RTP	*Revue de Théologie et de Philosophie,* Lausanne
Sab.	Sabean
Saf.	Safaitic
SAHG	A. Falkenstein-W. von Soden, *Sumerische und akkadische Hymnen und Gebete*
SAK	*Die sumerischen und akkadischen Königsinschriften,* ed. F. Thureau-Dangin (=*VAB,* I)
SAT	*Die Schriften des Alten Testaments in Auswahl,* trans. and ed. H. Gunkel, *et al.,* Göttingen
SAW	*Sitzungsberichte der Österreichischen Akademie der Wissenschaften in Wien*
SBM	*Stuttgarter Biblische Monographien*
SBS	*Stuttgarter Bibel-Studien*
SBT	*Studies in Biblical Theology*
SchThU	*Schweizerische Theologische Umschau,* Bern
ScrHier	*Scripta Hierosolymitana. Publications of the Hebrew University,* Jerusalem
SDAW	*Sitzungsberichte der Deutschen Akademie der Wissenschaften zu Berlin*
SEÅ	*Svensk Exegetisk Årsbok,* Lund
Sem	*Semitica*
Seux	J. M. Seux, *Epithètes Royales Akkadiennes et Sumériennes,* Paris, 1968
SgV	*Sammlung gemeinverständlicher Vorträge und Schriften aus dem Gebiet der Theologie und Religionsgeschichte,* Tübingen
SJT	*Scottish Journal of Theology,* Edinburgh
SL	A. Deimel, *Šumerisches Lexikon,* Rome, 1925-1937
SNumen	*Supplements to Numen*
Soq.	Soqoṭri
SSN	*Studia Semitica Neerlandica*
StANT	*Studien zum Alten und Neuen Testament,* Munich
St.-B.	H. L. Strack-P. Billerbeck, *Kommentar zum Neuen Testament aus Talmud und Midrasch,* 1923-1961
StOr	*Studia Orientalia,* Helsinki
StSem	*Studi Semitici*
StTh	*Studia Theologica,* Lund, Aarhus
subj.	subject
subst.	substantive
suf.	suffix
Sum.	Sumerian

SVT	*Supplements to Vetus Testamentum,* Leiden
Synt.	C. Brockelmann, *Hebräische Syntax*
Syr.	Syriac
Syr	*Syria. Revue d'Art Oriental et d'Archéologie,* Paris
TAik	*Teologinen Aikakauskirja*
TDNT	*Theological Dictionary of the New Testament,* ed. G. Kittel and G. Friedrich, trans. G. Bromiley
TDOT	*Theological Dictionary of the Old Testament*
Th.	Theologie
Theol.	Theology (of)
THAT	*Theologisches Handwörterbuch zum Alten Testament,* ed. E. Jenni and C. Westermann, Munich, 1971
ThB	*Theologische Bücherei*
ThLZ	*Theologische Literaturzeitung,* Leipzig, Berlin
ThR	*Theologische Rundschau,* Tübingen
ThSt	*Theologische Studien,* Zurich
ThStKr	*Theologische Studien und Kritiken,* Berlin
ThZ	*Theologische Zeitschrift,* Basel
Tigr.	Tigrīnya (Tigriña)
TigrWb	E. Littmann-M. Höfner, *Wörterbuch der Tigre-Sprache,* 1962
trans.	translated
TrThSt	*Trierer Theologische Studien*
TrThZ	*Trierer Theologische Zeitschrift*
TS	*Theological Studies*
TüThQ	*Theologische Quartalschrift,* Tübingen, Stuttgart
TW	J. Levy, *Chaldäisches Wörterbuch über die Targumim,* 1867f., 1881
UET	*Ur Excavations. Texts,* London, 1928ff.
UF	*Ugarit-Forschungen*
Ugar.	Ugaritic
Urk.	*Urkunden des ägyptischen Altertums,* ed. G. Steindorff
UT	C. H. Gordon, *Ugaritic Textbook,* Rome, 1965
UUÅ	*Uppsala Universitets Årsskrift*
VAB	*Vorderasiatische Bibliothek*
VAS	*Vorderasiatische Schriftdenkmäler der königlichen Museen zu Berlin*
VAWA	*Verhandeling der Akademie van Wetenschappen Amsterdam,* Afdeling Letterkunde
VD	*Verbum Domini,* Rome
VG	C. Brockelmann, *Grundriss der vergleichenden Grammatik der semitischen Sprachen,* 1908-1913
VT	*Vetus Testamentum,* Leiden
Vulg.	Vulgate
WbÄS	A. Erman-H. Grapow, *Wörterbuch der ägyptischen Sprache,* I-V
WbMyth	*Wörterbuch der Mythologie,* ed. H. W. Haussig
Wehr	H. Wehr, *A Dictionary of Modern Written Arabic,* ed. J. M. Cowan, 1961
Whitaker	R. E. Whitaker, *A Concordance of the Ugaritic Literature,* 1972
WMANT	*Wissenschaftliche Monographien zum Alten und Neuen Testament,* Neukirchen
WO	*Die Welt des Orients,* Göttingen
WTM	J. Levy, *Wörterbuch über die Talmudim und Midraschim,* ²1924=1963
WUS	J. Aistleitner, *Wörterbuch der ugaritischen Sprache,* ³1967
WZ	*Wissenschaftliche Zeitschrift*
WZKM	*Wiener Zeitschrift für die Kunde des Morgenlandes*
ZA	*Zeitschrift für Assyriologie* (Leipzig), Berlin
ZÄS	*Zeitschrift für Ägyptische Sprache und Altertumskunde* (Leipzig), Berlin
ZAW	*Zeitschrift für die Alttestamentliche Wissenschaft* (Giessen), Berlin
ZDMG	*Zeitschrift der Deutschen Morgenländischen Gesellschaft* (Leipzig), Wiesbaden
ZDPV	*Zeitschrift des Deutschen Palästina-Vereins* (Leipzig, Stuttgart), Wiesbaden

ZE	*Zeitschrift für Ethnologie*
ZEE	*Zeitschrift für Evangelische Ethik,* Gütersloh
ZNW	*Zeitschrift für die Neutestamentliche Wissenschaft* (Giessen), Berlin
ZRGG	*Zeitschrift für Religions- und Geistesgeschichte,* Cologne
ZS	*Zeitschrift für Semitistik und verwandte Gebiete,* Leipzig
ZThK	*Zeitschrift für Theologie und Kirche,* Tübingen
→	indicates cross-reference within this *Dictionary*

TRANSLITERATION OF HEBREW

CONSONANTS

Hebrew Consonant	Technical Usage	Nontechnical Usage
א	ʾ	ʾ
בּ	b	b
ב	bh	bh
גּ	g	g
ג	gh	gh
דּ	d	d
ד	dh	dh
ה	h	h
ו	v, w	v
ז	z	z
ח	ch, ḥ	ch
ט	ṭ	t
י	y	y
כּ	k	k
כ	kh	kh
ל	l	l
מ	m	m
נ	n	n
ס	s	s
ע	ʿ	ʿ
פּ	p	p
פ	ph	ph
צ	ts, ṣ	ts
ק	q	q
ר	r	r
שׂ	ś	s
שׁ	sh, š	sh
תּ	t	t
ת	th	th

VOWELS

Hebrew Vowel	Technical Usage	Nontechnical Usage
ַ	a	a
ֲ	a	a
ָ	ā	a
ֶ	e	e
ֱ	e	e
ֶי	ey	ey
ֵ	ē	e
ֵי	ê	e
ְ	e	e
ִ	i	i
ִי	î	i
ָ	o	o
ֳ	o	o
ֹ	ō	o
וֹ	ô	o
ֻ	u	u
וּ	û	u
ַי	ai	ai
ָיו	āv	av
ָ	āi	ai
ַה	h	h

גִּלּוּלִים *gillûlîm;* גִּלְּלִים *gillulîm*

Contents: I. Occurrences. II. Etymology. III. Scope of Usage.

I. Occurrences. This substantive, which is not found outside Israelite-Jewish literature and which always appears in the OT as an (abstract?) plural (the sing. occurs only in Sir. 30:19), belongs to a group of words used in the OT in mocking polemics against idols; cf. → אֱלִילִים *ʾelîlîm,* "idols," → שִׁקּוּצִים *shiqqûtsîm,* "detested things," and possibly also → תְּרָפִים *teᵉrāphîm,* "teraphim, idols." Accordingly, it is used in conjunction with these words in Dt. 29:16 (Eng. v. 17); Ezk. 20:7f.; 30:13 (where *ʾelim,* "pillars," should be read instead of *ʾelilim,* "idols"); and 37:23. *gillulim* is found 48 times in the OT: 39 times in Ezekiel (6:4,5,6,9,13; 8:10; 14:3,4,5,6,7; 16:36; 18:6,12,15; 20:7,8,16,18,24,31,39; 22:3,4; 23:7,30,37,39,49; 30:13; 33:25; 36:18,25; 37:23; 44:10,12); and nine times in Deuteronomy or material influenced by it, or in literature closely connected with Ezekiel (Lev. 26:30; Dt. 29:16[17]; 1 K. 15:12; 21:26; 2 K. 17:12; 21:11,21; 23:24; Jer. 50:2). Thus the word appears for the first time in the late preexilic and exilic period, seems to come from priestly circles (in Jerusalem?) (because of its frequent connection with "uncleanness"),[1] and is the predominant word for foreign gods in Ezekiel and the Deuteronomistic history (for Ezk., cf. also → שִׁקּוּצִים *shiqqûtsîm,* "detested things"). North and Wolff ask whether *gillulim* might not have been a word coined by Ezekiel himself. That Ezekiel was already using this word without explanation is not a valid argument against this, if its meaning was discernible to his hearers.

The LXX frequently renders *gillulim* by *eídōla,* "idols," twice by *bdelýgmata,* "detestable things," in Ezekiel also by *epitēdeúmata,* "pursuits, ways of living," or *enthymḗmata,* "thoughts," only in Ezk. 14:3,4 by *dianoḗmata,* "thoughts," and in 23:30 by *epithymḗmata,* "desires."[2] The Qumran texts also use this word (always in the pl.: 1QS 2:11,17; 4:5; 1QH 4:15,19; CD B 20:9; in a corrupt text 1Q 22:1,7; 4QFlor 1:17).

---

gillûlîm. D. Baltzer, *Ezechiel und Deuterojesaja. BZAW,* 121 (1971), 3, 9, 37f., 80ff.; W. W. Graf Baudissin, "Die alttestamentliche Bezeichnung der Götzen mit gillūlīm," *ZDMG,* 58 (1904), 395-425; H.-U. Boesche, *Die Polemik gegen die Verehrung anderer Gottheiten neben Jahwe im alten Israel* (diss., Göttingen, 1962), 104-120; C. R. North, "The Essence of Idolatry," *Von Ugarit nach Qumran. Festschrift O. Eissfeldt. BZAW,* 77 (²1961), 151-160; W. Paschen, *Rein und Unrein. Untersuchung zur biblischen Wortgeschichte. StANT,* 24 (1970), 67, 119ff.; H. D. Preuss, *Verspottung fremder Religionen im AT. BWANT,* 92 (1971), 58, 137, 156f., 173, 281; H. W. Wolff, "Jahwe und die Götter in der alttestamentlichen Prophetie," *EvTh,* 29 (1969), 397-416; W. Zimmerli, *BK,* XIII, 149f.; idem, *Grundriss der alttestamentlichen Theologie* (1972), 102f., 183.

[1] See below.

[2] In addition, see Baudissin, 396-405.

II. Etymology. In Baudissin's opinion, this noun is a qaṭṭūl/qiṭṭūl form of the root → גלל gālal, "to roll"[3] ("rolled" = block, log = shapeless logs?; Baudissin: originally a designation for sacred stones, then images). In this connection, reference should be made to gal I and Ugar. gl, "vessel."[4] This derivation, however, does not help us to understand the term, so that in this unexplained word, which is intended to evoke negative and derisive associations, we have rather an artificially created and cacophonous term of abuse which calls to mind and is analogous to → אלילים 'elîlîm, and especially to → שקוצים shiqqûtsîm, which originated with Hosea (9:10; cf. Dt. 29:16[17]). In this connection, one might consider a development of gel, "dung, manure" (cf. Ezk. 4:12,15; elsewhere only in Job 20:7; cf. also gll II, "to be dirty," Isa. 9:4[5]; 2 S. 20:12; and in the Qumran texts; also galal, "dung [balls]," 1 K. 14:10; Zeph. 1:17),[5] and thus the meaning, "dung things, dung idols,"[6] in conjunction with which, for Ezekiel, reference can be made to gelele ha'adham, RSV "human dung" (Ezk. 4:12,15). Akk. gallu (a demon) is a Sumerian loanword and certainly does not belong here. On the other hand, a connection with gullulu, "to commit a crime," gullultu, "hostile acts, crimes," etc., is conceivable.

III. Scope of Usage. The frequency of the occurrences of gillulim in Ezekiel leads one to suppose that he coined this word and also justifies our beginning this investigation with him. In Ezekiel gillulim is used mainly to denote a sin of idolatry committed by Israel in the past and also in the exilic present. He employs it in Demonstration Oracles[7] which contain announcements of judgment and the reasons for it. In Ezk. 6:2-10,11-14 (Demonstration Oracles with introductory expressions), Yahweh announces judgment. The primary reason for it is that Judah has turned back after gillulim (6:8-10; cf. 8:10; 16:36 as a late interpretation; and esp. chaps. 20 and 23), and when it takes place the Israelites will no longer fall down before "their" idols in worship (cf. 8:10, "idols of the house of Israel"; so also 18:6,15; cf. 14:5), but will fall down before them slain (6:4; cf. v. 13; on v. 5 [secondary], cf. Lev. 26:30). Furthermore, the idols that the people have served (Ezk. 6:13) and with which they have practiced "harlotry," i.e., cultic apostasy (6:9; cf. 16:36; 23:37; also 23:39; in addition earlier, Hos. 2:7[5]; 4:11-19; 9:1), will be destroyed as well (Ezk. 6:6). Yahweh will demonstrate the impotence of these idols by his historical acts (6:1-7: before 587 B.C.; vv. 8-10: after 587?), and the knowledge of Yahweh will stand in contrast to their end (6:13). The problem of idols is not limited to chap. 6, but also runs through chaps. (16), 20, and 23 "like a crimson thread"[8] (however, on 20:31 cf. the LXX; but see also 20:7,16,18). In 6:11-14 we also encounter the

---

[3] Baudissin, 405f.; R. Meyer, *Hebräische Grammatik*, II (³1969), 30f.

[4] Cf. also Ugar. gll, UT, No. 581; Akk. galālu; Palmyrenian stone stela, *DISO*, 50; and Baudissin, 418-423.

[5] See already the reference by W. Bacher, *ZAW*, 5 (1885), 140.

[6] North, Boesche, Zimmerli; Eichrodt, *TheolOT* (trans. 1965), I, 225; Wolff, 407, "shit-gods."

[7] Zimmerli.

[8] Wolff, 406.

more specific statement that Judah's apostasy to idols is a → תועבה *tôʿēbhāh*, "an abomination," to Yahweh—a common phrase in Ezekiel (cf. 8:9f.; 18:12; 22:1-4). This (possibly cultic) word is used especially in Deuteronomy, Jeremiah, and Ezekiel[9] as a more specific definition of syncretistic forms of worship that are foreign to Yahwism, and in Ezekiel it is a "collective noun for all cultically defiling sins."[10] The frequent connection between *gillulim* and → טמא *ṭāmēʾ*, "to be unclean, to defile oneself," in Ezekiel (20:7,18,31; 22:3f.; 23:7,30; 36:18,25; idols are uncleanness personified; 37:23; cf. *sheqets*, "detestable thing," in 8:10; 20:7; and also *gel*, "dung," in 4:12,15; 11:18 is a later addition; on this matter earlier, cf. Hos. 5:3; Jer. 2:23)[11] also emphasizes the fact that the very name *gillulim* indicates an essential feature of impurity,[12] so that the word denotes what is totally foreign to Yahweh, concretely defines Judah's preceding apostasy from Yahweh, and thus provides the reason for judgment. Yahweh will now deliver up the temple that has been defiled in this way (Ezk. 8:9f.) to complete defilement (9:7; cf. 20:26, referring to Israel).

This emphasis on uncleanness and defilement, which calls to mind the not infrequent priestly influence in Ezekiel, goes hand in hand with the prophet's basic insistence in his historical surveys on understanding the whole history of Israel as a struggle between Yahweh and idols.[13] The no less strongly priestly verses in Ezk. 14:1-11[14] also show how important the theme of idols was to Ezekiel: idolatry is *the* sin of Israel. Anyone who clings to idols (even if he is in exile) can expect to receive nothing but a corresponding word of judgment from Yahweh himself (14:7ff.; cf. 18:12), and even death, since idolatry carries its own punishment as one falls under its curse (18:12f.).[15] Yahweh calls for repentance, for separation from idols (14:6ff.; cf. 18:6,12,15). The righteous does not practice idolatry (18:6,15); hence he can and should "live." Israel's election involved the obligation to renounce the idols of Egypt, which could only make it unclean (20:7; cf. 23:30 and Dt. 29:16f.[17f.]: idols of the nations—Ezk. 30:13 is secondary).[16] But Israel was already disobedient at that time, and did not cast away its idols (so only Ezk.: 20:8; cf. 44:10,12 [secondary], concerning the Levites), and therefore Yahweh did not bring all Israel into the land (20:18). The history of apostasy to idols continued in the following generations (20:18; "to this day," v. 31;[17] also 23:7), so that Yahweh's judgment had to come again—this time as a dispersion among the nations (20:24; cf. 22:3f.; 23:49; 36:18). Accordingly (in a later addition to 20:1-31), the exilic generation is again called to turn away from idols (20:39; cf. v. 7), because the new exodus

---

[9] For additional information, cf. Preuss, 156.
[10] Zimmerli, *BK, XIII,* 154.
[11] See also Paschen, 65-68.
[12] Zimmerli, 150, 311; Boesche, 120.
[13] Wolff, 406f.
[14] On vv. 3f., see → בוא *bôʾ*, II.1.
[15] On this point, see Preuss, 316.
[16] On *'elilim* in this passage, cf. → אליל *'elîl,* I.
[17] On the text, see Zimmerli, *BK, XIII, in loc.*

will bring a judgment of separation, and Israel cannot receive the land back from Yahweh as its own if it is idolatrous (33:25). In 23:7b and 23:30 (from a later hand),[18] the *gillulim* are to a certain extent "representatives of the great political powers."[19]

When Ezekiel speaks about the gift of the new heart and spirit, it is obvious to him that this must be connected with a cleansing from the sin of idolatry, which makes one unclean (Ezk. 36:24-28). The new people will no longer defile itself with idolatry (37:23). It is clean (36:25), because it has put away its idols.[20]

It is also typical of the texts in Ezekiel which mock idols that they employ suffixes with *gillulim* ("thy," "your," "their"). The point is that idols neither have nor can have anything to do with Yahweh or faith in Yahweh (Ezk. 6:4-6, 13; 14:3-7; 20:16,18,31,39; 22:4; 23:37,39,49; 33:25; 36:18,25; 37:23; 44:10; cf. Dt. 29:16[17]). Idols are also identified with their images in a degrading manner (Ezk. 6:4-6,9,13; 22:3f.; 23:30,37,49; 30:13; 44:12), while Lev. 26:30; Jer. 50:2; and Sir. 30:19 make it clear that *gillulim* means graven *images*.

Lev. 26:30 (cf. Ezk. 6:5 [secondary]) is closely related to Ezekiel, for (like Ezk. 6; etc.) it uses *gillulim* for the graven images of Canaan on the high place sanctuaries, and speaks of them as a reason for judgment in connection with threats of punishment and announcements of destruction. The dead bodies of the Israelites will be thrown upon those of the idols (cf. Ezk. 5:10f.; then Ps. 82:7; Jer. 16:18; also Ps. 106:28). Dt. 29:16f.(17f.) too, with its reference to the idols of the nations, is close to the message of Ezekiel and his school (cf. Ezk. 23:30).[21] Dt. 29:15-20(16-21) are related to 29:1-8(2-9) as a historical survey leading to parenesis: Yahweh will not forgive the worship of these images (cf. 29:21-28[22-29]; 30:17f.). This early exilic Deuteronomistic text[22] resembles the Deuteronomistic reflection in 2 K. 17:12. Other Deuteronomistic examples[23] are associated with these texts (1 K. 21:26; 2 K. 21:11,21: idolatry as one of the main reasons for the judgment), while 1 K. 15:12 and 2 K. 23:24 contain a Deuteronomistic evaluation of reforming measures which include the exemplary removal of idols.

Jer. 50:2 (in the exilic chaps. 50f.) announces the end of the idols of Babylon, along with the fall of Babylon[24] and the deliverance of Israel which is made possible thereby (cf. Isa. 46:1f.; Jer. 51:44).[25] In this connection Jer. 50:2c continues the concrete line generally set forth in b, so that it resembles texts to which additions have been made in mockery of idols.[26]

---

[18] Cf. *ibid.*

[19] Wolff, 407.

[20] On these texts, cf. Baltzer, 80-82.

[21] See also above.

[22] So following L. Perlitt, *Bundestheologie im AT. WMANT,* 36 (1969), 23-30.

[23] On these, see also W. Dietrich, *Prophetie und Geschichte. FRLANT,* 108 (1972), 37, 44, 82, who assigns them to the Deuteronomistic stratum N.

[24] Cf. → בבל *bābhel,* III.

[25] See also Baltzer, 70.

[26] See also Preuss, 275.

According to the Qumran texts, idolaters, as apostates from the community's interpretation of the Torah, stand under curse and judgment (1QS 2:11,17; 1QH 4:19; CD B 20:9), and thus they must be separated from those who abhor unclean idols (1QS 4:5; cf. 1Q 22:1,7; 4QFlor 1:16f.). [27] One cannot seek Yahweh among idols (1QH 4:15).

Preuss

---

[27] See Paschen, 119-121, on this, and also on the typical construct expressions with *gillule* which are found here.

גָּלַח *gillach;* גִּבֵּחַ *gibbēach;* גַּבַּחַת *gabbachath;* קָרַח *qārach;*
קֵרֵחַ *qērēach;* קָרְחָה *qorchāh;* קָרַחַת *qārachath;* גַּלָּב *gallābh;* מֹרָה *mōrāh;*
תַּעַר *ta'ar;* זָקָן *zāqān;* שָׂפָם *śāphām;* שֵׂעָר *śē'ār;* שַׂעֲרָה *śa'ᵃrāh*

Contents: I. Etymology, Occurrences, Words Related to *glḥ*: 1. Etymology and Occurrences of *glḥ*; 2. Words Related to *glḥ*: a. *gazaz;* b. *gara';* c. *kasam;* d. *marat;* e. *saphah;* f. *hiqqiph;* g. *qarach, qereach, qorchah, qarachath;* h. *gabbachath, gibbeach;* i. *gallabh;* j. *ta'ar;* k. *morah;* l. *zaqan;* m. *sapham;* n. *se'ar, sa'arah.* II. Shaving the Hair of the Head and the Beard in the OT: 1. General Observations; 2. Sign of Humiliation and Dishonor; 3. Mourning Customs; 4. Hair Style of the Nazirite; 5. Commands and Prohibitions for Priests and Community; 6. Leprosy and Purification Rites; 7. Rite before Marriage to a Prisoner of War. III. In the LXX.

I. Etymology, Occurrences, Words Related to glḥ.

1. *Etymology and Occurrences of glḥ.* The root *glḥ* appears in the OT 18 times in the piel, 3 times in the pual, and 3 times in the hithpael (Lev. 13:33; Nu. 6:19; Gen. 41:14 conjec.). Probably the piel, "to shave," describes the cause of a condition which is denoted by an inferred intransitive of the original root

---

gillach. H. Bardtke, "Haar, Haupthaar," *BHHW,* II (1964), 617f.; E. Beurlier, "Cheveux," *DB,* II (1899), 684-692; J. Börker-Klähn, "Haartrachten, A. Archäologisch," *RLA,* IV (1972), 1-12; A. van den Born, "Bart," *BL²,* 169; *idem,* "Haar," *BL²,* 649; K. Budde, "Das alttestamentliche Nasiräat," *CW,* 44 (1930), 675-681; A. Büchler, "Das Schneiden des Haares als Strafe der Ehebrecher bei den Semiten," *WZKM,* 19 (1905), 91-138; G. Dalman, *AuS,* V (1937), (261-67), 267-274, (332-35), 335-39; R. Dussaud, *Les origines Cananéennes du sacrifice israélite* (Paris, ²1941), 199-203, 264-67; W. Eichrodt, *TheolOT* (trans. 1965), I, 303-306; W. Engelkemper, "Blut und Haare in der Totentrauer bei den Hebräern," *BZ,* 7 (1909), 123-28; F. C. Fensham, "The Shaving of Samson. A Note on Judges 16:19," *EvQ,* 31 (1959), 97f.; G. Fohrer, *History of Israelite Religion* (trans. 1972), 217f.; *idem,* "Scheren," *BHHW,* III (1966), 1690f.; K. Galling, "Haartracht," *BRL; HAT,* 1 (1937), 252-56; G. B. Gray, "The Nazirite," *JTS,* 1 (1900), 201-211; H. Gressmann, "Die Haartracht der Israeliten," *BZAW,* 34 (1920), 61-68; P. Heinisch, *Die Trauergebräuche bei den Israeliten. BZfr,* 13/7-8 (1931); J. Henninger, "Zur Frage des Haaropfers bei den

(continued on p. 6)

meaning "to be naked": [1] Middle Heb. and Targum/Galilean Aram. *glḥ*, as well as late Heb. *gallāḥ*, "shorn, shaven"; further Arab. *ǧaliḥa*, "to be or become bald *aǧlaḥ*, "baldheaded, bald," [2] Tigré *gaelḥa*, "to be naked, shave the head," adj. "naked, close shaved" > "without horns" (of an ox), "without jewelry on the head" (of women), Tigr. *gʷaelḥayae*, "to shave the head." [3] *glḥ*, "to shave," takes as its object the hair of the head (*ro'sh*, "head," Nu. 6:9; Dt. 21:12; 2 S. 14:26; Isa. 7:20; Ezk. 44:20; Jgs. 16:17 [inclusive]), the consecrated hair of the head (*ro'sh nizro*, Nu. 6:18; *nizro*, v. 19), the locks of a man's head (*machlephoth ro'sho*, Jgs. 16:19), all a person's hair (*kol se'aro*, Lev. 14:8; in addition, the beard and the eyebrows are specifically mentioned in v. 9), the hair of the genitals (*sa'ar haraghlayim*, Isa. 7:20), the beard (*zaqan*, Lev. 14:9; 21:5; 2 S. 10:4; cf. 1 Ch. 19:4; Isa. 7:20; Jer. 41:5), the eyebrows (*gabboth 'enav*, Lev. 14:9), and the scab of the head and of the beard (*netheq*, 13:33).

2. *Words Related to glḥ*. The following OT words are related to the idea of shaving the hair or the beard.

a. *gazaz*. The root *gzz*, which is found in almost all Semitic languages (Akk., Ugar., Syr., Arab., Old South Arab.), is used mainly in Hebrew of shearing sheep (10 times). It is applied to the Servant of Yahweh in Isa. 53:7 in the statement that he was "like a sheep before his shearers." *gazaz* is used only 3 times as a mourning rite: according to Jer. 7:29, Israel (fem.) is told to cut off her hair (*nezer*, not diadem) [4] and raise a lamentation. Similarly, according to Mic. 1:16, the daughter of Zion is told to make herself bald (*qarach*), cut off her hair (*gazaz*), and make herself bald (*harchibhi qorchathekh*) as the eagle. According to Job 1:20, Job rends his robe and shaves (*gazaz*) (the hair of) his head. Nah. 1:12 is uncertain. *gez* denotes the shearing (RSV "fleece") of sheep (Dt. 18:4;

---

[1] So also Jenni, *Das hebräische Piʻel* (1968), No. 52.
[2] Wehr, 130.
[3] Cf. *TigrWb*, 560f.; Leslau, *Contributions*, 15.
[4] Cf. Rudolph, *HAT*, 12 (³1968), 56.

Semiten," *Die Wiener Schule der Völkerkunde. Festschrift . . . des Institutes für Völkerkunde an der Universität Wien (1929-1954)*, ed. J. Haekel, *et al.* (1956), 349-368; M. Jastrow, "The 'nazir' Legislation," *JBL*, 33 (1914), 265-285; E. Kutsch, "'Trauerbräuche' und 'Selbstminderungsriten' im AT, *ThSt*, 78 (1965), 25-42; A. Mau, *PW*, III/1 (1897=1958), 30-34; B. Meissner, *BuA*, I (1920), Index *s.v.* Bart, Haartracht; E. Meyer, *Sumerier und Semiten in Babylonien. ABAW* (1906), *passim;* H. Mötefindt, *Zur Geschichte der Barttracht im alten Orient* (Leipzig, 1923); F. Nötscher, *HSAT*, III (1940), 62-64; J. Ölssner, *Benennung und Funktion der Körperteile im hebräischen AT* (diss., Leipzig, 1960); J. Pedersen, *ILC*, III-IV, 264-66; *ANEP*, Index *s.v.* Beard; G. von Rad, *OTTheol*, I (trans. 1962), 246-48; H. Salmanowitsch, *Das Naziräat nach Bibel und Talmud* (Vilna, 1931); H. Schäfer, *Von ägyptischer Kunst, besonders der Zeichenkunst* (Leipzig, ²1922); P. Thomsen, "Haartracht, C. Syrien-Palästina," *RLV*, V (1926), 6-11; E. Unger, "Fremdvölker, C," *RLV*, IV/1 (1926), 110-16; F. Vigouroux, *DB*, I (1895), 1450-56; Z. Weisman, "הנזירות במקרא—טיפיסיה ושרשיה" (The Biblical Nazirite, Its Types and Roots), *Tarbiz*, 36 (1966/67), 207-220.

Job 31:20) and the mowing of grass (Am. 7:1; Ps. 72:6), and *gizzah* means shearing, wool (Jgs. 6:37).

b. *gara'*. → גרע *gāra'* is used in Jer. 48:37 and Isa. 15:2 for shaving and cutting the beard.

c. *kasam*. *kasam* appears only in Ezk. 44:20, where it refers to cutting the hair.

d. *marat*. *marat* is used in Isa. 50:6; Ezr. 9:3; and Neh. 13:25 of pulling out the hair.

e. *saphah*. *saphah* is used in the threat in Isa. 7:20 of snatching away the beard as a sign of shame and dishonor.

f. *hiqqiph*. *nqp, hiqqiph,* "to surround," occurs with the meaning "to shave around, cut around," only in Lev. 19:27 in a decalog of ancient (now rejected as superstitious) cult practices, as a prohibition against rounding off (*hiqqiph*)[5] the corners of the hair (*pe'ath ro'sh*); cf. *qrḥ,* "to make a tonsure."

g. *qarach, qereach, qorchah, qarachath*. *qarach,* "to make bald," is found twice in the qal (Lev. 21:5; Mic. 1:16), and once each in the niphal (Jer. 16:6), hiphil (Ezk. 27:31), and hophal (29:18). Except in the prohibition of tonsures for the priest (Lev. 21:5), making oneself bald is a mourning rite. *qereach*[6] is the back part of a bald head where the hairs have fallen out (*nimrat,* 13:40). It is used as a mocking word against Elisha in 2 K. 2:23. *qorchah* (*qorcha'*, Ezk. 27:31) is the bald head as a sign of mourning (Am. 8:10; Isa. 3:24; 15:2; 22:12; Mic. 1:16; Jer. 47:5; 48:37; Ezk. 7:18; 27:31). It is prohibited as a mourning custom for the dead in Dt. 14:1, and Lev. 21:5 forbids priests in general to practice it. Three times *qarachath* is the bare portion at the back of the head, the back part of a bald head, where the hairs have fallen out (*nimrat*) from infection, leprosy, or rash (Lev. 13:42 [twice],43). Lev. 13:55 is the only passage where *qarachath* means the "back" of a garment which is frayed (leprous).

h. *gabbachath, gibbeach*. On the other hand, *gabbachath* denotes the front part of a bald head or forehead, "when the head is bare on the front" (Lev. 13:41, 42 [twice],43); Lev. 13:55 is the only passage where it means the front of a garment. *gibbeach,* "baldness of the forehead," occurs only in 13:41.

i. *gallabh*. *gallabh,* "barber," is a loanword from Akk. *gallābu,* "barber," *gullubu,* "to cut"; this root is also found in Ugar. (*glbm*),[7] Phoen., Galilean

---

[5] Cf. Kutsch, 26: edges of a tonsure.

[6] Cf. E. Y. Kutscher, *SVT,* 16 (1967), 159.

[7] *PRU,* II, 207; according to Aistleitner, *WUS,* No. 648, "shearer, barber"; according to others a cereal.

Aram., and Syr. According to Ezk. 5:1, Yahweh tells Ezekiel, the "son of man," to take a sharp sword (*cherebh chaddah*) to shave his head and his beard. In a postscript, the sword is more closely defined as a "barber's razor" (*ta'ar haggallabhim*), which calls to mind Isa. 7:20. [8]

j. *ta'ar*. With the exception of Jer. 36:23 (where it means a penknife that was used to sharpen the calamus), *ta'ar*, "razor" (cf. *'arah*, "to bare, strip"), is used only for shaving the hair of the head and the beard (Isa. 7:20; Ezk. 5:1; Nu. 6:5; 8:7; Ps. 52:4 [Eng. v. 2]); elsewhere, *ta'ar* also means the sheath of the sword (1 S. 17:51; 2 S. 20:8; Jer. 47:6; Ezk. 21:8,9,10,35[3,4,5,30]).

k. *morah*. *morah*, "razor" (Jgs. 13:5; 16:17; 1 S. 1:11) appears only in connection with consecrated persons (Samson, Samuel) who are not allowed to cut their hair.

l. *zaqan*. *zaqan*, "beard," which is found in all Semitic languages, appears 19 times in the OT: 5 times in Lev.; twice each in Isa. and Jer.; once in Ezk.; 5 times in 1 and 2 S.; twice in Pss.; and once each in Ezr. and 1 Ch.

m. *sapham*. *sapham*, "moustache," occurs only in Lev. 13:45; Ezk. 24:17,22; Mic. 3:7; and 2 S. 19:25(24).

n. *se'ar, sa'arah*. *se'ar*, "hair, hairy, hairy covering," which is found in Akk., Middle Heb., Aram., and Syr., occurs 27 times in the OT, 15 times in Lev. 12f. alone. *sa'arah*, "hair," appears 6 times in the OT.

II. Shaving the Hair of the Head and the Beard in the OT.

1. *General Observations*. Among the Semites and Israelites, hair, *se'ar, sa'arah*, and *ro'sh*, "(hair of the) head," is usually black (*shachor*, Cant. 4:1; 5:11). Auburn, reddish hair (*'adhmoni*) was much rarer, and therefore was considered to be especially beautiful. This is why it is mentioned in particular in the description of the young David, along with his "beautiful eyes" and "goodly appearance" (1 S. 16:12; cf. 17:42). White (*labhan*), golden or yellow (*tsahobh*), and thin (*daq*) hair were regarded as symptoms of leprosy (Lev. 13f.). A gray-headed person was revered (19:32; 2 Macc. 6:23). Long and full hair that was cut and groomed with oil or aromatics was regarded as ornamentation for a man. Thus, in his praise of the handsome Absalom, the author of 2 S. 14:26 emphasizes his full hair: "When he cut the hair of his head (or, had it cut, *yeghalleach*) (from time to time he used to cut it [or, to have it cut], for when it was heavy on him, he had to cut it [*veghillecho*]), he (one) weighed the hair of his head, two hundred shekels by the king's weight." This abundance of hair with its extraordinary weight of 200 (LXX 100) shekels, which is equivalent to 2,280 grams (figuring 1 shekel = 11.4 grams), is hyperbolic, and is obviously intended to depict the

---

[8] Zimmerli, *BK*, XIII/1, 128.

magnificent virility of Absalom. According to Cant. 5:2,11, the black locks (*qevutstsoth*) of the beloved are like *taltallim,* date panicles. Whether men in Israel also wore braids can hardly be proved from the *machlephoth* (RSV "locks") mentioned in Jgs. 16:13, since this word can also mean strands or locks of hair.

Men wore beards (*zaqan*) and moustaches (*sapham*). The beard was regarded as ornamentation and as an expression of manly strength. Whether men in Israel wore plaited beards in the Assyrian style [9] cannot be determined from the OT. When giving the kiss of greeting, a man took another man's beard, as when Joab deceitfully gave Amasa the ominous "kiss of Judas" (2 S. 20:9). Joseph had himself shaved (*yeghallach*) and changed his clothes before he went in to Pharaoh to interpret his dream (Gen. 41:14). This corresponded to Egyptian custom, especially in the case of an audience with Pharaoh. [10] Israelite women not only bound their hair together, they also knew artistic hair styles. Thus, we are told that Jezebel painted her eyes and fixed her hair beautifully (*hetibh*) in order to mock Jehu (2 K. 9:30); cf. also Jth. 10:3. The announcement of judgment against the haughty daughters of Zion in Isa. 3:17,18-23,24 lists a catalog of novelties, ornaments, and cosmetics for women, including headdresses (*pe'erim,* cf. Egyp. *pyr*), v. 20, and turbans (*tseniphoth*), v. 23. On account of this generally foreign and therefore heathen custom, instead of an artistically braided or plaited hair style [11] there will be baldness (*qorchah*), and instead of beauty, "shame" (v. 24).

2. *Sign of Humiliation and Dishonor.* According to 2 S. 10:4 (cf. 1 Ch. 19:4), Hanun, the king of the Ammonites, shaved off (half: this is missing in the LXX and 1 Ch.) the beard of David's servants, split their garments in half down to the hips, and sent them away. As is shown by parallelism between *yeghallach 'eth chatsi zeqanam,* "he shaved off half the beard of each," and *yikhroth 'eth madhvehem bachetsi 'adh shethothehem,* "he cut off their garments in the middle, at their hips," Hanun did these things in order to humiliate and dishonor David's servants. This was a deliberate provocation, and was to be punished as such in the campaign of Joab and Abishai. Cases of shaving off the beard are reported from Egypt by Herodotus (ii.121) and from Sparta by Plutarch (*Agesilaos* 30).

Isa. 7:20, which probably comes from the period of the Syro-Ephraimitic War, threatens the people with the utmost humiliation, shame, and bondage. As a symbol of this, the prophet warns that Yahweh will shave (*yeghallach*) the head and the pubic hair with a razor (*ta'ar*) which is hired beyond the River Euphrates, and will sweep away (*tispeh*) the beard (*zaqan*) also. As 2 S. 10:4 shows, shaving off the beard was regarded as dishonor and humiliation. Prisoners and slaves were also treated in this way. The degradation and shame is particularly intensified by shaving off the pubic hair. Shaving off the hair does not merely represent the destruction and depopulation of the land of Judah. Instead

---

[9] Cf. *AOB,* 117, 130; *ANEP,* 439ff.
[10] Cf. H. J. Heyes, *Bibel und Ägypten* (1904), 225ff.
[11] Cf. Wildberger, *BK,* X/1, 139.

the text is alluding with bitter irony to 2 K. 16:7f.: With the razor of the Assyrian soldiers whom Ahaz hired with a heavy tribute, the Lord will bring about the abasement of Judah, which will be disgraced and enslaved like a man whose head, beard, and pubic region have been shaved, and thus Ahaz's pledge of loyalty to Tiglath-pileser III, "I am your servant and your son," will be fulfilled in bitter earnest. [12]

The symbolic act in Ezk. 5:1ff. takes up this idea of abasement and bondage. The prophet, the "son of man," is to pass a sharp sword (*cherebh chaddah;* like a razor, *ta'ar haggallabhim*) over his head and his beard, divide the hair by weighing it on balances, and then burn a third of it with fire, cut up a third of it with a sword, and scatter the last third to the wind. In his own person, the prophet is supposed to represent the fate of the conquered city. Divested of dignity and freedom, shaved like a slave or a prisoner, the prophet illustrates in a realistic symbol the humiliation and subjection of the capital and its people. A later expansion [13] uses the cutting off of the prophet's hair as an illustration of the fate of the people: a third of the people perish when the city is burned, a third die by the sword, and the remaining third are scattered abroad or led into the diaspora.

3. *Mourning Customs.* The OT contains references to many customs that were used in Israel and among Israel's neighbors to express grief over the death of a close relative or friend or over an imminent calamity. Out of grief, people tore their clothes, took off their sandals, fasted, gashed themselves, and freely lamented and wept. [14] The hair and the beard also played a role in these mourning ceremonies. A person let his hair fall loose, untied his headband, shaved his hair so as to make a tonsure, shaved or cut his beard, covered his moustache, or sprinkled earth or sand on his head.

Thus, out of grief over the death of his children and the loss of all his possessions, Job rent his robe and shaved his head (*vayyaghoz 'eth ro'sho,* Job 1:20). We are also told that Ezra was grieved when he learned of the mixed marriages of the leaders and priests of Judah, and he rent his garments and pulled hair from his head and beard (*marat,* Ezr. 9:3).

The prophets speak of mourning customs with astonishing frequency. In the announcement of a funeral lament in Am. 8:9f., [15] Yahweh warns the Israelites that when he brings the end upon them, he will turn their songs into lamentation, make them wear sackcloth instead of festal garments, and bring baldness upon their heads (*ha'alethi ... qorchah*). When the Israelites broke out in wild rejoicing at the retreat of Sennacherib's soldiers, the prophet warned them: "In that day Yahweh calls to weeping and mourning, to baldness (*leqorchah*) and girding with sackcloth" (Isa. 22:12). In his lament over the destruction of Judah, Micah de-

---

[12] Cf. F. Feldmann, *Das Buch Isaias* (1925), 96f.; H. Wildberger, *BK,* X/1, 305f.

[13] Zimmerli, *BK,* XIII/1, 102ff.

[14] Detailed examples of these practices are given in Heinisch; cf. also Kutsch, 26, 38f.

[15] According to H. W. Wolff, *BK,* XIV/2, 373, from the school of Amos, but before 733 B.C.

clares: "Make yourselves bald and cut off your hair (*qorchi vaghozzi*), on account of your beloved sons! Make yourselves as bald (*harchibhi qorchathekh*) as the eagle, they are lost" (Mic. 1:16). According to Mic. 3:7, the seers and the diviners shall be put to shame when there is no answer from God; then "they shall all cover their moustaches" (*'atu 'al sapham*). Jeremiah is also familiar with the mourning rite: according to 7:29, Israel (fem.) is to cut off and cast away (*gozzi nizrekh vehashlikhi*) her consecrated hair and to raise a lamentation on the heights, because Yahweh has rejected his people. On the other hand, Jer. 16:6 says that in the time of the great catastrophe, when "great and small die," no one shall lament for them or cut himself or make himself bald for them (*lo' yiqqareach lahem*). Jer. 41:5 gives an account of the pilgrimage of 80 Samarians to the Feast of Tabernacles, who shaved their beards (*meghulleche zaqan*), tore their clothes, and gashed their bodies as signs of mourning. Finally, according to Ezk. 7:18, all the people will put on mourning garments and shave their heads bald (*bekhol ro'shehem qorchah*) when the day of Yahweh brings the sword, hunger, and pestilence upon all.

According to Ezk. 24:17, the prophet was not allowed to have mourning ceremonies, bind on the turban, cover his moustache, etc., on the sudden death of his wife. When the exiles receive the news of the capture of Jerusalem, they will be so terrified that they will forget to call for mourners, etc., and will not cover their moustaches (24:22). In the OT shaving the hair of the head and the beard as a mourning ceremony (which is often connected with wearing sackcloth and gashing oneself, lamenting and weeping) is by no means limited to Israel. Thus the Moabites, when their cities are destroyed, go on a pilgrimage to the high places of their gods with baldness (*qorchah*) and shorn beard (*kol zaqan geru'ah*) and girded with sackcloth, and they observe a period of mourning (Isa. 15:2ff.). Jer. 48:29-39 (which may be borrowed from Isa. 15f.) mention also the "gashes (*gedhudhoth*) upon all hands" (v. 37). In the oracle against the Philistines in Jer. 47:1-7, because of destruction and catastrophe, baldness will come upon Gaza (*ba'ah qorchah 'el 'azzah*), and Ashdod and the remnant of the Anakim gash themselves (v. 5). Similarly, in the lament over the fall of Tyre, the sailors, i.e., the inhabitants of the city depicted as a magnificent ship, wail aloud, "cast dust on their heads, wallow in ashes, ... make themselves bald (*hiqrichu qorchah*), and gird themselves with mourning clothes" (Ezk. 27:31). Finally, reference should be made to Bar. 6:30f.: in the temples of the gods, "the priests crouch down with torn clothes, with shaven heads and beards and bared head. They howl and scream before their gods, as many do in the funeral feast."

These funeral and mourning customs are variously interpreted and traced back to different origins. Some derive the rites from ideas of death which demand either care for and association with the dead, or defense against the spirits of the dead.[16] This view may be justified to the extent that in such rites we have fixed gestures or possibly survivals of actions of whose magical, superstitious significance the OT (especially in the prophets) is no longer aware. Others em-

---

[16] Cf. the survey in A. Bertholet, *RGG*[2], V, 1253-57.

phasize in these rites the elements of conversion, repentance, mortification, and humility as means of moving God (who has brought the calamity upon the man) to gentleness and reconciliation.[17] Kutsch tries to combine the rites of self-humiliation and mourning customs under the general heading of "castigation rites." A mourning custom occasioned by death or misfortune is in reality a means of expressing the idea of abasement, the fact that a man "is bowed down, that he has had a humbling experience."[18]

4. *Hair Style of the Nazirite.* The prohibition against using a razor and against shaving or cutting the hair plays a special role in the Nazirite vow (→ נזיר *nāzîr*). From the time of the Philistine wars, we know Samson as one who was "consecrated to God" (*nezir 'elohim*, Jgs. 13:5,7; 16:17), who had unusual physical powers (16:17,19,28ff.), and whose military acts are described as works of the Spirit of Yahweh (13:25; 14:6,19; 15:14). In an addition, 13:5aα,b,[19] Samson is included among the judges (*lehoshia'*, "to deliver"), even though Nazirites and judges are hardly identical. He himself reveals the secret of his strength to Delilah in 16:17: "A razor has never come upon my head (in conformity with the proclamation of the angel of Yahweh in 13:5), for I have been consecrated to God from my mother's womb. If I be shaved (*gullachti*), then my strength will leave me, and I shall become weak, and be like any (other) man." As he slept upon her knees, "she called a man, and had him shave off (*vatteghallach*) the seven locks (*machlephoth*) of his head, . . . and his strength left him" (*vayyasar kocho me'alav*, v. 19).

It is ultimately irrelevant to the interpretation of this text whether Delilah herself cut off Samson's locks, or whether she had it done by the man whom she called (*vatteghallach*),[20] or whether (following the LXX)[21] the man whom she called did it (reading *vayeghallach*). According to the birth story of Samuel, which calls to mind the birth story of Samson in Jgs. 13,[22] Hannah makes a vow (1 S. 1:11) that she "will give (*ntn*) (the male descendant she is requesting) to Yahweh all the days of his life (*kol yeme chayyav*), and no razor (*morah*) shall touch his head." According to v. 28, "as long as he lives, he is lent to Yahweh (*sha'ul layhvh*)." Even if the element of the War of Yahweh plays no role in the case of Samuel, still he is set apart as one who has been "consecrated"

---

[17] Cf. W. Frankenberg, "Israelitische und altarabische Trauerbräuche," *PJ*, 2 (1906), 64-74; J. Frey, *Tod, Seelenglaube und Seelenkult im alten Israel* (1898), 45ff., 80ff.

[18] Kutsch, 34f. The Ugaritic parallel in *CTA*, 5 [I* AB], VI, 11-22, cited by Kutsch is comprehensible only in the larger context of Ugaritic literature and is very much contested in its details. In addition to the translation of J. Aistleitner, *Die myth. und kult. Texte von Ras Schamra* (1959), 17, which Kutsch cites, cf. now the divergent interpretation of J. Gray, *SVT*, 5 (²1965), 62; J. C. de Moor, *UF*, 1 (1969), 227; *idem*, *AOAT*, 16 (1971), 190-93; T. L. Fenton, *UF*, 1 (1969), 70. On the question of offering hair, cf. under III.4, on Nu. 6:18 and the account of research in this area by J. Henninger.

[19] W. Richter, *BBB*, 18 (²1966), 140, n. 92.

[20] According to F. C. Fensham, 97f., causative?

[21] Cf. *BHK, BHS*, etc.

[22] Cf. J. Hylander, *Der literarische Samuel-Saul-Komplex (1 Sam 1-15)* (Uppsala, 1932), 31ff.

to the Lord all his life and whose hair is not to be cut, and he is associated with the Nazirites. This seems to apply also to Joseph in the Blessings of Jacob (Gen. 49:26) and of Moses (Dt. 33:16f.). Obviously at issue here is an ancient pre-monarchical institution of bearers of a divine charisma, which set them apart for a particular service throughout their lives, perhaps originally for the War of Yahweh. [23]

The prohibition against using a razor (*morah*, used only in connection with Samson and Samuel; outside Nu. 6:5, *ta'ar* is used in connection with the Levites in 8:7, and in only two other passages) and cutting (*gillach*) the hair, and the wearing of long flowing hair, indicate the consecrated status of those who are set apart for Yahweh. The prohibition against using a metal razor may go back to an old taboo against profaning by metal the hair of one who has been con-secrated, since metal was not to be used in circumcision (Ex. 4:25) or in making a stone altar (20:25; etc.). As far as growing hair is concerned, many scholars call attention to primitive manaistic ideas in which it is believed that divine power resides in a person's hair. In conjunction with regulations pertaining to abstinence, long hair could have been the external symbol of a lifelong commit-ment to the service of Yahweh, which was later expanded, perhaps, as a symbol of ancient Yahwism and of opposition to every form of Canaanization in faith, cult, and ethics. [24] When his hair was cut off, the Nazirite who had been set apart lost his consecration charisma. Then in the monarchy this ancient institution of the Nazirite lost its significance, perhaps because of the new forms of defense and warfare brought about by the raising of a levy of soldiers and by the hiring of mercenaries. [25] This led to the idea of the temporary Nazirite under specific ceremonial rules. In the exilic period, the Deuteronomistic passage Am. 2:11f. [26] laments because Israel had seduced the Nazirites into drinking wine, thus causing them to become unfaithful to the consecration which was a reminder of the wilderness period; they had also commanded the prophets not to prophesy. Yahweh raised up ('*aqim*) prophets and Nazirites to offer salvation to Israel.

A development and reconstruction of the ancient lifelong Nazirite vow is found in the regulations concerning Nazirites in Nu. 6:1-21, which still shows clear traces of this process of growth. [27] In the earlier stratum 6:2b-8, the prohibi-tion against allowing a razor to come upon (the hair of) a Nazirite's head (*ta'ar lo' ya'abhor 'al ro'sho*) forms the oldest nucleus of the text. [28] The original life-time service of a Nazirite is suddenly changed to a temporary vow by the expression, "all the days of his separation," or the like (vv. 4a,5aα,6a,8a). Further emphasis is then given to this aspect by the positive supplement which states that the Nazirite is to let the locks of his hair grow long (*gaddel pera' se'ar ro'sho*, v. 5) because he is holy to Yahweh for the entire period of his "vow of separation"

---

[23] Stade, Sellin, Eichrodt, von Rad, Fohrer, etc.
[24] Similarly Sellin, von Rad, Fohrer, etc.
[25] Fohrer.
[26] Cf. W. H. Schmidt, *ZAW*, 77 (1965), 180ff.; H. W. Wolff, *BK*, XIV/2, 172, 207.
[27] Cf. the careful literary-critical analysis in D. Kellermann, *BZAW*, 120 (1970), 83-95.
[28] A. Dillmann, K. Budde, D. Kellermann.

(*hazziro*), i.e., for the duration of his separation (*'asher yazzir layhvh*, v. 5, or *hazziro layhvh*, v. 6) he is in the state of holiness (*qadhosh hu' layhvh*, "he is holy to Yahweh," v. 8); the latter characterizes the special status of the priest in Lev. 21:7b. [29]

The command in Nu. 6:5bβ that the Nazirite must let the locks of his hair grow long, obviously presupposes that it was kept and cut short before the state of "separation," while the prohibition against allowing a razor to come upon his head in v. 5aβ presupposes that the hair was allowed to grow long and forbids or excludes shaving the head for specific reasons.

Abstinence from wine (and intoxicating drink, Nu. 6:3a) and the forbidding of defilement by a dead body (v. 6b) are enumerated along with the prohibition against cutting the hair as status regulations or symbols of "separation" and "holiness." While abstinence from wine is also mentioned in connection with a Nazirite in Am. 2:11f. and Jgs. 13:4,7 (at least for Samson's mother), the regulation concerning defilement might be a later expansion.

In case of accidental defilement by a dead body, the Nazirite, i.e., the person who is in a state of "separation" and "holiness," is automatically released from his vow. Hence he must "shave" (*gillach*) "the consecrated hair of his head" (*ro'sh nizro*) which has been thus defiled (Nu. 6:9bαβ, cf. v. 18) and upon which "the separation to his God rests" (v. 7b), on the day of his cleansing (v. 9bα) (and declaration of holiness), and consecrate himself to Yahweh again.

In later additions to the text (according to Kellermann, vv. 9bβ-11,13-21), the Nazirite vow is terminated ritually by a *torah*, "law" (vv. 13-21). After he offers certain sacrifices, the *nazir* is to shave his consecrated hair (*gillach 'eth ro'sh nizro*) at the door of the tent of meeting, and put it on the fire under the *zebhach hashshelamim* (RSV, "sacrifice of the peace offering," the community- or covenant-sacrifice(?), → זבח *zebhach*, v. 18). After he has shaved the hair of his "consecration" (*'achar hithgallecho 'eth nizro*, v. 19), his Nazirite vow is ended and he can again drink wine (v. 20). Occasionally the burning of the consecrated hair of the head (*ro'sh nizro*) in the fire of the community or peace offering has been regarded as a hair offering: "clearly a survival of hair offerings—a species of offerings widely spread in antiquity." [30] Dussaud, however, rejects the idea that the Nazir offers his hair in place of his person, and points to an entirely different intention: "The primary idea is that the nazir is leaving the state of holiness in which he was placed: this holiness was located particularly in the hair, and when he had it cut off and carried away, the only proper thing for him to do was to have his hair consumed in the fire of sacrifice. It is true that a spirit of life was surrendered in this way, but it was a special spirit of holiness that had been superimposed on the man's own spirit." [31] Just as, e.g., the remains of animals that had been used in the cult were burned in order to guard against profanation and misuse (Ex. 12:10; 29:34; Lev. 4:12; etc.), so "the hair of his consecration," upon which "the separation to his God rests" (Nu. 6:7b), was burned when the

---

[29] Cf. Pedersen, 266f.
[30] G. B. Gray, *Numbers. ICC* (Edinburgh, 1912), 68.
[31] Dussaud, 202f.; cf. also M. Noth, *Numbers. OTL* (trans. 1968), 55f.

Nazirite vow was ended. At the same time, the consecrated one, the *nazir,* was relieved of his sacral status and responsibilities in order that he might be restored to the normal status of secular life, a process some scholars have called a "rite of transition." [32]

5. *Commands and Prohibitions for Priests and Community.* In prohibitions and instructions relating to the wearing of hair and beards by the priests and the community of Yahweh, the wide variety of terminology is striking. An (originally ethico-cultic) You-Decalog of negative commands for the Israelite community in Lev. 19 forbids not only eating blood, augury, and witchcraft (v. 26), but also rounding off the hair on the temples (*lo' taqqiphu pe'ath ro'shekhem*) and marring the edges of the beard (*lo' thashchith 'eth pe'ath zeqanekha,* v. 27), or making any cuttings (*seret*) in the flesh or tattooing any marks (*kethobheth qa'-aqa'*) upon oneself on account of the dead (v. 28). It is by no means certain that v. 27 has reference to a mourning rite just because v. 28 contains a prohibition against making cuttings, i.e., marrings, on account of the dead (*lanephesh*). Rounding off the hair and corrupting (or destroying) the beard could relate to idolatrous and heathen practices, just like eating blood, augury, and witchcraft (v. 26).

This prohibition is found with differences in terminology in the second main stratum of the Holiness Code, [33] where it is applied to the priests: "They shall not make tonsures upon their heads (*lo' yiqrechu qorchah bero'sham*), nor shave off the edges of their beards (*pe'ath zeqanam lo' yeghallechu*), nor make any cuttings in their flesh (*ubhibhesaram lo' yisretu sarateth*)" (Lev. 21:5). According to Elliger, this prohibition for priests "looks very much like an application of 19:27f.," [34] so that 19:27f. may be the democratization of a rule which originally pertained only to priests. [35] It is doubtful whether the various terms for cutting the hair and the beard mean the same thing, as Elliger assumes. [36] Does *hiqqiph pe'ath ro'sh,* "round off the hair on the temples" (19:27), mean the same thing as *qarach qorchah bero'sh,* "make tonsures upon the head" (21:5)? Again, does *hishchith 'eth pe'ath zeqanekha,* "mar the edges of the beard" (19:27), mean the same thing as *gillach pe'ath zeqanam,* "shave off the edges of the beard" (21:5)? *hiqqiph,* "to round off," occurs with the obj. *pe'ah,* "edge, temple," only in 19:27, while *qarach,* "to make a tonsure, make bald," is found in Lev. 21:5; Mic. 1:16; Jer. 16:6; Ezk. 27:31; 29:18; and *qorchah,* "tonsure, baldness," appears 9 times in the prophets as a sign of mourning. Why did 19:27 not use the expression *qarach qorchah,* "to make a tonsure, make bald," if it meant the same type of haircut as that designated for priests in 21:5, or did it have in mind another type of haircut? Similarly, one may ask why 19:27 uses the word *hishchith,* "to mar," in describing the way the beard is to be cut, while 21:5 uses *gillach,* "to shave off," in connection with which "corruption" (clip-

---

[32] A. van Gennep, H. Lewy, etc.; cf. J. Henninger, 259.
[33] Elliger, *HAT,* 4 (1966), 278ff.: Ph².
[34] *Ibid.,* 281.
[35] *Ibid.,* 289.
[36] *Ibid.,* 261.

ping?) is particularly striking. Finally, it should be mentioned that the prohibition against cutting the hair and the beard is not characterized explicitly and in the original context as a funeral custom: *lanephesh,* "on account of the dead," occurs only in 19:28 in connection with making cuttings in the flesh, and nothing is said about a funeral custom in the insertion in 21:5f., although defiling oneself by touching a dead body is forbidden in the preceding section (21:1b-4).

The prohibition against rounding off the hair on the temples (*hiqqiph pe'ath ro'sh*) calls to mind Herodotus iii.8, which states that following the example of and out of respect for their God Orotal, the Arabs "round off their hair, as they shave the temples" (*keírontai peritróchala perixyroúntes toús krotáphous*), or that the Libyan Makers let their hair grow long in the middle and cut it off on both sides. Josephus, *Contra Apion.* i.173, characterizes the Nabateans near the Dead Sea as "shorn shaggily and around the crown of the head" (*auchmaléoi koryphás trochokourádes*). In Jer. 9:25(26); 25:23; and 49:32, the Arabs "that dwell in the desert" are called "those who cut the corners of their hair" (*qetsutse phe'ah*). Consequently, it is natural to see in Lev. 19:27 the prohibition of an originally heathen hair style, which possibly was in conflict with the worship of Yahweh because of its original cultic implication (imitating the heathen god or sacrificing hair, etc.),[37] and thus was forbidden to the Israelites. This applies particularly if 19:27 was originally a prohibition for priests which was later democratized and given universal force.[38] In this sense, then, the prohibitions in 19:26-28 against eating blood, augury, witchcraft, rounding off the hair on the temples, making cuttings in the flesh, and tattooing marks upon oneself form an integral unit directed against idolatrous and superstitious practices.

It is uncertain whether a specific pagan or foreign hair style also lies behind the prohibition against *qarach qorchah,* "making tonsures." Since this prohibition pertains to priests, it could indeed have served to distinguish the priest from other people. In Leviticus, the verb *gillach,* "to shave off," occurs in the prohibition against shaving off the edges of the beard (*pe'ath zeqanim*) only in 21:5, and in the cleansing rites in 13:33; 14:8f. Usually, scholars are too quick to connect tonsures and making tonsures in the context of mourning and funeral customs with the prohibition in 21:5 for priests and that in 19:27 (where it is expanded to all the people), and then to trace this back to pre-Islamic hair sacrifices on the graves of the dead.[39] But in this case it is striking that Pg says only that the Aaronides (Lev. 10:6) and the high priests (21:10) should not let the hair of their heads hang loose (heavy? unkempt?) (*ra'shekhem 'al tiphra'u*). Perhaps the OT prohibition of priestly tonsures is connected with the fact that foreign heathen priests wore tonsures. The tonsure is found, e.g., in Egypt from the eighteenth dynasty on,[40] and it is usually traced back to purification laws.[41]

---

[37] Cf. Heinisch, *Trauergebräuche,* 54f.

[38] Cf. Elliger, 289.

[39] Gray, Cooke, quite recently Zimmerli, *BK,* XIII/2 (1969), 1134, on Ezk. 44:20; and Elliger, *HAT,* 4, 261; cf. the survey in Henninger.

[40] Sethe, *ZÄS,* 57 (1922), 24.

[41] Cf. Bonnet, *RÄR,* 389.

Dt. 14:1 contains the prohibition against cutting oneself (*lo' tithgodhedhu*) and making any baldness between the eyes (RSV, "on the forehead") for the dead (*lo' thasimu qorchah ben 'enekham lameth*). Gressmann explains this as "cutting off a lock of hair at the edge of the forehead," and calls attention to the depiction of hired mourners on the coffin of Anchpechrod (9th century B.C.).[42] The prohibition against cutting oneself and making baldness on the forehead (v. 1) is connected with the prohibition against eating any *to'ebhah*, "abominable thing" (v. 3). This is followed by lists of clean and unclean animals (vv. 4-20), and a concluding prohibition against eating anything that dies of itself (v. 21a). The prohibition against eating "any abominable thing" in v. 3 also lends particular importance to the preceding prohibitions against cutting oneself and making baldness on the forehead;[43] these were incompatible with the worship of Yahweh.

According to the directions in Ezk. 44:20, priests are not to shave (the hair of) their heads (*ro'sham lo' yeghallechu*) or to let their locks grow long (*pera' lo' yeshallechu*), but are to trim (the hair of) their heads neatly (*kasom yikhsemu 'eth ra'shehem*). The different terminology used here from that which is found in Lev. 19:27; 21:5; and Dt. 14:1 is striking, since Ezk. 7:18 and 27:31 also show acquaintance with *qorchah*, "tonsure, baldness," but use it only in connection with mourning customs, whereas 44:20 uses *gillach*, "to shave," and *kasam*, "to trim, cut."

Various terms are also used for shaving the beard. Lev. 19:27 prohibits marring (or destroying) the edges of the beard (*hishchith 'eth pe'ath zeqanekha*), while 21:5 uses *gillach*, "to shave off." It is impossible to determine whether these two verbs refer to cutting the beard in the same style; they might even denote different procedures. Gressmann translates 19:27 in this way: "You shall not round off the hair on the face, neither that on the upper lip nor that on the lower lip nor the beard underneath the chin."[44] According to this view, the beard was not cut at all. But perhaps this interpretation is influenced too much by E. Meyer's hypothesis that in Egyptian depictions of foreign nations[45] the Bedouins always had short hair, a short pointed beard, and no moustache, which is a sweeping statement that cannot be proved. We cannot be sure, then, whether *gillach pe'ath zeqanim*, "to shave off the edges of the beard," means to trim the beard or to cut it off completely. The OT has no rule concerning moustaches (*sapham*) for priests or Israelites, except that a leper must cover his *sapham*, "moustache" (Lev. 13:45).

6. *Leprosy and Purification Rites.* In the torah (law) for lepers in Lev. 13f., shaving off the hair and the beard is determined case by case after examination (13:29-37,38f.,40-46), and is prescribed after appropriate purification rites (chap. 14). The first criterion that is used to determine whether Israelites had leprosy

---

[42] H. Gressmann, 62.
[43] Cf. Merendino, *BBB*, 31 (1969), 84-94.
[44] Gressmann, 63.
[45] See in addition Mötefindt, 25-28; and Thomsen, 6f.

(*tsara'ath*) is based on the fact that their hair is normally black (*shachor*), so that "yellow" (*tsahobh*) hair by loss of pigmentation is regarded as a symptom of illness; the same is also true of thin hair (*se'ar daq*). If the infection (*negha'*, RSV "disease") of an itch or a scab (*netheq*) is deeper than the skin and the hair is yellow and thin, the priest must pronounce the person unclean (*timme'*): it is an infection (disease), leprosy of the head or the beard (vv. 29-30). If all these criteria are not present in the infection, but there is merely no black hair, the person is put in quarantine for seven days. Then if the infection has not spread and the other symptoms are still absent (vv. 31f.), the person must shave himself (or have himself shaved, *hithgallach*), but he must not shave the itch (or have the itch shaved, *yeggalleach*, v. 33). If no negative symptoms appear after another seven-day interval, the priest shall pronounce him clean (v. 34). But if the itch or scab breaks out after the priest pronounces the person clean, it is unnecessary for the priest to look any longer for symptoms in the hair, it is leprosy (v. 36).

The redactional additions in Lev. 13:38f.,40-44,45f. also deal with becoming bald (*yimmaret ro'sho*, vv. 40-44). "Baldness of the back of the head" (*qereach*) and "baldness of the forehead" (*gibbeach*) are *tahor*, "clean." But if there is on the bald head or the bald forehead "a reddish-white diseased spot," it is "leprosy breaking out (blossoming)" (*tsara'ath porachath*), and thus the person is *tsarua'*, "leprous," and *tame'*, "unclean." Baldness on the back or front of the head is not a certain indication of leprosy and uncleanness. The leper shall let the hair of his head hang loose (*parua'*), cover his moustache (*sapham*), cry "Unclean, unclean," live apart (*badhadh yeshebh*), and have his habitation outside the camp (*michuts lammachaneh moshabho*, vv. 45f.). The acts of tearing the clothes, letting the hair of the head hang loose, and covering the moustache (*'atah 'al sapham*; cf. Ezk. 24:17,22; Mic. 3:7) are interpreted in different ways. Some scholars think their purpose is one of disguise for protection against the dead or against evil spirits by letting the hair of the head hang loose and by covering the lower half of the face. [46] According to Elliger, the moustache (*sapham*) was also covered "to prevent the spirits from entering into a person through the entrances in his head, the breathing passages." [47] Some think that shaving off the hair is a remnant of an original hair sacrifice, others that it is an essential cleansing precaution against itch or scab. Kutsch rejects these explanations. "Uncleanness" belongs to the realm of "humility." By practicing this rite, the leper "expresses his uncleanness, i.e., his lowliness, in ritual form." [48]

After the person who is being healed of leprosy submits to the rite of cleansing and exorcism, in which he is sprinkled with the water of cleansing, and a bird of cleansing (with the pathogenic agent) is released into the open field (cf. Azazel in the ritual of the great Day of Atonement, Lev. 16:10,20ff.), he is pronounced clean and he must then "wash his clothes, shave off all his hair, and bathe himself in water" (Lev. 14:8). According to Lev. 14:9, on the seventh day he must

---

[46] Cf. M. Noth, *Leviticus. OTL* (trans. 1965), 106.
[47] Elliger, *HAT*, 4, 185.
[48] Kutsch, 31.

shave off "the hair of his head, his beard, his eyebrows, and all his hair." Schneider thinks this shaving indicates that the hair of the body was regarded as "a hiding-place of uncleanness," and therefore had to be removed when a leper was cleansed, "in order that he might begin a new, clean growth and life; cf. Nu. 6:9; Dt. 21:12."[49] Others, however, think it contains the remnant of an original hair offering. After these rites of cleansing, the person who is healed is again accepted into the human community.

7. *Rite before Marriage to a Prisoner of War.* According to the rules in Dt. 21:10-14 concerning the marriage of an Israelite to a woman captured in war, the prisoner is to shave her head (*gillechah 'eth ro'shah*), pare her nails, and put off her captive's garb. Before the marriage is consummated, she is to bewail her father and her mother a full month. These ceremonies are hardly to be interpreted as mourning rites. It seems more likely that Junker is correct in seeing them as a change in outward appearance which was intended to symbolize new life relationships.[50] But an interpolator has probably inserted this as a cleansing ceremony for the prisoner,[51] intended to remove the alien and heathen stigma, and to offset the danger of foreign religious infection or infiltration when a person entered into the house of Israel (cf. Ezr. 9f.; Neh. 10:31[30]; 13:23).

III. **In the LXX.** In the LXX, *gillach*, "to shave," is translated 20 times by *xyrán*, "to shave," which is also used to translate *qarach*, "to make bald," 4 times. *gillach* is rendered by *keírein*, "to shear, cut one's hair," only 3 times in 2 S. 14:26; *keírein* usually translates *gazaz*, "to shear" (14 times). *gara'*, which means "to shave off the beard," is translated by *xyrán*, "to shave," in Jer. 48:37, and by *katatémnein*, "to cut in pieces," in Isa. 15:2. *kasam*, "to cut," is rendered by *kalýptein*, "to cover, hide." *marat*, meaning "to pull out," is translated once each by *hrápisma*, "a blow," *tíllein*, "to pluck," and *madaroún*, "to make bald." *saphah*, "to sweep away," which occurs only in Isa. 7:20 in conjunction with the beard, is translated by *aphaírein*, "to take away, cut off"; *hiqqiph* (*nqp*), meaning "to cut around," is rendered by *poieín sisóēn*, "to make a braid," in Lev. 19:27. *qarach* is rendered by *xyrán*, and in the hophal by *phalakrós*, "bald-headed"; *qereach*, "back part of the bald head," by *phalakrós; qorchah*, "bald head," 7 times by *phalákrōma*, "bald head," twice by *xyrán*, and once by *xýrēsis*, "baldness"; and *qarachath*, "the back part of the bald head," by *phalákrōma* or *siēmōn*, "a group of threads, chain, web." *gabbachath*, "a bald forehead," is translated by *anaphalántōma* or *phalántōma*, "baldness"; and *gabbachath* as the front of a garment is rendered by *krókē*, "the loose thread of the woof, web, garment" (Lev. 13:55). *gibbeach*, "baldness of the forehead," is translated by *anaphálantos*, "bald-headed"; *gallabh*, "barber," by *koreús*, "barber"; and *ta'ar*, "razor," 5 times by *xyrón*, "razor"; and as "the sheath of the sword" by *kolaiós* or *koleós. morah*, "razor," is rendered 3 times by *sídēros*, "iron, knife," and

[49] H. Schneider, *EB* on Lev. 14:8f.
[50] H. Junker, *EB, in loc.*
[51] Steuernagel, Horst, Merendino.

once by *xyrón. se'ar,* "hair," is translated 23 times by *thríx,* "hair," twice each by *dasýs,* "hairy," and *tríchōma,* "a growth of hair," and once by *tríchinos,* "from or of hair"; *sa'arah,* "hair," 7 times by *thríx; sapham,* "moustache," twice by *stóma,* "mouth," and once each by *cheílos,* "lip," and *mýstax,* "moustache"; and *zaqan,* "beard," 18 times by *pṓgōn,* "beard," and once by *phárynx,* "throat."

Botterweck

גָלַל *gll;* גַּל *gal*

Contents: I. Etymology, Occurrences. II. Meaning. III. Theological Meaning—"To Commit." IV. Stone Heap. V. Wave.

I. Etymology, Occurrences. In Akkadian the verb *gll* means "to roll, turn." It refers chiefly to a flood which brings high water (cf. Am. 5:24), and then to the (angry) rolling of the eyes.[1] In the Semitic languages, this root means a circle or something that can be rolled. In Ugaritic, *gl* is a vessel from which wine and honey are drunk.[2] Akk. *gullu* is a dish, a basin, or a small gold vessel.[3] Like Heb. *gullah,* it can also denote a bulgy vessel.[4] The Libyan root meaning "to be round" is also connected with this (in particular, the Arab. equivalent means "to be great, exalted").[5] Akk. *galālu,* which is probably cognate with *gelal,* the Aramaic term for "stone, stela," means "pebble, squared stone"[6] (cf. also Heb. *gal,* "stone heap"). The connection between the verb *gll* and subst. *gal* is very hard to establish. Halper tries to make a distinction between an active and a passive meaning of *gll.*[7] That which rushes and rolls is a wave, while that which is formed by rolling together (of stones) is a stone heap. But these two words never appear together in Hebrew in the sense that a *gal,* "stone heap," is formed by rolling stones (though cf. Gilgal in Josh. 5:9). *gal* is probably a primary noun that has nothing to do with "rolling."

---

gll. G. J. Botterweck, *Der Triliterismus im Semitischen, erläutert an den Wurzeln GL, KL, ḴL. BBB,* 3 (1952), 32-36, 51ff.; J. P. Brown, "The Mediterranean Vocabulary of the Vine," *VT,* 19 (1969), 146-170; M. Dahood, "Canaanite-Phoenician Influence in Qoheleth," *Bibl,* 33 (1952), 30-52, 191-221; idem, *Ugaritic-Hebrew Philology* (Rome, 1965); J. Gray, *The Legacy of Canaan. SVT,* 5 (Leiden, ²1965); E. Täubler, *Biblische Studien, Die Epoche der Richter* (1958).

[1] *AHw,* 273.

[2] Brown, 158; Gordon, *UT,* 380/581.

[3] *AHw,* 297.

[4] Gray, 275.

[5] See O. Rössler, "Der semitische Charakter der libyschen Sprache," *ZA,* 50 (1952), 121-150, 132; on Ethiopic parallels, cf. Leslau, *Contributions,* 15.

[6] *AHw,* 273.

[7] B. Halper, *ZAW,* 30 (1910), 105-107.

gll occurs 17 times in the OT: 10 times in the qal, twice each in the niphal and the hithpolel, and once each in the poal, hithpalpel, and pilpel (it is also read conjecturally in 5 passages).

II. Meaning. gll usually means "to roll, turn" a stone, either to shut a well (Gen. 29:3,8,10) or a cave (Josh. 10:18), or to build an altar (1 S. 14:33). The Wisdom Literature takes up the figure of rolling stones in order to show the connection between a deed and its consequences (Prov. 26:27). Apparently the point is that damage is done to others by the rolling of a stone.

In the niphal, the verb means "to roll up." At the end the heavens (skies) will be rolled up like a scroll (Isa. 34:4), or human life will be rolled up like a shepherd's tent (38:12). [8]

A group of cognate nouns shows that the original meaning of the root gll was "round." Thus, galgal means "wheel": the wheel of a war chariot (Isa. 5:28; Jer. 47:3; Ezk. 23:24; Ps. 77:19 [Eng. v. 18]), possibly the wheels underneath the cherubim (Ezk. 10:2,6,13), [9] a round thistle (Isa. 17:13; Ps. 83:14[13]), or the wheel at the cistern (Eccl. 12:6; unless the word used here is to be derived from Akk. gulgullu and means "bucket"); [10] cf. also gulgoleth, "skull"; gelilim, "round, revolving"; gelilah, "circuit, district"; and galal, "dung."

As in Akkadian, the root can refer to the "rolling" of a torrential river (Am. 5:24), or to thundershowers that "roll" down on a house (Job 20:28; conjec. based on LXX; MT has yighel, RSV, "to be carried away"). gll is also used in a figurative sense of dangers which "roll on," e.g., enemies who make slaves (Gen. 43:18), or demons that cause illness (Job 30:14). [11] The verb is farthest removed from its original meaning when it is used to refer to the bloodstained cloak of a soldier (Isa. 9:4[5]), or to a slain man wallowing in his blood (2 S. 20:12). In these cases, gll should be translated, "to roll in blood," a figure that is well suited to what these passages are describing. [12] KBL[3] assumes that we have in these two instances and in Sir. 12:14 a gll II, "to pollute, defile."

III. Theological Meaning—"To Commit." The Wisdom Literature advises man to commit his plans to God, because success comes from him (Prov. 16:3). This concept of the unbroken connection between a deed and its results is problematic when one considers the prosperity of the ungodly (Ps. 37:7). When the godly in this situation is advised to commit his way to God, i.e., to trust in his help (v. 5), this is an appeal for perseverance, which is supported by the reference to the speedy end of the ungodly (v. 10). Ultimately, this empirical principle can become an argument against the godly. It can be said that he turned his distress over to God, but nothing was changed. The enemies of the psalmist mock his trust in God (Ps. 22:9[8]).

---

[8] So J. Begrich, *Der Psalm des Hiskia* (1926), 27f.
[9] Cf. W. Zimmerli, *BK*, XIII, 232.
[10] Dahood, *Bibl*, 216f.; otherwise H. W. Hertzberg, *KAT*, XVII/4, 208.
[11] Cf. G. Fohrer, *KAT*, XVI, 419.
[12] H. P. Smith, *The Books of Samuel. ICC* (1912, [2]1953), 369.

God can also be the subject of *gll*. The psalmist prays that he will roll away (RSV "take away") scorn and contempt from him (Ps. 119:22). The OT states that the name "Gilgal" was given to a town because God had rolled away the reproach of Egypt from Israel (Josh. 5:9). The meaning of this expression is uncertain: it might refer to the reproach of slavery or of uncircumcision (in the eyes of the circumcised Egyptians?); but perhaps the precise meaning can no longer be determined. [13] The word Gilgal [14] does not mean "a circle of stones," as is often assumed, [15] but "rubble, stone heap." [16] It is thus a reduplication of *gl*.

IV. Stone Heap. In Gen. 31 the forming of a *gal* is described. Stones (*'abha-nim*) are gathered and the *gal* is set up with them. The stone heap is the place where the two partners in a covenant share in a common meal (v. 46). It also serves as a witness to the covenant (vv. 47f.: etiology of Galeed). [17] This passage is particularly significant, because some scholars believe that the secular prototype for the sealing of the Sinai covenant is to be found here. [18] If so, the meal at the stone heap would be the prototype for the meal at Sinai (Ex. 24:9-11).

gal 'abhanim, "heap of stones," is the expression used for a mound (Josh. 7:26; 8:29; 2 S. 18:17) which is set up over the dead body (of one who has been put to death). In Job 3:22, *gal* (MT *ghil*) is an isolated term for the grave for which the despairing yearn (it is impossible to regard *ghil* as a synonym of *qebher,* "grave," and thus we must read *gal* in the sense of "grave"). [19] Elsewhere *gal* means the stone heap that remains after a city is destroyed; it expresses the idea of complete destruction (Isa. 25:2; Jer. 9:10[11]; 51:37; cf. Dt. 13:17[16]—*tel*). Ruins of cities are dwelling places of demons like the wasteland; people avoid them (Isa. 13:20ff.). They become the haunt of jackals, places without inhabitant (Jer. 9:10[11]; 51:37).

Yahweh demonstrates his power in history by allowing fortified cities to be turned into *gallim* (RSV "heaps of ruins," 2 K. 19:25; Isa. 37:26), and he avenges his people by destroying the cities of their enemies (Jer. 51:37; Isa. 25:2); but he also can make Jerusalem a heap of ruins (Jer. 9:10[11]).

The altars in Gilgal shall also become stone heaps (Hos. 12:12[11]). Here there is clearly a wordplay between *gal* and Gilgal. But it is impossible to decide whether *gal* means heaps of ruins or stone heaps which the peasant farmer piles up in the corners of his field when he plows. [20]

---

13 M. Noth, *HAT,* 7², 25.

14 On the location of Gilgal, cf. M. Weippert, *The Settlement of the Israelite Tribes in Palestine. SBT,* 21 (trans. 1971), 22ff.

15 H.-J. Kraus, "Gilgal, ein Beitrag zur Kultusgeschichte Israels," *VT,* 1 (1951), 181-199; A. Kuschke, "Gilgal," *RGG³,* II, 1577ff.

16 Täubler, 27-29; K. D. Schunck, *Benjamin. BZAW,* 86 (1963), 46, n. 165.

17 Cf. M. Ottosson, *Gilead* (Lund, 1969), 22ff., 36ff.

18 W. Beyerlin, *Origins and History of the Oldest Sinaitic Traditions* (trans. ²1965), 33f.; otherwise L. Perlitt, *Bundestheologie im AT. WMANT,* 36 (1969), 187f.

19 Fohrer, *KAT,* XVI, 112; F. Horst, *BK,* XVI/1, 38.

20 Rudolph, *KAT,* XIII/1, 232; on the LXX reading *chelōnai* in conformity with Syr. *gallā*=Heb. *gll,* "tortoise," cf. *ibid.,* 223.

V. Wave. The word *gal* occurs only in the plural when it means "wave, billow" (read *gan,* "garden," in Cant. 4:12). [21] The predominantly later texts show that originally mythical power is ascribed to the sea and its waves. [22] But Yahweh is understood as the one who hushes the waves of the sea (Ps. 107:29) and crushes Rahab (Ps. 89:10f.[9f.]); by his word, he stills the waves (Job 38:11). He has set a bound for the sea, which it cannot pass over (Jer. 5:22). God not only subdues the waves; he also uses them as his instrument and causes them to rage (Jer. 31:35).

Old Testament writers use the waves of the sea as a figure for the power of Israel's enemies (Jer. 51:55) or God's attack against Tyre (Ezk. 26:3). They can be used to express the concept of destruction (Jer. 51:42) or to illustrate the coming salvation of God (Isa. 48:18).

Münderlein

---

[21] Dahood, *Philology,* 54.
[22] O. Kaiser, *Die mythische Bedeutung des Meeres in Ägypten, Ugarit und Israel. BZAW,* 78 (²1962).

גָּמַל *gāmal;* גָּמוּל *gāmûl;* גְּמוּל *gᵉmûl;* גְּמוּלָה *gᵉmûlāh;* תַּגְמוּל *taghmûl*

Contents: I. 1. Occurrences: a. In the Ancient Near East; b. In the OT; 2. Etymology; 3. Meanings. II. 1. *gamal/gamul* in the Context of Growth and Maturity; 2. *gamal/gemul* As Social Behavior: a. In General Usage; b. In the Reflection of the Wisdom Literature; c. In Statements Concerning Divine Judgment. III. *gamal/gemul* As Divine Activity: 1. In Proper Names; 2. In the Psalms; 3. In Prophetic Texts; 4. In the Qumran Literature.

I. 1. *Occurrences.*

a. *In the Ancient Near East.* Words built from the verbal root *gml* occur in several Semitic languages. The Akk. verb *gamālu* is the basis for a widely ramified and diffuse word group having the principal meanings "to recompense, requite, spare." [1] But the main meanings of the verb forms are: "to treat kindly, be kind to someone, be helpful," and "to spare, save." They are used, and

---

gāmal. P. A. H. de Boer, "Psalm CXXXI 2," *VT,* 16 (1966), 287-292; K. Koch, ed., *Um das Prinzip der Vergeltung in Religion und Recht des AT* (1972); L. Köhler, "Karmäl= Jungkorn," *ThZ,* 2 (1946), 394; also *JSS,* 1 (1956), 18; L. Kopf, "Arabische Etymologien und Parallelen zum Bibelwörterbuch," *VT,* 8 (1958), 168f.; M. Noth, *IPN,* 35f., 182, Index; L. Oppenheim, "Lexikalische Untersuchungen zu den 'kappadokischen' Briefen," *AfO,* 12 (1937-39), 350-54; J. Pedersen, *ILC,* I-II, 394f., 533; G. Quell, "Struktur und Sinn des Psalms 131," *Das ferne und nahe Wort. Festschrift L. Rost. BZAW,* 105 (1967), 173-185; G. Sauer, "גמל antun, erweisen," *THAT,* I (1971), 426-28; J. Scharbert, "ŠLM im AT," *Lex tua veritas. Festschrift H. Junker* (1961), 209-229, esp. 217-220; K. Seybold, "Zwei Bemerkungen zu גמול/גמל," *VT,* 22 (1972), 112-17; Stamm, *AN,* Index.

[1] *AHw,* 275f.

in part further specified, of men and gods, frequently also in proper names, commercial transactions, and prayer. [2] We also encounter the nouns *gimillu,* meaning "a kind deed as or for the purpose of doing recompense, kindness, an act of kindness," and *gimiltu,* "friendliness," both frequently in the expressions *šakānu g.eli/ina,* "to be friendly, kind to someone," the former with *epēšu, gamālu,* "to do good," and *turru* D, "to recompense," and the latter also with *šalāmu* D, "to complete, restore." [3] The noun forms with infixed *t* (*gitmālu*), which are used of gods, heroes, and men, but also of animals and plants, are connected with the concept of "completeness, perfection," [4] and "equality." [5] In West Semitic languages the verbal root appears only sporadically in certain Aramaic dialects with the meaning "to recompense, do violence to"—"blessing" (Jewish Aram. Targum), "to do good, be kind" (Palestinian Aram.), [6] "to reward," as a noun "deed" (Samaritan Aram.), [7] "to pay, reward, recompense" (Palestinian Syr.), [8] and in proper names of the Nabatean and Palmyrenian inscriptions. [9] Arabic has the verbs *ǧamala,* "to combine (collect), gather" (rarer), and *ǧamula,* "to be beautiful," III "be kind," IV "treat nicely, well," VI "be kind to each other," with more common derivatives (*ǧumla,* "entirety, sum, whole"; *ǧamīl,* "beautiful," also "friendliness, act of kindness"), [10] as well as *kamala* (with derivatives), meaning "to be whole, complete." [11] Tigré has an active participle meaning "to be thick-leafed," "grow well" (of plants), "have thick hair." [12]

b. *In the OT.* The OT contains the following forms built from the root *gml:* the verb in the qal and niphal, the qal passive participle as a subst. *gamul,* the noun of action *gemul* ($<$ *ga[u]i/mûl;* [13] sing. and pl.) with a vocal *sheva* in the first syllable, its fem. counterpart *gemulah,* a nominal form with prefixed *t* (in the pl.), and proper names (names of persons: Gamlî'el, Gᵉmallî, Gāmûl; names of places: Bêth Gāmûl). With the exception of two passages (Nu. 17:23 [Eng. v. 8]; Isa. 18:5), the verb has a personal subject, and a personal object connected by the accusative (sometimes a suffix; also with a double acc.), *le,* and *'al.* The noun also (which is frequently connected with *šlm* in the piel, "to complete, finish," and with *shubh* in the qal and the hiphil, "to pay back, return") always refers to a personal subject of the action. It is worthy of note that the

---

2 Oppenheim, 350ff.: "to pay, bring good, remit"; *AHw, CAD,* V, 21f.: "to reach an agreement."

3 Scharbert, 210, 213.

4 *AHw,* 294.

5 *CAD,* V, 110f.

6 Kutscher, in F. Rosenthal, ed., *Aramaic Handbook* (1967), I/2.

7 Ben-Ḥayyim, in *ibid.,* II/2.

8 Black, in *ibid.,* II/2.

9 *BDB,* 168; *KBL²*; not *DISO;* see *KBL³*.

10 Kopf, 168f.

11 *Wörterbuch der klassischen arabischen Sprache,* I (1970), 318ff.

12 *TigrWb,* 567a.

13 *BLe,* § 473c; R. Meyer, *Hebräische Grammatik,* II (³1969), 29.

passive verb forms (including *gamul*), the two occurrences of this verb with impersonal subject (and object), and the qal forms that take children as their object stand in contrast to the other occurrences of this root and form a semantic field of their own.

2. *Etymology.* The close contacts (and in part, overlappings) in Akkadian and Hebrew usage, and the intransitive meanings of "equality, completeness" (Akk.), "beauty, kindness," or "perfection" (Arab.), "good growth" (Tigré), and "maturity" (? Middle Heb.), which occur in various Semitic languages, some-times in different forms and relationships from the transitive usage, are worthy of note. There is much in favor, then, of the view that the words come from originally different roots. [14] The Hebrew words come from the roots *gml* and *kml* (inferred from a noun form *karmel* IV, [15] which probably arose by dis-similation, *mm* > *rm*, "[new] grain that has just gotten ripe" [Lev. 2:14; 23:14; 2 K. 4:42], and based on Arab. *kamala* [16]), which have become homonyms by phonetic convergence (*k* > *g*) [17] (otherwise in Arab., but cf. Tigré). This would explain the development of two distinctive types of usage and two semantic fields. [18] It is impossible to demonstrate connections between these words and the morphologically related root *gmr*, [19] which some scholars also connect with Arab. *kamala*. [20]

3. *Meanings.* Modern lexicons are increasingly hesitant about tracing these words to a common original Semitic meaning (perhaps "to complete"). [21] Even the attempt to trace the Hebrew verb back to a single original meaning (perhaps "to accomplish, prove") cannot get round the fact that in the passive and active usages (with an impersonal obj.) the verb has the specific meaning, "to wean, ripen," but in the other active forms (and the nouns of action) it has an additional range of meaning, viz., "to do violence to, prove, deal fully or adequately with." Since the two types of usage of these words are neither related to each other nor overlap in the OT, it is necessary, then, to begin with the assumption that they come from two relatively independent semantic fields. If the first field is clearly delineated, the second is defined as an "ethically relevant deed," as "the act of a man which affects other people favorably or unfavorably," [22] as we learn from the parallel *'asah*, "to do, act" (Jgs. 9:16; 1 S. 24:18ff.[17ff.]; Ps. 7:4f.[3f.]; 28:4; 103:10; Lam. 3:64), the construction with *yedhe*, lit. "according to the dealing of the hands" (Jgs. 9:16; Isa. 3:11; Prov. 12:14), the antithesis with *shicheth* (piel), "to deal corruptly" (Dt. 32:5f.), and *'akhar*, "to disturb, trouble, hurt" (Prov. 11:17), the direct objects (along with indirect objects) *tobh(ah)*,

---

[14] Cf. F. Zorell, *Lexicon Hebraicum et Aramaicum* (1966).
[15] *kammāl*, according to Köhler, 394, or 18; *KBL²*.
[16] Cf. *TigrWb*, 394.
[17] Cf. *KBL³*, 161.
[18] Cf. Seybold.
[19] *KBL³*.
[20] A. Guillaume, *Abr-Nahrain*, 1 (1959/60), 7, 21.
[21] *GesB, BDB* (?).
[22] Scharbert, 220, n. 68.

"good" (1 S. 24:18[17]; Prov. 31:12), ra'(ah), "evil" (Gen. 50:15,17; 1 S. 24:18 [17]; Isa. 3:9; Ps. 7:5[4]; Prov. 3:30; 31:12; cf. 11QPsª 3:7=col. 24:6), zo'th, "this, thus" (Dt. 32:6), kol, "all" (Isa. 63:7), the paronomastic gemulah, "dealing, recompense" (2 S. 19:37[36]; Ps. 137:8; 1QpHab 12:3), and finally the integration into constructions with šlm in the piel, "to recompense, reward" (1 S. 24:20 [19]; Isa. 59:18; 66:6; Jer. 51:6,56; Joel 4:4[3:4]; Ps. 137:8; Prov. 19:17), and shubh in the qal and hiphil, "to pay back, return" (Gen. 50:15; Joel 4:4,7[3:4,7]; Ob. 15 [qal]; Ps. 18:21,25[20,24] and par.; 28:4; 94:2; 116:12; Prov. 12:14; Lam. 3:64; 2 Ch. 32:25; cf. 11QPsª 3:7). It also follows from this that the meaning "to recompense" or "recompense," which is more or less emphasized in the lexicons, is acquired in the relevant passages from the context and cannot be derived from the inherent meaning of the word. Nevertheless, the nouns especially can in certain expressions take on the sense of "action as payment and retribution," as in Akkadian. [23] This also explains why the LXX, which usually keeps the two semantic fields separate (except in Ps. 131:2), with few exceptions translates half the verb and noun forms by antapodidónai, "to recompense," and antapódoma, "recompense," etc. (in the theological passages: Ps. 18:21[20] and par.; 103:2, 10; 116:7; 119:17; 142:8[7]; Isa. 35:4; 63:7; Jer. 51:6; Joel 4:4b[3:4b]; 2 Ch. 32:25). [24] Later Hebrew usage also reflects a development in meaning.

II. 1. *gamal/gamul in the Context of Growth and Maturity.* When the verb *gml* is used with a feminine subject or in the passive in speaking of the relationship between "mother and child," it means to wean the child from its mother's milk (Isa. 28:9), which was done at the end of a nursing period of about three years, according to ancient Near Eastern custom (2 Macc. 7:27). [25] As is shown by the threefold 'adh, "as soon as, until," and ka'asher, "when," in 1 S. 1:22-24, and the construction with yom, "day," in Gen. 21:8, weaning was done on a fixed date: this is regarded as the conclusion of the first phase of childhood. According to Gen. 21:8 (E), this event is celebrated with a feast, [26] and according to Hos. 1:8 it clears the way for another child. Weaning also means that the child leaves the immediate area around its mother and is set free to play with other children (Gen. 21:9), or is given over to further education outside the household (1 S. 1:22ff.). The same series of events is also in view in 1 K. 11:20aβ, which states that it was not the child's own mother, but her sister, the wife of Pharaoh, who weaned the son of the Edomite Hadad "in Pharaoh's house," where he was among the sons of Pharaoh (cf. the LXX). [27] gamul is the term used by the OT to describe the child who has completed the first phase of life as a yoneq, "suckling" (Isa. 11:8; 28:9), who plays (Isa. 11:8; Gen. 21:9), learns (Isa. 28:9f.; 1 S. 1:22ff.), rides on his mother's shoulders when travelling, is no

---

[23] Pedersen, 394f., 533; Seybold, 114ff.
[24] Büchsel, *TDNT*, II, 167-69.
[25] Meissner, *BuA*, I, 391f.; Erman-Ranke, *Ägypten und ägyptisches Leben* (²1923), 191ff.; G. R. Driver, *Festschrift A. Dupont-Sommer* (1971), 279, n. 4.
[26] Cf. G. Pfeiffer, *ZAW*, 84 (1972), 341ff.
[27] Noth, *BK*, IX/1, 253; also Erman-Ranke, 192f.

longer carried in a shawl or a pouch (Ps. 131:2), [28] and has thus begun a new phase of his life (gamul occurs as a person's name in 1 Ch. 24:17, [29] and in the place name Beth-gamul in Jer. 48:23). In Nu. 17:23(8) and Isa. 18:5, the verb k/gamal seems to be used in its original meaning, "to ripen": [30] the rod (of Aaron) puts forth buds, produces blossoms, and at last bears ripe almonds (Nu. 17:23[8]). The announcement of judgment in Isa. 18:4ff. describes Yahweh under the figure of the husbandman who waits quietly and then goes to work "when the blossom is over, and the flower becomes a ripening grape" (MT gomel is intransitive; only Sir. 14:18 uses this word to refer to the generations of mankind—here govea' is contrasted with gomel; 1QIs^a is different with gmwl[31] and gv').

2. gamal/gemul As Social Behavior.

a. In General Usage. When the verb gml is used to describe the relationship between human beings, it always has a personal subject and object to express the personal reference. Thus, it denotes the relationship between Joseph and his brothers (Gen. 50:15,17), Saul and David (1 S. 24:18[17]), the king and his host (2 S. 19:37[36]), the psalmist and his friend (Ps. 7:5[4]; cf. Prov. 3:30), a wife and her husband (Prov. 31:12), etc., i.e., a direct personal action in the milieu of concrete social relationships. Characteristically, either the paronomastic gemul or gemulah (2 S. 19:37[36]; Ps. 137:8; cf. 1QpHab 12:3), or the evaluative tobh, "good," or ra', "evil," separately or together (Gen. 50:15,17; Ps. 7:5[4]; Prov. 3:30; 1 S. 24:18[17]; Prov. 31:12), appear as a second object, thus qualifying the action as important and "ethically relevant." The former usage is of particular importance for the mediating of various nuances of meaning.

According to 2 S. 19:37(36), the aged Barzillai declines David's offer to spend his last years in the king's court, which was David's way of trying to show his gratitude to Barzillai for giving him provisions in the course of his flight from Jerusalem (vv. 32ff.[31ff.]). Barzillai says: "Why should the king recompense me (yighmeleni) with such a reward (gemulah)?" Undoubtedly David's offer was regarded as a recompense and a reward for the deeds of the rich patriarch (cf. v. 34[33] with v. 35[34]). It is very questionable, however, whether this was what Barzillai meant by the expressions which he used in his courteous question, especially since the deeds that he did are quite concealed by v. 37a(36a) and brought into question in v. 37b(36b). Moreover, the verb itself does not mean "to recompense" (cf. the clear contrast between action [gml] and reaction [šlm/ shubh] in Joel 4:4[3:4]). [32] This sense is extremely unlikely in the case of gemulah in Jer. 51:56 and especially Isa. 59:18 (pl.; cf. the Middle Heb., Jewish Aram. Targum gemuletha', "blessing, kindness"). [33] In harmony, then, with Akk. gimiltu,

---

[28] See also Quell, 178ff.; ANEP, 49.
[29] See III.1 below.
[30] See I.2 above.
[31] KBL³.
[32] See III.3 below.
[33] See III.3 below.

"kindness," or *gimillam gamālu*, "to do good,"[34] and the Middle Hebrew-Jewish Aramaic tradition, Barzillai's question should probably be translated: "Why should the king do me this favor?" with no specific reference to "recompense" or "reward." A comparison of the figurative use of *gml* in Prov. 11:17 and Isa. 3:9 also points to a certain basically positive sense of this verb, as in Akkadian. In these passages, *ra'ah*, "evil," is added to convey the negative thought (Isa. 3:9), but the verb stands alone (Prov. 11:17, ptcp.) to convey the positive meaning (which is determined by the context in Prov. 12:14; 19:17; cf. also 2 Ch. 20:11).

The passages that use the evaluative *tobh*, "good," and *ra'*, "evil," with *gml* present an alternative (either/or), thus indicating that *gml* is not neutral like *'asah*, "to do," but has a fundamentally ethical relevance. Consequently, *gamal* is an act that one performs intentionally and deliberately toward his fellow man, and the latter experiences and evaluates it as good and beneficial or as harmful and evil. In 1 S. 24:18(17), Saul admits to David, *'attah gemaltani hattobhah*, "you have repaid me good." But in vv. 19 and 20 (18 and 19), he further defines this as "doing good with him (*'itti*) and for him (*li*)" (and he says this within the context of a hostile relationship). He expresses the wish that David might receive a divine reward for this, while at the same time he is afraid that he himself might have to suffer the consequences (vv. 21f.[20f.]) of the evil he had repaid to David (*gamalti hara'ah*, v. 18[17]). As a deliberate and premeditated act (*chashabh ra'ah*, "to mean evil," Gen. 50:20), "repaying evil" (*gamal ra'[ah]*) could lead to judicial measures, whether in the form of bringing actual evidence against someone (Prov. 3:30), or in that of compelling him who is falsely accused to take an oath of purification in the process of divine judgment (Ps. 7:5[4]).[35] Explanations made before legal charges are brought (such as those found in Gen. 50:15-21 and 1 S. 24)[36] may make such drastic measures unnecessary (cf. 11QPs^a 3:7=col. 24:6: *gmwly hr' yšyb mmny dyn h'mt*).

b. *In the Reflection of the Wisdom Literature.* If it is true that the specification of *gml* as "good" and "evil," etc., is probably to be traced back to the influence of Wisdom thought (Gen. 50:15ff.; 1 S. 24; Prov. 3:30; 31:12) in the topical milieu of ethics and law (Prov. 3:30; Ps. 7:5[4]; 11QPs^a 3:7; and 1 S. 24:10ff.[9ff.]), this is even more certain of various characteristic uses of the word group which appear mainly in Proverbs. This explains its application to typical relationships in certain social situations (*'esheth chayil—ba'al*, "good wife—husband"; *'adham—dal*, "man—poor"; *'attah—rea'*, "you—friend") and also the establishment and preservation of stereotyped associations (*gamal ra'— rasha'*, "to do evil to"; *gamal tobh—chesedh—tsaddiq*, "to do good, steadfast love, righteousness to"; *šlm* in the piel, "to complete, finish"; *shubh* in the qal

---

[34] *AHw*, 288, 1 g.

[35] See W. Beyerlin, *Die Rettung der Bedrängten in den Feindpsalmen der Einzelnen. FRLANT*, 99 (1970), 96ff.

[36] On v. 18(17), cf. H. J. Boecker, *Redeformen des Rechtslebens im AT. WMANT*, 14 (²1970), 128f.

and hiphil, "to pay back, return"; *'asah* in the niphal, "to be done, performed"; *peri,* "fruit," in a simile or metaphor, etc.). The transition to the use of *gml* to express man's relationship to himself may also be laid to the account of Wisdom reflection: "A man who is kind (*'ish chesedh*) benefits himself, but a cruel man hurts himself" (Prov. 11:17). If this proverb (and 19:17) conveys the same idea as the Old Akkadian business expression *awīl gimillim:* a "man who reciprocates with kindness," [37] then Prov. 11:17; 12:14; and Isa. 3:10f. are probably based on the idea of a fateful action in the sense of a synthetic view of life. [38] Isa. 3:8f. uses *gml* figuratively to characterize words and acts which are obviously oriented to Yahweh as self-accusation and absurd self-destruction. The most far-reaching theological concept along the lines of Prov. 11:17; 12:14; and Isa. 3:10f. is advanced in Prov. 19:17, which harmonizes social and religious relationships by using ideas from business and economic life: [39] "Yahweh lends to him who helps the poor, and he repays him for his deed." [40] If here *gemul* in the positive sense is wholly set in a theological dimension, the same is true in a different way of the passage in the Joseph Story that is closely related to Wisdom thought, viz., Gen. 50:15-21 (E), which not only equates *gamal ra'ah,* "to do evil to," with *pesha',* "transgression," and *chatta'ath,* "sin," and connects it with *shubh* in the hiphil, "to pay back," but also traces it back to its inner source and affirms that it is reversed and transformed by the divine *chashabh,* "to mean, intend." [41] Of course, this peculiar meaning has not influenced the broader use of *gamal.*

    c. *In Statements Concerning Divine Judgment. gamal/gemul* as a responsible and significant act which ought to be repaid is especially clear in a series of passages which contain a construction with *šlm* in the piel, "to complete, finish," or *shubh* in the qal or hiphil, "to pay back, return," and whose dominant characteristic is the idea of divine judgment. Examples from prophetic oracles concerning foreign nations compose one group (Joel 4:4,7[3:4,7]; Ob. 15; Jer. 51:6, 56; Isa. 59:18b, internal enemies—59:18a; 66:6). These are supplemented by two statements in "vengeance" psalms, Ps. 94:2 and 137:8 (a reflection on 2 Ch. 20:11). Sometimes these passages implore or declare that the deeds of Israel's enemies will come upon their own heads. In all these texts, the idea of "recompense" in the sense of "payment, reward, recompense, or revenge" [42] comes, not from *gemul,* but from the verbs used with *gemul.* [43] Passages from Psalms of Individual Lament compose a second group (Ps. 28:4; 11QPsª 3:7; Lam. 3:64). In complete harmony with the first group, these contain prayers for a judicial and retributive intervention of Yahweh in the conflict with personal enemies (cf. Ps. 7:5[4]; Prov. 3:30). In all cases, the incriminating action is set in the light of the direct sphere of divine interest.

---

[37] Oppenheim, 351, n. 21; *CAD,* V, 75.
[38] Fahlgren, Koch.
[39] Differentiated as in *BWL,* 146f., 326.
[40] Gemser, *HAT,* 16, 76f.: "Yahweh lends to the one who. . . . "
[41] G. von Rad, *Wisdom in Israel* (trans. 1972), 199f.
[42] Scharbert.
[43] Contra *KBL*³.

III. gamal/gemul As Divine Activity. The following points of syntax are worthy of note in the use of the verb *gamal* and the noun *gemul* with a divine subject: the frequent combination with *'al,* "with" (Ps. 13:6; 103:10; 116:7,12; 119:17 [11QPsᵃ—*gmwr*]; 142:8[7]; 2 Ch. 32:25; cf. Joel 4:4[3:4]; conjec. Ps. 57:3b[2b] for *gomer,* "who fulfils his purpose," cf. the LXX), which conveys the idea of "protecting, inclining over, of adding and impressing, of binding obligation" [44] (cf. Akk. *gimillam šakānu eli/ina ṣēr*); the use in the absolute without a second object, with the characteristic exception of Isa. 63:7 (*kol,* "all"; *rabh tubh,* "great goodness"); the plural use of the nouns (with *kol,* "all," in Ps. 103:2, MT; and 116:12; Jer. 51:56); the distribution of examples in proper names, Psalms, and certain prophetic passages.

1. *In Proper Names.* Of the three proper names formed from the root *gml* in the OT, viz., Gamul (1 Ch. 24:17), Gemalli (Nu. 13:12), and Gamaliel (the son of Pedahzur, Nu. 1:10; 2:20; 7:54,59; 10:23), only the last can be defined more precisely. While the qal pass. ptcp. *gamul,* from *gamal,* "to wean," is not found elsewhere in this context, and the short form *gemalli* may come from *gāmāl,* "camel," the theophorous name of the Manassite *gamli'el* (LXX, NT, *Gamaliēl,* "Gamaliel") with the perfect plus noun (and infixed connective vowel) points to a distinctively Israelite structure. [45] As to type, it is to be classified as a name of thanksgiving, or better perhaps (in view of its character as witness), as a name of confession which is intended to express and affirm the divine blessing experienced in the birth of the child. Here *gamal* is a general term for the gracious act of the deity who intervenes directly and concretely in personal life. Further aspects of this confession, and especially of its theophorous elements, may be seen from the context of the ancient list of names in Nu. 1:5-15, [46] including the form of the name of Gamaliel's father, Pedahzur, from the ancient Near Eastern background of various compound Akkadian words containing *gml,* [47] and from the closest OT parallels in the poetry of the Psalms.

2. *In the Psalms.* In trying to determine the meaning of *gamal/gemul/gemulah/taghmul* when they are used with the divine subject, it is best to begin with the characteristic usage. With few exceptions, the striking construction of the verb *gml* with *'al,* "with" (*'al* is also used with nouns from the root *gml* in Ps. 116:12; 2 Ch. 32:25), gives the theological passages containing *gml* a particular emphasis by connecting the divine act with the pregnant concept of "coming upon someone from above." In the secular sphere, this construction is found only in one derived and figurative expression in 2 Ch. 20:11 (cf. v. 12), which has to do with the behavior of the Ammonites and Moabites as they "come against Judah." On the other hand, in religious usage Ps. 18:21(20) and par. and Isa. 63:7 (where

---

[44] *GK,* § 119aa-dd; Brockelmann, *Synt.,* § 110.

[45] *IPN,* No. 353.

[46] M. Noth, *Numbers. OTL* (trans. 1968), 18f.; called in question by D. Kellermann, *Die Priesterschrift von Numeri 1, 1 bis 10, 10. BZAW,* 120 (1970), 5f., 155ff.

[47] Stamm, *AN,* 168, 190, 220, etc.

gml takes the acc.) form the exception as the only two passages where it is not ordinary men (sing. or pl., Ps. 103:1ff.,10), but in all probability a king (Ps. 18) or Israel as a total community (beth yisra'el, "the house of Israel"—'ammi, "my people"—banim, "sons, children"—Isa. 63:7), who appears as the direct counterpart, and not so much as people indirectly subjected to the divine activity ('abhdekha, Ps. 119:17). In this light, a statement like that found in 2 Ch. 32:25 (kighemul 'alav, "according to the benefit done to him") seems to be a deliberate degradation of the proud king Hezekiah (gabhah libbo, "his heart was proud," vv. 25f.), while the perverted 'al that is applied to Yahweh himself in Joel 4:4(3:4) clearly indicates the writer's scorn for the grotesque actions of the coastal nations against Judah and Jerusalem. The emphasis that appears in this usage allows us to conclude that behind the group of words built from the root gml there usually lies the sense of an action on the same plane or of a reciprocal action, as is common between partners who meet one another on the same footing (cf. the secular usage with the acc., rarely with le, "to," once with 'al, "with"), but that this is corrected and relativized in theological passages which use gml with the 'al construction (but cf. the LXX and the later development of meaning). The absolute use of gml is also significant for the religious use. It leaves no place for the ambivalent meaning of gml found in the secular realm, and it regards the qualitative character of the personal act as determined by the divine subject, even when a seemingly arbitrary standard is applied to it, as in Ps. 18:21(20) and 103:10 with the particle ke, "according to": an act of punishment can also be expressed by using gamal, according to Ps. 103:10 (cf. Isa. 35:4; Jer. 51:56).[48] The use of the root gml in plural forms, statements containing "all" (kol, Ps. 103:2; 116:12; Isa. 63:7), and the plerophoric expressions in Isa. 63:7 indicate that religious statements with gml have a tendency to be abstract, and also to fill out and overextend the emotional dimension which is inherent in the root from the outset.

The scope of the use of the root gml determines decisively its nuances of meaning. Apart from Isa. 63:7, but under the influence of forms of theophorous names, gml always describes an event out of the personal realm of individual people, which is verified by gamal and implored or declared as a divine act both relating to them and executed for them: deliverance from death and from the danger of death (Ps. 13:6,4[3], illness [?] and danger from enemies; 18:21, 17ff.[20,16ff.], threat of enemies; 103:2[10],3-5, sickness and sin; 116:7,12,3,8, danger of death; 119:17, 'echyeh, "that I may live"; 142:8,4,7[7,3,6], oppression by enemies; 2 Ch. 32:25,24, fatal illness).[49] Isa. 63:7ff. is also immersed in this warm personal light by the double use of gamal with the direct accusative (v. 9). Furthermore, this act is related in each context to gratitude and response in the form of praise. If this is implicit and actual in Ps. 18 and par. (vv. 2ff.,25[1ff.,24]), the gamal statement in Ps. 13:6 (qal perf. 3rd masc. sing.) contains the explicit reason for singing a song, and in Ps. 142:8(7), as a part of the psalmist's promise to praise God, it is the prerequisite of his doing so in the community of the

---

[48] See 3 below.
[49] See 1 above.

righteous (qal impf. 2nd masc. sing.). In Ps. 103 (v. 10—negative statement); Ps. 116; and Isa. 63:7ff. this may be seen clearly from the expressions found in the context: "Forget not" (Ps. 103:2), "I will recount" (Isa. 63:7), and the answer to the question, "What shall I render (*'ashibh*) to Yahweh for all his bounty to me?" (Ps. 116:12; cf. vv. 13ff.). In Ps. 119:17, the poet promises to "observe God's word" because he is grateful that God has given him new life, while the author of 2 Ch. 32:25 criticizes Hezekiah for not having reciprocated the benefit done to him (*gemul 'alav*), and for not having "returned" (*heshibh*) thanks to Yahweh. Here again it is evident that the word group includes as one of its elements the obligation of grateful response, or at least carries the association and suggestion of reciprocal exchange and equalization in the sphere of personal relationships, initiative being especially denoted by *gamal*.

3. *In Prophetic Texts.* The reproachful question in Dt. 32:6 (at the beginning of a text that can be called "prophetic" in the light of its form and function): [50] "Do you thus requite Yahweh?" uses *gamal* to emphasize the incredibly unnatural behavior (cf. Isa. 3:9 and Ps. 7:5[4]) of a child who rebels against his father or of a creature who rebels against his creator (vv. 5,15ff.), and it accuses the Israelites of deliberately insulting God personally. Joel 4:4-8(3:4-8) offers the clearest definitions of the meaning of *gamal/gemul*. [51] On the one hand, this passage plainly differentiates *gamal* from the expressions *shillem gemul* and *heshibh gemul*, "to pay back, recompense" (4:4,7[3:4,7]), so that its original meaning, viz., an action "that grows out of the wilfulness of the wrongdoer," [52] is brought out clearly. On the other hand, the use of *gamal* with *'al* in 4:4(3:4) makes the alternate question somewhat absurd, since the thought communicated by *gamal* and *shillem gemul* makes it seem out of place. [53] Among the key phrases which, according to Isa. 35:4, are to be spoken to "those who are of a fearful heart," "(God) will come with vengeance (*naqam*)," "the recompense (*gemul*) of God," and "he will come and save you" stand side by side. Nevertheless, it is neither certain nor even likely that these expressions are synonymous and therefore that *gemul* means "recompense." [54] Instead, the prophet is here using dramatic diction to express the fact that divine vengeance on Edom will also be a saving act of the God who is about to appear personally. Isa. 59:18a, which has textual difficulties (the second *ke'al* [RSV "so"] should probably be understood distributively; cf. the Targ.: perhaps interpreted as *b'l* following Jer. 51:59), means that when Yahweh appears, he will repay ("wrath to his adver-

---

[50] O. Eissfeldt, *Das Lied Moses Deuteronomium 32,1-43 und das Lehrgedicht Asaphs Psalm 78. BSAW,* 104/5 (1958); G. E. Wright, "The Lawsuit of God: A Form-Critical Study of Deuteronomy 32," *Israel's Prophetic Heritage. Festschrift J. Muilenburg* (1962), 26ff.

[51] See 2.a above; cf. H. W. Wolff, *Joel. BK,* XIV/2, 93ff.; W. Rudolph, "Wann wirkte Joel?" *Das ferne und nahe Wort. Festschrift L. Rost. BZAW,* 105 (1967), 193-98; B. Reicke, "Joel und seine Zeit," *Wort—Gebot—Glaube. Festschrift W. Eichrodt. AThANT,* 59 (1970), 133-141.

[52] Wolff, 94; Scharbert, 218.

[53] On 4:4bβ,7 (3:4bβ,7) and Ob. 15, see II.2.c.

[54] *KBL³.*

saries, requital to his enemies") each person what he deserves ("according to individual works, according to ... he will repay"), i.e., he will settle accounts according to the *jus talionis* (the law of retribution). *gemulah* as "individual payment" (fem.) (in the figure of restoring the equivalent) [55] stands in contrast to the completed "act," which in turn is distinguished from the attitude of "anger." Finally, there are several possible interpretations of *gemulah* in Jer. 51:56. In analogy to v. 6 (*gemul*), *'el gemuloth*, RSV "a God of recompense," may be understood in relation to the deeds of the Babylonians which God in his omniscience records and requites, or it may again be translated as a predicate, "God of (good) deeds," after the analogy of the Bab. *bêl gimilli,* [56] the reference being to the saving deeds of Yahweh which have been experienced and which are to be anticipated. In both cases, however, the idea of retribution is based on the context (*shallem yeshallem,* "he will surely requite"). The context first puts the deeds denoted by *gemuloth* in this perspective, which undoubtedly dominates v. 56 as well as v. 6. [57]

4. *In the Qumran Literature.* In the extracanonical Qumran literature, the use of *gml* and its derivatives does not appear to be essentially different from that of the OT. This material has the paronomastic construction (1QpHab 12:2f.), the construction with *ra'ah,* etc. (1QM 6:6; 1Q37; cf. 11QPs^a 3:7 = col. 24:6), and the expression *heshibh/shillem gemul,* "to recompense, avenge a deed" (1QM 6:6; 1QpHab 12:2f.; 1QS 2:6f.; 10:17ff.; 4QpPs37 4:9f.). The following occurrences of the root *gml* in the Qumran literature are worthy of note: the theological usage in the watchword written on standards, *gemul 'el,* "Revenge (Exploit) of God," in 1QM 4:12 (cf. Isa. 35:4), and in the plural in 1Q36: *gmwly 'mtk(h)* (actually the plural of *gemul* appears frequently, 1QS 2:6f.; 1Q36, 28b; 6Q16; 11QPs^a 3:7), and the construction with *'al* with reference to the *'ebhyonim,* "poor" (1QpHab 12:2f.). Yet beyond the more general meaning "to do to, to prove"—"deed," there is no discernible narrowing of the meaning to that of "retribution."

Seybold

---

[55] Scharbert, 221f.
[56] *CAD.*
[57] On the prophetic oracles concerning foreign nations, see II.2.c above.

Contents: I. In the Ancient Near East: 1. Mesopotamia; 2. Egypt. II. In the OT: 1. Distribution; 2. Secular Usage; 3. Translation of gan in the LXX; pardes; 4. Ideas Concerning Paradise: a. The Geography of Paradise; b. gan As the Garden of God; c. Gen. 2; d. Ezk. 28.

I. In the Ancient Near Eeast.

1. *Mesopotamia.* The most common word for "garden" in Akkadian is *kirû*.[1] In addition, we also find *mūšaru,* "bed, garden," and the loanwords *gannu* (pl. *gannāti,* Aram.) and *pardēsu* (Old Persian).[2] The kings of Mesopotamia tell of their gardens, where they had fruit trees, cedars, and other kinds of trees planted.[3] These gardens were planned with great skill and often attained the size of a park. Assyrian emperors like Tiglath-pileser I, Ashurnasirpal II, Sargon II, and Sennacherib made sure that the horticulture of their land was well known far beyond their own borders. Usually, too, the Babylonian sanctuaries were surrounded by gardens.[4] According to Sumerian and Babylonian creation stories, man's purpose and task consisted of "making the field of the gods grow."[5]

In a figurative sense, the king and prince is given the rule over a "garden of plenty" (*kirī nuḫši*) when he worships the god Ashur and celebrates his holy New Year Festival.[6]

The Sumerian myth speaks of the paradisiacal land called Tilmun, where no beast of prey tore asunder and no illness reigned. After the sun-god brought forth water, the land became a luxuriant garden. This caused eight herbs to spring forth, which Enki ate and which made him sick.[7]

---

gan. A. Brock-Utne, *Der Gottesgarten, eine vergleichende religionsgeschichtliche Studie.* ANVAO, 2/2 (1935); E. Ebeling, "Garten," *RLA,* III (1959), 147-150; J. de Fraine, "Paradisus apud Sumeros?" *VD,* 25 (1947), 161-171; W. Fuss, *Die sogenannte Paradieserzählung: Aufbau, Herkunft und Bedeutung* (1968); H. Gressmann, "Mythische Reste in der Paradieserzählung," *ARW,* 10 (1907), 345-367; E. Haag, *Der Mensch am Anfang. TrThSt,* 24 (1970); S. N. Kramer, "Die Suche nach dem Paradies. Dilmun und die Indus-Zivilisation," *WZ Halle,* 12 (1963), 311-17; J. Kroll, "Elysium," *AFNW, Geisteswissenschaft,* 2 (1952), 7-35; G. Pettinato, *Untersuchungen zur neusumerischen Landwirtschaft,* I (Naples, 1967), 27-37; E. A. Speiser, "The Rivers of Paradise," *Festschrift J. Friedrich* (1959), 473-485; O. H. Steck, *Die Paradieserzählung. BSt,* 60 (1971); Th. C. Vriezen, *Onderzoek naar de Paradijsvoorstelling bij de oude semietische volken* (Wageningen, 1937); C. Westermann, *BK,* I, 283-306 (with additional literature); G. Widengren, *The King and the Tree of Life in Ancient Near Eastern Religion. UUÅ,* 4 (1951).

[1] *AHw,* 485; *CAD,* VIII, 411ff.
[2] See II.3 below.
[3] Meissner, *BuA,* I, 201-212.
[4] *Ibid.,* 201.
[5] G. Pettinato, *Das altorient. Menschenbild. AHAW* (1971), 1, 25.
[6] *ZA,* 43 (1936), 18, 64; cf. *BuA,* II, 142.
[7] *ANET*[3], 37-41; cf. also G. Lambert-R. Tournay, *RA,* 43 (1949), 105ff.

The hero of the Sumerian flood narrative, Ziusudra, is represented as a deified man who, with his wife, has been placed on a mountain in Tilmun. [8] This has reference to the mysterious island on the other side of the river of death, which, according to the Gilgamesh Epic, is located at the mouth of the streams. In modern times, Tilmun is usually identified with the island of Bahrein in the Persian Gulf and the coastal region south of it, [9] but it is obvious that the description itself exhibits purely mythical features.

According to Gilg. IX, V.48ff., Gilgamesh finds a mythical garden on the sea, whose trees bear precious stones, at the place where the female donor, Siduri-Sabitu, lives. But this garden does not seem to be identical with the place where the herb of life grows (Gilg. IX, 304ff.).

Sumerian texts speak of a temple garden where the herb of life grows. [10] Widengren compares these statements with the presence of a *kiškanû* tree, which "is spread out over the Apsû," in the temple garden of Eridu. [11] It is likely that the temple garden had a mythical-symbolic significance. But it should be noted that the former source speaks of an herb while the latter speaks of a tree, and that neither uses the expression "tree of life." [12]

The concept of a happy ideal state in the Primeval Age appears in the Sumerian Epic of King Enmerkar, which speaks of a time in which there was no snake or scorpion, no hyena, lion, or wolf, and with one voice men praised Enlil without fear. [13]

2. *Egypt.* Garden-parks (Egyp. *kȝn.w*, later *kȝm;* [14] cf. Heb. *kerem*, → כֶּרֶם *gephen*) with trees and flowers were popular in ancient Egypt. [15] In particular, the garden was regarded as a place of love; love poetry likes to speak of meetings among the flowers of the garden. [16]

In the text accompanying a relief depicting a beautiful garden (from the 18th dynasty), the owner expresses the wish that after his death he might "walk through the garden in the west, refresh himself under its sycamores, and admire its large and beautiful plantations." [17] The idea of a wonderful garden as the distant abode of happiness, which was widespread in the ancient Near East, was also given distinctive emphasis in Egypt. It was connected here with the idea of the realm of the dead. Under the partly contradictory concepts of the realm of the dead, Egyptian texts frequently speak of a country northeast of heaven. It is the fruitful "country of food or sacrifice" (*śḫt ḥtp*), or the country of Earu ("rushes") (*śḫt iȝrw*), which has been called "the idealized hereafter of Egyptian

---

[8] *ANET*³, 43f.
[9] Kramer.
[10] Widengren, 9f.
[11] *Ibid.*, 5f.
[12] H. Genge, *AcOr,* 33 (1971), 321-334.
[13] S. N. Kramer, *The Sumerians* (1963), 285; A. Falkenstein, *CRRA,* 2 (1951), 16.
[14] *WbÄS,* V, 106f.
[15] Erman-Ranke, *Ägypten und ägyptisches Leben im Altertum* (²1923), 203-211.
[16] *Ibid.,* 209f.; A. Hermann, *Altägyptische Liebesdichtung* (1959), 121.
[17] *Urk.,* IV, 73.

peasants."[18] The Egyptians believed that the dead lived there in security and abundance. The rich crops of this heavenly country, e.g., the tall grain, served as food for the dead. The island realm of the gods was certainly not without the attractions of the garden. We may assume this from the Egyptians' delight in flowers and gardens.[19]

The concept of a happy Primeval Age characterized by the rule of *maat* or right order may also be found in Egyptian literature.[20]

II. In the OT.

1. *Distribution.* The word *gan* does not occur very often in the OT. It is found in very specific writings, viz., in Genesis and Deuteronomy, in the historical books 1 and 2 Kings, in the prophets Isaiah, Jeremiah, Ezekiel, and Joel, and in the late writings Canticles, Lamentations, and Nehemiah.

2. *Secular Usage.* A wholly secular use of *gan* appears in Dt. 11:10 and 1 K. 21:2, which speak of a vegetable garden (*gan hayyaraq*); in 2 K. 9:27, where it probably occurs in a proper name; and in 2 K. 21:18,26; 25:4; Jer. 39:4; 52:7; Neh. 3:15, which speak of the king's garden. The simile in Isa. 58:11 speaks of a *gan raveh,* "a watered garden," while Cant. 4:12 refers to a *gan naʻul,* "a locked garden," as a symbol of the inaccessible and unassailable beloved.

From antiquity Palestine has had many gardens. Gardens were not owned merely by the king. People liked to plant gardens, usually fruit gardens, near fountains or springs. These fruit gardens were true oases for man and beast when the ground was parched, especially in late summer. Canticles contains a detailed description of an Israelite garden with its abundant growth of trees.[21]

3. *Translation of gan in the LXX; pardes.* When *gan* is used to describe the garden of Eden and the garden of God, the LXX translates it with the foreign word *parádeisos,* "paradise." The cognate word in Hebrew, *pardes,* occurs only three times in the OT, and that in late passages (Cant. 4:13; Eccl. 2:5; Neh. 2:8). It is an Iranian loanword (Old Persian *paridaida;* Avest. *pairidaēza,* lit. "enclosure") and means "orchard, park."[22] Thus, it has the same secular meaning as *gan.* The LXX was the first to lift this word out of the secular into the religious sphere.[23] It was introduced into the Vulgate by Jerome, and consequently became the usual term for the garden of God.[24] This elevated religious meaning does not

---

[18] *RÄR,* 161.

[19] Kroll; cf. *RÄR,* 161f.; R. Weill, *Le champ de roseaux et le champ des offrandes dans la religion funéraire et la religion générale. Études d'égyptologie,* 3 (Paris, 1936).

[20] S. Morenz, *Egyptian Religion* (trans. 1973), 114.

[21] An instructive and detailed investigation of Palestinian gardens may be found in Brock-Utne, 8ff.

[22] Cf. *pardēsu,* which seldom appears in late Bab. texts, *AHw,* 833.

[23] But cf. Westermann, 287: "the same ideas that we connect with the foreign word 'paradise'."

[24] *TDNT,* V, 766.

apply to Gen. 2:8, but all other passages reflect what we call the OT concept of paradise.

4. Ideas Concerning Paradise.

a. *The Geography of Paradise. gan* is also the term used for the first garden of the world, which Yahweh himself planted according to the Yahwistic account of creation: Gen. 2:8f.,10(?),16; 3:1-3,8,10. According to 2:8, Yahweh planted this garden in → עֵדֶן *'ēdhen*, lit. *be'edhen miqqedhem*, "in Eden, in the east." Since the reader would understand *miqqedhem* as a direction, according to Gressmann Eden is the proper name of a land which the speaker locates in an easterly direction, i.e., in the far east. According to Westermann, the writer uses the term *miqqedhem* to indicate that the place where the events in Gen. 2 occurred was "far away in an unknown land." [25] In fact we do not have here specific historico-geographical ideas, although the garden was obviously located in Mesopotamia where the Euphrates and Tigris rivers originate (cf. 2 K. 19:12; Isa. 37:12). [26] For modern scholars the material sense of *'edhen* in Gen. 2:8 is no more clear than *miqqedhem*, but *'edhen* is undoubtedly a geographical term in this passage. The same cannot be said for the other passages in which *gan* and *'edhen* appear together, e.g., Gen. 2:15; 3:23,24; Ezk. 36:35; Joel 2:3. Usually it is assumed that in these passages the name of the territory in which the garden was located has been transferred to the garden itself. Since Eden was obviously the name of a fruitful territory, the garden of Eden can hardly mean anything other than a particularly fruitful garden. This idea of a beautiful, well-watered orchard was reinforced for the Israelite by the name Eden, for in this word he caught an echo of the Hebrew word *'eden*, "delight."

b. *gan As the Garden of God. gan*, the garden of the Primeval Age, receives a second very specific interpretation in the expression "garden of Yahweh" (Gen. 13:10), which Ezekiel changes to "garden of God" (Ezk. 31:8). "Garden of God" can stand for Eden (28:13; 31:9); "garden of Yahweh" is used in parallelism with Eden in Isa. 51:3.

The expression "garden of God" emphasizes the close connection between God and the garden of the Primeval Age. While the name "garden of Eden," at least originally, derives from the location of the primeval garden, the name "garden of God" refers to the planter and owner of the garden. This seems to be rooted in ancient Canaanite ideas, for the fruitful land which was watered by natural springs and abounded in trees "was from early times regarded as a land of Baal in the specific sense." [27] This ancient Canaanite idea was then transferred

---

[25] *BK*, I, 287.

[26] Cf. further Gressmann. He bases his thesis of the foreign, i.e., Mesopotamian origin of the geography of Paradise partly on the pericope concerning the rivers of Paradise in Gen. 2:10-14 (which is not original in the context of the Yahwistic account of creation), and more especially on v. 14, which mentions the Tigris and Euphrates rivers.

[27] Gressmann, 349.

to Yahweh. While the geography of Paradise, as we saw above, points to elements which lead to Mesopotamia, the idea of the garden of God seems to suggest a Canaanite ancestry.

c. *Gen. 2.* There is no uniform concept of Paradise in the OT. In Gen. 2, the idea of Paradise is identical with the description of the earliest history of mankind. Vv. 9,15-17 in particular constitute the basis for the idea of Paradise in Gen. 2. Paradise is a part of God's creation, at the center of which is man. To be sure, in v. 9 the interest is still entirely in the garden itself: God makes trees grow in the garden of Paradise. But the reminiscence of the garden of God should not be overlooked here. Gen. 3:8 is based on the original idea that God lives in the garden of Paradise. Unmistakably, then, the garden has a significance of its own connected with its beauty and its relationship to God. Indeed, this independent significance is the main reason why it is possible to speak of a concept of Paradise from Gen. 2:9 on. (By way of contrast, 2:8 speaks only of a garden called Eden located in the east, which was planted for man to keep.) The concept of the beginning of human history is interwoven into this concept of Paradise. The first man (→ אדם *'ādhām*) is allowed to live in the garden of Paradise and he finds his sustenance in this garden. His task is to till and to keep this garden. The OT, then, does not represent Paradise as a place of blissful enjoyment. This must be stated unconditionally, for there are commentators who, because of a false, or at least nonbiblical understanding of man, have regarded v. 15bβ as a later insertion. [28] The work of man is a task which he is given by God, not service of God. On the other hand, man's work is not related to God mythically; it grows out of the environment in which God has placed him.

According to Gen. 2, man's relationship to his creator is determined by the command which he is given (vv. 16f.). This command of God defines the paradisiacal relationship of man to his creator. In Paradise, man lives in such close communion with God that he simply does what God wills. It is only when man transgresses God's commandment that he loses the paradisiacal dimension of his existence. (More precise textual analysis indicates that God's prohibition does not refer directly to the acquisition of knowledge [*da'ath,* → ידע *yādha'*, "to know"], but to the preservation of man from death.) But after he is driven out of Paradise, man yearns for the Paradise that he has lost.

d. *Ezk. 28.* The original mythical material in the funeral dirge over the king of Tyre originated in pre-Israelite contexts. If it is taken into account that Ezk. 28:13a might be an addition, vv. 11ff. do not simply contain the earlier concept of the garden of God. The earlier form of the tradition may also be discerned in the reference to a single human figure, the Primeval Man. For all the points of contact between Ezk. 28 and J's account of primeval history, which speaks of a first human couple, other deviations may be found at detailed points.

---

[28] Cf. in addition Westermann, *BK,* I, 300, where he enters into discussion with K. Budde and H. Gunkel, and shows that the ordinary idea of "blissful enjoyment" in Paradise may be found in the Koran and in Hesiod, but not in the Bible.

The concept of Paradise in Ezk. 28 begins with the mountain (→ הַר *har*) of God. [29] This mountain is the remote dwelling place of God, the place where the cherub stays and which he guards. As in Gen. 2, this passage clearly distinguishes between creator and creature. Man, from whose vicinity the dwelling place of God is far removed, is set in premises on the mountain of God. The additional characterization of the mountain of God as "holy" shows the late exilic origin of this verse about the prince of Tyre. In contrast to Gen. 2, Ezk. 28 distinguishes between the divine-heavenly and the human-earthly realms.

The primeval being with whom the king of Tyre is compared is described fully in all his beauty. The picture of this magnificent being is rounded off by an allusion to his irreproachable behavior at the dwelling place of God. The implicit assumption in Gen. 2 that man's original abode was in Paradise is explicitly emphasized here in Ezk. 28 in the manner of P. The wrong that the king of Tyre commits later is the reason for his ruin. Yahweh condemns him and hurls him down from the height of the mountain of God to the earth. The one who carries out God's decree of expulsion is the cherub, who appears here in the singular, in contrast to Gen. 3:24.

Jacobs-Hornig

[29] On locating Paradise on the cosmic mountain in the north, which seems to be in the background here, cf. also W. Zimmerli, *BK*, XIII, 685.

גָּנַב *gānabh*

Contents: I. Ancient Near Eastern Law. II. Philological Considerations: 1. Distribution and Meaning of *gnb*; 2. Use in the OT. III. Judicial and Historical Examples: 1. Stealing People (Kidnapping): a. In the Decalog and Book of the Covenant; b. In Narrative Texts; 2. Stealing Possessions (Theft): a. In the Decalog and Book of the Covenant; b. In Narrative Texts. IV. Ethical and Religious Use of *gnb*: 1. Later Passages; 2. Ethical Evaluation.

I. **Ancient Near Eastern Law.** Ancient Babylonian law, in the Code of Hammurabi, frequently speaks of "stealing," and goes into much greater detail on this subject than does the OT. "Stealing" includes several kinds of embezzle-

---

gānabh. A. Alt, "Das Verbot des Diebstahls im Dekalog," *KlSchr*, I, 333-340; T. Delleman, "Het zevende gebod," *De thora in de thora. Een Boek van de tien geboden*, ed. T. Delleman, II (1964), 56-88; F. Horst, "Der Diebstahl im AT," *Festschrift P. Kahle* (1935), 19-28=*Gottes Recht. ThB*, 12 (1961), 167-175; B. S. Jackson, *Theft in Early Jewish Law* (1972); E. Nielsen, *The Ten Commandments in New Perspective. SBT*, N.S. 7 (trans. 1968); A. Phillips, *Ancient Israel's Criminal Law* (1970); H. Presker, "κλέπτω," *TDNT*, III, 754-56; H. Graf Reventlow, *Gebot und Predigt im Dekalog* (1962), 79-81; H. Schulz, *Das Todesrecht im AT. Studien zur Rechtsform der Mot-Jumat-Sätze. BZAW*, 114 (1969); J. J. Stamm-M. E. Andrew, *The Ten Commandments in Recent Research. SBT*, N.S. 2 (²1967), 101-107.

Special Literature on I: G. R. Driver-J. C. Miles, *The Babylonian Laws* (Oxford, 1952-55); C. H. Gordon, "Nuzi Tablets Relating to Theft," *Or*, 5 (1936), 305-330; I. M. Lurje, *Studien zum altägyptischen Recht. Forsch. z. Röm. Recht*, 30 (Weimar, German trans. 1971); M. San Nicolò, "Diebstahl," *RLA*, II, 212-15, with literature.

ment (cf. Ex. 22:8-14 [Eng. vv. 9-15]). In the Code of Hammurabi, the death penalty is required for kidnapping children (§ 14). More serious types of theft, such as stealing things that belong to the temple or to the king, are also punishable by death (§ 6). A later stratum in this Code requires that a thief make thirtyfold restitution for things stolen from the temple or the king, and tenfold for things stolen from a citizen. If the thief cannot make this payment, he is to be put to death (so also § 256). At an earlier time, all serious thefts and burglaries seem to have been punished by death (§§ 7,9-11,21,25), and embezzlement of seed or fodder, by cutting off the hands (§ 253), while assessment of fines for theft (§§ 259f.) was a later practice. If a herdsman steals a cow entrusted to him, he must restore it tenfold (§ 265).

In Assyrian law, stealing in certain cases was punished by death (e.g., stealing by a wife, § 3),[1] but other penalties include the mutilation of ears and nose (§§ 4f.), fines, beating with rods, and forced labor.[2] In a later period (8th/7th century B.C.), only fines in cash or kind are mentioned.[3]

Hittite law lists various kinds of stealing, all of which are punished by fines in cash or kind (§§ 57ff.).[4] In cases of stealing livestock, the age of the animals is also taken into consideration. Frequently these laws state that the earlier very high price for recompense is now reduced to half the original amount. The only kind of theft punishable by death in Hittite law is stealing a bronze lance on the palace gate (§ 126). §§ 19-21 deal with kidnapping people of varying worth. Regulations concerning theft in Nuzi are also more humane than those in Old Babylonia and Assyria.[5]

The essential difference between these laws and those of the OT is that the punishments for crimes of theft in extrabiblical laws are much more rigorous. In the early period especially, punishment by death and mutilation was not rare in the ancient Near East, even for stealing possessions. In spite of similarities in form and content, it is not likely that the laws of the OT are dependent directly on ancient Near Eastern laws. Instead, both probably come from a "common legal culture."[6]

No law codes from ancient Egypt have been discovered. Records from the New Kingdom, however, reveal that, in addition to making restitution, a thief had to pay a fine of more than twice or three times the value of the stolen item in cases of theft of personal possessions. Thefts of temple property were regarded as serious crimes and were punished by a hundred lashes and a hundred-fold restitution. Thieves who stole temple livestock were threatened with mutilation of the nose and ears, and also with enslavement. Anyone who plundered tombs in the Necropolis was to be put to death by impalement.[7]

---

[1] *ANET*, 180.

[2] *ANET*, 187.

[3] San Nicolò, 214.

[4] *ANET*, 192-94.

[5] Cf. Gordon, 313.

[6] A. Alt, "The Origins of Israelite Law," *Essays on OT History and Religion* (trans. 1966), 98 (= *KlSchr*, I, 290).

[7] Cf. Lurje, 154-160.

II. Philological Considerations.

1. *Distribution and Meaning of gnb.* The root *gnb* appears in almost all Semitic languages. [8] It has not yet been found in Ugaritic. [9] The Akkadian word for "to steal" is *šarāqu*, and the Arabic word is *saraqa*. If there is a connection between Heb. *gnb* and Arab. *ǧanb*, "side," Aram. and Syr. *gab(b)*, the original meaning of this root was "to remove, keep away (secretly)" (so Arab. *ǧanaba*). (*ǧanb*, however, could be a primary noun independent of the verbal root *gnb*.) In its original meaning, the verb can be ethically neutral, as in Job 21:18; 27:20: chaff which the wind carries away; cf. also 2 S. 19:4,42(3,41); 21:12; 2 K. 11:2.

2. *Use in the OT.* The root *gnb* is found 55 times in the OT: 36 times as a verb, 17 times (besides Sir. 5:14) as a noun *gannabh* = the (habitual) thief (whence the Yiddish word "ganove"), in contrast to the participle *gonebh* = the actual thief (these two words appear in the same context in Zec. 5:3f.). The technical term *genebhah*, "that which is stolen," appears only in Ex. 22:2f.(3f.). Probably the proper name Genubath (1 K. 11:20) also should be regarded as coming from this root. [10]

The root *gnb* appears most frequently in the qal, where it has a transitive meaning. The niphal, which has a passive meaning, is found only in Ex. 22:11 (12). The piel contains the idea of result in this root: [11] "to acquire by stealing" [12] (2 S. 15:6; Jer. 23:30—both times with a figurative meaning: "Absalom stole the hearts of the men of Israel"; "the prophets stole my words from one another"). Moreover, the pual appears in Gen. 40:15 and Ex. 22:6(7), where it means "to be stolen," and in Job 4:12, where it means "to be stolen away to" (*'el*) = to be brought secretly. [13] The hithpael occurs only in 2 S. 19:4(3), and means "to steal aside" = to go away secretly. In all these cases, the original meaning is retained. It is not necessary to assume additional semasiological derivatives after the analogy of the Arabic. [14] The semantic field of the root, however, extends from "removing (secretly)" to "cheating": Gen. 31:27: "you cheated me" (*'othi*). The use of *gnb* with *lebh*, "heart," conveys a similar thought: "you cheated my heart" (Gen. 31:20,26; so similarly the piel in 2 S. 15:6). [15] The Greek words *kléptein*, "to steal," [16] and *kléptōn*, "secret (stealthy)" (Tob. 1:18), form a parallel to this use of *gnb*.

The element of secrecy distinguishes stealing from robbing. Again, robbery is often carried out by larger or smaller bands, and in the early period included plundering foreign peoples [17] (→ גזל *gzl*, "to rob," cf. also Ex. 3:22). Never-

---

[8] *KBL³*, 190.
[9] However, cf. PN *bn gnb*, CTA, 93, 7; 133, I, 1; *UT*, 598.
[10] *KBL³*, 191.
[11] E. Jenni, *Das hebr. Pi'el* (1968), 190f.
[12] *KBL³*.
[13] *GesB*.
[14] L. Kopf, *VT*, 8 (1958), 169; 9 (1959), 250f.
[15] See above.
[16] Cf. *GesB; TDNT*, III, 754.
[17] Jackson, 6-14.

theless, the distinction between these two words is fluid: "thieves and robbers" stand side by side in Ob. 5; Ep. Jer. 57; Jn. 10:1,8. Occasionally the verb → לקח lāqach, "to take," can also mean "to steal" or "to rob" (e.g., in Jgs. 17:2; 18:17f., 24; cf. Josh. 7:11; also Gen. 6:2[?]).

III. Judicial and Historical Examples.

1. Stealing People (Kidnapping).

a. *In the Decalog and Book of the Covenant.* Stealing people (kidnapping) is mentioned in the Book of the Covenant (which is probably Elohistic, but which goes back into the period of the judges from a traditio-historical perspective). It occurs in Ex. 21:16, in the very ancient form of a *"moth*-statute" (a statute in which the penalty for a crime is death),[18] and similarly in Dt. 24:7. The victim here is a free Israelite citizen (*'ish,* "man"); that Ex. 21:16 originally had in mind only kidnapping members of one's *own* family[19] would seem to be too narrow. Such kidnapping and selling is not much less than murder.

Since the work of Alt, many exegetes assume that what is known as the seventh (eighth) commandment: "you shall not steal" (Ex. 20:15; Dt. 5:19), was directed originally against stealing people (kidnapping). In the three brief homogeneous commands, "you shall not kill, you shall not commit adultery, you shall not steal," the first two clearly have to do with crimes against basic personal rights. Furthermore, the law against coveting (Ex. 20:17; → חמד *ḥmd*) a neighbor's possessions (including his wife, manservant, and maidservant) was listed separately when the Decalog was (later) given its form as a total unit.

Of course, one might expect the verb "to steal" to have an object after it. The etymology of *gnb* and all the examples in which the root occurs oppose the view that it once meant "to steal persons."[20] Moreover, that *'ish,* "man," or something similar, was at one time used with *gnb* is only a hypothesis. Thus Alt's conjecture can indeed be inferred from the context and from Ex. 21:16, but it cannot be proved absolutely.[21] In any case, the short prohibition was open to a general interpretation at a later time. It is interesting that the Rabbis still interpreted Ex. 20:15 as a prohibition against stealing persons (kidnapping).[22]

b. *In Narrative Texts.* In the narrative texts, there is a clear example of kidnapping in the account of the Egyptian Joseph, where the pual, "to be stolen" (Gen. 40:15), mentioned in II.2 above, refers back to the unlawful act of his brothers in "putting him away" by selling him to the Midianites (37:28). The verb "to steal" is not used in the special case of the joint abduction of the

---

[18] See esp. Schulz, 36-40; also G. Liedke, *Gestalt und Bezeichnung alttestamentlicher Rechtssätze. WMANT,* 39 (1971), 120-138.

[19] Liedke, 132f.

[20] A. Jepsen, *ZAW,* 79 (1967), 294.

[21] Cf. Jackson, 148f.; and *HUCA,* 42 (1971), 198-207.

[22] Gottstein, *ThZ,* 9 (1953), 394f.; Petuchowski, *VT,* 7 (1957), 397f.; also Jackson, 148, n. 5.

women in Jgs. 21:15-23. [23] In 2 S. 19:42(41), the men of Israel refer to David's hasty return to Jerusalem as "stealing" (kidnapping), and 2 K. 11:2 (=2 Ch. 22:11) uses the word "steal" to describe the way in which Jehosheba secretly took away the prince Joash and hid him.

2. *Stealing Possessions (Theft).*

a. *In the Decalog and Book of the Covenant.* In contrast to the penal law of ancient Babylonia, in Israel the death penalty was required only in cases of kidnapping. At most, only persons, not things, enjoyed legal protection. [24] Even though death is sometimes suggested as a punishment for theft in exuberant emotional statements in narrative texts (Gen. 31:32; 44:9; 2 S. 12:5), this does not mean that there was a basis for this in ancient legal practice. We have already dealt with the problem of Ex. 20:15 and 17 above. Stealing livestock was a particularly acute problem from earliest times. The casuistic legal maxim in Ex. 22:1(2) contains the general rule: "If a thief is found breaking in, and is struck so that he dies, there shall be no bloodguilt for him." Verse 2(3) indicates that this law applies to a thief who broke in during the night: "but if the sun has risen upon him, there shall be bloodguilt for him." The difference is that at night the situation is more uncertain and dangerous, and usually no helpers are available, so that an urgent need for self-defense may be assumed. Verse 2b(3b) decrees: "A thief shall make restitution; if he has nothing, then he shall be sold for his theft" (and not be put to death, as is required in the Code of Hammurabi). Just before this we find the general precept (Ex. 21:37[22:1]): "If a man steals an ox or a sheep, and kills it or sells it, he shall pay five oxen for an ox, and four sheep for a sheep" (the idea of restoring "fourfold" also occurs in 2 S. 12:6). [25] Such multiple compensation is adequate punishment, and since an ox is much more valuable than a sheep, the restitution made for a stolen ox must be higher than that for a stolen sheep. Full proof is provided by slaughter or sale. On the other hand, if the animal is still alive in the thief's possession and thus it is still possible to return it to its owner, the customary double restitution is sufficient (22:3[4]). Daube thinks that 22:3(4), and the phrase "or is found in possession of him" in 21:16, are later expansions, [26] contra Noth, [27] while Jackson takes a middle position, [28] not wanting to rule out the possibility that in all ages possession alone was evidence of theft. Ex. 22:6-8(7-9) again deals in general with money or valuables that are brought to another person's house for safekeeping. If some of these are stolen and the thief is found, he must pay double (v. 6[7]). If the thief is not found, the owner of the house shall "come near to God" (v. 7[8]), which means that he shall swear by an oath of cleansing that he has not embezzled the

---

[23] See H. J. Boecker, *Redeformen des Rechtslebens im AT. WMANT,* 14 (²1970), 36f.

[24] Cf. Phillips, 141.

[25] Cf. A. Phillips, *VT,* 16 (1966), 242-44.

[26] D. Daube, in *Von Ugarit nach Qumran. Festschrift O. Eissfeldt. BZAW,* 77 (²1961), 33f.

[27] M. Noth, *Exodus. OTL* (trans. 1962), 180, 183.

[28] Jackson, 47f.

things himself (cf. also the oath of malediction in the case of unsolved theft at Qumran, CD 9:11f.). Verse 8(9) lays down similar laws for the theft of property of all kinds. [29] In private complaints another means of redress was to pronounce a public curse against the unknown thief: Jgs. 17:2; Prov. 29:24; cf. Lev. 5:1. Ordinary theft was also committed to the judgment of God by subsidiary devices of this kind (1 K. 8:31f.).

b. *In Narrative Texts.* Occasionally narrative texts contain accounts of theft. Rachel stole her father's teraphim (Gen. 31:19,30,32). Joseph's brothers were charged with stealing his silver cup (44:4[LXX],8). Josh. 7:11 uses the word "steal" in describing Achan's embezzlement of the devoted thing (→ חרם *ḥrm*). Such a flagrant theft had to be punished by death, not so much because of the act of stealing itself, as because the entire people had come under a curse through Achan's transgression. According to Jgs. 17:1-4, Micah stole 1100 pieces of silver from his mother. Moved by her curse, he confessed that he was the thief and restored the amount to her without making any additional restitution in this internal family affair. According to 2 S. 21:12, the citizens of Jabesh secretly "removed," i.e., carried away, the bones of Saul. The idea that eating a neighbor's grapes and standing grain while one is in his neighbor's vineyard or field does not constitute stealing (Dt. 23:25f.[24f.]) is magnanimous and humane.

IV. Ethical and Religious Use of gnb.

1. *Later Passages.* In addition to laws and concrete examples, the verb "to steal" and in particular the substantive "thief" are often used to denote a criminal act. Hos. 4:2 contains the list: "swearing, lying, killing, stealing, and committing adultery." A similar list appears in Jer. 7:9: "steal, murder, commit adultery, swear falsely." These lists are connected with the prohibitions in the ethical Decalog, but in the days of Hosea and Jeremiah, of course, the fixed form of the whole Decalog was not yet established. In these descriptions of ethical corruption, "stealing" is probably intended in a general sense, [30] and the same is true of the list of prohibitions in the Holiness Code (Lev. 19:11; cf. also Ps. 50:18). The sudden invasion of enemies is compared to thieves that come in the night (Jer. 49:9; Ob. 5; cf. 1 Thess. 5:2; Job 24:14). Isaiah calls the leading circles of Jerusalem "rebels and companions of thieves" (Isa. 1:23). When a thief is caught, he reaps public shame and contempt (Jer. 2:26; 48:27; Job 30:5; Prov. 6:30; Sir. 5:14). Surprisingly only Prov. 6:31 speaks of punishment for theft. Here, "sevenfold" and "all his goods" are intended only in a hyperbolic and proverbial sense. The Israelites seem to have abandoned restitution to the victim and to have turned a blind eye, especially if the thief was poor (Prov. 6:30; cf. 30:9).

---

[29] For a detailed investigation of Ex. 22:8(9), cf. R. Knierim, *Die Hauptbegriffe für Sünde im AT* ([2]1967), 143-174.

[30] Cf. W. Richter, *Recht und Ethos. StANT,* 15 (1966), 128, n. 23; contra Phillips, 131.

2. *Ethical Evaluation.* The ethical consciousness of all men concurs that stealing is wrong. An additional point in the OT is that it is a social crime against the tribal and national community and a sin against God himself. Therefore the verb *gnb,* which is almost always used negatively when referring to morals, is never applied to God in the OT. It is hardly possible to discern a gradual alleviation or aggravation of the seventh commandment, whether with reference to kidnapping or theft, even if social and legal development in general gives the impression that an increasing effort was made to establish security and order, especially in the monarchical period. [31] The prophets in particular opposed moral decay of every type. Zec. 5:3f. states explicitly that a "curse" goes out from God to consume the house of the thief and the one who swears falsely. Only personified "folly" subscribes to the frivolous statement: "Stolen water is sweet, and bread eaten in secret is pleasant" (Prov. 9:17), although these statements are, of course, to be understood figuratively of all deeds performed in secrecy, especially adultery. Theft is not a theme of traditional Wisdom teaching. Everyone sees that it is reprehensible.

Hamp

---

[31] Cf. Jackson, 151-53.

גָּעַל *gāʿal;* גֹּעַל *gōʿal;* גַּעַל *gaʿal*

Contents: I. 1. Etymology; 2. Occurrences in the OT. II. On Inscriptions: 1. Aramaic and Canaanite; 2. South Arabic. III. In the OT: 1. Semantic Field; 2. In the Niphal and Hiphil; Vestiges of the Original Usage; 3. In the Qal; A Technical Term Connected with the Covenant.

I. 1. *Etymology.* The root *gʿl* appears only in West Semitic languages, and even here is missing in Geʿez and Ugaritic.

It seems fairly certain that the Heb. verb *gaʿal* is related to Arab. *ǧaʿara,* "to drop dung" (of animals), [1] but probably not to *ǧaʿala,* "to make, place, lay";

---

gāʿal. J. Barth, *Wurzeluntersuchungen zum hebräischen und aramäischen Lexicon* (1902); J. Blau, "Über homonyme und angeblich homonyme Wurzeln," *VT,* 6 (1956), 242-48; R. Dussaud-Fr. Macler, *Voyage archéologique au Ṣafâ et dans le Djebel ed-Drūz* (Paris, 1901); idem, *Mission dans les regions désertiques de la Syrie moyenne* (Paris, 1903); A. Guillaume, "Hebrew and Arabic Lexicography," *Abr-Nahrain,* 1 (1959), 3-35 (repr. *Hebrew and Arabic Lexicography* [Leiden, 1965]); A. R. Johnson, "The Primary Meaning of √ גאל," *SVT,* 1 (1953), 66-77; R. Kilian, *Literarkritische und formgeschichtliche Untersuchung des Heiligkeitsgesetzes. BBB,* 19 (1963); Th. Nöldeke, *Beiträge zur semitischen Sprachwissenschaft* (1904); H. Graf Reventlow, *Das Heiligkeitsgesetz formgeschichtlich untersucht. WMANT,* 6 (1961); N. Rhodokanakis, *Studien zur Lexikographie und Grammatik des Altsüdarabischen,* I. *SAW,* 178/2 (Vienna, 1915); J. Scharbert, *Fleisch, Geist und Seele im Pentateuch. SBS,* 19 (1966).

[1] Guillaume, 8; Wehr, 127; → גער *gāʿar,* "to rebuke."

cf. also Tigré geʿel.[2] Jewish Aram. geʿal, which means "to soil, stain," in the pael,[3] is influenced by Heb. gʿl. gaʾal is found in conjunction with gaʿal in the Qumran texts (1QM 9:8; CD 12:16). Johnson's attempt to trace this form back to a common root, "to cover" > "cover with dirt" and "protect," "release, redeem" (→ גאל gāʾal),[4] may be regarded as incorrect; cf. Blau.[5]

2. *Occurrences in the OT.* The verb gaʿal appears 12 times in the OT.

a. It occurs 9 times in the qal: Lev. 26:11,15,30,43,44; Ezk. 16:45 (twice, in the acc.); Jer. 14:19 and Zec. 11:8 (with be, "in"). The translation of this form in the LXX is heterogeneous: Lev., *prosochthízō*, "to be angry, offended, provoked," and *bdelýssomai*, "to abhor, detest" (11 times); Jer., *aphístamai*, "to put away, stand aloof"; Ezk., *apōthéomai*, "to push aside, reject"; and Zec., *epōrýonto ep' emé*, "they rushed violently upon me."

b. It is found twice in the niphal: 2 S. 1:21 (the LXX translates *prosochízomai*, "to be angry, offended, provoked"); Sir. 31:16, if the text here is not emended[6] (the stich in which this word is found does not appear in the LXX).

c. It appears once in the hiphil: Job 21:10 (the LXX translates differently). The words found in the OT that are derived from the root gaʿal are goʿal, "abhorrence, abomination" (Ezk. 16:5; LXX *skoliótēs*, "crookedness, perversity, deceit"), and the proper name Gaal (Jgs. 9:26-41).[7] The LXX transliterates this as *Gaal;* cf. Josephus *Ant., Gyálēs.*[8]

II. On Inscriptions. In addition to the occurrences cited under I.1 above, outside the OT the root gʿl is found several times on inscriptions in personal names and place names.[9]

1. *Aramaic and Canaanite.* An Aramaic inscription speaks of a [bb]l šhd gʿlʾ,[10] and two Neo-Punic inscriptions speak of a lqy bn gʿlgst[11] and a "citizen of gʿl."[12]

2. *South Arabic.* On South Arabic inscriptions, we encounter the proper name Guʿal or Giʿal (Ḥaḍr. and Saf.).[13] gʿl is also preserved in the place names (Saf.) Guʿalat and (Sab.) Gawʿal.[14]

---

2 *TigrWb,* 594a.

3 Levy, *WTM,* I, 350.

4 Johnson, 72.

5 Blau, 244.

6 In agreement with Peters, Charles, etc.

7 Cf. Noth, *IPN,* 230, n. 17; contra Nöldeke, 88.

8 Schlatter, 38.

9 *KAI,* II, 277, in agreement with Noth, *IPN,* 230; etc.

10 *KAI,* 277.6.

11 *KAI,* 145.34.

12 *KAI,* 140.2.

13 Cf. Rhodokanakis, *WZKM,* 37 (1930), 295; Dussaud-Macler, *Voyage,* 22b; *idem, Mission,* 551, 740; Ryckmans, *Les noms propres sud-sémitiques* (1934), I, 62.

14 Ryckmans, I, 328, appealing to Grohmann, *Historisch-geographische Bemerkungen zu Glaser 418-419,* 1000, A, B.

III. In the OT.

1. *Semantic Field.* The following words belong to the same semantic field as *gaʿal: mr'* I, either as a denominative of *re'i,* "dung" (Zeph. 3:1), [15] or as a subordinate form of *mar* II (cf. *marah* II, "body of water with unpalatable water"); *šwṭ* II, "to treat with despite, despise" (cf. *shot,* "concentration of water"); and *tso'i,* "soiled with dung" (RSV "filthy," Zec. 3:3f.). [16] We may also mention *t'b,* "to treat or regard as a *to'ebhah,* an abomination," and *shiqqats,* "to detest as cultically unclean." Usually, → מאס *mā'as,* "to spurn, reject," appears in parallelism with *gaʿal* (Lev. 26:15,43,44; Jer. 14:19; Sir. 31:16).

2. *In the Niphal and Hiphil; Vestiges of the Original Usage.* In order to determine the specific meaning of *gaʿal,* it is best to begin with the niphal and hiphil, because it is still possible to recognize remnants of the original usage in these forms. The so-called Song of the Bow speaks of the "shield of the mighty" that is defiled (niphal, 2 S.1:21). The conclusion of this curse, which condemns the places of calamity to eternal barrenness, is textually doubtful. Therefore it cannot be decided with certainty whether the shields of the slain are "soiled" with their own blood, [17] or whether, since they are now lying around idle without the usual care, they are "corroded" with rust and filth. In any case, the emendation to *nigh'al,* "to be redeemed," [18] is unnecessary, and Hertzberg's translation, "was rejected," [19] is incorrect. Job 21:10 seems to have in mind a defilement connected with the impregnation of a cow. The text is disputed. Kittel and others emend it. Delitzsch assumes a causative meaning for the hiphil ("does not cause to pass over," i.e., semen). [20] Here *'ibbar,* "to impregnate" (RSV "breeds"), stands in parallelism with *gaʿal.* Probably the meaning is that the bull does not defile when he impregnates the cow, i.e., the impregnation does not fail. [21]

3. *In the Qal; A Technical Term Connected with the Covenant.* The qal describes the feeling which results from being soiled and unclean: loathing, abhorrence, disgust. This affective-intransitive meaning of *gaʿal* has been abandoned almost completely in the OT. Remnants of this original meaning still appear in the regular use of *nephesh,* "soul" (as the seat of feeling and emotion), [22] as the subject of *gaʿal* (with the exception of Ezk. 16:45), and in the construction with *be* in Jer. 14:19 and Zec. 11:8. *gaʿal,* however, has a transitive meaning in the OT: "to consider someone or something as dung and filth,"

---

[15] *KBL²,* 563, following Graetz.
[16] *KBL²,* 790.
[17] Leimbach, Kittel, etc.
[18] *BHK.*
[19] Hertzberg, *ATD,* X, 192; not in *OTL* (trans. 1964), 235.
[20] Cf. also Driver, *ICC,* 184: "causeth not (the cow) to loathe."
[21] Cf. Fohrer, *KAT,* XVI, 337.
[22] Cf. Scharbert, *SBS,* 19, 68.

(idiomatically:) "to regard someone as dirt." Accordingly, it takes a direct object when it has this meaning.

a. Israel regards Yahweh's ordinances as dung and filth (Lev. 26:43); it abhors them, since it runs after other gods and sacrifices on their high places (26:30; etc.). *gaʿal* here is very close to *tʿb,* "to regard as a *toʿebhah,* an abomination," and to the *toʿebhah*-lists (lists of abominations, as in Dt. 16:21–17:1), which, in sharp opposition to Canaanite religion, were designed to safeguard Yahweh's *berith* or covenant community against a complete Canaanization. [23] Instead of abhorring the gods of the land and their cults as dung and filth according to the statutes of Yahweh, Israel treats Yahweh and his ordinances as something to be loathed. Ezekiel takes up this thought when he holds up before Jerusalem and her inhabitants their heathen origin, which they never really overcame in spite of all Yahweh's efforts: "You are the daughter of your mother, who loathed her husband and her children; and you are the sister of your sisters, who loathed their husbands and their children" (Ezk. 16:45). The connection of *gaʿal* with *tʿb* and *toʿebhah* is particularly clear if the conjectural emendation of *ʾeghraʿ,* "I will withdraw," to *ʾeghʿal,* "I will loathe," in Ezk. 5:11 is justified. [24]

b. Yahweh will deal with his people accordingly; he will destroy their high places, cut down their incense altars, cast their dead bodies upon the dead bodies of their idols, and abhor them (Lev. 26:30), "as they also detested me" (Zec. 11:8). Yahweh will devastate the land, so that Israel's enemies will be astonished (Lev. 26:32), and the people will be scattered among the nations (Lev. 26:33). In view of this judgment, which Yahweh actually brought upon his people later, the lament of Jeremiah remains: "Hast thou utterly rejected Judah? Does thy soul loathe Zion?" (Jer. 14:19). On the other hand, when Israel obeys Yahweh's statutes and does not abhor them, Yahweh will make his abode among them and will not abhor them (Lev. 26:11). On the contrary, "I will walk among you, and will be your God, and you shall be my people" (Lev. 26:12).

c. Accordingly, *gaʿal* is part of the covenant theology of the OT, no matter how the covenant may be understood. *gaʿal* indicates that the *berith* or covenant relationship between Yahweh and his people has been utterly destroyed. The people have treated Yahweh and his statutes as *gʿl.* The result is that now Yahweh for his part treats his people as *gʿl.*

Fuhs

---

[23] Cf. J. L'Hour, "Les interdits Toʿeba dans le Deutéronome," *RB,* 71 (1964), 481-503; R. P. Merendino, *BBB,* 31 (1969), 326-336; etc.

[24] Cf. Elliger, *HAT,* 4 (1966), 377, n. 58 (contra Hitzig, Ewald, Cornill; Eichrodt and Zimmerli persist in arguing that *ʾeghraʿ* comes from → גרע *gāraʿ*): "since you have defiled my sanctuary with all your abominations (*toʿabhothayikh*), I will also abhor (you). . . ."

גָּעַר **gā'ar;** גְּעָרָה **ge'ārāh;** מִגְעֶרֶת **migh'ereth**

Contents: I. 1. Etymology; 2. Occurrences and Meaning. II. Secular Usage. III. Religious Usage.

I. 1. *Etymology.* Classical Arabic uses the root *ğ'r* in a wide variety of senses. Thus, we find *ği'ār,* "rope that is stretched around the waist to climb into a well." The denominative *tağa''ara,* "to gird oneself with a *ği'ār,*" is derived from this. The Arabic also has a verb *ğa'ara,* "to have a bowel movement," which can also mean "to scream, cry out," in the postclassical period. Then a verb *ğa'ar* develops in the Arabic dialects meaning "to roar, bleat, low," denoting various sounds of animals. We also encounter this root in Ethiopic as *ga'ara/ğě'ěra,* meaning "to sigh, weep, cry out for help." The meaning of the root *ğ'r,* which phonetically is very similar to *ğ'r* and in Classical Arabic means "to bleat, scream," or "to shout at someone," corresponds to this. It is very doubtful whether one may assume a relationship between these two roots, nor can the transfer of the meanings of *ğ'r* to *ğ'r* be clarified etymologically.

In the Aramaic dialects, Syr. *ge'ar* presents almost the same problems as the Biblical Heb. *g'r* (which it translates occasionally), but a subst. *ge'artā,* "lament," also occurs. The verb *ge'ar* is used in Christian Palestinian to translate *krázein,* "to cry out, scream" (Mk. 9:24).

The Ugaritic use of *g'r* deserves consideration. In a hippiatric text,[1] *g'r* denotes a disease of horses, possibly "wheezing" (which is characterized by abnormally noisy breathing). The other occurrences of *g'r* are in mythological texts. In RS 24.256,[2] line 14, *g'r b* is used to express the rebukes of a member of the divine assembly against the goddess; these rebukes are then communicated verbatim. Similarly, in *CTA,* 2 [III AB], I, 24, Baal reproves the gods because of their cowardice toward Yam, and in *CTA,* 2 [III AB], IV, 28, Baal rebukes 'Athtart in order to shame her for her behavior. In these three passages *g'r* denotes the vehement sound of a reproving speech.

2. *Occurrences and Meaning.* In Biblical Hebrew the verb *ga'ar* occurs 14 times, always in the qal. Ten times it is construed with the preposition *be* to denote the recipient of the invective; in the four remaining passages (Ps. 9:6 [Eng. v. 5]; 68:31[30]; 119:21; Mal. 2:3) the verb is transitive. The substantive

---

gā'ar. P. Joüon, "Notes de lexicographie hébraïque," *Bibl,* 6 (1925), 318-321; H. C. Kee, "The Terminology of Mark's Exorcism Stories," *NTS,* 14 (1968-69), 232-246; A. A. Macintosh, "A Consideration of Hebrew גער," *VT,* 19 (1969), 471-79; J. Pedersen, *Der Eid bei den Semiten* (1914), 82; S. C. Reif, "A Note on גער," *VT,* 21 (1971), 241-44; F. M. Seely, "Note on G'RH with Especial Reference to Prov. 13:8," *BT,* 10 (1959), 20f.; P. J. van Zijl, "A Discussion of the Root *gā'ar,*" *Biblical Essays. Proceedings of the 12th Meeting of De Ou Testamentiese Werkgemeenskap in Suid Afrika* (1969), 56-63.

[1] *CTA,* 161, 23.
[2] *Ugaritica,* V, 545f.

geʿarah is found 15 times in the OT; it is usually construed with a genitive or a possessive suffix to denote the one acting; it appears in the absolute only 3 times in Proverbs (Prov. 13:1,8; 17:10). The other substantive derived from this root, *mighʿereth*, occurs only in Dt. 28:20 (in the absolute). Provisionally, the etymology of the root *gʿr* suggests that *gaʿar* should be translated "to scream, cry out," and *geʿarah,* "scream, cry." But the context alone can establish this meaning and give it greater precision.

II. Secular Usage. In three passages the verb *gaʿar* has a human subject. In this connection, Ruth 2:16 is particularly enlightening, because it seems to reflect daily usage. The reapers are instructed by Boaz not "to rebuke Ruth" when she joins them to pluck ears of grain. Here *gaʿar* conveys more the idea of "rebuff" than "reproof"; the reapers are more inclined to drive Ruth away with their cries than to reprove her because of her behavior. On the other hand, the nuance "reproof" can clearly be seen in Gen. 37:10, where Jacob "cries out against" Joseph in condemnation of his arrogant dreams concerning his own greatness. Jacob's affection for Joseph might justify one's softening the meaning of *gaʿar* to "reprimand," but this does not exclude the fact that the author used this verb to emphasize the severity of the reprimand. Gen. 37:10 is the only passage that implies clear moral disapproval. Jer. 29:27 is more difficult; a prophet among the Babylonian exiles is astonished that the priest Zephaniah, who has thrown the prophet in prison, has not "cried out" against Jeremiah. Does this mean that he has not given vent to his anger against Jeremiah, or that he has not lifted up his voice against Jeremiah? The LXX, which renders *gaʿar* by *epitimán,* "to reprimand," in Ruth 2:16 and Gen. 37:10, translates it by *loidoreín,* "to reproach," in Jer. 29:27, which favors the former interpretation.

Nor is the meaning of the substantive *geʿarah* entirely clear when it is used in connection with a noun or a possessive suffix and carries a human reference. The military figures in Isa. 30:16 would allow one to translate *geʿarah* in v. 17 (twice) "battle-cry," but it is also possible to render it "threat." In Eccl. 7:5, "the *geʿarah* of the wise" is contrasted with "the *shir* of fools." If we translate *geʿarah* here as "reproach," then we must render *shir* "hymn of praise," which is not entirely certain; *geʿarah* here could mean simply "grunt." It is necessary, however, to consider the special nuance of the word in the language of the Wisdom Literature. Two passages in the book of Proverbs show that it is certainly possible for *geʿarah* to mean "reproach" or "reproof." In Prov. 13:1, *geʿarah* is used in synonymous parallelism with *musar,* "instruction" (the verb *shamaʿ,* "to hear," appears in both halves of this verse); and 17:10 teaches that a *geʿarah* addressed to a wise man is more effective than a hundred blows inflicted on a fool. The third passage in Proverbs is problematic. If we do not wish to emend the text of Prov. 13:8, the second line contains an elliptical sentence, and it is difficult to reconstruct the author's train of thought. It is impossible to accept the interpretations proposed by Rashi ("the rich man can ransom himself for eternal life because he gives alms, provided that he does not *wrong* the poor man to whom he gives them," or "in contrast to the rich man, the poor man is not able to prevent evil, because he does not know the *threats* of the law"). Modern commentators understand the contrast between rich and poor in the sense that the rich must pay a ransom, while the poor "hears no threat," i.e., is not in any danger of being taken captive. [3] Other hypotheses could be considered, e.g., "the rich buys his freedom with money, for the poor (thief) does not hear the cry (of the captive)." The text, however, is too obscure to be of use in defining the word geʿarah.

III. **Religious Usage.** The religious use of gaʿar and geʿarah is concentrated in the lyric and prophetic literature of the OT. These words have a strong anthropopathic thrust, and almost always denote a threatening manifestation of the anger of God. When it is said that God "cries out," what is in mind is certainly not his mild judicial action in handing down a sentence. On the contrary, God is viewed as a fierce warrior who "cries out" in anger to drive away his enemies. Here God's appearances as a gentle judge and loving teacher are no longer in the forefront. Those who are addressed in the invectives containing gaʿar are various enemies of Yahweh, everything that is symbolized by chaos in nature and revolt in history.

The waters and the sea represent the primeval powers of chaos, which Yahweh (like the Ugaritic Baal) had to conquer in order to ensure the establishment of the universe. The derivatives of gaʿar frequently appear in poetic references to the victory that God won over the waters; so Ps. 18:16(15)(=2 S. 22:16), where the parallelism between Yahweh's geʿarah and "the blast of the breath of the nostrils" shows that "crying out" and "panting" refer here to a physical demonstration of the divine anger and not to the giving of a reprimand. The adjoining figures of "arrows" and the "lightning" indicate that the manifestation of the geʿarah is hardly to be distinguished from the phenomena that accompany a storm. This interpretation is confirmed by Ps. 104:7, where geʿarah is used in parallelism with "thunder." In the epiphany of world judgment in Isa. 66:15, where the motif of Ps. 18:16(15) is eschatologically refashioned, geʿarah is connected with the figure of flames of fire. Elsewhere, the divine geʿarah is closely related to the releasing of a (strong) wind that can dry up the sea (Isa. 50:2). Nah. 1:4 and Isa. 50:2 both connect geʿarah with a hurricane. The close connection between Yahweh's geʿarah and a storm is still perceptible in a marginal reading of manuscript B from the Cairo Genizah and in the Masada fragment of Sir. 43:13 (the text itself reads gebhurah, "strength, might"): the geʿarah of Yahweh brings hail and lightning, it activates cosmic storms.

By the well-known process of historicization, the metaphors of the cosmic battle could be used to express the motif of Yahweh's war against the enemies of his people. The Egyptians who were slain at the Red Sea are the primeval type of these enemies. Therefore the "beast in the reed" (which appears as the obj. of gaʿar) in Ps. 68:31(30) may also mean Egypt or another historical enemy with Egyptian characteristics. But this verse poses a special problem. It is not certain that Yahweh is the subject here. The subject could also be the earthly

---

[3] Cf. Seely.

king (called *'elohim*) whom the psalmist summons in v. 29(28). If this is the case, the poet has here transferred a divine predicate to the sacral king. On the other hand, in Ps. 76:7(6) Yahweh's *geʿarah* puts to flight the aggressors (the Assyrians) under the symbol of horses and chariots (cf. the Egyptians in Ex. 15:1,21). In Ps. 80:17(16), the author prays for the divine *geʿarah* to come upon an enemy that has destroyed Jerusalem. Here *geʿarah* is qualified by *paneykha,* "thy countenance," which indicates the operative side of the phenomenon which can as such be experienced. What the psalmist has in mind is the cry or breath of God's countenance, not its threatening features. The "nations" in general, who must vanish before Yahweh's omnipotence, are the object of *gaʿar* in Ps. 9:6(5) (cf. Isa. 17:13).

Occasionally the divine wrath also comes upon Israel. Isa. 51:20 says that "the daughters of Jerusalem" have become victims of the *geʿarah* of Yahweh; it uses the word *chemah,* "wrath," parallel with *geʿarah.* Ps. 119:21 says that *geʿarah* also rages against the insolent who do not believe in the word of God. The Wisdom tone of Ps. 119 is not sufficient reason to give *gaʿar* the softer meaning "to reprove," as in the secular examples in the book of Proverbs. Similarly, in Dt. 28:20 Yahweh threatens Israel with *mighʿereth* (RSV "frustration") in case of disobedience. It is difficult to determine the exact meaning of this hapax legomenon, but it may be observed that it is used with expressions that are surprisingly very general, viz., *meʿerah,* "curse," and *mehumah,* "confusion," to introduce the list of concrete calamities which follows. Thus *mighʿereth* would seem to refer to the wrath of Yahweh and not to a simple "reprimand." The LXX translation *análōsis,* "devastation," is less apt than that of Aquila, *epitímēsis,* "rebuke, reproof."

gaʿar also denotes Yahweh's enmity against other, random enemies. In Mal. 3:11, the verb *gaʿar* seems to mean that, by his "cry," God drives back the "devourer" (*'okhel*), which personifies an agricultural disaster. Zec. 3:2 is the passage which seems to have guaranteed the verb *gaʿar* a certain reviviscence in the later literature. In the vision of the heavenly installation of the high priest Joshua, the prophet hears the angel say to the accuser (→ שָׂטָן *śāṭān*): "Yahweh will reproach you, *hassatan.*" Nothing indicates that the author here is using a familiar curse formula. But in a later period, this verse became an incantation, as the references in Jude 9, the Babylonian Talmud *Berakhoth* 51a, and the quotations of Zec. 3:2 in the Jewish Aramaic magical bowls [4] show. *gaʿar* is found in the Qumran texts in connection with the exorcism of demons: in 1QM 14:10, Heb. *gaʿar* takes "the spirits of destruction" as its object; and in 1QGenAp 20:28, the passive form of Aram. *geʿar* has "evil spirit" as its subject (cf. also 1QH 9:11; 1Qf 4:6; 4QMᵃ 7; *geʿarah,* 1QH 10:18). In the Talmud, *gʿr* is used in paraphrases of Zec. 3:2. It is not impossible that the use of *epitimán,* "to rebuke," in the exorcism stories in the Gospels goes back to this special meaning of *gʿr*; [5] cf. also Mk. 4:39.

---

[4] Cf. J. A. Montgomery, *Aramaic Incantation Texts from Nippur* (1913), Nos. 3, 5, 16, 26.
[5] Kee.

Mal. 2:3 is a *crux interpretum*. The LXX has a completely different text from that found in the MT. It reads *godheaʿ*, "cut off," instead of *goʿer*, "rebuke," and *zeroaʿ*, "arm," instead of *zeraʿ*, "seed, offspring," so that the terms used in 1 S. 2:31 appear again here. The Syriac and the Targum translate the MT faithfully, interpret *zrʿ* as a verb, "to sow," and suggest that Yahweh threatens the land with famine by spoiling the seed. A translation of *gaʿar* more in harmony with its usual meaning is achieved if it is assumed that the prophet is here threatening with divine wrath the descendants (*zeraʿ*) of the priests attacked in the book of Malachi. Furthermore, the fact that in Mal. 2:3 *gaʿar* is closely connected with the word *peresh*, "dung," raises the question whether this passage does not preserve as a secondary sense something of the meaning attested by Arab. *ğaʿara*, "to have a bowel movement."

When the etymology and secular use of *gaʿar* ("to utter a cry") are taken into account, it seems that the central point in the religious use of *gaʿar* and *geʿarah* lies in the fearful and threatening voice of Yahweh, which he utters in the thunder, and which functions as a battle cry when he puts various enemies to flight.

Caquot

גֶּפֶן *gephen*

Contents: I. The Grapevine in the Ancient Near East: 1. Viticulture in the Ancient Near East, especially in Syria and Palestine; 2. Distribution and Meaning of the Root *gpn* in Ancient Near Eastern Languages. II. The Grapevine in the Secular Usage of the OT: 1. Concrete Meaning; 2. Hebrew Terminology Used in Connection with Cultivating Grapes. III. The Grapevine in OT Theological Statements: 1. As a Sign of the Fruitfulness of Canaan, of Blessing, or of Yahweh's Judgment; 2. As a Symbol for Israel.

I. The Grapevine in the Ancient Near East.

1. *Viticulture in the Ancient Near East, especially in Syria and Palestine.* Until approximately the beginning of the twentieth century, the predominant

---

gephen. K. Albrecht, "Das Geschlecht der hebr. Hauptwörter," *ZAW*, 16 (1896), 106f.; F. Altheim-R. Stiehl, *Die Araber in der alten Welt*, II (1964), 105-107; L. Anderlind, "Die Rebe in Syrien, insbesondere in Palästina," *ZDPV*, 11 (1888), 160-177; E. Baumann, "Die Weinranke im Wald. Hes 15,1-8," *ThLZ*, 80 (1955), 119f.; J. Behm, "ἄμπελος," *TDNT*, I, 342f.; R. Bultmann, *The Gospel of John* (trans. 1971), 529ff.; E. Busse, *Der Wein im Kult des AT. FreibThSt*, 29 (1922); Dalman, *AuS*, IV (1935), 291-416; J. Döller, "Der Wein in Bibel und Talmud," *Bibl*, 4 (1923), 143-167, 267-299; G. R. Driver, "Problems of the Hebrew Text and Language," *Festschrift F. Nötscher. BBB*, 1 (1950), 46-61; O. Eissfeldt, "Neue keil-alphabetische Texte aus Ras-Schamra-Ugarit," *SDAW, Kl. für Sprache, Literatur und Kunst* (1956/66), 34, on No. 489,1-10; J. Finkel, "An Interpretation of an Ugaritic Viticultural Poem," *The Josh. Starr Memorial Volume* (New York, 1953), 42f.; G. Fohrer, "Wein, Weinberg," *BHHW*, III (1966), 2149-2151; V. Hehn, *Kulturpflanzen und Haustiere* (⁸1911=

(continued on p. 54)

view was that viticulture (the cultivation of grapes) originated in the region south
of the Caspian Sea, gradually spread over the Near East, and finally was brought
into Greece and Italy by the Phoenicians. [1] Today, this view has been largely
replaced by the theory that viticulture was developed independently in several
regions around the Mediterranean Sea. In Egypt, it can be traced back to the
pre-dynastic period (4th millennium B.C.). Its dissemination, of course, remained
relatively limited because of unfavorable soil conditions. Usually, the Egyptians
must have elevated their vineyards artificially in order to protect them from the
annual flooding. The OT reference to the vine as one of the common cultivated
plants of Egypt (Nu. 20:5) reflects the Israelite ideal of a fruitful cultivated land [2]
more than the actual conditions in ancient Egypt, where grape juice (Gen. 40:9ff.)
and wine were indeed prized very highly, but were not daily and popular bever-
ages. The soil in southern Mesopotamia was just as unfavorable for viticulture as
was that in Egypt. The Gudea Cylinder (A, XXVIII, 10f.,23f.), which dates
ca. 2100 B.C., contains the earliest reference to viticulture in this region. It mentions the planting of a vineyard in the temple garden. This must have had cultic
significance. The natural prerequisites for viticulture were more favorable in Asia
Minor, Assyria, and especially Syria-Palestine. In these areas, viticulture not only
attained great economic significance; it also affected strongly the religion of these
countries (cultic drinking of wine, ecstasy, wine libations). Syria and Palestine
were already known in the Old Kingdom as excellent regions for viticulture (the
Tomb Inscription of Uni, line 25, in Abydos *ca.* 2350 B.C.). [3] The Egyptian,
Sinuhe (*ca.* 1950 B.C.), praises the abundance of wine in Palestine in the account
of his journey (lines 81, 87) [4] with words which are just as extravagant as those
used by Thutmose III in his military records (*ca.* 1450 B.C.; [5] cf. Gen. 27:28;
49:11f.; Dt. 6:11; 8:8). From the New Kingdom on, wine is one of the coveted
products of Syria and Palestine, and was brought to Egypt as booty, tribute, or

---

1963); P. Humbert, "En marge du dictionnaire hébraïque," *ZAW,* 62 (1949/50), 200; A.
Jirku, *Kanaanäische Mythen und Epen aus Ras Schamra-Ugarit* (1962); H. Kees, "Kulturgeschichte des alten Orients I. Ägypten," *HAW,* 3:1:3:1 (1933), 50-52; W. Krenkel, *Lexikon
der alten Welt* (1965), 3263-66; C. Leonardi, *Ampelos. Il simbolo della vite nell'arte pagana
e palecristiana. Ephemerides Liturgicae,* 36 (Rome, 1947); O. Loretz, *Studien zur althebräischen Poesie,* 1. *Das althebräische Liebeslied. AOAT,* 14/1 (1971), 7, 19, 52, 65; I. Löw, *Die
aramäischen Pflanzennamen* (Vienna-Leipzig, 1884=Hildesheim, 1967); *idem, Die Flora
der Juden,* I (1928); H. F. Lutz, *Viticulture and Brewing in the Ancient Orient* (1922); M.
Mansoor, "Some Linguistic Aspects of the Qumran Texts," *JSS,* 3 (1958), 40-57; J. B. Pritchard, "Industry and Trade at Biblical Gibeon," *BA,* 23 (1960), 23-29; J. F. Ross, "Vine,
vineyard," *IDB,* IV (1962), 784-86; L. Rost, "Noah der Weinbauer," *Festschrift A.Alt. BHTh,*
16 (1953), 169-178; A. E. Ruethy, *Die Pflanze und ihre Teile im biblisch-hebräischen Sprachgebrauch* (diss., Basel, 1942); C. Seltman, *Wine in the Ancient World* (London, 1957); H.
Torczyner, "Dunkle Bibelstellen," *Vom AT. Festschrift K.Marti. BZAW,* 41 (1925), 278;
V. Zapletal, *Der Wein in der Bibel. BSt,* 20/1 (1920), 103-106.

[1] Hehn, 65-95.
[2] Cf. III.1.
[3] *ANET,* 228; *AOT,* 81.
[4] *ANET,* 19f.; *AOT,* 57.
[5] *ANET,* 234-241; *AOT,* 82-90.

merchandise. [6] Certain viticultural regions of Syria and Palestine were favored in ancient times: Lebanon (Hos. 14:8 [Eng. v. 7]), the territory around Helbon (north of Damascus, Ezk. 27:18), and the southern and western portions of Judah (Gen. 49:11f.; Jgs. 14:5), especially the district around Hebron (Nu. 13:23f.). But vineyards were also cultivated in the Philistine coastal plain (Jgs. 15:5), the plains of Sharon and Jezreel (1 K. 21:1), the regions around Shechem (Jgs. 9:27), Shiloh (Jgs. 21:20f.), and Gibeon, where large areas were set aside for the production and storage of wine, [7] and the oasis of Engedi (Cant. 1:14) near the Dead Sea. In the Transjordan, a place called Sibmah (near Heshbon in Moab) was known for its vineyards (Isa. 16:8f.; Jer. 48:32f.). In analogy to the numerous compound Judean place names using *kerem* (vineyard), the name of the city *'abhel keramim* (RSV "Abel-keramim," Jgs. 11:33, probably in the vicinity of *'Ammān)* can also be interpreted as a reference to the viticulture that was carried on in the central region of Transjordan. The ancient Near Eastern and OT sources concur, therefore, in describing Canaan (in which Israel settled in the last half of the 2nd millennium B.C.) as the center of an ancient viticulture (Gen. 9:20; Nu. 13:23f.).

2. *Distribution and Meaning of the Root gpn in Ancient Near Eastern Languages.* In Akkadian, *gapnu* and its Late Babylonian form *gupnu* occur only in Late Babylonian texts and in Assyrian Royal Inscriptions from the time of Tiglath-pileser III on (the middle of the 8th century B.C.). [8] The relatively late appearance of these words in Akkadian and their distribution in other Semitic languages would suggest that the root *gpn* originated in West Semitic languages. [9] The following are designated as *ga/gupnu* in Akkadian: (1) trees in general, especially in mountain forests and as homes for birds; (2) (a) fruit-bearing trees and bushes in orchards (Akk. *bīt* ᵍⁱˢ*ga-pan*), including the grapevine; (b) sometimes *gapnu* followed by a more specific term (like *ša titti*, "fig," *ša karāni*, "vine") is used to denote different kinds of fruit-trees and fruit-bushes. On the basis of this usage and the frequent use of the determinative for trees and objects of wood (*giš*), it can be assumed with a great deal of probability that the primary meaning of *ga/gupnu* in Akkadian was "any type of branched tree-trunk or bush." In the Akkadian semantic field, which can no longer be defined temporally or spatially, this general meaning took on the special connotation of cultivated fruit-trees and fruit-bushes. Apparently the root did not take on the narrower meaning of "vineyard" in Akkadian.

gpn has a double meaning in Ugaritic. (1) It means grapevine, and possibly vineyard. A definitive decision is not possible on the basis of the relevant texts. A fragmentary list of groups of people dwelling at different places [10] mentions not only people "in the house of cattle," but also spinners, potters, and those who are *b.gpn*, which can mean "in the vineyard" or "beside the grapevine."

---

6 Additional examples are given by Lutz, 22-26.
7 See Pritchard, *BA*, 23.
8 *CAD*, V, 44f.; *AHw*, 281, 298.
9 So *CAD*.
10 *PRU*, V, 103, 7=*UT*, 2103, 7; Eissfeldt, 34.

Certainly *gpn wʔgr,* [11] the name of the first of the two divine messengers of Baal, who always appear together, would seem to mean "vineyard, grape plantation," rather than "grapevine," because of the meaning of the second name, *ʔgr* ("irrigated land"), [12] but this is not certain. (2) The meaning "saddle paraphernalia, packsaddle," of riding animals is clearly illustrated by the Ugaritic texts *CTA*, 19 [I D], 53,[13] and *CTA*, 4 [II AB], IV, 5, 7, 10, 12, where *gpn* appears in synonymous parallelism with *ṣmd* ("yoke, pole") and *nqbnm* ("saddle paraphernalia," etc.). However, the translation of *gpn* in the cultic-liturgical text concerning the birth of the gods *šḥr* and *šlm* (Dawn and Dusk) [14] is problematic, since both meanings are possible in this passage. [15] When the meanings of the root *gpn* in Akkadian and Ugaritic are compared, it seems very probable that they can be traced back to a common original idea, viz., that of an object which has branches, boughs, or shoots, but which otherwise can have very different features (branches, implements with tendrils or runners, something that has branched out). The fact that in Mandean *gūpnā* generally means both "grapevine" and "climbing plant" [16] favors this hypothesis. It is true that Syr. and Aram.-Modern Heb. *gūphnā, gephetta,* and *gephen,* when they stand alone, mean "grapevine, vine, grape," but when they are used with *tsemer* or *ʿamar* ("cotton"), these forms of the root *gpn* serve to denote the cotton plant. This suggests an originally more general meaning (climbing plant, bush).

The meaning of the Arabic words *ǧafn* and *ǧifn,* which undoubtedly are related to the root *gpn* etymologically, is highly varied. Not only do they mean the grapevine and its parts and fruits, any climbing plant, and a certain kind of aromatic tree, but also the sheath of a sword, the eyelid, the eye socket, a bowl, a key, and a surface area. Arabic lexicographers regard *ǧafn* and *ǧifn* as specifically Yemenite expressions which are synonymous with the Classical Arabic word for grapevine and its parts and fruits, for vine, and for vineyard (*karm*). They try to derive all senses of the words *ǧafn* and *ǧifn* from the supposed basic meaning "grapevine and everything pertaining to it," although this hardly yields conclusive explanations. The tradition of the South Arabic origin of the root *ǧfn* seems to be correct. A borrowing from Akkadian is not unlikely. It is probable that from this the differentiations of meaning in Arabic arose. As a root meaning "grapevine," *gpn* is not used as frequently as the root *krn* (Akk.) or *krm* (Arab., Ugar., Heb.), which frequently has the same sense, nor is it as widely disseminated in the Semitic languages (cf. Egyp. *kʔn*; → גַּן *gan*). Occasionally *gpn* is used in contrast to *krn/m* to denote the piece of land on which grapevines grow, or to denote their fruits and the products derived from them. *gpn* in the sense of "grapevine" is found in religious texts only sporadically in Ugaritic,

---

[11] *CTA*, 4 [II AB], VII, 54; *CTA*, 8 [II AB Var.], 6-7; *CTA*, 5 [I* AB], I, 12, etc.

[12] Cf. *CML*, 146; *WUS*, No. 67, 686; *UT*, Glossary, No. 69, 609.

[13] There is no parallel here with Gen. 49:11; contra *UT*, Glossary, No. 609, and *KBL*³, s.v. *gephen.*

[14] *CTA*, 23 [SS], 9, 10, 11.

[15] Cf. *UT*, Glossary, No. 69, 609; *CML*, 120; Finkel, 42f.; Jirku, 81; *WUS*, No. 685.

[16] *MdD*, 84b; on the grapevine symbolism of the Nasoraic-Gnostic systems, see R. Macuch in Altheim-Stiehl, *Die Araber . . .*, II, 105-107; cf. also Behm, *TDNT*, I, 342f.

relatively often in the OT and Jewish literature related to the OT, and also in the Mandean writings and the related Gnostic systems, but not in Akkadian and Arabic literature. It would seem, then, that the root *gpn* became a part of the religious vocabulary only in its home region, i.e., in the West Semitic-Canaanite linguistic realm.

II. The Grapevine in the Secular Usage of the OT.

1. *Concrete Meaning.* gephen occurs 55 times in the OT. It has the general meaning "climbing plant, bush," in only 3 instances. [17] In Nu. 6:4 and Jgs. 13:14 it means the grapevine, the fruit of which (*gephen hayyayin*) one who is consecrated to God (a Nazirite) is not to eat in any form. That *gephen* is defined more precisely by the gen. *yayin*, "wine," shows that in these passages it simply means a bush or a climbing plant in general. It is doubtful whether *gephen sadheh* (2 K. 4:39; text?) means a "wild grapevine," i.e., a grapevine that grows wild, as is usually assumed (cf. Mal. 3:11). [18] The name of its fruits (*paqqu'oth,* "colocynth"), the way it is cooked, and the harmful effects of eating it seem to favor a different kind of plant. *gephen* in the usual OT sense of "grapevine" is used repeatedly in parallelism with *soreq/soreqah,* "vine" (Gen. 49:11; Isa. 16:8; Jer. 2:21; cf. Isa. 5:2); the expressions in which it occurs in these passages indicate that it means some sort of grapevine bearing light red grapes. In Israel it was regarded as the best kind of grapevine (*zera' 'emeth,* RSV "of pure seed") and in figurative speech it is contrasted to a degenerate (*suri*) and wild (*nokhriyyah*) grapevine (Jer. 2:21). *gephen* is used in parallelism with and as a synonym of *kerem* ("vineyard") in lists of cultivated plants and fruits which represent the fruitfulness of the arable land (2 K. 18:31f. = Isa. 36:16f.).

2. *Hebrew Terminology Used in Connection with Cultivating Grapes.* As with most subjects that play an important role in daily life, OT Hebrew has numerous special expressions for the parts and fruits of the grapevine, its alterations, and the things that were done in connection with its cultivation. However, the exact meaning of these words and expressions cannot always be determined. [19] The appearance of the grapevine changes several times during the year: its leaves (*'aleh*) wither (*nabhel,* Isa. 34:4; Jer. 8:13) and fall off in late autumn (November/December); in the spring (April/May) it puts forth (*parach,* Cant. 7:13[12]; *perach,* "bud, blossom," Isa. 18:5) new leaves and very fragrant blossoms (*nets,* Gen. 40:10; *semadhar,* Cant. 2:13,15; 7:13[12]). The grapes (*'eshkol,* actually the vine-stalk or the tendril on which the grapes hang, Gen. 40:10; Nu. 13:23f.) begin to ripen (*hibhshil,* Gen. 40:10) in July. The Hebrew word for grape is *'enabh* (Gen. 40:11; Nu. 6:3), but this word can also mean clusters of grapes (Lev. 25:5; Dt. 32:32; *'eshkol 'anabhim,* Nu. 13:23; cf. Arab. *'inab*). The people particularly enjoyed eating grapes that were still in an unripe stage (sour grapes or wild grapes, *boser,* Jer. 31:29; Ezk. 18:2). These were distinguished from the

---

[17] Cf. I.2.
[18] So recently *KBL*[3].
[19] Dalman, *AuS,* IV, 299-307, 319-335, 339-344; cf. Döller.

riper "full" sour grapes (*boser gomel,* Isa. 18:5). Sometimes the grapevine "suppressed" (*chamas,* Job 15:33; Lam. 2:6) the further ripening of sour grapes, or yielded bad, "stunted" grapes (*be'ushim,* Isa. 5:2,4, usually translated incorrectly by "rotten"). Depending on the location and weather, grapes reached the stage of full maturity in the period between July and November. The main harvest (*batsir,* verb *batsar,* Lev. 26:5; Jgs. 8:2; Jer. 48:32; Mic. 7:1) usually occurred in September/October. It ended with a joyful festival (*hillulim,* Jgs. 9:27; *hedhadh,* Isa. 16:9f.; cf. Jgs. 21:21; Isa. 24:7-11; 32:12-16), which included orgiastic elements among the Canaanites and also sometimes among the Israelites. The grapes that were left on the vine, because they were not ripe or through oversight, were gathered in a later gleaning (*'oleloth,* Jgs. 8:2; Isa. 24:13; Jer. 6:9; Mic. 7:1), although this was forbidden by the law (Lev. 19:10; Dt. 24:21). The grape-gatherers (*botser,* Jer. 6:9; 49:9; Ob. 5; *mebhatstser,* Jer. 6:27?; *korem,* Joel 1:11f.) plucked the grapes off the vines with their hands (Jer. 6:9, so also on Egyp. pictures). The use of the sickle in gathering grapes is mentioned for the first time in Rev. 14:8. Pruning hooks (*mazmeroth,* Isa. 18:5; cf. 2:4; Mic. 4:3) were used to cut off excess grapes, a process called pruning or trimming (*zamar, zamir,* Lev. 25:3f.; Isa. 5:6; Cant. 2:12; and the Peasant Calendar of Gezer, line 6, 10th/9th century B.C.); this was usually done before and after the vines bloomed. Grapevines were planted in hilly country on terraced slopes and in the plains on level fields (cf. Isa. 5:1-7; → כרם *kerem*). In the OT it is usually assumed that a grapevine will spread out on the ground (Ps. 80:10,12[9,11]; Isa. 16:8; Jer. 48:32). Accordingly, in OT times (as today) when the vines bloomed the branches were raised about 0.5-1 meter off the ground to prevent the grapes from rotting. The Israelites, of course, must have had grapevines that stood or climbed upward also, for this is presupposed in the stereotyped expression, "every man dwelt under his vine and under his fig tree" (1 K. 5:5 [4:25]; Mic. 4:4; similarly Zec. 3:10). Since grapevines and fig trees are mentioned together in this expression and frequently elsewhere (Cant. 2:13), [20] it may be assumed that the process of making a grapevine climb on a fig tree planted beside it, which is a favorite practice today among Palestinian Arabs, was already used frequently in ancient Israel. On the other hand, training grapevines on poles, trellises, and arched pergolas, which was common in Egypt from time immemorial, cannot be traced back before the Hellenistic period in Palestine. In ancient Israel, nonchalantly tying a riding animal to a grapevine was regarded as the sign of a blessing of extraordinary fruitfulness (Gen. 49:11). This practice is also worthy of note because the trunk of the grapevine in Palestine usually attains a diameter of only 6 to 10 centimeters. Hence it cannot stand upright without support and it certainly cannot be used for tying riding animals.

III. The Grapevine in OT Theological Statements.

1. *As a Sign of the Fruitfulness of Canaan, of Blessing, and of Yahweh's Judgment.* Theologically speaking, the grapevine, its fruit, and the luxuries that it produces, such as grape juice, wine (→ יין *yayin*), grape honey, and grape

---

[20] Cf. III.1.

cakes (often together with other typical agricultural products), are viewed positively as visible signs of the blessing of Yahweh and of the fruitfulness he brought about in the land Israel inhabited.

The highest notes are struck in Gen. 49:11f., where the abundance of wine in the land belonging to the tribe of Judah, along with its military efficiency, is regarded as a guarantee of the choice of Judah to rule over the Israelite tribes. Here the grapevine represents the prosperity of the land in general. In similar passages, however, the grapevine is not usually mentioned alone but along with other cultivated plants. When every Israelite can call a grapevine and fig tree his own, [21] the ideal condition of secure possession of the promised land has been attained (1 K. 5:5[4:25]). The prophets again make this an object of promises (Mic. 4:4; Zec. 3:10). The envoy of the king of Assyria tries to make the idea of deportation appealing to the inhabitants of besieged Jerusalem by promising them that they will have their own grapevines, fig trees, and cisterns (2 K. 18:31 = Isa. 36:16). In the OT such lists of typical plants and other agricultural achievements usually consist of two elements, and four different variants can be found.

1. The pairing of "grapevine" or "vineyard" (kerem) and "fig tree" (te'enah) is firmly anchored in cultic and daily usage from the eighth century B.C. on: Hos. 2:14(12) (confession formula); Joel 1:7; 2:22 (liturgical texts); Isa. 34:4 (lament); Mic. 4:4; Zec. 3:10 (prophetic oracles of salvation); 1 K. 5:5(4:25); Jer. 8:13; Cant. 2:13; Ps. 105:33; 78:47 (mulberry figs; both psalms are cultic songs). Since cisterns are mentioned only once in connection with these two terms (2 K. 18:31 = Isa. 36:16), it must be assumed that we have in this instance an expansion of the two-membered formula. The expression "grapevine and fig tree" reflects the custom of planting these two plants close together—a custom that was widespread in Palestine both in OT times and later. [22]

2. The pairing of "field" (sadheh) or "grain seed" (zera') or "bread" (lechem) and "vineyard" occurs already in the Book of the Covenant (Ex. 22:4[5]), in ancient narratives (Nu. 16:14, J; 20:17; 21:22, E; 1 S. 8:15; 22:7; 2 K. 18:32 = Isa. 36:17), and in preexilic prophetic oracles (Isa. 32:12). Postexilic texts also use these expressions to designate the cultivated land: Ps. 107:37 (a Thanksgiving Liturgy); Mal. 3:11; Neh. 5:4f.; Zec. 8:12 (grapevine and fruit of the land); Job 24:6; Prov. 31:16. They are presupposed in Am. 9:13.

3. The pair "houses and vineyards" can also represent the prosperity of the cultivated land. This formula appears from the eighth century B.C. on: Am. 5:11; 9:14 (cities without houses); Zeph. 1:13b; Ezk. 28:26; Isa. 65:21; Eccl. 2:4.

4. The terms "grapevine" or "vineyard" and "olive tree" (zayith) appear together only rarely, and mainly in postexilic texts: Dt. 6:11; Ps. 128:3 (instruction and blessing); Isa. 24:13 (indirectly); Job 15:33 (wisdom comparison). Earlier texts seem to presuppose this expression, but do not use it unambiguously: Hos. 14:7f.(6f.) (text?); 2 K. 5:26 (contains later expansions?). Hence one can only

[21] Cf. II.2.
[22] See II.2.

conjecture that it is an earlier stereotyped expression from the cultic realm. On the other hand, the expression "grapevines and pomegranates" (*rimmon*), which is found only in Cant. 6:11 and 7:13(12), is undoubtedly a spontaneous formulation of love poetry.

Lists with three or more elements are rarer and much more variable than those with two. Jotham's Fable mentions the olive tree, the fig tree, and the grapevine (Jgs. 9:8-13). Since elsewhere these three elements appear together only in Hab. 3:17, and that in a different sequence, the expression cannot be regarded as a stereotyped formula. The list, "field or grain seed, vineyard/fig tree, and pomegranate or date palm (*tamar*) or olive tree," seems to reflect a secondary combination and expansion of the first and second two-membered formulas. This list occurs in Nu. 20:5 (P); Joel 1:11f.; and Hag. 2:19. There seems to be a secondary expansion of the second formula on the basis of the fourth in the lists with three members in Dt. 28:38-40; 1 S. 8:14; Dt. 24:19-21 (the order of the last two elements is reversed in the last passage). Formulas which vary frequently in structure and order arise by a free combination of various two-membered formulas: Jer. 32:15; 35:7 (houses, fields, and vineyards); 35:9 (houses, vineyards, and fields); Neh. 5:11a (fields, vineyards, olive orchards, and houses); 9:25 (seven elements); Dt. 8:8 (eight elements); and Jer. 5:17 (four pairs of words). In sum, it may be said that the two-membered formulas 1-3 were used side by side in ancient Israel as representative terms for the cultivated land. Presumably they had already come into use in the pre-Israelite-Canaanite period. The existence of the two gods, "Grapevine (or Vineyard) and (Watered) Field," in the Ugaritic pantheon [23] favors this view. The Egyptians Uni (line 25) and Sinuhe (line 81) also use the pairings "fig trees and grapevines" or "figs and grapes" or "bread and wine" (Sinuhe, line 87) to describe the richness of Canaan. In the OT, the cultic use of the grapevine is reflected in the comparison of the righteous man with a fruitful grapevine and his children with the shoots of the olive tree (Ps. 128:3), as also of the evildoer with a grapevine that "suppresses" its sour grapes (i.e., does not let them ripen) and an olive tree that casts off its blossoms (Job 15:33). The spreading grapevine of Sibmah, which Yahweh destroys, occurs as a symbol of the richness and arrogance of Moab in the lament in Isa. 16:8f. (=Jer. 48:32f.). Esteem for the grapevine and its fruit is assumed even in passages where its destruction is depicted as a sign of Yahweh's judgment: Hos. 2:14(12); Isa. 7:23; 32:12; 34:4; 24:7,13; Jer. 5:17; Dt. 6:11; Ps. 105:33; 78:47 (cf. Ex. 9:13-35).

In an almost allegorical address (Ezk. 17:6,8) and then again in the interpretation of a lament which contains motifs from fables about plants and animals (19:10ff.), Ezekiel uses the grapevine as a figure for Zedekiah, or for the Davidic royal house and the calamity about to overtake it. This use of the figure of the grapevine, which occurs this once in the OT, is probably a carryover of its use as a symbol for Israel. The figurative use of the grapevine in OT love poetry (Cant. 2:13; 6:2 [conjec.]; 7:9,13[8,12]) is not as developed as that of the vineyard (*kerem*, cf. Isa. 5:1-7; Cant. 1:6; 8:11f.; Isa. 27:2f.). Everywhere in the OT

---

[23] See I.2.

where the grapevine occurs as a symbol of fruitfulness, wealth, and greatness, it is clearly subordinated to the sovereign power of Yahweh. Clearly, then, one catches in the use of this figure a polemic against the Canaanite fertility cults (so explicitly in Hos. 2:14[12]) and against the high self-esteem of man or the people (Isa. 16:8f. = Jer. 48:32f.). [24]

2. *As a Symbol for Israel.* The figurative comparison of Israel with a grapevine which Yahweh transplanted from Egypt to Canaan, and which he there caused to grow into a cosmic tree, has an unbroken positive significance in the preexilic lament of the people in Ps. 80:9-16(8-15) (from the time of Josiah?). This indicates the cultic use and probably also the origin of the grapevine as a figure for the election of Israel and its privileged position. This figure is oriented to the valuable fruit of the grapevine. [25] In their polemic against Israel's self-confident consciousness of its election, the prophets freely and poetically reinterpret the figure of the grapevine. They use the luxuriant grapevine as a metaphor for Israel's prosperity in Canaan, through which the people is tempted to participate in the Canaanite fertility cults and thus to fall away from its God (Hos. 10:1f.; cf. 9:10). When Isaiah compares Israel with a vineyard that yields only inedible grapes (*be'ushim*) (Isa. 5:1-7), and when Jeremiah compares himself or Yahweh with a grape-gatherer who searches the grapevine in vain for grapes (Jer. 6:9; 8:13), they have in mind the produce of the vineyard (*kerem*). The comparison of Israel with a choice grapevine which Yahweh has planted in Canaan, but which has become totally degenerate there (Jer. 2:21), [26] points further in a negative direction. Perhaps this variation of the metaphor of the grapevine originated in the Wisdom observation of history and nature. The figurative reference to the grapevine of Sodom which bears poisonous and bitter grapes favors this view, since it is used to illustrate the complete hopelessness of the nations and their total inability to understand (Dt. 32:32). Ezekiel is even more radical than Jeremiah when he changes the meaning of the grapevine figure into a brutal and offensive statement, for "in an astonishing shift in perspective" he turns attention away from the fruit of the vine to its wood (Ezk. 15). [27] Seen in this way, the grapevine appears just as useless as any other climbing plant of the forest. In spite of the prophets' increasingly sharper polemical reinterpretation of the metaphor of the vine and their attack on the excessive drinking of wine (Hos. 4:11; Isa. 28:7f.; cf. Gen. 9:20-27 [J]), the grapevine never became so characteristic a feature of the Canaanite cults as cultic prostitution did. Accordingly, neither the prophets nor the law voice any fundamental opposition to producing and drinking wine. Only the sect of the Rechabites radically rejected it, as they did agriculture in general, on religious grounds (Jer. 35).

Hentschke

גֵּר *gēr* → גור *gûr*

---

[24] Cf. III.2.
[25] Cf. III.1 and Zimmerli, *BK,* XIII on Ezk. 15:1ff.
[26] Cf. II.1.
[27] See Zimmerli, *BK,* XIII, 328.

גֹּרֶן gōren

Contents: I. Etymology, Occurrences. II. Meaning. III. Figurative Meaning. IV. Cultic Site?

I. Etymology, Occurrences. In Ugaritic, *grn* occurs several times in the plural forms *grnm* and *grnt*. The meaning "threshing floor," i.e., a place where grain is gathered and stored, fits well in the context of *CTA,* 14 [I K], 112, 215, and is defended by many scholars.[1] *grn* is also a place of legal transactions (*CTA,* 17 [II D], V, 7; 1 K. 22:10).[2] The Akkadian equivalent *gurunnu* means a "pile" of tribute or of dead persons.[3] The cognate verb means "to heap up, pile up" stones, tribute, barley, or grain in general,[4] but this cannot be considered here because the word is strictly *qurunnu*. The meaning "to rub away, crush, grind" lies behind the Arabic root, and so *ğurn* can mean a stone mortar in which fruits or medicines are crushed, but also a threshing or drying place.[5] In Ethiopic and Syriac, the word means "threshing place."[6]

gōren occurs 36 times in the OT: 7 times in the Prophets, 9 in the Deuteronomistic Work, 8 in the Chronicler's Work, 6 in the Pentateuch, 4 in the book of Ruth, and once in Job (its occurrence in Jer. 2:25 is a scribal error).

II. Meaning. a. *gōren* is the threshing place where grain is threshed and winnowed (Ruth 3:2). Before the harvest, the threshing floor is trodden down (Jer. 51:33) to make it suitable for threshing. The sheaves are brought to the threshing floor and threshed (Job 39:12), possibly by an animal (Hos. 10:11).

---

gōren. G. W. Ahlström, "Der Prophet Nathan und der Tempelbau," *VT,* 11 (1961), 113-127; Dalman, *AuS,* III, 67-139; E. Fuchs, "σινιάζω," *TDNT,* VII, 291f.; J. Gray, "Tell El Far'a by Nablus: A. 'Mother' in Ancient Israel," *PEQ,* 84 (1952), 110-13; *idem,* "The Goren at the City Gate," *PEQ,* 85 (1953), 118-123; H. H. Rowley, "The Marriage of Ruth," *The Servant of the Lord and Other Essays on the OT* (Oxford, ²1965), 169-194; J. Schreiner, *Sion-Jerusalem, Jahwes Königssitz. StANT,* 7 (1963); S. Smith, "The Threshing Floor and the City Gate," *PEQ,* 78 (1946), 5-14; *idem,* "On the Meaning of Goren," *PEQ,* 85 (1953), 42-45; H.-J. Stoebe, "Tenne," *BHHW,* III (1966), 1952; A. J. Wensinck, "Some Semitic Rites of Mourning and Religion," *VAWA,* N.R. 18/1 (1917), 1-12; *BRL,* 137f.

[1] Aistleitner, *WUS,* No. 69; A. Jirku, *Kanaanäische Mythen und Epen aus Ras Schamra-Ugarit* (1962), 130; Gordon, *UT,* 622.

[2] Gordon, *ibid.;* otherwise S. Smith, PEQ, 85, 43.

[3] *CAD,* V, 142.

[4] *CAD,* V, 46f.

[5] Smith, *PEQ,* 85, 44f.; but Gray, *PEQ,* 85, 121, wants to retain the meaning "open place" for the Arabic also; cf. Gray, *PEQ,* 84, 113; W. W. Müller, *ZAW,* 75 (1963), 308.

[6] H. Möller, *Vergleichendes indogermanisch-semitisches Wörterbuch* (²1970), 99f.; Leslau, *Contributions,* 15.

The threshed grain is thrown up in the air with the winnowing-fork, and the chaff is blown away by the wind (Ps. 1:4). This is done in the evening or at night, because this is the time of day when the wind is most favorable for threshing (Ruth 3:2). The owner remains all night at the end of his heap of grain so as to prevent theft (3:7). In order to take full advantage of the wind, it was customary to build threshing floors near or on a hill; but there were also threshing floors to which it was necessary to descend (Ruth 3:6). [7] At the end of the harvest, a heave-offering from the threshing floor was supposed to be offered, i.e., a tax from the freshly harvested grain was to be paid. This law is mentioned in the OT only at Nu. 15:20 and it must be distinguished from the exaction of the tithe, which had to be paid out of the wine press and the threshing floor (Nu. 18:27,30).

b. *goren* can mean not only the threshing place, but also the produce that is obtained from the threshing floor. When a slave is set free, his master must give him something out of his threshing floor (Dt. 15:14; cf. the earlier law in Ex. 21:2-6, which states that a slave is not to be set free without remuneration), i.e., out of the yield of grain that the master gathered on the threshing floor (Nu. 15:20; 2 K. 6:27).

c. When *goren* is used with → יֶקֶב *yeqebh*, "wine press," it can mean the entirety of the harvest yield or of the food (Nu. 18:27; Hos. 9:2; 2 K. 6:27). The end of the harvest is celebrated in the Feast of Booths (Tabernacles), when the Israelites make an ingathering from the wine press and the threshing floor (Dt. 16:13). Joel speaks of a future time of salvation in which the threshing floors shall be full of grain and the wine presses shall overflow with wine and oil (Joel 2:24).

d. *goren* is a place name in the instances of the "Threshing floor of Thorns" (*goren ha'atadh*), where Jacob's family made lamentation for him (Gen. 50:10f.), and of the "Threshing floor of Nacon" (*goren nakhon*, 2 S. 6:6; *goren kidhon*, 1 Ch. 13:9), where the ark almost toppled over on the ground. The place name Migron (1 S. 14:2; Isa. 10:28) is also connected with *goren,* and originally meant "threshing place." [8]

III. **Figurative Meaning.** The various activities that took place on the threshing floor can be used figuratively for the acts of God in history. The chaff that is driven away when the grain is winnowed on the threshing floor is used as a metaphor for the quick destruction and the swift disappearance without a trace of the ungodly and graven images (Ps. 1:4; Hos. 13:3). Yahweh gathers Israel's enemies and brings them to the threshing floor like sheaves (Mic. 4:12).

---

[7] Cf. W. Rudolph, *KAT*, XVII/1-3, 53.

[8] Cf. M. Noth, *ZDPV*, 73 (1957), 14f.; Z. Kallai-Kleinmann, *IEJ*, 6 (1956), 180ff.; H. Donner, *ZDPV*, 84 (1968), 46-54.

But Yahweh can also call Israel "the son of my threshing floor" (*ben gorni*; the suf. does not go with *goren*, but with the whole expression), because the other nations had threshed him (Isa. 21:10). Similarly, Jer. 51:33 compares Babylon with a threshing floor that is trodden, i.e., prepared for the time of harvest. The calamity that is about to come upon Babylon, however, is not this "treading" but the harvest that follows it. The text could be interpreted to mean that the threshing floor, i.e., Babylon, will be affected by the harvest. The passage is clear, however, if one assumes that the text originated at a time when the harvest had already become established as a stereotyped figure for God's lawsuit, so that the preparation for harvest was understood as a preparation for judgment (Mic. 4:12; Joel 4:13 [Eng. 3:13]; Isa. 27:12; 63:3).

IV. **Cultic Site?** On the basis of certain OT texts, some scholars have supposed that the OT knows the threshing floor as a cultic site in the religions of surrounding nations. If so, *goren* would mean a threshing place in some passages and a cultic site in others. Gray tries to eliminate the difficulties connected with this theory by translating *goren* as "open place." He argues that the *goren* was left open for various uses, including that of the cult. [9] But such an interpretation is not convincing, because *goren* is connected too clearly with threshing and winnowing, and finally can even mean the produce of the threshing floor. [10] Some scholars, then, try to interpret the threshing floor itself as a cultic site where a group of cultic acts was performed alongside the rites associated with the harvest. [11]

A careful examination of the individual passages that are used to support this theory shows that it is highly doubtful whether the OT contains reminiscences of an earlier use of threshing floors as cultic sites. 1 K. 22 (2 Ch. 18) describes an interrogation of certain prophets at the gate of the threshing floor, but this is in no sense an event connected with a cultic site.[12] It is possible to suppose that cultic prostitution lies behind the events related in the book of Ruth (chap. 3)[13] but this idea is alien to the author of the narrative as we now have it (cf. Gen. 38). The sign which Gideon uses to try to ascertain God's will (Jgs. 6:37) is not connected with a sanctuary (Gen. 24:12-14; 1 S. 14:8-10).[14] *goren* is linked to a place name in Gen. 50:10 and 2 S. 6:6. Hence, it is not possible to determine the original meaning of the word directly from these passages. Furthermore, one must question whether the events recorded in these verses are connected with a cultic site. Hosea reproves Israel because it has disloyally forsaken its God and loved a harlot's hire upon all threshing floors (Hos. 9:1). This does not necessarily mean, however, that these threshing floors

---

[9] J. Gray, *PEQ*, 84, 112f.; *VT*, 2 (1952), 210, n. 1.
[10] Cf. II.b.
[11] Gray, *PEQ*, 85, 120; Ahlström, 115f.
[12] Gray, 121.
[13] *Ibid.*, 120; May, *JRAS* (1939), 76f.; otherwise Rowley, 189, n. 2.
[14] Cf. W. Zimmerli, *Gottes Offenbarung. ThB*, 19 (²1969), 92f.

were the cultic sites of foreign gods. [15] When Hosea paints a positive picture of the early history of his people, he characterizes it as a trained heifer that loved to thresh (10:11). This comparison would be inconceivable if Hosea thought of the threshing floor as a place where Israel had fallen away to foreign gods. Hos. 9:1 says that the people had anticipated a reward for their apostasy from Yahweh on the threshing floors (and in the wine presses, v. 2). But the cult at issue did not have to be practiced on the threshing floor. [16] The story of David's building of the altar (2 S. 24; 1 Ch. 21) is a *hieros logos* ("holy oracle") regarding the location of the temple. [17] The narrator describes the place as a very ordinary threshing floor which was not used for any cultic purposes before David built his altar there (the Chronicler strengthens this point by stating that Ornan was threshing wheat when David came to him, 1 Ch. 21:20).

Thus no text in the OT warrants the conclusion that *goren* was an ancient cultic site. At the same time, however, the well-known religio-historical continuity of the holy place, and the detailed description of David's purchase of the threshing floor of Araunah (2 S. 24:21-24), favor the conjecture that Solomon's temple was built on an ancient cultic site. [18] The tradition calls it "the threshing floor of Araunah." The threshing floors of cities were common property, and so it is hardly conceivable that Araunah owned the Jerusalem threshing floor. Hence David could have bought a Jebusite cultic site from Araunah in order to build his altar on it. Later generations could not tolerate the idea that the temple was built on what had once been the site of a heathen cult, and so the story went that the temple was built on a wholly secular site, viz., on a threshing floor. [19] If it is assumed that the threshing floor of Araunah was located "near" (*'im*, 2 S. 24:16) the holy place, which was the highest portion of land in or around the city, [20] the secular character of the threshing floor is again ensured.

Münderlein

---

[15] H. W. Wolff, *Hosea* (trans. 1974), 154.
[16] W. Rudolph, *KAT*, XIII/1, 175.
[17] Schreiner, 57ff.
[18] Ahlström, 117ff.
[19] H. Gressmann, *Älteste Geschichtsschreibung und Prophetie Israels. SAT*, II/1 (²1921).
[20] Noth, *BK*, IX/1, 108f.

גָּרַע gāra'

Contents: I. Etymology. II. Usage in the OT: 1. "To Shave"; 2. "To Diminish, Lessen"; 3. "To Take Away"; 4. Sir. 51:15.

I. Etymology. The root gr' occurs in Jewish Aramaic and Syriac, where it means "to shave." Old South Arabic also has a gr' that means "to shave." [1] Possibly Arab. taqarra'a, "to have shaved the head," is connected with this. [2] gr' is found in Middle Hebrew and Jewish Aramaic with the meaning "to diminish," "take away." It must be assumed that the original meaning was "to cut (off)." [3]

II. Usage in the OT.

1. "To Shave." gr' means "to shave" or "trim" the beard in Jer. 48:37 and Isa. 15:2: the shaved head and the trimmed beard are signs of mourning. Both of these passages describe the destruction of Moab. The passage in Isaiah (where certain Heb. mss. and the LXX read gedhu'ah, "is shaved off," instead of geru'ah) is the obvious basis of the statement in Jeremiah. Ezk. 5:11 is disputed. Zimmerli understands the verb absolutely [4] and translates: "I will 'have a shearing,' and my eye will not be grieved, and also I will have no pity." [5] Be this as it may, the context indicates that Yahweh will not spare his people in view of the desecration of the sanctuary, but will execute the punishment without any deduction (→ גלח gillach).

2. "To Diminish, Lessen." gr' also means "to diminish, lessen." Thus, the Egyptians refuse to "lessen" the fixed number of bricks that the Israelites are to make each day (Ex. 5:8,19—qal; v. 11—niphal), and the Book of the Covenant requires a man who marries a second wife not to "lessen" or "diminish" the food, marital rights, and clothing of the first wife (Ex. 21:10). Similarly, Ezk. 16:27 states that God has "lessened" or "diminished" the allotted portion (the right, choq) of the people, which is depicted as Yahweh's wife. Lev. 27:18 requires that a "deduction" be made from that which is dedicated to Yahweh. Job 15:4 probably also belongs here. Eliphaz says to Job: "you shatter (tapher; → פרר prr) the fear of God, and 'diminish' devotion (sichah, RSV meditation) before God," i.e., Job denies God the full measure of godly respect that he deserves. The rendering "take away" might also be considered in this case.

---

1 Leslau, Contributions, 16.
2 KBL³.
3 Cf. E. F. Sutcliffe, Bibl, 30 (1949), 80.
4 Zimmerli, BK, XIII, in loc.
5 For Zimmerli's proposed emendations, see BK, XIII, 98.

3. *"To Take Away."* In some typical passages, *grʿ* appears in antithesis to *ysp,* "to add to," and thus means "to take away; subtract." In this sense we may refer first to the Deuteronomic law that forbids anyone to add to or take away from the commandments of God (Dt. 4:2; 13:1 [Eng. 12:32]). Yahweh speaks similarly to Jeremiah concerning the prophetic oracle: "Speak all the words that I command you to speak; do not 'leave out' a word (RSV, do not hold back a word)" (Jer. 26:2). The authority of God's commandments or word is so great that no one is to change them in any way. Qoheleth uses similar words to emphasize the omnipotence of God: nothing can be added to or taken from that which God does (Eccl. 3:14).

The same meaning appears in a juridical context in Nu. 36:3f., a passage that deals with taking away or adding to the portion of the inheritance. Job 36:7 is of an entirely different type. Here Elihu maintains that God does not "withdraw" (take away) his eyes from the righteous, but gives them a place of honor.

On the other hand, Eliphaz denies that man can "draw wisdom (*chokhmah;* → חכם *chākham*) unto himself" from the secret council of God (Job 15:8). In this allusion to the myth of the First Man, who desired to appropriate to himself the wisdom of God, the inferiority of man is emphasized. [6] Related is Job 36:27: God "draws up" (piel) the drops of water and pours them out as rain over the earth. [7]

In yet another connection Nu. 27:4 says that the name of Zelophehad will not be "taken away" from his family, although he has no son, but only daughters. It is presupposed, then, that the customary practice hitherto was that a man's name (→ שם *shēm*) would not live on if he had no male heir. Along different lines again Nu. 9:7 speaks of the unclean being "excluded from" the sacrificial cult.

4. *Sir. 51:15.* Finally, *grʿ* is used in a very peculiar way in a Qumran fragment of Sir. 51:15, which says: "And when the flower falls off (*garaʿ*), when the grapes ripen...." [8] The text of this fragment differs greatly from the Cairo text and the translations, but it preserves the alphabetic structure of the psalm well. Here *garaʿ* seems to be used intransitively in the sense "to go away," a sense which is also attested in Middle Hebrew. [9]

Ringgren

---

[6] See H. Ringgren, *Word and Wisdom* (Lund, 1947), 90f.
[7] Cf. Sutcliffe, 79f.
[8] *DJD,* IV, 80ff.
[9] On *grʿ*, cf. A. J. Brawer, *BethM,* 13 (1968), 148f.

גָּרַשׁ gārash

Contents: I. Etymology, Occurrences. II. Usage. III. In the Law.

I. Etymology, Occurrences. Outside its occurrences in Hebrew and Jewish Aramaic (where it is borrowed from the Bible), a root grš, "to drive out (away)," is found in Ugaritic[1] and Moabite.[2] The alleged example in Punic[3] is uncertain.[4] Soq. grś, "to move, draw, drag,"[5] Arab. ǧaraša II, "to expose publicly," ǧašara, "to surrender," and zaǧara, "to drive away,"[6] may be remotely related to this root. grš appears in the Old Babylonian letter from Mari as a Canaanite loanword.[7]

Hebrew also has a grš that means "to toss up (about)" (Isa. 57:20; Am. 8:8), which is usually interpreted as a variant meaning of grš, "to drive out (away)." But Blau thinks[8] that this is a different, homonymous root.[9]

The verb garash is found in the qal (8 times), niphal (3), piel (33), and pual (twice).

II. Usage. Primarily the word garash means "to chase away" or "drive out (away)," without implying anything other than interrupting an existing relationship. Abraham casts out Hagar and her son Ishmael (Gen. 21:10), Zebul drives Gaal and his brothers out of Shechem (Jgs. 9:41), the priest Abimelech drives David out (of Gath?) when he feigns madness (Ps. 34:1 [Eng. heading]; cf. 1 S. 21:13f.), and Solomon expels Abiathar from his priestly office (1 K. 2:27).

The verb garash acquires special secondary emphases from the context. Adam and Eve are driven out of Paradise (Gen. 3:24), excluded from their original nearness to God, and transferred into present human existence. Cain is driven away from the cultivated land (Gen. 4:14) and must live in the wilderness under a curse. David is driven into exile (1 S. 26:19), and must "serve other gods," because he is no longer in the land of Yahweh. Jonah says in the psalm he sings: "I am cast out from thy presence" (Jonah 2:5[4]).

The statements that Yahweh drove out the peoples of Canaan before Israel (Ex. 23:28; 33:2 [piel]; 34:11 [qal] [sometimes these peoples are listed differently]; Josh. 24:12,18; Dt. 33:27; Ps. 78:55) are theologically significant. In this

---

1 There are several examples; see *WUS*, No. 704.
2 *KAI*, 181.19, "Then Chemosh drove him (i.e., the king of Israel) out before me."
3 *CIS*, I, 144, 2, 7; see Albright, *BASOR*, 83 (1941), 19.
4 *KAI*, 46 and *DISO*, 286 read the text differently.
5 Leslau, *Contributions*, 16.
6 *KBL*³.
7 *ARM*, II, 28.9, 19.
8 Blau, *VT*, 6 (1956), 245f.
9 So also *KBL*³.

connection Ex. 23:28 and Josh. 24:12 refer to the *tsir'ah*, which probably should not be translated "hornets" with the LXX, but rather denotes the terror that God sends among Israel's enemies. Ex. 23:28-30 emphasizes the slow and gradual conquest of the land, while Jgs. 2:3 says that Yahweh will not drive the nations out of Canaan because of the disobedience of the Israelites, and 6:9 states that Yahweh drove out the nations before Israel and gave them the land, and yet the people had become disobedient.

Ps. 78:55 contains a theological evaluation of the conquest. It states that God drove out the nations (*goyim*) before Israel and gave them to the people of Israel as an inheritance. Ps. 80:9(8) uses a metaphor to say the same thing: "Thou didst bring a vine out of Egypt, thou didst drive out the nations (*goyim*) and plant it." Similarly, in his concluding prayer in the Chronicler's Work (1 Ch. 17:16ff.), David says that Israel is the only people that God redeemed for himself (→ פדה *pādhāh*), "since thou didst drive out nations" (*goyim*) (v. 21). On this ground, when Jehoshaphat is attacked by neighboring nations, he says to God: "Behold, they reward us by coming to drive us out of thy possession, which thou hast given us to inherit" (2 Ch. 20:11), and he prays for God's intervention.

The text of Ezk. 31:11 is doubtful. [10] The present MT says that the haughty Egyptians will be cast out or driven out by Yahweh because of their wickedness. [11] In Hos. 9:15, Yahweh warns Israel that he will drive them out of his land ("Yahweh's house"). Micah accuses the rich of driving women and children out of their houses (Mic. 2:9). Zephaniah announces that the people of Ashdod will be driven out of their city (Zeph. 2:4).

III. In the Law. *grš* is used 5 times in legal contexts: 4 times in P (Lev. 21:7, 14; 22:13; Nu. 30:10[9]), and once in Ezekiel (Ezk. 44:22). In all these passages, it refers to the "putting away" of a wife by her husband. [12]

Ringgren

גֶּשֶׁם *geshem* → מטר *māṭār*

---

[10] Zimmerli, *BK*, XIII/2, 749.
[11] Driver, *Bibl*, 19 (1938), 178f. argues that *grš* here should be translated "to expose to public contempt," in conformity with Arab. *ǧaraša*.
[12] Elliger, *HAT*, 4, 289.

דֹּב dôbh

Contents: I. Etymology; The Appearance of the Bear in the Canaanite Region. II. The Bear in the OT.

I. Etymology; The Appearance of the Bear in the Canaanite Region. The words for "bear" in the West Semitic languages come from a common root (which is used indiscriminately for the male and the female): Heb. *dobh,* Aram. *deb(b)ā,* Arab. *dubb,* Ethiop. *děb(b).* Akkadian has a very similar form, *dabû, dabbu,*[1] which alternates with the word *asu,* derived from Sum. *as.* Apparently inspired by the association of the bear with taboo in certain Indo-European languages (German and Balto-Slavic), many attempts have been made to explain the word *dobh* etymologically as a metaphorical term for the bear. Gesenius,[2] followed by *KBL* and Ben Yehuda, connects *dobh* with the root of the Arabic verb *dabba,* "to move (walk) slowly." Haupt thinks it comes from a verb meaning "to growl"[3] (cf. Isa. 59:11). Cohen supposes a possible connection with Egyp. *db,* "hippopotamus."[4] This would represent a peculiar use of the Hamito-Semitic word for a "large animal" in the Semitic languages.[5]

Discoveries of bones in the strata at Levalloisie and Mousterie[6] show that the bear (*ursus arctus syriacus*) existed in the Syro-Palestinian area as early as the prehistoric period. Iconographic witnesses are very scarce. A bear tied with a rope around its neck and led by Asiatics who are bringing tribute to Pharaoh Sahure (5th dynasty) is depicted on a relief in Abusir.[7] The animal represented on the orthostat in Tell Ḥalaf has been identified as a bear but this is disputed.[8]

II. The Bear in the OT. There are few references to the bear in the OT (it appears in only 12 passages)[9] and these give the impression of being literary

---

dōbh. F. S. Bodenheimer, *The Animals of Palestine* (Jerusalem, 1935); A. Caquot, "Les quatre bêtes et le 'Fils d'Homme'," *Sem,* 17 (1967), 37-71; J. Feliks, *The Animal World of the Bible* (Tel Aviv, 1962), 39.

[1] Cf. B. Landsberger, *Die Fauna des alten Mesopotamien* (1934), 82f.; *AHw,* 148f.

[2] Cf. Landsberger, 80-83.

[3] P. Haupt, *JAOS,* 32 (1912), 19, n. 1.

[4] M. Cohen, *Essai comparatif sur le vocabulaire et la phonétique du chamito-sémitique* (Paris, 1947), 153.

[5] Cf. already Ember, *ZA,* 28 (1914), 303, n. 4.

[6] Bodenheimer, 21f.

[7] Gressmann, *AOB,* No. 36.

[8] A. Moortgat, *Tell Ḥalaf. III. Die Bildwerke* (1955), 70f.; cf. also Hilzheimer, *RLA,* I, 398f.; E. D. van Buren, *The Fauna of Ancient Mesopotamia As Represented in Art. AnOr,* 18 (Rome, 1939), 20-22; L. Keimer, "Altägyptische, griechisch-römische und byzantisch-koptische Darstellungen des syrischen Bären," *AfO,* 17 (1956), 336-346.

[9] Feliks, 39.

clichés rather than zoological observations. The bear is primarily a wild, carnivorous, and untameable animal like the lion, with which it is often connected, or
like the leopard, which is mentioned along with the lion and the bear (Isa. 11:6f.;
Hos. 13:7). Like the lion, it lives in the woods (ya'ar): the two bears that tear
the boys who mocked Elisha come out of the woods (2 K. 2:24—a children's
story). Presumably the bear attacks flocks of sheep: the shepherd boy David
snatches the sheep from the jaws "of the lion and of the bear" which had seized
them (1 S. 17:34-37; cf. Sir. 47:3 ["he made a fool of the lion and the bear," not
"he played with the lion and the bear"] and Ps. 151:3 in the Syriac translation).
Lam. 3:10 compares Yahweh with a bear which (like a lion) lies in wait for his
prey. Am. 5:19 pictures the bear as even more dangerous than the lion: "as if a
man fled from a lion, and a bear met him" means the same thing as "out of the
frying-pan into the fire" (in Am. 5:19, the bear represents the inescapable peril
of the day of Yahweh). The cliché of the distress and ferocity of a she-bear
robbed of her whelps, which is used by classical authors, occurs 3 times in the
OT: to describe David's bitterness (2 S. 17:8), God's wrath (Hos. 13:8), and a
severe calamity (Prov. 17:12). Prov. 28:15 compares a wicked ruler with a greedy
bear (and a roaring lion). Wisd. 11:17 mentions the bear before the lion and
before mythical monsters in its description of the fearsome animals created by
God. The "paradisiacal" figure in Isa. 11:7 tells how the carnivorous bear will
be changed into a herbivorous animal which (like the lion) shall feed together
with the cow. The OT also uses the figure of the "growling" bear to describe a
forsaken and grumbling man (Isa. 59:11). The Greek text of Sir. 25:17 compares
the quarrelsome wife with a bear, but the Hebrew text says that she makes the
face of her husband "dark like that of a bear."

The allegory of the beasts in Dnl. 7:3-7 uses the bear (which is always described as a carnivorous animal) as a symbol for the Median Empire, while the
lion represents the Babylonian, the leopard the Persian, and the unnamed beast,
the Greek. [10] The origin of this figurative language should perhaps be sought in
an astrological geographical system which is comparable to that of Teukros of
Babylon (2nd millennium B.C.). According to Teukros, dominion over a portion
of the world is attributed to a constellation, which is symbolized by a beast. In
the system of Teukros, the bear controls the regions of the north, to which Media
belongs (as Babylon does to the south, Persia to the east, and Greece to the
west). If one wants to see a figure of the Roman Empire in the fourth beast of
Dnl. 7, the bear must represent Persia. For this reason the Talmud (*Yoma* 77a)
gives the "prince of the kingdom of Persia" in Dnl. 10:13 the name of *dobi'el*.

Caquot

---

[10] Cf. A. Caquot, *Sem,* 5 (1955), 5-13; M. Delcor, *Le livre de Daniel* (Paris, 1971), 143ff.

דִּבָּה dibbāh; זְבוּב zᵉbhûbh

Contents: I. Etymology. II. In Extrabiblical Literature: 1. *dīnu u dabābu*; 2. *bēl dabābi*—Beel-zebub. III. Usage in the Bible: 1. Occurrences; 2. Syntactical Use of *dibbah;* 3. Parallel Expressions, Synonyms; 4. In the LXX. IV. 1. Defamation, Slander; 2. Hostile Plot; 3. Evil Report. V. In the Qumran Literature.

I. Etymology. The root *dbb* does not appear very often in West and South Semitic languages. It is found only in Hebrew, Middle Hebrew, Mandean, the Talmud, the Targumim, Aramaic, Egyptian Aramaic, and Arabic. It is derived from Akk. (esp. Neo-Assyr. and Late Bab.) *dibbu,* "word, speech, report, idle talk," then also "event, thing, matter," in the juridical sphere "lawsuit, accusation, treaty, contract,"[1] which in turn is connected with Old Bab. *dabābum,* "speech, talk, wording (of a document), treaty, lawsuit, accusation, objection" (technical term *dīnu dabābu*), occasionally also the inarticulate "sound made by an animal,"[2] and frequently in the pejorative sense "untruthful, evil, presumptuous slander, idle talk." This should also be compared with Akk. *dabbibu,* "slanderer," and *dābibu,* "defense lawyer."[3] The verb *dabābu* lies behind this substantive. It has a wide range of meaning: its basic meaning is "to speak, relate" (partially synonymous with *atwûm*), which can suggest different things depending on the intention and the situation. It can be intensified beyond normal speaking (or praying) in the direction of "discussing, protesting, complaining, accusing, going to law against," or in the direction of "whispering, muttering,

---

dibbāh. W. F. Albright, "Zabûl Yam and Thâpiṭ Nahar in the Combat between Baal and the Sea," *JPOS,* 16 (1936), 17-20; H. Birkeland, *Die Feinde des Individuums in der israelitischen Psalmenliteratur* (Oslo, 1933); F. C. Fensham, "A Possible Explanation of the Name Baal-Zebub of Ekron," *ZAW,* 79 (1967), 361-64; W. Foerster, "Βεεζεβούλ," *TDNT,* I, 605f.; L. Gaston, *ThZ,* 18 (1962), 247-255; R. Gordis, *VT,* 5 (1955), 89; B. Halper, *ZAW,* 30 (1910), 108; E. Jenni, *BHHW,* I, 175f.; A. S. Kapelrud, *Baal in the Ras Shamra Texts* (Copenhagen, 1952), 60; J. Kohler-A. Ungnad, *Assyrische Rechtsurkunden* (1913), 455-58; P. Koschaker, *Neue keilschriftliche Rechtsurkunden aus der El-Amarna-Zeit* (1928), 28-31; I. Löw, "טובתיו Neh 6,19," *ZAW,* 33 (1913), 154f.; Y. Muffs, *Studies in the Aramaic Legal Papyri from Elephantine. Studia et Documenta,* 8 (Leiden, 1969); H. Petschow, *Die neubabylonischen Kaufformulare. LRSt,* 118 (1939), 2-31; G. von Rad, *Die Priesterschrift im Hexateuch. BWANT,* 4/13 (1934), 40f.; L. Ruppert, *Die Josepherzählung des Genesis. StANT,* 11 (1965), 31f.; M. San Nicolò, *Die Schlussklauseln der altbabylonischen Kauf- und Tauschverträge. MBPAR,* 4 (1922), 39-137; idem, *Beiträge zur Rechtsgeschichte im Bereiche der keilschriftlichen Rechtsquellen* (Oslo, 1931); M. San Nicolò-H. Petschow, *Babylonische Rechtsurkunden aus dem 6.Jahrhundert v.Chr. ABAW,* N.F. 51 (1960); K. Schwarzwäller, *Die Feinde des Individuums in den Psalmen* (diss., Hamburg, 1963); U. Skladny, *Die ältesten Spruchsammlungen in Israel* (1962); D. Sperling, "The Accadian Legal Terms *dīnu u dabābu,*" *JANES,* 1 (1968), 35-40; R. Yaron, *Introduction to the Law of the Aramaic Papyri* (Oxford, 1961), 78-92, esp. p. 86.

[1] *CAD,* III, 132f.; *AHw,* 168.
[2] *CAD,* III, 2f.
[3] *AHw,* 148.

slandering, conspiring, plotting," [4] "scheming against someone," [5] all of which is condensed in the expression *bēl dabābi*, "defense lawyer, enemy, adversary."

The West and South Semitic languages use this root almost entirely to convey the aspect of "defamation," thus Arab. *dabūb*, "slanderer." [6] In Egyptian Aramaic, *dbb* is found only in the juridical sense "accusation, lawsuit," [7] and the same is true of Mandean *dbb*, "to accuse," [8] Aram. *debhabha*, "enemy," *debhabhutha*, "enmity," [9] and Middle Heb. *dibbā*, "slander," "woman with a bad reputation."

II. In Extrabiblical Literature.

1. *dīnu u dabābu*. Frequently we encounter Akkadian terms involving the root *dbb* in legal documents, especially in documents containing contracts for the transfer of property. Thus a person can threaten to bring charges before the king or before his officer against a contracting party if the latter does not comply with the terms of the contract (*di-ib-b[i-šu]* ... *ina pān qīpi ša Esagila idabbub;* cf. *ša dib-bi-šú ina pān šarri bēliya adbubu*). [10] But much more frequently we find these terms in bills of sale and exchange in releases and waivers. [11]

Usually this kind of contract has the following structure: (1) names of the contracting parties; (2) description of the subject of the contract; (3) cost (or terms of exchange); (4) clause stating purchase agreement: "A has acquired and received ... from B for X shekels of silver"; (5) receipt: "The money has been paid in full, the (respective) commodity has been bought and received." This concludes and validates the sale or exchange agreement. But in order to assure even further protection, there follows (mainly in later formulations) [12] (6) the waiver, in which both contracting parties declare: *tu-a-ru de-e-nu dabābu la-aš-šu,* "There shall be no return, lawsuit, or complaint." In Neo-Assyrian bills of sale, this release is to be given only by the seller. [13] The waiver can be extended to relatives and descendants or to any third party by a release clause: "If any one rises up and brings a complaint or causes a complaint to be brought (*idabbub, ušadbab*—from Nebuchadnezzar on, replaced by *ragāmu*) against the contract, he shall restore twelve-fold." [14] Frequently this clause stands in synonymous parallelism with *enû*, "to change a contract," and *paqāru*, "to bring a judicial complaint." [15] These clauses declare all subsequent claims to be legally invalid.

---

[4] *CAD*, III, 4ff.; *AHw*, 146f.

[5] Birkeland, 374.

[6] Lane, I/3, 841: "one who creeps about with calumny or slander," "one who calumniates or slanders"; *'adabba 'alā*, "to spread abroad an evil rumor," Kopf, "Arabische Etymologien und Parallelen," *VT*, 8 (1958), 169.

[7] *DISO*, 54.

[8] *MdD*, 101b.

[9] Dalman, 90.

[10] *ABL*, 792, 6.

[11] Kohler-Ungnad, 455ff.; San Nicolò, *Schlussklauseln*, 39-125; idem, *Beiträge*, 170; Petschow, 2-31.

[12] Petschow, 2.

[13] Koschaker, 31.

[14] Petschow, 30.

[15] San Nicolò-Petschow, 14; Texts 8-12.

The same waiver clause occurs in numerous documents from Elephantine, [16] where we encounter the stereotyped expression *dyn vdbb* in conjunction with *l' 'khl 'grnk* or *l' 'khl 'ršnky*, "I can no longer bring a lawsuit and a complaint." [17] Here also the waiver can be extended to a third party and combined with penal regulations. [18] At the same time, the incontestability of a contract is sometimes declared more intensively by an additional *'pm* clause, [19] which states that the status quo created by the drawing up of the contract is irrevocable. [20] At Elephantine, *dbb* has already gone so far toward becoming a technical term that it does not appear outside this juridical clause. Possibly there is a direct line of development from Akkadian by way of Egyptian Aramaic to Greco-Egyptian papyri, where we find the formula *áneu díkēs kaí kríseōs*, "without penalty and punishment." [21]

2. *bēl dabābi—Beel-zebub*. In Akkadian documents from Middle Babylonian on, we encounter the *bēl dabābi*, [22] who is the "legal opponent" in juridical texts. [23] He functions here as the "accuser, public prosecutor," although the texts give no information about his official function. In Neo-Babylonian texts, he is the "enemy, slanderer," the instigator of controversies, [24] and one who speaks lies. Paradigmatically, his behavior represents hostile, injurious behavior. [25] The texts explicitly distinguish him from "friends" (*bēlē ṭābti*). [26] In contrast, he is mentioned along with the *bēl ikki*, "adversary," *bēl ṣirri*, "enemy," *bēl ridi*, "persecutor," *bēl dîni*, "accuser," *bēl amâti*, "slanderer," *bēl egirrê*, "schemer," and *bēl limutti*, "evildoer." [27] He stands on the same level as the *bêl dīktiya*, "murderer." [28] Outside the Bible he also appears in Aram. *ba'al debhabha*, "enemy," [29] and in Mandean *bildbaba*. [30]

The extent to which this concept has been influenced by the deformation of the name of the Philistine god "Baal-zebul" to "Baal-zebub" (2 K. 1:2ff.) can no longer be ascertained. Many recent attempts have been made to explain the connection between these two names: (1) Because of the fire motif in 2 K. 1, some scholars connect the name *Ba'al zebhubh* with the difficult Ugar. *dbb*, [31]

---

16 *DISO*, 54.
17 *AP*, 6, 12; 14, 7; etc.; Muffs, 30-37; 182ff.
18 *BMAP*, 10, 12; *AP*, 8, 20; 9, 13.
19 *AP*, 13, 9f.; 20, 16; 25, 10.
20 Joüon, *MUSJ*, 18 (1934), 29ff.; Yaron, *Bibl*, 41 (1960), 269ff.; *idem, The Law*, 88ff.
21 San Nicolò, *Beiträge*, 170; Kutscher, *JAOS*, 74 (1954), 239f.
22 *CAD*, III, 3f.
23 *KAR*, 96, 35=*BWL*, 144-47; *BIN*, I, 73, 31.
24 *ABL*, 326, 4.
25 CT 22, 144, 6.
26 *ABL*, 326, r. 11.
27 G. Meier, *Die assyrische Beschwörungssammlung Maqlû* (1937), 10, 14.
28 *AfO*, 18 (1957/58), 289, line 5.
29 Dalman, 90; H. Zimmern, *Akkadische Fremdwörter* (²1917), 24.
30 *MdD*, 60b.
31 *CTA*, 3 [V AB], III, 42f.

Aram. *shebhibha*, "flame," which would point to a god of fire. [32] (2) Others connect the "original" name *Ba'al zebhubh* with Arab. *dubāb*, "flight," and look upon this deity as a "god of flight" (cf. Zeus Apomyïos). [33] (3) The most likely theory is that the Philistine deity originally had the name *b'l zbl**, corresponding to Ugar. *zbl b'l-'rṣ*. [34] If this is so, the name means "Baal is prince." [35]

The contrast between Yahweh and Baal completely dominates the Elijah narrative in 2 K. 1, and thus it is easy to see how the author or a later redactor might try to intensify this antithesis by a cacophemistic deformation of the name of Baal to *Ba'al zebhubh*. Here a conscious contamination of the name with the idea of *bêl dabābi*, "enemy, slanderer, schemer," is not out of the question. There is no difficulty in identifying these two terms, especially since *d* frequently assumes the fricative sound *z* and *dbb* becomes *zbb* in *BMAP*, 3, 17. [36] The author or redactor shows his fidelity to Yahweh and his opposition to Baal simply by changing his name, characterizing Baal as the enemy, and thus separating him from any possible Israelite observance.

This designation was still known in NT times (cf. the Mandeans and the NT variant readings in Mk. 3:22 par.), but in the meantime the concept of the demon who is the slanderer, accuser, and adversary had been transferred to the figure of the → שָׂטָן *śāṭān*, "Satan." [37]

The NT *Beelzeboul* probably is not to be connected with *ba'al zbl* (2 K. 1). [38] This name may well be of Rabbinic origin, with a derivation from *zabhal*, "to have a bowel movement," *zibbul*, "dung." [39] If one wishes to see in it a traditio-historical development of *ba'al zebhubh*, it could perhaps be interpreted as an even more intensified and extremely pejorative cacophemy which in terms of the radicals comes very close to the Ugaritic prototype. The sequence in the tradition would then run from *zbl* (Ugar.) by way of *zebhubh* (2 K. 1) to *zebhul* (Rabbinic literature, NT). [40]

III. Usage in the Bible.

1. *Occurrences.* *dibbah* occurs 9 times in the OT: 4 times in P (Gen. and Nu.), twice in Proverbs, and once each in Jeremiah, Ezekiel, and Psalms.

2. *Syntactical Use of dibbah.* *dibbah* is used as the object of *yatsa'* in the hiphil, "to bring, bring up, utter" (Nu. 13:32; 14:36,37; Prov. 10:18), or of *bo'*

---

[32] Cassuto, Driver, J. Gray, Miller, van den Born in Haag, *BL*, 158; Albright, *BASOR*, 84 (1941), 14-17; recently again Fensham, *ZAW*, 79, 361-64.

[33] Montgomery-Gehman, *ICC*; Klauser, *RAC*; van den Born in Haag, *BL*, 158.

[34] *CTA*, 5 [I* AB], VI, 10, etc.; epithet of *b'l 'lȝyn;* → בעל *ba'al*; cf. Zebulun and Jezebel; also David, *VT*, 1 (1951), 59f.

[35] *UT*, 815; *WUS*, No. 878; Albright, *JPOS*, 16, 17; Kapelrud, 60f.; Tsevat, *VT*, 4 (1954), 322; Jenni, *BHHW*, I, 175f.; Gaston, *ThZ*, 247ff.; Fohrer, *Elia* (²1968), 82f.

[36] Kutscher, *JAOS*, 235.

[37] Cf. F. Horst, *BK*, XVI/1, 13f.; N. and H. W. Schnaper, "A Few Kind Words for the Devil," *Journal of Religion and Health*, 8 (1969), 107-122.

[38] Contra St.-B., I, 632.

[39] Van den Born, *BL*, 178.

[40] But cf. more recently M. Limbeck, "Beelzebul—eine ursprüngliche Bezeichnung für Jesus?" *Festschrift K. H. Schelkle* (1973), 31-42.

in the hiphil, "to bring" (Gen. 37:2), and conversely of *shamaʿ*, "to hear" (Jer. 20:10; Ps. 31:14 [Eng. v. 13]). Twice P characterizes *dibbah* as *raʿah*, "evil" (Gen. 37:2; Nu. 14:37). In half the occurrences of *dibbah* in the OT, it appears as the *nomen regens* (governing noun) of the construct in the sense of a subjective genitive: *dibbath rabbim*, "the whispering of many" (Jer. 20:10; Ps. 31:14 [13]), or *dibbath ʿam*, "the gossip of the people" (Ezk. 36:3); in P only in the sense of an objective genitive: *dibbath haʾarets*, "an evil report of the land" (Nu. 13:32 [Pᴬ]; 14:37 [Pᴮ]), which corresponds to *dibbah ʿal haʾarets*, "an evil report against the land" (Nu. 14:36 [Pᴬ]). A man or certain men always appear as the subject in these instances.

3. *Parallel Expressions, Synonyms.* *dibbah* is used in connection with the following parallel expressions and synonyms: *sephath lashon*, "talk" (Ezk. 36:3), *neʾatsoth*, "revilings" (Ezk. 35:12), *siphethe shaqer*, "lying lips" (Prov. 12:22), *dabhar ʿathaq*, "insolent speech" (Ps. 31:19[18]), *rakhil*, "slander" (RSV "gossiping") (Prov. 20:19; Ps. 31:21[20], conjec.), *raghan*, "to slander" (RSV "whisperer") (Prov. 26:20,22), and *higgidh*, "to denounce" (Jer. 20:10). Another synonym is **ṭibbah*, "rumor" (Neh. 6:19, conjec.).[41] We must reject a similar conjectural reading in Hos. 14:3(2),[42] because the MT (+ LXX) gives a good sense.

4. *In the LXX.* The LXX translates *dibbah* in various ways: *psógos*, "blame, censure" (3 times), *kateipeín*, "to accuse, charge," *loidoría*, "abuse, reproach, reviling" (elsewhere for *ribh*, "strife, dispute"), *oneídisma*, "reproaches, insults" (elsewhere for *cherpah*, "reproach"), *hrḗmata ponerá*, "evil words," and (interpreting greatly) *ékstasis*, "distraction, confusion, ecstasy" (Nu. 13:32) (once each).

IV. 1. *Defamation, Slander.* The earliest occurrences of *dibbah* are found in the axioms of the book of Proverbs and reach back into the earlier (Prov. 10:18) and later (25:10) monarchical period.[43] *dibbah* is found here in connection with *sheqer*, "lying" (10:18; 12:22), *tahpukhoth*, "perversity" (10:31,32), *raghan*, "whisperer" (26:20,22), *rakhil*, "slander, gossip" (RSV "talebearer") (11:13), etc. These are paradigms on the false use of words, which in contrast to the righteous (wise) is a characteristic of the fool (→ כְּסִיל *keṣîl*), who speaks indiscreetly in his garrulousness (10:8) and thus causes strife and violence (10:11). The formula in 10:18 is particularly pregnant: "He who conceals hatred has lying lips, and he who utters *dibbah* (slander) is a fool." It is not stupidity as a defect of the intellect that makes a man a *kesil*, "fool," but wrong behavior in ethics and religion. In Prov. 10–24 (but not in 25ff.), the *kesil* is identical with the *rashaʿ*, "guilty criminal (evildoer)." Accordingly, *dibbah* does not mean here a rumor about someone which arises out of ignorance, but a calculated

---

[41] *KBL*³, 352; M. Wagner, *Aramaismen. BZAW*, 96 (1966), 111; Gordis, *VT*, 89f.; Rudolph, *HAT*, 20, 137ff.

[42] Contra Wolff, *Hosea* (trans. 1974), and Rudolph, *KAT*, XIII/1, *in loc.*

[43] Skladny, 80f.; but cf. Eissfeldt, *The OT* (trans. 1965), 474, although he considers it possible that some proverbial sayings date back into the preexilic period, p. 475.

rumor which is conceived for the purpose of hurting someone and concerning whose truth or falsity no precise statement is made. It is, then, "defamation." The fact that *dibbah* is used with *sin'ah*, "hate," and *sheqer*, "lying," may perhaps indicate that falsehood is inherent in *dibbah*, so that its meaning can be narrowed down to "slander." Similarly, in Prov. 25:10 *dibbah* means a rumor which is spread abroad to hurt someone, specifically in this case the blabbing out of another's secret (*galah sodh 'acher*, v. 9; cf. Am. 3:7; Prov. 20:19). The warning against disclosing secrets is based on the idea of the connection between action and condition, for he who discloses *sodh* (a secret) reaps shame and his *dibbah* comes back (*shubh*) upon himself, i.e., he himself becomes the object of the *dibbah* of others and suffers the harm he had intended for someone else. This is not to disregard the possibility that in this passage *dibbah* means a rash legal accusation [44] which brings on the plaintiff the charge of slander when the innocence of the accused is established.

2. *Hostile Plot*. In a complaint in one of his confessions (Jer. 20:10) Jeremiah uses *dibbah* to describe the conniving scheming of his enemies, who seek an occasion against him. [45] This passage (in the form of a direct address) also contains an example of the use of *dibbah* to convey the idea of the conspiratorial preparation of a complaint by legal opponents, who scornfully take up the message of the prophet ("Terror on every side!" 6:25; 20:3; 46:5; 49:29), bring accusations against (*higgidh*, "denounce," cf. 1 S. 27:11) him, and want to take revenge on him (*laqach neqamah*). The passage is characterized by the "deadly hate" [46] of the many, even including some former friends of the prophet. But the prophet knows that he will be protected from this *dibbah* by Yahweh's help, so that ultimately it will come back upon his adversaries as shame and dishonor (*kelimmah*, v. 11; cf. Prov. 25:10, *chissedh*, "to bring shame upon"). Additional statements concerning words and plans of enemies occur in Ps. 41:6-8(5-7), where *'amar ra'*, "to speak evil (malice)," and *hithlachesh*, "to whisper together," are used as synonyms of *dibbah*. Possibly Ps. 31:14(13), "a late pre-exilic cultic song" [47] which shows several affinities with the confessions of Jeremiah, [48] is influenced by Jer. 20:10. Here *dibbah* [49] stands in parallelism with the *behissodham*, [50] "secret speech" of the "many" (*'oyebhim*, "enemies," and *rodhephim*, "persecutors," v. 16[15]), which the psalmist identifies with *sheqer*, "lying," and *dabhar 'athaq*, "insolent speech," in v. 19(18), and with *rakhil*, "slander, gossip," in v. 21(20). [51] Schwarzwäller thinks *dibbah* has here the sense of false accusations systematically initiated and contrived. [52] The threatening aspect of the *dibbah* is expressed clearly when the psalmist, in the parallel

---

44 Ringgren, *ATD*, XVI, 102; Hamp, *EB, in loc.*
45 Cf. *KAR*, 71 r. 27.
46 Weiser, *ATD*, XX-XXI, 172.
47 Sellin-Fohrer, *IntrodOT* (trans. 1968), 287.
48 Kraus, *BK*, XV/1, 248.
49 Birkeland, 197: "evil report," here the "scornful, triumphant words of the enemy."
50 Conjectural reading with *BHS*.
51 Conjectural reading with Kraus, *et al.*
52 Schwarzwäller, 100.

passage in v. 5(4), compares persecution by his enemies to a net (*resheth*) that has been secretly spread out for him.

The redactor who inserted v. 3 in Ezk. 36 [53] speaks of the *dibbath 'am*, "evil gossip of the people," in which Israel engaged (*'alah* in the niphal). This is equivalent to what Ezekiel calls "the words of the enemy" (*'omer ha'oyebh*) in v. 2b. Quoting these words, he makes them part of the basis of his oracle of salvation: "Aha, Aha! Wilderness for ever! It has become our possession!" [54] Here, contrary to first impressions, *dibbah* is not primarily a contemptuous utterance or an expression of "malicious pleasure," [55] as the same (?) redactor states on his own authority in vv. 4,5, but the plotting of enemy nations against devastated Israel as they plan its final overthrow. Yahweh does not consent to this *dibbah* for it expresses the scornful intention of neighboring countries which finally "shall themselves suffer reproach (*kelimmah*)" (v. 7b).

3. *Evil Report*. The Priestly Code uses *dibbah* in two senses. In Gen. 37:2 the reason P gives for the dissension between Joseph and his brothers is that Joseph "brought an ill report of them (*vayyabhe' dibbatham*) to their father" [56] (in contrast to J and E, which attribute the dissension to the brothers' jealousy of Joseph). Here, to be sure, *dibbah* can mean "an ill report of them," "tale-bearing," [57] but in the light of what has already been said, it seems better to interpret the line to mean that "Joseph took back a bad account of them." [58] The verb *hebhi'* "to bring," certainly does not allow us to suppose that Joseph was innocent in contriving this *dibbah*, but conversely *hotsi'* (Nu. 13:32; 14:36, 37) does not imply guilt. [59] *hebhi'* may have been chosen by the author of Gen. 37:2 to indicate a singular object, in contrast to *hotsi'*. P makes some excuse for what Joseph did by referring twice to his young age. Peck attempts to exonerate Joseph by referring *dibbatham* to a "slander" of the brothers against Joseph: "Joseph brought their slander against him to their father." [60] But there is nothing in the text to support this view. In Nu. 13:32; 14:36,37 P uses *dibbah* in a special sense, for these passages speak of a *dibbah*, "evil report," not against man, but against *ha'arets*, "the land." The story of the return and report of the spies is found in several versions. J introduces the more positive account in Nu. 13:27a with the words *vayesapperu lo vayyo'meru*, "and they related to him and said" (RSV, "and they told him"). The Deuteronomic wording in Dt. 1:25aβ is similar, *vayyashibhu 'othanu dhabhar vayyo'meru*, "and they brought us word again and said." But when the spies say in P, "the land devours its inhabitants" (Nu. 13:32), they are giving a negative and horrifying description, which obviously did not correspond to the actual circumstances, but was distorted in order to stir up the people (Nu. 14:36,37). Thus the *dabhar*, "word,"

53 Zimmerli, *BK*, XIII/2, 858, following Hölscher.
54 Zimmerli.
55 Contra Birkeland, 197.
56 Von Rad, *Priesterschrift*, 41.
57 Von Rad, *Genesis. OTL* (trans. 1961), 343, 345 (*ATD*, II/4 [⁹1972], 284ff.).
58 Cf. D. B. Redford, *A Study of the Biblical Story of Joseph. SVT*, 20 (1970), 14f.
59 Contra Ruppert, 31f.
60 J. Peck, "Note on Genesis 37,2 and Joseph's Character," *ExpT*, 82 (1970/71), 342.

becomes a *dibbah,* "false report," "defamation." This false report is directed against a promise and therefore against the God who made this promise, and Yahweh's answer to it is the death of the spies who brought it (Nu. 14:37; cf. Prov. 10:31) and the threat that the people will die in the wilderness.

V. In the Qumran Literature. The concepts of "defamation" and "hostile plot" are also found in the Qumran literature. In 1QH 2:11, the worshipper (the Teacher of Righteousness?) says that he has become a *dibbah* (an object of slander) "upon the lips of the violent" (*bisephath 'aritsim*). He is the man by whom the spirits of others are separated. He is "healing" and a banner (*nes*) for the elect and for those that are converted, but an object of "mockery" (*qeles*) and of "defamatory songs" (*neghinah*) for the ungodly and sinners. They throw "slime and mud"[61] at him (v. 13). By repeating that "the wicked" "roared against him like great waters" (vv. 12,16), he shows that he is exposed to great persecution, which takes on very dangerous forms in the *dibbah* of the rulers and the systematic attack of the Jerusalem orthodoxy (?). As may be seen from the additional phrase, *'al 'avon resha'im,* "the affronts of the wicked" (v. 10), he is accused of crimes that he has not committed.

Fabry

דְּבִיר *debhîr* → היכל *hêkhāl*

---

[61] J. Maier, *Die Texte vom Toten Meer* (1960), *in loc.*

> דָּבַק *dābhaq;* דֶּבֶק *debheq;* דָּבֵק *dābhēq*

Contents: I. 1. Etymology, Meaning; 2. Use in the OT. II. Figurative Use: 1. In Interpersonal Relationships; 2. In Internal, Spiritual Matters. III. Theological Use: 1. In Deuteronomy and the Deuteronomistic Work; 2. In OT Cultic Literature.

I. 1. *Etymology, Meaning.* In the OT the root *dbq* occurs 55 times in Hebrew and once in Aramaic. The derivatives *dabheq* and *debheq* appear 3 times each. This root is used with the prepositions *be,* "in," *le,* "to," *'el,* "unto," *'im,* "with," and *'achare,* "after." Outside the OT, it is found only in West Semitic dialects (but cf. Ethiop. *ṭabaqa* with the same meaning).[1]

---

dābhaq. H. J. Franken, *The Mystical Communion with JHWH in the Book of Psalms* (Leiden, 1954), 34-36, 90-92; E. Jenni, "דבק," *THAT,* I (1971), 431f.; S. Liebermann, "Forgotten Meanings," *Lešonenu,* 32 (1968), 89-102, esp. pp. 92-94; N. Lohfink, *Das Hauptgebot. Eine Untersuchung literarischer Einleitungsfragen zu Dtn 5–11.* AnBibl, 20 (Rome, 1963), 79; K. L. Schmidt, "κολλάω, προσκολλάω," *TDNT,* III, 822f.

[1] Leslau, *Contributions,* 16.

According to Bauer, *dbq* is a "concealed infixed t-form with a reflexive meaning," from a root reflected in Arab. *baqiya* ("to remain"), in which the *t* is assimilated to the *b* sound for the sake of euphony. [2] But the suggestion of Fraenkel
is better. [3] He thinks Arab. *dibq, dābūq,* and *dābūqā'* ("glue, bird-lime") are
loanwords from Aram., and that the verb *dabiqa* is a denominative. S. Liebermann thinks that *dbq* is related to Aram. *bdq* (Mandean *ptk*), which the Talmud
uses sometimes as a translation for *dabhaq*.

The verb *dabhaq* is intransitive in all West Semitic idioms: "to cling together,
stick together" (of various things or materials that are usually differentiated
according to their substance). [4]

In antithesis to → חָשַׁק *chāshaq,* which emphasizes more strongly the idea of
conscious adhesion or attachment, [5] "to adhere to someone in love," [6] the root
dbq has a medial-passive character, which is especially suitable in statements
concerning objects or things. The LXX has attempted to express this idea by
always using *kolláō* and *proskolláō* (which are rarely used in profane Greek) in
the middle or passive (19 and 11 times respectively, in contrast to 3 and 2 times
respectively in the active, usually translating the Heb. hiphil). Formally this is
in complete agreement with the NT use of these Greek verbs. [7] At the same time,
the LXX uses 13 other verbs to translate *dabhaq,* some of which are employed
only once for this purpose.

2. *Use in the OT.* The meaning "cling to, stick to, cleave," which must be
considered original and which is narrowly limited in content, is relatively rare in
OT-biblical usage. It denotes the cleaving together of wet clods (pual, Job 38:38)
and the joining together of the scales of the crocodile (pual, Job 41:9 [Eng v. 17]).
Corresponding to this, the segholate noun *debheq* means the soldering of the
scales on a breastplate (1 K. 22:34 = 2 Ch. 18:33), [8] or the fastening together of
the parts of a graven image (Isa. 41:7). *dbq* can also be applied to living creatures
to denote fish fastening themselves to the scales of a crocodile (Ezk. 29:4). It is
also used in the description of living creatures. Thus we read concerning the cherubim on the lid of the ark that their outspread wings are joined together (2 Ch.
3:12; 1 K. 6:27 speaks only of the wings touching one another, → נגע *nāgha'*).
But the waistcloth that a man puts on his loins is also said to cling to him (Jer.
13:11), and the clenched hand of a warrior cleaves to his sword (2 S. 23:10).
dbq is not used to denote a material joining or merging.

II. Figurative Use.

1. *In Interpersonal Relationships.* The Hebrew root *dbq* is used figuratively

---

[2] H. Bauer, *ZS,* 16 (1935), 174-76, esp. p. 175.

[3] S. Fraenkel, *Die aram. Fremdwörter im Arabischen* (Leiden, 1866), 120f.

[4] Franken, 34; for Ugar.-Akk. *dubbuqu,* "to join together, unite," cf. von Soden, *UF,* 1
(1969), 191.

[5] Franken, 36.

[6] G. Quell, *TDNT,* I, 22.

[7] Schmidt.

[8] Cf. *BRL,* 416f.

in passages that have to do with relationships between people. These relationships can be friendly or hostile in nature. (a) *dbq* is used in a positive sense of a man cleaving to his wife (Gen. 2:24). Shechem's desire (*dbq*) for Dinah (Gen. 34:3, in connection with → אהב *'āhabh,* "to love") expresses the passionate element of love more strongly. Dnl. 2:43 uses *dbq* (Aram.) to denote a marital relationship. *dbq,* however, does not denote a sexual relationship as *kolláō* does in the NT (Mt. 19:5; Eph. 5:31 = Gen. 2:24 in the LXX). It expresses rather a strong erotic or even a friendly affection toward someone. *dabhaq* does not connote sexual union because it can also describe the relationship between members of the same sex or human relationships in general. Thus, Ruth clings to her mother-in-law Naomi (Ruth 1:14). As she works in the field, she keeps close to the gleaners of Boaz (2:21), but she also keeps close to his maidens (2:8,23). The Wisdom Literature uses *dbq* to denote friendship among men (Prov. 18:24; here it stands in parallelism to *'ahabh,* "to love"). (b) With wholly unfriendly intentions, Laban follows close (hiphil) on the heels of Jacob in order to overtake him (Gen. 31:23). Finally, *dbq* is used in this sense as a technical term for immediate military pursuit (Josh. 23:12; Jgs. 18:22; 20:42,45; 1 S. 14:22; 31:2; 2 S. 1:6; 20:2; 23:10; 1 Ch. 10:2). The basic difference between *dabhaq* and its synonym → רדף *rādhaph,* "to pursue," is that *dabhaq* seems to express the idea of directly annihilating pursuit more strongly.

2. *In Internal, Spiritual Matters.* In a deeper sense the root *dbq* is also applied figuratively in the OT to the sphere of internal, spiritual matters. Poetry employs the idiom "cleaving to the roof of the mouth" as a figure of suffering (Lam. 4:4; Ps. 22:16[15]; 137:6; Job 29:10). The idioms "(dried up) flesh of a sufferer cleaving to the bones" (Ps. 102:6[5]) and "bones cleaving to the skin" (Job 19:20) are expressions of need or distress. From another angle the sufferer describes his distress as a cleaving to the dust (Ps. 119:25) or to the ground (44:26[25]). Various sufferings which cling to man or which God has caused to cleave to man are illness (2 K. 5:27), pestilence (Dt. 28:21), evil or disaster in general (Gen. 19:19), plagues in general (Dt. 28:60), curses (CD A 1:17), famine (Jer. 42:16), devoted things (Dt. 13:18[17]), and much else (Job 31:7).

III. Theological Use. In the light of all that has been said, *dbq* is very well suited (in its original and figurative sense) to denote theological matters. It has already been pointed out above[9] that the root can be used when Yahweh threatens that various things will cleave to man such as pestilence (Dt. 28:21), devoted things (13:18[17]), and the plagues of Egypt (28:60). But the godly man can also use the word to express his relationship to Yahweh. The simile of Jeremiah (Jer. 13:11) is significant in describing the relationship between Israel and Yahweh: here, Israel's inner relationship to Yahweh (hiphil) is symbolized by the waistcloth cleaving to a man's loins (qal).[10]

1. *In Deuteronomy and the Deuteronomistic Work.* The book of Deuteronomy has a certain preference for the root *dbq* to denote Israel's relationships to God

---

9 II.2.
10 See I.2 above.

as these are characteristically described by various series of expressions.[11] The word → עבד ʾābhadh, "to serve" (Dt. 10:20), along with → ירא yārēʾ, "to fear," and nishbaʿ bishemo, "to swear by his name" (cf. 10:20; 13:5[4]), frequently appears at the head of these series. 11:22 adds → אהב ʾāhabh, "to love" (cf. 30:20). 13:5(4), however, moves on to verbs which denote observance of the law: keep (→ שמר shāmar) his commandments (mitsvah); walk (→ הלך hālakh) in all his ways; walk after Yahweh, listen to (obey, → שמע shāmaʿ) his voice (qol) (cf. 30:20).[12]

The speech of Joshua to the Transjordanian tribes (which is all composed in Deuteronomistic style) has the same characteristics. It uses several terms to explain what Israel's relationship to Yahweh means. It must act in keeping with his commandment (mitsvah), observe his law (torah), love (ʾahabh) him, walk (halakh) in all his ways (derekh), and serve him with all its heart (lebh) and with all its being (nephesh). dabhaq is used in a similar way in Joshua's valedictory address. Israel must be very steadfast to keep and to do all that is written in the book of the law of Moses so as not to turn aside (sur) from it, but to cleave to Yahweh as it has done thus far (Josh. 23:6-8).

Such admonitions and vetitives, which contain a series of synonyms and antonyms of dabhaq, remove man's relationship to Yahweh from the realm of involuntary and unsubstantial connection and establish it on a wholly concrete decision to serve Yahweh and to reject other gods, i.e., on conscious action, which is the only appropriate response to the wholly practicable demand that man obey the divine law. Deuteronomy does not seek to bring about this obedience by imposing laws and injunctions on the people. Instead, it seeks to motivate the people to obey the law through persuasive sermons which to some extent employ stereotyped expressions. "Deuteronomy was, in fact, the first place where such far-reaching efforts were made to gain a theoretical understanding of the relationship to Yahweh."[13] Indeed, in these series Lohfink calls dabhaq an expletive.[14] In any case, the scroll of the Rule (Manual of Discipline) at Qumran (1QS 1:3-11) contains a series of commandments related in form and content to the Deuteronomic/Deuteronomistic style. Clinging (dbq, v. 5), not directly to Yahweh himself, but to all good works, to the practice of truth (ʾemeth), righteousness (tsedhaqah), and justice (mishpat), is adopted here as a constant element in the broad depiction of God's requirements. It is noteworthy that dabhaq is not used to denote the relationship on Yahweh's side either in the Deuteronomic/Deuteronomistic Work or anywhere else; chesedh, "steadfast love," is the appropriate term for this[15] (Ps. 63:4a[3a]).

The Deuteronomist finds a shining example of obedience to God in the figure of king Hezekiah. He tells how he trusted completely in Yahweh, and did not depart (sur) from him, but kept the commandments which Yahweh commanded

---

[11] Lohfink, 73-80.
[12] Additional expressions that convey this idea without dbq are given in Lohfink, 64-72.
[13] G. von Rad, Deuteronomy. OTL (trans. 1966), 84.
[14] Lohfink, 79.
[15] See 2 below.

Moses (2 K. 18:5-7). All the more disturbing is it, then, when a member of the people of Yahweh clings more tenaciously to other things than to Yahweh himself, so that finally he is inwardly separated from him. In this sense, the Deuteronomist considers it to be fundamentally sinful for Solomon not only to permit foreign cults in his realm, but to begin to cling (dabhaq; cf. hittah lebh 'achare, "to turn away the heart after") to them himself, and ultimately to love (→ אהב 'āhabh) them (1 K. 11:2). This was the reason for the internal and external decay of the Israelite kingdom.

2. *In OT Cultic Literature.* The use of dabhaq in Israel's cultic songs falls less in the realm of theologico-ethical decision and more in the realm of godly living. Thus the whole of Ps. 63 is in fact a meditation on this concept by one who is confident that he is an adherent of Yahweh.

The psalmist remembers this in his outward and inward distress (v. 10[9]). It is precisely on this presupposition that he seeks (shachar in the piel) Yahweh, thirsts (→ צמא tsāmā') for him, and faints for him like a dry land where there is no water (v. 2[1]). In the sanctuary he looks upon (→ חזה chāzāh) him to behold his power and glory. This communion with Yahweh finds its ultimate expression in the psalmist's vow to praise (→ הלל hillēl, v. 6[5]; → רנן rinnēn, v. 8[7]) Yahweh as long as he lives (v. 5[4]). This feeling grows until it becomes an assurance that he will be satisfied (sabha') with Yahweh (v. 6[5]) when he thinks of (→ הגה hāghāh; → זכר zākhar) him upon his bed at night (v. 7[6]), so that he can sing for joy in the conviction that he is safe under Yahweh's wings (v. 8[7]). This certainty of communion with God is based on faith in Yahweh's chesedh, "steadfast love" (v. 4a[3a]) and only indirectly on the concept of the covenant. [16] Thus the divine counterpart to man's dabhaq is Yahweh's chesedh. "This remarkably high esteem for communion with God is the real center of this profound psalm." [17] Kraus rightly opposes a spiritualizing and mystical interpretation. [18] Franken also rejects any mystical absorption of the psalmist in God. [19] What the psalmist is trying to express is not a mystical experience of the nearness of Yahweh or of union with him, but the assurance of safe keeping in the basic promise of his saving acts. This consciousness of union with Yahweh and his promise is the poet's pledge of inner security against his oppressors. At the same time, the feeling of security, which is repeated again and again in the Psalms, [20] extends far beyond all material and forensic qualities, and reaches maturity in the joy of the righteous at the divine favor which gives meaning and content to his life, even in distress. As a consequence the righteous refuses to have communion with evildoers and evil deeds (Ps. 101:3).

Although the root dbq has different nuances in the various literary genres of the OT, when it is used theologically the original middle-passive idea is

---

[16] Franken, 36.

[17] H.-J. Kraus, *BK*, XV/1, 444.

[18] G. von Rad, "Gerechtigkeit und Leben in der Kultsprache der Psalmen," *Festschrift A. Bertholet* (1950), 418-437, esp. p. 431 = GSAT (1958), 225-247, esp. p. 240.

[19] Franken, 35.

[20] H. Ringgren, *The Faith of the Psalmists* (1963), 47-60, esp. p. 58.

preserved to the extent that the reality of man's relationship to God is always expressed, even when a decision is made against God. The relationship of Israel or of the righteous individual to Yahweh is primary; separation from God can only be a disastrous secondary step. Loose though it may be, the link between *dbq* and the sacral, cultic realm (cf. Deuteronomy/the Deuteronomistic Work; Psalms) [21] may perhaps explain why the earlier classical prophets did not use the term. Jeremiah, Ezekiel, and Deutero-Isaiah are the first prophets to use the root theologically in its original and figurative sense. There seems to be no explanation for the absence of the root in P (except at Nu. 36:7,9).

Wallis

---

[21] *Ibid.*, 6f.

| דָּבַר *dābhar*; דָּבָר *dābhār* |

Contents: I. In the Ancient Near East: 1. Egypt: a. General Observations; b. In Cosmogonies; c. In the Literature for the Dead; d. In the Royal Ideology; e. In Oracles; 2. Mesopotamia. II. The Root: 1. Etymology: a. "To Be Behind"? b. "To Add Up"? c. A Biliteral Root? 2. Occurrences; 3. Derivatives; 4. Verb Forms. III. The Verb: 1. Use with Prepositions; 2. In Phrases; 3. The Relationship Between *dibber* and *'amar*; 4. Use in the Prophetic Literature: a. Reception of the Word; b. Proclamation; c. Phrases; 5. Application to God: a. Formal Expressions; b. Main Occurrences in the Pentateuch. IV. The Substantive: 1. Meaning: a. Word; b. Thing; c. "Something"; 2. Verbs That Take *dabhar*, "Word," As an Object: a. Verbs of Speaking; b. Verbs of Hearing; c. Verbs of Scorning; d. Verbs of Doing; e. Verbs of Trusting; 3. Use of *dabhar* in Legal Terminology; 4. In the Wisdom Literature; 5. In the Prophetic Literature: a. *dabhar* As a Term Meaning "Prophecy"; b. Formal Expressions. V. The Word of God: *1. debhar Yahweh*: a. Occurrences; b. *debhar (ha)'elohim*; c. Phrases; 2. Other Constructions; 3. Characteristics of the Word of God; 4. Verbs That Affirm the Fulfilment of the Word: a. *dabhar* As Object; b. *dabhar* As Subject; 5. *dabhar* in the Sense of "Commandment": a. A Technical Term for Apodictic Commandments? b. Use in Deuteronomy and the Deuteronomistic Work; 6. Occurrences in the Psalms; 7. History and the Ancient Near East; 8. Beginnings of Hypostatization: a. In the Psalms; b. In the Prophetic Literature.

I. In the Ancient Near East.

1. *Egypt*.

a. *General Observations.* The common Egyptian word for "word" is *mdw,* which later usually appears in the form *mdw.t.* [1] Frequently the expression

---

dābhar. P. R. Ackroyd, "The Vitality of the Word of God in the OT," *ASTI,* 1 (1962), 7-23; B. Albrektson, *History and the Gods* (Lund, 1967), esp. pp. 53ff.; *idem,* "Gudsordet enligt Gamla Testamentet," *TAik,* 72 (1967), 57-69; L. Alonso-Schökel, *The Inspired Word* (London, 1967); R. Asting, *Die Verkündigung des Wortes im Urchristentum* (1939), esp. pp. 9ff.; D. Baltzer, *Ezechiel und Deuterojesaja. BZAW,* 121 (1971), esp. pp. 100ff.; J. Barr, *The Semantics of Biblical Language* (Oxford, 1961); *idem,* "Hypostatization of Linguistic

(continued on p. 85)

[1] *WbÄS,* II, 180ff.

ₔₔ *dd mdw* is used to denote spoken words: it always introduces the oracles of the gods in ritual scenes (*dd mdw in N*, "oracle of the god N"), and denotes proverbs that are to be recited. Moreover, the expression *mdw-ntr*, "word(s) of God," is common. It can refer to the spoken word, [2] but often it is used for the word of God contained in the hieroglyphics and is thus a technical term for the ancient holy literature handed down in hieroglyphic writing. This development in meaning, which is significant for the literary culture of Egypt, is also indicated by the close connection between the "words of God" and the god Thoth, the scribe of the gods and of men: he is called "Lord of the Words of God," etc. [3] A solemn ritual note says: "According to this writing of the words of God, which Thoth

---

Phenomena in Modern Theological Interpretation," *JSS*, 7 (1962), 85-94, esp. pp. 88ff.; P. Benoit, *RB*, 70 (1963), 337f.; K. Beyer, *Spruch und Predigt bei den vorexilischen Propheten* (diss., Erlangen, 1933); T. Boman, *Hebrew Thought Compared with Greek* (trans. 1960), esp. pp. 56ff.; G. Braulik, "Bedeutungsnuancen der Ausdrücke für Gesetz im deuteronomischen Sprachgebrauch," *ZDMG Supplement*, 1 (1969), 343f.; idem, "Ausdrücke für Gesetz im Buch Deuteronomium," *Bibl*, 51 (1970), 39-66, esp. pp. 45ff.; H. Brunner, "'Was aus dem Munde Gottes geht'," *VT*, 8 (1958), 428f.; F. Buhl, "Über die Ausdrücke für: Ding, Sache u. ä. im Semitischen," *Festschrift V. Thomsen* (1912), 30-38; R. Bultmann, "Der Begriff des Wortes Gottes im NT," *Glauben und Verstehen*, I (⁶1966), 268-293; H. Cazelles, "Loi israélite," *DBS*, 5 (1957), 497-530; idem, *DBS*, 7 (1966), 751ff.; V. Christian, "Über einige Verben des Sprechens," *WZKM*, 29 (1915), 438-444; A. Deissler, *Psalm 119*. MThS, 1/11 (1955); W. Dietrich, *Prophetie und Geschichte*. FRLANT, 108 (1972); Z. W. Falk, "'Words of God' and 'Judgments'," *Studi in onore di E. Volterra*, 6 (1969), 155-59; J. de Fraine, "L'efficacia della parola di Dio," *BeO*, 8 (1966), 3-10; W. J. Gerber, *Die hebräischen Verba denominativa* (1896), esp. pp. 217-230; G. Gerleman, "Wort und Realität," *Donum natalicium H. S. Nyberg* (1954), 155-160; idem, *THAT*, I (1971), 433-443; K. Gouders, *Die prophetischen Berufungsberichte Moses, Isaias, Jeremias und Ezechiel* (diss., Bonn, 1971), esp. pp. 220ff.; A. Greiner, "Trois études bibliques. I. La Parole créatrice," *RevRéf*, 19 (1968), 1-16; O. Grether, *Name und Wort Gottes im AT*. BZAW, 64 (1934), esp. pp. 59ff.; V. Hamp, *Der Begriff "Wort" in den aramäischen Bibelübersetzungen* (1938); J. Hänel, *Das Erkennen Gottes bei den Schriftpropheten*. BWAT, N.F. 4 (1923), esp. pp. 100ff.; F. Häussermann, *Wortempfang und Symbol in der alttestamentlichen Prophetie*. BZAW, 58 (1932); P. Heinisch, *Das "Wort" im AT und im alten Orient*. BZfr, 10/7-8 (1922); idem, *TheolOT* (trans. ²1957), 122-26; J. Hempel, "Wort Gottes und Schicksal," *Festschrift A. Bertholet* (1950), 222-232; P. van Imschoot, "Wort (Gottes)," *BL²*, 1896-99; idem, *TheolOT*, I (trans. 1965), 188-195; E. Jacob, *TheolOT* (trans. 1958), 127-135; E. Jenni, *Das hebräische Pi'el* (1968), esp. pp. 164ff.; J. Jeremias, "Die Vollmacht des Propheten im AT," *EvTh*, 31 (1971), 305-322; O. Kaiser, "Wort der Propheten und Wort Gottes," *Tradition und Situation. Festschrift A. Weiser* (1963), 75-92; C. A. Keller, "Wort," *BHHW*, III (1966), 2182-84; K. Koch, "Wort und Einheit des Schöpfergottes in Memphis und Jerusalem," *ZThK*, 62 (1965), 251-293; I. Lande, *Formelhafte Wendungen der Umgangssprache im AT* (1949); J. Z. Lauterbach, "The Belief in the Power of the Word," *HUCA*, 14 (1939), 287-302; F. J. Leenhardt, "La signification de la notion de parole dans la pensée chrétienne," *RHPR*, 35 (1955), 263-273; G. Liedke, *Gestalt und Bezeichnung alttestamentlicher Rechtssätze*. WMANT, 39 (1971); J. Lindblom, "Die Vorstellung vom Sprechen Jahwes," *ZAW*, 75 (1963), 263-288; N. Lohfink, *Das Hauptgebot. Eine Untersuchung literarischer Einleitungsfragen zu Dtn 5–11. AnBibl*, 20 (1963); E. Lohse, "Deus dixit," *EvTh*, 25 (1965), 567-586; D. J. McCarthy, "Gottes Anwesenheit und das Wort des Propheten," *Concilium*, 5 (1969), 735-741; J. L. McKenzie, "The Word of God in the OT," *TS*, 21 (1960), 183-206=*Myths and Realities* (1963), 37-58; J. D.

(continued on p. 86)

[2] Cf. Pyr. 333c, 2047.
[3] Cf. P. Boylan, *Thoth* (Oxford, 1922), 92-97.

himself has produced." Another noteworthy expression is *wd.t-mdw*, "command." [4] The verbs *mdw*, "to speak," and *wd*, "to command" (and cognate substantives), often appear in parallelism. This is calculated to show that the word has power according to Egyptian thought. Thus Maspero speaks of the "omnipotence of the word," [5] and Sauneron emphasizes its creative cosmic power. [6] In particular the cosmogonies and the literature of the dead testify to this power, which especially transforms the words of the gods and of the king, as well as those of sorcerers and celebrants of the ritual, into commands which carry their own power within them. [7] *mdw(.)t* never seems to be used as a personification,

---

A. Macnicol, "Word and Deed in the NT," *SJT*, 5 (1952), 237-248=*ABR*, 1 (1951), 44-56; U. Mauser, *Gottesbild und Menschwerdung* (1971), esp. pp. 83ff.; F. Montagnini, "Parole e realtà nella Bibbia," *PV*, 10 (1965), 337-345; S. Mowinckel, "'The Spirit' and the 'Word' in the Preexilic Reforming Prophets," *JBL*, 53 (1934), 199-227; *idem, The OT As Word of God* (1959), esp. pp. 42ff.; *idem, Die Erkenntnis Gottes bei den alttestamentlichen Propheten* (1941); *idem*, "Loven og de 8 termini i Sl 119," *NTT*, 61 (1960), 95-159, esp. pp. 111ff.; P. K. D. Neumann, "Das Wort, das geschehen ist," *VT*, 23 (1973), 171-217; O. Procksch, "λέγω," *TDNT*, IV, 91-100; C. Rabin, *BethM*, 6 (1961), 73-76; R. Rendtorff, "Geschichte und Wort im AT," *EvTh*, 22 (1962), 621-649; E. Repo, *Der Begriff "RHEMA" im Biblisch-Griechischen*, I (1951); L. Richard, "The Word and the Sacraments," *JES*, 2 (1965), 234-250, esp. pp. 244ff.; G. Rinaldi, "Alcuni termini ebraici relativi alla letteratura," *Bibl*, 40 (1959), 267-289, esp. pp. 271ff.; A. Robert, "Logos II. La Parole divine dans l'AT," *DBS*, 5 (1957), 442-465; W. R. Roehrs, "The Theology of the Word of God in the OT," *CTM*, 32 (1961), 261-273; L. Rost, "Gesetz und Propheten," and "Bemerkungen zu *dibber*," *Studien zum AT. BWANT*, 101 (1974); K. H. Schelkle, "Wort Gottes," *Wort und Schrift* (1966), esp. pp. 11ff.; O. Schilling, "Das Wort Gottes im AT," *ErfThSt*, 12 (1962), 7-26; W. H. Schmidt, *Die Schöpfungsgeschichte der Priesterschrift. WMANT*, 17 (³1973), esp. pp. 169ff.; K. Schwarzwäller, *Theologie oder Phänomenologie* (1966), esp. pp. 130ff.; I. P. Seierstad, *Die Offenbarungserlebnisse der Propheten Amos, Jesaja und Jeremia* (²1965), esp. pp. 183ff.; *idem*, "Wort Gottes," *EKL*, III (1959), 1846-48; A. Strobel, "Wort Gottes und Mythos im AT," *Catholica*, 17 (1963), 180-196; C. Stuhlmueller, "The Prophets and the Word of God," *Thomist*, 28 (1964), 133-173; *idem, Creative Redemption in Deutero-Isaiah. AnBibl*, 43 (1970), esp. pp. 169ff.; A. Szeruda, *Das Wort Jahwes* (1921); W. Thiel, *Die deuteronomistische Redaktion von Jeremia 1-25. WMANT*, 41 (1972); P. Troadec, "La Parole vivante et efficace," *BVC*, 11 (1955), 57-67; B. Vawter, "God Spoke," *The Way*, 7 (1967), 171-79; C. Westermann, *BK*, I/1, 52ff.; W. Zimmerli, "Wort Gottes," *RGG*³, VI, 1809-1812.
On I: A. Barucq, "Oracle et divination," *DBS*, 6 (1960), 752-787; S. G. F. Brandon, *Creation Legends of the Ancient Near East* (London, 1963); L. Dürr, *Die Wertung des göttlichen Wortes im AT und im Antiken Orient. MVÄG*, 42/1 (1938); F. Ellermeier, *Prophetie in Mari und Israel* (1968); G. Lanczkowski, *Altägyptischer Prophetismus* (1960) (on this, cf. H. Brunner, *ThLZ*, 87 [1962], 585ff.; S. Morenz, *DLZ*, 83 [1962], 601ff.; S. Herrmann, *OLZ*, 58 [1963], 124ff.); S. Morenz, *Egyptian Religion* (trans. 1973); A. Moret, "Le verbe créateur et révélateur en Égypte," *RHR*, 59 (1909), 278-298; F. Nötscher, "Prophetie im Umkreis des alten Israel," *BZ*, N.F. 10 (1966), 161-197; H. W. Obbink, *De magische beteekenis van den naam inzonderheid in het Oude Egypte* (Amsterdam, 1925); L. Ramlot, "Prophétisme I/1. Prophétisme et politique en Orient," *DBS*, 8 (1970), 812-908; H. Ringgren, *Word and Wisdom* (Lund, 1947); S. Sauneron-J. Yoyotte, *La naissance du monde selon l'Égypte ancienne. Sources orientales*, 1 (Paris, 1959), 17ff.

[4] *WbÄS*, I, 396.
[5] G. Maspero, *RT*, 24 (1901), 168-173.
[6] S. Sauneron, *Les prêtres de l'ancienne Égypte* (Paris, 1957), 123ff.
[7] See below.

although *wḏ* is used in this way when it occurs alone.[8] Hu (*ḥw*, "utterance, saying") and Hike (*ḥkꜣ*, "incantation, spell") are to be found frequently as personifications of the divine word. Since their prominent place derives from the speaking of the creator-god, they will be treated in the section on cosmogony below.

Another frequently used term is *ts*, "saying, utterance, sentence,"[9] which is employed for all kinds of sayings (judicial speech or judgment, wisdom speech, proverb, incantation). In the later period, it appears as *ḏꜣyś*,[10] and plays a role in the cosmogonies.

Wordplays, which are very abundant in Egyptian texts, also show that in Egyptian thought "word" and "thing" are identical[11] and that giving a name is a creative act: word becomes reality. What we might regard as an accidental kinship of sound reveals to the Egyptian a deeper identity of being, which he expresses in stereotyped formulas.

Several wisdom sayings or rules of life, which can be called "sentences of good words," i.e., "maxims,"[12] testify to the high regard for words and speeches in Egypt. To be sure, "the righteous silent person" is set up as an ideal (compare the fact that more than a fourth of the sins in chap. 125 of the Book of the Dead are "sins of words"), but a series of statements emphasizes that there is a time for speech too. Merikare gives this admonition: "Be skillful in speech that you may maintain the upper hand, for the tongue is the power of man, speaking is more effective than any fighting." The story of the "Eloquent Peasant," whose speech "delights the heart of his majesty more than anything else in the land" (B 2,131f.), is an exquisite testimony to the value of good speech.

b. *In Cosmogonies.* Statements of the creator-god often play a decisive role in the cosmogonies, and in some cases the word occurs as the absolute creative power without which there can be no existence at all.[13] The so-called Memphitic theology of the Shabaka Stone, whose prototype is dated in the fifth-sixth dynasty,[14] occupies a special position. Here we find a developed theological and scientific teaching concerning creation through the word or, more accurately, through the cooperation of the heart and tongue: "It is the heart that is responsible for all knowledge, it is the tongue that repeats that which is conceived in the heart." There then follows a polemic against the Heliopolitan teaching that the nine original gods originated from the phallus and the hand. "But (in reality) the nine gods are the teeth and lips in this mouth, which named the name of all things, from which came Shu and Tefnut, which created the nine gods. Yea, every word of God (*mdw-nṯr*) came from that which the heart conceived and the tongue commanded." The expression "through the word"

---

[8] Hornung, *Amduat*, II, 23.
[9] *WbÄS*, V, 403.
[10] *WbÄS*, V, 521.
[11] Morenz, *Egyptian Religion*, 8f.; Sauneron, *loc. cit.*
[12] *The Teaching of Ptah-hotep*, 42.
[13] Sauneron-Yoyotte, 39f.; Morenz, 163ff.
[14] Morenz, 153ff.

appears repeatedly in designation of the various works of the creator, and the final statement in the teaching is: "And thus Ptah was content after he created all things and all the words of God." The following points should be noted in evaluation of this doctrine of "creation through the word," which logically characterizes creatures as "words of God." (1) The action of Ptah, which apparently can be explained on a purely spiritual plane, is at the same time to be understood very concretely in a physiological sense.[15] Moreover, "heart" and "tongue" (at least according to Junker's interpretation) are equated with the gods Horus and Thoth. These two details sharply differentiate this teaching from the corresponding teaching in the OT. (2) The Memphitic theology stands apart as an accomplished teaching. Only certain reminiscences of this teaching are found among the numerous later witnesses to Ptah theology. On the other hand, all sorts of wordplays and name formulas which are attributed to utterances of the creator-god play an important role in a late papyrus which contains fragments of the Memphitic theology.[16]

The teaching of the Shabaka Stone is opposed to the Heliopolitan idea of the creative activity of Atum through "phallus and hands"—or "semen and fingers." But in several texts of Heliopolitan provenance we encounter a pair of gods, Hu and Sia, who as the firstborn of Atum vie with Shu and Tefnut for the position of the first duality in connection with the origin of the world.[17] Scholars who regard Hu and Sia as "the divine utterance" or "the divine understanding," which is a good parallel to the pair "tongue and heart" in Ptah theology, frequently assume that there is a connection between these two teachings.[18] It is just as possible, however, that these ideas arose independently of one another in several places. In any case, the personifications Hu and Sia enjoy a wide dissemination: not only Atum and Re, but also Amun, Shu, Horus, Sobek, etc., are furnished with these effective creative organs and in the literature of the dead and the royal ideology their mighty help is claimed.

Coffin Text 325[19] deals with Hu. Its title is "Change into Hu," and it ends with the words: "Hu belongs to me. That which I said was good, that which came out my mouth, and the good which I say happens accordingly. I am Hu. (I am) the Lord of Hu" (156d-157b). Similar statements appear in the famous dialog between Re and Osiris in chap. 175 of the Book of the Dead (lines 40ff.):[20]

"Then Osiris said: 'I did it as an utterance (*ḥw*) of my mouth; how good is a king in whose mouth is the utterance (*ḥw*).' Then said Re: 'Behold, the good

---

[15] For a rather crass interpretation of the "teeth" and the "lips," see Schott, *ZÄS,* 74 (1949), 94-96.

[16] Berlin Papyrus 13603; see Erichsen-Schott, *Abhandlungen der Akademie der Wissenschaften* (Mainz, 1954), 7.

[17] A. Gardiner, *PSBA,* 37 (1915), 43-54, 83-95; Ringgren, 9-27; Bonnet, *RÄR,* 318ff., 715.

[18] Gardiner thinks Heliopolis has priority in this, while Bonnet, e.g., believes the influence probably is the reverse.

[19] *CT,* IV, 153ff.

[20] See H. Kees, *ZÄS,* 65 (1930), 74.

which came to you out of my mouth: your primeval (abode) came out of it, its name shall stand as such for millions and millions (of years?).'"

The last statement indicates that name giving and creation are identical (here there is an etymological explanation of Heracleopolis as the primeval abode of Osiris). The absence of corresponding formulas concerning Sia indicates that the central role was allotted to the utterance. That the normal sequence is Hu-Sia, and not Sia-Hu (which is physiologically more natural), favors this view.

A figure of even greater significance than Hu is Hike (*ḥkɜ*), who personifies in particular the mysterious-magical element in the nature of the word. [21] Hike is incantation, magical power, and creative power all at the same time. Coffin Text 261, [22] which has the title "Change into Hike," contains a detailed Hike theology, from which we cite the most important lines: [23]

"I am he whom the one lord created before the duality arose in this land, when he sent out his one eye, and was alone with that which came out of his mouth, when his millions of Ka (*ḥḥ . . . k* can be explained as *ḥkɜ*) formed the protection of his subjects, when he spoke (*mdw*) with the one who arose together with him, but how mighty he would have been if he had claimed the utterance (*ḥw*) which was in his mouth! I am the son of the father of all, I am the protection of all that the one lord commanded (*wḏ*). I am the giver of life to the nine gods, . . . a venerable god who speaks (*mdw*) with his mouth, and eats with his mouth. . . . Everything belongs to me before you came into existence, gods, you are the last to have come. I am Hike."

At issue here is Hike's right of primogeniture. Not only the gods in general, but all the dualities (whether Shu-Tefnut, Hu-Sia, or Heaven-Earth) originated later than he and are thus subordinate to him. The role which is attributed to "speaking," "commanding," and "uttering" in this line of argumentation is significant.

Amon theology adopted the concepts of Hu and Sia. Amon is "Lord of Sia, and on his mouth is Hu" (Greater Cairo Hymn to Amon, 4, 5); indeed, "Sia is his heart and Hu his lips" (Leiden Hymn to Amon, 5, 16). A later text (*Urk.,* VIII, No. 142, 3) gives the following explanation: "He prophesied that which was to come, and it received existence immediately, he established (?) that which he called forth with his voice." But the Leiden Hymn to Amon also contains special elements which testify to the decisive significance of the first word/sound in the primeval beginning: "He made his voice cackle like 'the Great Cackler' (Amon is thus identified with the primeval bird). . . . He began to speak (*mdw.t*) in the midst of the silence. He began to cry out while the earth was still in idleness. His cry spread abroad when there was as yet none other" (4, 5-8). The cosmogony of the Esna temple, [24] which acquires its special structure from the

---

[21] Gardiner, *PSBA,* 37 (1915), 253-262; Ringgren, 27-37; Bonnet, *RÄR,* 301f., cf. 435-39, 875-880; H. Te Velde, *JEOL,* 21 (1970), 175-186.

[22] *CT,* III, 382-89.

[23] A translation of this entire text appears in H. Kees, *Ägypten. Religionsgeschichtliches Lesebuch,* ed. A. Bertholet, 10/2 (1928).

[24] Sauneron, *Esna,* V, 253ff., esp. 268f.

seven statements (*ḏ³ yśw*) of the goddess Neith, says in summary fashion (Text No. 206, 12f.):

"Thus the seven statements came out of the mouth (sc. of Neith) and became seven divine beings, for that which she had uttered had given to the seven statements, to the word of God (*mdw-nṯr*), and to the city of Sais their names (i.e., their existence)."

"Creation through the word" never appears in total isolation from other processes and activities, but the "inclusive attitude" of the Egyptian, his joy in a "multiplicity of approaches," is revealed in the cosmogonies. [25] It is impossible to deny some sort of relationship to a magical act which is based on the magical power of the name. "The god conceives the names of things and causes them to become reality by uttering these names. Hence he acts no differently from a human sorcerer." [26] Morenz, too, correctly calls attention to the validity of a command in a divine kingship; as the people understands it such a command is carried out automatically and compulsorily. [27]

c. *In the Literature for the Dead.* The vast Egyptian literature for the dead is also dominated both in form and in content by "words" or "sayings." The texts cited in the section on cosmogonies belong for the most part to this genre. In it the creative word functions as a life-giving word. The dead want to be identified with Hu and Hike. The attitude reflected in the following Pyramid Text is typical of the literature for the dead: "It is not Pepi who says this to you, O gods; it is Hike who says this to you, O gods!" The Pyramid Texts, like the Coffin Texts and the Book of the Dead, mostly represent collections of sayings, and *ḏd mdw*, "reciting a word," usually indicates the beginning of sayings that are treated as independent. On the coffins and in the Books of the Dead, frequently this formula is made more specific by the addition of the phrase, "of Osiris N. He says: . . . ." The "chapters" of the Book of the Dead contain rubrics which begin with a stereotyped formula, *r³ n . . .*, "Formula for. . . ." The Books of the Underworld (Amduat, the Book of Gates, the Book of Caves, etc.) [28] do not exhibit the same "saying character," but are more uniform literary works. Nevertheless, sayings of the gods play an important role in them; thus the first two sections of the Book of Caves are composed entirely of sayings of the sun-god. [29] In the nocturnal journey of the sun ship through the underworld, Hu and Sia are naturally on board the ship, and the same is often true of Hike, who (together with Isis) intervenes at the turn of the night (Amduat, the seventh hour). Two very important words, which are varied again and again, have to do with Osiris: the decisive word of judgment, "the great and powerful word, which came out of the mouth of Thoth for the benefit of Osiris," [30] and "the great word that Horus says to his father Osiris," [31] which

---

[25] → בּרָא *bārā'*, I.1.

[26] Bonnet, *RÄR,* 866; cf. 615.

[27] Morenz, 165.

[28] See the translations in E. Hornung, *Die äg. Unterweltbücher* (1972).

[29] *Ibid.,* 311-340.

[30] Pyr. 1522f.

[31] *CT,* I, 298j; cf. Pyr. 1558.

is part of the embalming ritual. Since the sayings are supposed to help the dead acquire new life and divine status, and to protect them from all kinds of danger, naturally the guarantee of the ability to speak in the underworld is of vital interest. [32]

d. *In the Royal Ideology.* The word plays an important role in several respects in the royal ideology. The Pyramid Texts and the Amduat, as royal texts, illustrate one side of this. According to the birth legend, at conception the name of the future king was already determined and his dominion prophesied by a divine statement. [33] Hike plays a role in the birth scenes of Mammisi. Hu and Sia are supposed to serve the king, as is well illustrated by a statue of Sesostris I. In the familiar throne scene of the "union of the two lands," Hu and Sia appear in place of Horus and Seth. Like the gods, the king has Hu and Sia at his disposal.[34] As one educated by Thoth, the king is experienced in the "word of God," and as the only legitimate celebrant of the ritual he can be characterized in this way: "With glorious mouth and beautiful sayings (*ḏ³yš*), who delights the gods with his voice." [35]

e. *In Oracles.* In relation to some kings, we hear of an oracular saying which is regarded as the choice of the future king. It is said of Thutmose III: "An oracular word (*tp.t-r³*) of the god himself, like a word (*mdw*) of Re in the first primeval time, and Thoth gives the words of the writing." [36] This formulation emphasizes the fact that the same creative power that once brought the world into being through words is still active in the oracular word. The judgment of God is often called a "command" (*wḏ*), as, e.g., the oracle which was regarded as the occasion of the famous Punt expedition of Hatshepsut: "A command of the High Seat, an oracular word (*nḏw.t-r³*) of the God himself." [37] That words, even in written form, were given at the place of the oracle is clear; but it is not clear how they occurred or what the exact practice was in each case. [38]

Bergman

2. *Mesopotamia.* The question of the "word of God" in ancient Mesopotamia cannot be separated from men's endeavors to come into contact with the gods who, they believe, determine events in individual and social life, and thereby to get information concerning these events. The extant textual material indicates that the sayings of the gods, which are, of course, common in myth, actually seem to have played only a small role in daily life. In this connection, reference should be made to the conversations of the gods with heroes in the epics; these are probably intended to emphasize their special position. Thus Inanna speaks

---

[32] Cf. *CT*, II, 247f.

[33] *Urk.*, IV, 221.

[34] Ringgren, 22.

[35] Junker, *Philä*, I, 64, 12f.

[36] *Urk.*, IV, 165, 13-15.

[37] *Urk.*, IV, 342, 11f.; cf. further 157, 2; 565, 12; 566, 13; etc.

[38] Blackman, *JEA*, 11 (1925), 249-255; 12 (1926), 176-185; Bonnet, *RÄR*, 560-64; Roeder, *Kulte und Orakel im alten Ägypten* (1960), 191-272, offers a German translation of a group of oracles.

to Lugalbanda "as to her son, the lord of Šara," [39] and the divine mother of Gilgamesh, Ninsun, interprets a dream for him in literal speech. [40]

The intentions and commands of the gods were transmitted to men mainly through signs. These could be fortuitous (behavior of animals, peculiarities in the fetus and in physiognomy) or sought out deliberately (by inspecting the intestines, esp. the liver, and by black magic, and white magic). [41] Large collections or lists of such signs and their effects on private and national affairs (usually related to the king in the latter case) were used by the priestly interpreter of omens in translating the divine message into specific statements. Nevertheless, it is worthy of note that in Akkadian spoken utterances play an important role even in descriptions of the process. The god (usually Shamash and Adad) is asked (*šâlu*) and summoned to give a "certain, affirmative answer," e.g.: "O Shamash, great Lord, give me what I ask thee, a certain (affirmative) answer" (*ša ašallū-ka anna kīna apul-anni*). [42] To be sure, the scanty Sumerian material [43] simply says that the sacrificial animal was good (*máš-a šu ì-gíd máš-a-ni ì-ša₆*, "He stretched out his hand to the sacrificial animal, his [report on the] sacrificial animal was good"), [44] but shortly before this we read: "Before the words of Ningirsu, he bowed his head" (*du₁₁-du₁₁-ga-ᵈnin-gír-su-ka-šè sag-sig ba-ši-gar*); before the description of the inspection of the sacrifice, another passage says: "The words of the gods are highly esteemed" (*inim-dingir-re-e-ne nì-kal-kal-la-àm*). [45] Against this background are to be seen also the numerous instances in the late collection of the so-called Prayers with Uplifted Hands in which the deity is requested "to speak good, life, well-being, to cause them to go out of the mouth, 'to place' them upon his lips," e.g., "may mouth and tongue speak good for me" (*pû lišānu liqbû damiqtī*); [46] "may well-being be 'placed' upon your lips" (*ina šaptē-ka liššakin šalāmu*); [47] "may life come forth out of your mouth" (*ina pî-ka lūṣā balāṭu*). [48] The rest of the literature, too, says frequently that oral utterances of the gods create positive or negative reality. [49] Many statements emphasize the power, nobility, and significance of the word of God. [50] It is said of Enlil: "No god invalidates the word of his lips." [51] That which a god speaks

---

[39] C. Wilcke, *Das Lugalbandaepos* (diss., Heidelberg, 1969), 123ff., 352ff.

[40] See A. L. Oppenheim, *The Interpretation of Dreams* (Philadelphia, 1956), 246f.

[41] Cf. also *idem, Ancient Mesopotamia* (Chicago, 1964), 206-227; *La divination en Méso-potamie ancienne. CRRA*, 14 (1965).

[42] G. Klauber, *Politisch-religiöse Texte aus der Sargonidenzeit* (1913), XII; see further *CAD*, I, *apālu*, A 2a 2′; d 1′, 3′.

[43] See A. Falkenstein, *CRRA*, 14, 45-68.

[44] *Ibid.*, 49.

[45] *Ibid.*, 48.

[46] E. Ebeling, *Die akkadische Gebetsserie 'Handerhebung'* (1953), 38, 38.

[47] *Ibid.*, 38, 24.

[48] *Ibid.*, 38, 23; see 18, 35-37; 16, 25f.; 103, 16; 109, 22.

[49] On this see the new lexicons, e.g., *s.v. annu*, "affirmation, promise"; *awātum/amātu*, "word"; *apālu*, "to answer"; *malāku*, "to give advice"; *milku*, "counsel, advice"; *nabû*, "to name, call"; *pû*, "mouth, saying"; *qabû*, "to speak"; *qību, qibītu*, "saying, command"; *ṣīt pî*, "utterance, command"; *zakāru*, "to speak, name, decide"; *zikru*, "saying, command."

[50] Dürr, 53ff.; cf. p. 56: "His word is exalted, his word cannot be stayed."

[51] *Ibid.*, 578.

comes true. The naming of something calls it into being. [52] In EnEl IV, 19-26 Marduk by his word destroys a garment and then creates it anew. [53] Finally, the divine word appears in a number of hymns as cosmic power which creates and destroys. [54] Thus, it is said of Sin:

> Thy word goes out from above like a wind, it makes pasture and watering place luxuriant.
> Let thy word come down upon the earth, it will produce green plants.
> Thy word makes stable and fold fat, it spreads abroad living creatures.
> Thy word causes justice and righteousness to arise, so that men speak uprightness. [55]

It is said of Enlil:

> His word is a torrential flood against which there is no resistance.
> His word splits the heavens, it shakes violently the earth.
> His word destroys both mother and child like a reed.
> The word of the Lord breaks off the reed in its full growth. [56]

On the other hand, accounts of a god speaking directly with men are rare in the ancient Near East. We learn from the Sumerian tradition that in dreams gods command princes of cities to build a temple or promise them military success. [57] Nabonidus tells of a dream in which Marduk spoke to him. [58] A Neo-Assyrian letter speaks of a dream containing the literal words of the god Ashur. [59] But for the most part the dream is in pictures, and then it is the task of the interpreter of dreams (*šabrû*) to give the meaning. Thus a collection of interpretations of dreams has been preserved from Assyria and this also subjects the possibility of divine speaking to magic. [60]

Examples of the gods speaking in ways that are comparable with prophecy in Israel are found in ancient Babylonian Mari and in Assyria. [61] In a group of letters from the archives at Mari, accounts are given to the king of the proclamations of different gods through the mouth of men or women who are called *āpil(t)um*, "male or female answerers," and *muḫḫûm/ûtum*, perhaps ecstatics

---

[52] *Ibid.*, 33.

[53] *Ibid.*, 368.

[54] *Ibid.*, 6ff.; Ringgren, 66f.

[55] Dürr, 68.

[56] *Ibid.*, 9. On the theme "word, utterance of God" in name giving, cf. for Sumerian names H. Limet, *L'anthroponymie sumérienne* (Paris, 1968), 230-34 (e.g., *Inim-dba-ba₆-zi*, "the word of Baba is reliable"); for Akkadian names, cf. on the type *Ikūn-pī-DN*, "the promise of DN has come to pass," Stamm, *AN*, 146f.; on the type *DN-balāṭa-iqbi*, "DN has uttered life," *AN*, 188, 206; on the type *Rabât-awāt-DN*, "great is the word of DN," *AN*, 232-34; further Dürr, 82ff.

[57] See Falkenstein, *CRRA*, 14, 56-64.

[58] See Oppenheim, *Dreams*, 250.

[59] See *ANET³*, 450b.

[60] See Oppenheim, *Dreams*, 256ff.

[61] See Ellermeier.

of some sort, and we also encounter a simple young man (ṣuḫārum). Probably the former were closely connected with a temple. The texts do not give any clear information concerning the exact circumstances of the experience; dreams, visions, and ecstasy are mentioned. The proclamations deal with practical things such as the erection of buildings and behavior toward subjects or enemies. The king is promised success if he follows these instructions. But it is possible that only oracles pertaining to the king have been preserved in the palace archives. [62] In the Neo-Assyrian period, commands and instructions are delivered to the king through the priestesses of Ishtar at Arbela, who in part speak representatively for the goddess in the first person. [63] Ashurbanipal also tells of this several times.

It is crucial, however, that in this material, in contrast to prophetic speech in Israel, the subject is never a historical act of God, either as an interpretation of the past or as a plan for the future. Furthermore the moral claims of the deity, which are familiar enough to the Babylonians elsewhere (cf. the Prayers with Uplifted Hands and esp. the Šurpu series of incantations), [64] are never mentioned in this material.

Lutzmann

II. The Root.

1. *Etymology.* Thus far, no etymology of *dbr* has met with general approval.

a. *"To Be Behind"?* Every etymological explanation of this root is faced with the difficulty that in addition to *dabhar,* "word, thing," and *dibher,* "to speak," other words with a wide variety of meanings are formed from the radical *dbr,* e.g., → דביר *dᵉbhîr,* "back room, most holy place," *dobher,* "pasture," *dobheroth,* "raft," → מדבר *midhbār,* "desert, steppe," etc. Scholars generally derive this last group of words from a root *dbr,* "to be behind" (cf. Arab. *dubr,* "back," *dabara,* "to be behind"). They cannot agree, however, on whether *dabhar,* "word, thing," should be connected with this original meaning.

Several scholars favor this connection. [65] Accordingly, "a dynamic and energetic motion forward from that which is behind" [66] is thought to be the idea lying behind *dbr*. The verb is explained differently: "to be occupied with the *dabhar* of something, to develop a *dabhar,*" [67] "to set words in motion, to cause words to follow each other," [68] "to drive forward that which is behind; the verb thus portrays in some sense the function of speaking." [69] The *tertium compara-*

---

[62] See G. Dossin, *CRRA,* 14, 77-86; W. L. Moran, *Bibl,* 50 (1969), 15-56.

[63] Cf. *ANET³,* 449.

[64] E. Reiner, *Šurpu. BAfO,* 11 (1958).

[65] *GesB,* 153; Procksch, 90; Grether, 60ff.; Boman, 65; E. Jacob, *TheolOT,* 128; J. T. Milik, *Bibl,* 38 (1957), 252, n. 4; cf. Repo, 57ff.; W. Leslau, *Language,* 25 (1949), 316; etc.

[66] Schilling, 9.

[67] Procksch, 90.

[68] *GesB,* 153.

[69] Boman, 65.

tionis (third element of comparison) of a forward motion is, however, a postulate. Thus these derivations are unsatisfactory and artificial.

KBL², then, assumes that two different roots are involved here, and Barr emphasizes [70] "that 'hinterground of meaning' is a semantic indication which is quite unreconcilable with any use of the Hebrew *dabar*," i.e., "that the connection of *dibber* 'speak' with the root *d-b-r* 'behind' is not certain." [71] On this basis *KBL²* and *KBL³* (in opposition to *GesB*) propose a verb, *dbr* I, piel, "to turn the back, turn away from, drive away, pursue," pual passive, hiphil, "to subjugate, subject," cf. Akk. *dubb/ppuru*. [72] Schmuttermayr even divides the questionable occurrences of *dbr* into two roots, one meaning "to drive away," and the other "to treat violently." [73]

Finally, some scholars suspect to some degree a *dbr* piel III, "to have descendants," at Prov. 21:28. [74]

b. *"To Add Up"?* On the basis of earlier attempts to explain the original meaning of *dbr*, [75] *KBL²*, 199, and *KBL³*, 201 argue with some reservations that the original meaning of *dibber*, "to speak," was "to add up" (understood as an onomatopoeic sound) (cf. *debhorah*, "bee"). Notwithstanding the quantitative occurrences of both word groups, however, this derivation is also highly uncertain.

c. *A Biliteral Root?* Gerleman seeks to solve the problem by assuming an etymological connection between *dbr* and Akk. *dabābu*, "to speak right or the right thing." [76] "The semantic isolation of the northwest Semitic word *dbr* indicates that the idea that there was a root *dbr* is only apparent, and that this word should be understood as a word formed by analogy, i.e., an original *dbb* was assimilated to *'mr*, 'to say,' which is related to it semantically and is partly synonymous with it." [77] It might be possible to go a step beyond this and purely hypothetically to posit an original two-radical root *db*, which could be expanded in different ways (cf. also *ndb*, Arab. "to cry out," Heb. "to incite, do voluntarily"; *'db*, "to invite to a meal"). [78]

---

[70] Specifically against T. F. Torrance.

[71] Barr, *Semantics*, 131, 135; cf. *JSS*, 7, 88ff.

[72] *AHw*, 147a; *CAD*, III, 186ff.; also *DISO*, 55. In addition to the literature on the OT meaning of *dbr* mentioned in *KBL³*, 201, see G. R. Driver, *JTS*, 35 (1934), 382; H. Junker, *BZAW*, 66 (1936), 171f.; M. Dahood, *TS*, 14 (1953), 87f.; *Bibl*, 42 (1961), 385; 45 (1964), 401; Jenni, 231; J. Barr, *Comparative Philology and the Text of the OT* (Oxford, 1968), 324.

[73] G. Schmuttermayr, *Psalm 18 und 2 Sam 22. Studien zu einem Doppeltext. StANT*, 25 (1971), 196f.

[74] B. Gemser, *HAT*, 16 (²1963), 113; *KBL³*, 202; Jenni, 270.

[75] E.g., Gerber, 230.

[76] *AHw*, 146f.; *CAD*, III, 2-14; → דבה *dibbāh*.

[77] *THAT*, I, 434.

[78] *KBL³*, 11. On the original two-radical basis of three-radical roots in Semitic words, cf. A. S. Marmardji, *La lexicographie arabe à la lumière du bilittéralisme et de la philologie sémitique* (1937) (on this see F. Rosenthal, *Or*, N.S. 8 [1939], 148-150); G. J. Botterweck, *Der Triliterismus im Semitischen. BBB*, 3 (1952); W. von Soden, *Grundriss der akkadischen Grammatik* (1952), 96, § 73b; S. Moscati, *An Introduction to the Comparative Grammar of the Semitic Languages* (²1969), 72ff.; Barr, *Comparative Philology*, 166ff.

2. *Occurrences.* The root *dbr* occurs not only in OT Hebrew, the Lachish Ostraca, and the Siloam Inscription, but also in Phoenician-Punic as a verb, "to speak," and a substantive, "word, thing," [79] and again in Official Aramaic. [80] In Biblical Aramaic we encounter only *'al dibhrath*, lit. "upon the word" (Dnl. 2:30; with *'adh* in 4:14 [Eng. v. 17]), which comes from the vocabulary of Canaanite officialdom. [81] On the other hand, in Ugaritic this root does not occur, at least with any certainty, in the sense of "word, to speak." [82] *WUS*, No. 724 mentions the meanings "to follow, yield or submit," and "pasture, pasture land"; and *UT*, 641 understands *dbr* as a place name. Gordon says further, "*dbr* in the sense of Hebr. *dbr*, 'thing, word' may possibly occur in *kl dbrm* (1022:7 [*PRU*, II, 22, 7]) 'all things = everything', but the context is broken." [83]

3. *Derivatives.* In addition to the verb *dabhar* and the substantive *dabhar*, Biblical Hebrew also contains the rare substantival derivatives *dibhrah* (Job 5:8, "legal cause or suit"; 3 times *'al dibhrath*, "because of, for the sake of"; once *'al dibhrathi*, "after the order [or manner] of"), *dabbereth* (Dt. 33:3, "word"), [84] and *midhbar*, "probably not an instrumental noun (= mouth), but an action noun (= speaking)." [85]

4. *Verb Forms.* The piel of the verb *dbr* (*dibber*) occurs in the OT much more frequently than the qal (the piel is found about 20 times as often as the qal). [86]

In the piel imperfect, *yedhabber* may be the remnant of an extinct qal durative or present-future. [87]

dabhar always appears in the qal active participle (39 times) with two exceptions: once it occurs in the infinitive construct (Ps. 51:6[4]), and once in the passive participle (Prov. 25:11).

In agreement with Nyberg, [88] Gerleman has made this distinction: "The frequently used active participle usually denotes someone who speaks by habit, who says something out of or because of his innermost nature." [89] On the other hand, according to Jenni, "the distinction is not to be sought in terms of the indefinite or definite situation but in terms of the object: the actuality is limited to the act and to the general manner of speaking as such without any idea of a specific wording, whereas the result is always a specific word content, whether

---

[79] Cf. Z. S. Harris, *A Grammar of the Phoenician Language* (1936), 95.

[80] *DISO*, 55; *KAI*, III, 6.

[81] See below, IV.1.b.

[82] Cf. the examples in Whitaker, 179.

[83] *UT*.

[84] Otherwise I. L. Seeligmann, *VT*, 14 (1964), 80: "behind you."

[85] E. Würthwein, *HAT*, 18 (²1969), 51, in agreement with *KBL²*, 495.

[86] *THAT*, I, 434f., gives a statistical analysis of the occurrences of the verb and the substantive.

[87] Cf. R. Meyer, *Festschrift O. Eissfeldt. BZAW*, 77 (1958), 118-128; *SVT*, 7 (1960), 309-317; *Hebräische Grammatik*, I (³1966), § 3, 2d; II (³1969), §§ 63, 2; 70, 1g.

[88] H. S. Nyberg, *Hebreisk Grammatik* (1952), 221.

[89] *THAT*, I, 436.

this is stated or silently presupposed.... The qal means 'to speak words in general (spontaneously or intentionally),' while the piel means 'to speak specific words.'"[90]

dbr also occurs very few times in the niphal, pual, or hithpael (participle).

III. **The Verb.** Within the general meaning "to speak," the verb *dibber* also receives more specific and developed meanings according to the contexts: "to demand or desire" (Ex. 12:31f.), "order, command" (Gen. 12:4; Ex. 1:17; 23:22), "threaten" (Ex. 32:14; Jer. 18:8), "promise" (Gen. 18:19; 21:1f.; Dt. 1:14; 6:3), "recite" (Jgs. 5:12; cf. Ps. 18:1 [Eng. heading]), and perhaps even "write poetry" (1 K. 5:12[4:32]).

1. *Use with Prepositions.* The verb *dibber* can be used in the absolute (Gen. 18:5,30,32; Ex. 4:14; Isa. 1:2; etc.) but it can also be connected with the most diverse prepositions.[91]

dibber is used as follows to denote "speaking to or with a person": *'el* (Gen. 8:15; 12:4; 18:27; 19:14; 24:50; 41:17; Ex. 4:10; qal—Gen. 16:13), *'eth* (Gen. 17:3,22ff.; 23:8; 35:13ff.; 41:9; 42:30), *be* (Nu. 12:2,6,8; 1 K. 22:28; esp. 1 S. 25:39, "to woo"; qal—Zec. 1:9,14; etc.),[92] *le* (Gen. 24:7; Jgs. 14:7; 1 K. 2:19), *'al* (= *'el*? Jer. 6:10; 26:2; in the sense of "concerning": 1 K. 2:19; 5:13[4:33]; cf. Gen. 18:19; Hos. 7:13, "concerning, against"?), *'im* (Gen. 31:24,29; Ex. 19:9; 20:19; Dt. 5:4; Hos. 12:5[4]). It is possible that *dibber* is used also with *liphne* in this sense (Ex. 6:12), and in exceptional cases it can even take a suffix instead of a preposition (Gen. 37:4; cf. Nu. 26:3). *dibber* is also used with several prepositions for "to speak to one's heart, i.e., to oneself," "to think": *'el* (Gen. 24:45), *be* (Eccl. 2:15), *'al* (1 S. 1:13), and *'im* (Eccl. 1:16) (cf. Ps. 15:2).

In addition, *dibber be* means "to speak of, concerning" (1 S. 19:3f.; Dt. 6:7; Ps. 119:46), and "to speak against" (Nu. 12:1,8; 21:5,7; Ps. 50:20; 78:19; cf. Jer. 31:20). *be* also appears in the following constructions with *dibber*: *dibber be'ozne*, "to speak in someone's ears, i.e., in his presence, so that he hears" (Gen. 23:13, 16; Ex. 11:2; 1 S. 8:21), *dibber beghe'uth*, "to speak haughtily, arrogantly" (Ps. 17:10; cf. 73:8; → גאה *gā'āh*), *dibber battephillah*, "to speak in prayer" (Dnl. 9:21), and *dibber beshem*, "to speak in someone's name, by someone's order or authority" (Ex. 5:23; Dt. 18:20; Jer. 26:16; Dnl. 9:6).[93]

2. *In Phrases.* The verb *dibber* receives a specific meaning in certain combinations (with objects, adverbs, etc.) which in some cases solidify into stereotyped phrases. *dibber (tobh) tobhah* means "to speak good in behalf of, intercede for" (Jer. 18:20; cf. Est. 7:9; otherwise in Nu. 10:29; 1 S. 25:30; Jer. 32:42, where it means "to promise good"), *dibber tobhoth,* "speak kindly to" (2 K. 25:28 = Jer.

---

[90] Jenni, 165.

[91] On this construction, in addition to the lexicons, cf. the exhaustive treatment in Gerber, 217ff.

[92] On *be* and *beyadh,* see III.4.a.

[93] Cf. H. A. Brongers, *ZAW,* 77 (1965), 7f.; → שֵׁם *shēm.*

52:32; 12:6), *dibber ra' 'o tobh,* "speak neither good nor bad, say neither yes nor no, raise no objection" (Gen. 24:50), and *dibber mittobh 'adh ra',* "say good or bad, i.e., anything at all" (Gen. 31:24,29; cf. 2 S. 13:22). [94] *dibber shalom* (Jer. 9:7[8]; Ps. 35:20; qal—Ps. 28:3; cf. 122:8, "to wish peace"; also 85:9[8]; Zec. 9:10; Est. 10:3) or *dibber leshalom* (Gen. 37:4) means "to speak kindly, friendly to." [95] *dibber 'al lebh,* "to speak to the heart," takes place between brothers (Gen. 50:21), in various situations (1 S. 1:13; 2 S. 19:8[7]; 2 Ch. 30:22; 32:6), and is particularly at home in OT love language, where it characterizes the relationship between a man and his wife (Gen. 34:3; Jgs. 19:3; Ruth 2:13). Hosea (Hos. 2:16[14]) and Deutero-Isaiah (Isa. 40:2) transfer the expression to the relationship between God and his people. [96]

dibber qashoth, "to speak harshly, roughly" (Gen. 42:7,30; cf. 1 S. 20:10; 1 K. 12:13; 14:6), has the opposite meaning. *dibber 'emeth,* "speak truth" (Jer. 9:4[5]; Zec. 8:16; cf. 1 K. 22:16; Jer. 23:28; Ps. 15:2), *dibber mishpat,* "speak justice" (Isa. 32:7), *dibber tsedheq,* "speak righteousness" (Ps. 52:5[3]; 58:2[1]; cf. Isa. 45:19), and *dibber mesharim,* "speak uprightly" (Prov. 23:16; cf. Isa. 33:15; Prov. 16:13), stand in contrast to *dibber kazabh,* "speak lies" (Zeph. 3:13; Dnl. 11:27; cf. Jgs. 16:10,13; Hos. 7:13; Ps. 5:7[6]; 58:4[3]), *dibber sheqer,* "speak lies" (Isa. 59:3; Jer. 9:4[5]; 29:23; 43:2; cf. 40:16; Ps. 63:12[11]; 101:7), *dibber shav',* "speak lies" (Isa. 59:4; Ezk. 13:8), [97] and *dibber sarah,* "speak rebellion (or malicious lies)" [98] (Dt. 13:6[5]; Jer. 28:16; 29:32; cf. Isa. 59:13).

In other passages, *dibber mishpat* (2 K. 25:6) or *dibber mishpatim* (in the parallel passage to 2 K. 25:6 in Jer. 52:9; cf. Jer. 1:16; 4:12; 39:5) means "to pass sentence, judgment" (the meaning is different in 12:1, "to discuss, plead, a legal case"). [99]

Occasionally *ken dibbarta,* "What you say is quite right" (As you say) (Ex. 10:29; cf. Nu. 27:7; 36:5), and frequently *'asah ka'asher dibber,* "Do as you have said" (Gen. 18:5; 27:19; etc.), appear as corroborating, affirmative answers. [100]

3. *The Relationship Between dibber and 'amar.* How does *dibber* differ from → אמר *'āmar?* Jenni writes: "Unlike the resultative *dbr* in the piel, 'to utter specific words,' where the object is already implied, *'mr* in the qal (present) needs to be supplemented in direct or indirect discourse." [101] Gerleman has carried this distinction of Jenni further: In the case of the verb *'mr,* "to say, speak," which is semantically connected to and partly synonymous with *dbr,* "the primary concern is with the content of what is said," whereas "*dbr* in the piel

---

[94] On this merismus, cf. E. König, *Syntax* (1897), §§ 91f.; A. M. Honeyman, *JBL,* 71 (1952), 11-18; P. Boccaccio, *Bibl,* 33 (1952), 173-190; H. A. Brongers, *OTS,* 14 (1965), 100-114.

[95] Cf. W. Eisenbeis, *Die Wurzel* שׁלם *im AT. BZAW,* 113 (1969), 84f., 157.

[96] Cf. H. W. Wolff, *Hosea* (trans. 1974), 42; J. Vollmer, *BZAW,* 119 (1970); 87, n. 166.

[97] Cf. M. A. Klopfenstein, *Die Lüge nach dem AT* (1964), *passim;* Jenni, 168ff.

[98] Cf. J. van der Ploeg, *OTS,* 5 (1948), 142ff.

[99] Cf. H. W. Hertzberg, *ZAW,* 41 (1923), 23; Liedke, 83, 86.

[100] Cf. Lande, 63.

[101] Jenni, 165, n. 192.

denotes primarily the activity of speaking, the uttering of words and sentences. While *'mr* requires that the content of what is said (in direct discourse) be stated and sufficiently defined by the context, so that *'mr* does not occur in the absolute, *dbr* in the piel can occur in the absolute without any more specific statement about what is imparted (e.g., in Gen. 24:15; Job 1:16; 16:4,6)." [102] Perhaps this distinction can be brought into sharper focus here simply by citing some examples. When "Abraham's servant" arrives at the house of Laban (Gen. 24:32ff., J), he is told: "Speak on" (*dabber,* v. 33b). The servant's account itself is introduced by *vayyo'mer,* "so (and) he said" (v. 34; cf. vv. 39f.). It contains a monolog with verbatim statements. This, too, is introduced by *'amar* (vv. 42-44), but it is then summed up in retrospect (v. 45a; cf. v. 15): "Before I had done speaking in my heart (*dibber*), behold...." Then the new conversation again begins with *'amar* (v. 45b). Similarly in Gen. 34:6,8,13, *dibber* is used to denote the act of speaking, whereas *'amar* is necessary before the direct discourse that follows (vv. 8,14). Conversely, the verbatim statements recorded in Gen. 27:1-4; 29:4-8; or 39:7-9 are all introduced by *'amar* but are then summed up at the end in terms of *dibber* (27:5f.; 29:9; 39:10; cf. 18:27ff. following 18:23-26; Ex. 1:17 following 1:15f.; Jgs. 8:2f.; 12:6; etc.).

Thus, in contrast to *'amar, dibber* has a more comprehensive and overarching sense, i.e., it sums up a conversation as a whole at the beginning or at the end, so that generally speaking it should be translated, "to speak, have a conversation, converse with." (Rost now agrees with this. He argues that, in contrast to direct discourse, *dibber* means primarily to converse, discuss, confer with, utter words.) The substantive *dabhar* and constructions involving the substantive and the verb can also function in a similar way (e.g., in Gen. 39:19; 44:2; cf. Jer. 38:24,27, *debharim* or *dabhar,* "conversation"). In such instances, the content of the speech itself is not suggested by *dibber* (e.g., in Jgs. 14:7), but is presupposed on the basis of what precedes or follows (e.g., in Gen. 27:5f.), or is only roughly indicated (e.g., in Gen. 42:7; 1 S. 1:16). *dibber,* then, must always be supplemented by a finite verb form of *'amar* (Gen. 19:14; 32:20f.; 43:19f.; Dt. 20:2f.; Ezk. 14:4; etc.), or by the infinitive *le'mor* (Gen. 34:8,20; 39:17; 41:9; 42:14; 50:4; Ex. 13:1; Dt. 1:6; Jgs. 9:1; 1 K. 12:3,7,9f.; etc.), as long as it is not followed by an impersonal statement (Ex. 6:11; 11:2; 14:2,15; cf. 25:2 in contrast to 25:1; etc.). The general meaning of *dibber* may also be seen perhaps in the contrast between "speaking and doing" (Ezk. 17:24; etc.), or in expressions like "speaking a language" (Isa. 19:18; cf. 36:11; Neh. 13:24) or "knowing how to speak" (Jer. 1:6), which refer to speaking as a whole (cf. Job 34:35; Jer. 5:15; 44:25; etc.).

Sometimes, to be sure, this general meaning is lost, so that *dibber* can introduce the words that are spoken directly (Gen. 41:17; Ex. 32:7; 1 K. 12:10; 21:5f.; 2 K. 1:3,6f.,9-13,15f.; Ezk. 40:4; cf. Jgs. 9:2; Isa. 1:2; etc.). *dibber* and *'amar* can also stand in synonymous parallelism (Isa. 40:27; cf. 45:19).

In view of this, the distinction that Koch makes between *dibber* and *'amar* in

---

[102] *THAT,* I, 435f.

the Priestly Code[103] is questionable. A speech introduced by 'amar (Gen.17:15ff.) can be summed up later by dibber (17:22f.; cf. 35:13ff. following 35:10ff.; also Ex. 6:9,13), or a statement can be introduced by dibber + 'amar (Gen. 8:15; 17:3; 23:3,8,13; Ex. 6:2,10,12,29; etc.). Thus Gen. 1 may use only an introductory vayyo'mer [104] (and not the more general vayedhabber, etc.) but one cannot conclude from this "that for the Priestly Work the creation of the world is comparable to the general words of God to man but not the emphatic salvation statements which are first found in the making of covenants." [105] In any case no one has as yet made a special study of the use of dibber and 'amar in their historical development. [106]

4. *Use in the Prophetic Literature.* In the prophetic literature, the verb dibber denotes both the reception of the word (a) and also its proclamation (b).

a. *Reception of the Word.* "The lion has roared; who will not fear? The Lord Yahweh has spoken; who can but prophesy?" (Am. 3:8; cf. 1 S. 3:9f.; etc.). In both "authentic" and redactional prophetic texts, Yahweh "speaks" (dibber) "with" ('eth), "to" ('el), or (partly in the same sense) "in" (be) the prophet (Isa. 8:5; Jer. 36:2,4; Ezk. 2:1f.,8; 3:10; etc.; with be: Hos. 1:2; Hab. 2:1; Zec. 1:9; etc.).[107] The expression "speak through (by)" (beyadh, 1 K. 12:15; Isa. 20:2; Jer. 37:2; 50:1; Ezk. 38:17; cf. Ex. 9:35 with 9:12; also Hag. 1:1; Mal. 1:1; Hos. 12:11[10]; etc.) seems to view the prophet as the "instrument" or mouthpiece of God. This makes it possible for us to understand the reception and transmission of the word as a single act (similarly dibber be: 2 S. 23:2; 1 K. 22:28; cf. also Isa. 7:10; etc.). By way of contrast, it is denied that Yahweh speaks to the "false" prophet (Jer. 14:14; 23:21; Ezk. 13:7; 22:28; cf. Jer. 5:13).

b. *Proclamation.* As oral speaking, etc., prophetic proclamation can also be called dibber (Jer. 20:8f.; 6:10; Ezk. 14:4; 20:3,27; etc.). The prophet receives the commission to "speak" what Yahweh commands (Dt. 18:18; Jer. 1:7,17; 26:2,8; Ezk. 3:1; cf. Ex. 7:1f.; also Nu. 22:20,35,38; 23:12,26; 24:13; etc.), "to speak in the name of Yahweh" (Dt. 18:19; Jer. 26:16; 44:16; cf. 20:9), or even "to speak the words" of Yahweh (Jer. 43:1; Ezk. 2:7; 3:4; 11:25; etc.). "Thus you shall say to the prophet, 'What has Yahweh answered you?' or 'What has Yahweh spoken?'" (Jer. 23:37,35). "Let him who has my word speak my word faithfully" (23:28). These passages assume that one encounters the word of God in the mouth of the prophet. The message of the prophet, however, is often rejected; those who are addressed are not willing to hear what Yahweh says (6:10; 7:13; 23:17; 35:14,17; Isa. 65:12; 66:4).

c. *Phrases.* In the prophetic writings the verb dibber occurs especially in various phrases, although, to be sure, these are not as common as formulas using 'amar or ne'um.

---

[103] Koch, *ZThK,* 62, 282.
[104] → אמר 'āmar, III.1.a.
[105] Koch, 282.
[106] Cf. now the observations of L. Rost.
[107] Cf. also Hänel, 108ff.; Wolff, *Hosea,* 13; W. Rudolph, *KAT,* XIII/1 (1966), 37.

The phrase *ki yhvh dibber*, "for Yahweh has spoken (determined) (it)," usually stands at the end (1 K. 14:11; Isa. 22:25; 25:8; Joel 4:8[3:8]; Ob. 18; supplemented by the divine name *'elohe yisra'el*, "the God of Israel," in Isa. 21:17; and by an object in Isa. 24:3). This formula is also found, however, at the beginning after the summons to hear the word of God (Isa. 1:2) or of the prophet (Jer. 13:15).

It also occurs in an expanded form: *ki pi yhvh dibber*, "for the mouth of Yahweh has spoken," which comes at the end (Isa. 1:20; 40:5; 58:14; supplemented by *tsebha'oth*, "of hosts," in Mic. 4:4; cf. Jer. 9:11 [12]). Both forms could be called a "confirmation formula." "Their function is everywhere the same: to emphasize the authority of the preceding or following oracle as the word of God, whether it is styled a word of Yahweh or not; this explains the inverted position in the verbal clause, so that emphasis is placed on the subject." [108]

The phrase *zeh haddabhar 'asher dibber yhvh*, "this is the word that Yahweh spoke" (Isa. 16:13; 37:22; cf. 38:7), produces a solemn effect. [109]

The self-assertion *'ani yhvh dibbarti*, "I, Yahweh, have spoken (it)," which calls to mind the so-called Formula of Self-Presentation (*'ani yhvh*, "I am Yahweh," etc.), [110] appears in the book of Ezekiel with certain variations, and always as a concluding formula. This phrase occurs independently (Ezk. 5:15,17; 21:22 [17]; 30:12; 34:24), or is connected with the preceding context by *ki*, "for" (21:37[32]; 26:14; without the divine name, 23:34; 26:5; 28:10; 39:5; cf. 12:25; 13:7). It is used especially with the verb "know" ("know that": 17:21; 37:14), and with other additions (5:13; 6:10). In an expanded form, this formula emphasizes the efficacious power of the word: "I, Yahweh, have spoken (it), and I will do (it) (*ve'asithi*)" (17:24; 22:14; 36:36; cf. 24:14; 37:14; also Nu. 14:35; Isa. 46:11).

5. *Application to God.* In the most varied literary contexts the OT says of God: *dibber*, "he speaks." "God speaks once and twice—(only) no one pays heed thereto" (Job 33:14). In addition to occurrences in the prophetic literature, [111] (a) some formal expressions and (b) a few examples in the Pentateuch may be singled out from the large number of witnesses.

a. *Formal Expressions.* *dibber ra'ah 'al* denotes God's resolution to bring calamity: "to pronounce evil, announce calamity against" (1 K. 22:23; Jer. 11:17; 18:8; 19:15; 26:13,19; cf. 16:10; 35:17; with *'el*, 36:31; 40:2; similarly 36:7; Ex. 32:14; Jonah 3:10), while God's intention to save can be announced by *dibber shalom*, "to speak peace" (Ps. 85:9[8]), or *dibber tobh*, "to speak good" (Nu. 10:29; cf. 1 S. 25:30; Jer. 32:42).

The phrase *ka'asher dibber yhvh*, "as Yahweh has spoken (determined, commanded, promised, threatened)," refers back to a word which God has uttered

---

[108] K. Elliger, *BK*, XI, 7; cf. Hänel, 30ff.; W. Dietrich, 80.
[109] On *ka'asher dibber yhvh*, "as Yahweh has spoken" (Jer. 27:13), cf. III.5.a.
[110] Cf. W. Zimmerli, *Gottes Offenbarung* (²1969), 17; *BK*, XIII (1969), 40*, 98f., 134.
[111] III.4.

previously (Gen. 12:4; 24:51; Ex. 7:13,22; 8:11,15 [15,19]; 9:12,35; Nu. 5:4; 17:5 [16:40]; 27:23; Jer. 27:13; cf. Gen. 17:23; 21:1f.; Ex. 12:25; Nu. 22:8; Dt. 1:11,43; 6:3; 10:9; 18:2; 27:3; Jer. 40:3; of Moses, Lev. 10:5; Nu. 17:12 [16:47]; of Balaam, Nu. 23:2; etc.).

'asah ka'asher dibber, "he did as he had said" (Gen. 21:1), and 'asah 'eth 'asher dibber, "he did what he said" (28:15; Jer. 51:12), denote the fulfilment of God's intimation of the future, whether it be a promise or a threat. "Has he (Yahweh) said ('amar), and will he not do ('asah) it? Or has he spoken (dibber), and will he not fulfil (heqim) it?" asks Balaam (Nu. 23:19; cf. Isa. 46:11). The same or similar expressions (dibber—'asah) can be used on the other hand for Israel's obedience to the word of God (Ex. 19:8; 23:22; 24:3,7; Nu. 5:4; cf. 14:35; Ezk. 17:24; etc.). [112]

Among the various formulas used to introduce cultic laws, [113] vayedhabber, "and he said," occurs frequently, always as Yahweh's speech to Moses (Lev. 1:1; 4:1; 5:14,20 [6:1]; 17:1; Nu. 1:1; etc.), to Moses and Aaron (Lev. 11:1; 13:1; 14:33; 15:1; Nu. 19:1), or to Aaron alone (Lev. 10:8; Nu. 18:8), or on occasion as Moses' speech (Lev. 10:12; Nu. 30:2 [1]). In Deuteronomy especially Moses can appear as proclaimer of the divine statutes (dibber—Dt. 4:45; qal, 5:1). [114]

Sometimes the introductory formula vayedhabber yhvh 'el . . . le'mor, "and Yahweh spoke unto . . . , saying," is used as an introduction to a commissioning formula, dabber 'el . . . , "Speak to . . . ," ve'amarta 'el . . . , "and say to . . . ," especially in the Holiness Code (Lev. 1:1f.; 17:1f.; 18:1f.; 19:1f.; 22:17f.; 23:1f., 9f.; 25:1f.; 27:1f.; pl. 15:1f.; cf. with le'mor, 4:1f.; 6:17f. [24f.]). [115]

Twice (Ex. 16:23; Lev. 10:3) we find before a quotation the explanatory formula, hu' 'asher dibber yhvh, "This is that which (or, In this is fulfilled that which) Yahweh has said." Its function is to interpret an existing situation by a divine word (cf. similar explanatory statements in Ex. 16:15f.; etc.).

In Zec. 2:2 (1:19)–6:4, the interpreting angel is called hammal'akh haddobher bi, "the messenger (angel) who talked with me" (cf. Gen. 16:13).

In the polemic against images or idols the argument peh lahem velo' yedhabberu, "they have mouths, but do not speak," is used (Ps. 115:5; 135:16; cf. Jer. 10:5). This antithesis, among other things, helps us understand a motif which led the exilic prophet Deutero-Isaiah to emphasize so strongly in his debates Yahweh's ability to predict the future (Isa. 45:19; 46:11; 48:16; 52:6; etc.). [116] Ability to announce what is to come is a sign and a proof of the power of God, and one is to hope in this rather than what appears to be reality.

---

[112] Cf. IV.2.d.

[113] Cf. H. Holzinger, Einl. in den Hexateuch (1893), 349; R. Rendtorff, Die Gesetze in der Priesterschrift (1954), 67ff.; also L. Rost.

[114] See Lohfink, 59, 297; cf. pp. 86f., etc.

[115] See K. Elliger, HAT, 4 (1966), 223f.

[116] Cf. H. D. Preuss, Verspottung fremder Religionen im AT. BWANT, 92 (1971), 23ff., 215ff., 251ff.

b. *Main Occurrences in the Pentateuch.* The earlier Sinai pericope, in describing the natural phenomena that accompany the theophany, observes only cautiously and therefore ambiguously: "Moses spoke, and God answered *beqol* (in a voice)" (Ex. 19:19: probably E), i.e., either "in the thunder," [117] or "with an audible, understandable voice"(?). [118] Be this as it may, Dt. 4:33 clearly interprets the tradition in the latter sense, and in so doing emphasizes the uniqueness of God's relationship to his people: "Did any people ever hear the voice of God speaking out of the midst of the fire?" (*qol 'elohim medhabber;* cf. v. 12, *qol debharim,* "the sound [lit. voice] of words"; also Ezk. 10:5). The statement that Yahweh "speaks from heaven" (Ex. 20:22; cf. Dt. 4:36; also Gen. 21:17 [E]; etc.) conveys a similar thought. It might well be a correction of the earlier Sinai tradition (cf. Ex. 19:17; etc.), and in contrast to it emphasizes more strongly the transcendence of God, which then can become the basis of the first or second commandment (Ex. 20:23). The axiom, "man shall not see me and live" (Ex. 33:20; cf. 19:21; Jgs. 13:22; Jer. 30:21; etc.), which strongly distinguishes between God and man, is occasionally extended even to hearing God speaking: "Let not God speak (*dibber*) to us, lest we die" (Ex. 20:19; cf. Dt. 18:16; 5:5, 24f.). Such a sense of distance between God and man presupposes the existence of a mediator to whom this rule does not apply and who lives in a close relationship to God: "Yahweh spoke (*dibber*) to Moses face to face (*panim 'el panim*), as a man speaks to his friend" (Ex. 33:11). To be sure, the view that *panim bephanim dibber yhvh 'im makhem,* "Yahweh spoke with you face to face," is still possible at a later time (Dt. 5:4; cf. Nu. 14:14). Nevertheless, this recollection of the directness of the encounter (Ex. 24:11) is restricted or even abolished by the person of Moses, who "stood between Yahweh and you to declare to you the word of Yahweh" (Dt. 5:5). Nu. 12:6,8 even contains a contrast formula, which exalts Moses above prophecy and in doing so certainly does not do justice to prophecy: with the prophet "I speak (only) in a dream" (*bachalom 'adhabber bo*), whereas "I speak with Moses *peh 'el peh,* mouth to mouth," i.e., directly (Jer. 32:4; 34:3). [119]

IV. The Substantive.

1. *Meaning.*

a. *Word. dabhar* can mean either a single word (e.g., *lo' 'anah dabhar,* "to answer not a word," 2 K. 18:36) or speech: *dabhar tobh,* "a friendly word" (Prov. 12:25) or "a pleasant speech" (Ps. 45:2 [1]), *debharim 'achadhim,* "the same words, i.e., a common language" (Gen. 11:1), *dibhre davidh ha'acharonim,* "David's last words" (2 S. 23:1), *berobh debharim,* "in a fulness of words, i.e.,

---

[117] Cf. recently H. Schmid, *Mose* (1968), 57f.

[118] So recently Jeremias, 308.

[119] Cf. F. Nötscher, *"Das Angesicht Gottes schauen" nach biblischer und babylonischer Auffassung* (²1969), 23, 54f.; J. Reindl, *Das Angesicht Gottes im Sprachgebrauch des AT* (1970); L. Perlitt, *EvTh,* 31 (1971), 592ff.; W. H. Schmidt, in *Festschrift G. Friedrich* (1973), 28f.

in much speaking" (Prov. 10:19), *debharim,* "conversation" (Jer. 38:24; sing., 38:27).

An *'ish debharim,* lit. "man of words," is an "eloquent man" (Ex. 4:10; differently in 24:14). Among the good qualities of a young man is his ability to be *nebhon dabhar,* "skilled in speech" (1 S. 16:18). [120]

The same meaning also follows from construct expressions using *dabhar: debhar sether,* "secret word (message)" (Jgs. 3:19), *debhar sephathayim,* "mere word(s)" (2 K. 18:20 = Isa. 36:5), or "empty (idle) talk" (Prov. 14:23), *debhar sheqer,* "lying speech" (Prov. 13:5 [RSV "falsehood"]; cf. 22:12; 30:8; Ex. 5:9; 23:7), [121] *dibhre ruach,* "windy words" (Job 16:3; cf. 15:2), *dibhre hassepher,* "the wording, content of the document (letter)" (Isa. 29:11; Jer. 29:1).

Like the verb, [122] the substantive *dabhar* can also be given by the context a more specific meaning than the general one of "word, speech": thought (Ezk. 38:10), promise (1 K. 2:4), threat (12:15), commission, command (Gen. 24:33; Est. 1:12,19), rule, regulation (Est. 9:31), order (1 K. 13:1), precept (Ps. 50:17; 119:57), suggestion, counsel (Nu. 31:16; 2 S. 17:6), request, wish (2 S. 14:15), news, information (Gen. 37:14), attitude, refusal (Est. 1:17; but cf. also the much debated passage in Job 41:4 [12]), etc. Whereas the phrase *debhar ... hayah 'im,* "to reach an agreement, decision" (2 S. 3:17; pl., 1 K. 1:7), "denotes obviously questionable conspiracies," [123] *dabhar 'en lahem* means "they have no association (dealing) with" (Jgs. 18:7,28).

The nominal form *kidhebhar,* "according to, in conformity with the word of," is analogous to the verbal expression *ka'asher dibber,* "as (he) said" (cf. Lev. 10:5 with 10:8; also Gen. 44:2; Nu. 14:20; 1 K. 12:24; Jer. 32:8; 1 Ch. 15:15; etc.). *kidhebharekha,* "according to your wish" (Ex. 8:6 [10]; 1 K. 20:4), can express a reply of consent. In particular *'asah ka'asher dibber,* "to do as one has said," [124] corresponds to the parallel phrase *'asah kidhebhar,* "to do according to the word of ... " (Gen. 47:30; Ex. 8:9,27 [13,31]; 32:28; Lev. 10:7; etc.). [125]

b. *Thing.* Frequently, *dabhar* means "thing, matter" (e.g., in Prov. 11:13; 17:9; Eccl. 7:8). According to F. Buhl, who refers to similar developments in other Semitic languages (e.g., Aram. *millah,* "word," which also means "thing" in Dnl. 2:10ff.), "very comprehensive ideas, which do not have concrete characteristics, belong to the later linguistic development." [126] He considers "whether these words, at least in part, could not have been borrowed from the language of law, so that strictly speaking they denoted a case that was handled in legal proceedings and in popular assemblies." [127] On the other hand, the fact that the

---

[120] Cf. L. Köhler, *Hebrew Man* (trans. 1956), 27, 67.
[121] Cf. III.2 above.
[122] Cf. III above.
[123] M. Noth, *BK,* IX/1 (1968), 16.
[124] Cf. III.2.
[125] Cf. Lande, 66f.
[126] *Festschrift Thomsen,* 30.
[127] *Ibid.,* 33.

general meaning "thing" is very widespread, ancient, and unusually variable in the OT argues against this conjecture in the case of *dabhar*.[128]

bidhebhar 'uriyyah means "in the matter of Uriah" (1 K. 15:5; cf. Nu. 17:14 [16:49]; 25:18; otherwise in Nu. 31:16; 2 S. 3:17). *dabhar* has the same meaning not only in conjunction with proper names, but also in connection with things and ideas: *debhar hammizbeach*, "the matter of the altar" (Nu. 18:7), *debhar hammelukhah*, "the matter of the kingdom" (1 S. 10:16), etc. *shoresh dabhar* means the "root of the matter" (Job 19:28), and *pesher dabhar* either "the interpretation of a thing" or "the interpretation of a statement" (Eccl. 8:1).[129] *kabhedh haddabhar* means "the task is too difficult" (Ex. 18:18).

debhar yom beyomo, "the thing of a day to its day," is that which is appropriate to a day or that which is necessary on a given day (Lev. 23:37; 1 K. 8:59; Ezr. 3:4; Neh. 11:23; 12:47; 1 Ch. 16:37; 2 Ch. 8:14; 31:16), i.e., the task, duty, or job of a day (Ex. 5:13,19) and also the need of a day (16:4; 2 K. 25:30 = Jer. 52:34; Dnl. 1:5). The similar phrase, *debhar shanah beshanah*, means "year by year, every year" (1 K. 10:25).

dibhre hayyamim, lit. "words of the days," are the "events of the day," or "current events," which were recorded in a royal chronicle according to 1 K. 14:19,29; 15:7,23,31; 16:5,14,20,27; etc. [130] The phrase *sepher dibhre shelomoh*, "the book of the events (RSV acts) of Solomon" (1 K. 11:41), also has reference to annals. [131] Some commentators also interpret *dibhre yirmeyahu* (Jer. 1:1; cf. Neh. 1:1; etc.) as "the history of Jeremiah." [132] The superscription *dibhre 'amos* (Am. 1:1), however, introduces "the *words* of Amos." [133]

'achar haddebharim ha'elleh, "after these events" (Gen. 15:1; 22:1,20; 40:1; 48:1), establishes a "loose connection with the past." [134] Like the singular, the plural too can mean "matter, business" (Josh. 2:14; cf. the disputed passages 1 S. 10:2; Jer. 5:28), and some scholars translate *debharav* in 1 K. 6:38 as "parts of the temple." [135]

vezeh debhar, "and this is the situation, what is to be done" (Dt. 15:2; 19:4; 1 K. 9:15), is designed "to explain what procedure to follow in a particular situation." [136] The similar phrase, *vezeh haddabhar 'asher*, "and this is the thing which" (Ex. 29:1; Josh. 5:4; 1 K. 11:27; cf. the pl. in Ex. 19:6), which is to be translated "in this way, for this reason," etc., also serves to explain the more detailed circumstances of a situation. Elliger calls the expanded form, *zeh haddabhar 'asher tsivvah yhvh*, "this is the thing which Yahweh has commanded" (Ex. 16:16,32; 35:4; Lev. 8:5; 9:6; 17:2; Nu. 30:2[1]; 36:6; cf. the pl. in Ex.

---

[128] On juridical language, cf. IV.3.
[129] Cf. H. W. Hertzberg, *KAT*, XVII/4, 160; cf. p. 140 on Eccl. 7:8.
[130] Cf. M. Noth, *Überlieferungsgeschichtliche Studien* (³1967), 72ff.; A. Jepsen, *Die Quellen des Königsbuches* (²1956), 54ff.
[131] Cf. Noth, *Überlieferungsgeschichtliche Studien*, 66f.
[132] E.g., W. Rudolph, *HAT*, 12 (³1968), 2f.
[133] Cf. IV.4.
[134] O. Kaiser, *ZAW*, 70 (1958), 110.
[135] Noth, *BK*, IX/1, 97, 128: "matters, conditions."
[136] R. P. Merendino, *Das deuteronomische Gesetz. BBB*, 31 (1969), 107f.

35:1; also Lev. 8:36), an "introductory statement by which Moses disclaims any arbitrariness and attributes his actions to Yahweh's express command. It may be conjectured that this phrase is a liturgical formula which is adopted from the living cult and which is used in various ways as an introit in the various strata of P (and here alone)." This formula "is not native to the legal literature, but is taken over from Pg, from which it also penetrates into the later P literature." [137]

Like *'al debhar* (Gen. 12:17; 20:11,18; Ex. 8:8 [12]; Nu. 17:14 [16:49]; 2 S. 18:5; Ps. 45:5 [4]; one Lachish Letter) [138] and *'al dibhrath* (Eccl. 3:18; 7:14; 8:2; [139] cf. the Biblical Aram. expression in Dnl. 2:30), *'al dibhre* (2 K. 22:13; Jer. 7:22; 14:1; cf. Dt. 4:21) means "in the matter of, with regard to, for the sake of, because"; cf. *'al dibhrathi* (Ps. 110:4), [140] "after the manner of." This is a technical term in the language of Canaanite officialdom. [141] *'al debhar 'asher* expresses the reason "why, because" (Dt. 22:24; 23:5 [4]; cf. with *be*, Ex. 18:11; etc.).

c. *"Something."* Finally *dabhar* has the general and colorless meaning "something," so that this substantive seems merely to function as an indefinite pronoun. In this sense *dabhar* rarely stands alone, but usually appears in specific expressions: *'asah dabhar*, "to do something" (Am. 3:7), *sim dabhar be*, "to reproach someone for something, charge someone with something (RSV impute something to someone)" (1 S. 22:15), *yesh dabhar*, "there is something" (Eccl. 1:10), *dabhar ra'*, "something bad (evil, harmful)" (Dt. 17:1; cf. 2 K. 4:41; also Dt. 23:15 [14], *'ervath dabhar*, "something disgraceful [RSV indecent]"), *kol dabhar*, "everything" (Nu. 31:23), *kol dabhar tame'*, "anything unclean" (Lev. 5:2; cf. Ex. 22:8 [9]), *debhar mah*, "what" (Nu. 23:3; cf. interrogative sentences like those in Ex. 18:14; Gen. 18:14), *lo' dabhar*, "nothing" (Ex. 9:4; Dt. 22:26; 2 K. 20:13,15,17; Jer. 32:17), *lo' tobh haddabhar*, "this is not good" (Ex. 18:17; 1 S. 26:16; cf. 1 K. 18:24; etc.), *'en dabhar*, "it is of no consequence" (Nu. 20:19; 1 S. 20:21), *haddabhar hazzeh*, "this" (Gen. 20:10; 22:16; Ex. 9:5f.), *kaddabhar hazzeh*, "such a thing, such" (Gen. 18:25; 44:7; pl., 1 S. 2:23). The plural can have the same meanings, e.g.: *kol haddebharim*, "everything" (Gen. 20:8; 24:66), *debharim tobhim*, "something good" (2 Ch. 12:12; 19:3); etc.

In view of the diverse and often stereotyped use of *dabhar*, one should exercise caution in relation to interpretations like the following: In both meanings, "word" and "thing," "an intellectual element is almost without exception connected with the idea of *dabhar*.... *dabhar* arises only when one is occupied with something intellectually." [142] "There is always connected with *dabhar* something of the activity of the verb." [143]

---

[137] Elliger, *HAT*, 4, 116, 223, n. 16.
[138] *KAI*, 194.5.
[139] Cf. M. Dahood, *Bibl*, 33 (1952), 47f.; Hertzberg, *KAT*, XVII, 4f., 101, 152.
[140] *BLe*, §§ 526k, 603g.
[141] *KBL²*, 1063; *KBL³*, 203a.
[142] Grether, 59.
[143] *THAT*, I, 437.

2. *Verbs That Take dabhar, "Word," As an Object. dabhar* (sing. and pl.), "word," is used in the OT as the object of a large number of verbs. Only a partial list of the passages that illustrate this use of *dabhar* can be given here, and for the sake of clarity the respective verbs are grouped together on the basis of similarity of thought.

a. *Verbs of Speaking. dabhar* frequently appears as the object of verbs of speaking, etc., which express the communicability, transmission, or reproduction of the word: *dibber,* "to speak" (Gen. 20:8; Ex. 4:30; 20:1; Nu. 11:24; 22:7,20,35,38; Jer. 30:2,4; 43:1; Job 42:7; cf. Hos. 10:4; Isa. 58:13, "merely to make speeches, to make empty words"; 8:10, "to reach an understanding, agreement"; Gen. 24:33, "to carry out a commission"), *higgidh* (→ נגד *nāghadh*), "to proclaim, tell" (Ex. 4:28; 19:9; Dt. 17:9f.; 1 S. 10:16; 2 S. 1:4; Ps. 147:19), *sipper* (→ ספר *sāphar*), "to tell, relate" (Ex. 24:3), *'amar,* "to say" (1 S. 8:10), → קרא *qārā',* "proclaim" (RSV "read") (Jer. 36:6,8), → צוה *tsivvāh,* "to command" (Ex. 35:1,4), *sim,* "set before" (Ex. 19:7),[144] → כתב *kāthabh,* "write" (Ex. 24:4; 34:1,27f.; Jer. 30:2), *heshibh* (→ שוב *shûbh*) with various meanings, as "render an account, report" (Gen. 37:14; Nu. 13:26; Ezk. 9:11; cf. Ex. 19:8), "give instruction, advise" (Nu. 22:8; 1 K. 12:6,9), or "answer" (1 S. 17:30; 2 S. 3:11; Prov. 18:13; 24:26; Isa. 41:28; cf. Job 13:22; etc.),[145] → ענה *'ānāh,* "to answer" (1 K. 18:21; 2 K. 18:36; Jer. 42:4; 44:20; Ps. 119:42; cf. Isa. 50:4).

b. *Verbs of Hearing. dabhar* is also used as the object of verbs of hearing, which depict the word as intelligible, understandable: → שמע *shāma',* "to hear" (Ex. 33:4; Nu. 12:6; Am. 8:11; Jer. 23:18,22; 29:19; 36:11; 37:2; 44:24; Ezk. 3:17; 33:7),[146] *hiqshibh* (→ קשב *qāshabh*), "give heed to" (Jer. 6:19), → חזה *chāzāh,* "see" (Isa. 2:1; cf. Am. 1:1; Mic. 1:1), *her'ah* (→ ראה *rā'āh*), "cause to see, show" (Jer. 38:21; Ezk. 11:25; negatively: → הפך *hāphakh,* "to pervert" (Jer. 23:36). "Stealing" (*ginnebh*) the word (Jer. 23:30; pual, Job 4:12) may in the first instance refer simply to the secrecy of the revelation, which creeps in like a thief in the night, but Jeremiah uses the expression polemically: the false prophets steal (self-invented) words of Yahweh from one another.[147]

c. *Verbs of Scorning. dabhar* can also be the object of verbs of scorning which attest to the rejection of the word: → בזה *bāzāh,* "to scorn, despise" (Nu. 15:31), → מאס *mā'as,* "reject" (1 S. 15:23,26; Jer. 8:9; Isa. 30:12; cf. 5:24; etc.).

d. *Verbs of Doing. dabhar* occurs, too, as the object of verbs of doing which express the fulfilment or execution of the word:[148] → שמר *shāmar,* "to keep" (Ex. 12:24; Ps. 119:17,57,101; 2 Ch. 34:21; cf. Dt. 33:9; etc.). When combined with *'asah,* "to do," *dabhar* is ambiguous: "to do something or do this" (Ex. 1:18; 9:5), or "perform or carry out a word" (Nu. 22:20; Ps. 103:20), "keep

---

[144] On the phrase *sim/nathan bephi,* cf. IV.5.b.
[145] Cf. W. L. Holladay, *The Root šûbh in the OT* (1958), 99f.
[146] On the so-called Call to Attention, see IV.5.b.
[147] Cf. R. J. Z. Werblowski, *VT,* 6 (1956), 105f.
[148] Cf. V.4.a.

commandments" (Ex. 24:3), "fulfil a wish or desire" (Ex. 33:17; 2 S. 14:15), "honor a promise" (Nu. 32:20), etc. If *dabhar* is not defined more precisely, it is sometimes hard to decide whether it has retained the meaning "word" or has the weaker sense of "something." Nonfulfilment of the word can be expressed by *hechel* (→ חלל *chālal*), "to make invalid, break" (Nu. 30:3 [2]).

e. *Verbs of Trusting*. Finally *dabhar* is used as the object of verbs of trusting or hoping which extol the reliability of the word (cf. Ps. 56:5 [4]; 106:12; 119:42, 81,114,147; 130:5; but also Isa. 66:2,5).

3. *Use of dabhar in Legal Terminology*. The root *dbr* also has various functions in the realm of law.

The uncovering of a trespass affecting the community (e.g., the destruction of the altar of Baal) necessarily raises the question of the offender: *mi 'asah haddabhar hazzeh*, "Who has done this thing?" After the required investigation the guilty party is identified with the words: Gideon *'asah haddabhar hazzeh*, "has done this thing" (Jgs. 6:29). Analogous to this is the so-called Accusation Formula, *mah haddabhar (hara') hazzeh ('asher) 'asah*, "What is this (evil) thing that thou hast/you have done?" (Jgs. 8:1; 2 S. 12:21; Neh. 2:19; 13:17; similarly Ex. 1:18). This formula, which varies slightly in form, is usually followed by an account of the precise situation. [149] After an investigation, a disputed state of affairs can be confirmed by the formula *nakhon haddabhar*, "the matter is correct, this is how things are" (Dt. 13:15 [14]; 17:4). [150]

In place of the general meaning "thing, matter," *dabhar* often takes on the special and more precise meaning "dispute, legal case" (Ex. 18:16,22,26; Dt. 1:17; 19:15; Isa. 29:21; pl. Ex. 18:19; 23:8; Dt. 16:19). The "matter of the two" (Ex. 22:8 [9]) [151] is the lawsuit of the parties involved in the case. *ba'al debharim* means "one who has a legal case" (Ex. 24:14). *haddabhar*, "controversy," is a familiar fact of experience (2:14f.). *debhar (ham)mishpat*, lit. "word of judgment," is the verdict (Dt. 17:9; 2 Ch. 19:6), just as *dibber mishpat(im)* means "to declare a verdict." [152] In Isa. 41:1 *dibber* is used in the summons to a lawsuit. [153]

4. *In the Wisdom Literature*. *dabhar* also has its place in the Wisdom Literature, although it does not have the same significance in this area as certain parallel words. Collections of proverbs have the superscription: the words (*dibhre*) of the wise (Prov. 22:17; cf. 1:6; Eccl. 9:16f.; 12:11; 2 S. 20:16f.), of Agur (Prov. 30:1), of Lemuel (31:1), of Qoheleth (Eccl. 1:1); similarly: the words of Job (Job 31:40), and of Jeremiah (Jer. 51:64). Accordingly, *dibhre yirmeyahu* in Jer.

---

[149] Cf. Lande, 99f.; H. J. Boecker, *Redeformen des Rechtslebens im AT. WMANT*, 14 (²1970), 20, 26ff., 66f.; W. Schottroff, *Der altisraelitische Fluchspruch. WMANT*, 30 (1969), 78f.

[150] Cf. F. Horst, *Gottes Recht. ThB*, 12 (1961), 37, n. 33.

[151] Cf. recently B. S. Jackson, *Theft in Early Jewish Law* (1972), 241f.

[152] See III.2 above; Lieke, 83.

[153] On *dabhar* in the sense of "commandment" (Ex. 20:1; etc.), see V.5.

1:1 is not to be interpreted as "the history of Jeremiah,"[154] but as "the words of Jeremiah."[155] The corresponding introduction to the book of Amos, *dibhre 'amos,* may also come from a wisdom background if one excludes the statements that follow concerning his occupation and the place and time.[156] The admonitions of the father (Prov. 4:4,20) and the teaching of personified wisdom (1:23) are also "words." In the book of Proverbs *dabhar* (sing. without an article) seems to mean the word of God two or three times at the most (cf. 30:5f.), even if it is not expressly defined more closely as such: "He who gives heed to the word (*dabhar*) will prosper, and happy is he who trusts in Yahweh" (16:20; cf. 13:13; 19:16—conjec.).[157] Another view in this case is that "the instruction of the wise ... is regarded as possessing divine authority and as being equivalent to the word of God."[158] The words of the wicked or the fool stand in contrast to the words of the wise (Prov. 12:6; cf. Eccl. 10:12ff.; also Isa. 32:4,6). The Wisdom Literature contains warnings against effusive, rash, flattering, or false speech, and therewith also against unwarranted confidence in a person's words (Prov. 10:19; 13:5; 14:15,23; 18:8,13; 22:12; 26:22; 29:12,19f.; 30:8; cf. 23:8; Eccl. 5:1f.,6[2f.,7]; 6:11; 7:8,21; 10:12ff.,20). Conversely, a fitting word is praised: "a word in season, how good it is!" (Prov. 15:23 in contrast to 15:1). "A word fitly spoken is like apples of gold in a setting of silver" (25:11; cf. 12:25; 18:4; 24:26; 27:11; Eccl. 12:10f.; Job 15:3).

5. In the Prophetic Literature.

a. *dabhar As a Term Meaning "Prophecy." dabhar* is to a special degree a typical and specific term for prophecy. Together with intercession (Gen. 20:7; Jer. 7:16; etc.), imparting the word of God is the essential task of the prophet. Just as cultic-legal instruction (→ תורה *tôrāh*) characterizes the priest and counsel ('*etsah*) the wise man, so the word (*dabhar*) characterizes the prophet (Jer. 18:18).[159] One may thus expect information from a prophet. To seek (→ דרש *dārash*) God through the prophet (1 S. 9:9; 2 K. 3:11; etc.) is "to ask a word from" the prophet (1 K. 14:5; 22:5; cf. Jer. 37:17; 38:14; 42:2ff.; Am. 8:12; also 2 S. 16:23). Thus the OT can speak of the "word of the prophet" (*debhar nabhi',* Jer. 28:9; pl. 1 K. 22:13; Jer. 23:16; cf. Isa. 44:26).

One meets the prophet's word with confidence, and with the proviso that it is not a word invented by the prophet himself, but one heard and transmitted by him. Reception of the word counts as a mark of genuine prophetic sending (Jer. 27:18; cf. 23:18,22,28ff.; 36:2ff.; 37:17; etc.). "Thy words were found, and I ate them" (15:16). The proclamation of salvation is regarded as the "good word" of Yahweh (29:10; cf. Zec. 1:13). In retrospect a promise of Jeremiah can be cited as the "word of Yahweh" (2 Ch. 36:21f.; cf. Ezr. 1:1).

---

154 See IV.1.b above.
155 Thiel, 36ff.
156 Wolff, *BK*, XIV/2, 149 with literature.
157 Cf. J. Fichtner, *Die altorientalische Weisheit in ihrer israelit.-jüd. Ausprägung* (1933), 86ff.; E. G. Bauckmann, *ZAW*, 72 (1960), 38f.
158 B. Gemser, *HAT*, 16, 71.
159 On Zec. 1:6; 7:12, cf. L. Rost.

Conversely the "false" prophets of salvation are reproached because they steal the words of Yahweh (Jer. 23:30), their message does not come from Yahweh (23:16f.; Ezk. 13:6; cf. Dt. 18:20; etc.), and they are even deceived by him (Ezk. 14:9). The people is urged, then, not to trust the words of the lying prophets (Jer. 23:16; 27:14,16; cf. 7:4,8). At the same time the complaint is made that the words of the "true" prophets encounter unbelief, doubt (17:15; cf. Ezk. 12:21ff.; etc.), and disobedience (Jer. 29:19; 37:2; 44:16; Ezk. 33:30f.; cf. Isa. 30:12; Jer. 6:19; 35:13; etc.). Indeed, the prophet himself can suffer under the word which is laid upon him (Jer. 20:8; 23:9).

In the history of prophecy, the word increasingly displaces other means of revelation such as the dream, [160] and reception of the word takes the place of possession by the Spirit. [161]

b. *Formal Expressions.* The relationship between the word of God and the prophetic word is also expressed in certain fixed expressions.

In the phrase *sim/nathan dabhar/debharim bephi,* "to put/give a word/words in the mouth," God (Yahweh or Elohim) is always the subject of the sentence (Nu. 22:38; 23:5,12,16 [E?]), even when it is not incorporated in the divine I-oracle (Isa. 51:16; 59:21; with *nathan,* "to give," Dt. 18:18; Jer. 1:9; 5:14). Occasionally, however, this formula is used in connection with the instruction of one person by another, since in this instance the point at issue is the exact rendition of what is said (2 S. 14:3). If in Ex. 4:15 Moses is the speaker and Aaron the recipient of the word, Aaron is subordinate to Moses; Moses holds divine rank as it were, while Aaron must be content with being his mouth (v. 16).

The so-called Call to Attention, "Hear thou (ye) the word of Yahweh!" [162] transfers the summons to hear, as it is used in instruction in wisdom (Prov. 1:8; 4:1; 5:7; 7:24; 8:32; Job 34:2,10; etc.), [163] before the singing of a song (Gen. 4:23; Jgs. 5:3; 9:7; cf. Lam. 1:18; 2 S. 20:17), or in the cult (Dt. 6:4; 9:1; etc.), to prophetic proclamation (cf. Nu. 12:6; Ps. 50:7; 81:9 [8]; also Am. 3:13; 8:4; Mic. 6:2; Jer. 28:15; etc.). Often, but not always (cf. Isa. 1:10), the summons "Hear the word of Yahweh!" seems not to be the original introduction of the prophetic word, but a redactional insertion, which was intended to point emphatically to the proclamation that followed and to cause the reader to understand it as the word of God (Hos. 4:1; Am. 3:1; 5:1; 7:16; Jer. 10:1; etc.). [164] Nevertheless, a word of Yahweh does not have to follow this summons unconditionally (cf. Am. 5:1). In part the formula is closely connected syntactically with the accusation (Am. 4:1; Isa. 1:10; 66:5; etc.). According to Lindblom, [165] Wildberger, [166] and others, the Appellation Formula introduces a legal summation or a judgment.

---

160 Cf. Grether, 84ff., 97ff.; also V.8.b below.
161 Cf. perhaps Mowinckel, *JBL,* 53, 199ff.
162 Cf. Grether, 69.
163 Cf. Wolff, *Hosea* (trans. 1974), 97; J. von Loewenclau, *EvTh,* 26 (1966), 294ff.
164 Cf. *ZAW,* 77 (1965), 173; Wolff, *Hosea,* 67; *BK,* XIV/2, 362, in contrast to pp. 213, 276; K. von Rabenau, *WZ* Halle-Wittenberg, 5 (1955/56), 678.
165 J. Lindblom, *ZAW,* 75, 283.
166 H. Wildberger, *BK,* X/1, 9.

The summons to hear may be addressed to individuals (1 K. 22:19; 2 K. 20:16 = Isa. 39:5; Am. 7:16; Jer. 22:2; 34:4; cf. 28:7), certain groups (2 K. 7:1; Am. 4:1; Hos. 5:1; Isa. 1:10; 7:13; 28:14; 66:5; Jer. 9:19 [20]; 21:11; 42:15; 44:24; Ezk. 13:2; 34:7,9), to an entire group, such as the people (Am. 3:1; 5:1; Hos. 4:1; Isa. 1:10; Jer. 2:4; 7:2; 10:1; 17:20; 19:3; 29:20; 44:26; Ezk. 18:25; 37:4; cf. 25:3; Jer. 31:10), to the city (Isa. 51:21; Ezk. 16:35), or to the land or the earth (Jer. 6:19; 22:29; cf. Ezk. 6:3; 21:3 [20:47]; 36:1,4). [167]

V. The Word of God.

1. debhar Yahweh.

a. *Occurrences.* The expression *debhar yhvh,* "word of Yahweh," appears approximately 240 times in the OT. [168] "With few exceptions this expression means only one specific type of divine speech," viz., "the word of Yahweh to the prophet, or the word which the prophet proclaims to his contemporaries as the word of Yahweh." This means that "almost everywhere it occurs, *debhar Yahweh* is a technical term for the prophetic word of revelation." [169]

It is understandable, then, that *debhar yhvh* should occur so rarely in the Pentateuch (Gen. 15:1,4; Ex. 9:20f.; Nu. 15:31; Dt. 5:5 [uncertain]). Surprisingly, however, the expression also occurs only rarely in the genuine words of the early literary prophets. On the other hand it is found in superscriptions (Hos. 1:1; Mic. 1:1; etc.), redactional transitions (as in Hos. 4:1), accounts concerning the prophet (Am. 7:16), or in oracles whose genuineness is disputed (as in Am. 8:11f.; Isa. 2:3 = Mic. 4:2); but cf. Isa. 1:10; etc.

On a statistical basis Stuhlmueller has drawn this general conclusion: "The Deuteronomist ... did not invent the term ..., but he seems largely responsible, directly or indirectly, for its popularity in the prophetic literature and preaching contemporaneous with himself and immediately after." [170] Köhler has called attention to the following facts: the words of the prophets "are not parts of a jig-saw puzzle; they are historical phenomena each with its own context in time and place. ... That which the prophets have to declare is always called *the* word of God. It is never called *a* word of God. Indeed, the latter expression would seem never to have occurred." [171]

By way of exception, in 2 Ch. 19:11 *debhar yhvh* means "the matter(s) of Yahweh"; cf. 1 Ch. 26:32.

b. *debhar (ha)'elohim.* In a few earlier texts, *debhar (ha)'elohim* perhaps means an oracle.

In Jgs. 3:20 and 1 S. 9:27, "the purpose is to arouse the attention of the hearer.

---

[167] Cf. Zimmerli, *BK,* XIII/1, 360.

[168] Cf. the statistics in Grether, 63ff.; also Gerleman, *THAT,* I, 439; Stuhlmueller, 175.

[169] Grether, 62, 66, 76.

[170] C. Stuhlmueller, 175.

[171] L. Köhler, *OT Theol* (trans. 1957), 106; cf. *ThR,* 7 (1935), 257; also von Rad, *OT Theol,* II (trans. 1965), 87f.

Behind the ambiguous *debhar 'elohim* there is something mysterious (cf. *debhar sether*, 'secret word [RSV message],' Jgs. 3:19). . . . In this sort of context, 'word of God' or 'oracle' is much closer to the idea than is the meaning of *debhar yhvh;* namely, a specific revelation, a specific command of Yahweh. . . . The best proof that *debhar 'elohim* is not the word of a specific God is that in Jgs. 3:20 *debhar 'elohim* is used with reference to a heathen." [172] The address to Saul, "I will make known to you a word of God" (1 S. 9:27), seems in this earlier narrative stratum to be the introduction to the proclamation of the signs (10:2ff.) and not to the anointing (10:1). [173]

According to 2 S. 16:23, the counsel of Ahithophel is given the same status as a reply received when inquiry is made of God (*sha'al bidhebhar ha'elohim*). [174]

1 K. 12:22 (which is part of the later section, vv. 21-24), [175] in its introduction of the word of God to the man of God, Shemaiah, simply contains a modification of the familiar [176] (and here also perhaps original) formula, *vayehi debhar yhvh 'el*, "and the word of Yahweh came to."

In the phrase *debhar 'elohim*, "word of God" (1 Ch. 17:3), the Chronicler has replaced *yhvh* (2 S. 7:4) with *'elohim*, as he frequently does elsewhere. *debhar ha'elohim* occurs in 1 Ch. 26:32 in the sense of "matter(s) of God."

With his unusual expression *debhar 'elohenu*, "word of *our* God" (Isa. 40:8), an exilic prophet, in the framework of his message of comfort, emphasizes the special relationship between God and his people (which exists again after the judgment, cf. Hos. 1:9; 2:25 [23]). [177]

The unusual expression *debhar kol chazon* should probably be interpreted, "what all visions say" (Ezk. 12:23), after the analogy of *debhar yhvh*, "the word of Yahweh." [178]

c. *Phrases*. It is worthy of note that in the overwhelming majority of cases, *debhar yhvh* appears in more or less fixed phrases, [179] only some of which can be listed here. [180]

Approximately half of all the occurrences of *debhar yhvh* (more than 110) appear in the so-called Word-Event formula, a construction of *debhar yhvh* as subject with the verb *hāyāh* (*'el*). [181] This construction is found in different variations, e.g., *vayehi/hayah debhar yhvh 'el*, "(and) the word of Yahweh came unto," or *haddabhar 'asher hayah 'el*, "the word that came unto." It can also include

---

[172] F. Baumgärtel, *Elohim ausserhalb des Pentateuch* (1914), 45; but cf. the objections of Grether, 74, 87.

[173] Cf. L. Schmidt, *Menschlicher Erfolg und Jahwes Initiative. WMANT*, 38 (1970), 71ff.

[174] Cf. C. Westermann, *KuD*, 6 (1960), 13.

[175] Noth, *BK*, IX/1, 279f.

[176] See below.

[177] Cf. V.8.b.

[178] Cf. Zimmerli, *BK*, XIII/1, 274, 277.

[179] Grether, 67ff.

[180] Cf. also IV.5.b above on the so-called Call to Attention, "Hear thou (ye) the word of Yahweh!"

[181] Cf. the summary in Grether, 67f., 73; also C. H. Ratschow, *Werden und Wirken. BZAW*, 70 (1941), 34f.

supplementary material, e.g., chronological statements. It is surprising that the earlier literary prophets (Amos, Hosea, Isaiah, Micah) did not use this formula themselves, although it appears in the accounts of early prophecy and is especially common in the literature of later prophecy.[182] Zimmerli has summarized the relevant data concerning the distribution of the Word-Event formula:

> Outside the actual prophetic sphere, ... one should compare Gen. 15:1; 1 K. 6:11; 18:31. The expression is undoubtedly rooted in the vocabulary of prophecy. In fact, it is first used with frequency in the prophetic stories of the earlier monarchical period, which are thought to have been handed down in prophetic groups (Samuel—1 S. 15:10; Nathan—2 S. 7:4=1 Ch. 17:3; Gad— 2 S. 24:11; Shemaiah—1 K. 12:22=2 Ch. 11:2; 12:7; the prophet of Bethel— 1 K. 13:20; Jehu—1 K. 16:1 [7]; Elijah—1 K. 17:2,8; 18:1; 21:17,28). It is missing in the actual words of the earlier writing prophets. It is found only in the redactional superscriptions (Hos. 1:1; Zeph. 1:1; also Joel 1:1) and the narrative traditions (Isa. 38:4=2 K. 20:4) of the older prophetic books. Even among the 30 instances in the book of Jeremiah, a considerable number fall in secondary passages (46:1; 47:1; 49:34) or in sections narrated by later disciples (Baruch?) (28:12; 29:30; etc.). Nevertheless, one should not fail to recognize that the formula had in fact made its way into the oracles of Jeremiah himself (1:4,11,13; 2:1; etc.). It then achieved a fixed place in Ezekiel, Haggai (Hag. 2:10,20; cf. 1:1,3; 2:1), and Zechariah (Zec. 1:1,7; 4:8; 6:9; 7:1,4,8; 8:1,18) and it also occurs in later writings (cf. Jonah 1:1; 3:1; Dnl. 9:2). As far as content of the formula is concerned, it is clear that it has its origin in a knowledge of the "word of Yahweh" which is already well developed. ... The word is not spoken out of a direct confrontation with the personal address of the personal God, but "the word" is understood as an almost objective entity that has its own power.... Again, when reference is made to the word of Yahweh taking place, what is in mind is the eminently historical character of the word of God, its character as an event.[183]

In its different versions, this formula is what gives the superscriptions of the prophetic books their distinctiveness and it is therefore discussed at length in the commentaries. Since the phrase comes (at least for the most part) from Deuteronomistic circles, some scholars have inferred from it that the prophetic books were edited in the exilic period.[184] This view has been opposed, however, on the ground that pre-Deuteronomistic passages use the phrase (Gen. 15:1; 1 S. 15:10; 2 S. 7:4; 24:11; 1 K. 6:11; 13:20; 16:7,34; 17:2,8; 18:1,31; 21:17; 2 K. 20:4; also Jer. 1:4,11,13; etc.).[185] Still, Gen. 15:1 should probably be excluded,[186]

---

[182] Approximately 30 times in Jeremiah; cf. H. Wildberger, *Jahwewort und prophetische Rede bei Jeremia* (1942), 19ff.; Thiel, 77f.; Neumann; 50 times in Ezekiel: cf. Zimmerli, *BK*, XIII/1, 36*, 38*, 88ff.

[183] *BK*, XIII/1, 89.

[184] So Wolff, *Hosea*, 4; cf. J. Jeremias, *ZAW*, 83 (1971), 352f.

[185] W. Rudolph, *KAT*, XIII/1, 35.

[186] O. Kaiser, *ZAW*, 70 (1958), 110; L. Perlitt, *Bundestheologie im AT. WMANT*, 36 (1969), 70.

and the other passages are disputed; not one of them is unequivocally ancient. The following view, then, has much to commend it: "The occurrence of the formula in the prophetic narratives of the early monarchical period ... is ... hardly original then, but is to be explained as Deuteronomistic redaction." [187] The problem of authenticity in the sayings of Jeremiah [188] has not yet been solved to the satisfaction of all, but in any case these come from a time very near the exilic period. [189]

In the Deuteronomistic history, the fulfilment of the word of God proclaimed by the prophet is frequently affirmed by the phrase: *kidhebhar yhvh 'asher dibber beyadh hannabhi'*, "according to the word which he spoke by the prophet ..." (1 K. 14:18; 15:29; 16:12,34; cf. 2 S. 24:19; 2 K. 1:17; 2:22; 4:44; etc.). Again, there is no unanimity as to whether this formula is an original part of the conclusion of the prophetic narratives or is (rather) to be attributed to (Deuteronomistic) redaction. [190]

The phrase *bidhebhar yhvh*, "by the word of Yahweh," is used repeatedly in the story of the man of God from Judah (1 K. 13:1f.,5,9,17f.,32). It "also occurs in 1 K. 20:35 and 1 S. 3:21 (which is of doubtful authenticity); the *be* should probably be understood in an instrumental sense (Brockelmann, *Synt.*, § 106k), and accordingly should be translated: 'by virtue of the word of Yahweh'." [191] Commenting on the commission given to the prophet Ezekiel, *vedhibbarta bidhebharai*, "speak my words" (Ezk. 3:4), Zimmerli asks whether "the formula from the vocabulary of the prophetic schools, which is obviously present in this didactic story of the prophet ... does not work itself out in an obvious assimilation to Yahweh's speaking in the first person ... ," so that the phrase might be rendered somewhat as follows: "in prophetic mission, officially." [192] One can also find an echo of this expression in the statement made in 2 Ch. 30:12 (cf. 29:15; 1 Ch. 15:15 in the LXX) that a royal command was given *bidhebhar yhvh*, "according to the word of Yahweh," and was thus in agreement with this word. Finally, Ps. 33:6 says that the heavens were made *bidhebhar yhvh*, "by the word of Yahweh" (cf. also 17:4).

2. *Other Constructions*. The plural construct expression *dibhre yhvh 'elohim*, "the words of Yahweh God," is much rarer (20 occurrences) and less specific (Ex. 4:28; etc.). [193] It can refer both to legal proclamation (Ex. 24:3f.; Ezr. 9:4) and also to prophetic words (Jer. 36:4,6,8,11; 37:2; 43:1; Ezk. 11:25).

---

[187] G. Fohrer, *Elia* (²1968), 53f.; but cf. the doubt expressed by O. H. Steck, *Überlieferung und Zeitgeschichte in den Elia-Erzählungen. WMANT*, 26 (1968), 41f., n. 3; 21, n. 7; differently again W. Dietrich, 71f.

[188] Cf. the differentiations in Thiel, 77f.

[189] On the peculiarities of this formula in the books of Haggai and Zechariah, cf. W. A. M. Beuken, *Haggai-Sacharja 1-8. SSN*, 10 (1967), 138ff., 347.

[190] Cf. A. Jepsen, *Die Quellen des Königsbuches*, 6ff.; G. von Rad, *Problem of the Hexateuch* (trans. 1966), 208ff.; O. H. Steck, *EvTh*, 27 (1967), 547, n. 7; H. C. Schmitt, *Elisa* (1972), 100f.; etc.; Dietrich, 88.

[191] Noth, *BK*, IX/1, 296.

[192] Zimmerli, *BK*, XIII/1, 11; cf. 65*.

[193] Cf. Grether, 76ff.

Aside from the construct expressions, *dabhar* or *debharim* refers to God more than 300 times. Approximately three-fourths of these passages relate to the prophetic word of revelation, and approximately one-fifth to the legal words of God. [194]

3. *Characteristics of the Word of God.* Frequently, but not until the later period, certain characteristics are attributed to the word of God. *dabhar* (sing. or pl.) is *tobh,* "good, full of promise, comforting" (Josh. 21:45; 23:14f.; 1 K. 8:56; Isa. 39:8; Jer. 29:10; 33:14; Zec. 1:13; cf. 2 S. 7:28; 1 K. 12:7; 22:13; Prov. 12:25; Ps. 45:2 [1]; it is also *ra'*, "evil," Ex. 33:4), *yashar,* "upright" (Ps. 33:4; cf. 19:9 [8]; Neh. 9:13), *'emeth,* "true" (2 S. 7:28; 1 K. 17:24; cf. Gen. 42:16,20; 1 K. 10:6; 22:16; Jer. 23:28; Ps. 119:43,160; Prov. 22:21; Eccl. 12:10; 2 Ch. 9:5; etc.), [195] and *ne'eman,* "true, reliable" (1 K. 8:26; 1 Ch. 17:23; 2 Ch. 1:9; 6:17; cf. Ps. 19:8 [7]; 93:5; etc.).

4. *Verbs That Affirm the Fulfilment of the Word.* The word that announces the future is connected with the expectation that it will be fulfilled. This idea of the fulfilment or realization of the word is expressed by the greatest variety of verbs. [196] In this sense, *dabhar* appears both as the object (a) and also as the subject (b) of these verbs.

a. *dabhar As Object.* According to Szeruda, the expression *mille'* (→ מלא *mālā'*) *dabhar,* "to fulfil, accomplish, complete a word" (1 K. 1:14; 2:27; 2 Ch. 36:21; cf. 1 K. 8:15,24; etc.), is based on the idea that the word "attains its totality through fulfilment; it must be filled up by God, as it were, to its full content." [197] Noth, however, understands this phrase "not in the sense of 'materially filling up' or 'completing' but in that of 'fully executing'" [198] (cf. → כלה *kālāh*). *'asah dabhar* [199] can also mean "to carry out (accomplish) the word" (Nu. 22:20; Isa. 38:7; Jer. 1:12; cf. Nu. 23:19; Jer. 28:6; Ezk. 12:28; etc.).

"The expression *haqim dabhar,* 'to confirm (establish) the word,' is predominantly if not exclusively Deuteronomic-Deuteronomistic" [200]: Dt. 9:5; 1 S. 1:23; 2 S. 7:25; 1 K. 2:4; 6:12; 8:20; 12:15; Isa. 44:26; Jer. 28:6; 29:10; 33:14; Dnl. 9:12; Neh. 9:8; 2 Ch. 6:10; 10:15; piel, Ezk. 13:6; of men: 1 S. 15:11,13; Jer. 34:18; Neh. 5:13; also 2 K. 23:3,24; hophal, Jer. 35:14; cf. also Nu. 23:19; 1 S. 3:12; Jer. 11:5; Ps. 119:38; etc.

b. *dabhar As Subject.* That word and event do not have to appear as two independent phenomena, but can be regarded as a unit, is evident from the use of *dabhar* as subject with the same meaning. The word itself can *yatsa',* "go out"

---

194 Grether, 79; cf. *THAT,* I, 440.
195 Cf. III.2 above.
196 Cf. Szeruda, 24f.; Dürr, 66f.
197 Szeruda, 24.
198 Noth, *BK,* IX/1, 20.
199 See IV.2.d.
200 Noth, *BK,* IX/1, 276; cf. Dietrich, 77f.

(Gen. 24:50; cf. Isa. 2:3; 45:23; 55:11), *bo'*,[201] "come true" (Dt. 18:22; Josh. 23:15; Jgs. 13:12,17; Jer. 17:15; 28:9; Ezk. 33:33; cf. Josh. 21:45; 1 S. 9:6; Isa. 5:19; 46:11; Hab. 2:3; etc.), → היה *hāyāh*, "come to pass" (Dt. 18:22; Isa. 55:11; cf. Jer. 32:24; etc.),[202] *kalah*, "come to completion, be accomplished" (Ezr. 1:1; 2 Ch. 36:22), *qum*, "endure" (Isa. 8:10; 40:8; Jer. 44:28f.), *ruts*, "run" (Ps. 147:15), *qarah*, "happen, occur" (Nu. 11:23), *hissigh*, "reach" (RSV "overtake") (Zec. 1:6), and *naphal*, "fall upon" (RSV "light upon") (Isa. 9:7 [8]).

The following phrase appears in the negative: *naphal* (*'artsah*), "to fall (to the earth)" (Josh. 21:45; 23:14; 1 K. 8:56; 2 K. 10:10; cf. the hiphil in 1 S. 3:19). "This expression is probably derived from the idea of ears of grain falling dead to the earth, or from the net of the hunter that falls on the prey (Am. 3:5)."[203] *shubh*, "to return," is also used with *dabhar* in the OT (Isa. 45:23; 55:11; cf. Jer. 4:28; hiphil, Nu. 23:20; Isa. 43:13; Am. 1:3; etc.).

Other passages (such as Isa. 31:2; Jer. 23:29; 51:12; Ps. 89:35 [34]; Lam. 2:17) might be mentioned too.[204] The OT says almost summarily: the word is not *req*, "empty" (Dt. 32:47) or "unfruitful" (Isa. 55:11; cf. 2 S. 1:22).

In the main there can be no question that frequently (cf. esp. Nu. 23:19), although not always, the fulfilment of the word is regarded as a decisive and sufficient criterion of truth, irrespective of the fact that this criterion applies only in retrospect and therefore is useless in the situation of the hearer. Jer. 28:8f. (unlike Dt. 18:21f.) judges only the prophet of salvation by the standard of fulfilment, and Dt. 13:2ff. (1ff.) sets the first commandment to worship Yahweh alone above the prophetic sign or wonder. The OT canonized a prophet like Deutero-Isaiah even though his expectation that the kingdom of God was near (Isa. 40:9; 52:7) was not fulfilled and the living conditions of the returned exiles turned out to be quite different from what he had promised.

5. *dabhar in the Sense of "Commandment."*

a. *A Technical Term for Apodictic Commandments?* According to Grether, *dabhar* is "the proper term for a commandment in the covenant law of Israel which stands at the beginning of the people's history. In the period before Deuteronomy, the term *dabhar* is used only rarely to denote legal revelation and it appears only in the plural, since the laws consisted of many regulations. In the first instance it serves to denote the demands of the decalog." "Only the ancient commands of the Sinaitic law, which go back to the immediate revelation of God and on the basis of which God made his covenant with the people, count as *debharim*."[205]

Meanwhile this view has run up against serious objections both historically and linguistically. To be sure, the reference of the texts in Ex. 19:6ff.; 20:1;

---

201 → בוא *bô'*, V.
202 On the so-called Word-Event formula, see V.1.c.
203 Dürr, 67.
204 On the phrase *kidhebhar*, cf. V.1.c above.
205 Grether, 80f., 83.

24:3f.,8; 34:1,27f., not all of which belong to P, is to words of God in various forms; from all appearance, however, these passages do not belong to the oldest stratum of the Sinai tradition, although this cannot, of course, be demonstrated in detail here. [206]

Again, the thesis that *debharim* is the genuine technical term for apodictic commands (cf. also Dt. 4:13; 5:22; 10:4; Josh. 24:26; Ps. 50:17), although it is often defended, [207] does not seem to be tenable.

Moran thinks, instead, that *debharim* means the "stipulations" of the treaty (cf. *awātē*) in Josh. 24:26, and appeals to v. 14 in support of this. [208]

The expression "ten words" itself can hardly be old.

"In all these passages, *debharim* is to be understood as 'words of God.' But this means that *debharim* can come to denote a covenant commandment only where Yahweh has become the giver of that commandment. Since Alt's thesis does not hold up that the form of commandment stands in genuine connection with Yahweh, *dabhar*, which in any case belongs more to prophecy, cannot be an original technical term to denote the commandments." [209] Alt himself [210] and Gerstenberger [211] have expressed similar doubts. "The only passages that explicitly use the expression 'the ten words' are Ex. 34:28; Dt. 4:13; 10:4. Since Ex. 34:28 is uncertain..., the first literary evidence is Deuteronomic." [212]

Besides, the commandments are not only called *debharim*, but also *dibhre yhvh*, "the words of Yahweh" (Ex. 24:3f.; etc.), [213] and occasionally even *debhar yhvh*, "the word of Yahweh" (Dt. 5:5; 1 Ch. 15:15; etc.). [214]

b. *Use in Deuteronomy and the Deuteronomistic Work.* Recently Braulik has investigated the use of *dabhar* in Deuteronomy and reached the following conclusions: "The *debharim* in Dt. 4:10,13,36; 5:5,22; 9:10; 10:2,4 denote the decalog. *dabhar* in 15:15; 24:18,22 and *debharim* in 12:28 mean concrete individual regulations. *dabhar* in 4:2; 13:1 [12:32]; 30:14, and *debharim* in 1:18; 6:6; 11:18 have reference to the entire Mosaic 'law,' viz., the parenetic portion and the related individual commandments. In 28:14, *debharim* denotes this 'law' probably together with the decalog." [215] Accordingly, Deuteronomy does not

---

[206] Cf. recently Perlitt, *Bundestheologie im AT,* 156ff. with literature; also W. H. Schmidt, *Alttestamentlicher Glaube und seine Umwelt* (1968), 38ff.; E. Zenger, *Die Sinaitheophanie. FzB,* 3 (1971), esp. pp. 109f.; otherwise W. Zimmerli, *Festschrift W. Eichrodt* (1970), 171-190; *idem, Grundriss der alttestamentlichen Theologie* (1972), 39ff.

[207] Cf. the literature in Liedke, 194, n. 8.

[208] W. L. Moran, *Bibl,* 43 (1962), 105.

[209] So Liedke, 194f.

[210] A. Alt, *KlSchr,* I, 323, n. 1.

[211] E. Gerstenberger, *Wesen und Herkunft des "apodiktischen Rechts." WMANT,* 20 (1965), 77, n. 1.

[212] *Ibid.;* cf. Perlitt, *Bundestheologie,* 229f.; otherwise W. Beyerlin, *Origins and History of the Oldest Sinaitic Traditions* (trans. ²1965), 24f., 80f., 149; E. Nielsen, *The Ten Commandments in New Perspective. SBT,* N.S. 7 (trans. 1968), 27ff.

[213] Grether, 76f.

[214] *Ibid.,* 71f.

[215] G. Braulik, *Bibl,* 51, 49; cf. also Grether, 120ff.; Lohfink, 54ff.

seem to use the different expressions for commandment indiscriminately. [216]

Predominantly at least in Deuteronomic-Deuteronomistic and later texts, plural construct expressions containing *dabhar* are used to refer to the commandments: *dibhre habberith* (→ ברית *berith*), "the words of the covenant" (Ex. 34:28; Dt. 28:69 [29:1]; 29:8 [9], cf. v. 18 [19]; 2 K. 23:3; Jer. 11:2,6,8; 2 Ch. 34:31), *dibhre hattorah (hazzo'th)*, "the words of (this) law" (Dt. 17:19; 27:3,8,26; 28:58; 29:28 [29]; 31:12,24; 32:46; Josh. 8:34; 2 K. 23:24; Neh. 8:9,13; 2 Ch. 34:19), *dibhre (has)sepher (hattorah/habberith)*, "the words of (the) book (of the law/ of the covenant)" (2 K. 22:11,13,16; 23:2; 2 Ch. 34:21,30).

Under the stimulus of prophecy, the Deuteronomistic history "depicts Israel's history as a history of Yahweh's effective word": [217] Josh. 21:45; 23:15; 1 S. 1:27; 15:11,13; 1 K. 2:4,27; 6:12; 8:20,56; etc.

The later use of *dabhar* in the sense of "commandment, law," etc., is demonstrated in the Priestly Code (Ex. 16:16,32; 29:1; 35:1,4; Lev. 8:5,36; etc.), [218] and in Ps. 119 (vv. 9,17,57,130,139) with the confession: "Thy word is a lamp to my feet" (v. 105).

6. *Occurrences in the Psalms.* The Psalms do not speak of the word of God often (outside Ps. 119, only 18 times), [219] but they do so in many different ways. *dabhar* is at work in the history of the people (Ps. 105:8,42; 106:12,24), in the life of individuals (56:5,11 [4,10]; 130:5; cf. 51:6 [4]), and in nature (33:6; 147:15,18; 148:8; cf. 103:20f.). It can also refer to God's commandments.

Express reference should be made to a special use of *dabhar*. Begrich has detected in the OT a "priestly oracle of salvation" "which promised the worshipper in the name of his God that God would hear his prayer, and which [in the Individual Lament] came after the lament and the petition and before the affirmation of the certainty of hearing and the vow." [220] In three psalms (parts of which may well be later), the word *dabhar* is used of this oracle of salvation. The original situation in which this oracle functioned comes out most clearly in Ps. 107:19f. (cf. Wisd. 16:12): those sick unto death "cried to Yahweh in their trouble...; he sent forth his word, and healed them." [221] The anthological Ps. 119 [222] contains not only the confession, "My soul languishes for thy salvation; I hope in thy word" (v. 81; cf. vv. 74,114,147), but also the petition, "Revive me according to thy word!" (v. 25; cf. v. 37). In the confession of trust in Ps.

---

[216] On ancient Near Eastern parallels to the so-called Text or Canon formula (Dt. 4:2; also 13:1[12:32]; Prov. 30:6; Rev. 22:18f.), cf. recently S. Herrmann, *Festschrift G. von Rad* (1971), 165, n. 24 with literature.

[217] Von Rad, *OT Theol*, II, 94; cf. I, 341ff.; *Problem of the Hexateuch*, 208ff.; Grether, 128ff.

[218] On the formal use of *dabhar*, see IV.1.b.

[219] Cf. Deissler, 83f.

[220] J. Begrich, "Das priesterliche Heilsorakel," *ZAW*, 52 (1934), 81-92 = *ThB*, 21 (1964), 217-231, esp. p. 217; cf. H. Gunkel-J. Begrich, *Einl. in die Psalmen* (1933), 246; also C. Westermann, *EvTh*, 24 (1964), 355-373; *idem, Forschung am AT* (1964), 117ff.; J. Schüpphaus, *ThZ*, 27 (1971), 161-181; A. Schoors, *SVT*, 24 (1973), 32ff.

[221] Cf. V.8.a below.

[222] Cf. Deissler.

130:5, "in his word I hope," the hope is no longer directed especially toward deliverance from a concrete distress; *dabhar* is no longer the saving, but "only" the forgiving word. Furthermore, it is no longer the promise of the priest that God will hear; rather, the worshipper supplies his own answer with his hope. [223]

On the basis of the fact that *dabhar* characterizes the prophet elsewhere, [224] Würthwein "traces back the *dabhar* which is sought and received in the Psalms, not to priests, but to cult prophets." [225] Jeremias, however, opposes this view. [226] But perhaps one may also see an effect of this encouragement that God will hear in the commissioning of the Servant of the Lord (Isa. 50:4), "to answer (?) him that is weary with a word (*dabhar*)."

7. *History and the Ancient Near East.* The God of the fathers is already "a God in whom one trusts because one has been addressed by God. He is a God who *says* he will lead a person." [227] Just as he promises the patriarchs a prosperous future, viz., protection, descendants, and possession of the land, so at the call of Moses he promises him deliverance from Egypt (Ex. 3:7ff.). Later at least, then, the Exodus tradition is also interpreted in the light of the divine promise. Nevertheless, the concept of "the word of God" (*debhar yhvh/'elohim*) is not firmly anchored in any important passage in these Pentateuchal traditions. Passages like Gen. 15:1,4; Ex. 4:28,30; 9:20f.; Nu. 11:23f.; 14:39; 15:31 are, if not late, then at least not characteristic, i.e., they are peripheral and not central to the tradition. [228] It is even doubtful whether the Sinai pericope in its earliest form knew the concept of *dabhar*. [229] A word of God which precedes the event and announces the future also plays a decisive role in the War of Yahweh tradition (Jgs. 3:28; 7:9,15; etc.). This possibly goes back into Israel's early period (cf. Ex. 14:13ff.), but it actually takes its shape only in the promised land. In the period of the judges, the concept of *dabhar* is attested occasionally with different nuances of meaning (Josh. 3:9; Jgs. 3:20; 1 S. 3:1,7; 9:27; 15:1,10; etc.), but its true appearance is only from the age of the monarchy onward in prophecy (1 K. 14:5; 22:5ff.; etc.). [230] Perhaps it is no accident, then, that *dabhar* already appears frequently in the Balaam pericope (Nu. 22:20,35,38; etc.).

The basic traditions of Israel's faith are thus developed already when the people comes into contact with the religious ideas of the cultures of the ancient Near East. It is understandable, therefore, that Grether could delineate a development almost completely within the OT itself, [231] and could look upon

---

[223] Cf. W. H. Schmidt, *ThZ*, 22 (1966), 241-253, esp. pp. 248f.

[224] Cf. IV.5.a above.

[225] E. Würthwein, *Festschrift A. Weiser* (1963), 125ff.=*Wort und Existenz* (1970), 154ff., esp. p. 157.

[226] J. Jeremias, *Kultprophetie und Gerichtsverkündigung in der späteren Königszeit Israels. WMANT*, 35 (1970), 159.

[227] M. Buber, *Werke*, II (1964), 273.

[228] Cf. also Grether, 85.

[229] Cf. V.5.a above.

[230] Cf. IV.5; V.1.

[231] Grether, 126ff., 135; cf. 144.

"the positing of a relationship between *dabhar* and nature as the final consequence of typical Israelite ideas." [232]

This view would seem to be too one-sided now that Dürr has collected a large number of ancient Near Eastern testimonies to the existence of the concept of the divine word outside the OT: as "physical-cosmic power," giver and sustainer of life, as creative, irresistible, and irrevocable and constant energy. [233] In his criticism of Grether, who argues that ancient Near Eastern religions "do not know and cannot know the word as a principle of history," [234] Albrektson has adduced additional testimonies to the operation of the word of God in history. [235] No one, however, has undertaken a study which combines the historical question of Grether with the phenomenological-comparative investigation of Dürr, a study which focuses strictly on the history of form and tradition. Thus far only similarities and possibly identical concepts can be shown, but dependences and also differences have not yet been established with certainty. "In Israel, ancient Near Eastern concepts of the creative power of the divine word have been transferred to Yahweh." [236] This view is possible or probable for certain texts, but can hardly claim general validity. It is worth noting that the texts which most clearly suggest a relationship to ancient Near Eastern ideas all appear late in the OT. [237]

In Ps. 29 there is an especially close connection with ancient Near Eastern ideas about the weather god, although this psalm, of course, extols the *qol* ("voice") of God and not his word.

A most important point is that the theory that foreign concepts are borrowed is not in itself a negative judgment, since the statements concerned are to be interpreted in their respective contexts. Characteristic differences remain. On the one hand we may refer to the exclusiveness of Yahweh and the opposition to images. Implied here is the transcendence of God, i.e., the sharp distinction between God and world. On the other hand we may refer to the OT relationship of the one God to history. [238]

8. *Beginnings of Hypostatization.* Of the many texts on the hypostatization of the word which Grether in particular has collected, [239] only a few leading examples can be mentioned here. [240]

According to Dürr, "there appears already in the OT at the end of its development the concept of the 'divine word' which proceeds from the deity but operates independently, moving silently and surely in its course, a piece of the deity, the

---

[232] *Ibid.,* 139.

[233] See I.2 above.

[234] Grether, 139; cf. 144.

[235] Albrektson, 53ff.

[236] H.-J. Kraus, *BK,* XV ([3]1966), 958 on Ps. 147:15ff.; cf. pp. 263f. on Ps. 33:6,9.

[237] Cf. V.8.b above.

[238] Cf. also Albrektson, 115; Koch, 289ff.

[239] Grether, 150ff.

[240] Cf. the following works on the phenomenon of the hypostatization of the word of God: Szeruda, 51ff.; P. Heinisch, *Personifikationen und Hypostasen im AT und im Alten Orient* (1921); Dürr, 122f.; Hamp, 129ff.; Ringgren, 157ff.; Deissler, 297ff.; G. Pfeiffer, *Ursprung und Wesen der Hypostasenvorstellungen im Judentum* (1967), 72f.; etc.

bearer of divine power, clearly distinguished from it and yet belonging to it, a hypostasis in the real sense of the word." [241] In the OT, however, *dabhar* does not represent a personified force which exists more or less independently of God, "a natural, tangible substance"; [242] it contains only certain beginnings of hypostatization (but cf. Wisd. 18:15ff.). These may be found (a) in the Psalms, and (b) in the prophetic literature, especially in Jeremiah and Deutero-Isaiah.

a. *In the Psalms.* In Ps. 107:20, "he sent forth his word, and healed them" (cf. Wisd. 16:12), and 147:15, "he sends forth his command (*'imratho*) to the earth, his word (*dabhar*) runs swiftly" (cf. v. 18, *yishlach debharo,* "he sends forth his word"), the word is "represented as having the function of a messenger of God." [243] While Ps. 107:20, with its backward glance at deliverance from distress, sees the function of the word as that of an oracle of salvation, [244] 147:15, 18a are incorporated in statements concerning the rule of Yahweh in nature. Thus events in nature may be understood as operations of the word of God, even if this is not explicitly stated in the text (but cf. 1 K. 17:1; etc.), so that "the *dabhar* also appears as the creative and formative principle in the consideration of nature." [245] The author of Ps. 33:6, while not ascribing independence to the word, confesses in relation not merely to the world's preservation, but also to its creation: "By the word of Yahweh (*bidhebhar yhvh/ /beruach piv,* by the breath of his mouth) the heavens were made."

In Ps. 147:19 there is a sudden transition from the *dabhar* that controls nature to the *debharim* (*qere;* the *kethibh* has the sing. *dabhar*), the statutes and ordinances which Yahweh declared to Israel. "This sort of juxtaposition is possible only because the concept of *dabhar* in these relatively late passages has already been hypostatized to the extent that it means the God who reveals himself." [246] On the other hand, Kraus argues: "Yet there is certainly no conflicting or twofold concept of *dabhar* in Ps. 147. Rather, one must interpret this passage to mean that the *dabhar* that controls nature has become known to Israel in the revelation of the *debharim.* ... That is, Israel does not understand the creative *dabhar* mythically and naturalistically, but after the analogy of the word of law and government which was imparted to the chosen people." [247] In any case, "all statements in Ps. 147 concerning the creative *dabhar* that is sent forth are completely integrated into the concept of the sovereign majesty of the subject, Yahweh." [248]

Beginnings of personification or hypostatization may also be found in Ps. 119:89; etc. Still, according to 103:20, the word itself is not the divine messenger; it needs heavenly creatures to deliver it.

---

[241] Dürr, 123; adopted by Ringgren, 157.
[242] Dürr, 123.
[243] *Ibid.,* 125.
[244] Cf. V.6 above.
[245] Grether, 138f.
[246] *Ibid.,* 156.
[247] H.-J. Kraus, *BK,* XV/2, 958.
[248] *Ibid.*

b. *In the Prophetic Literature.* The inevitability of coming judgment, which means that even those who seek God will no longer find him (Hos. 5:6), is described in a revised but not secondary oracle in the book of Amos as an insatiable hunger "to hear the words of Yahweh" (*dibhre yhvh;* LXX has the sing. *dabhar*). People will run to and fro through the land or the earth in all directions "to seek the word of Yahweh (*debhar yhvh*), but they shall not find it" (Am. 8:11f.). This threat refers either to a pilgrimage to a sanctuary (cf. Hos. 5:6; Am. 5:5; Zec. 8:21f.) or to seeking God through a prophet. [249] In any case, the statement has been detached from the concrete situation and generalized into a fundamental principle. The absence of the word of God does not merely bring about but already is itself the situation of inescapable judgment (cf. 1 S. 28:15f.; Mic. 3:6; Ezk. 7:26).

dabhar is the subject of the retrospective saying in Isa. 9:7(8): "A word (*dabhar*) the Lord sent against Jacob, and it alighted upon Israel."

> This passage speaks of *dabhar* in a remarkably objective way. It alights upon Israel like an object and... is now dangerously and destructively at work in the history of the northern kingdom. The translation 'word' does not seem to be suitable here, since *dabhar* has little affinity with what we understand by the word 'word.' There is nothing at all to indicate that this word was addressed to anyone, nor are we told who said it or what was its content. It is sent and it is at work—that is all. [250]

dabhar, however, seems to be used here only formally, "for the first time without having a specific content in view and exclusively as the bearer of a power," [251] for according to the context the word of judgment (which was no doubt promulgated by the prophet, cf. Hos. 6:5) is the cause of the catastrophe. It may be doubted, then, whether the antithesis which follows is really in keeping with the meaning of the text: "It is a word, not as the bearer of a message that one is to *hear,* but of an event that one is to *experience,* a word that creates history and thus shapes the future." [252] Against Grether's view that *dabhar* "here is not a prophetic word of revelation..., but... an independent quantity, a hypostasis," [253] Dürr can say already: "At issue here is the spoken prophetic word," not a hypostasis, because "the element of personal activity is missing." [254]

There may be an echo of Isa. 9:7(8) in the controversial introduction of Zec. 9:1: "An Oracle. The word of Yahweh (*massa' debhar yhvh*) in the land of Hadrach, and Damascus is its resting place." [255]

Jer. 5:14 explicitly affirms that the word of God is the prophetic proclamation which has a part in the power of God: "Behold, I am making my words in your

---

[249] Cf. IV.5.a above.
[250] Rendtorff, 642; cf. von Rad, *OT Theol,* II, 90.
[251] Grether, 104.
[252] Wildberger, *BK,* X (1972), 213.
[253] Grether, 105; cf. p. 153.
[254] Dürr, 124 with n. 5; cf. Wildberger, 213; recently J. Vollmer, *BZAW,* 119 (1971), 132.
[255] Cf. recently M. Saebø, *Sach 9-14. WMANT,* 34 (1969), 141f.

mouth a fire, and this people wood, and the fire shall devour them." But the word of God in the mouth of the prophet not only announces judgment; it also causes it to happen.

In the controversy with his prophetic opponents, Jeremiah makes a distinction between the means of revelation, criticizes dreams on the basis of the word, and attains "perhaps for the first time a definition of the word of Yahweh." "This is not given, however, for its own sake but has a purely polemic point": [256] "Let the prophet who has a dream tell the dream, but let him who has my word (*debhari*) speak my word faithfully. What has straw in common with wheat? says Yahweh. Is not my word like fire, says Yahweh, and like a hammer which breaks the rock in pieces?" (Jer. 23:28f.).

The power of the word expressed in this figurative comparison reminds us how alien it was when he received it (15:16; 20:7ff.; etc.). Thus Jeremiah seems "to set forth the forceful nature of the word of Yahweh when he reflects theologically on his own experiences. . . ." [257] What we have here, then, is reflection on prophetic preaching. In these sayings he simply makes explicit what earlier prophets had already experienced (Am. 3:8; etc.). In Jeremiah we find "the beginning of meditation on the meaning of Yahweh's speaking, and this with such intensity and breadth that it is possible to speak of a Jeremianic theology of the word of God." [258] Other scholars like to reserve the concept of a "theology of the word" for Deutero-Isaiah. [259]

Two affirmations concerning the power of the word of God form the framework (Isa. 40:8; 55:10f.) of the book of this exilic prophet. The transitoriness of human power in general and of the Babylonian oppressor in particular ("all flesh is grass," Isa. 40:6ff.; cf. 51:12f.) is contrasted with the statement: "The word of our God will stand for ever" (*yaqum le'olam,* 40:8), i.e., it maintains its stability and durability when all else decays, it establishes itself against a very different form of reality, and it therefore merits confidence as compared with external appearance.

Von Rad calls this "an almost gnostic view" in which the word of God stands on the one side as that which alone is creative, while history with all its peoples stands on the other side as the realm of the transient. [260] The statement should not be understood timelessly, however, but concretely in terms of the situation in which Deutero-Isaiah finds himself. As the formula "word of *our* God" (*debhar 'elohenu* instead of *debhar yhvh*) indicates, and as the context suggests, *dabhar* here does not refer in general to all prophetic revelation, but in particular to the promise of the end of the exile (40:1ff.). [261]

In the concluding sentences of his work (Isa. 55:6ff.), where Deutero-Isaiah

---

[256] Jeremias, 319.

[257] *Ibid.*

[258] Mauser, 83.

[259] Cf. Procksch, 96; von Rad, *OT Theol,* II, 94, 91, n. 20, 265f.; Rendtorff, 643; also Zimmerli, *BK,* XIII/1, 89; Baltzer, 117ff. on Ezekiel.

[260] Von Rad, *OT Theol,* II, 243.

[261] Cf. recently Elliger, *BK,* XI/1, 126ff.

again seems to affirm his message in a summary, we find "prophecy's most comprehensive statement about the word of Yahweh and its effects...; the dimensions are extended to the furthest limits of thought and even to the very foundations of theology."[262] Nevertheless, the exilic situation again shines through these statements. The contrast between "my thoughts and your thoughts, and my ways and your ways" (vv. 8f.) is to be explained in terms of the polemical or apologetic debate with the self-understanding of his contemporaries (cf. 40:27; 49:17; Ezk. 37:11).

> "As the rain and the snow come down from heaven,
>   and return not thither but water the earth,
> making it bring forth and sprout,
>   giving seed to the sower and bread to the eater,
> so shall my word be that goes forth from my mouth;
>   it shall not return to me empty,
> but it shall accomplish that which I purpose,
>   and prosper in the thing for which I sent it." (Isa. 55:10f.)

When it is said that the rain "fructifies" the earth, this may call to mind the myth of Father Heaven impregnating Mother Earth with the semen of rain, but here the idea is simply a figure which in the form of a simile (ka'asher—ken, "as—so") is intended to illustrate the efficacy of the word (cf. Isa. 45:23, lo' yashubh, "shall not return"). No natural or even magical power is attributed to the word, nor does this passage have in mind an objectified word, but the word proclaimed by the prophet (cf. 44:26, meqim debhar 'abhdo, "he confirms the word of his servant"). Here then, as in 9:7(8) (cf. Ps. 107:20; 147:18), the term shalach, "to send," which is borrowed from the accounts of prophetic calling (Ex. 3:10; Jgs. 6:14; Isa. 6:8; 61:1; Jer. 1:7; 14:14; 26:5; Ezk. 2:3f.; etc.; cf. Isa. 42:19; 48:16), can also be transferred to the word. Thus it can even take on something of the character of the prophet himself, and (as in Jer. 23:29 and Isa. 40:8) it becomes the subject of the sentence, so that it is possible to speak of its own activity.[263] But it is not (yet) a substantial being or a personally independent mediating figure which appears alongside or in place of God (cf. Isa. 45:19; 48:3; etc.).

Dürr also concludes: "The word is still an impersonal, even if a real, power."[264] Baltzer comments: "The word is described as a subject who has been sent out by his master to accomplish a mission."[265] Similarly, Pfeiffer says that the word is "like a person acting by Yahweh's authority."[266]

Furthermore, Isa. 55:6ff. takes up the promise of Jer. 29:10ff., so that the word

---

[262] Von Rad, *OT Theol*, II, 93.
[263] Cf. V.4.b.
[264] Dürr, 124.
[265] Baltzer, 128.
[266] Pfeiffer, 72.

of Yahweh (*debhari,* "my word") in Isa. 55:11 is to be interpreted as the "good, i.e., comforting word of promise" (*debhari hattobh*) of Jer. 29:10. [267]

As in Isa. 40:8, *dabhar* in 55:10f. is not an indefinite "proclamation uttered by God with no specific content...", the divine factor that permeates the whole of history and also the life of nature." [268] Instead, it is the promise of deliverance (cf. 55:12f.). Even in such texts, the historical situation and the material function of the word are only apparently lost behind its more dynamic function.

According to Rendtorff, there is "now no question but that these passages express an idea of the powerful word of God which has parallels throughout the ancient Near East. By no means, then, was this idea originally created by the prophets themselves to express their peculiar understanding of the word of Yahweh." [269] But if Jer. 23:29 and Isa. 55:10f. are modelled after ancient Near Eastern prototypes, then we must ask (as we did in our remarks on the concept of the word as creator) [270] why these passages appear so remarkably late in the prophetic literature. Apparently the ancient Near Eastern views aided the prophets in describing their experiences, and the prophets seem to have been able to make what sound like mythical or objective statements about an independently functioning word of God only after it has been made clear by the context that these statements retain their relationship to history and man and therefore their character as personal address. [271]

W. H. Schmidt

---

[267] Cf. W. H. Schmidt, *Festschrift G. Widengren,* I (1972), 135ff.; Baltzer, 117ff., refers to Ezk. 37:4, where the word "announces Yahweh's new creation and also sets in motion the process by which it will become reality."

[268] Grether, 133f.

[269] Rendtorff, 643; cf. Baltzer, 132f.

[270] Cf. V.7 above.

[271] On the translation of *dabhar* in the LXX, cf. Procksch, 91f.; Repo; G. Bertram, *ThR,* 10 (1938), 152ff.; on the Aramaic translation, cf. Hamp; and on the treatment of *dabhar* in the Talmudic literature, cf. Lauterbach.

דֶּבֶר *debher*

Contents: I. Meaning, Etymology. II. Use: 1. Prophetic-Deuteronomistic Explanatory Scheme; 2. Hab. 3:5.

I. **Meaning, Etymology.** As is indicated by the change from *debher* to *maveth,* "death," in Jer. 15:2 and the consistent LXX rendering by *thanatos*

---

debher. K. Elliger, *HAT,* 4, 367-377; F. C. Fensham, "Malediction and Benediction in Ancient Near Eastern Vassal-Treaties and the OT," *ZAW,* 74 (1962), 1-9; *idem,* "Common Trends in Curses of the Near Eastern Treaties and *kudurru*-Inscriptions Compared with Maledictions of Amos and Isaiah," *ZAW,* 75 (1963), 155-175; D. R. Hillers, *Treaty Curses and the OT Prophets. BietOr,* 16 (1964); M. Noth, *A History of Pentateuchal Traditions* (trans. 1971); M. Weinfeld, *Deuteronomy and the Deuteronomic School* (1972); H. W. Wolff, *BK,* XIV/2, 247-266.

(except in Hab. 3:5, where *logos* goes back to the reading *dabhar,* and in passages which omit the word), *debher* denotes a fatal pestilence (Jer. 27:13; Ezk. 33:27; etc.) which comes upon men and domestic animals (Ex. 9:3). It is not possible to identify the precise disease on the basis of information given in the Bible. Scholars usually connect *debher* with Akk. *dibiru,* "calamity," [1] but this is disputed by *CAD.* [2] Only S. R. Driver connects it with Ugar. *dbr,* "death." [3] Arabic has the words *dabrah,* "calamity," and *dabarah,* "running sore, abscess" (in camels). [4]

II. Use.

1. *Prophetic-Deuteronomistic Explanatory Scheme. debher* is not used in a secular setting in the OT. According to the usual translation, pestilence is always a divinely sent punishment for disobedience. It can come upon the people of Israel, foreign nations (Ex. 9:15; Ezk. 28:23), groups (Jer. 42:17,22; 44:13), or individuals (Ezk. 38:22). Before God sends it (cf. *shillach,* Jer. 24:10; Ezk. 14:19; Am. 4:10), it can be said almost mythologically to abide with him (Hab. 3:5).

The word never appears alone, but always as a part of a list, or at least in parallelism (Nu. 14:12; Hab. 3:5). It occurs in *multipartite lists:* the Egyptian plagues—contamination of the water, frogs, insects, pestilence, hail, locusts, darkness (Ex. 7:8–10:29 with 5:3; cf. Ps. 78:50); pestilence, famine, sword, dispersion (Ezk. 5:12); famine, wild beasts, pestilence, blood, sword (5:17); famine, wild beasts, sword, pestilence (14:12-23; cf. Jer. 15:1-3); sword, pestilence, blood, hail, fire, brimstone (Ezk. 38:22); famine, drought, damage to crops, fall of cities, locusts, pestilence, sword (Am. 4:6-11); lack of rain, famine, pestilence, damage to crops, locusts, enemies, misfortune, disease (1 K. 8:36-40; cf. also 2 Ch. 6:24ff.; 7:11ff.; 20:6ff.); disease, enemies, lack of rain, famine, wild beasts, sword, pestilence (Lev. 26:16ff.); pestilence, disease, damage to crops, lack of rain, enemies (Dt. 28:21ff.). *debher* also appears in *tripartite lists:* sword, famine, pestilence (Jer. 14:12; 21:6,7,9; 24:10; 27:8,13; 29:17,18; 32:24,36; 34:17; 38:2; 42:17,22; 44:13; Ezk. 6:11,12; 7:15; 12:16; 2 S. 24:13,15 = 1 Ch. 21:12,14); war, calamity (RSV famine), pestilence (Jer. 28:8); pestilence, blood, sword (Ezk. 28:23); sword, wild beasts, pestilence (33:27). This survey shows that the lists are concentrated in prophetic and deuteronomistic passages. They explain God's judgment, which (except when it refers to foreign nations) has been brought on by Israel's breaking of the divine covenant. To some extent they are even appended to specific texts or terms in the form of a commentary. An eloquent example of this is Ezk. 5:12, which elucidates 5:1f. The LXX has removed the discrepancy between the three elements listed in the "text" and the four elements listed in the "commentary" by inserting a fourth element into the "text."

---

[1] *AHw,* 168b.
[2] *CAD,* III, 135a.
[3] *CML,* 154b.
[4] However, cf. Wehr, 270.

The tripartite list—hunger, pestilence, sword—is connected with the downfall of the Judean state in 587 B.C. and its ramifications, and it describes the war in its most fearful consequences. When we set this alongside the triad—sword, wild beasts, pestilence—of the word of judgment in Ezk. 33:27, which came upon those who were left behind after the fall of Jerusalem, and Jeremiah's summary of the genuine prophetic message as "war, calamity, pestilence" in 28:8, we must obviously conclude that under the formal pressure of the number three these lists arose on the basis of life's experiences and existing conditions. Consequently the multipartite lists were not expansions of the tripartite lists, but conversely the tripartite lists (and the parallelism in the Deuteronomistic insertion in Nu. 14:12) constituted only a selection from the repertoire represented by the multipartite lists. The execration tablets of the ancient Near Eastern boundary stones and vassal treaties, which threaten a fixed consequence for breaking a treaty (e.g., famine, calamity, disease, flooding, vermin, locusts, lack of rain, slaughter, and pestilence),[5] support this supposition. To be sure, in Wiseman no form of the root *dbr* is used for "pestilence," but the word *mūtānu*.[6] In the prophetic-Deuteronomistic explanatory scheme, these lists of curses were adapted to conditions in Israel. They were used, however, not merely in descriptions of the judgment of Yahweh but also in the story of the Egyptian plagues leading up to the Passover[7] and then again in the description of a pestilence as the punishment of David in 2 S. 24.

2. *Hab. 3:5.* In the description of the vision in Hab. 3, where Yahweh appears for battle accompanied by pestilence and plague, there is an echo of ancient Near Eastern portrayals of deities, as in Ps. 89:15 (Eng. v. 14). Ishtar also appears with her footmen beside, before, and behind her.[8] Probably we should read *debher* instead of *dabhar* in Hos. 13:14, following Hab. 3:5.

Mayer

---

[5] Cf. *KAI*, 222 A.14ff.; D. J. Wiseman, *The Vassal-Treaties of Esarhaddon. Iraq*, 20 (1958), lines 418ff.

[6] Wiseman, lines 455f.

[7] Noth, 65ff.

[8] E. Schrader, *Die Keilinschriften und das AT* (³1902), 455f.

דְּבַשׁ   dᵉbhash

Contents: I. Etymology and Meaning. II. Use: 1. Secular; 2. Religious. III. "Honey" As a Figure and a Symbol.

I. Etymology and Meaning. The word *debhash* is part of the common vocabulary of the Semitic languages. It has cognates in Aramaic (Syr. *debšā,* Jewish Aram. *dûḇšā,* Mandean *dupšā*), Arabic (*dibs*), and certain South Ethiopic dialects (Gafat *dēbsä,* Argobba *dims,* Harari *dūs*). Akk. *dišpu*[1] is simply a variant that came about through metathesis. The translation of *debhash* by "honey," which goes back to the ancient versions, can be retained here only as the traditional interpretation. It would be more correct to render the term "sweet substance," because it does not always seem to denote only the product of bees. For several reasons, it is advisable to treat with skepticism the identification of *debhash* with honey, which Armbruster and others defend.

First, in Biblical Hebrew *debhash* is connected with words that could be more specific terms for bee honey, viz., *yaʿar* (Cant. 5:1), which is related to Ethiop. *maʿar,* and *nopheth* (Ps. 19:11 [Eng. v. 10]; Prov. 24:13; Cant. 4:11), which corresponds to Ugar. *nbt,* "honey," but also to Akk. *nub/p-tu* and Ethiop. *nĕhĕb,* "bee." When the ancient versions frequently translate *nopheth* by "honeycomb" (the Vulgate also translates *yaʿar* by "honeycomb" in Cant. 5:1), possibly they are attempting to find an acceptable parallel to *debhash,* which they render "honey."

Second, Arab. *dibs* does not mean bee honey, but a honey-like syrup derived from grapes and made thick by cooking. Until recently, this product was exported from Palestine to Egypt by large caravans. Akk. *dišpu* can refer to a sweet substance which is obtained from dates (*dišip suluppi*). Josephus (in *Wars* iv.468) says that in Jericho a "honey" of good quality was made from dates which were trodden with the feet. Thus, postbiblical Hebrew correctly distinguishes between the *debhash* of bees and the *debhash* of dates or figs.

Third, relevant OT texts hardly ever make more precise statements about the actual nature and origin of *debhash.* The only passage where it is necessary to translate "bee honey" is Jgs. 14:8f., which describes the background for Samson's riddle (v. 14). The text here is obviously speaking of a product of bees. But it must be asked whether *debhash* has not in this case replaced an original *yaʿar,* which would have formed a wordplay with "lion" (*ʾaryeh*). The narrative in 1 S. 14:26-30 is not entirely clear. It is usually assumed that when Jonathan was weary and

---

deḇhash. L. Armbruster, "Die Biene im Orient," "Bibel und Biene," *Archiv für Bienenkunde,* 13 (1932), 1-43; F. Blome, *Die Opfermaterie in Babylonien und Israel,* I (Rome, 1934), 298-304; R. Chauvin, ed., *Traité de biologie de l'abeille. V: Histoire, ethnographie et folklore* (Paris, 1968), 38-60; Dalman, *AuS,* IV, 382-88; R. J. Forbes, *Studies in Ancient Technology,* V (Leiden, ²1966), 80-111; W. Michaelis, *TDNT,* IV, 552-54.

[1] *AHw,* 173.

was wandering about lost in the forest, the *debhash* which he collected with the tip of his staff was honey produced by wild bees, but the word *ye'arah* (RSV "honey-comb"), which precedes *debhash* in v. 27, is an obscure hapax legomenon whose established translation by "honeycomb" is by no means certain. Since bees are not mentioned in the narrative, and since the staff which Jonathan uses does not seem to be suitable for scattering a swarm of bees, it could be that the substance called *debhash* is a sweet secretion of plant parasites. In any case, it is a wild product and not honey made by domesticated bees. There is no certain evidence that bees were domesticated in Israel during the biblical period, [2] although we know they were domesticated in Asia Minor before the fourteenth century B.C. [3] and in Egypt from the third century B.C. on. [4] In the Mesopotamian region, the introduction of beekeeping is mentioned by a certain Šamaš-rēš-uṣur. [5] In Israel, it is first attested for certain in the Mishnah and the Talmud. It would be absurd to conclude from Dt. 32:13 (cf. Ps. 81:17[16]) that wild honey was collected in the rocks. "Honey out of the rock" was not something to be collected any more than the "oil out of the flinty rock" which is connected with it. The Song of Moses is using a figure here which contrasts the liquid of an edible product with the solid substance which produces it. According to Lev. 2:11 and 2 Ch. 31:5, the firstfruits of *debhash* were brought (*hiqribh*) to Yahweh. Since firstfruits were offered from what was gained through working, Blome is right when he argues that in these two passages *debhash* cannot mean "wild honey." [6]

II. Use.

1. *Secular.* The OT contains only isolated instances of the use of "honey." It does not mention its use as a medicine, which is well known in Mesopotamia for healing diseases of the ears and eyes, etc., and which is also attested in the Mishnah and the Talmud. 1 S. 14:26-30 refers to the invigorating character of *debhash,* but this applies to all sweet substances. If the expression "to have the eyes enlightened" means the same thing as "to see more clearly" (v. 27), it is possible that this passage also has in mind the supposed healing quality of bee honey.

debhash is a food which is often taken along with grain and oil and also milk products. Sir. 39:26 lists it among the staples of life. Honey is a product of Palestinian farming (Gen. 43:11; Dt. 8:8; 2 K. 18:32; Ezk. 16:13), and is used for food (2 S. 17:29). It can be stored up (Jer. 41:8), brought as a gift (Gen. 43:11; 1 K. 14:3), and traded as merchandise to Tyre (Ezk. 27:17).

2. *Religious. debhash* is not used in religio-cultic functions. The only allusion to it in this context is negative: Lev. 2:11 forbids the use of *debhash* or leaven

---

[2] Otherwise Armbruster; F. Nötscher, *Bibl. Altertumskunde* (1940), 42.
[3] J. Friedrich, *Die Hethitischen Gesetze* (1959, 1971), §§ 91-93.
[4] W. Wreszinski, *Atlas zur altaegyptischen Kulturgeschichte,* I (1914), 378.
[5] Meissner, *BuA,* I, 273f.
[6] Blome, 303f.

as a vegetable offering by fire to Yahweh. Armbruster, who regards *debhash* as a cultivated product, assumes that poorly refined honey could cause the cake mixture to which it was added to ferment. [7] If *debhash* includes grape syrup, the prohibition in Lev. 2:11 may be a polemic against the heathen sacrifice of cakes of raisins (Hos. 3:1). In both cases, the prohibition against sacrificing *debhash* could be a reaction against the use of "honey" in the ancient Near Eastern cult.

Sacrifices of honey to the deity are known in ancient Egypt: honey, "the tears of Re," is sacrificed to Amon-Re in Karnak. Babylonian texts command the use of "honey" (*dišpu*) in purification rites, and prescribe sacrifices of honey in consecration rites, in connection with the rebuilding of temples, and in the rites of *bît rimki*. In these rituals, *dišpu* is often mixed with grain (*mirsu*) and butter (*ḫimētu;* cf. Heb. *chem'ah*). Sacrifices of honey (*nbt*) are also mentioned in the Ugaritic texts. [8] Possibly there is a sarcastic allusion to these heathen practices in Ezk. 16:19, where Jerusalem is reproved because she offered to idols the flour, "honey," and oil which Yahweh had given her. The same might be true of the well-known oracle in Isa. 7:15, which refers to *debhash* and butter (*chem'ah*) as the food of Immanuel. These two words are used together only rarely (the only other instance is Job 20:17). They so vividly call to mind the *dišpu u ḫimētu* of the Akkadian rituals that Isa. 7:15 must be interpreted as a warning to Ahaz, who was tempted to make an alliance with the Assyrians and to embrace their customs.

III. "Honey" As a Figure and a Symbol. The figurative use of *debhash* is derived from the natural characteristics of a product which, economical though it may be, is tasty and invigorating. The lips of one's beloved are compared with honey (Cant. 4:11). "Honey" is often used figuratively for pleasant and encouraging words: the words of a friend (Prov. 16:24), perhaps of a flatterer (which seems to be the meaning in Prov. 25:16,27; cf. 5:3), and finally the words of God which are "sweet" to the godly (Ps. 19:11 [10]; 119:103; cf. Ezk. 3:3).

debhash is used in conjunction with milk (*chalabh*) as a symbol of the abundance and fruitfulness which Yahweh gives Israel in Palestine. The promised land is the "land that flows with milk and honey" (*'erets zabhath chalabh udhebhash*). This expression occurs more than 20 times in connection with the conquest. [9] The exact meaning and origin of this formula have long been discussed. On the basis of a parallel in pre-Islamic poetry, Guidi understood this expression to mean "milk *with* honey," i.e., sweetened milk, as a strong symbol for grace. [10] Many scholars have found in the expression very ancient "mythological" concepts and not an allusion to the actual products of the land. According to Benzinger, [11] who further develops an idea of Stade, [12] the expression

---

[7] Cf. also M. Noth, *Leviticus. OTL* (trans. 1965), 28f.; K. Elliger, *HAT,* 4, 46.

[8] *CTA,* 14 [I K], I, 72; *Ugaritica,* V, 582.

[9] J. G. Plöger, *BBB,* 26 (1967), 90f.

[10] I. Guidi, *RB,* 12 (1903), 241-44.

[11] I. Benzinger, *Hebräische Archäologie* ([3]1927), 67, n. 1.

[12] B. Stade, *ZAW,* 22 (1902), 321-24; in agreement with H. Usener, *Rheinisches Museum,* 57 (1902), 177-192.

"land that flows with milk and honey" has no more to do with the products of the ground than the nectar and ambrosia of the Greeks; milk and honey are divine, paradisiacal foods.[13] In contrast, Krauss[14] sees in the phrase a literal reference to the products of dairy farming (milk) and agriculture (grape "honey").[15] In the meantime, it has been discovered that the OT is simply repeating a cliché of Canaanite origin in a somewhat modified form. In the Ugaritic Baal Epic,[16] El discovers that Aliyan Ba'al is alive when he sees in a dream that "heaven rains fat and the streams gush forth honey (nbt)." Thus, the "land that flows with milk and honey" is a traditional, easily intelligible, literary formula,[17] which is used to denote fertility. But this formula does not prove a mythological background or an accompanying description of "paradise," nor does it help toward a more precise definition of debhash, which is still a matter of debate.

In postbiblical Jewish literature, the motif of the "land that flows with milk and honey" is connected with the classical motif of milk and honey as the food of paradise and of initiation. In the Slavonic Book of Enoch (8:5), the four rivers of Paradise have become rivers of honey, milk, oil, and wine.[18] The comparison of the divine word with honey is connected with the description of manna, which tasted like honey (Ex. 16:31), in order to make honey a symbol of the spiritual food that comes from the heavenly storehouses. According to the Book of Joseph and Asenath (chap. 16), the illumination of Asenath takes place when she discovers a honeycomb in her locked room with supernatural bees coming out of it.

Caquot

---

[13] Cf. also H. Gressmann, *Der Messias. FRLANT*, 26 (1929), 155-58.
[14] S. Krauss, *ZDPV*, 32 (1909), 151-164.
[15] Cf. H. Gross, *Die Idee des ewigen und allgemeinen Weltfriedens im Alten Orient und im AT* (1956), 70-78; F. C. Fensham, *PEQ*, 98 (1966), 166f.; H. Wildberger, *BK*, X, 295f.
[16] *CTA*, 6 [I AB], III, 6f., 12f.
[17] Plöger, *BBB*, 26, 91: "Sermon Tradition."
[18] Cf. the Koran 47:17.

דָּג dāgh; דָּגָה dāghāh

Contents: I. In the Ancient Near East: 1. Egypt; 2. Mesopotamia. II. 1. Etymology; 2. Occurrences in the OT; 3. In the LXX. III. Exegetical Evidence: 1. Distribution in the OT; 2. Fishing; Fishing Equipment, Actual and Figurative; 3. The Connection of Fish with Creation and Destiny; 4. The Abundance of Fish As a Blessing of Salvation; 5. Jonah and the "Great Fish"; 6. Fish Entrails in Magic and Medicine.

I. In the Ancient Near East.

1. *Egypt.* According to Erman-Grapow [1] and Gamer-Wallert, the Egyptians knew 50 names of specific species and types of fish, and had terms for whole classes of fish, as *rmw mḥyt, tpw, tpyw,* etc.

As early as the Pharaonic period, Egyptian sources allude to sea ashes, many-colored perch, Nile perch, carp, Nile pike, etc. Fishing with fishhooks, nets, baskets, weir-baskets, and harpoons was one of the earliest occupations of the poorer inhabitants of the Nile Valley. Harpooning fish was originally reserved for the king, but later was the sport of the nobles. Fish (raw, cooked, baked, or dried) was the principal food. Occasionally kings gave fish to their servants as wages. Fish and grain were used to pay subjects. Pickled or dried fish were familiar exports. Fats, entrails, gall, fish-bones, etc. were used in the manufacture of medicinal ointments and as dressings for the hair and eyelashes.

---

dāgh. F. S. Bodenheimer, *Animal and Man in Bible Lands* (Leiden, 1960), 68-72; H. Bonnet, "Fische, heilige," *RÄR,* 191-94; E. D. van Buren, "Fish-Offerings in Ancient Mesopotamia," *Iraq,* 10 (1948), 101-121; *idem, The Fauna of Ancient Mesopotamia as Represented in Art. AnOr,* 18 (1939), 104-108; cf. also *idem, AnOr,* 23 (1945); M. Civil, "The Home of the Fish, A New Sumerian Literary Composition," *Iraq,* 23 (1961), 154-175; Dalman, *AuS,* VI (1939), 343-370; F. Dunkel, "Die Fischerei am See Genesareth," *Bibl,* 5 (1924), 375-390; E. Ebeling, E. Unger, M. Lambert, "Fisch, Fischen, Fischer(ei)," *RLA,* III (1957-1971), 66-70; J. Engemann, "Fisch, Fischer, Fischfang," *RAC,* VII (1969), 959-1097; H. Frehen, "Fisch," *BL²,* 481; M. C. Gaillard, *Recherches sur les Poissons représentés dans quelques tombeaux Égyptiens de l'Ancien Empire. MIFAO,* 51 (1923); K. Galling, "Fischfang," *BRL,* 167f.; I. Gamer-Wallert, *Fische und Fischkulte im Alten Ägypten. ÄgAbh,* 21 (1970); E. R. Goodenough, *Jewish Symbols V/VI, Fish, Bread and Wine* (New York, 1956); W. Heimpel, *Tierbilder in der sumerischen Literatur. Studia Pohl,* 2 (Rome, 1968); O. Kamlós, "Jona Legends," *Études Orientales à la mémoire de P. Hirschler* (Budapest, 1950), 41-61; J. M. Roy, "Le Poisson dans la Bible," *Actualités marines,* 9/2 (Quebec, 1968), 13-23; A. Salonen, *Die Fischerei im alten Mesopotamien nach sumerisch-akkadischen Quellen. Eine lexikalische und kulturgeschichtliche Untersuchung. AnAcScFen,* B, 166 (1970); S. Sarig, *Bibliography of Fishponds and Inland Waters in Israel. Limnologorum conventus 17 in Israel* (Tel Aviv, 1968); J. Scheftelowitz, "Das Fischsymbol in Judentum und Christentum," *ARW,* 14 (1911), 1-53, 321-392; W. von Soden, "Fischgalle als Heilmittel für Augen," *AfO,* 21 (1966), 81f.; D. Sperber, "Some Observations of Fisheries in Roman Palestine," *ZDMG,* 118 (1968), 265-69; H. W. Wolff, *Studien zum Jonabuch. BSt,* 47 (1965).

[1] *WbÄS.*

The role the fish plays in the cult is most varied. Apparently there have been fish cults among simple people from time immemorial. Official religion, however, avoided them because they were largely regarded as unclean; the Pyramid Texts even avoid the sign for a fish. Evidences of fish cults increase in the Late Period, but they are limited for the most part to figures, coffins, and mummies of sacred animals. In the provincial capital of Latopolis, the Nile perch (latos) had its own cult. It was connected with Neith, who at the creation of the world momentarily assumed the form of a latos in the primeval waters in order to penetrate the *Nwn.* [2] In Latopolis, but especially in Oxyrhynchus, the capital of the nineteenth province of Upper Egypt, the Nile pike (oxyrhynchus) was worshipped; it was the holy animal of Hathor. In the Greco-Roman period it even had its own temple. According to Plutarch, the oxyrhynchus was one of the fish that had eaten the phallus of Osiris. The Nile carp (lepidotos) was consecrated to the pair of gods *Onuris* and *Mḥyt;* it was worshipped in Lepidotonpolis, where archeologists have discovered a chapel dating from the Saitic Period with numerous bronze figures of a fish. The fish *Ant* and *Abdu* appear as attendants and protectors of the sun barque. They had a special relationship to Re and were regarded to some extent as the incarnation of Re; *Abdu* also must have indicated the imminence of the serpent enemy.

Fish were considered cultically unclean, an "abomination." Priests refrained from eating fish, particularly before certain ceremonial acts. Similarly, kings and princes seem to have abstained from fish food; the Nubian king Pianchi would not allow princes from Lower Egypt to come into his palace, because they had not been circumcised and because they ate fish. From the New Kingdom on, the eating of fish was prohibited on certain days of the year.

It is remarkable how rarely fish are mentioned as gifts for the dead and as offerings to the gods, although cf. the offering and carrying of fish in the Cairo Museum. [3]

In Egyptian beliefs concerning the dead, fish were regarded as protectors of the dead, but also as guarantors of their revival. The Egyptians also believed that a dead person was changed into a fish, so that he lived on in the fish. [4] A person was protected from the new dangers of fishermen and nets if he knew their names and was justified before Osiris.

2. *Mesopotamia.* In Babylon, along with the general words for fish, Sum. *ku(a),* Akk. *nūnu,* numerous types of fish were known: carp (*arsuppu*), swallow-fish (*sinûntu*), turbot (?) or eel (?) (*kuppû*), sturgeon (*singurru*), sprat (*uruttu*), etc. [5] Fish were eaten raw, cooked, baked, salted, dried, or preserved. In ancient Babylonian times, the right to fish belonged to the king or to the privileged temple personnel. Fishermen were divided into groups and registered, then they were given wages or a piece of land. Fresh-water fish were caught with fish

---

[2] Gamer-Wallert, 88f.
[3] H. Kees, *Der Götterglaube im Alten Ägypten. MVÄG,* 45 (²1956), 64.
[4] Cf. Gamer-Wallert, 131-34.
[5] Cf. Ebeling, 66; Salonen, *passim.*

fences, weir-baskets, and harpoons, while salt-water fish were caught with nets, harpoons, and hooks. [6] Archeologists have discovered remains of copper fish-hooks and clay weights to hold down nets. [7]

Nanše (also read *Nazi*) was regarded as the tutelary goddess of fishing and as the friend of fish; *Ḥaya* was also regarded as the patron of fish. The goddess *Nanše* is depicted with the ideogram meaning "house of the fish," she is clothed with fish from head to foot, and has a fish in her hand as a scepter. [8] She was a goddess of watercourses, but she did not have the form of a fish. The fish-centaur (a fish with the raised upper body of a bearded god) brings water from heaven to earth and is also regarded as one of eleven monsters created by *Tiamat*.

In Babylonian religion the fish seems to have been regarded in part as a symbol of life and fertility, and therefore it was popular to portray a fish on amulets. [9] Babylonian literature usually speaks of fish only incidentally; exceptions to this are found in Civil [10] and in certain Nanše Songs.

Fish were very important as offerings to the gods, as may be inferred from the vast remains of fish and the Sumerian documents. [11] In his essay on "Fish-Offerings," van Buren has investigated and summarized the pertinent material on fish-offerings and fish meals. In Eridu, the main location of the Enki cult, in the E-anna district of Uruk, and in Lagash or Girsu, many places of sacrifice have been found with vast remains of fish, which testify to fish-offerings. In the light of this, van Buren [12] has conjectured a transition from burnt-offerings to offerings of decomposing flesh, and he believes that in Lagash there were chthonic-type rites in conjunction with burial rites.

Art and documents from the Early Dynastic Age and from the Akkad Period attest to fish-offerings, and show or mention fish and fishermen frequently. The fish is often part of the cult meal; two fish form the footstool of the male deity in the scene of a reigning pair of gods which van Buren [13] identifies with the chthonic goddess Nanše and her consort; other artistic works show people carrying fish. [14] Van Buren thinks that without exception these refer to a rite for the dead. [15] Fishermen were respected and esteemed as a social class; blessing could be achieved by extending charity and hospitality to them; [16] the opposite behavior was punished by the gods. [17] After the Akkad Period, fish-offerings are not mentioned as frequently in literature and art. A *suḫur* fish is listed among the wedding gifts of Gudea to the goddess Ba-ba. Fish are offered to Enlil, Nanše, Ishtar, and Hadad. Assyrian seals depict food motifs in which a fish is brought to a reigning

---

[6] Salonen, 51ff.
[7] On the fish in representative art, cf. van Buren, *Fauna*, 104-107.
[8] *ZA*, 47, 210.
[9] Van Buren, "Fish-Offerings," 102, 106.
[10] Civil, 154ff.
[11] Ebeling, 67.
[12] Van Buren, "Fish-Offerings," 105.
[13] *Ibid.*, 110.
[14] *Ibid.*, 106f.
[15] But cf. Engemann's doubts.
[16] Van Buren, 110f.
[17] Güterbock, *ZA*, 42 (1934), 54ff.

figure by a servant or worshipper; sometimes it is laid on a table or altar. Usually this figure can be interpreted as a deity (on Neo-Babylonian seals it can be replaced by symbols of deities). When a meal motif is depicted on a tomb relief, it is certainly to be understood as a funeral feast. [18] Van Buren thinks the use of the fish as a religious symbol reached its zenith in the Achaemenid Period. [19] A small clay tablet from Nippur depicts falcons pulling a large fish out of the water. The water represents the underworld from which all life springs, and the birds are represented in the same manner as they are elsewhere on tomb reliefs.

In Mesopotamia, as in Egypt, fish were used in the preparation of various kinds of medicine. [20] They were also used as a defense against demons. Omens were also taken from fish. In Assyrian hemerology, there were certain days on which "fish were not to be eaten if a person did not want to become sick." [21]

II. 1. *Etymology. dagh* (*da'gh*, Neh. 13:16), fem. *daghah*, [22] "fish," appears in the ancient Semitic languages only in Ugar. *dg*, "fish" (sing. and pl.). [23] Middle and Modern Hebrew also have a word *dagh* meaning "large fish," and *daghah* with a more collective meaning "small fish." [24] It is doubtful whether *dagh* is cognate with Arab. *daǧaǧ*. Heb. *davvagh*, pl. *davvaghim*, "fisherman," should be read *dayyaghim* (Jer. 16:16; Ezk. 47:10; cf. 1QH 5:8); cf. Ugar. *dgy*, "fisherman." [25] Heb. *digh*, "to fish for" (Jer. 16:16), is probably a denominative verb from *dagh. daghah*, "to multiply, become numerous" (Gen. 48:16), is obscure. [26]

2. *Occurrences in the OT. dagh* occurs 18 times in the OT, 15 times in the plural. It is found in the following expressions: "fish of the sea" eight times, "Fish Gate" three times, and *tsiltsal daghim*, "fish harpoons," once. *daghah* occurs 15 times in the OT. It always has the collective meaning "fish," except in Jonah 2:2 (Eng. v. 1), where we should probably read *haddagh*, "the fish." [27] *daghah* appears twice each in the expressions "fish of the sea" and "fish of your Nile."

3. *In the LXX*. The LXX translates *dagh, da'gh, daghah* predominantly (24 times) by *ichthýs*, "fish." In Jonah, however, *kêtos*, "whale" (which is used elsewhere also to render *livyathan*, "Leviathan," *rahabh*, "Rahab," and *tannin*, "sea monster, serpent"), appears 4 times. *ópsos*, "fish," is used to translate *dagh*

[18] Klauser-Engemann.
[19] Van Buren, 121.
[20] *BuA*, II, 308f.; von Soden, 81f.
[21] *BuA*, II, 279; R. Labat, *Hémerologies et ménologies d'Assur* (Paris, 1939), 190.
[22] Cf. Th. Nöldeke, *Neue Beiträge zur semitischen Sprachwissenschaft* (1910), 122f.
[23] *CTA*, 23 [SS], 63; *PRU*, V, 1, verso, 16; V, 4, 12; cf. Whitaker, 179; *UT*, 642; *WUS*, 725.
[24] Levy, *WTM*, 375; cf. *dēget*, A. Murtonen, *StOr*, 24 (1960), Glossary, 89.
[25] *CTA*, 3 [V AB], VI, 10; *CTA*, 4 [II AB], II, 31; IV, 3; Whitaker, 179; *UT*, 642; *WUS*, 725.
[26] On Jerome's erroneous interpretation of Dagon as *dagh-'on*, cf. → דָּגוֹן *dāghôn*.
[27] Cf. Nöldeke, *Neue Beiträge*, 122, n. 3.

only in Nu. 11:22. *halieús,* "fisherman," is always used to render *davvagh/dayyagh. ichthýs,* "fish," is found 14 times in Tobit.

III. Exegetical Evidence.

1. *Distribution in the OT.* The OT does not mention any zoological types of fish. *deghath/deghe hayyam* is used not only of "fish of the sea" but also of fresh-water fish, e.g., those of the Sea of Chinnereth (the Sea of Tiberias) (cf. Nu. 34:11; Josh. 12:3; 13:27; *thálassa,* Mt. 4:18; 15:29), which was famous for its abundance of fish. In the laws concerning clean and unclean animals in Lev. 11:9-12 and Dt. 14:9f., aquatic animals with fins and scales are distinguished from those without fins and scales; the latter are regarded as *tame',* "unclean" (Dt. 14:10). Within the category of "unclean" aquatic animals, Lev. 11:10-12 makes a further distinction between "small animals (RSV swarming creatures) of the water" and "living creatures in the water," and states that they are a *sheqets,* "an abomination." It is possible that this expansive statement is connected with the exilic home of the author, "for in the many canals of Babylon, the danger of contamination by aquatic animals played an entirely different role than in Palestine." [28]

2. *Fishing; Fishing Equipment, Actual and Figurative.* The OT says very little about fishing, and what it does say appears predominantly in figurative expressions. However, it uses several terms for fishing tackle and nets. The terms for fishing tackle are as follows: *chakkah,* "fishhook," "fishing tackle" (Isa. 19:8; Hab. 1:15; Job 40:25 [41:1]), was "cast" or "drawn up"; *tsiltsal daghim* (? cricket-like, *tselatsal*), "fish harpoon" (Job 40:31 [41:7]; Isa. 18:1), and *sukkah,* "prong," "harpoon" (Job 40:31 [41:7]), are probably more poetic terms, [29] because *tsiltsal* and *sukkah* are unsuitable for catching Leviathan; other terms for fishhooks are *siroth* (Am. 4:2; Job 40:31 [41:7]), *chach,* pl. *chachim* (Ezk. 29:4), and *tsen* (Am. 4:2). The terms for fish nets are: *cherem,* "dragnet" or "throw net" (?) (Ezk. 26:5,14; 32:3; Hab. 1:15,17; etc.), and *mikhmereth,* "casting net" (Isa. 19:8; Hab. 1:15f.), which were "spread," "thrown," and "emptied" over the water. After fishing (*digh;* occasionally also *tsudh,* "to hunt, lie in wait," Mic. 7:2), fishermen (*dayyaghim—qere; davvaghim—kethibh;* Jer. 16:16; Ezk. 47:10) spread out their nets on a *mishtach* or *mishtoach,* "drying-ground" (Ezk. 26:5,14; 47:10).

The importance of fishing (*dughah*), the fishing business, and the fish market is seen in the fact that one of the city gates in Jerusalem was called the *sha'ar haddaghim,* "Fish Gate" (Neh. 3:3; 12:39; 13:16; 2 Ch. 33:14; Zeph. 1:10); this was located in the center of the north wall and gave free access to the new city (Zeph. 1:10). Evidently there was a fish market near the "Fish Gate," where

---

[28] Elliger, *HAT,* 4, 144. On the priestly division of animals according to their various environments of water–air (heaven)–earth in Gen. 1, cf. → אֶרֶץ *'erets,* II.1. Cf. also the list of animals in 1 K. 5:13 (4:33), concerning which Solomon wrote proverbs and songs.

[29] *AuS,* VI, 360.

merchants from Tyre did a considerable business selling salted (cf. Taricheae, "Pickle Place," on Gennesaret) or dried fish (even on the Sabbath) (Neh. 13:16). Zeph. 1:10 announces that when Israel's enemies attack, great destruction from the hills will come upon these Tyrian merchants too.

In the imagery of the OT some figures of speech are taken from fishing. Thus the threat of judgment against Pharaoh and the inhabitants of Egypt is presented in the form of a grotesque picture of a sea monster or crocodile (→ תַּנִּין *tannîn = tannîm*), in whose scales the fish of the Nile streams have been caught and to whose scales they cling (Ezk. 29:4). Yahweh will put hooks (*chachim*) in the jaws of this Nile beast with all the fish that cling to its scales, draw them up out of the Nile, and cast them forth into the wilderness or upon the open field, where they will be food for the beasts and the birds (29:4,5). The sea monster or crocodile represents the tyrannical Pharaoh, and the fish that stick to his scales are the inhabitants of Egypt who will be affected by Pharaoh's fate; after its inhabitants are carried into exile (cf. v. 12), the land will become a desolation.

According to Jer. 16:16, when Yahweh brings penal judgment on his people, he will send "many fishers" and "many hunters," i.e., enemies, against Judah, who will "catch" them and "hunt" them. In Hab. 1:14-17, the people lament because God has made a leaderless swarm like the fish of the sea, which the enemy will catch with a "hook" (*chakkah*), a "net" (*cherem*), and a "seine" (*mikhmereth*). Here the fish represent men and nations which have no ruler and are oppressed, and the fishermen represent their enemies. According to Eccl. 9:12, the person who does not know his evil time is like fish that are caught "in an evil net" (*bimetsodhah ra'ah*). The heart of the seductive woman is like *charamim*, "dragnets," because it attempts to draw men into it (Eccl. 7:26). As a sign of dishonor, the pleasure-seeking women of Israel are taken away with *tsinnoth*, "hooks," and *siroth dughah*, "fishhooks" (Am. 4:2).

3. *The Connection of Fish with Creation and Destiny.* In the creation theology of the Priestly Code, man indeed has dominion (→ רדה *rādhāh*) over the entire animal world, over the fish of the sea, the birds of the air, and the beasts upon the earth (Gen. 1:26,28; cf. Ps. 8:9 [8]). But it is only when God renews his blessing after the flood that fish, birds, and land animals are divinely given to Noachite man as food and may thus be killed for nourishment (Gen. 9:2). According to Job's prudent reply to Zophar, all living creatures, including fish, testify to the power and wisdom of the creator (Job 12:8). According to Isa. 50:2, Yahweh's creative power can even dry up the sea and the rivers so that the fish perish for lack of water (cf. also Ps. 107:33).

In an addition from the Late Exilic Period, the prohibition of graven images in Dt. 4:9-28 is defined more specifically by detailed prohibitions against making "the likeness of any fish that is in the water under the earth" (v. 18), etc. This excludes fish emblems or representations of fish gods according to the heathen custom.

In Egypt, where fish abounded, and where the Israelites got fish to eat for nothing (Nu. 11:5—J), one of the plagues also affected the fish: Yahweh struck the water of the Nile, the fish died, and the water of the Nile became foul and polluted (Ex. 7:18,21a–J). Along with the other plagues, the death of the fish was a proof of the superiority of the God of Israel.

The fateful connection of beasts and fish with the destiny of man appears in the judgment of Yahweh when he brings a great drought over the land so that men, beasts of the field, birds, and fish of the sea are destroyed (Hos. 4:3). According to Zeph. 1:3, on the day of Yahweh man and beast, birds and fish will be swept away; the animals are inseparably connected with the destiny and judgment of "evildoers." In connection with the destruction of Gog (Ezk. 38:17-23), all (men and animals) will be shaken by the terrible earthquake.

4. *The Abundance of Fish As a Blessing of Salvation.* Ezk. 47:9,10 tells of a wonderful abundance of fish as Yahweh's gift of salvation: a great river goes out of the temple fountain and brings salvation everywhere. The waters of the salty sea will become fresh water, in which "very many fish" will move; on both sides of the Dead Sea, from En-gedi to En-eglaim, there will be fishing villages and drying-grounds for fish nets. In this time of salvation, the abundance of fish in what had been called the "Dead Sea" will be no less than that in the "Great Sea," the Mediterranean.

5. *Jonah and the "Great Fish."* The story of the "great fish" that swallowed Jonah and after three days and nights vomited him out on the dry land (Jonah 2:1f.,11[1:17–2:1; 2:10]) contains no textual criteria that would justify identifying the fish zoologically with a whale, a shark, or any other aquatic animal. Perhaps the author has adapted an ancient seafaring narrative that was handed down from time immemorial at the port in Joppa, and has put it in the service of his own wisdom narrative. Research into the book of Jonah has postulated different phases of a prehistory of the narrative. In a sun myth the sun is swallowed up by the western part of the sea and then rises again. This myth is "historicized and re-neutralized in Jonah, as ...Jonah replaces the sun and the 'great fish' plays the role of the sea."[30] On the other hand, the period of time Jonah stayed in the belly of the fish suggests a moon myth, and calls to mind, among other things, Inanna's descent into the underworld. The "great fish" recalls the sea monster in the story of Heracles and Perseus, who went into the innermost parts of the monster, killed it, and then came out into the light again. Wolff thinks this Greek saga is "the bridge between the sun myth and the Jonah narrative; the sun becomes the legendary hero who came out of the sun, and the sea becomes the sea monster."[31] These and similar motifs, which Kamlós cites, were probably known in different variations, and may have been told by sailors even in Joppa, although no dependence can be proved. This narrative serves to animate and dramatize a wisdom story about the universality of the divine compas-

---

[30] Wolff, 22.
[31] *Ibid.,* 24.

sion. It is directed against a particularistic or "Israelo-centric eschatology," [32] as this is critically represented in the figure of the prophet Jonah. [33]

6. *Fish Entrails in Magic and Medicine.* According to Tob. 6:2-9; 8:2f.; and 11:7-13, fish entrails were used in exorcising demons and as medicine. The warm dung of sparrows fell into the eyes of the young Tobit and caused white films (*macula cornea*) to form on his eyes (2:10). When fish gall was rubbed on his eyes, the white films scaled away from them and Tobit was able to see again (11:11-13). Von Soden cites five examples of the use of the gall of a *kuppû* fish (an eel?) as one ingredient of an eye salve which was used to treat an illness (the nature of which cannot be determined specifically) in which a *šišîtû,* "film," impaired the ability to see. [34] In order to drive out the demon on the wedding night, the heart and liver of a fish were laid on the ashes of incense, and the demon fled at the smell (8:2f.).

Botterweck

---

[32] Moltmann.
[33] Cf. the literature in Wolff, 127, and Kamlós, 41-61. On the NT references to Jonah in Mt. 12:40,41; Lk. 11:32, cf. the pertinent comms. and *TDNT,* III, 406-410.
[34] Von Soden, 81f.

| דָּגָן *dāghān;* דָּגוֹן *dāghôn* |

Contents: I. Etymology. II. The God Dagon. III. *daghan* As a Sign of Fertility and As a Gift of God. IV. *daghan* As Firstfruits and Tithes.

I. Etymology. The subst. *daghan* is found exclusively in the Canaanite-Aramaic region. In Ugaritic, *dgn* appears in the Nikkal Text, [1] where the Kāṭirāt are implored to take care of (*zd*) the newborn child and to give him grain (*dgn*), and in the Keret Epic, [2] where the tillers of the field turn to those who supply grain (*dgn*) because the bread, wine, and oil are exhausted. *dgn* also occurs several times as a divine name (Dagan). [3]

The only occurrence of this word in Phoenician is disputed. The Ešmun'azar Inscription [4] speaks of *'rṣt dgn,* either "grain fields" or "fields of the god Dagon," which "the Lord of kings" has given. Since this has reference to the Palestinian

---

dāghān. M. Delcor, "Jahweh et Dagon," *VT,* 14 (1964), 136-154; E. Dhorme, "Les avatars du dieu Dagon," *RHR,* 138 (1950), 129-144; J. Fontenrose, "Dagon and El," *Oriens,* 10 (1957), 277-79; H. Gese, *Die Religionen Altsyriens. RdM,* 10/2 (1970), 107-113; F. J. Montalbano, "Canaanite Dagon. Origin, Nature," *CBQ,* 13 (1951), 381-397; M. J. Mulder, *Kanaänitische Goden in het OT* (Den Haag, 1965), 71ff.; H. Schmökel, "Dagan," *RLA,* II, 99ff.

[1] *CTA,* 24 [NK], I, 14.
[2] *CTA,* 16 [II K], III, 13.
[3] Cf. II below.
[4] *KAI,* 14.19.

coastal plain, where the worship of Dagon was especially prominent, [5] there is much to be said for the latter interpretation. [6]

dgn also appears in Official Aramaic in a passage in the Ahikar Text (129) which speaks of "grain and wheat." Examples of the word in Middle Hebrew and Jewish Aramaic were undoubtedly influenced by biblical usage.

These facts have led to the conjecture that *daghan* is connected with the divine name Dagan/Dagon, or was even derived from it. [7] Nielsen defends this derivation, [8] but his argument that the divine name came from Arab. *dağn,* "overcast sky, rain," [9] is to be rejected. Others do not consider the connection between Dagon and *daghan* to be certain. [10]

II. The God Dagon. The god Dagan is well attested in Akkadian sources and especially in the Mari Texts. At Ugarit, the name of the god *Dgn* frequently appears in the texts, but remarkably only in the combination "Ba'al, son of Dagon." We hear nothing of Dagon himself in these texts. Since Ba'al is regarded elsewhere as the son of El, Gese conjectures that Dagan "is an El-type deity." [11] Others believe that Ba'al replaced Dagan as the god of fertility and that this is why *dgn* occurs as the father of Ba'al, i.e., his predecessor. A proper name *Dagan-takala* is found in the Amarna Letters, [12] and two stelae devoted to Dagan have also been discovered at Ugarit. [13]

In Philo of Byblos, Dagon (Phoenician form), the father of Demarus, is identical with Siton, "grain field," and is called Zeus Arotrios, because he invented grain and the plow. [14] Here also, then, Dagon's connection with grain is certain.

Dagon is mentioned several times in the OT as god of the Philistines. At a sacrificial festival in Gaza, which the Philistines hold for "Dagon their god" (Jgs. 16:23), Samson is brought forth and demonstrates his strength by pulling down the house upon himself and the Philistines who were gathered in it. This proves the superiority of the Israelite God over Dagon. The same point is made in the narrative in 1 S. 5:1-7: the image of Dagon in the temple at Ashdod is twice thrown down after the ark of Yahweh is brought into the temple. The head and hands of the divine image are broken off, and "only *daghan* is left" (v. 4). At one time, this expression was taken to mean that Dagon was represented in the form of a fish (*dagh*) and only the body of the fish was left, [15]

---

[5] See below.

[6] So *DISO,* 55; *ANET,* 505.

[7] So W. F. Albright, *Yahweh and the Gods of Canaan* (London, 1968), 161f.; cf. Gese, 111; Dhorme, 133; and *KAI,* comm. on 14.19.

[8] D. Nielsen, *Der dreieinige Gott,* II/1 (1942), 138-145.

[9] *Ibid.,* 141.

[10] W. von Soden, *RGG*³, II, 18f.; Montalbano; M. J. Dahood, "Ancient Deities in Syria and Palestine," *StSem,* 1 (Rome, 1958), 78f.

[11] Gese, 107.

[12] *Ibid.*

[13] R. Dussaud, *Syr,* 16 (1935), 177ff.; *UT,* Nos. 69 and 70.

[14] Gese, 109f.

[15] Delcor, 145.

which made Dagon comparable with the goddess Derketo and the Babylonian fish-man Oannes. This interpretation assumes the reading *dagho,* "his fish," instead of *daghon,* and it must in any case be regarded as very uncertain. Fontenrose thinks that since Dagon was worshipped by the maritime Canaanite people, at a later time he came to be connected with *dagh,* "fish."

Dagon is also mentioned as god of the Philistines in 1 Ch. 10:10. This passage tells how the Philistines hung up the head of Saul in the temple of Dagon after his death. The parallel passage in 1 S. 31:8-10 speaks only of the Philistines announcing the good news of Saul's death "in the house of their idols" (*beth 'atsabbehem*) and of their putting the weapons of Saul in the temple of Astarte. 1 Macc. 10:83 and 11:4 mention a temple of Dagon in Azotus, i.e., Ashdod. Also two place names, Beth-dagon in Judah (Josh. 15:41) and Beth-dagon in Asher (19:27), preserve the memory of the worship of Dagon. [16]

III. daghan As a Sign of Fertility and As a Gift of God. *daghan* occurs 40 times in the OT. It is found in narrative, legal, and prophetic texts, and also in the Psalms. Thus Speiser's statement that *daghan* (like *tirosh,* "wine") is found especially in ritual and poetic contexts [17] is not entirely true. On the one hand, the other word for "grain," *shebher,* is found not only in narrative literature (Gen. 42:1,2,19,26; 43:2; 44:2; 47:14), but also in Am. 8:5 (to be sure, in a secular context) and Neh. 10:32 (Eng. v. 31) (with a ritual hue). On the other hand, *daghan* occurs, e.g., in Neh. 5:2,3,10,11, in an entirely prosaic context.

daghan frequently appears in lists in the OT, the most frequent of which is "grain, wine, and oil" (Nu. 18:12,27; Dt. 7:13; 11:14; 12:17; 14:23; 18:4; 28:51; 2 Ch. 31:5; 32:28; Neh. 5:11; Jer. 31:12; Hos. 2:10,24 [8,22]; Joel 1:10; 2:19; Hag. 1:11). This three-membered list belongs "to the body of Deuteronomistic formulas," [18] but it is not exclusively Deuteronomistic. It appears quite naturally as a list of agricultural products. One cannot be certain whether Wolff is correct in suggesting a Canaanite prototype, because *dgn* is found in the Keret Text outside the list *lhm, yn, šmn,* "bread, wine, oil." The two-membered list "grain and wine" also occurs fairly frequently (Gen. 27:28,37; Dt. 33:28; Hos. 2:11 [9]; 7:14; Zec. 9:17; Isa. 62:8; Ps. 4:8 [7]; Lam. 2:12). 2 K. 18:32 = Isa. 36:17 is exceptional in that it contains three pairs of words: grain and wine, bread and vineyards, olive trees and honey.

The two oldest examples, Gen. 27:28 and Dt. 33:28, are both poetic, and both refer to grain as a sign of divine blessing. Isaac blesses Jacob and prays that God might give him "the dew of heaven, the fatness of the earth, and plenty of grain and wine." And the hymnic framework of the Blessing of Moses says that Israel lives "in a land full of grain and wine," and that its "heavens drop down dew." Thus both passages contain a two-membered list. It is worth noting that dew (→ טל *tal*) plays an important role in both passages.

---

[16] Cf. J. Simons, *Geographical and Topographical Texts of the OT* (Leiden, 1959), § 332.
[17] E. A. Speiser, *Genesis. AB,* I (1964), on Gen. 27:28.
[18] Plöger, *BBB,* 26 (1967), 172; Wolff, *Hosea* (trans. 1974), 37.

Grain also appears frequently as a sign of fertility in various linguistic and ideological contexts. Deuteronomy, among other OT books, promises increase of "grain, wine, and oil" (Dt. 7:13; 11:14) as rewards for keeping the commandments, while disobedience results in the destruction of these same products by enemies (28:51—conversely, in Isa. 62:8 God says that he will not again give Israel's grain to enemies and Israel's wine to foreigners). The Rabshakeh speaks enticingly to the Israelites and promises that the king of Assyria will bring them into a good land, where there is "grain and wine, bread and vineyards, olive trees and honey" (2 K. 18:32 = Isa. 36:17). Jer. 31:10-14 describes the fertility of the land after the return of the dispersed Israelites. It mentions, among other things, grain, wine, oil, and plentiful flocks (v. 12). In the Oracle of Salvation in Joel 2:19f., Yahweh says: "I am sending to you grain, wine, and oil, and you will be satisfied." Other passages too connect grain with the idea that no one need go hungry (e.g., Neh. 5:2f.; Ezk. 36:29). Ps. 4:8(7) connects plentiful grain with joy, and Zec. 9:17 says that in the coming age of salvation "grain will make the young men flourish, and new wine the maidens" (is the text correct?). Ps. 65:10(9) emphasizes that grain is a gift of God; Ps. 78:24 describes manna as "the grain of heaven." A major theme of Hosea is that it is Yahweh and not Baal who gives grain, wine, oil, etc. (Hos. 2:10[8]). Thus he also has the power to take all these things away (2:11 [9]) and then to give them back again to the restored people (2:24[22]; cf. 14:8[7]).

This idea is expressed negatively in descriptions of calamity in which the lack of products such as grain appears as a sign of misfortune and of divine wrath. Joel 1:17 says: "The storehouses are desolate; the granaries are ruined because the grain has failed," and the whole three-membered list is found in v. 10: "the ground mourns (→ אבל 'ābhal), the grain is destroyed, the wine fails, the oil languishes." According to Hos. 7:14, the Israelites lament (read yithgodhedhu, "gash themselves," instead of yithgoraru, "assemble themselves") for the grain and wine. This verse may contain a reminiscence of the mourning rites of the Baal cult over the dying away of vegetation. In Lam. 2:12, hungry children lament: "Where is bread and wine?"

IV. daghan As Firstfruits and Tithes. In the laws concerning firstfruits and tithes, grain appears as one of the most important agricultural products. According to Nu. 18:12, the firstfruits of oil, wine, and grain belong to the priests (cf. v. 27). Dt. 18:4 prescribes the same thing in the ordinary sequence: grain, wine, and oil. According to Dt. 12:17 and 14:23, the tithes of grain, wine, and oil are not to be eaten at home but are to be eaten "before the face of Yahweh." When Hezekiah renews the cultic institutions, he also provides that the people of Israel should give the firstfruits of their grain, wine, oil, and honey (2 Ch. 31:5); 2 Ch. 32:28 mentions storehouses for these taxes. Neh. 10:40(39); 13:5,12 also speak of tithes of grain, wine, and oil. Here provision is made that when the covenant is renewed, the Levites should receive their portion.

Ringgren

Contents: I. Etymology. II. Usage: 1. In the East Semitic Languages; 2. In the West Semitic Languages; 3. In the Bible: a. Occurrences in the OT; b. In the Law and Related Texts; c. In the Prophets and Wisdom Literature; d. In Canticles. III. Significance: 1. Theological; 2. Anthropological.

I. Etymology. Little can be said with certainty about the etymology of Heb. *dodh*, pl. *dodhim*. It is possible that *dodh* is an onomatopoeic word (*dad[u]*) which arose out of repetition of the *da*, as is often the case with words that denote kinship. It is quite likely that *dodh* is a nominal form derived from the root *w/ydd*, "to love" (→ ידד *yādhadh*). The question whether *w/ydd* can be traced back to an original onomatopoeic word (cf. Hurrian *tat[t]*, "love") must remain open, [1] as must also that of a possible connection between *dodh* and *š/dad*, "breasts." [2]

II. Usage.

1. *In the East Semitic Languages.* The equivalent of *dodh* in Akkadian literature is *dādu(m)*. In the singular it means "beloved, darling," and denotes a (personal) object of love. It is used of men because they are regarded as children

dôdh. G. W. Ahlström, *Psalm 89* (Lund, 1959); W. F. Albright, "Northwest-Semitic Names in a List of Egyptian Slaves from the Eighteenth Century B.C.," *JAOS*, 74 (1954), 222-233; L. Alonso-Schökel, *El Cantar de los Cantares. Los Libros Sagrados*, X/1 (Madrid, 1969); D. R. Ap-Thomas, "Saul's 'Uncle'," *VT*, 11 (1961), 241-45; G. Buccellati, *The Amorites of the Ur III Period* (Naples, 1966); P. Cersoy, "L'apologue de la vigne," *RB*, 8 (1899), 40-49; E. Ebeling, "Aus den Keilschriften aus Assur religiösen Inhalts," *MDOG*, 58 (1917), 48-50; *idem*, "Das HL im Lichte der assyrischen Forschungen," *ZDMG*, 78 (1924), LXVIII-LXIX; A. Feuillet, "La formule d'appartenance mutuelle (II 16) et les interprétations divergentes du Cantique des Cantiques," *RB*, 68 (1961), 5-38; *idem*, "Einige scheinbare Widersprüche des HL," *BZ*, N.F. 8 (1964), 216ff.; P. Garelli, *Les Assyriens en Cappadoce* (Paris, 1963); I. J. Gelb, "La lingua degli Amoriti," *AANLR*, 8/13 (1958), 143-164; *idem, et al., Nuzi Personal Names* (Chicago, 1943); G. Gerleman, *Das Hohelied. BK*, XVIII (1965); J. Gray, *The Legacy of Canaan. SVT*, 5 (²1965); Gröndahl, *PNU;* M. Held, "A Faithful Lover in an Old Babylonian Dialogue," *JCS*, 15 (1961), 1-26; 16 (1962), 37-39; A. Hermann, *Altägyptische Liebesdichtung* (1959); A. Hoffmann, *David. Namensdeutung zur Wesensdeutung. BWANT*, 100 (1973); A. Jamme, *The Al-'Uqlah Texts* (Washington, 1963); D. F. Kinlaw, *A Study of the Personal Names in the Accadian Texts from Ugarit* (1967, microfilm); W. G. Lambert, "Divine Love Lyrics from Babylon," *JSS*, 4 (1959), 1-15; H. Limet, *L'anthroponymie sumérienne dans les documents de la 3ᵉ dynastie d'Ur* (Paris, 1968); O. Loretz, "Zum Problem des Eros im HL," *BZ*, N.F. 8 (1964), 191-216; *idem, Studien zur althebräischen Poesie, 1. Das althebräische Liebeslied. AOAT*, 14/1 (1971); T. J. Meek, "Canticles and the Tammuz Cult," *AJSL*, 39

[1] Gelb, 263.
[2] Cf. Ugar. *ṯd, WUS*, No. 2842; and Akk. *dīdu, AHw*, 169, 149.

of the deity: "her beloved father (abu dadiša) Anu."[3] This meaning is attested very early; the word appears already in Old Akkadian as a royal epithet of Šarkali-šarri, "beloved son (mar'um dādi) of Enlil";[4] and in the Old Babylonian period Samsuiluna is called "Beloved (dādi) of Shamash and Aya,"[5] with the variant narām, "darling," and the Sumerian equivalent ki-ág, "beloved."[6] Within the family circle, dādu(m), "darling," continues to be used to denote descendants in general: "May the gods destroy his descendants (daddašu)!"[7] or concretely: "my own little child ... my darling" (dādūa).[8] The spelling daddu suggests the onomatopoeic character of dwd. dādu(m) is also used in an erotic sense as "beloved, partner," especially in love poetry. In a catalog of hymns dating ca. 1100 B.C., we encounter a song that begins with the words, "You are the darling, the affectionate one, our beloved" (dādini).[9] The pl. dādū is constantly used in this erotic sense. It can be used abstractly with the meaning "to love," "love," or concretely with the meaning "the art of love," "the pleasure of love." Thus Tašmetu is described as the "goddess of sexual joy (kuzbu) and of 'love' (u dadi),"[10] and the love song says, "I am made for your love" (ana dadika).[11] The same is true of Gilg. I, IV.15 (cf. also 20), where admittedly the word dādū could have a more specific meaning, "genitals": "his 'love' (physical body? dādūšu) will press itself upon you."[12] The meaning "genitals" is certain in the

---

(1922/23), 1-14; idem, "Babylonian Parallels to the Song of Songs," JBL, 43 (1924), 245-252; idem, "The Song of Songs and the Fertility Cult," The Song of Songs: A Symposium, ed. W. H. Schoff (Philadelphia, 1924); idem, "The Iterative Names in the Old Akk. Texts from Nuzi," RA, 32 (1935), 131-155; W. L. Moran, review of G. W. Ahlström, Psalm 89, Bibl, 42 (1961), 237ff.; F. Ohly, Hoheliedstudien (1958); N. Peters, Der jüngst wiederaufgefundene hebr. Text des Buches Ecclesiasticus (1902); H. Ranke, Early Babylonian Personal Names from the Published Tablets of the So-Called Hammurabi Dynasty (Philadelphia, 1905); H. Ringgren, Das Hohe Lied. ATD, XVI/2 (1958); H. H. Rowley, "The Song of Songs: An Examination of Recent Theory," JRAS (1938), 251-276; idem, "The Interpretation of the Song of Songs," The Servant of the Lord and Other Essays on the OT (²1965), 197-245; W. Rudolph, Das Hohe Lied. KAT, XVII/2 (1966), 19-62; G. Ryckmans, Les noms propres sud-sémitiques, I-II (Louvain, 1934); H. Schmökel, "Zur kultischen Deutung des HL," ZAW, 64 (1952), 148-155; idem, Heilige Hochzeit und das Hohelied. AKM, 32/1 (1956); A. Schott, "Zu meiner Übersetzung des Gilgameš-Epos," ZA, 42 (1934), 93-143; W. von Soden, "Ein Zwiegespräch Hammurabis mit einer Frau," ZA, 49 (1950), 151-194; idem, "Eine altassyrische Beschwörung gegen die Dämonin Lamaštu," Or, 25 (1956), 141-48; J. J. Stamm, "Der Name des Königs David," SVT, 7 (1960), 165-183; F. J. Stephens, Personal Names from Cuneiform Inscriptions of Cappadocia (New Haven, 1928); K. Tallqvist, Assyrian Personal Names (Helsingfors, 1918); idem, Akkadische Götterepitheta. StOr, 7 (1938); L. Waterman, "דודי in the Song of Songs," AJSL, 35 (1918), 101-110; W. Wittekindt, Das Hohelied und seine Beziehungen zum Ištarkult (1926).

3 Archiv für Keilschriftforschung, 1, 21, II.3.
4 BE I, 2.2.
5 CT 37, 3, II.63.
6 See SL, 461, 120b; RA, 39 (1942/44), 5ff.
7 MDP, 6, 39, VII.27.
8 VAB, IV, 62, III.11.
9 KAR, 158; see also Lambert, 6; further von Soden, ZA, 151-194; Held.
10 L. W. King, Babylonian Magic and Sorcery (1896), 1.37; 33.30; see Schott, 101.
11 KAR, 158, VII.11.
12 See von Soden, Or, 146.

expression, "her love (*dādūša*) is uncovered," [13] and possible in the phrase, "your body (*da-du-ú-ka*) is sweet." [14]

dādu(m) also occurs with comparative frequency as a component of Akkadian proper names. Here, however, the exact sense cannot always be determined with certainty. The greatest caution must be used in interpretation in such cases, if for no other reason than that in a linguistic region encompassing so wide a geographical area and extending over such a long historical period, the origin and local color must always be taken into consideration.

The problem of the use of *dādu(m)* in Akkadian names is of the greatest relevance in attempting to determine the meaning of *dwd* in the OT. On the basis of the existence of a deity called *Dudu/i* in the Akkadian pantheon, which is conjectured from the Akkadian onomasticon, some scholars have assumed the existence of the same deity in the OT, although not without severe criticism. [15] *Dada/u* appears already in Neo-Sumerian names. Although the literary witnesses exhibit a strong mixture of East Semitic, West Semitic, and genuine Sumerian elements, it must be taken into account that the deity played an important role at Ur III (see, e.g., PN *Da-da-ḪA.MA.TI*, "may Dada give me life"; *Lú-ᵈDa-da*, "man of Dada," etc.). [16] The same applies to *Dudu*. In such cases, of course, neither *ᵈDa-da* nor *ᵈDu-du* has anything to do with *dodh*. *Dada* is simply a doubling of *da*, [17] and already in Fara can even occur as the deity *ᵈDa* (PN *A.BA.ᵈDA*). Moreover, *Dada* obviously lost his independence very quickly and came to be identified with the Akkadian deities Adad, Ninurta, and Etallak. [18] *Dudu*, interpreted as "leader (*muttarrû*) of the gods," became an appellative of Marduk. [19]

In personal names like *Šu-da-da* [20] the meaning is uncertain, especially since they can be read simply either as Sumerian or as mixed Sumerian-Akkadian forms. This raises the question of the extent to which West Semitic (Amurritic) elements appear in the onomasticon of Ur III. It is as good as certain that not all proper names containing the element *dada/u* have in mind the Sumerian deity. This is true of *Da-dum-pi₅-DINGIR* (Amurritic: **Dādumpī'ēl*, "the word of El is my darling"), [21] and *Zu-da-dum* (Amurritic: *dū-dādum*, "he is the beloved" [or *dū-dādim*, "the one who is of the beloved"?]), [22] where the element *dādum* no longer denotes the Sumerian deity, but is the Semitic "beloved, darling," [23] and in fact functions as the predicate of a nominal sentence. Also in the case of the Old Bab. PN *A-bu-da-di* ("the father is my darling"), [24] *dādi* is clearly

---

[13] *Ibid.,* 143.
[14] BE 40294, 32f.=*MIO,* 12:48:9, 11; see *AHw,* 149.
[15] See Moran, 239.
[16] For additional examples cf. Limet, 149.
[17] See *SL,* 335, 3=Akk. *idu,* "side"; 15=Akk. *le'ū,* "strong."
[18] See Tallqvist, *Akk. Götterepitheta,* 278.
[19] *Ibid.,* 283, 491.
[20] See the examples in Limet, 530.
[21] *BIN,* IX, 316.29.
[22] *BIN,* IX, 388.10; see Buccellati, 207.
[23] See above.
[24] See Ranke, 211.

a predicate. *A-ba-ᵈDa-di*[25] is merely its Old Akkadian variant. Here again we do not have a theophorous element (in spite of the divine determinative) but merely an equivalent name,[26] where the deceased and then deified relative is called "divine beloved." The same seems to apply to the later expression *PN Da-di-i-lu,* "my beloved is God" (Annals of Tiglath-pileser III, 152). The Old Assyrian names contain the element *dādu* in hypocoristic forms, shortened names in which only one of the original components remains: *Da-da, Da-da-a(-a), Da-da-nim, Da-tim, Da-ti-a,* etc.[27] Hypocoristica which appear already in Ur III and Old Babylonian (*Da-du-ša,* "her [Ishtar's] beloved"),[28] are especially common in the Akkadian border regions: Nuzi (*Da-da, Šu-da-da,* cf. Ur III *Zu-da-dum,* etc.), Mari (*Da-da-tum, Da-da-num* [cf. Old Assyr. *Da-da-nim*], *Da-di-im* [cf. Old Assyr. *Da-tim*], *Da-di-ya,* etc.), Ugarit,[29] etc. Spellings like EA *Du-u-du Du-ú-du* (EA 164, *passim;* 167, 28; 158, *passim*) or Nuzi *Du-ú-du-a-bu-šu*[30] show that we have here the Semitic element *dā/ī/ūdu,* "beloved," and not the Sumerian deities *Dada/u.*[31] Moreover, in hypocoristic forms the theophorous element is usually omitted, so that the predicate alone is left. But in East Semitic names a concrete divine figure cannot function as a predicate. In a case like, e.g., *Dādu-Sin,*[32] the god Sin is always the subject, and *dādu* can only be the predicate even though it comes first. Thus the element *dādu(m)* in the predicate position cannot possibly denote a deity, not even if it has the determinative as in *ᵈDādu.*

The situation is different when *Dādu* is the subject (e.g., at Nuzi: *Dūdu-Abu-šu;* at Mari: *Da-di-ḫa-du-un*).[33] But the examples are less common. Here one might speak hypothetically of a deity, but there is no certain example of this figure in the Akkadian pantheon. According to the materials that have been discovered and collated thus far, as a subject *dādu(m)* can at best be an appellative but it cannot be a divine *name.* In other words, the word retains its original meaning "beloved, darling," and is thus used as an adjective for a specific figure that is not named more specifically. Nor is this function as an epithet by any means limited to deities; *dādu(m)* in particular is also used for kings.[34] In this sense, *dādu(m)* is simply an epithet like the more common words *narāmu(m), râmu,* and *ra'ūmu/rûmu* ("beloved, darling"),[35] or like the terms for relatives, *abu(m),* "father," *aḫu(m),* "brother," and *ḫālu(m),* "maternal uncle,"[36] which can also function sometimes as divine epithets without thereby being divine names.

---

[25] See the examples given in I. J. Gelb, *Glossary of Old Akkadian* (Chicago, 1957), 104.
[26] See Stamm, *AN,* 301-305.
[27] See the examples in Stephens, 27, 31ff., 83; see also Garelli, 128-133.
[28] *OIP,* 43, 139.
[29] See II.2 below.
[30] See Gelb, *et al, Nuzi Personal Names,* 161, 303.
[31] See also Meek, *RA,* 154.
[32] *UET,* V, 577, 6.
[33] *ARM,* XV, 143; VI, 73.7; cf. Gelb, 155, etc.; *APNM,* 181f.
[34] See above; see Seux, 65.
[35] See the examples in Tallqvist, *Akk. Götterepitheta,* 166ff.
[36] See Huffmon, *APNM,* 154, 160, 194.

2. *In the West Semitic Languages*. In the Northwest Semitic literature, *dwd* occurs less often, except in names. In the literary texts from Ugarit, *dd*, pl. *ddm*, means "love(s)"; in *CTA*, 3 [V AB], III, 1-4, it is used in synonymous parallelism with *rỉmt / yd / hbt* twice. Usually, different nuances of meaning should not be attributed to such synonyms; rather, Ugar. *dd* seems to mean "sexual relationship" and not merely "friendship." *CTA*, 3, III, 12-14 shows that *dd* is part of the erotic vocabulary of Ugarit. This text, which describes a fertility ritual, is characterized by strong erotic references. In it *dd*, which stands in parallelism with *mlḥmt*,[37] *šlm*, and (*'rb*)*dd*, simply means "love-making"; the sexual sense is established by the words *lkbd 'rṣ/šdm*, "(Love) into the heart of the ground/ the fields (to give)." In ancient Near Eastern literature, the "field" (*šd*) is often used poetically to refer to the female body,[38] and this is true at Ugarit, where the love poem *CTA*, 24 [NK], 23 says: "I will make her 'field' (*šd*) a vineyard, the field of her love (*šd ddh*) an orchard." Thus, in the text mentioned above, *CTA*, 3, III, 12ff., *dd* means the consummation of the love relationships (by a liturgically [*nsk šlm*] symbolized sexual union) between mankind and Mother Earth (*'rṣ*) in the milieu of a fertility ritual. In *Ugaritica*, V, 558: RS 24.245 verso, lines 7f., where the "love" (par. *'hbt*) of Ba'al is extolled, *dd* has the same erotic sense of "to love."

dd is also well attested in the Ugaritic onomasticon with the meaning "beloved" (syllabic: *Da-da; [Bin-]Da-de₄-ya; Da-di-ya; Da-di-ni; Du-du-nu;* etc.; alphabetic: *ddy*).[39] It should be noted that here it appears only in hypocoristic (predicate) forms.

In the Moabite Mesha Inscription *dwd* is in all probability a divine epithet of Yahweh.[40]

From the standpoint of semantics the essentially later Aramaic and Old Arabic materials are important because they all use *dwd* in the sense of "(paternal) uncle."[41] *Dād* (*dd*) and its feminine counterpart *Dādat* (*ddt*) are also used frequently in theophorous proper names of the North and South Arabic regions as divine epithets for deities that are not described more specifically. Parallel forms with **'mm*, "uncle," make this meaning of *dd* as good as certain, although one cannot entirely exclude the translation "friend of the father" or "of El" in the case of proper names like *dd'b* (Sabean) and *dd'l* (Thamudic).[42] A comparison of the proper names shows that *dd* must be interpreted as an epithet and not as a divine name: see *ddkrb*, "the 'uncle' is near" (Sabean), and *krb'l*, *'lkrb*, "(the god) Il is near"; cf. further *ntndd* (*liḥy*) and *nt(n)b'l*. It is most likely that the

---

[37] See Gray, *Legacy*, 45, n. 9.

[38] See II.3.d below.

[39] See Gröndahl, *PNU*, 112; also Kinlaw, 278.

[40] *KAI*, 181.11f., cf. 17f.; see S. Segert, *ArOr*, 29 (1961), 241; also A. H. van Zyl, *The Moabites* (Leiden, 1960), 174, 190.

[41] For the Aramaic, see *DISO*, 55f.: *dd* I, *dwd* I; for Syr. *dd'*, cf. Brockelmann, *LexSyr*, 144.

[42] See recently Jamme, 36.

hypocoristica *dd* and *ddy,* as well as *ḥydd,* mean "uncle." For the feminine form *Dādat,* one should note the proper name *'bdddt.* [43]

Until better information is available on the family structure of the Semites in the early period, it is impossible to know why these peoples chose to use the appellative "uncle" when they spoke of a particular god such as Il. Again, the semantic shift [44] from the word "darling, beloved," to "uncle" can be only partly explained with the help of hypotheses. One must assume a development from an original onomatopoeic word, perhaps **dādā,* "darling," to a verbal root *(w/y)dd,* "to love," from which the substantives *dwd* and *ydd* arose. If one assumes that the "uncle" played an important role in the Semitic family as provider and helper, the shift to uncle is easily understandable. [45] Different social conditions caused the meaning of this word to develop in different ways in different areas. In the East and Northwest Semitic region, *dd* retained the meaning "darling." But among the Aramean and Arabian tribes, where the way of life was influenced for a longer time by (semi-)nomadism and the family ties were stronger, the meaning "uncle" became predominant.

It cannot be established clearly that *dwd* was used as a divine name in the East, West, or South Semitic region. In these areas, where it appears as a theophorous element in proper names (which is not always the case), it functions simply as the appellative of another deity. In the material presently at our disposal there is no evidence, then, that *Dwd* was a god.

3. *In the Bible.*

a. *Occurrences in the OT.* The word *dôdh* (defectively written *dōdh,* Lev. 10:4; Est. 2:15), pl. *dodhim,* fem. *dodhah,* occurs 56 times in the MT: 13 times in the Pentateuch and historical books, 8 times in the Prophets and Wisdom Literature, and the other 35 times in Canticles. Sir. 40:20 (in Heb.) should be added to this. An initial survey makes it clear that in the OT two different meanings of *dodh* come together. [46] One coincides with the Aramaic and Old South Arabic usage; here *dodh* means "(paternal) uncle" (LXX *adelphós toû patrós,* "father's brother," Lev. 25:49; Jer. 39:7ff. = 32:7ff. in MT; *syngenḗs,* "kinsman, relative," Lev. 20:20; *oikeíos,* "kinsman, relative," Am. 6:10). The other corresponds to the meaning of the word among the old, sedentary, and civilized peoples of Mesopotamia and Syria, viz., "darling, beloved" (LXX *agapētós,* "beloved," Isa. 5:1). In all probability, this was the original meaning of *dd* in the ancient Hebrew (Canaanite) language, [47] while the meaning "uncle," which is found only in the Pentateuch and in traditions dependent on it, must be assigned to a later stage of the language.

b. *In the Law and Related Texts.* The meaning "uncle," and not merely "relative," is assured by 1 S. 14:50f., where Ner is said to be Saul's uncle. Appar-

---

43 All occurrences are given by Ryckmans.
44 See K. Baldinger, *Revue de Linguistique Romane,* 28 (1964), 249-272.
45 See Stamm, 174ff.
46 See *KBL³,* 206f.
47 See the proper name *Dūdu* in EA under I.1 above, and Albright, 229.

ently the meaning of *dodh* was not sufficiently clear here, because the text goes on to explain that Kish, the father of Saul, and Ner were brothers. 1 Ch. 27:32 mentions a certain Jonathan, who is otherwise unknown, [48] and calls him *dodh davidh*, "David's uncle" (not "relative" or "nephew"), [49] and counsellor. Thus, the uncle seems to have a prominent position as spiritual leader of the tribe, especially if the father is no longer alive. In this case, the uncle or his son (*ben dodh*, "cousin") is the logical guardian ('*omen*; cf. Akk. *ummānu*, "to experience, come to know, undergo," "workman") of the widow, and according to the law takes the place of the deceased (Est. 2:7,15). This sort of context may explain why the weak king Jehoiachin was replaced by his uncle Mattaniah/Zedekiah (2 K. 24:17). In view of 1 S. 10:13-16, it is very probable that the uncle also had a certain political responsibility. It has even been suggested that *dodh* means "commander of a garrison" in this passage, [50] a meaning that would fit best in the context. Unfortunately, there is not a single passage outside or inside the Bible that supports this proposal of Ap-Thomas. It is highly improbable that *dwd* means "deputy ruler, governor," in the Mesha Inscription; [51] it is difficult to understand why the commander of a garrison should be understood as the owner of the vineyard in Isa. 5:1. [52] Nevertheless, this meaning must be kept in mind for 1 S. 10:13ff.

The great responsibility of the uncle for his relatives in the Hebrew *mishpachah*, "clan, family," becomes especially clear in difficult circumstances. P shows that he must act as a deliverer of the tribe in connection with the law of redemption (*ge'ullah*, → גּאל *gā'al*), i.e., in a case of slavery for debt. In particularly serious cases the closest relatives are mentioned individually: his brother and "his uncle or his cousin" (*dodho 'o bhen dodho*, Lev. 25:48f.). The cohesiveness of the Israelite family (*mishpachah*) provides the framework for such a regulation. Men and possessions must be defended and kept undivided. After the father and the brother, responsibility for seeing that this is done falls on the uncle and his sons, who are properly "brothers" ('*ach*, Lev. 25:25) in the family circle. Whether redemption was a duty or only a right in the time of Jeremiah is another question. In any case, the prophet responds positively to the call of his cousin (*ben dodh*) Hanamel, and thus the family possession in Anathoth remains intact (Jer. 32:7ff.). Again, when the daughters of Zelophehad, who had died without leaving behind any male descendants, claim the right of succession, it is granted to them on the condition that they marry men who are members of their father's tribe. This requirement is satisfied when they marry their own cousins (*bene dhodhehen*) within the family (*mishpachah*) circle (Nu. 36:11).

In case of death, the uncle is even responsible for burying the deceased relative. Aaron and his sons, as priests, are not to touch the corpses of Nadab and Abihu in order that they might not become unclean (Lev. 10:4ff.). Therefore Moses commissions Mishael and Elzaphan, the sons of Uzziel, Aaron's father's brother

---

[48] See Rudolph, *HAT*, 21, 182.
[49] See E. L. Curtis, *Chronicles. ICC*, 294.
[50] See Ap-Thomas.
[51] See above.
[52] Ap-Thomas, 245.

(*dodh*) (cf. Ex. 6:18,22), to bury his relatives (*'achim*, lit. "brothers"). This custom is confirmed by Am. 6:10. The text is badly preserved and does not come from Amos himself, but the word *dodh* is certain from a text-critical point of view (LXX translates *hoi oikeíoi* [*autōn*], "[their] kinsmen, relatives," in the broader sense), and the meaning is intelligible: when all in the house are dead, the uncle must come and take away the corpses. (Perhaps we should read *uphatseru*, "and they compel [the uncle to bring the corpses out of the house]," instead of the MT *umesarepho*, "and his cremator [RSV he who burns him]"). [53]

All these passages show that under the influence of a (semi-)nomadic past the paternal uncle was an important member of the Israelite family. The significant role of the paternal uncle is expressed in the Holiness Code. The entire *mishpachah*, "family," must be preserved whole in its natural foundations (Lev. 20:7, *qadhosh*) and protected against sexual crimes. In this context Lev. 20:20 puts the uncle too under the protection of the law.

c. *In the Prophets and Wisdom Literature.* Not only is *dodh* used in the Pentateuch and in traditions related to it, but it also appears in the prophetic and Wisdom books, and therefore in (predominantly) poetic texts, in the sense of "beloved." In spite of the efforts of orthodox Yahwism, these texts reflect the linguistic usages and thought patterns of the pre- and non-Mosaic people which were still alive in preexilic Israel.

In these passages the sing. *dodh* means "beloved/darling" in an erotic sense, as in the Syrian and Mesopotamian literature. It is worthy of note that outside Canticles, which is a unique phenomenon in biblical literature, [54] this word appears only in Isa. 5:1: "Let me sing for my friend (*lidhidhi*) the song of my 'beloved' (*shirath dodhi*) concerning his vineyard." It seems clear in the context of the Song of the Vineyard that "beloved" in this instance is to be interpreted as an epithet of Yahweh. It is thus a divine epithet used by the prophet, exactly like its parallel *yadhidh*. Both words are used in an erotic sense: they characterize Yahweh as being in love with his girlfriend Israel, who here again is described allegorically under the well-known literary figure of the vineyard (*kerem*).

The question how Isaiah could use "so familiar a term" [55] for the Holy One (cf. Isa. 6:1-8) has frequently caused difficulties for exegetes. For this reason, Marti, [56] Schmidt, [57] and others have followed Cersoy [58] in reading *shirath dodhim*, "love song," in Isa. 5:1 in order to avoid the expression "song of my 'beloved'" (*shirath dodhi*). Others suggest that the MT *dodh* has a milder meaning, such as "friend." [59] From a text-critical viewpoint, however, Isa. 5:1 has been handed down faultlessly and there is no reason to deviate from the MT. Furthermore, the prophet is here using "beloved" ambiguously. On the one

---

[53] See recently H. W. Wolff, *BK*, XIV/2, 324f.

[54] See II.3.d below.

[55] G. B. Gray, *Isaiah. ICC* (1912, 1947), 82; also J. Steinmann, *Le prophète Isaïe* (²1955), 69.

[56] K. Marti, *KHC*, IX, 52.

[57] H. Schmidt, *Die grossen Propheten. SAT* (1923), 40.

[58] Cersoy, 40-49.

[59] E.g., R. B. Y. Scott, *IB*, V, 197.

hand, Yahweh is *his* beloved insofar as Isaiah tells of him and speaks on his commission as a prophet. On the other hand, Yahweh is actually the "beloved" within the erotic allegory of the vineyard. [60] To translate *dodh* by "friend" here would falsify the meaning and purpose of Isaiah's composition. In this context *dodh* means "beloved" in its fullest sense.

In addition, there is relatively good evidence that *dodh* was used as a divine epithet in the Israelite onomasticon. Noth's misgivings [61] about this can be eliminated if we take note of the aforementioned distinction between appellative and name. [62] *dwd* is used as a theophorous element in the following proper names: *dodhai*, "Dodai" (*dadhai*, hypocoristically "darling," 1 Ch. 27:4), *dodho*, "Dodo" (*dadhahu*, "he is my/the beloved," Jgs. 10:1; 2 S. 23:24; 1 Ch. 11:12, 26; 2 S. 23:9 [*qere*]), *dodhihu*, "Dodihu" (2 Ch. 20:37, *kethibh ddwhw*, *qere dodhavyahu*),[63] and *'eldadh*, *'elidhadh*, "Eldad," "Elidad" (Nu. 11:26; 34:21). It is to be assumed, then, that *dodh* was not unknown to Isaiah as a divine epithet for Yahweh or El.

The pl. *dodhim* always means "love" in the OT, specifically the "physical sexual relationship." This is the case in Ezk. 16:8, where the expression "the age for love" (*'eth dodhim*) denotes the sexual maturity of the girl (Israel). The word has the same meaning in Ezk. 23:17: the girl Oholibah is defiled because she has sexual relationships with the Babylonians, who came to her to the "bed of love" (*mishkabh dodhim*). Prov. 7:18 is obviously describing sexual intercourse as "getting drunk (*ravah*) with *dodhim*," which stands in parallelism with "becoming intoxicated (*hith'alles*) with *'ohabhim*": here *dodhim* means "the pleasure of love, sensual pleasure" (cf. Hos. 8:9; Prov. 5:19).

d. *In Canticles.* Canticles is a lyric poem; thus, its vocabulary is determined by the subject matter and form of the genre "Love Song." The strikingly frequent occurrence of *dodh* in Canticles is to be explained first of all by the genre. The sing. *dodh*, "beloved/darling," is the consistent term for the lovesick young man. But it is worthy of note that the girl is variously called "companion" (RSV "my love") (*ra'yah*, Cant. 1:9,15; 2:2,10,13; 4:1,7; 5:2; 6:4), "bride" (*kallah*, 4:8,9,10,11,12), and "my sister" (*'achothi*, 4:12). In Old Babylonian love poetry, nicknames for the beloved are more varied: *mārum* ("son, little one") and *bêlum* ("lord") appear most frequently, [64] and *šarru* ("king") [65] and the inevitable *libbī* ("my heart") [66] are also used. Egyptian love songs use the appellatives *ḥnmś*, "friend" (also in the sense of "beloved"), and especially *śn*, literally "brother," but in love poetry always with the figurative meaning "beloved." [67]

The young man in Canticles is not only called *dodh*, but also "king" (*melekh*). The passages where this term appears, however, are textually very doubtful.

---

[60] Cf. also A. Bentzen, *AfO*, 4 (1927), 209f.

[61] M. Noth, *IPN*, 79.

[62] See II.1 above.

[63] But see Albright, 229.

[64] See Held, 1-16.

[65] *KAR*, 158, VII.28, 50.

[66] *Ibid.*, line 27.

[67] See Hermann, 75-78; and the examples in *WbÄS*, III, 294; IV, 150f.

melekh is a later addition in 1:4 and a gloss which probably replaced an original *dodh* in 1:12; 7:6 (Eng. v. 5). *melekh* is also secondary in 3:9,11, where even "Solomon" is added. [68] In 2:16 and 6:3, the young man is also described as *haro'eh bashshoshannim,* one who "pastures his flock among the lilies." But this phrase stands in apposition to *dodh* and is not a nickname "shepherd" (note the article with *ro'eh*).

As one would expect, in Canticles the word *dodh* has a strong erotic meaning. It is never used without a suffix, but always appears in the forms *dodhi,* "my beloved," or *dodhekha,* "your beloved," or *dodhah,* "her beloved." In the syntactical framework of Canticles, the possessive suffixes with the subst. (lexem) *dodh* form a completely new semantic unit: he is "Her-Beloved." In comparison with the intensity of this personal use of *dodh,* everything else is only stage and symbol, emanation and presence. [69] *dodhah,* "her beloved," occurs only once in the chorale, 8:5; *dodhekha,* "your beloved," is found in 5:9 and 6:1 in the mouth of the "daughters of Jerusalem"; in the other pertinent passages, only *dodhi,* "my beloved," appears on the lips of the girl (24 times): as an address (2:8,17; 7:12,14[11,13]; 8:14), as the subject of a description (almost always in a simile or a metaphor: 1:13,14; 2:3,9; 5:5,16), or as a simple, obvious designation.

The beloved is described from two different points of view: various people speak of him in the third person (the girl as his lovesick partner, the choir and the Jerusalemite maidens as third parties standing outside the love relationship), or he is involved in a dialogue (thou-form). Both styles are familiar ones in love literature outside the Bible and they simply provide the poet with better possibilities of expression. In the song describing the young man in 5:(9),10-16, which follows his body in sequence, the girl sings of the ideal of manhood personified by her beloved. For this song, the poet chooses objects from nature and art. Thus he combines the description of a statue with the topics and symbols of love poetry. He uses for this purpose figures that very clearly originated in a milieu emotionally charged with eroticism. The same is true of the other metaphors and similes found in Canticles. The figure of "a gazelle or a young stag" (2:9,17; 8:14) breathes speed and haste and presents the topic of the waiting maiden longing for her beloved (note the intensive forms *medhallegh,* "leaping," and *meqappets,* "bounding," in 2:8). On the other hand, according to 1:13f., the beloved is "a bag of myrrh, that lies between her breasts." Here the poet describes the union and trust that exist between the lovers, their sleeping together on the fragrant bed of love, and the slowly passing night hours (cf. *KAR,* 158, VII.48: "after I have slept in the bosom of my beloved"). To the maiden, the young man is "more wonderful (*daghul*) than ten thousand" (5:10). In his joy-inspiring manhood, he is as unique as a magnificent fruit tree (*tappuach,* "apple tree") among common trees of the wood (2:3). He is "beautiful, truly lovely" (*yapheh 'aph na'im,* 1:16), words which in the first instance are to be understood erotically and sensuously as expressions of a girl longing for a hand-

---

[68] See Loretz, *Liebeslied,* 61.
[69] Alonso-Schökel, 15.

some young man. It is important not to overlook the strongly erotic allusions in the dream narrative in 5:2-8 (note the myrrh in v. 5), even if one cannot accept Haller's suggestion of a metaphorical use of *yadh* (="phallus") and *chor* (="vagina").[70] The calls of the young man to his maiden (2:10), his "coming into the 'garden'" (4:12ff.) to eat its "choicest fruits" (4:16) or to "feed among" and "gather" the "lilies" (cf. 2:1f.; 4:5; 6:2; 7:3[2]), his "knocking" and "putting his hand to the latch" (5:2ff.), are all lyrical representations of love, which have nothing to do either with a divinization of the sexual or with the idea of conjugal procreation, and which are to be understood in the framework of the literary parodies of the "shepherd" and the "gardener."[71] This is the only way the threefold occurrence of the expression, "my beloved is mine and I am his" (2:16; 6:3; 7:11[10]), can be brought into this context. This phrase expresses the mutual devotion of the lovers and their desire to keep themselves only for one another. Nevertheless, we are far removed from idealized love. In the eyes of the maiden, the feeling that the young man has in their relationship is genuine, passionate sexual desire (*teshuqah*, 7:11[10]; cf. Gen. 3:16). The reciprocal character of this love relationship, which enables the maiden to call the young man "my beloved" (vocative), is also attested with the same clarity. Canticles is a lyrical representation of sensual love without moral reservations. It does not do away with the personal and once-for-all element, but embodies it.

The pl. *dodhim* means "loves." The LXX detects the erotic undertones of the Hebrew prototype, but translates the word incorrectly (except in 5:1, it always reads *mastoí*, "breasts" [*dadda'im*]). The same is true of the Syriac in 4:10 and 7:13(12). But there is no reason to deviate from the MT. The parallelism with *re'im*, "friends," in 5:1 could cause one to interpret *dodhim* as a concrete plural in this case (so already the LXX *adelphoí*, "brothers," Vulgate *carissimi*, "beloved ones," Siegfried,[72] Aalders,[73] etc.). But the plural use of *dodh* in the concrete sense of "friends" appears with certainty only in Middle Hebrew,[74] while *dodhim* in Canticles always means "loves."[75] In addition, the themes of "drinking" and "loving" are frequently combined in love poetry. Thus, the speakers in Cant. 1:4 say: "we will become drunk with thy love (*dodheykha*) more than with wine."[76] In this context, the maiden compares the kisses of the young man with the sweetness of perfume and wine (1:2), which again is a well-known topic in love poetry.[77] The desire for the "sweet pleasure of love" often

---

[70] Haller, *HAT*, 18, *in loc.*

[71] Gerleman, 60ff.; Hermann, 111-124; cf. *KAR*, 158, VII.35; "O gardener of the love garden," line 38 (→ גַּן *gan*).

[72] K. Siegfried, *GHK* (1898), *in loc.*

[73] G. C. Aalders, *COT* (1952), *in loc.*

[74] See M. Jastrow, *Dictionary of the ... Talmud* (1903, 1950), I, 283; also cf. below on Sir. 40:20.

[75] See Rudolph, *KAT*, XVII/2, *in loc.*

[76] Read with Budde and Rudolph *nishkerah* instead of the allegorizing MT *nazkirah*, "we will exult."

[77] E.g., *KAR*, 158, VII.18, where the maiden is called "sweet darling(?)," *laḥanatu dašuptu*, and line 21, which speaks of love for the "fragrance of cedar," *sammūt erini*. On Ugar. *ṭb*, "sweet," see *WUS*, No. 1110.

causes the lovesick maiden to go into the "garden," where (*sham*) she gives the young man her love (7:13 [12]). The garden in its secularity is the typical, ideal setting for love in ancient Near Eastern poetry, [78] and a figure for the sensual attractions of the maiden. [79] Thus expressions like "going down into the garden," "coming into the garden," etc., are to be interpreted as ambiguous allusions of the poet and belong to the common language of ancient Near Eastern love poetry. In the sphere of nature, as a source of beauty and an expression of unrestrained freedom, love rises to the limits of aesthetic joy; this love is "beautiful" (verb *yaphah,* 4:10) in its very search for sensual happiness (4:11).

This exhausts the occurrences of *dodh/dodhim* in the OT. The simple statistical fact stands out that in its original erotic sense *dodh* occurs rarely in the rest of the OT in comparison with its frequent use in Canticles. A natural conclusion is that *dodh* was the victim of a thorough purging of the text. The word was retained only in Isa. 5:1 (thanks to its parallelism with *yadhidh* and its clear Yahwistic meaning) and in Canticles, where its erotic undertone was weakened by a shift of sense (a procedure that can be traced to an early period; see the canonical title of this book in 1:1 and the glosses using "king" [Solomon]), and also by allegorization. The Israelite onomasticon shows that it was used more frequently in preexilic and postexilic Israel than the concordances indicate. Sir. 40:20 proves indirectly that its disappearance was no natural death, but the result of deliberate attacks on the text.

The Hebrew prototype (ms. "B") of Sir. 40:20 has *'ahabhath dodhim,* but the LXX has *agápēsis sophías,* "the love of wisdom." Leaving aside the literal meaning of the Hebrew expression, it is clear that *dodhim* has nothing to do with "wisdom." Thus the LXX represents a tendentious emendation [80] of the original text. Admittedly, the Hebrew text is not immediately clear. The text of Prov. 7:18 [81] shows that *dodhim* here could mean "physical love." But the construct expression *'ahabhath dodhim* is suspect. Possibly *'ahabhath* should be translated "inclination, eager desire, lust," if it is not a gloss on *dodhim*. The translation "love of friends" is hardly possible, especially since this meaning of *dodhim* is late, and other clearer words (*'achim, re'im,* etc.) were at the writer's disposal.

III. Significance.

1. *Theological.* A direct theological evaluation of the word *dodh* can be made only if one considers it to be a term which is endowed with a second higher sense, especially in Canticles. If, however, it is simply interpreted within the framework of a (lyrical) representation of purely human love, its theological value is only indirect. In other words, the problem is whether *dodh,* especially in Canticles, is a statement about God or a statement about man. If it is a statement about God, it must be understood allegorically.

---

[78] In *KAR,* 158, VII.28, the lover is the *a-ri-id GIŠ.SAR,* "the one who goes down into the garden"; on the motif of "love among the trees" in Egypt, see Hermann, 121f.

[79] *KAR,* 158, VII.26: "garden of your charms," *GIŠ.SAR la-li-ka;* this figure is quite at home in Canaan, see *CTA,* 24 [NK], 22f.; Isa. 5:1f.

[80] Peters, 182.

[81] See II.3.c above.

Canticles was interpreted allegorically at a very early period. Jewish exegesis understood the *dodh* of Canticles as God the "beloved of Israel" (Midrash Rabba Shir hash-Shirim on Cant. 1:4). In the Middle Ages, this theological approach was developed by Rashi and Ibn Ezra, while other Jewish scholars sought an explanation in the philosophical realm (*dodh* = *noús poiētikós,* "the creative mind," in its relationship to men). The same is true of early and medieval Christian exegesis beginning with Origen. In modern times, allegorical exegesis is defended by Feuillet, among others.

What the allegorical interpretation of Canticles was for the past, the mythico-cultic interpretation is for modern scholarship. Many modern critics take the view that Canticles is a literary residue of the Old Hebrew New Year liturgy, in which the marriage of the young god with a goddess was celebrated. Thus *dodh* in Canticles is none other than the Israelite form of the Mesopotamian god Dumuzi/Tammuz, the "beloved—brother" of Ishtar. This thesis, which was suggested by Ebeling, [82] became well known through Meek's publications. Meek was followed by Wittekindt, Ringgren, Schmökel, *et al.,* while Rowley, Rudolph, Gerleman, and Loretz rejected the thesis. The mythico-cultic interpretation is based on two main arguments: 1. the literary parallels between the love songs of Mesopotamia (interpreted in a basically cultic sense) and those of Canticles; and 2. the appearance of the god *Dodh* in the OT, which is the Israelite version of Dumuzi. In the intervening years, the first argument has been shown to be invalid: Mesopotamian love poetry does not have an absolutely, consistently, and principally cultic-liturgical character. Even if the beginnings of certain hymns in *KAR,* 158 [83] were used in the cult (and this has not been proved), it must be assumed that their modes of expression were borrowed from human love songs, and not vice versa. Moreover, the literary parallels usually consist of topics and motifs that are still used in modern love poetry. The second argument, that in the OT *Dodh* was originally a name or epithet of the god of vegetation, [84] is by no means convincing.

In Isa. 5:1, the only passage in the OT where *dodh* is used as a divine appellative, the prophet is undoubtedly thinking of Yahweh. At any rate this is the final meaning of the allegory on the lips of Isaiah. If one assumes that the Song of the Vineyard had a prehistory, its pre-Isaianic setting could be explained in purely erotic terms. [85] In Canticles *dodh* is simply the appellative of the young man, elevated almost to the category of a proper name. Because of their theme, the love songs, which originally were undoubtedly independent of each other, could have been used to some extent in extra-Yahwistic fertility liturgies (possibly among the adherents of Ishtar-Tammuz). But this is the fate of every love song (cf. the mystical use of Spanish folksongs by John of the Cross). Schmökel's desperate attempt to discover in *dodh* the god Tammuz is one of those hypotheses

---

[82] Ebeling, *ZDMG.*
[83] See II.1 above.
[84] See recently Ahlström, 169ff.
[85] Cf. Bentzen under II.3.b above.

which find in Canticles "what they bring to it." [86] As far as Israelite names are concerned, the conclusion is again negative. In practice the element *dodh* appears only as a hypocoristic residue and therefore as a predicate, which would be impossible in a divine name. Furthermore, the sentence-name *Dodhihu* (2 Ch. 20:37) [87] does not mean "Yahu is Dodh," [88] but "he is my darling." [89]

A final attempt to read a god *Dodh* into the OT appears in connection with Am. 8:14. Here some scholars propose a conjectural reading: "by your God, O Dan! by your *Dodh* (MT has *derekh*, "way"; BH³ says to read perhaps *dodhekha*), O Beer-sheba!" The parallelism favors this conjecture: *'eloheykha— dodhekha* (LXX reads *ho theós sou*, "your God"). But in light of Ugar. *drk*, "strength, might," [90] this sort of emendation is not necessary, for *drk* could be the desired appellative. [91]

2. *Anthropological.* The word *dodh*, then, is to be evaluated only in the sphere of the human *dodh*, either in its original erotic meaning "beloved, lover," or in its secondary meaning "uncle"; in and of itself, this word denotes purely interhuman relationships. The type of love that this word suggests is sexual love as such, irrespective of any further particulars about the lovers and in contrast to the somewhat broader meaning of *'ahabhah* (→ אהב *'āhabh*). Thus Ezekiel uses *dodhim* to denote the sinful and unfaithful intercourse of the prostitute Israel. In Canticles, however, the word unites two young people who experience their passions in the purest absoluteness. In this case eros emerges as simple human reality with no moral or sociological undertones. Love (*dodhim*) and loving (*dodh*) are presented naturally and sung lyrically in their sensuality. No mention is made of fertility or even of marriage. The lovers are not described as a bridal couple or a married couple. The writer does not praise the pleasure of love as a gift of God. A religious atmosphere is entirely absent. Nothing at all is said about God and his relationship to his people. The love of which the writer speaks is consummated in the most radical manner in this world. It expresses itself in a secular way, wants to be understood in its secularity, and makes no attempt to convey a deeper, more mysterious meaning. In Canticles, love is desacralized and demythologized; it has neither prerequisites nor consequences. This is the main significance of Canticles. For the experience of sex in its sensual depth and sheer radicality traces in the love between man and wife an appropriate symbol for illustrating the other feelings of relationship which shape human life. For example, fertility myths and liturgies on the one hand, and the metaphorical concept of the deity as the sexual partner of an unfaithful people on the other hand (Jer. 3:1-5; Ezk. 16:1-63; 23:1-49; Hos. 1-3; etc.), may be explained in this way. Yahweh's appellative *dodh* in Isa. 5:1 is also to be understood in this context.

Sanmartin-Ascaso

---

[86] Rowley, *JTS,* 38 (1937), 362.
[87] See II.3.c above.
[88] So, e.g., Meek, *IB,* V, 96.
[89] Albright.
[90] See *WUS,* 792.
[91] Another reading is proposed under → דור *dôr.*

דָּוִד *dāvidh;* דָּוִיד *dāvîdh*

Contents: I. Etymology of the Name. II. David in the Deuteronomistic History. III. David in the Psalms. IV. David in the Prophets. V. David in the Chronicler's Work.

I. Etymology of the Name. The name "David" (*dāvidh,* later *dāvîdh*) occurs 790 times in the OT. Like the names of the patriarchs, *Davidh* is con-

---

dāvidh. G. W. Ahlström, *Psalm 89* (Lund, 1959); *idem,* "Der Prophet Nathan und der Tempelbau," *VT,* 11 (1961), 113-127; S. Amsler, *David, roi et Messie* (Neuchâtel, 1963); G. Beer, *Saul, David, Salomo* (1906); G. J. Botterweck, "Zur Eigenart der chronistischen Davidsgeschichte," *TüThQ,* 136 (1956), 402-435; W. Brueggemann, "David and his Theologian," *CBQ,* 30 (1968), 156-181; *idem,* "The Trusted Creature," *CBQ,* 31 (1969), 484-498; *idem,* "On Trust and Freedom," *In,* 26 (1972), 3-19; P. J. Calderone, *Dynastic Oracle and Suzerainty Treaty, 2 Sam 7,8-16* (Manila, 1966); A. Caquot, "Les 'grâces de David'. A propos d'Isaïe 55/3b," *Sem,* 15 (1965), 45-59; R. A. Carlson, *David the Chosen King. A Traditio-Historical Approach to the Second Book of Samuel* (Stockholm, 1964); *idem,* "Profeten Amos och Davidsriket," *RoB,* 25 (1966), 57-78; H. Cazelles, "David's Monarchy and the Gibeonite Claim (II Sam XXI,1-14)," *PEQ,* 87 (1955), 165-175; *idem,* "La titulature du roi David," *Mélanges Bibliques A. Robert* (Paris, 1957), 131-36; L. Delekat, "Tendenz und Theologie der David-Salomo-Erzählung," *BZAW,* 105 (1967), 26-36; L. Dürr, *Ursprung und Ausbau der israelitisch-jüdischen Heilandserwartung* (1925); O. Eissfeldt, *Das Lied Moses Deut 32,1-43 und das Lehrgedicht Asaphs Ps 78 samt einer Analyse der Umgebung des Moseliedes. BSAW,* 104/5 (1958); H. Gese, "Davidsbund und Zionserwählung," *ZThK,* 61 (1964), 10-26; J. H. Grønbaek, *Die Geschichte vom Aufstieg Davids* (Copenhagen, 1971); A. H. J. Gunneweg, "Sinaibund und Davidsbund," *VT,* 10 (1960), 335-341; E. Hammershaimb, "Ezekiel's View of the Monarchy," *Studia Orientalia J. Pedersen* (Copenhagen, 1953), 130-140; A. Hoffmann, *David. Namensdeutung zur Wesensdeutung. BWANT,* 100 (1973); U. Kellermann, "Der Amosschluss als Stimme deuteronomistischer Heilshoffnung," *EvTh,* 29 (1969), 169-183; E. Kutsch, "Die Dynastie von Gottes Gnaden," *ZThK,* 58 (1961), 137-153; J. Mauchline, "Implicit Signs of a Persistent Belief in the Davidic Empire," *VT,* 20 (1970), 287-303; D. J. McCarthy, "2 Samuel 7 and the Structure of the Deuteronomic History," *JBL,* 84 (1965), 131-38; R. Mosis, *Theologie des chronistischen Geschichtswerkes. FreibThSt,* 92 (1973); S. Mowinckel, *Psalmenstudien,* VI (1924); M. Noth, "David und Israel in II Samuel 7," *Mélanges Bibliques A. Robert* (Paris, 1957), 188-229; Pedersen, *ILC,* I-IV; G. von Rad, *Das Geschichtsbild des chronistischen Werkes. BWANT,* 4/3 [54] (1930); *idem,* "Der Anfang der Geschichtsschreibung im alten Israel," *AfK,* 32 (1944), 12-42 = *ThB,* 8 ([2]1961), 148-188, esp. 159-188; *idem, OT Theol,* I (trans. 1962), II (trans. 1965); M. Riehm, *Der königliche Messias* (1968); L. Rost, *Die Überlieferung von der Thronnachfolge Davids. BWANT,* 3/6 (1926) = *Das kleine Credo und andere Studien zum AT* (1965), 119-253; L. Schmidt, *Menschlicher Erfolg und Jahwes Initiative. WMANT,* 38 (1970); K. Seybold, *Das davidische Königtum im Zeugnis der Propheten. FRLANT,* 107 (1972); J. J. Stamm, "Der Name des Königs David," *SVT,* 7 (1960), 165-183; F. Stolz, *Strukturen und Figuren im Kult von Jerusalem. BZAW,* 118 (1970); M. Weinfeld, "The Covenant of Grant in the OT and in the Ancient Near East," *JAOS,* 90 (1970), 184-203; *idem, Deuteronomy and the Deuteronomic School* (1972); A. Weiser, "Die Legitimation des König David," *VT,* 16 (1966), 325-354; R. N. Whybray, *The Succession Narrative: A Study of II Samuel 9-20 and I Kings 1 and 2. SBT,* N.S. 9 (London, 1968); G. Widengren, "King and Covenant," *JSS,* 2 (1957), 1-32; T. Willi, *Die Chronik als Auslegung. FRLANT,* 106 (1972); G. E. Wright, "The Lawsuit of God," *Israel's Prophetic Heritage. Festschrift J. Muilenburg* (1962), 39ff.

nected exclusively with David, the founder of the dynasty. The epic tradition in 1–2 Samuel gives *Davidh* the meaning "darling." David is *'ish kilebhabho*, "a man after his (Yahweh's) heart" (1 S. 13:14); he is chosen because Yahweh "looks on the heart" (16:7); and his heir to the throne is given the name *yedhidhyah*, "Jedidiah," "Yahweh's darling" (2 S. 12:25; cf. *veyhvh 'ahebho*, "and Yahweh loved him," v. 24). In other words, the tradition connects the name *Davidh* with the root *ydd*, "to love," and the appellative *dodh* (→ דּוֹד *dôdh*). This tradition would seem to be correct on linguistic and contextual grounds. In the present context, it need only be mentioned that the proposed connection between *Davidh* and the *dāvidûm* of the Mari texts is incorrect (*dāvidûm* is a variant of *dabdû* in the expression *dabdâ(m) dâku*, "to inflict a defeat"). [1] In form, *Davidh* is connected with *dodh*, "darling," "paternal uncle." In Ugaritic one encounters *dd* (*dādu), *yd* (*yuddu), "love," and the adj. *ydd* (*yadīdu); the latter also occurs as a proper name (cf. also *mddb'l*). In Amoritic-Akkadian, the word *dādu* means "beloved, darling." [2] In some proper names, however, the translation "uncle" might be preferable. [3] Hence Stamm interprets the name *dādānum* and the related *dāvidānum* [4] as "little uncle." Comparisons with South Arabic and later Arabic materials shed light on the important social function of the uncle in ancient Israelite society, and lead Stamm to conclude that *Davidh* is a "substitute name," i.e., "the one who bore this name was regarded by those who gave it to him as the substitutionary reincarnation of a deceased member of the family." [5]

Some scholars have interpreted *Davidh* as a "playful form" of *dodh* and have translated it by "paternal uncle." [6] But the traditional interpretation, "darling," is more probable. [7] The numerous proper names from the root *ydd* in Hebrew and Ugaritic, and the ordinary meaning of *dādu* in Akkadian favor this view. *dādānum* and *dāvidānum* could also be understood as hypocoristica of *dādu* interpreted in this sense. It is significant that the youngest brother often receives the name "darling." [8] In the OT, Solomon's name "Jedidiah" reflects this custom (2 S. 11:27; 12:24f.). The youngest of the Jacob tribes, Benjamin, receives the epithet *yedhidh yhvh*, "the beloved of Yahweh" (Dt. 33:12). Therefore, it is understandable that the eighth (1 S. 16:10f.; 17:12; according to 1 Ch. 2:13-16, the seventh) and youngest son of Jesse is given the name *Davidh*, "darling."

From a linguistic point of view, the name *Davidh* can be understood as an imitation of *yadhidh* (homophony). It is less likely that *Davidh* is a passive

---

[1] See H. Tadmor, *JNES*, 17 (1958), 129-141; *AHw*, I, 148.

[2] *CAD*, III, 20; *AHw*, I, 149.

[3] Stamm, 181, nn. 3, 4; Å. Sjöberg, *SEÅ*, 25 (1960), 105ff.

[4] T. Bauer, *Die Ostkanaanäer* (1926), 17; R. Harris, *JCS*, 9 (1955), 76, No. 19:6.

[5] Stamm, 180; cf. D. R. Ap-Thomas, *VT*, 11 (1961), 241ff.

[6] So already G. B. Gray, *Studies in Hebrew Proper Names* (London, 1896), 83; Nöldeke; etc.

[7] Noth, *IPN*, 183, 223; so also Gesenius, Sayce, König, etc.

[8] Cf. *CAD*, s.v. *dādu*, 2b.

participle of a verb *dudh*, [9] or that *dodh* was changed to *davidh* after the pattern of *mashiach*, "anointed one, messiah," [10] or *nasi'*, "chief, prince." [11]

The interpretation suggested above assumes that *Davidh* is the real name of the son of Jesse. The attempts to interpret *Davidh* as a name given to the son of Jesse at a later time [12] must be characterized as purely hypothetical. They are occasioned partly by the statements in the OT concerning Elhanan of Bethlehem who killed Goliath (2 S. 21:19; 23:24b), and partly by the assumption that there was a fertility-god named Dod side by side with Yahweh in Jerusalem. [13] As to the former, it is assumed that Elhanan-David is a double name similar to Solomon-Jedidiah. But the double name Solomon-Jedidiah is clearly established in the OT and therefore is not analogous. Furthermore, Elhanan has an entirely independent place in the tradition as one of "the thirty" (2 S. 23:24b). As to the latter assumption, the evidence is hard to interpret (→ דּוֹד *dôdh).* The names *'Eldadh* (Nu. 11:26f.) and *Dodhihu* (2 Ch. 20:37) show that *dodh-dadh* can be used as a divine epithet as in Akkadian. [14] The same is true of *dwdh* in the Mesha Inscription. [15] The expression *ledhavidh* (lit. "to or for David") in the superscriptions of the Psalms and the cultic interpretation of Canticles play a critical role in the very controversial [16] hypothesis that there was a fertility-god named Dod in Jerusalem, with whom *Davidh* was connected. [17] Furthermore, the name of the stronghold on Zion, *'ir davidh*, "the city of David" (2 S. 5:7-9), clearly indicates that the son of Jesse was called David before his conquest of Jerusalem (cf. 2 S. 12:28). Thus the interpretation of the name *Davidh* advocated by the tradition can be considered correct.

II. David in the Deuteronomistic History. The traditions in 1 S. 16–1 K. 2, which describe David and the time he reigned as king, have a central function in the Deuteronomistic history from both a literary and a theological point of view. As far as literary analysis is concerned, Rost's division into (1) a description of the relationship between Saul and David and (2) a "Succession History" is generally accepted. The extent of the "History of David's Rise" varies with different scholars. [18] Greater unity prevails with regard to the extent of the Succession History: it includes 2 S. 9–20 + 1 K. 1f. [19] The important unit 2 S. 7 is especially controversial. In its present form, this chapter has a clear Deuteronomistic stamp in vocabulary, [20] composition, and content. [21] This suggests that

---

[9] Gesenius, Noth.
[10] Gressmann.
[11] Wittekindt.
[12] Böttcher: in Saul's court; Cook: after David's conquest of Jerusalem.
[13] I. Engnell, *Studies in Divine Kingship* (Uppsala, 1943), 176f.; Ahlström, 183ff.
[14] But cf. Sjöberg, 106f.
[15] *KAI,* 181.12.
[16] Cf. Stamm, 172ff.
[17] Ahlström, *Psalm 89,* 183ff.
[18] Nübel: 1 S. 16–2 S. 9; Mildenberger: 1 S. 13–2 S. 7; Grønbaek: 1 S. 15–2 S. 5.
[19] Noth, von Rad, Whybray; but cf. J. W. Flanagan, *JBL,* 91 (1972), 172ff.
[20] Weinfeld, *Deuteronomy,* 320ff.
[21] Wellhausen; Pedersen, *ILC,* I-II, 235f.; Carlson, *David,* 97ff.; McCarthy, 131ff.

comparative material like "the Egyptian Royal Novella" [22] is less relevant than the vassal treaty texts, which evidently influenced the Deuteronomistic language and thought world. [23] Therefore the evaluation of the figure of David in the Deuteronomistic history can begin with 2 S. 7, since the view of David before and after this chapter is directly dependent on chap. 7. 2 S. 7 gives a summary interpretation of the role of David in Israel's life as a nation and as the people of God. This theme is presented in the light of Deuteronomistic theology and reflection. The writer emphasizes the inseparable connection between the house of David, the people of Israel, and the hereditary land. This connection is rooted in the will of God and has the character of revelation (Dt. 29:28 [Eng. v. 29], *vehannighloth lanu ulebhanenu 'adh 'olam*, "but the things that are revealed belong to us and to our children for ever"; cf. 2 S. 7:27, *galithah 'eth 'ozen 'abhdekha le'mor bayith 'ebhneh lakh*, "thou hast made this revelation to thy servant, saying, 'I will build you a house'"). The solid anchoring of the figure of David in this theological context explains both its positive idealizing use and also its negative typological use in the Deuteronomistic history.

From the standpoint of composition 2 S. 7 retrospectively combines the results of the preceding history of David and prepares the reader for what follows. The central theme is the "blessing" (*berakhah*) that David had received through the events described in 1 S. 16–2 S. 5 [24] and that is now given to him in full measure through the promise of an everlasting dynasty (2 S. 7:11b-16). According to 2 S. 7:1-3, the state of blessing in which David finds himself gives rise to the idea of building a temple for Yahweh. The manner in which this *bayith* ("house") motif is presented in this introduction betrays a harmonization of the Deuteronomistic picture of David with that which precedes. At the same time genuine Deuteronomistic ideas which characterize this picture are also evident. The earlier tradition sketches the picture of the young war hero (1 S. 16:18), who with the help of Yahweh (*yhvh 'immo*, 1 S. 16:18; 18:12,14,28; 20:13; cf. 17:37; 2 S. 5:10) [25] rises out of poverty and contempt (1 S. 18:23) to wealth and honor. All this is captured in 2 S. 7:2 by the pregnant expression *beth 'arazim*, "house of cedar," as a contrasting term to *'ohel*, "tent," in 1 S.17:54. This formulation of the *berakhah*, "blessing," is strengthened by the Deuteronomistic phrase, "rest from all his enemies round about" (*veyhvh heniach lo missabhibh mikkol 'oyebhav*, 2 S. 7:1b), which is connected with the Deuteronomistic idea of cult centralization and points to an inheritance from the time of Joshua which expects its fulfilment in David (cf. Dt. 12:9f.; 25:19; Josh. 1:13,15; 21:44; 22:4; 23:1). [26] The account of the transfer of the ark to Jerusalem in 2 S. 6 together with 2 S. 7 follows the main Deuteronomistic thesis of the place "which Yahweh will choose" (Dt. 12:5, 11,14). [27] This appears once in the following expression, but then especially in the

---

[22] S. Herrmann, *WZ* Leipzig, 3 (1953/54), 51ff.
[23] Calderone; Weinfeld, *Deuteronomy*, 74ff.
[24] Pedersen, *ILC*, I-II, 183ff.
[25] See Grønbaek, 79f., 123.
[26] See below.
[27] Cf. Carlson, 86ff.

fact that the building of the temple was hardly a reality in the time of David. [28] But the Deuteronomistic history tries very hard to connect the building of the temple with David in order to emphasize the exclusiveness of Jerusalem as a cult place from the very beginning, which is in keeping with the Deuteronomistic interpretation of history. Another idealizing element is evident when David suggests the possibility of building a temple to Yahweh early in his reign. The present account would suggest that David began to contemplate building a temple just after his decisive victory over the Philistines (2 S. 5:17-25). The idea of David taking the initiative in building Yahweh a temple may be understood as a Deuteronomistic attempt to make good use of the figure of David for the Deuteronomistic interpretation of history. Viewed from a literary perspective, 2 S. 7:13a forms a counterpart to v. 5b, [29] while the author's main interest is in Yahweh's intervention in v. 11b. The postponement of building the temple is presented in words that clearly emphasize Yahweh's acknowledgment of David and preference for him. [30]

David is indeed rejected as the builder of the temple, but instead he receives in 2 S. 7:9b-11b the commission to finish the work of Joshua and thus fulfil the promises to the fathers. Allusions here to the Abraham traditions (2 S. 7:9; cf. Gen. 12:2; 2 S. 7:12; cf. Gen. 15:4) indicate a conscious effort to connect them with David. The Deuteronomistic form of 2 S. 7 makes it hard to determine how this relationship was originally defined. [31] In vv. 10f. David appears in the role of a second Joshua who will finally defeat Israel's enemies and give the people rest in the promised land. The conquests in the time of Joshua (Josh. 11:17; 12:7) did not correspond to the promise to Abraham (Gen. 15:18). Only through David were the lands subjugated to Israel. This is expressed in 2 S. 7:10f. by a reference to the victory chronicle in 2 S. 8. The passage in 2 S. 7:8f. emphasizes retrospectively David's function in this conquest and his glorification of the name of Yahweh by a victorious execution of the holy war. Of particular interest is the use of the technical term *nāghîdh* (→ נגיד), [32] "prince," in v. 8 and its independent use in the description of David's rise. [33] It is clear that the title *naghidh* is identical with the term *melekh*, "king," when it is used of David. But it was chosen in order to emphasize the unconditional loyalty which David always showed to Yahweh according to the Deuteronomistic interpretation. [34] Even if Yahweh will not allow David to build the temple, he will make for him "a great name" (*shem gadhol*, v. 9b). This expression reflects the powerful political position David is to attain by his successful wars. [35] Ancient Near Eastern treaty texts often men-

---

[28] See Pedersen, *ILC*, III-IV, 237-240; Carlson, 221f.

[29] Caspari; Mowinckel; Noth, 122ff.

[30] Carlson, 109ff.; there is no evidence of nomadic or Jebusite dislike for building the temple.

[31] Cf. R. E. Clements, *The Covenant People of God* (1968), 41ff.

[32] W. Richter, "Die *nāgîd*-Formel. Ein Beitrag zur Erhellung des *nāgîd*-Problems," *BZ*, N.F. 9 (1965), 71-84.

[33] Schmidt, 120ff.

[34] Carlson, 52ff.

[35] Calderone, 44ff.

tion, next to the land, "the house," i.e., the dynasty, as the second main promise.[36] *bayith,* "house," appears in 2 S. 7:11b-16 in this sense; the promise of the dynasty is given "for ever" (*'adh 'olam,* v. 16). 2 S. 23:1-7 uses the expression *berith 'olam,* "everlasting covenant" (v. 5) for Yahweh's covenant with David. Here Yahweh's covenant with David is evidently to be understood as a "grant covenant."[37] This is suggested by the formal and material similarities between this passage and comparative material outside the Bible. The dynastic promise is given on the basis of David's unbroken loyalty to Yahweh, as the Deuteronomistic redactors characteristically emphasize (1 K. 3:3,6; 8:25; 9:4; 11:4,6,33,38; etc.). This agrees with the consistent emphasis on the loyalty and righteousness of Yahweh's servant, David, in the history of his rise. In keeping, too, is the repetition of the formula *yhvh 'immo,* "Yahweh was with him" (1 S. 16:18; etc.), and especially the emphasis that David sought Yahweh's oracle at the beginning and end of his career (1 S. 23:1-4; 2 S. 5:17-25). David's fear of "shedding innocent blood" and his punishment of those who committed such crimes (cf. 1 S. 25:28-31) should be mentioned as a third important element. The epic function of the unit 2 S. 7 in the Deuteronomistic history as a whole helps to explain why the dynastic promise was expressed in an unconditional form. But the conditional character of the promise is emphasized in the Deuteronomistic sections of the history of Solomon (1 K. 2:3; 8:25; 9:4ff.); the king's relationship to the "Law of Moses," i.e., to Deuteronomy, is decisive. It should not be surprising that this is emphasized especially with regard to Solomon (1 K. 2:3; cf. 2 K. 21:8f.). The downfall of the kingdom of David is the result of his apostasy and syncretism according to the Deuteronomistic interpretation. Nevertheless, the loyalty of David and the choice of the city of David are the two factors which sustained the mutilated kingdom of David until its fall.[38]

It is likely that the promise of the "eternal" continuation of the dynasty (2 S. 7:16; cf. 23:5) was understood as a real, Messianic hope in the exilic situation in which the Deuteronomistic history arose. The formulation in 1 K. 11:39 and the concluding paragraph concerning the pardon of Jehoiachin in 2 K. 25:27-30 would seem to indicate this.[39] Possibly the prayer in 2 S. 7:18-29 is also to be understood in terms of the exilic situation. The combination of Yahweh, the people of God, and the Davidic dynasty is a necessity in the Deuteronomistic conception in order to express fully the greatness of Yahweh.

The Deuteronomistic description of "David under the blessing" serves as a framework around the narrative concerning "David under the curse" (2 S. 10–24). In an epic tradition the story of a great man's rise and fall is often illustrated by climaxes (cf. Samson and Saul). The twofold aspect was probably present in the original Davidic narrative. However, the Deuteronomistic redaction of the Bathsheba episode made 2 S. 10–12 a key section in the description of David

---

[36] *Ibid.,* 50ff.; Weinfeld, 78f.
[37] Weinfeld, *JAOS,* 184ff.; *Deuteronomy,* 74ff.; → ברית *berîth,* VI.
[38] Cf. above and 2 S. 13:32,36; 15:4f.; 2 K. 8:19; von Rad, *OT Theol,* I, 334ff.
[39] Von Rad, 343, 345; Carlson, 263ff.

under the curse. [40] It is basic to an understanding of this episode to see that the punishment which David unknowingly pronounces upon himself is sevenfold (so the LXX), while the *'arba'tayim,* "fourfold," of the MT of 2 S. 12:6 is a secondary construction connected with Ex. 21:37 (22:1). [41] The guilt of David is accentuated by the poor-rich motif, which makes his conduct even more unpardonable. [42] The following description of David under the curse fits the original order of the tradition, but material of a different origin is also inserted in chaps. 21–24. In this way, two seven-year periods of calamity are created in chaps. 13–14 on the one hand and in 15:1–21:14 on the other. [43] Moreover, the Deuteronomistic combination of traditions depicts three disasters that came upon David and his people. First, chaps. 15–20 describe devastation by the sword (wars); second, 21:1-14 tells of a famine which ends with the sacrifice of seven descendants of Saul; and third, chap. 24 describes a pestilence which kills 70,000 men. [44] According to the usual interpretation, the three afflictions from which David was allowed to choose reach their culmination in the harsh punishment of pestilence (24:12-14). [45] But it is more likely that the intention of this description is to emphasize Yahweh's mercy in spite of everything, since Yahweh stops the pestilence before it reaches Jerusalem. Nevertheless the description of three disasters emphasizes not only this theological concept but also a cultic idea of Jerusalem-Zion as the chosen cult place. The three disasters which the Bathsheba episode introduces are not arrested until David prays at the future location of the temple and builds an altar on the threshing floor of Araunah; this expresses a typical Deuteronomistic idea. [46] It is also evident that the generation to which the Deuteronomistic proclamation is directed was responsive to the emphasis on God's mercy. The exilic character of the number three is illustrated by its frequent occurrence in Ezekiel, Jeremiah, and Lamentations. The figure of David takes on a typological significance in this description. Just as the series of calamities in the life of David finally comes to an end through prayer and sacrifice at the future location of the temple, so also the exilic generation will be saved from utter destruction by confession of sins, conversion, and prayer in Zion-Jerusalem (cf. 1 K. 8).

Carlson

III. David in the Psalms. Seventy-three Psalms are connected with David by the superscription *ledhavidh.* This expression was usually understood as a statement concerning authorship (and that already at an early time, as is shown, e.g., by Ps. 34:1; 51:1f.; 52:1f. [the headings of Pss. 34, 51, and 52 respectively]). But this interpretation has also been called into question; Mowinckel, e.g., thinks that *ledhavidh* must mean "for David," i.e., for the king, [47] while in light of the

---

[40] Carlson, 152ff.; Weinfeld, 130f.
[41] Carlson, 153f.
[42] U. Simon, *Bibl,* 48 (1967), 226ff.
[43] Carlson, 163ff.
[44] *Ibid.,* 194ff.
[45] Von Rad, *OT Theol,* I, 318.
[46] Cf. Cazelles, *PEQ,* 165ff.
[47] Mowinckel, 72ff.

discovery of the Ugaritic documents, many scholars have compared the super-scriptions to the Psalms with the registry notes *lb'l,* "belonging to the Baal Epic," and *lkrt,* "belonging to the Keret Epic," and have interpreted *ledhavidh* to mean "belonging to the David collection." [48] Be this as it may, it is obvious that the tradition of David as a great poet and singer lies behind this term.

In the other references to David in the Psalms, the continuity between the founder of the dynasty and the reigning king is almost always present. Thus, e.g., in the thanksgiving vow of the Royal Psalm 144 (v. 10) we read: "who givest salvation (*teshu'ah,* RSV victory) to kings, who rescuest (*patsah*) David his servant." "The original act of rescuing David is reflected in each of the saving acts (pertaining to the kings of his dynasty)." [49] It is worthy of note that David is called the servant of Yahweh. The concluding verse (v. 51 [50]) of Ps. 18 cites the *yeshu'oth,* "triumphs, saving acts," and *chesedh,* "steadfast love," which Yahweh had shown to the anointed king as the reason for the thanksgiving: here "David and his descendants" is used as an explanatory synonym for "king." Thus the same saving deeds that David himself experienced are experienced by his descendants. (Ps. 122:5 speaks of thrones of judgment for the house of David in Jerusalem, and thus alludes to the judicial function of the king.)

Three psalms deal at great length with the role of David and his significance for the reigning king: Pss. 78, 132, and 89. Ps. 78 carries its resumé of Israel's history up to David (vv. 65ff.), and presents him as the chosen (verb *bachar*) servant of Yahweh (v. 70), whom God establishes as shepherd of his people (v. 72; cf. 2 S. 7:8). The choice of David is connected with the choice of Judah and of Mount Zion (again using the verb *bachar,* v. 68); in this connection, it is worthy of note that the poet states that Yahweh "rejected (→ מאס *mā'as*) the house of Joseph" and did not choose Ephraim (v. 67). Surprisingly the building of the temple is mentioned *before* the choice of David, which does not corre-spond to the actual historical sequence of events. In any case, dynasty and city or sanctuary are intimately related here. The Davidic traditions and the Zion traditions are interwoven. The choice of the city of God and the choice of David probably became the common theme of a cultic celebration which was the actual setting of this psalm. [50]

Psalm 132 deals with David almost exclusively. First, it tells of David's inten-tion to build God a dwelling place and mentions the transfer of the ark to Jeru-salem (vv. 2-9). This is followed by a solemn oath of Yahweh to preserve the Davidic dynasty for ever (vv. 11f.; reference is made here to Nathan's oracle in 2 S. 7:12-16). It is striking that these verses refer not only to David's son Solomon, but to his descendants in general, and that the permanence of the dynasty is said to be dependent on the covenant faithfulness of the kings. The condition is more stringent here than it is in 2 S. 7:14f.: "my *chesedh* (steadfast love) will not depart from him (in spite of everything)." The next two verses of

---

48 Kraus, *BK,* XV, XX.

49 *Ibid.,* XV/2, 944.

50 Kraus: "the Royal Zion Festival"; others: the New Year Festival, the Enthronement Festival, the Covenant Festival; cf. on this psalm Wright, 39ff.; Eissfeldt, 26-43.

Ps. 132 again speak of Yahweh's choice of Zion (vv. 13f.). The connection between the Davidic tradition and the Zion tradition is clear; one gets the impression that the temple is the goal of the psalm and vv. 7f. indicate that the ark played a major role in the cultic activity that took place there. It is not without good reason that 2 Ch. 6:41f. connects Ps. 132 with the consecration of the temple. The merits of David (v. 1) serve as a basis for the petition on behalf of the anointed one who is now reigning (v. 10). The horn and the lamp (v. 17) are symbols for the continuation of the dynasty, which is clearly represented by the reigning king.

Ps. 89 also refers to the prophecy of Nathan (vv. 20-38 [19-37]) as a background for a petition on the king's behalf in a desperate situation (vv. 39-52 [38-51]). Here the oracle is quoted in greater detail than it is in 2 S. 7, and it relates to David himself rather than to Solomon as in 2 S. 7, or David's descendants as in Ps. 132. The father-son relationship between Yahweh and David (the king) is described in terms similar to those found in 2 S. 7:14, and the conditional understanding of the permanence of the dynasty agrees with 2 S. 7: "If his children forsake my law (note the Deuteronomistic terminology: *torah*, "law," *mishpat*, "ordinance," *choq*, "statute," *mitsvah*, "commandment," etc.),... then I will punish their transgression with the rod..., but I will not remove from him my *chesedh* (steadfast love)" (Ps. 89:31-34 [30-33]). Possibly this emphasis on *chesedh* is connected with the particular situation of the psalm. Ps. 89:23f. (22f.) also promises victory over enemies, which has no parallel in 2 S. 7. Whether Ps. 89 refers to a historical defeat (as most scholars think) or to a cultic humiliation of the king[51] is disputed. But it is certain that the hope in the eternal permanence of the dynasty was traced back to the divine choice of David, and played an important role in critical situations.

IV. David in the Prophets. There is no common prophetic attitude toward the figure of David. Furthermore, occasional references do not always have ideological significance; the influence of the Davidic tradition is perceptible even when the name of David is not explicitly mentioned.

The book of Amos contains only two allusions to David, both of which are probably secondary. In Am. 6:5, "like David they invent for themselves instruments of music," *kedhavidh* is probably an addition (cf. *kele Davidh*, "the instruments of David," in 2 Ch. 29:27).[52] Am. 9:11 contains the promise of the restoration of the fallen booth of David (*sukkath davidh hannopheleth*). This passage is generally considered to be spurious, because it seems to assume that the Davidic dynasty has already fallen. Carlson defends its genuineness on the ground that the statements in Am. 1–2 are directed to the different parts of the ancient Davidic kingdom, and thus hope in the restoration of this kingdom can also be genuine.[53] The prosperity of the time of salvation is contrasted with the calamities that befall the apostate northern kingdom (4:6ff.).

---

[51] A. R. Johnson, *Sacral Kingship in Ancient Israel* (Cardiff, ²1967), 103f.; Ahlström.
[52] Wolff, *BK*, XIV/2, 320f.
[53] Carlson, *RoB*, 77f.

Hosea mentions David only once at 3:5: "the children of Israel shall return and seek Yahweh their God, and David their king." But either the reference to David or the entire verse should probably be understood as a Judean addition. [54] What is in mind is either the Davidic king or a coming David redivivus. The expression is also found in Jer. 30:9.

In Isaiah the Davidic tradition and the Zion tradition are combined, just as they are in the Psalms. [55] The Immanuel prophecy [56] is explicitly directed to "the house of David" (7:13); in harmony with this, the narrative section earlier refers to the threatened dynasty as the "house of David" (7:2). Similarly, the oracle concerning the Prince of Peace in 9:1-6(2-7) explicitly refers to "the throne of David and his kingdom" (v. 6[7]). Similar ideas are expressed in 37:35: Yahweh will defend Jerusalem from the king of Assyria and save it "for my own sake and for the sake of my servant David." Thus the chosen city is defended by God because it is the seat of the chosen Davidic dynasty. Similarly, the narrative concerning Hezekiah's illness combines city and dynasty (or king): "Thus says Yahweh, the God of David your father: ... behold, I will add fifteen years to your life. I will deliver you and the city out of the hand of the king of Assyria, and defend this city" (38:5f.). (The promise of a religious Messianic ruler, who "will sit in the tent of David" [16:5], is probably spurious.)

On the other hand, the woe oracle concerning Ariel (29:1ff.) has a negative emphasis: just as David once "pitched (*chanah*) his camp, encamped," in Jerusalem in order to settle there, so now Yahweh will pitch his camp against the city and fight against it.

In the book of Jeremiah the king is often designated as "the one who sits on the throne of David." This designation is used in direct address (22:2; cf. 29:16, "thus says Yahweh concerning ... "), but it appears more frequently in statements concerning the king and the people, as in 13:13, where Yahweh says that the king and the people will be filled with drunkenness, or in 17:25 and 22:4, where Yahweh promises that the king will rule securely if he and the people do righteousness and keep the Sabbath. But this neutral use shows indirectly what significance Jeremiah ascribes to the dynasty. Consequently he regards it as a punishment that no descendant of Jehoiachin or Jehoiakim will "sit on the throne of David" (22:30; 36:30). We also encounter this high evaluation in the Messianic statement in 23:5f., where Yahweh promises to "raise up for David a genuine (or righteous) Branch." Thus Jeremiah expects a new king from the lineage of David who will fulfil the ideal of the good and righteous king. The same promise is repeated in 33:15 (which is secondary) but is now applied to a successive line of Davidides. In this context, it is emphasized that the permanence of the dynasty will guarantee the continuation of the kingdom (33:17), and that Yahweh's covenant with David will not come to an end (v. 21). The statement in 30:9, which calls to mind Hos. 3:5, is probably a later addition. [57]

---

[54] Wolff, *Hosea* (trans. 1974), 57, 63; Rudolph, *KAT*, XIII/1, 95.

[55] Von Rad, *OT Theol*, II, 169-175.

[56] → את *'ēth*, III.

[57] Rudolph, *HAT*, 12, 161.

The book of Ezekiel also contains the hope of a new king (here called *nasi'*) who will rule over the reassembled and reunited people of God as one (→ אחד *'echādh*) shepherd, viz., "my servant David" (34:23f.). This passage probably does not have in mind the return of David, but is speaking of a David redivivus, for the prince is certainly viewed as a righteous ruler similar to David, as is also emphasized by the epithet → עבד *'ebhedh,* "servant." [58] The same thought is repeated once again in 37:24f., although here the new David is called "king" (*melekh*). [59]

The concept of David experiences remarkable reinterpretation in a passage in Deutero-Isaiah. In Isa. 55:3 Yahweh promises that he will make a new and everlasting covenant with the whole people (pl. suf. *lakhem*), but this is defined more precisely as Yahweh's "steadfast, sure love for David" (*chasdhe Dhavidh hanne'emanim*). The next two verses, clearly alluding to Ps. 18:44 (43), state that the people will rule in the world as David once did. Thus the people as a whole receives the inheritance of David. (Caquot understands *chasdhe Dhavidh* to mean "David's faithfulness," and thinks that in this passage Yahweh promises that the good reign of David will return. [60] But the generally accepted interpretation is preferable, because *chasdhe Dhavidh* has reference to the covenant that Yahweh will make with Israel, and the idea here is parallel to the thought expressed in Ps. 89:50 [49]; cf. also Ps. 18:51 [50].)

Finally, Zec. 12:8,10 (cf. v. 12; 13:1) speaks in lavish words of the restoration of the Davidic dynasty (*beth Davidh,* "house of David"). In the coming age of salvation, the citizens of the kingdom will be like David, and the dynasty like a divine being (*'elohim*) and a *mal'akh yhvh,* "angel of Yahweh." (According to Otzen, this passage points to a penitential liturgy whose atoning character is indicated by the reference to the royal ritual [the "piercing"]; the restoration of the people and the nation is included in the revivification of the king.) [61]

V. David in the Chronicler's Work. The very fact that 19 of the 65 chapters in the books of Chronicles (viz., 1 Ch. 11–29) are devoted to the history of David shows what significance the Chronicler ascribes to him. But it is of greater interest to see how the Chronicler's work deviates from its Deuteronomistic prototype. One thing that immediately attracts attention is that narratives which put David in an unfavorable light are omitted. Thus, e.g., the story of Uriah (2 S. 11) and the civil wars with Absalom and Sheba (2 S. 15-18,20) are missing. Furthermore, all events connected with David's youth are omitted. As the story now stands, David becomes king over all Israel immediately after Saul's death (his war with Eshbaal is not mentioned). In 1 Ch. 22-29, interest is concentrated on the organization of the priests and especially the Levites, the preparations for building the temple, and instructions to Solomon pertaining to the temple. In this way, the Chronicler makes David an ideal figure who not only founded the dynasty,

---

[58] Cf. Zimmerli, *BK,* XIII, *in loc.*
[59] Cf. Hammershaimb, 137f.
[60] Caquot, 45ff.
[61] B. Otzen, *Studien über Deuterosacharja* (Copenhagen, 1964), 173ff.

but also prepared everything that was necessary for the building of the temple and made arrangements for the organization of the cult by divine commission (1 Ch. 28:19) and with divine authority (2 Ch. 29:25). (Thus the musical instruments are also *kele Davidh,* "the instruments of David," 2 Ch. 29:27, or *kele shir Davidh 'ish ha'elohim,* "the musical instruments of David the man of God," Neh. 12:36.)

The Chronicler made three changes in the prophecy of Nathan (2 S. 7) which are also important in his revision of the picture of David (1 Ch. 17). First, he retains the promise that Yahweh will be the king's father, then omits the statements concerning the sin and punishment of the king, and continues immediately with the promise of the permanent divine *chesedh,* "steadfast love" (2 S. 7:14f.; 1 Ch. 17:13). The Chronicler's emphasis is not on an empirical succession of rulers with their good qualities and weaknesses, but on an ideal picture in which Yahweh's relationship to the ruler is established solely on the basis of Yahweh's grace. [62] Second, whereas 2 S. 7:12 speaks directly of Solomon, "who shall come forth from your (David's) body" (*'asher yetse' mimme'eykha*), 1 Ch.17:11 speaks of an offspring, "who will be from your sons" (*'asher yihyeh mibbaneykha*), and thus of the posterity of David's sons. In this way, the Chronicler extends the promise to David "to a much more distant future." [63] Third, 2 S. 7:16 says: "your (David's) house and your kingdom shall be made sure for ever before me," while 1 Ch. 17:14 says: "I will confirm him in my (Yahweh's) house and in my kingdom," thus elevating the kingdom of the Davidides into the theocratic realm (cf. also the expression "throne of Yahweh," or something similar, in 1 Ch. 28:5; 29:23; 2 Ch. 9:8). [64]

It is worthy of note, however, that in the two other instances where the Chronicler refers to the Nathan oracle, these ideas are not carried out consistently. In 1 Ch. 28:6-8 David refers to the prophecy of Nathan and says that Yahweh will establish Solomon's kingdom if he keeps his commandments (*mitsvoth*) and ordinances (*mishpatim*); thus, his success will depend on his fidelity to the law. We encounter similar ideas in Solomon's speech at the dedication of the temple: the permanence of the dynasty depends on the successors of David "walking in Yahweh's law (*torah*)" (2 Ch. 6:16; but cf. 1 K. 8:25, where the law is not mentioned). These passages express the high estimate of the law which is characteristic of the postexilic period.

The decisive new element in the Chronicler's work, however, is a Messianic tendency. [65] Hope for the restoration of the royal house is connected with the idea of the *chasdhe Davidh,* "steadfast loves of David," i.e., the *chesedh,* "steadfast love," which Yahweh showed and promised to David, perhaps in conjunction with passages like Isa. 55:3; Ps. 89:2,3,50(1,2,49). [66] The expression itself occurs in 2 Ch. 6:42 at the end of Solomon's address at the dedication of the temple,

---

[62] Von Rad, *Geschichtsauffassung,* 123.
[63] *Ibid.,* 124.
[64] *Ibid.,* 125.
[65] *Ibid.,* 126; Freedman.
[66] Von Rad, *ibid.*

where Ps. 132:8f. is quoted. The importance of the Davidic covenant to the Chronicler's interpretation of the kingdom is expressed several times. Thus 2 Ch. 21:7 says that Yahweh will not destroy the house of David because of the covenant which he made with David (2 K. 8:19 says that he will not destroy Judah for the sake of David his servant). Similarly, 2 Ch. 13:5 says that Yahweh gave the kingship over Israel for ever to David and his sons by a covenant of salt. Thus, "the kingdom of Yahweh" is "in the hand (*beyadh*) of the sons of David," and therefore the rebellious northern kingdom cannot withstand it (2 Ch. 13:8). This emphasis on the covenant is also expressed in 2 Ch. 7:18, where the *dibbarti* ("I promised") of 1 K. 9:5 is changed to *karatti* ("I covenanted"). There may also be in 2 Ch. 7:18 an allusion to the Messianic statement of Mic. 5:1(2) when the *meʿal kisseʾ yisraʾel* ("upon the throne of Israel") of 1 K. 9:5 is emended to *moshel beyisraʾel*, "to rule Israel." [67]

Ringgren

---

[67] *Ibid.*, 124.

Contents: I. 1. Etymology; 2. Occurrences; 3. Meaning. II. Concrete Uses in the OT. III. Usages in Theological Contexts: 1. The Assembly of Yahweh; 2. The Assembly of Sheol; 3. Generations and Historical Continuity; 4. Degenerate Generations; 5. Generations and Historical Discontinuity in the Cult and in the Court.

I. 1. *Etymology.*

a. The basic meaning underlying Heb. *dor* is "circle." According to Albright, the meaning of *dor* is to be explained on the basis of the older *dahru* (> *dâru*

dôr. P. R. Ackroyd, "The meaning of Hebrew *dôr* Considered," *JSS*, 13 (1968), 3-10; W. F. Albright, "The Song of Deborah in the Light of Archeology," *BASOR*, 62 (1936), 30; *idem*, "Abram the Hebrew: A New Archaeological Interpretation," *BASOR*, 163 (1961), 50f.; J. Barr, *Biblical Words for Time* (London, 1962); J. Blau, *On Pseudo-Corrections in Some Semitic Languages* (Jerusalem, 1970), 101; F. Buchsel, "γενεά," *TDNT*, I, 662-65; G. R. Driver, "Linguistic and Textual Problems. Isaiah 40-66," *JTS*, 36 (1935), 396-406, esp. 403; L. R. Fisher, *Ras Shamra Parallels*, I. *AnOr*, 49 (1972), Index *dr*; P. Fronzaroli, "Studi sul lessico commune semitico," *AANLR*, 20 (1965), 143, 148; G. Gerleman, "*dōr* Generation," *THAT*, I (1971), 443-45; Ch. Krahmalkov, "Ps 22,28-32," *Bibl*, 50 (1969), 389-392; F. Neuberg, "An Unrecognized Meaning in Hebrew DOR," *JNES*, 9 (1950), 215-17; C. von Orelli, *Die hebräischen Synonyma der Zeit und Ewigkeit* (1871), 34-36; J. L. Palache, *Semantic Notes on the Hebrew Lexicon* (Leiden, 1959), 21; Pedersen, *ILC*, I-II, 490f.; M. H. Pope, *El in the Ugaritic Texts*. *SVT*, 2 (1955), 48; D. W. Thomas, "A Consideration of Is 53 in the Light of Recent Textual and Philological Study," *ETL*, 44 (1968), 79-86, esp. 84; W. A. Ward, "Some Egypto-Semitic Roots," *Or*, 31 (1962), 397-412, esp. 398f.

> *dôr*), meaning "lap in a race," "cycle of time," "lifetime";[1] *doher* is a "driver in a chariot race" and *daharot* "chariot racing."[2] *dor*, "lifetime," is an exact parallel to *dārum* in an inscription of Shamshi-Adad I (18th century B.C.), who says that "seven *dāru*" had elapsed between the *šulum Akkadîm* and his own time. The cognate noun *dûr* took the meaning "circle" or "ball," while *dor* refers more specifically to a "circle of people," viz., an assembly or generation. A denominative verb also developed meaning either "to move in a circle" or "to belong to an assembly."[3]

Freedman-Lundbom

Although Ackroyd too believes that the meaning of the root *dwr* developed from "circle" (with special reference to "circular hut") to "assembly" or "community," he still points to the OT use of *dor* for "generation" in support of the rather different idea of group membership, perhaps in relation to *bayith*, "dwelling and those associated with it."[4] On the other hand, *GesB, KBL*[2,3], *CAD*, and *AHw* cite two separate roots. Fronzaroli argues that the Akkadian emphasizes "continuity and duration," while the West Semitic languages indicate "the duration of life of a group of people, a generation."[5] *CAD, AHw*, and Fronzaroli deny any connection between *dūru(m)*, "town wall," "city wall," "fortress," and *dārum, dārū(m)*, "duration," "eternity."[6]

b. In Akkadian we encounter *dāru(m)* from the Old Akkadian period on with the meaning "duration," "eternity,"[7] "ever," "continuously";[8] *ištu dār*, "from time immemorial," *ana dār*, "for ever," *dār dūr* or *ana dār dūr* and *dūr dār* or *ana dūr dār*, etc., "for ever";[9] Ugar. *ana dāri dūri*, "for ever and ever."[10] Akk. *dārū(m)*, fem. *dārītu*, "enduring," "eternal," "unceasing," is used of the name or memory, of gods and temples, the kingdom, an "eternal" life, divine protection, etc.[11] Von Soden argues that *dārū(m)* is derived from a verb *dārû(m)*, "to endure (eternally)," which in turn may be a denominative from *dāru(m)*, "duration," "eternity." Like *dāru(m)*, *dārû(m)*, and *daru(m)*, *dūru(m)* II also means "duration," "a long time," *ištu dūrim*, "for a long time," *dūr ūmī* or *ana dūr ūmī*, "for all (future) time," "for ever," *ana dūr u pala*, "for ever and for all time," *dūr dār(i)*, "for ever and ever."[12] Apart from the general meaning "duration," "a long time," "eternity" for the roots *dāru(m)*, *dārû(m)*, *dūru(m)*, Akkadian

1 Albright, *BASOR*, 163, 50f.
2 Albright, *BASOR*, 62, 30.
3 Neuberg.
4 Ackroyd, 8; cf. also Ward, who thinks a connection with Egyp. *tr* is possible.
5 Fronzaroli, 143.
6 *CAD*, III, 107b-108b; *AHw*, I, 164; Fronzaroli, 143.
7 *AHw*, 164.
8 *CAD*, III, 107b-108b.
9 Cf. the examples in *CAD, AHw*.
10 *PRU*, III, 161a, 13; 169, 7; etc.
11 *CAD*, III, 115b-118a.
12 *CAD*, III, 197bf.; *AHw*, 178b.

also has a substantive *dūru(m),* "town or city wall," "fortress," etc. *dūr* is also used in a figurative sense in connection with parts of the body: *dūr appi,* "cheek," *dūr libbi,* "diaphragm"(?), *dūr naglabi,* "hip bones"(?), etc.[13] *dūru,* "cane fence around a settlement of shepherds,"[14] "settlement [of shepherds or nomads],"[15] is probably connected with this root too. Old Bab. *dārum,* "generation," "age" (of 60 [*AHw*] or 70 [*CAD*] years) is a West Semitic loanword;[16] cf. Heb. *dor,* Ugar. *dr. dāru(m)/dūru(m)* and *(ana) dūr dār* are used only in poetic texts in Akkadian dialects, and only in juridical texts in Elamite, Nuzi, and related dialects.

c. Ugar. *dr*[17] means "assemblage,"[18] while Aistleitner prefers the translation "house, dynasty," for *CTA,* 15 [III K], III, 18f.; 34 [1], 7; 32 [2], 2, 17, 25, 34.[19] *dr ʾl,* "the family of El," is found in parallelism with *ʾlm,* "gods."[20] Cf. also *'b//dr,* "father//generation," in *CTA,* 32 [2], 25, Heb. *'abh//dor* in Ps. 95:9f., or *dor//ʾabh* in Job 8:8; Ps. 49:20 (Eng. v. 19). On *dr bn ʾl//(m)pḫr(t)* or *pḫr* in *CTA,* 15 [III K], III, 15-19, cf. Am. 8:14, *dorekha,* "thy generation."[21] Like Heb. *dor (va)dhor,* Ugar. *dr dr* also means "from generation to generation," "for all generations,"[22] "for ever and ever,"[23] or "everlasting."[24] On *'lm//dr dr* in *CTA,* 4 [II AB], III, 7; 2 [III AB, A], IV, 10; 19 [I D], 154, 161f., 167f., cf. *'olam//dor (va)dhor,* "for ever//from generation to generation, throughout all generations," in Ex. 3:15; Dt. 32:7; Isa. 34:10,17; 51:8; Ps. 33:11; 85:6(5); Prov. 27:24; etc., as well as *dor vadhor//le'olam va'edh,* "from generation to generation, in all generations//for ever and ever," in Ps. 45:18(17).[25] According to Gordon, the place name *dr khnm* in *PRU,* V, 90, 17 means "Abode of Priests,"[26] like Arab. *dair,* "cloister, convent," *dār,* "residence, city," Syr. *dārṯā,* "home," and Aram. *dūrā',* "village."

d. The root *dr* also appears in Phoen.-Pun. *dr* with the meaning "family," "generation."[27] The curse formula of the Karatepe Inscription[28] refers to *kl dr*

---

13 *CAD,* III, 192a-197a; *AHw,* 178.
14 *AHw,* 178b.
15 *CAD,* III, 115b.
16 *AHw,* 164b; *CAD,* III, 115b.
17 *CTA,* 34 [1], 7; 32 [2], 17, 34; 30 [53], 2.
18 Gordon, *UT,* 697; Neuberg, 125.
19 Aistleitner, *WUS,* 785; cf. also *CTA,* 33 [5], 6; 140 [87], 1, 6; *PRU,* II, 105, 3; *CTA,* 54 [13], 16.
20 Cf. M. Dahood, *Bibl,* 52 (1971), 344, n. 2; Fisher, 112.
21 Cf. Fisher, 14f., literature.
22 Pritchard, *ANET*³, 154f.
23 Driver, *CML,* 64f.
24 Gordon.
25 Cf. Fisher, 294f.
26 Gordon, *UT,* 697.
27 *DISO,* 60.
28 *KAI,* 26 A III.19; cf. also Neuberg, and M. Dahood, "Ancient Deities in Syria and Palestine," *Le Antiche Divinità Semitiche,* ed. Moscati (1958), 66.

bn 'lm, "the whole family (circle) [29] of the sons of the gods" (cf. Ugar. *dr bn ʒlm//mpḫrt bn ʒl*) as a group of subordinate deities [30] at the end of the imprecatory gods "Baʿal of the sky," "El, who created the earth" (*'el qn 'rṣ*), and the "sun god of eternity" (*šmš 'lm*), who will obliterate (*mḥh*) the kingdom of the foolish evildoer. The reading of the incantation of Arslan Tash, [31] *wrb dr kl qdšm*, "and the chief of the generation of all holy ones (among the gods of heaven and earth)," is "very uncertain." [32] The formula *skr dr' l'wlm l'b*, "memorial of the family to their father for ever," appears in Punic on tombs. [33] Also important is the statement, "the unity which belongs to the generations that built the sanctuary" (*hmzrḥ 'š ldrt 'š bn' mqdš*). [34] The meaning of Pun. *drh, drt* is uncertain. [35] The same is also true of *mr dr*, [36] which is usually equated with Heb. *mar deror*, "lumpy myrrh," thick anointing oil, in Ex. 30:23. [37]

e. The meanings of Official Aram. *dr*, pl. const. *dry*, [38] and *dwrh*, [39] are uncertain.

dār, "generation," is found in Aramaic, Biblical Aramaic, Samaritan, [40] and Mandean. [41]

Brockelmann renders *dār* "to live," *dairā* "dwelling, home," *dārtā* "court, temple," "house, dwelling"; but for *dārā* he also gives the meaning "age, time, period." [42]

f. Arabic cognates are divided into various roots: (1) *dāra* (median w), "to turn, move in a circle, V. be round," etc., [43] *daur*, "circle, recurring change, phase, epoch, age," fem. *daura*, "rotation, revolution, cycle," etc., adj. *daurī*, "recurring, occurring at specific intervals," *dawwār*, "turning intensely and continuously"; (2) *dār*, "house, building, dwelling," etc., fem. *dāra*, "halo (of the moon), circle," [44] *dair*, "convent, cloister"; [45] (3) *dahr*, "time, a long while, endless time, eternity,"

---

[29] *KAI, in loc,* but the meaning given in the glossary is "generation, family."

[30] *KAI, in loc.*

[31] *KAI,* 27.12.

[32] *KAI,* II², 45.

[33] *KAI,* 128.2; 165.7f.; and *JA,* 11; 10 (1917), 30, 3f.

[34] *KAI,* 145.1, and also the commentary in II, 141; otherwise J.-G. Février, *Sem,* 6 (1956), 15-31, who calls attention to the corresponding Syr. *dārtā,* "dwelling place," "temple."

[35] *DISO,* 60, "house"; Février, "sanctuary."

[36] Février, *RA,* 45 (1951), 146.

[37] *KBL³,* 221.

[38] Cowley, *AP,* 26, 20; "board," "file, succession, generation"? *DISO,* 60.

[39] Cowley, *AP,* 79, 2-4; "thickness"? *DISO,* 56; otherwise *LidzEph,* II, 218: *dwr* + 3rd fem. sing. suf., "its [a board's] circumference, perimeter."

[40] Cf. Ben Hayyim, *Literary and Oral Tradition of Hebrew and Aramaic amongst the Samaritans,* II (Jerusalem, 1957), 445.

[41] *MdD,* 100b.

[42] Brockelmann, *LexSyr.*

[43] Wehr, 298.

[44] Wehr, 299f.

[45] Wehr, 300.

"destiny, fate," also in the expressions *dahra 'd-dāhirīna* and *ilā 'āḥiri 'd-dahri,* "for all eternity, for ever" (cf. Akk. *ana dūr dār* and Ugar. *ana dāri dūri*).

g. According to Leslau, Ethiop. *dar, dor,* "age," are Hebrew loanwords;[46] for Tigr. *dora,* "go around," he refers to Heb. *dor;* cf. also Amharic *dᵉro,* "formerly," which originally meant "time period," and Ge'ez *dar,* "generation."[47]

2. *Occurrences.* Heb. *dor* occurs 167 times in the OT (discounting Isa.38:12): 116 times in the sing., 48 in the fem. pl., and 3 in the masc. pl. The sing. *dor* is found in the following texts in JE: Gen.7:1; 15:16; Ex.1:6; 3:15 (double form); 17:16 (double form); Nu.32:13; and 10 times (or 11: double form in Dt.32:7) in Deuteronomy. The phrase *ledhoroth* + suffix is found 40 times in P alone; in 15 of these passages it occurs in the formula *chiqqath 'olam ledhorothekhem,* "eternal (permanently binding) statute for your generations."[48] The occurrences of *dor* in the prophetic books are late: Isa.34:10,17; 7 times in Deutero- and Trito-Isaiah; Isa. 13:20 (postexilic); 5 times in Joel (double form in two verses); Jer. 2:31 (gloss?);[49] 50:39 = Isa.13:20 (cf. Joel 2:2; 4:20 [Eng. 3:20]); Jer. 7:29 (Mowinckel's source C). Double forms of *dor* occur 36 times in different variations: the earliest examples are *middor dor,* "from generation to generation" (Ex. 17:16, J), and *ledhor dor,* "throughout all generations" (Ex. 3:15, E). In the Psalms, *ledhor vadhor,* "of (for) all (many) generations," is found 10 times, and modified forms of this phrase occur 11 times. Similar expressions appear once each in Lam., Prov., Dt. 32:7; 4 times in promises of salvation in Deutero- and Trito-Isaiah, once each in Isa. 34:10, in the oracle concerning Babylon in Isa.13:20 = Jer. 50:39, in the warning cry against Israel's enemies in Joel 2:2, in the post-script in 4:20 (3:20), and in Est. 9:28.

Botterweck

3. *Meaning.* The OT meanings of *dor* are as follows: (a) "Assembly" of people[50] or "congregation"; in Ps.14:5 the assembly of the righteous stands opposed to the assembly of the wicked. Ps.73:15 speaks of the *dor* of God's children, i.e., the community of the faithful.[51] In the problematic verse Ps. 24:6 it is possible to read *zeh dor* as an archaic appellation of Yahweh, "One of the Assembly," similar to *zeh sinai,* "One of Sinai," found in Jgs. 5:5.[52]

---

[46] Leslau, *Contributions,* 16.
[47] Leslau, *Hebrew Cognates in Amharic* (1969), 38.
[48] Cf. K. Elliger, *HAT,* 4, 50.
[49] Cf. Duhm, Rudolph, *in loc.*
[50] Neuberg.
[51] A. Weiser, *Psalms. OTL* (trans. 1962), 511.
[52] W. F. Albright, *BASOR,* 62, 30; M. Dahood, *Psalms,* I. *AB,* XVI (1966), 151f., translates "The One of Eternity," and calls attention to *'l d 'lm,* "El, the One of Eternity," in the Sinai Inscription (F. M. Cross, *HThR,* 55 [1962], 225-259, esp. 238f.), and the divine appellative *'olam* (F. M. Cross and D. N. Freedman, *JBL,* 67 [1948], 201f.).

Ps. 49:20(19) speaks of the assembly of one's fathers residing in Sheol.[53]
(b) "Family" or "descendants," as in Isa. 38:12;[54] Ps. 112:2; and Prov. 30:11-
14. (c) "Generation," which is by far its most common meaning, and less specifically "age." With this meaning *dor* becomes a measure of time or a period
of time. Like other ancient peoples, the early Hebrews dated long periods by
lifetimes. They divided long periods of time into segments corresponding to the
life-span of a generation. This is the meaning of *dor* in Gen. 15:16.[55] The difficulty came in attaching numerical values to a generation, and the *'arbaʿ meʾoth*
in Gen. 15:13 were reckoned as 400 years (4 generations of 100 years each). The
idea that four generations equals 400 years, which lies behind Gen. 15:13, is undoubtedly based on an artificial scheme which assigns 100 years to a generation.

Freedman-Lundbom

Recently Lohfink has called attention to two different ideas concerning the
length of a *dor:* a longer period of 100 years, and a shorter period of 30.[56]
Accordingly, he believes that the 400 years of Gen. 15:13 refers to the length
of time from Abraham to the exodus from Egypt, while the four generations of
v. 16 refer to the length of time from the exodus to David's conquest of Jerusalem.

Botterweck

But as written records come closer to contemporary events, numerical values
diminish. In the Wilderness, a period of 40 years was allowed for the cursed
generation to die off (Nu. 32:13). But when we come down to royal history, the
four generations of the Jehu dynasty reign for only 70 years (815-745 B.C.),
which by any count reduces the number of years in a generation considerably
(2 K. 10:30; cf. 15:12). In Job 42:16 the 140 years (the LXX says 170) for four
generations is schematic. Job's years are doubled (the normal life being 70 years;
cf. Ps. 90:10; Jub. 23:12), as are his possessions (42:10,12; cf. 1:3) when his
ordeal is ended. We may also note that Herodotus reckons three generations to
a century (ii.142). In this latter period in Israel when the number of years in a
generation is reduced (post-10th century B.C.), it is usual to assume that they
refer to the time between a man's birth and that of his son.[57] This need not be
the case. In the Wilderness, those 20 years and older constituted the cursed generation, which would make a generation to mean those years between, say, 20
and 60.

We should also remember that the Hebrews began with the son and not the
father in counting generations. The sons (*banim*) are the first generation; the
grandsons (*bene bhanim*) the second, followed by the third (*shilleshim*) and

---

53 Neuberg, 216.
54 Otherwise *KBL*[3], 209a, "camp, city of residence."
55 Albright, *BASOR*, 163, 50f.
56 N. Lohfink, *Die Landverheissung als Eid. SBS,* 28 (1967), 85f., with abundant literature.
57 *KBL*[3], 209a.

fourth (*ribbe'im*) generations (Ex. 34:7). Thus, Joseph's great-grandchildren (sons of Machir) are the third generation (Gen. 50:23), and the fourth generation of Jehu's family is Zechariah, following Jehoahaz, Jehoash, and Jeroboam II (2 K. 10:30; cf. 15:12).

More generally a generation consists of the people who collectively become a man's contemporaries in any age (Gen. 6:9; 7:1; Ex. 1:6; Jer. 7:29; Isa. 53:8). In a less personal sense, *dor* can simply mean "age" (*doroth 'olamim*, "generations of primeval time," Isa. 51:9; *dor ri'shon*, "the earlier generation," Job 8:8).

The stereotyped phrase *dor vadhor* is commonly used in the OT to mean "generation upon generation"; like *'olam* it is frequently to be translated "for ever" (Ps. 10:6; Joel 2:2). The two terms are often found in parallelism (Joel 4:20 [3:20]), and like *'olam*, *dor* can refer either to former time or latter time. In the priestly material we have the phrases *ledhorothav, ledhorothekhem*, and *ledhorotham*, which are also stereotyped formulas meaning "throughout all generations" (Lev. 25:30; Ex. 12:14,42).

II. Concrete Uses in the OT. Because a generation assumes primary importance in the OT as a means whereby historical time is reckoned, much is made of the discontinuity resulting when one generation dies off and another comes to life. Discontinuity is caused by death, whereas life (especially long life) makes for continuity. The Preacher says, "a generation goes and a generation comes" (Eccl. 1:4), but this rather detached point of view is not normative. The death of a generation is in all cases a cause for concern, which on the one hand can cause fear, while on the other it can give rise to a faith that transcends the vicissitudes of time.

The fear of discontinuity was well founded. Israel found itself enslaved shortly after Joseph and "all that generation" died and a new king arose in Egypt who did not know Joseph (Ex. 1:6,8).

One of the best contributors to continuity was longevity. When a man lived to old age he could bridge the gap of generations. If one would be wise, say the sages, let him inquire of the fathers (Dt. 32:7; Job 8:8). They will instruct you from the wealth of their own experience besides passing on the wisdom bequeathed to them.

III. Usages in Theological Contexts.

1. *The Assembly of Yahweh.* In the Canaanite pantheon, El was the head of a *dor* consisting of lesser gods who together with him co-inhabited the heavens. By Amos' time, Canaanite religion was well established in Israel and we hear Amos crying out against those who use oaths that name such foreign deities. Am. 8:14 reads, *veche dhorekha be'er shabha'*, which is translated, "and by the life of thy Pantheon, O Beer-sheba," [58] where *dorekha* stands in parallelism with *'eloheykha*, "thy Pantheon." [59] Yet in Ps. 24:6 Yahweh is also called *zeh dor*

---

[58] Neuberg, 215.
[59] Cf. also Ackroyd, 4; *KAI*, 26 III.18; contra H. W. Wolff, *BK*, XIV/2, 372.

doreshav, "One of the Assembly of those who seek him," and thus, as in Ps. 29:1, he too may have been recognized in Israel as heading the divine assembly. In other cases, though, viz., Ps. 14:5 and 73:15, Yahweh's assembly consists of people gathered to worship him. Ps. 14 is a song directing its invective against a godless ruling class which exploits the poor. It is a slightly different version of Psalm 53 and alters a key phrase *ki 'elohim pizzar 'atsmoth chonakh,* "for God scatters the bones of your besiegers" (53:6[5]) to *ki 'elohim bedhor tsaddiq,* "for God is in the assembly of the righteous" (14:5). The result is a contrast of righteous and wicked assemblies, a step in the direction of Ps. 1. The context of Ps. 73:15 also depicts a worshipping assembly in whose presence the aims of the wicked are made clear; the psalmist says that he will not sin against the *dor baneykha,* "assembly of thy children" (vv. 17f.), since the end of wicked-doers has become clear to him. The assembly of Yahweh is not always reckoned as righteous, however. An editorial introduction in Jer. 2:31 reads: *haddor 'attem re'u dhebhar yhvh,* "And you, O assembly, consider the word of Yahweh!" after which comes a poem of rebuke not unlike the sermon found in Jer. 7. This insertion, then, attests to the fact that Jeremiah spoke at least one other time to a temple audience.

2. *The Assembly of Sheol.* Ps. 49 is a wisdom song which reflects—with a bit of irony perhaps—on the fate of wealthy and oppressive rulers. Justice will come to them in death; and in the balanced verses of the psalm's parallel strophes the psalmist plays upon *dor* in describing Sheol: there the wasted forms will remain *ledhor vadhor,* "from generation to generation," in the *dor,* "assembly," of their fathers (vv. 12,20[11,19]).

3. *Generations and Historical Continuity.* If the transition from one generation to another causes discontinuity in human life, it is no wonder that guardians of the faith view this with healthy concern. In Israel the chief guardians were the priests. Consequently, the bulk of passages expressing both concern for and affirmation of the continuity of faith are found in P material and the Psalms. The stereotyped phrases *doroth* and *ledhorothekhem* (*-tham, -thav*) are acknowledged P phrases, and *ledhor vadhor* occurs repeatedly in the Psalms.

a. *Continuity of Yahweh.* Prior to God's revelation of himself as Yahweh, he went by different names, some of them being coterminous with the generations of the patriarchs. With the name "Yahweh," however, it would be different. This was to remain the same "throughout the generations" (Ex. 3:15). We hear this echoed in the Psalms. In addition to his name (Ps. 102:13[12]; 135:13), his years (102:25[24]), his divine counsel (33:11), and above all his kingship (145:13; 146:10; plus the addendum in Lam. 5:19) endure through all generations. Yahweh is also a refuge to be counted on in all generations (Ps. 90:1).

b. *Continuity and Holy War.* Even Yahweh's holy wars transcend the generations. Following the bitter war which Israel fought and won against the tribe of Amalek, Moses swears on behalf of Yahweh a perpetual state of war with Amalek

(Ex. 17:16). Later on, after the major wars of conquest had been fought, the theology of Jgs. 3:1ff. justifies the continued existence of Israel's enemies in the land saying "it was only that the generations of the people of Israel might know war," viz., the new generations who had not fought before. Yahweh himself had left these people in the land to test Israel periodically.

c. *Continuity and Worship.* In Josh. 22 the Reubenites, Gadites, and half-tribe of Manasseh show concern lest the descendants of the remaining tribes of Israel cut off their descendants from the worship of Yahweh. Since they were settled east of the Jordan, it is conceivable that subsequent generations would view the Jordan as Yahweh's boundary line (v. 25). To prevent this from happening, and also to witness to the solidarity of worship having just taken place among all the tribes at Shiloh, the Transjordanian tribes build an altar of witness for subsequent generations to see (vv. 27f.). The fear was that continuity would be lost in a generation or more (cf. the priestly view of the restored boundary in Ezk. 47:18). The building of this altar was an occasion of some misapprehension, however, and the Transjordanian tribes were called upon to explain their motives. This they did, and approval was given by Phinehas the priest, one who had gained respect in his own right from an earlier generation (Ps. 106:31; cf. Nu. 25).

It was also a matter of concern that the mighty acts of Yahweh would be forgotten. We are told that when Joshua died along with his generation, "there arose another generation (*dor 'acher*) after them, who did not know Yahweh or the work he had done for Israel" (Jgs. 2:10). Thus the importance is stressed of remembering Yahweh's past deeds and passing them on to future generations. Again the theology is embodied in the hymns. One generation shall tell of Yahweh's mighty acts to another (Ps. 145:14[13]; 22:31[30]; 102:19[18]). The fathers are commanded to tell their children (78:4,6). In one psalm the supplicant even prays for old age and gray hairs so he can pass on the might of Yahweh to subsequent generations (71:18). Even the city of Zion—God's city—must be described to the next generation (48:14[13]). Alas, Yahweh also performs acts of judgment, a much less joyous thing to remember; nevertheless, this too will be passed on to future generations (Dt. 29:21[22]; Joel 1:3).

Continuity also exists within the worshipping community. Ps. 79:13 and 89:2 (1) contain words of thanks and praise to be sung to Yahweh over the generations.

d. *Covenantal Continuity.* Continuity is constitutive for the covenant. This is true of the conditional covenant which depends on the fulfilment of specific requirements. It is also true of the unconditional covenant. In both Yahweh's promise to his people is for all generations. Dt. 7:9 says regarding the Mosaic covenant: "Know therefore that Yahweh ... keeps covenant and steadfast love to those who love him and keep his commandments, to a thousand generations." Yet the real covenant of continuity is the unconditional covenant given to Noah (Gen. 9:12; the "Noachic commandments" in 9:1-7 are given first, completely detached from the covenant, and do not function as conditions on which the covenant is based), Abraham (Gen. 17:7,9; Ps. 105:8 = 1 Ch. 16:15), and David (Ps. 89:5[4]). This covenant was a unilateral covenant of divine commitment for all generations. [60] Basic to Yahweh's covenant is his "steadfast love" (chesedh) and "faithfulness" ('emunah). The Psalms also affirm that these will last through all generations (Ps. 100:5; 119:90), although Yahweh's anger occasionally brings the psalmist to ask rhetorically if the opposite might not be true (Ps. 77:9[8]; 85:6[5]).

e. *Continuity of Religious Duty.* Although the Priestly tradition reflects the unconditional covenant of divine commitment, there is no lack in P material of legislation concerning religious duty. Numerous obligations existed for the people and even more for the priests themselves. This legislation is found in Genesis-Numbers where the stereotyped phrases *ledhorothekhem/ledhorotham* occur no fewer than 34 times. It is important from the priestly point of view to celebrate the feasts throughout the generations. In so doing, the important events of the past (notably the exodus) can be kept alive for those generations far removed in time from those events. The celebration is given as much continuity as possible with the event: as the night before escape was a night of watching in Egypt, so shall the Passover celebration be a night of watching "throughout the genera-tions" (Ex. 12:42; cf. also vv. 14,17). The Feast of Booths has a similar rationale. By dwelling in booths for seven days, the generations will vicariously join in the exodus event at which time Yahweh made the people live in booths (Lev. 23:41, 43). (Note, too, the later injunction to keep Purim *bekhol dor vadhor*, "through-out every generation," Est. 9:28.) From the days of wilderness wandering, some manna was kept to show to subsequent generations (Ex. 16:32f.).

Once settled in the land of Canaan, the people pursued an agricultural way of life which culminated in the harvest celebration. Included together with the Feast of Booths in this larger harvest festival was the Feast of Weeks and the Day of Atonement. Both were placed before the people as perpetual observances for all generations (Lev. 23:14; Ex. 30:10). Included in these festivals were convoca-tions. The convocation of Weeks (Pentecost) and the Day of Atonement were days like the Sabbath on which no work could be done—again to be observed throughout the generations (Lev. 23:21,31). The observance of the Sabbath was, of course, the special concern of the priests. The importance they gave to it was out of proportion when compared with the other commandments. For them it was a sign of the perpetual covenant between Yahweh and his people (Ex. 31:13,16).

The priests were also guardians of the law. By them the people were admon-ished to sew tassels on the corners of their garments that they might be aided in remembering the commandments of Yahweh (Nu. 15:38).

The priests controlled the activities of the sanctuary. The rite of circumcision, which for Abraham was the mark of Yahweh's covenant, became later an injunc-tion for all generations (Gen. 17:12). Joshua's reason for performing his act of mass circumcision after crossing the Jordan was expressly in order to include the new generation born in the wilderness (Josh. 5:2ff.).

---

60 Cf. → בְּרִית *berîth*, and recently E. Kutsch, *Verheissung und Gesetz. Untersuchungen zum sogenannten "Bund" im AT. BZAW,* 131 (1973).

The priests controlled the sacrifices (Lev. 17:1-7) and various other offerings (Nu. 15) which were to be carried on through the generations. For this they received portions of food and tithes in perpetuity (*choq ʿolam*) (Lev. 6:11[18]; 7:36; Nu. 18:23). They also saw to it that no one ate the fat or the blood from the sacrificial animals (Lev. 3:17), and they condoned ritual uncleanliness for the celebration of Passover only when one was far off on a journey (Nu. 9:10). [61] The priesthood itself was conceived of as a perpetual institution (*likhunnath ʿolam ledhorotham*, Ex. 40:15; cf., e.g., of Phinehas, Ps. 106:30f.; Nu. 25:7ff., 13) with rules governing its life to be perpetually kept. There were daily house-keeping chores such as keeping the lamps lit and supplied with oil (Ex. 27:21; Lev. 24:3), burning incense (Ex. 30:8), and presenting burnt-offerings (Ex. 29:42). All these functions were to be performed morning and evening. Then, of course, the priests were the ones commissioned to blow the trumpets (Nu. 10:8). Of a more personal nature were the regulations of sanctification. No descendant of a priest could officiate if he had a physical defect (Lev. 21:17). Neither could any priest come into the sanctified places if he were ritually unclean (Lev. 22:3). Priests must wash hands and feet before entering the Tent of Meeting as well as before offering sacrifices (Ex. 30:21). Along with the rest of the sacred furniture, they received an anointing of oil (Ex. 30:31). They were also not permitted to drink wine or strong drink when on duty (Lev. 10:9). All these religious duties were to be carried on throughout the generations. Indeed, it appears as if the entire priestly corpus of the Tetrateuch was intended as instruction for all generations; the concluding formula of Nu. 35:29 reads like a summary: "And these things shall be (*vehayu ʾelleh*) for a statute and ordinance to you throughout your generations (*ledhorothekhem*) in all your dwellings."

f. *Continuity in Yahweh's Blessing.* Ps. 112:1-2 says of the man who fears Yahweh that he will be blessed along with his family (*dor*) after him. One of the signs of Yahweh's blessing was longevity. When Job's fortunes were restored twofold, so also were his years doubled as a sign of Yahweh's blessing (Job 42:10-16). Thus he was able to see children of the fourth generation. In the case of Hezekiah, he says, "My family (*dori*—others translate "house, dwelling") is plucked up (*nissaʿ*) and removed from me" (Isa. 38:12), [62] i.e., taken away from me prematurely. He was scarcely 40 years old and no doubt lamenting because death would take him in the prime of life (v. 10). When he was delivered, his thoughts turned to his children, saying, "the father makes known to the children thy faithfulness" (v. 19). The king's hope for a long life is also voiced in the Psalms (Ps. 61:7[6]; 72:5). In addition, a king blessed by Yahweh will be remembered "in all generations" (*bekhol dor vadhor*) (45:18[17]).

g. *Restored Continuity in Deutero-Isaiah.* Deutero-Isaiah presupposes a major break in the covenant between Yahweh and Israel and thus a major break in

---

[61] But cf. M. Noth, *Numbers. OTL* (trans. 1968), 71.
[62] Cf. also H. S. Nyberg, *ASTI*, 9 (1973), 90f.

continuity. But this prophet foresees a new exodus. This causes him to look back into the ancient past—to the times when Yahweh did mighty works among generations of old—and to compare with the past this new thing about to happen. After all, it was Yahweh who called forth the generations from the beginning (Isa. 41:4). [63] The beginning for Israel was the exodus, and in one sense the first exodus will be a prototype for the second. But the prophet goes back even further—to the creation of the world—and he brings to mind the myths of primordial time. Isa. 51:9f. brings both events together. Yahweh is asked to awake as in "generations long ago" (*doroth 'olamim*) when he conquered the primordial Rahab and later dried up the Red Sea. When the people return to the homeland continuity with the past will be furthered when the ancient cities are reconstituted (Isa. 58:12; 61:4). The deliverance, moreover, will be for all generations (Isa. 51:8; 60:15).

4. *Degenerate Generations.*

a. *Bad Descendants.* Four successive proverbs are contained in Prov. 30:11-14 which speak of bad generations. They are presumably the second generation of a family who brings that family shame. The LXX correctly translates *dor* in these verses with *ékgonon kakón*, "bad descendant." It is a bad descendant who curses his parent (v. 11); it is a bad descendant who is self-righteous (v. 12) and proud (v. 13); it is a bad descendant whose vitalities are expended in despoiling the poor (v. 14). Note too the assumption here, especially in the first proverb, that good parents can have bad descendants. This assumption was also held by Ezekiel in his preaching of individual retribution (Ezk. 18). [64] Each generation is to be judged on its own merits.

b. *Bad Communities.* Ps. 12 judges an entire community as being degenerate. No doubt the psalmist is engaging in a bit of hyperbole; nevertheless, he wishes deliverance from this generation (v. 8[7]), from which the godly and the faithful have vanished and in which lying and oppression are widespread (vv. 2-6[1-5]).

5. *Generations and Historical Discontinuity in the Cult and in the Court.*

a. *Discontinuity and Worship.* Deuteronomic Law prohibits certain people from attending worship (*qahal*). Children born of an incestuous union (*mamzer*) along with Ammonites and Moabites—who themselves are similarly derived through Lot (Gen. 19:30-38)—are not allowed into the sanctuary "even to the tenth generation" (Dt. 23:3,4[2,3]), which amounts to "never" (note how *dor 'asiri*, "the tenth generation," in v. 3[2] is expanded to *'adh 'olam*, "for ever," in v. 4[3]). The Edomites and Egyptians are allowed entrance in the "third generation." The Edomites rank as brothers to Israel and the Egyptians attain preferred status because Israel sojourned in their land (Dt. 23:8f.[7f.]).

---

[63] On the interpretation of this passage, cf. K. Elliger, *BK*, XI, 124f.
[64] Cf. W. Zimmerli, *BK*, XIII/1 (1969), 391-416.

b. *Discontinuity and Judgment.* Discontinuity comes in judgment, especially when this judgment results in death. One does, however, live on in the lives of his children, which means the discontinuity is lessened when one has descendants. Ps. 109:13 voices the ultimate curse: "may his name be blotted out in the second generation." Curses of no less intensity are directed against foreign cities. To consign them in perpetuity to the wild animals is to wish for them a permanent break with the past. May they never be reconstituted and thereby share in their former glory. Such curses are imposed upon Edom (Isa. 34:10,17) and Babylon (Isa. 13:20; Jer. 50:39).

Yahweh on occasion views an entire generation as degenerate with sweeping judgment to follow. In the primordial history, Noah alone was singled out as righteous in an otherwise evil generation (Gen. 6:9; 7:1). So also in the Wilderness wanderings, a period of 40 years had to elapse in order that a generation might die off (Nu. 32:13). Dt. 2:14 qualifies this to mean only the "men of war." This generation gained much notoriety in Israelite history; the tradition became firmly embedded in their songs. It is the central theme of Dt. 32 (cf. vv. 5,20), and is recounted in Ps. 78:8 and 95:10. As in the case of Noah, so also in this case Yahweh did maintain some continuity by allowing Joshua and Caleb to enter Canaan (Dt. 1:35-38). Among the prophets, the wilderness tradition is carried on by Jeremiah. In Jeremiah's famous temple sermon, he states that Yahweh is about to cut off the "generation of his wrath" (Jer. 7:29). Some of the faithful in his time, e.g., Baruch (45:5) and Ebed-melech (39:18), would be thankful to escape with their lives alone as a prize for war. Finally, we view the servant of Isa. 53 as one who stood out in his generation. Only in his case there was no deliverance; instead, he was the one to suffer judgment while his *dor* looked on and lived on (v. 8). *dor* here is understood by some as "generation," "period of time," or "descendants," while others believe it means "destiny" or "fate." [65]

Freedman-Lundbom

---

[65] L. Köhler, G. R. Driver, O. Kaiser, D. W. Thomas, *et al.;* cf. G. R. Driver, *JTS,* 403; V. de Leeuw, *De Ebed Jahweh-Profetieën* (Assen, 1956), 244f.; O. Kaiser, *Der königliche Knecht. FRLANT,* 70 (²1962), 112; C. Westermann, *Isaiah 40-46. OTL* (trans. 1969), 265; Thomas, 84.

דּוּשׁ *dûsh;* דַּיִשׁ *dayish;* מְדֻשָׁה *meᵈhushāh*

Contents: I. 1. Etymology; 2. Extrabiblical Parallels; 3. Occurrences in the OT. II. "To Trample Down": 1. General Linguistic Usage; 2. As a Figure for the Destruction of Countries and Nations. III. "To Thresh": 1. In Everyday Life; 2. As an Expression for Cruel Military Acts; 3. As a Figure for the Destruction of Enemies; 4. Israel As a "Threshing Heifer."

I. 1. *Etymology. dwš* or *dyš*[1] is a common Semitic biliteral root with a long medial vowel. Its cognate in Akkadian is *diāšum* or *dâšu* (with *dīšu* I and its derivatives), "to trample down, thresh";[2] hence Aram. *dwš* and Old South Arab. *dws,* Arab. *dāsa,*[3] sometimes with the same meaning; cf. also Tigré *dawšaša,* "to dash in pieces, pulverize,"[4] possibly also Tigr. *dawāsa,* "to mix together thoroughly"(?), and Amharic *dasa,* "to dash in pieces, pulverize," or *dassasa,* "to rub (away), grind (down), pulverize," "to demolish."[5] It is quite possible that this root is related to Egyp. *dš,* "knife (made out of flint)," and *tʒš,* "to cut in pieces, divide,"[6] but in the final analysis this must remain uncertain. It is possible, however, to point with some certainty to Ugar. *dt,* "to trample down," as a cognate,[7] and this undoubtedly corresponds to Arab. *dyṯ* (Arab. *dṯṯ,* "to beat violently," is also simply a variant root). The Ugaritic root, of course, presupposes a proto-Semitic *ṯ,* while the Aramaic-Arabic root seems to assume that the proto-Semitic *š* is the last radical. Therefore, *KBL*³, 209 assumes a combination of Ugar. *dt,* Arab. *dṯṯ,* and Old South Arab. and Arab. *dāsa.* The Akkadian-Hebrew and Ugaritic roots can be regarded as one and the same.

2. *Extrabiblical Parallels.* This assumption is supported by the fact that the scope of meaning and range of application of this word are constant in all Semitic languages. In general, the element of "treading down" is constitutive for its meaning. This original meaning appears repeatedly. In the second place, this root comes to be a technical term in agriculture for treading down grain = threshing. For both meanings there are important Akkadian and Ugaritic parallels which are of no small interest for the use and meaning of the root in the OT.[8]

---

1 *GesB,* 146; *KBL*³, 209.

2 *CAD,* III, 121; *AHw,* 168.

3 J. Obermann, *Ugaritic Mythology* (New Haven, 1948), 77, 89.

4 *TigrWb,* 537b.

5 W. Leslau, *Hebrew Cognates in Amharic* (1969), 38.

6 *WbÄS,* V, 486 and 236.

7 *WUS,* 803; M. Dahood, *Ugaritic-Hebrew Philology* (1965), 56.

8 On threshing grain with oxen with and without threshing sledges, cf. *CAD,* III, 121; *AHw,* 168.

a. The root is used figuratively in a text of Shalmaneser III (Monolith, verso, 52): "I trod down his land like a wild bull," or when Tiglath-pileser III says: "I pulverized DN as with a threshing sledge."[9]

b. The root is used in its original sense in a text from the Gilgamesh Epic: she-asses trample down their young,[10] and in an inscription of Esarhaddon: "I tread down serpents. ..."[11] The Annals of Sennacherib tell how the Assyrian soldiers in flight trampled down the bodies of their wounded or dead companions in order to save themselves.[12] The root also appears frequently as a figure for the destruction of countries and nations,[13] or of a single opponent. Thus in a mythological text from Ugarit El allows the goddess ʿAnat to punish the warriors of Aqhat when he says: "he who lies in wait for thee shall surely be trampled down."[14]

3. *Occurrences in the OT.* dwš occurs 17 times in the OT: (a) 13 times in the qal: Dt. 25:4; Jgs. 8:7,16 (conjec.); 2 K. 13:7; Isa. 28:28; 41:15; Jer. 50:11; Hos. 10:11; Am. 1:3; Mic. 4:13; Hab. 3:12; Job 39:15; 1 Ch. 21:20; (b) once in the pual (ptcp.): Isa. 21:10; (c) twice in the niphal: both times in Isa. 25:10; and once in the hophal (or qal):[15] Isa. 28:27.

The LXX translates dwš and its derivatives in various ways: *katapatéō*, "to trample down (with the feet)" (2 K. 13:7; Isa. 25:10 [twice]; 28:28; Job 39:15), *kataxaínō*, "to scratch, tear to pieces" (Jgs. 8:7,16; Hab. 3:12), *kathairéō*, "to pull down, demolish" (Isa. 28:27), *aloáō*, "to thresh" (Dt. 25:4; Isa. 41:15; Mic. 4:13; 1 Ch. 21:20), and *prízō*, "to cut in pieces" (Am. 1:3). It translates *medhu-shah* by *odynṓmemoi*, "those who cause pain," in Isa. 21:10, and by *agapán neíkos*, "to love strife," in Hos. 10:11. *dayish*, "threshing, time of threshing" (Lev. 26:5), can possibly be regarded as a derivative (cf. Aram. *dîshā, deyāshā,* and Arab. *dōs*),[16] if it is not to be read simply as an infinitive construct. The LXX translates *ho aloētós*, "threshing, time of threshing."

II. **"To Trample Down."** The original meaning of *dush*, "to trample down," is found in three or possibly four passages in the OT.

1. *General Linguistic Usage.* The first speech of God (Job 38:1–40:5) in the concluding theophany of the book of Job (38:1–42:6) says of the ostrich, among other things, that Yahweh has given her no understanding and she carelessly leaves her eggs anywhere in the sand so that "the wild beast can trample them"

---

[9] P. Rost, *Die Keilschrifttexte Tiglat-Pilesers III* (1893), 29, 12.

[10] R. C. Thompson, *The Epic of Gilgamesh* (Oxford, 1930), 97, 7.

[11] R. Borger, *Die Inschriften Asarhaddons. BAfO,* 9 (1956), § 76, verso, 6.

[12] D. Luckenbill, *OIP,* II, 47, 29.

[13] Cf. *CAD,* III, 121; *AHw,* 168.

[14] *CTA,* 18 [III D], I, 19; cf. J. Haspecker–N. Lohfink, *Scholastik,* 36 (1961), 363.

[15] *BL,* 397a.

[16] Dalman, *AuS,* I, 560; *BHHW,* I, 355 (Kapelrud); *KBL*³, 212.

(39:15). This passage raises many difficulties in text and form and therefore many scholars think it is a later insertion.[17] Perhaps it means something like this: In spite of the already proverbial stupidity of this animal (which is not limited to the ancient Near East), in spite of the carelessness with which it exposes its offspring to destruction, its species survives, because the wisdom of its Creator takes care of it and protects it from ultimate extinction.

2. *As a Figure for the Destruction of Countries and Nations.* Isa. 25:10 uses *dush* in an entirely different area of life, viz., for treading down straw in dung,[18] which was probably part of the building process.[19] Isa. 25:10b-12 uses this procedure as a dramatic figure for the destruction of Moab. The Moabite city of Madmen (cf. Jer. 48:2) certainly forms the basis for this oracle,[20] which in announcing the final judgment upon Moab refers to *madhmenah*, "dung-pits." The offensive nature of the figure has led to many emendations of the text, all of which are quite arbitrary. The entire oracle, of course, is regarded as a later addition to Isa. 25:6-10a by the majority of scholars: in the description of the joyful eschatological feast, to which Yahweh invited all nations on Zion, a later glossator missed a special saying concerning the hereditary foe, Moab.[21]

Yet not only Moab (as the later glossator wished), but Israel itself had also to suffer the fate of shameful destruction. Thus the prophet turns to his "pulverized and trodden down" people to give them comfort and new hope by announcing the destruction of Babylon (Isa. 21:10).

III. "To Thresh." Apart from these few passages, *dush* means "to thresh" in the OT.

1. *In Everyday Life.* Ornan is threshing wheat when David comes to him and desires to buy his threshing floor in order to appease Yahweh's wrath by building him an altar there (1 Ch. 21:20). Threshing was usually done simply by driving oxen (or asses) over the scattered grain, so that they trampled it with their hooves.[22] This work is easy and the animals do it gladly (Hos. 10:11; Jer. 50:11). The Israelites were specifically forbidden to muzzle the ox while it was treading out the grain (Dt. 25:4; cf. 1 Cor. 9:9), so that it could eat without hindrance. At a very early period, however, certain kinds of machines drawn by oxen or horses were used to thresh grain (Isa. 28:28). Am. 1:3 (and possibly also 2 S. 12:31 = 1 Ch. 20:3) mentions a threshing slate trimmed with iron (*charutsoth habbarzel*); *moragh* in Isa. 41:15 probably refers to the same implement.[23] Al-

---

[17] Fohrer, *KAT*, XVI, 493; etc.
[18] Cf. Dalman, *AuS*, II, 142f.; III, 114.
[19] Procksch, *KAT*, IX/1 (1930), 321.
[20] But cf. Procksch, *ibid.*
[21] J. Lindblom, *Die Jesaja-Apokalypse. LUÅ*, N.F. 34/3 (1938), 34-40; O. Plöger, *Theokratie und Eschatologie. WMANT*, 2 (²1962), 79f.
[22] Dalman, *AuS*, III, 104, 107.
[23] *Ibid.*, 82-84, 114; *BRL*, 138f.; *AOB*, fig. 169.

though a threshing *sledge* (as these words are often translated) is not found in the OT, Isa. 28:7f. is describing an implement very similar to a threshing sledge (hence the LXX rendering of Isa. 41:15 "wheels of a chariot, threshing, new, sawlike"). [24]

Whether the threshing was done with oxen or with special machines, the harvested plants were in any case cut in pieces, trampled down, and crushed. The violence of this process is frequently used as a figure for the destruction of enemies or as an expression for cruel military acts.

2. *As an Expression for Cruel Military Acts.* Jgs. 8:7,16 certainly has in mind cruel military acts, although these verses do not specify in detail how Gideon punished the elders of Succoth. It is clear that he did not actually use threshing disks. [25] We will have to be content to say with Myers: "What threshing with thorns and briers meant we do not know, but we may imagine that it meant death by torture." [26]

3. *As a Figure for the Destruction of Enemies.* Am. 1:3-5 announces that Yahweh will punish Damascus "because they have threshed Gilead with threshing slates of iron." A passage like 2 K. 8:12 shows how cruel warfare was in ancient times (and not only among the Syrians). The statement in Am. 1:3, however, is not to be interpreted literally, [27] but as a figure for especially cruel treatment of land and people (cf. also 2 K. 13:7b; Mic. 4:12f.; Isa. 21:10). Because of this inhumanity, Syria will be punished by Yahweh, and this punishment is irrevocable (v. 3a). Of course, one is not to think that the prophet envisioned a direct intervention of Yahweh, but rather an Assyrian invasion ordained by him.

In the eschatological hymn in Hab. 3:3-15, it is Yahweh himself who intervenes on behalf of his oppressed people and his anointed one, and who threshes "the nations" in his anger (v. 12), so that "their leaders are scattered like chaff" (v. 14). It is quite obvious here that the concrete punishment of Babylon has been set on the horizon of the eschatological judgment of the nations (note the change from "the nations" in v. 12 to "the house of the wicked" in v. 13b). Echoes of the destruction of Egypt at the time of the exodus of Israel may also be detected (vv. 14b,15).

Some scholars would take Isa. 41:15 in the same sense: "I will make of you a threshing slate, ... you shall thresh the mountains and crush them, and you will make the hills like chaff," as if Israel were about to be given new political strength and to execute judgment on the nations as Yahweh's instrument. It is true that Deutero-Isaiah uses the traditional figure of threshing for the destruc-

---

[24] Cf. Dalman, *AuS,* III, 88ff.; on this whole problem, see the discussion in S. R. Driver, *Joel and Amos. CBSC,* 227f.

[25] W. Rudolph, *KAT,* XIII/2, 130; but cf. Dalman, *AuS,* III, 114, who refers to Wetzstein, *ZE,* 5 (1873), 283ff., and 2 S. 12:31 = 1 Ch. 20:3, where admittedly the text is not in order; cf. W. Rudolph, *HAT,* 21, *in loc.;* and G. C. O'Ceallaigh, *VT,* 12 (1962), 179-189.

[26] J. M. Myers, *IB,* II, 747.

[27] W. Rudolph, *KAT,* XIII/2, 130.

tion of enemy powers, but the mountains and hills here are not metaphorical representations of the nations.[28] The meaning of the salvation oracle in Isa. 41:14-16 is different, as a comparison with vv. 8-13 clearly shows: Yahweh makes Israel an instrument that is capable of overcoming the obstacles that stand in its way as it returns home to Yahweh.[29]

4. *Israel As a "Threshing Heifer."* The idea of Israel as a threshing heifer has its origin in the election tradition as it is expressed by Hosea in a new set of images.[30] Ephraim, a "stubborn heifer" for a long time (Hos. 4:16), was once a threshing heifer that loved to do this easy work (10:11) and therefore seemed to be suited for hard field work under the yoke. What is meant is that when Yahweh had found Israel to be good and willing in the early period, he entrusted it with higher tasks in a new phase of its development and summoned it to be an active instrument in his plan of salvation.[31]

The concept then finds its way into OT eschatology (as in Isa. 41:15,[32] although naturally with a different emphasis), and it is dramatically worked out in Mic. 4:9-13. The figure of the assault of the nations against Jerusalem (v. 11), where their power is ultimately shattered, is a familiar one (Ps. 46:5ff. [Eng. vv. 4ff.]; Joel 4:12 [3:12]; Zec. 12:3; 14:2; Ezk. 38f.) which is emphasized especially in Isaiah (Isa. 17:12ff.; 28:16ff.; 29:1ff.; etc.). But Yahweh gathers the nations "as sheaves to the threshing floor" (Mic. 4:12b) in order to demonstrate his power to them. In living anticipation of this End Time event, which the cultically assembled community already experiences as present, the word of God preserved in v. 13 summons the daughter of Zion, as the uniquely empowered and elected instrument of Yahweh (cf. Hos. 10:11), to execute this divine judgment on the nations. Yet even here the ultimate meaning of this final judgment is not Israel's victory and fame, but the honor and glorification of Yahweh, to whom all nations, including Israel, will ultimately subject themselves, paying homage to him as the Lord of the whole earth.[33]

Fuhs

---

[28] As Volz, *KAT*, IX/2 (1932), 21f., has rightly seen.

[29] Cf. E. J. Hamlin, "The Meaning of 'Mountains and Hills' in Isa. 41,14-16," *JNES*, 13 (1954), 185-190; also C. Westermann, *Isaiah 40–66. OTL* (trans. 1969), 74-78.

[30] H. W. Wolff, *Hosea* (trans. 1974), 185.

[31] W. Rudolph, *KAT*, XIII/1, 203.

[32] See above.

[33] On this cf. also H. Gottlieb, "Den taerskende Kvie Mi 4,11-13," *Dansk Teologisk Tidsskrift*, 26 (1963), 161-171.

דִּין dîn

Contents: I. Distribution and Meaning: 1. *dyn*: a. In Extrabiblical Literature; b. In the OT; 2. Synonyms; 3. Derivatives: a. *dayyān*; b. *mādhôn*; c. *mᵉdhînāh*; d. Proper Names. II. Judging in the OT: 1. Earthly Judgment; 2. God Judges: a. God Judges the Individual and His People; b. God Judges All Nations; 3. Theological Relevance: a. The God-Man Relationship; b. The Genre "Lawsuit."

I. Distribution and Meaning.

1. *dyn*.

a. *In Extrabiblical Literature.* The root *dyn* is found in all Semitic languages.[1] In Akkadian, e.g., *dânu (diānum)* means "to judge,"[2] *dīnu* denotes both the "verdict" and the "legal maxim," and then also the "legal case" and the "lawsuit,"[3] and *dayyānu* means "judge."[4] *dn* also appears in Ugaritic as a verb and a substantive: *ydn dn 'lmnt*: "He *(Dnʾl)* procured judgment (justice) for widows."[5] Along with the forensic meaning, *dnt* occurs, too, in the more general sense of "dissension."[6] The very frequent employment of this root in the Sumerian and Akkadian legal literature,[7] and its occurrences in Ugaritic, show that the forensic use goes back to the earliest period.

b. *In the OT. dyn* is found only 25 times in the OT (Heb. and Aram.) as a verb, always in the qal with the exception of 2 S.19:10 (Eng. v. 9) (niphal), where it has a reciprocal meaning: "they strove with each other." The subst. *dîn* occurs

---

dîn. H. J. Boecker, *Redeformen des Rechtslebens im AT. WMANT*, 14 (²1970); H. Cazelles, "Loi israélite," *DBS*, 5 (1957), 497-530; A. Gamper, *Gott als Richter in Mesopotamien und im AT* (1966); B. Gemser, "The RÎB- or Controversy-Pattern in Hebrew Mentality," *SVT*, 3 (1955), 120-137; J. Harvey, *Le plaidoyer prophétique contre Israël après la rupture de l'alliance* (1967); *idem*, "Le 'Rîb-Pattern,' réquisitoire prophétique sur la rupture de l'alliance," *Bibl*, 43 (1962), 172-196; V. Herntrich, "κρίνω, B. The OT Term מִשְׁפָּט," *TDNT*, III, 923-933; J. Jeremias, *Kultprophetie und Gerichtsverkündigung in der späten Königszeit Israels. WMANT*, 35 (1970); B. Landsberger, "Die babylonischen Termini für Gesetz und Recht," *Festschrift P. Koschaker* (Leiden, 1939), 219; G. Liedke, *Gestalt und Bezeichnung alttestamentlicher Rechtssätze. WMANT*, 39 (1971); I. L. Seeligmann, "Zur Terminologie für das Gerichtsverfahren im Wortschatz des biblischen Hebräisch," *SVT*, 16 (1967), 251-278; E. von Waldow, *Der traditionsgeschichtliche Hintergrund der prophetischen Gerichtsreden. BZAW*, 85 (1963); E. Würthwein, "Der Ursprung der prophetischen Gerichtsrede," *ZThK*, 49 (1952), 1-16=*Wort und Existenz* (1970), 111-126.

[1] Cf. the Lexicons, esp. *KBL³*, 211.

[2] *AHw*, 167f.

[3] *AHw*, 171f.

[4] *AHw*, 151.

[5] *WUS*, No. 766; the etymological figure is typical in all languages.

[6] *WUS*, No. 722; *wdbḥ dnt*, "a banquet of dissension"; cf. also Prov. 17:1: *zebhche ribh*, "feasting with strife."

[7] See Gamper.

24 times. The original meaning "judgment" embraces all individual acts of supportive or punitive justice. In Prov. 22:10, where *din* appears in parallelism with *madhon,* "strife," and *qalon,* "abuse," it has almost lost its juridical sense, and simply means "quarreling" (cf. 2 S. 19:10[9] above). Also in the maxim in Eccl. 6:10, "a man is not able to dispute (go to law) with one stronger than he," the original meaning "judge" seems to have taken on the expanded meaning of "dispute, go to law." [8]

2. *Synonyms.* When it has the comprehensive meaning "to judge," "to do justice," etc., *dyn* is to a great extent synonymous with other roots, especially → שׁפט *shāphaṭ,* "to judge," and → ריב *rîbh,* "to conduct a lawsuit." This is often shown by their parallel use in the pertinent OT passages. *dn* and *ṭpṭ* already appear in parallelism in Ugaritic. [9] While *dīnu(m)* is predominant in the Akkadian literature, [10] in the OT (West Semitic!) *špṭ* is much more frequent. [11] *špṭ* denotes first of all the act of arbitration, the legal decision, while *dyn* refers more to the formal judicial process as a whole. Hence Boecker [12] and Liedke [13] interpret *din* in the overwhelming number of cases as an act of the judge and *mishpat* as "the decision stated by the judge." [14] Thus *dinu mishpat* in Jer. 21:12 means "carry out the legal decision," "do justice" (*shiphtu din* should probably be translated, "decide concerning the execution of justice").

Hamp

Recently Liedke has tried to show that the predominant meaning of *din* is the "authoritative, binding decision in a lawsuit." [15] In addition to God, a king (Jer. 21:12; 22:16; Ps. 72:2; Prov. 20:8; 31:5,8,9), a tribal leader (Gen. 49:16), or a high priest (Zec. 3:7) is the subject who gives justice to the oppressed. On the other hand, *shaphat* [16] denotes "the action that restores the disturbed *shalom* (peace) of a community . . . ; for the one who suffers under the disrupted order, *shaphat* means 'to deliver, to aid in bringing about justice'—for the one who is the cause of the disruption, the *shaphat*-action is judgment that brings about exclusion and destruction." [17] With a royal subject, *'asah mishpat utsedhaqah,* "to do justice and righteousness," [18] denotes "the establishment and preservation of the realm of salvation which surrounds a man." [19]

Botterweck

---

[8] Cf. Gemser, 124, n. 4; but Boecker, 87, n. 7, thinks it means "conducting a lawsuit as a whole."

[9] *WUS,* Nos. 766 and 2921.

[10] Cf. Landsberger, 223 on *dīnum* and *šipṭum.*

[11] *KBL²*: 180 times in the qal.

[12] Boecker, 85, n. 7.

[13] Liedke, 84.

[14] *Ibid.*

[15] *Ibid.;* cf. *THAT,* I, 446f.

[16] For a survey of the research that has been done on this root, cf. Liedke, 62f.

[17] *Ibid.,* 73.

[18] On the transmission of this formula, cf. H. W. Wolff, *BK,* XIV/2, 287f.

[19] Liedke, 76f.

Job 36:17 contains the pleonastic expression *din umishpat*, "judgment and sentence." *mishpat* often takes on the moral quality of "justice," most clearly in the formula "righteousness and justice." In contrast to the always sing. *din*, the *mishpatim* in the plural are "legal regulations, statutes." *ribh* has in mind the opposing parties (cf. Ex. 21:18) and denotes the dispute during or before a lawsuit, the litigation, and then also the legal case as a whole. According to Wolff, *ribh* "denotes the succession of speeches before the court (with *'im*, "with," [Hos.] 4:1; 12:3[2]) and thus the judicial procedure as a whole. In a narrower sense, combined with *be*, it means a speech that calls one to account, that assails with rebuke (Gen. 31:36; Jgs. 6:32), or that makes an accusation." [20] Frequently it denotes private disputes, quarrels, and accusations, which would seem to indicate that originally it was not used juridically. [21] A person might dare to quarrel with God, but never to pass sentence on him. In Dt. 17:8f. one can still, with difficulty, distinguish between *mishpat*, "legal decision," *din*, "case," and *ribh*, "contention." But often in synonymous parallelism, and in other contexts too, it is hardly possible to differentiate between their meanings; cf., e.g., Ps. 140:13(12): *din 'ani mishpat 'ebhyonim*, "the judgment of the afflicted, the legal claim of the poor" (RSV, "the Lord maintains the cause of the afflicted, and executes justice for the needy"). All three of these roots appear together in 1 S. 24:16(15); Isa. 3:13f.; Ps. 9:5(4). In the Qumran texts *din* appears in parallelism with *mishpat* (1QH 9:9) and *ribh* with *mdnym* (1QH 5:23,35). The Targumim and the Peshitta always render the OT *spt* by *dyn* and in this way they come closer again to the almost exclusive use of *dānu* in Akkadian. [22]

3. *Derivatives.*

a. *dayyān. dayyan*, "judge," which is found in Akkadian, Arabic, Aramaic, and Syriac, appears in the OT only in 1 S. 24:16(15); Ps. 68:6(5) (in both cases referring to God); and (in Aram.) Ezr. 4:9; 7:25 (the text of Job 19:29 is uncertain). Elsewhere in the OT the unusually frequent *shophet* is predominant.

b. *mādhôn. madhon* is not used forensically and simply means strife and contention. [23] In the OT, this word is limited almost entirely to the book of Proverbs (14 out of 17 occurrences; it is used in parallelism with *din* in Prov. 22:10). [24] It appears with *ribh* in Prov. 15:18; Hab. 1:3; and 1QH 5:23,35. [25] Jeremiah is a man of strife (*ribh*) and contention (*madhon*) to the whole land (Jer. 15:10). *midhyanim*, "contentious persons," which appears only in the plural, is identical with *madhon* in meaning, and frequently occurs in its place in the

---

[20] H. W. Wolff, *Hosea* (trans. 1974), 33.
[21] Seeligmann, 256.
[22] For pre-Christian Aramaic cf. E. Vogt, *Lexicon Linguae Aramaicae* ... (Rome, 1971), 42f.
[23] Cf. Seeligmann, 256f.
[24] See above.
[25] See above.

textual tradition. It is found only in Proverbs (10 times), mostly with reference to the contentious wife.

c. *mᵉdhînāh*. *medhinah* means literally a judicial district, i.e., a province. [26] It is used frequently in the book of Esther as a technical term for the 127 Persian satrapies. Then in late texts it has the more general meaning of "district" and "land": Lam. 1:1 (RSV "cities"); Eccl. 5:7(8); Dnl. 11:24; Ezk. 19:8 (controversial); Eccl. 2:8. The narrower meaning of "city" (the equivalent of *'ir*), which the word takes on in Aramaic and Syriac, is not the sense in Dnl. 2:48f.; 3:1,12, 30; Ezr. 7:16 ("province of Babylon"). [27]

d. *Proper Names*. Mention should be made of certain proper names derived from the root *dyn*: Dinah, Abidan, Dan, and frequently Daniel. A similar name appears in Ugaritic in the person of King *Dnʒl* in the Aqhat Epic. The Akkadian name Dan(n)ilu could come from *danānu*, "to be mighty." [28] But the name Dan is explicitly connected with "judging" in Gen. 30:6 and 49:16; the OT prophet Daniel has a special role of judging, especially in the story of Susanna; and the Ugaritic Dnʒl executes justice for widows and orphans. [29] A Daniel appears in Ezk. 14:14,20 as a righteous man of antiquity and in Ezk. 28:3 as an exemplary wise man. It is very probable, then, that not only in Ezekiel but also in the book of Daniel this name goes back to a legendary figure. But this is not to say that in the OT the name must have been borrowed directly from Ugarit. [30]

II. Judging in the OT.

1. *Earthly Judgment*. The lawsuit was carried out in the early nomadic period by the tribal chief, later by the elders at the gate of the city, and then by the king as the highest court and by his official judges. [31] In difficult and uncertain cases the priests had to render a divine decision (Dt. 17:8). When Yahweh says to the high priest Joshua, "you shall judge my house" (Zec. 3:7), the context shows that *din* does not denote an exclusive judicial activity but more broadly the administration and management of the temple. Of course, it was always the moral responsibility of the judge to execute justice and especially to defend the socially disadvantaged; in Sumeria the protection of widows and orphans is already a traditional formulation. [32] Frequently, then, when *din* stands alone (again like *shaphat*) with no more precise specification it can mean "to secure justice," or as a noun "(righteous) judgment," "justice," "legal claim": Prov. 29:7: the righteous man is concerned about the lawsuit (the rights) of the poor; Prov. 31:9:

---

26 Cf. C. C. Torrey, "Medina and Polis," *HThR,* 17 (1924), 83ff.
27 Cf. *KBL²*, 1092; Vogt, 97.
28 Cf. the literature in *KBL³*, 218f.
29 Cf. M. Noth, *VT,* 1 (1951), 253.
30 Cf. M. Delcor, *Le livre de Daniel. Sources Bibliques* (Paris, 1971), 63f.
31 On legal procedure and legal terminology, cf. Boecker, and Gamper, 195ff.
32 Gamper, 47.

maintain the rights (*din*) of the poor and needy; Prov. 31:5,8: the legal claim (the case, the rights) of all the afflicted; Jer. 5:28: evildoers are not concerned about justice (*din lo' dhanu*), the cause of the fatherless (*din yathom;* in synonymous parallelism with *mishpat 'ebhyonim,* the rights of the needy); Jer. 22:16: Josiah was concerned about the cause of the poor (*dan din 'ani*); Jer. 22:15: he did justice and righteousness; Jer. 21:12: (righteous) judgment (justice) is executed (*dinu mishpat*) in the morning; [33] Isa. 10:2: to turn aside the needy from judgment (justice, *middin;* note the parallel phrase, to rob the poor of their right, *mishpat*); Jer. 30:13: there is none to uphold your cause (*'en dan dinekh*); Prov. 20:8: the king's tribunal (*kisse' dhin*); Ps. 72:2: the ideal king judges (*din*) thy people with righteousness; Est. 1:13: all who were versed in law and judgment (*kol yodhe'e dath vadhin*).

2. God Judges.

a. *God Judges the Individual and His People.* In the OT (as elsewhere in ancient Near Eastern literature), we frequently encounter the statement that God "judges." And he never judges unjustly, even though it is impossible to ignore the difficulties and doubts in Job, Ecclesiastes, and Jeremiah. His judicial acts consist of punishment of heathen nations and sinners and protection and help for those who are faithful to him. The examples (here only for *din,* which very often is parallel to *shaphat*) can be classified. First, an individual begs God for judgment (justice) or receives it from him: Gen. 30:6; Ps. 9:5(4); 54:3(1) (par. to "help me"; RSV "save me"); 140:13(12) (par. to *mishpat*). It is noteworthy that God appears to the individual only in the role of a merciful judge. Then Yahweh judges his people Israel both in the sense of helping or vindicating them (Dt. 32:36; Ps. 135:14; Job 35:14 [the text here is disputed]) and also in that of punishing them (Isa. 3:13f.; Ps. 50:4).

b. *God Judges All Nations.* Yahweh's judgment comes, too, upon the nations and the whole earth: Gen. 15:14; 1 S. 2:10; Ps. 7:9(8); 9:9(8); 76:9(8); 96:10; 110:6; Job 36:31 (the text here is disputed). The phrase "the (heavenly) judgment took place" (*dina' yethibh*) is characteristic of the book of Daniel (Dnl. 7:10,22,26).

3. Theological Relevance.

a. *The God-Man Relationship.* Whereas in the social sphere of civic life *din* denotes the legal process, or more rarely private disputation, in a wholly literal sense, it can be used of God's judicial action only in an anthropormorphic and metaphorical sense, especially when it refers in general to the nations or the whole earth. Yahweh's appearance in the theophany is a type of judicial intervention. His just rule in righteousness and grace is a favorite motif in Is-

---

[33] See I.2 above.

rael's songs of praise and petition. [34] The use of forensic terminology shows how highly personal the God-man relationship was understood to be. If this was true already for the ancient peoples of Mesopotamia, it was true even more for Israel, where the covenant with Yahweh reflects a certain legal relationship. [35] Yahweh and his law are guiding principles for man in all legal practice and social behavior. No Israelite king could issue laws by his own power and competence, with the exception of administrative measures. Moses himself was only a mediator of divine law.

b. *The Genre "Lawsuit."* Recent exegetical literature discusses the extent to which the major genre of the prophetic "lawsuit" had its original setting in the secular legal system or in the temple cult, more specifically the dramatic celebration of the Covenant Festival.

Hamp

Against earlier scholars who thought that the prophetic accusations against Israel were borrowed from secular law, [36] Würthwein believes they were derived from a "cultic act of trial" in which "the accusation was proclaimed by a cultic official speaking in the name of Yahweh." [37] By examining certain prophetic lawsuits (Hos. 4:1f.; 12:3f.[2f.]; Isa. 3:13f.; Mic. 6:1ff.; Jer. 2:5ff.; 25:30ff.; Mal. 3:5), he shows that "the covenant faith is ... the spiritual home of these lawsuits." [38] In his view, the prophetic oracles in which Yahweh makes accusations through the prophet cannot be understood very well as an imitation of the secular lawsuit. A further observation concerning certain psalms that speak of "the appearance of Yahweh to judge" (Ps. 76:11-13 [10-12]; 98:1-9; 76:8-10 [7-9]; 50:1-7; 75; etc.) leads Würthwein to conclude that the prophetic lawsuits must have had their origin "in a cultic trial scene." [39] This thesis of the cultic origin of the prophetic lawsuit is adopted by Gunneweg. [40]

But Würthwein's thesis has also received strong opposition from Hesse, [41] and especially from Wolff, [42] Westermann, [43] Boecker, [44] and Jeremias, [45] and from others as well. Westermann contends that the psalm texts which speak of Yahweh appearing to judge should not be used as evidence for the origin of the prophetic lawsuit, because no oracles of accusation are found in these psalms.

---

[34] Gamper, 221ff.
[35] Cf. for further details *TDNT*, III, 924f. and Gamper, 233f.
[36] Gunkel, Begrich, W. Schmidt, *et al.*
[37] *ZThK*, 15 = *Wort und Existenz*, 125.
[38] *ZThK*, 8 = *Wort und Existenz*, 118.
[39] *ZThK*, 15 = *Wort und Existenz*, 125.
[40] A. H. J. Gunneweg, *Mündliche und schriftliche Tradition der vorexilischen Propheten-bücher. ... FRLANT*, 73 (1959), 81ff., esp. 114ff.; cf. also *ZThK*, 57 (1960), 1-16.
[41] F. Hesse, *ZAW*, 65 (1953), 45-53.
[42] H. W. Wolff, *EvTh*, 15 (1955), 460f.; *Hosea*, 65ff.
[43] C. Westermann, *Basic Forms of Prophetic Speech* (trans. 1967), 77-80.
[44] Boecker, esp. 91ff., 156ff.
[45] Jeremias, 151ff.

Moreover, Würthwein took into consideration only the element of accusation and disregarded the element of judgment or the announcement of judgment. Boecker develops Gunkel's understanding of Yahweh's lawsuit as a prophetic form of the reproach [46] and he traces the genre of the so-called reproach back to the accusation oracle or process accusation. [47] "The reproach establishes the sin, while the threat announces the punishment. The order can also be reversed." [48] According to Boecker, the combination of reproach and threat, which is so characteristic of the prophets, [49] had "its origin in the structure of the legal verdict, which in its complete form consists of the verdict and the ensuing sentence." [50] The identity of plaintiff and accuser, e.g., in Isa. 3:14b-15, does not indicate a cultic setting, but simply shows the special character of the accusation, [51] in which the prophet uses "I" for Yahweh (Isa. 1:2bβ; 5:4; Jer. 2:11b; Isa. 3:15). On the other hand, when, e.g., the "reproach" appears in the form of a prophetic oracle, but the "threat" in the form of an oracle of Yahweh, it must be assumed that Yahweh is the real judge. Boecker follows Wolff [52] in removing the difficulty of this juxtaposition by arguing that it is due to the "pastoral and homiletic concern" [53] of the prophet "to make Yahweh's acts acceptable to the people." [54] This is why the prophet has in many passages abandoned the pure form of the "lawsuit." [55]

E. von Waldow takes a mediating position in his historical investigation of the tradition. He thinks that prophetic lawsuits were a heterogeneous collection of accusation oracles (appeal of the plaintiff, the plaintiff's speech before the court), pleas (appeal of the defendant, speech of the accused or his special defender), and speeches of the judge. [56] There is no justification, then, for a separate genre called the "prophetic lawsuit." If prophetic lawsuits follow in expression and form the types of speech that were used in secular law at the city gate in the context of the Hebrew judiciary, the prophets must have had reasons for taking over different forms of legal address. "It can hardly be assumed that Yahweh is listed among the participants in a legal process, as plaintiff, accused, or judge, only when the prophets take over secular genres." [57] The "viewing of Yahweh's covenant with Israel in legal categories" made it possible for the prophets "to imitate in their oracles the genres which were commonly used in legal circles and in this way to initiate a process against the people and to call it to account for

---

[46] Introduction to H. Schmidt, *Die grossen Propheten. SAT*, II/2 (²1923), LXIII.
[47] Boecker, 92.
[48] *Ibid.*, 156.
[49] Cf. already H. W. Wolff, *ZAW*, 52 (1934), 1-22 = *ThB*, 22, 9-35; and Westermann, *passim*.
[50] Boecker, 157.
[51] *Ibid.*, 90f.
[52] *ZAW*, 52 (1934), 19 = *ThB*, 22, 31.
[53] Boecker, 159.
[54] Wolff.
[55] Boecker, 159.
[56] Von Waldow, 9-11.
[57] *Ibid.*, 11.

its wrongdoing as the people of God either through guilt (as defendant) or through arrogance (as plaintiff)." [58] Von Waldow, too, rejects a cultic setting, a cult liturgy with cult prophet announcing the divine judgment that is about to come on Israel. Developing the concept that the prophetic lawsuit is rooted in the covenant both legally and theologically, Huffmon understands Yahweh's accusations as covenant accusations and views one portion of the prophetic lawsuit as a covenant lawsuit; historical reflection on Yahweh's saving acts on Israel's behalf is equivalent to a historical prologue to the covenant formula, which may be regarded as the basis of the accusation. [59] Because of its form, vocabulary, and phraseology, J. Harvey sees in the rîbh-pattern of the prophetic lawsuits adaptations of the covenant formula to the particular situation of the covenant disloyalty of a vassal in contrast to the covenant loyalty of his suzerain. The Israelite tribes which settled in Palestine seem to have been familiar with these forms; and they must have been taken over at an early period (Jgs. 2:1-5; 1 S. 2:27-36) to bring the people to repentance, conversion, and covenant renewal.

Botterweck

It is best, then, to take a mediating position on this issue. In both form and content the prophetic lawsuits of the OT were dependent on the religious covenant traditions and perhaps also on the cultic covenant festivals. This does not rule out the possibility that secular legal practices and legal terminology (which were also influenced by religion) provided an additional background for the lawsuits and even perhaps for covenant theology itself. [60]

Hamp

---

[58] *Ibid.*, 42.

[59] H. B. Huffmon, "The Covenant Lawsuit in the Prophets," *JBL*, 78 (1959), 285-295.

[60] A good review of the discussion of this problem is given by H. Wildberger, *BK*, X/1, 10f., and Jeremias, 151-54; cf. → רִיב *rîbh*.

דָּכָא *dākhā'*; דָּכָה *dākhāh*; דּוּך *dôkh*; דַּךְ *dakh*; דקק *dqq*; דַּק *daq*

Contents: I. The Semantic Field "To Crush, Pulverize" in Hebrew: Verb and Noun Forms, Synonyms, Word Combinations, Occurrences: 1. *dk'*; 2. *dkh*; 3. *dkk*; 4. *dwk*; 5. *dqq*. II. Etymology. III. Usage and Meaning of *dqq* and *dk'* in the OT: 1. General Survey; 2. *dqq*: a. In Everyday Usage; b. As a Figure for the Destruction of Enemies; 3. *dk'/h*: a. As a Figure for Yahweh's Victory Over the Powers of Chaos; b. As an Expression Meaning Social Oppression and Defeating the Ends of the Law; c. Yahweh, the Savior of "Those Who Are Broken"; d. The Oppressed Community As "Distressed" and "Broken"; e. The "Broken Heart"; f. The Suffering Servant of God, the "Bruised One" of Yahweh.

I. The Semantic Field "To Crush, Pulverize" in Hebrew: Verb and Noun Forms, Synonyms, Word Combinations, Occurrences.

The semantic field "to crush, pulverize > to break (dash to pieces)[1] > to oppress, abuse,"[2] is expressed in Hebrew by a group of four or five verb forms.

---

dākhā'. Chr. Barth, *Die Errettung vom Tode in den individuellen Klage- und Dankliedern des AT* (1947); E. Baumann, "Strukturuntersuchungen im Psalter I," *ZAW*, 61 (1945/48), 131-36; W. Beyerlin, *Die Rettung der Bedrängten in den Feindpsalmen der Einzelnen auf institutionelle Zusammenhänge untersucht. FRLANT*, 99 (1970); G. J. Botterweck, → אביון *'ebhyôn; idem*, "Die soziale Kritik des Propheten Amos," *Festschrift Höffner* (1970), 39-58; S. T. Byington, "Hebrew Marginalia III," *JBL*, 64 (1945), 339-347; F. M. Cross-D. N. Freedman, "A Royal Song of Thanksgiving," *JBL*, 72 (1953), 16ff.; M. Dahood, "Ugaritic-Hebrew Syntax and Style," *UF*, 1 (1969), 15-36; St. Damaskinos, "Ps. 51 As a Result of the Prophetic Proclamation," *Festschrift Vellas* (in modern Greek) (1969), 226-239; G. R. Driver, *Problems of the Hebrew Verbal System* (Edinburgh, 1936); J.-B. Dumortier, "Un Rituel d'Intronisation: Le Ps. LXXXIX 2-38," *VT*, 22 (1972), 176-196; O. Eissfeldt, "Gott und Meer in der Bibel," *Festschrift J. Pedersen* (1958), 76-84; G. Fohrer, "Stellvertretung und Schuldopfer in Jesaja 52,13–53,12 vor dem Hintergrund des Alten Testaments und des Alten Orients," *Das Kreuz Jesu. Theologische Überlegungen*, ed. P. Rieger (1969), 7-31; E. J. Hamlin, "The Meaning of 'Mountains and Hills' in Isa. 41,14-16," *JNES*, 13 (1954), 185-190; J. G. Harris, *Prophetic Oracles in the Psalter* (diss., Princeton, 1970); P. Humbert, "*qānā* en Hébreu biblique," *Festschrift A. Bertholet* (1950), 259-266; O. Kaiser, *Die mythische Bedeutung des Meeres in Ägypten, Ugarit und Israel. BZAW*, 78 (²1962); O. Keel, *Feinde und Gottesleugner. Studien zum Image der Widersacher in den Individualpsalmen. SBM*, 7 (1969); C. van Leeuwen, *Le développement du sens social en Israël avant l'ère chrétienne. SSN*, 1 (1955); L. J. Liebreich, "The Parable Taken from the Farmer's Labors in Isaiah 28,23-29," *Tarbiz*, 24 (1954/55), 126-28; E. Lipiński, *Le poème royal du Ps 89,1-5.20-38. CahRB*, 6 (1967); S. Moscati, "Il biconsonantismo nelle lingue semitiche," *Bibl*, 28 (1947), 113-135; S. Mowinckel, *Psalmenstudien*, III (1923), 34ff.; G. von Rad, "Erwägungen zu den Königspsalmen," *ZAW*, 58 (1940/41), 216-222; E. Rohland, *Die Bedeutung der Erwählungstraditionen Israels für die Eschatologie der alttestamentlichen Propheten* (diss., Heidelberg, 1956), 216ff.; H. Schmidt, *Das Gebet der Angeklagten im AT. BZAW*, 49 (1928); A. Schoors, "Arrièrefonds historique et critique d'authenticité des textes deuteró-isaiens," *Orientalia Lovaniensia Periodica*, 2 (1971), 105-135; H.-M. Weil, "Exégèse d'Isaïe 3,1-15," *RB*, 49 (1940), 76-85.

[1] *KBL³*, 212.
[2] *GesB*, 161f.

1. *dk'*. The verb *dk'* appears 18 times in the OT: twice each in Isaiah and Trito-Isaiah, once in Jeremiah, 4 times in the Psalms, 6 times in Job, and once each in Proverbs, Ecclesiastes, and Ben Sirach. Two noun forms are built on the root: *dakkā'* I, "crushed, contrite" (twice in Deutero-Isaiah, Ps. 34:19 [Eng. v. 18])—"crushed > dust > land of death(?)" (Ps. 90:3; cf. Gen. 3:19),[3] and *dakkā'* II in *petsua'-dakka'*, "he whose testicles are crushed" (Dt. 23:2[1]). Thus *dk'* and its derivatives are found only in prophetic and poetic texts, most of which are relatively late (exilic/postexilic)—except in Isaiah (Isa. 3:15 is certainly old, but 19:10 is very controversial), in the old *mashal* in Prov. 22:22 (cf. Amenemope 4:4f.),[4] and in Ps. 72 and 89 (once). *dakka'* II in Dt. 23:2(1) is also an exception, as it has been handed down in a small corpus of ancient Yahwistic sacral laws (Dt. 23:2-9[1-8]).[5] The frequent occurrence of this root in Trito-Isaiah (4 times), Job (6 times), and Psalms (6 times) is striking. The following roots appear in parallelism with or as synonyms of *dk'* in the OT: *tachan*, "to grind" (Isa. 3:15; cf. Nu. 11:8—E); → שבר *shābhar*, "to break in pieces, break, crush" (Ps. 34:19[18]; 51:19[17]); → נכה *nākhāh*, "to smite" (Isa. 53:4—in the sense of a very serious injury);[6] → נגע *nagha'*, "to strike, smite" (Isa. 53:4); → חלל *chālal* II[7] = *chālal* I, "desecrated, defamed" (RSV "wounded") (Isa. 53:5; cf. Ps. 89:11[10]);[8] → עשק *'āshaq*, "to oppress" (Ps. 72:4); → ענה *'ānāh* II, "to oppress, humble" (RSV "afflict") (Isa. 53:4; Ps. 94:5); and → שפל *shāphal*, "to bring low, humble" (Isa. 57:15—twice). Fixed formulas with *dk'* are: *lebh nidhka'im*, "the heart of the contrite" (Isa. 57:15—par. to *ruach shephalim*, "the spirit of the humble"), *lebh (nishbar ve)nidhkeh*, "a (broken and) contrite heart" (Ps. 51:19[17]—par. to *ruach nishbarah*, "a broken spirit"), and *dakke'e ruach*, "crushed in spirit" (Ps. 34:19[18]—par. to *nishbere lebh*, "brokenhearted"). The LXX uses a wide variety of renderings: *tapeinoún*, "to humble" (always in the Psalms), *paíein*, "to strike, hit," *titrṓskein*, "to wound, injure," *kathaireín*, "to bring down, lower, destroy," *syntríbein*, "to break, crush," *malakízesthai*, "to be soft, weak," *kolabrízesthai*, "to mock, ridicule," *kakeín*, "to harm, mistreat," *adikeín*, "to do wrong, injure," and *atimázein*, "to dishonor, insult."

2. *dkh*. *dkh* is identical with *dk'*.[9] *dkh* appears only in the Psalms (6 times), and possibly also in Prov. 26:28, if *dakkayv* can be connected with *dokhi*, "crushing, pounding" (Ps. 93:3; cf. 1QS 3:9)[10]—the text is uncertain. The derivatives

---

3 H. W. Haussig, *WbMyth*, I (1965), 131.

4 *ANET*, 422a.

5 Cf. K. Galling, "Das Gemeindegesetz in Dt. 23," *Festschrift A. Bertholet* (1950), 176ff.

6 Cf. J. Scharbert, *Der Schmerz im AT. BBB*, 8 (1955), 98, n. 39.

7 *KBL*.

8 Hertlein, *ZAW*, 38 (1919/20), 127; Gunkel, *Einl. in die Psalmen* (1933), 390f.

9 *KBL*³, 212; on the formation of the weak roots III. *h* < III.' < III. *y*, cf. V. Christian, *Untersuchungen zur Laut- und Formenlehre des Hebräischen* (1953), 101f.; but this may simply be a matter of an orthographic variant.

10 Ringgren; otherwise Gemser, who reads *b'lyv*.

of *dkh* are *dakkah*, "crushed" (Ps. 10:10, but the text is uncertain)[11]—*dakka'* I,[12] and *dky* (*dokhi*, "crushing, pounding," Ps. 93:3; 1QS 3:9).[13] The LXX translates *dkh* uniformly by *tapeinoún*, "to humble"; Ps. 9:30 = 10:10 in the MT reads *enedreúein*, "to lie in wait for," and *dky* in Ps. 93:3 is not translated.

3. *dkk*. *dakh* is the noun form of an inferred verbal root *dkk*. It occurs five times in the OT: four times in the Psalms, and once in Ben Sirach. Thomas' conjecture that *derakhim*, "ways," should be emended to *dekhakhim*, and then translated: "On (every) sand-flat shall they graze . . . ,"[14] should be treated with some caution. The following words appear in parallelism with or as synonyms of *dk(k)* in the OT: → עָנִי *'ānî*, "the afflicted" (Ps. 10:12; 74:21); → יתום *yāthôm*, "the fatherless" (Ps. 10:18); and → אביון *'ebhyôn*, "the needy" (Ps. 74:21). The LXX translates *dkk* by *tapeinós*, "the poor," *tetapeinōménos*, "the humbled," and *pénēs*, "the needy."

4. *dwk*. *dwk*, "to pulverize," occurs three times in the OT: Nu. 11:18 (E); Job 40:12 (conjec.), and in *medhokhah*, "(that in which something is pulverized) > mortar" (Nu. 11:8). The LXX translates *dwk* by *tríbein*, "to grind down," and *sḗpein*, "to cause to rot or decay."

5. *dqq*. It is very probable that *dqq* and its derivatives are connected with these four verbs. The verb *dqq*, "to crush > to be ground up fine > to pulverize," appears 13 times in the OT: twice in Exodus, once in Deuteronomy, once in 2 Samuel, twice in 2 Kings, 3 times in Isaiah, once in Micah, and 3 times in Chronicles. The noun form *daq*, "flat, even, thin > fine > delicate," is found 14 times in the OT: 6 times in Genesis, twice in Exodus, 3 times in Leviticus, and once each in 1 Kings, Isaiah, and Deutero-Isaiah. The origin and meaning of *doq* (Isa. 40:22) is as uncertain as ever; it is usually translated "(something thin) > veil, gauze."[15] The LXX translates *dqq* by *leptýnein*, "to make thin," *katakóptein*, "to beat, bruise" (2 Ch. 15:16; 34:7), *daq* always by *leptós*, "thin," and *doq* by *karáma*, "having an arched cover."

II. Etymology. The etymology of these verbs, and especially the task of determining how they are related to one another, is very problematic and is much debated among scholars.

It is fairly certain that *dqq* is related to Akk. *daqqu* or *duqququ*.[16] According

---

[11] Cf. Kraus, *BK*, XV/1, 76.
[12] Not *dakka'* II, as *KBL*[3], 212 assumes.
[13] On this form cf. *BL*, 577h, i; cf. perhaps also Phoen. *dky*, *LidzEph*, III, 109; *DISO*, 57, which, of course, is very controversial.
[14] D. W. Thomas, *JTS*, 19 (1968), 203f.
[15] *KBL*[3]; cf. the comms.
[16] *CAD*, III, 190.

to *CAD*,[17] the latter should be connected with *dakāku* B.[18] *dqq* also is probably related to Ugar. *dqq*,[19] Pun. *dq*,[20] Egyp. *dqq*(?),[21] Arab. *daqqa*, Soqotri *dqq*, Mehri *duqq*, Šḫauri *deqq*,[22] Ethiop. *daqqaqa*,[23] Amharic *daqaqa*, and Tigr. *daqqa*.[24] It is interesting that Heb. *dqq* in Ex. 30:36; Lev. 16:12; and Isa. 28:28 has the same meaning as *dukh*;[25] cf. also Akk. *duqququ* in the expression *ana bulluṭišu Ú ḫašâna SIM.GAM.GAM. ina abatti tu-daq-qaq*,[26] and Pun. *dq*.[27]

dukh, "to pulverize (in a mortar),"[28] is, according to *AHw*,[29] related to Akk. *dâku* or *duâku*, but these Akkadian words have a different meaning.[30] For this reason one should consider the possibility that *dukh* is related to Akk. *sâku* or *zâku*.[31] Then Heb. *medhokhah* would correspond to Akk. *mas(z)ūktu* (cf. Akk. *madakku*, but this word is to be derived from *dakāku* I or B[32] rather than from *dâku*),[33] and Arab. *midakk*. Possibly Arab. *dāka*, "to pulverize," also belongs here.

dakh is a noun form of a verb *dakhakh* (which does not occur in Hebrew), and means "oppressed, miserable,"[34] cf. Aram. *dakhdekh*, "struck down, humbled," and Ethiop. *dgdg*, "miserable, thin." Heb. *dak(k)* corresponds to Akk. *dakāku* I[35] or B,[36] "to pulverize," which, interestingly, in the D stem means the same thing as Heb. *dwk*: *ina urṣi tu-dak(-kak)*.[37] Tigr. *dakäka*[38] and Arab. *dakka*, "to crush, destroy," probably also belong here.

dk' and *dkh* correspond to Old South Arab. *dkw*,[39] and possibly also to Ugar. *dky*: *yṣhd b'l bn 'ṯrt rbm ymḫṣ bktp dkym ymḫṣ bṣmd*.[40] *dky*, a divine epithet,[41] is a noun form of a verb *dk*, "to compound."[42]

---

17 *CAD*, III, 34.
18 See below.
19 *CTA*, 34, 1, 15; 35, 3, 29; 36, 9, 12; App II, 15; App II, 32; etc.
20 *KAI*, I, 76 B.6.
21 *WbÄS*, V, 494.
22 W. Leslau, *Lexique soqotri* (Paris, 1938), 133.
23 Dillmann, *Lexicon Linguae Aethiopicae* (1865), 1099.
24 *TigrWb*, 525.
25 See below.
26 *AMT*, 41, 36; cf. *CAD*, III, 190.
27 *KAI*, I, 76 B.5f.
28 *KBL*³, 207f.
29 *AHw*, 152.
30 Cf. *CAD*, III, 35-45.
31 *CAD*, III, 43.
32 See below.
33 Cf. *CAD*, III, 43.
34 *KBL*³, 212.
35 *AHw*, 151.
36 *CAD*, III, 34.
37 *AMT*, 24, 3, 14.
38 W. Leslau, *Contributions*, 17.
39 A. Jamme, *Sabaean Inscriptions from Maḥram Bilqîs [Mârib]* (Baltimore, 1962), 631.27; 665.17, 19.
40 *CTA*, 6 [I AB], 5, 1-3.
41 Dumortier, 180, n. 5.
42 Cf. *CTA*, 5 [I* AB], 3, 8; 6 [I AB], 5, 3; 160 [55], 5, 7, 9, 14; etc.

III. Usage and Meaning of dqq and dk᾽ in the OT.

1. *General Survey.* A survey of the occurrences and uses of the verb and noun forms of the root *dk/dq* in the OT gives the following picture.

a. *dq* and its derivatives are found predominantly in the Pentateuch and the books of Samuel and Kings (in Chronicles in parallel passages). The root appears a few times in the prophetic literature (only in Isaiah, Deutero-Isaiah, and the isolated Zion oracle in Mic. 4:13, which presumably is influenced by Deutero-Isaiah),[43] and only once in the proverbial and psalm poetry, viz., at 2 S. 22:43 (=Ps. 18:43 [42]) in a thanksgiving hymn whose poetic form and content date it in the early monarchical period.[44] The term does not seem to be known in the rest of the poetic literature of the OT. By way of contrast, it is precisely in this literature that *dk* and derivatives are especially frequent, above all in the Psalms, where 16 of the total 35 OT instances are to be found. Apart from Pss. 72 and 89 the occurrences are in exilic and postexilic psalms. Corresponding to these findings is the striking frequent use in Trito-Isaiah. This raises the question whether Trito-Isaiah borrowed liturgical formulas here (perhaps the "heart of the contrite" in Isa. 57:15), or whether he for his part influenced the liturgical language of the Psalms (cf. Ps. 51:19[17]), a question that has not yet been answered convincingly either way.[45] In early prophecy, *dk* is found only once in Isaiah (Isa. 3:15), or possibly twice (19:10) if, with Procksch *et al.*, we assign the oracle against Egypt in 19:1-15 to Isaiah, which is, of course, very controversial. Apparently these terms are unknown in the Pentateuch (with the exception of Nu. 11:8 [E] and Dt. 23:2[1]) and in the two great historical works, those of the Deuteronomistic school and the Chronicler.

b. An examination of the nouns built from the verb forms of the roots *dk* and *dq* sheds light on the semantic difference between *dk᾽*, *dkh*, *dk(k)*, and (*dwk*) on the one hand, and *dqq*, *dq*, and (*dwk*) on the other. If a form of *dk* is used as a verbal phrase in a sentence, a personal term usually appears as its subject, referring to a small, specifically defined group, viz., Yahweh (Ps. 44:20[19]; 51:10 [8]; 89:11[10]—addressed as "thou" in Job 6:9; 34:25), the king as Yahweh's representative (Ps. 72:4; cf. Job 40:12), and on the other side enemies (of the people—Lam. 3:34; or of the individual—Ps. 143:3), the arrogant and evil-doers (Ps. 94:5), and leaders who stand over against the people as enemies (Isa. 3:15; cf. Mic. 2:8). As an apparent exception one might cite the friends in Job 19:2, but in this context these are in some sense to be understood as enemies of the individual. In any case, the object of *dk* is a personal term which always represents a specific group through its nominal references to the person of the subject and which is then placed in a whole concrete relationship to the subject

---

[43] Cf. Th. Lescow, "Redaktionsgeschichtliche Analyse von Micha 1-5," *ZAW*, 84 (1972), 66f.

[44] W. F. Albright, *Archaeology and the Religion of Israel* (⁴1956), 129. Cross-Freedman, 16ff., call attention to Canaanite parallels.

[45] Cf. Elliger, *BWANT*, 4/11 (1933), 281f.

by the particular form of *dk,* which can be determined semantically by the characteristics of the verb form of *dk.* This object of *dk* may be the people (Isa. 3:15—with the 1st person sing. suf. "my people"; Ps. 94:5—with the 2nd sing. suf., indicating the poet's participation in the collective lament, "thy people"; 44:20[19]—1st pl. "us"; Lam. 3:34), specific groups of people (Job 22:9—widows and fatherless), an individual (Ps. 51:10[8]—"the members" [RSV "bones"] as a portion of the body standing for the whole; similarly Ps. 143:3—"my life"; Job 6:9;19:2), and on the other side oppressors (Ps. 72:4), evildoers (Job 34:25;40:12), and Rahab as the embodiment of demonic powers hostile to God (Ps. 89:11[10]; cf. 87:4; Isa. 51:9f.; Job 9:13; 26:12). [46] Thus, the following subject-object relationships can be ascertained which are always characterized in a particular way by a form of *dk:* enemies → people/individual; Yahweh → enemies; and finally Yahweh (thou) → people/individual (us/me). The only exception to this is the use of *dwk* in Nu. 11:8 (E), where the subject is a group of persons (the people) and the object is inanimate (the manna). This passage is the only existing literary indication in the OT that originally *dk* may have been used of concrete objects, and it also establishes the semantic bridge to the verb form *dqq.* The relationship between the subject and the object of *dq* is considerably different from that of *dk.* To be sure, the subject of *dq* too is usually a personal term representing a larger circle of persons who have no strong relationship to one another, viz., Moses (Ex. 32:20; cf. Dt. 9:21), the king as a type of ruler (2 S. 22:42 = Ps. 18:43 [42]), Josiah (2 K. 23:6,15 = 2 Ch. 34:4,7), Asa (2 Ch. 15:16), the maggot Jacob and the worm Israel (Isa. 41:15), [47] and the daughter of Zion (Mic. 4:13), but never Yahweh (in contrast to *dk*). In most cases, however, the object of *dqq* is inanimate: grain (Isa. 28:28), incense (Ex. 30:36; Lev. 16:12), the golden calf (Ex. 32:20; cf. Dt. 9:21), an Asherah (2 K. 23:6,15 = 2 Ch. 34:4,7), and the mountains and hills (Isa. 41:15). It is only in metaphorical language that *dqq* can also take a personal object: enemies (2 S. 22:43 = Ps. 18:43[42]) and many peoples (Mic. 4:13). But in each case the relationship between the subject and the object is not produced by nominal characteristics, but only by the projective power of *dqq,* which in selective ways puts different terms for totally unrelated and independent persons and things into a specific relationship to each other (e.g., "the worm Jacob" and "the mountains and hills"). This differs from the use of *dk,* because the relationships between the personal subjects and the personal objects in sentences where forms of *dk* appear as verbal phrases already indicate well-established relationships by their nominal characteristics (e.g., "Yahweh"— "people," or with a suf., "my people," "thy people"), relationships that in turn are characterized in a specific way for a particular case by the specific form of *dk.*

c. It should also be noted that the verb and noun forms of *dk* no longer have their original meaning (except in a single instance). Referring to God and his

---

[46] Cf. Kraus, *BK,* XV/2, 620; Gunkel, *Schöpfung und Chaos* (1895, ²1921), 33ff.

[47] Cf. Thexton, *VT,* 2 (1952), 81-83; J. Begrich, *ZAW,* 52 (1934), 87; Westermann, *ThB,* 24 (1964), 284.

people or the individual and his enemies, they now give rise to statements of specific theological relevance, whereas *dq* and its derivatives largely reflect the concrete usage of everyday life.

2. *dqq.*

a. *In Everyday Usage.* The cows that eat up the seven sleek and fat cows in Pharaoh's dream (Gen. 41:1-57) are described as *daqqoth,* i.e., they are thin, lean, impoverished, so that they are "very poor and hideous of form" (RSV "thin and gaunt," v. 20). The ears of grain that swallow up the seven plump and full ears are also called *daqqoth,* i.e., they are blighted by the east wind (vv. 6,23,27), their stalk is thin and withered, without strength or support, and the ears are empty and unfruitful. Like the other dreams in the Joseph story (37:5-10; 40), this dream contains no deeper symbolic meaning (such as the mythological idea that the cows are holy animals of the goddess Hathor and symbols of fertility, etc.). On the contrary, the cows and the ears of grain must be understood as real symbols and figurative, anticipatory representations of coming events, and the dream itself (in contrast to real dreams) must be characterized as an "artistic dream," in which what is seen is greatly stylized and lifted to a rational dimension. [48]

The latest edition of *BHK* still proposes the emendation of *daqqoth* in Gen. 41:3,4 to *raqqoth* ($<$ *rqq* II, "to be thin") as in vv. 19,20,27, but this is unnecessary in view of Ugar. *dqt,* "small cattle." [49] On the contrary, it is better to read *daqqoth* in vv. 19,20,27 with the majority of Hebrew manuscripts, the LXX, the Syriac Peshitta, and the Targum, since it is evident that a ר, *resh,* has been written by mistake for ד, *daleth.*

The manna (→ מן *mān*) with which Yahweh feeds the people in the wilderness (Ex. 16:1-36; cf. Nu. 11:4ff.) has for the Israelites the appearance of something "thin, fine" (Ex. 16:14), which lies on the ground like hoarfrost.

In order to determine cultic impurity as a result of "leprosy" (→ צרעת *tsāra'ath*), the priest is instructed to inspect the suspicious sore and to regard a reddish-white thin hair as a certain sign of the disease (Lev. 13:1-59). Again, in the list of bodily defects that exclude one from the priestly office (Lev. 21:18b-20), a *daq* (RSV "dwarf") is mentioned along with a hunchback, a leper, etc. This probably refers to a man who suffers from consumption or phthisis. His condition and his appearance call to mind the impoverished cows of Gen. 41.

In the preparation of incense, various fragrant substances are taken and ground (Ex. 30:36) (presumably in a mortar, cf. Nu. 11:8) to powder, to "small dust" (Isa. 29:5). Ex. 30:34-38 gives the formula for preparing the incense to be used in the cult. It consists of equal parts of stacte, onycha, galbanum, and frankincense. Rabbinic tractates mention mixtures of up to 16 substances.

---

[48] G. van der Leeuw, *Phänomenologie der Religion* (²1955), 528; J. Bérard, "De la légende greque à la Bible. Phaéton et les sept vaches maigres," *RHR,* 151 (1957), 221-230.
[49] *CTA,* 4 [II AB], I, 42; cf. Driver, *CML,* 92f.; etc.

According to Ex. 32:20, Moses takes the golden calf, burns it, and grinds what is left to powder (cf. Dt. 9:21). 2 K. 23:6,15 = 2 Ch. 34:4,7 use the same words to describe the destruction by Josiah of the Asherah in Jerusalem and of the Asherah and altar of Bethel. Josiah burns the Asherim and the altar and beats what is left to dust (cf. 2 Ch. 15:16).

b. *As a Figure for the Destruction of Enemies.* The grinding of spices in a mortar, and especially the violent nature of the process, can then be used as a figure for the complete and final destruction of enemies. This figure is a common one in the tradition, has a long history which extends far back into the pre-Israelite period, [50] and is widespread in the whole ancient Near East. It is often connected with a singular figure, viz., the threshing of grain (→ דוש *dûsh*) (cf. Isa. 28:28; 29:5; 41:15; Mic. 4:13). These two figures seem to overlap in Isa. 28:28. Procksch notices the discrepancy, and correctly recognizes that *dqq* is not identical with *dwš,* and that this passage cannot mean that grain "was ground before it was threshed." [51] Of course, there is no reason to emend *dqq* to *dwš.* Here, as in Isa. 41:15 and Mic. 4:13, two different figures or ideas are connected with each other or have been interchanged. [52] An undoubtedly very old example of the use of *dqq* as a figure for the destruction of enemies is found in the king's Song of Thanksgiving or of Victory in 2 S. 22 = Ps. 18. Yahweh intervenes in a powerful theophany (2 S. 22:8-16 = Ps. 18:8-16[7-15]), delivers the worshipper (who calls himself *tsaddiq,* "righteous," 2 S. 22:21ff. = Ps. 18:21ff.[20ff.]) [53] from his great oppression, and gives him a complete victory over his enemies, who, represented as foreign powers, oppress the people of God and his chosen king. Because of Yahweh's powerful intervention and gracious gift, the worshipper can now say of his enemies: "I beat them fine as dust before the wind; I cast them out (*'adhaqqem*) like the mire of the streets" (Ps. 18:43[42] = 2 S. 22:43).

This figure, combined with that of threshing, is then adopted in prophecy, where it occurs alongside a motif taken from the cult tradition, namely, that of the battle against the nations (cf. Ps. 46:5ff.; Joel 4:12[3:12]; Zec. 12:3; 14:2; Ezk. 38f.). [54] For example, in the eschatological portion (Isa. 29:5-8) of the Woe Oracle against Ariel in Isa. 29:1-8 we read that "the multitude of your foes shall be like small dust (*'abhaq daq*), and ... like passing chaff" (v. 5). Mic. 4:11-13 takes up this motif and shapes it in accordance with ideas from the election tradition, carrying over even the new type of imagery in which Hosea expresses it (Hos. 4:16; 10:11). [55] The word of God in Mic. 4:13 calls upon the daughter of Zion as Yahweh's especially equipped and chosen instrument (cf. Hos. 10:11) to execute his judgment on the peoples: "Arise and thresh (→ דוש *dûsh*), O daughter of Zion, for I will make your horn iron and your hoofs bronze; you shall beat in

---

[50] Cross-Freedman, 16ff.
[51] Procksch, *KAT,* IX/1 (1930), 367.
[52] Thexton, 81-83; Liebreich.
[53] Cf. Kraus, *BK,* XV/1, 146f.
[54] Cf. G. Wanke, *Die Zionstheologie der Korachiten. BZAW,* 97 (1966), 81-83.
[55] Cf. H. W. Wolff, *Hosea* (trans. 1974), 185.

pieces (hiphil of *dqq*) many peoples. . . . " But the goal of this final judgment is not (as, e.g., in the cultic tradition) Israel's victory and honor but simply and solely the glorification of Yahweh, to whom all peoples (including Israel) will be subjected, and whom they will honor as the Lord of the whole earth.

Some scholars have tried to understand the Deutero-Isaianic oracle of salvation in Isa. 41:14-16 in the same way. Certainly Deutero-Isaiah takes up the traditional figure of the destruction of Israel's enemies, but if he uses the same verbs "to thresh . . . to crush . . . to make like chaff," he does not have the same objects. Possibly in contrast to vv. 11ff., vv. 14-16 do not refer to enemies but to "the mountains and the hills." Volz has correctly seen that "the mountains and the hills" here are not a metaphorical representation of Israel's enemies but that Deutero-Isaiah has consciously changed the traditional picture and placed a different emphasis on the statement, as a comparison with vv. 8-13 clearly shows. [56] At the same time there is undoubtedly an intentional allusion to 40:4. Yahweh makes Israel a suitable instrument that can overcome all obstacles—which enemies have certainly set up too but above all Israel itself—and in this way return home to Yahweh. [57]

There is no doubt that in these texts *dqq* is synonymous with *dk'*. In other words, beyond its concrete everyday usage, in some texts *dqq* has taken on a theological significance such as elsewhere is true only of *dk'*. To be sure, this is limited to a few texts where *dqq* is used metaphorically for the destruction of Israel's enemies (but cf. Isa. 40:15 and 41:15!). For the rest, a variegated pattern of theological statements is produced by *dk'* and its derivatives in this sense.

3. *dk'/h.*

a. *As a Figure for Yahweh's Victory Over the Powers of Chaos.* Ps. 89:11 (10) speaks of the destruction of enemy powers. This verse is part of a hymn about Yahweh's great deeds (89:2-19[1-18]). [58] Yahweh's great deeds are, first, his choice of the Davidic dynasty (vv. 3ff.,18f.[2ff.,17f.]; cf. Isa. 55:3; Ps. 132), and then, second, his works of creation. Again and again the powerful rise of the chaos floods (Ps. 46:3ff.[2ff.]; 75:4[3]; 96:10) violently shakes the earth and threatens its stability. The entire destructive power of this primeval force is expressed by *dokhyam*, "their roaring" (Ps. 93:3), which undoubtedly is equivalent to Ugar. *dkym*. [59] Here, as in Ps. 89, we catch an echo of the motif of the mythological dragon and the battle with chaos. [60] Yahweh demonstrates his power by conquering the surging Primeval Sea (Ps. 89:10[9]). Rahab (v. 11[10]) is the monster of the Primeval Age (cf. Ps. 87:4; Isa. 51:9f.; Job 9:13; 26:12) and also the embodiment of the enemy powers that are hostile to God. Since Yahweh completely

[56] Volz, *KAT*, IX/2 (1932), 21f.
[57] Cf. Hamlin; Schoors.
[58] Cf. Kraus, *BK*, XV/2, 616; on the composition and theological conception of Ps. 89, cf. Mowinckel, 34ff.; von Rad.
[59] Cf. *CTA*, 6 [I AB], V, 1-3; Dumortier, 180, n. 5.
[60] Gunkel, *Schöpfung und Chaos*, 106ff.

destroys them (dk' in Ps. 89:11[10] is strengthened by the simile kechalal, "like a carcass,"[61] which conveys the idea that Rahab was destroyed by being mortally wounded, as in Isa. 53:5, cf. Ps. 18:15f.[14f.], he is Lord of heaven and earth and reigns on high in sovereign authority over the mighty powers of chaos (Ps. 93:4).[62]

b. *As an Expression Meaning Social Oppression and Defeating the Ends of the Law.* The wisdom teaching in Prov. 22:22 already depicts the elders and princes in their function as guardians of justice and admonishes them not to rob the poor (→ דל *dal*) (cf. Ex. 22:20f.,22,24f.[21f.,23,25f.]; Lev. 19:13; Ezk. 18:7ff.; etc.) nor to crush (piel of *dk'*) the afflicted (→ עני *'ānî*) when he seeks justice at the gate (cf. Ex. 23:1-9 [esp. v. 6]; Dt. 27:25; etc.). There can be no doubt that Prov. 22:22 carries direct reference to a maxim of ancient Near Eastern official wisdom as it was handed down, for example, in the Egyptian Wisdom of Amenemope (4:4f.).[63] Ps. 72:4 calls upon the king to defend the cause of the poor, to help the needy (→ אביון *'ebhyôn*), and to destroy (*dk'*—RSV "crush") anyone who exploits or threatens them; and then 72:2,12-14 draws a picture of the ideal ruler, who takes an interest in the poor and weak of the people and delivers them from oppression and violence. The reality, however, was very different. Under the monarchy the ruling upper classes succeeded in gaining increasing economic power, in depriving independent farmers of their original possessions, and in making these farmers dependent on them by putting them in their debt and eventually enslaving them.[64] The social criticism of the prophets (esp. Amos and Micah, but also Isaiah) then breaks out against these intolerable abuses. Isa. 3:13-15, which in vv. 14b-15 hands down a word of Yahweh in the form of an indictment before the court,[65] clearly refers to Prov. 22:22, and connects with it ideas from the Song of the Vineyard (Isa. 5:1-7). Instead of carefully tending Yahweh's vineyard, the house of Israel (v. 7), the leaders of the people have "devoured" (→ בער *b'r* IV) it. Like wicked shepherds (Jer. 12:10), they have filled their houses with things they have stolen from the poor. Oracles like Mic. 2:1ff.; Am. 2:6,7a; 5:6,10; etc., describe the complete brutality and ruthlessness of the rich toward the poor (but cf. also Isa. 5:8; 10:2). The oracle in Isa. 3:15 is no less clear and impressive. The rich crush the people as between millstones, and grind the poor as spices are ground in a mortar. In English one might say that they catch the people in the wheels of their legal trickeries and by their economic power the poor are pushed to the wall. Ps. 94 speaks of the resha'im (→ רשע

---

61 Cf. Gunkel, *Psalmen*, 386f.; Hertlein, 127.

62 Cf. J. Gray, *VT*, 6 (1956), 268ff.; Eissfeldt; Kaiser.

63 *ANET*, 422a.

64 On the historical and sociological background, cf. A. Alt, "Der Anteil des Königtums an der sozialen Entwicklung in den Reichen Israel und Juda," *KlSchr*, III (1959), 348-372; H. Donner, "Die soziale Botschaft der Propheten im Lichte der Gesellschaftsordnung in Israel," *OrAnt*, 2 (1963), 229-245; G. J. Botterweck, → אביון *'ebhyôn*, with extensive literature; *idem*, "Soziale Kritik," with additional literature.

65 Wildberger, *BK*, X/1, 131.

rāshā‘), "the wicked" (v. 3), the *ge'im* (→ גאה *gē'eh*), "the proud" (v. 2), and the *po‘ale 'aven* (→ און *'āven*), "the evildoers" (v. 4), who trample upon Yahweh's people by slaying the widows and aliens and murdering the fatherless (vv. 5f.). In addition to economic exploitation and social oppression, bending the law and judicial murder destroy the people of God.

c. *Yahweh, the Savior of "Those Who Are Broken."* Ps. 9:10(9) calls the one who is exploited and deprived of his rights *dakh*, "the oppressed." In the Individual Laments in the Psalms, "the oppressed" appears in a list with the → עָנִי *'ānî*, "afflicted" (Ps. 10:12; 74:21—elements of the Individual Lament are taken up into this National Lament; cf. also 9:19[18]; 10:2,9; 14:6[5]; 18:28 [27]; 68:11[10]; 72:2; 74:19; etc.), the → אביון *'ebhyôn*, "needy" (74:21; [66] cf. 40:18[17]; 70:6[5]; 72:4; 86:1; 109:22), and the → יתום *yāthôm*, "fatherless" (10:18; cf. 10:14; 109:12). In a more intimate or more remote context, the → ענו *'ānāv*, "afflicted or meek" (9:13[12]; 10:17; etc.), the → דל *dal*, "poor or needy" (41:2[1]; 72:13; 82:3f.), and the *chelkhah*, "innocent or hapless" (10:8,10,14), also belong to this group.

chelkhah appears in the OT only in Ps. 10:8,10(pl.),14. The origin and meaning of this word are still uncertain. Even the Masoretes did not understand its meaning and pointed it artificially *chelekha*, "thy army" (v. 8), or *chel ka'im*, "army of weary ones" (v. 10). Most scholars maintain the pointing *chelkhāh* and conjecture with the LXX that it means "poor, miserable." Gunkel derives it from a root *hlk*, "poor, miserable," [67] but this root does not occur anywhere. Recently attempts have been made to connect it with Arab. *halaka* [68] <*hilikkā'u*, [69] "to be black," whence Heb. **hlk*, "dark, miserable," [70] but this does not shed much light on the matter. Even less convincing is the argument of Komlós, [71] who, in agreement with Wallenstein, tries to determine the meaning of the word in Ps. 10 on the basis of its occurrences in the Qumran texts. There, however, *chelkhah* is synonymous with *resha‘im*, "evildoers." To conclude from this that *chelkhah* means "miserable" poses real difficulties. Perhaps it is best to assume that *chelkhah* or *chelkha'im* is corrupt. Then any attempt to restore the original reading will have to begin with the more intimate or more remote context. There is a verb form of *dk'* in 10:10a, though the text is not in order. If we agree with Gunkel's view that 10:10 deals with the fate of the oppressed, who are forced to suffer under the violent acts of evildoers, and in accordance with this we follow his restoration of the text, then v. 10a says: "the (righteous one?) will be struck down...." In vv. 12 and 18, *dakh* is used in synonymous parallelism with *‘anayim*, "the afflicted," and *yathom*, "the fatherless." But in vv. 14 and 8, *chelkhah* is used in parallelism with *yathom*, "the fatherless," and *naqi*, "the in-

---

[66] See above.
[67] Gunkel, *Psalmen*, 38.
[68] Wallenstein, "Some Lexical Material in the Judean Scrolls," *VT*, 4 (1954), 213f.
[69] Cf. Peters, *OLZ*, 45 (1942), 274ff.
[70] *KBL*³, 360.
[71] O. Komlós, "The Meaning of חלכאים־חלכה," *JSS*, 2 (1957), 243-46.

nocent." In light of this, it may be conjectured with some caution that *chelkhah* or *chelkha'im* is a corrupt form from *dk'/h*, and thus it may be better to read *dakhah* or *nidhkah*, "bruised or crushed," in vv. 8 and 14 (cf. Isa. 53:10), and *nidhka'im*, "contrite," in v. 10 (cf. Isa. 57:15; Sir. 12:5).

These "broken," "miserable," "helpless," "small," "weak," and "poor" people certainly do not compose separate groups, much less factions in Israel, [72] but, as Mowinckel has argued, they are "real suffering people," the victims of their "enemies." According to Ps. 143:3, it is the enemy (→ אויב *'ôyēbh*) who pursues the psalmist and crushes (*dk'*) his life to the ground. He appears in many forms: as the evildoer or the wicked (Ps. 9:6,17f.[5,16f.]; 10:4; etc.), as the hater (9:4 [3]; etc.), the persecutor (35:3), etc. Figures and concepts from the spheres of hunting, war, chaos, and the underworld are used to characterize and to illustrate the dangerous and wholly malicious nature of his actions. The affliction that the enemy brings on the psalmist is also portrayed in many different forms, especially oppression and illness (40:13[12]; 69:18[17]; 109:22; etc.), loneliness and nearness to death (9:14[13]; 86:13; etc.). Since there is no one to see that justice is done to him, or to help him in his affliction, and since his closest relatives regard him as a stranger (69:9[8]) and he hopes in vain even for a word of comfort (69:21[20]), in his distress he turns to Yahweh, flees like all the poor and afflicted to the temple, and entreats Yahweh for help, for mighty intervention against his enemies, and for a reversal of his distress. What binds the poor, the miserable, and the broken to one another is their turning to Yahweh, and their knowledge that he alone gives help and deliverance—salvation. This knowledge of all the poor and afflicted, of all the miserable and broken in all ages, is based on the certainty of faith that Yahweh is good (86:5) and gracious (9:14[13]), abounding in steadfast love (69:14,17[13,16]) and faithfulness (86:15), slow to anger (86:15), and merciful (69:17[16]; 86:15). Therefore Yahweh is a refuge of deliverance (RSV "strong deliverer," 140:8[7]), the hope of the miserable, who does not forget the weak (9:13,19[12,18]), a stronghold of the broken (RSV "oppressed," 9:10[9]).

d. *The Oppressed Community As "Distressed" and "Broken."* Along with material from the ancient cultic tradition, ideas and concepts from the Individual Lament then make their way into the Laments which were sung in the regular celebrations of repentance and lamentation of the exilic and postexilic community (cf. Jer. 41:5ff.; Zec. 7:1ff.; 8:18ff.). The catastrophe of 587 B.C. and the bleak circumstances in the land after the return are reflected in these songs. The community sees itself exposed to the caprice of its enemies without any defense or help. These enemies are described in ideas and figures borrowed from the Individual Laments (Ps. 74:18,22; etc.). Everywhere they "crush" prisoners under foot (Lam. 3:34) and they oppress the people without any reason. The community sees itself exposed to the derision and scorn of its neighbors (Ps. 44:14-17 [13-16]) and a general condition of injustice prevails. But much more serious than this external affliction is the internal religious distress of the community, for all

---

[72] → אביון *'ebhyôn* with literature.

this takes place unhindered "in the presence of the Most High" (Lam. 3:35), whose powerful deeds in primeval times and in history had once been told by the fathers (Ps. 44:2-4[1-3]; cf. 78:3f.; also Ex. 10:1f.; 12:26f.; Dt. 6:20ff.). But now, it seems, God has forsaken and rejected the "sheep of his pasture" (Ps. 74:1; cf. Jer. 23:1ff.; Ps. 79:13; 95:7; 100:3), his "chosen people" "of old" (Ps. 74:2). So there are not absent in the community voices that call into question God's sovereign power (78:18; cf. 14:1). In this distress, which is characterized by external affliction and internal religious turmoil, the community turns to Yahweh for help with complaints and petitions. This community, which is afflicted and troubled in faith, sees itself now as the "poor," the "needy," and the "downtrodden" (74:21), for whom Yahweh is at all times—and therefore now also—a stronghold (9:10[9]) and a strong deliverer (140:8[7]).

e. *The "Broken Heart."* In the theological reflection of exilic and postexilic prophecy, especially in Trito-Isaiah, the idea of being broken takes on an added dimension which is then preserved in the Laments (e.g., Lam. 1:18,20; 3:40-42; 4:22) and especially in the Individual Penitential Psalms. The suffering of man, whether it be the individual or the nation, is ultimately and properly separation from God. In affliction at the hand of enemies, in sickness, and in nearness to death, he experiences remoteness from God and abandonment by him at the deepest level. He recognizes that the reason for this is sin, his sins against God and man. These stand clearly before the eyes of the psalmist (Ps. 51:5[4]; cf. Isa. 59:12); they weigh down heavily upon him like a heavy burden (Ps. 38:5[4]; cf. Ps. 32); they hang over his head (38:5[4]). The psalmist sees his sin radically interwoven with his existence (51:8[6]; cf. Gen. 8:21; Jer. 17:9; Job 14:4; 15:14f.; 25:4ff.; Ps. 143:2). Standing under the heavy burden of sin, he turns to Yahweh with an unrestricted confession of his guilt and a prayer that it might be blotted out (Ps. 51:3[1]; cf. Nu. 5:23; Isa. 43:25; Ps. 109:14) [73] and cleansed (51:9[7]). Coupled with this petition is another for a wonderful new creation, for a clean heart and a steadfast spirit (51:12[10]; cf. Jer. 24:7; 31:33; 32:39; Ezk. 11:19; 36:25ff.). Only God's free, creative act (→ ברא *bārā'*, cf. Gen. 1:1; Isa. 65:18) can overcome the intolerable situation of man's separation from God through sin and renew the heart of man. This new disposition of the man who has been set free from sin and guilt and reconciled to God consists in a complete surrender to Yahweh with a broken spirit and contrite heart, which is much more acceptable to Yahweh than all sacrifices (Ps. 51:19[17]; cf. Am. 5:22; Isa. 1:11; Jer. 6:20; etc.).

f. *The Suffering Servant of God, the "Bruised One" of Yahweh.* The idea of man's complete surrender to Yahweh with a broken spirit and contrite heart finds a distinctive development and new significance in the figure of the suffering Servant of the Lord (Isa. 52:13–53:12). It does so through its combination with the motif of vicarious suffering. This servant takes upon himself the sin of

---

[73] H. Zimmern, in E. Schrader, *Die Keilinschriften und das AT* (³1903), 402.

others and sickness and suffering as its consequences. He who is disfigured by sickness and bowed down and bruised by the burden of an excruciating suffering bears the sin and guilt of others and thus procures salvation for them by his vicarious atonement. Yahweh is pleased "to bruise him" (53:10), [74] and causes his work to prosper (52:13); this is unprecedented and incredible. Yahweh will lift up this bruised and broken one (52:13). [75]

Fuhs

---

[74] Cf. Elliger, 7f.
[75] Cf. E. Fascher, *Jes. 53* (1958); H. W. Hertzberg, "Die 'Abtrünnigen' und die 'Vielen', ein Beitrag zu Jes 53," *Festschrift W. Rudolph* (1961), 97-108; S. Mowinckel, *He That Cometh* (²1959), 187-260; J. Scharbert, "Stellvertretendes Sühneleiden in den Ebed-Jahwe-Liedern und in altorientalischen Ritual-texten," *BZ*, N.F. 2 (1958), 190-213.

דַּל *dal;* דָּלַל *dālal;* דַּלָּה *dallāh;* זָלַל *zālal*

Contents: I. 1. Etymology; 2. Extrabiblical Occurrences; 3. *zll*; 4. Biblical Occurrences; 5. Word Combinations; 6. In the LXX. II. 1. *dal* As a Term for a Psychosomatic Constitution of Men and Animals; 2. *dal* As a Social Concept in the Book of the Covenant and the Priestly Code; 3. Form of the Tribal Ethos in the Wisdom Thought of the Early Monarchical Period. III. 1. Intensification of Socio-Ethical Statements by Amos; 2. Wrong Social Behavior As a Consequence of Human Hubris in Isaiah; 3. a. Israel As *dallim* in Post-Isaianic Traditions; b. "The Remnant" in Zephaniah. IV. 1. *dallim* As the "Lower Stratum of the People" Detached from the Social Ethos in Jeremiah; 2. *dallim* and *dallah* in the Post-Jeremian Exilic Tradition. V. 1. The *dallim* Under the Protection of Yahweh, King, and Fellow Men (Psalms); 2. The *dallim* Under the Protection of the Righteousness of God (Job); 3. In Ben Sirach. VI. *dalal*.

I. 1. *Etymology.* The root *dl(l)*, Heb. *dll* I (to be distinguished from *dll* II, "to hang," *dll* III, "to praise," *dlh* I, "to draw," and *dlh* II, "to hang" [1]), is found in most Semitic languages. In the East Semitic languages, Old Assyrian (like Old Babylonian) already has the noun *dullu(m)*, "trouble, toil, misery," then "obligation to work, work, compulsory labor," [2] probably a derivative of a verb

---

dal. E. Bammel, "πτωχός, etc.," *TDNT*, VI, 885-915; G. J. Botterweck, "Die soziale Kritik des Propheten Amos," *Festschrift Höffner* (1970), 39-58; *idem*, "'Sie verkaufen den Unschuldigen um Geld'. Zur sozialen Kritik des Propheten Amos," *BiLe*, 12 (1971), 215-231; H. Brunner, "Die religiöse Wertung der Armut im Alten Ägypten," *Saeculum*, 12 (1961), 319-344; T. Donald, "The Semantic Field of Rich and Poor in the Wisdom Literature of Hebrew and Accadian," *OrAnt*, 3 (1964), 27-41; H. Donner, "Die soziale Botschaft der Propheten im Lichte der Gesellschaftsordnung in Israel," *OrAnt*, 2 (1963), 229-245; H. Ehinger, *Die Armen und die Reichen. Biblische Katechesen zu einem aktuellen Thema.*

---

[1] *KBL³*, 214ff.
[2] *AHw*, 157; *CAD*, III, 173-77.

dalālu, "to be miserable," [3] which appears in stem I only in Old Babylonian; Late Babylonian has the causative "to oppress," *dullulu,* "oppressed, oppression"; [4] and Neo-Babylonian has the variant *dullu,* "work, duty." [5] The adj. *dallu* can be demonstrated in only two passages (Neo-Assyrian and Old Babylonian) with the meaning "needy, miserable." [6] The derivation and meaning of the Late Babylonian forms *dalilu* II and *dallālu* are disputed. It is questionable whether *dallālu* I is related to Sum. *dul,* "to cover, overcome," and *dul,* "depth, sinking depression." [7] In the Canaanite sphere we find Ugar. *dl* and *dll,* [8] Heb. and Middle Heb. *dl,* "poor, needy," and *dldl,* "to become poor," causative "to weaken," *dalluth,* "poverty, need," [9] Phoen.-Pun. *dl;* [10] similarly in the Aramaic dialects: Jewish Aram. *dldl,* "to become poor," *dalīl,* "thin, sparse," [11] Syr.

Werkhefte zur Bibelarbeit, 14 (1971); J. Ellul, "Der Arme," *EvTh,* 11 (1951/52), 193-209; F. C. Fensham, "Widow, Orphan and the Poor in Ancient Near Eastern Legal and Wisdom Literature," *JNES,* 21 (1962), 129-139; A. Gamper, *Gott als Richter in Mesopotamien und im AT* (Innsbruck, 1966), esp. 156-172; A. George, "La pauvreté dans l'AT," *Lire la Bible,* 27 (Paris, 1971), 13-35; J. Gray, *The Legacy of Canaan. SVT,* 5 (²1965); *idem,* "Social Aspects of Canaanite Religion," *SVT,* 15 (1966), 170-192; W. Grundmann, "ταπεινός, etc.," *TDNT,* VIII, 1-26; E. Häusler, *Sklaven und Personen minderen Rechts im AT* (diss., Cologne, 1956); J. Hempel, *Das Ethos des AT. BZAW,* 67 (²1964); J. Jocz, "God's 'Poor' People," *Jud,* 28 (1972), 7-29; J. Kelly, "The Biblical Meaning of Poverty and Riches," *The Bible Today,* 33 (1967), 2282-2291; K. Koch, "Die Entstehung der sozialen Kritik bei den Profeten," *Probleme biblischer Theologie. Festschrift G. von Rad,* ed. H. W. Wolff (1971), 236-257; H. J. Kraus, "Die prophetische Botschaft gegen das soziale Unrecht Israels," *EvTh,* 15 (1955), 295-307 = *Biblisch-theologische Aufsätze* (1972), 120-133; *idem,* "'Anī und 'Anāw," *BK,* XV/1 (⁴1972), 82f.; A. Kuschke, "Arm und reich im AT mit besonderer Berücksichtigung der nachexilischen Zeit," *ZAW,* 57 (1939), 31-57; E. Kutsch, "Armut," *RGG³,* I (1957), 622ff.; J. A. Lucal, "God of Justice—The Prophets as Social Reformers," *The Bible Today,* 32 (1967), 2221-28; J. W. McKay, "Exodus XXIII 1-3,6-8: A Decalogue for the Administration of Justice in the City Gate," *VT,* 21 (1971), 311-325; H. van Oyen, *Ethik des AT* (1967), 75-84; J. van der Ploeg, "Les pauvres d'Israël et leur piété," *OTS,* 7 (1950), 236-270; G. von Rad, *Wisdom in Israel* (trans. 1972), 74-96; L. Ruppert, *Der leidende Gerechte. Eine motivgeschichtliche Untersuchung zum AT und zwischentestamentlichen Judentum. FzB,* 5 (1972); J. Schmidt, "Armut," *LThK,* I (1957), 878-881; A. van Selms, "Akkadian DULLU(M) as a Loan-Word in West Semitic Languages," *JNWSL,* 1 (1971), 51-58; W. S. Udick, "Reflections on the Poor of Yahwe," *The Bible Today,* 32 (1967), 2258-2262; H. E. von Waldow, "Social Responsibility and Social Structure in Early Israel," *CBQ,* 32 (1970), 182-204; G. Wanke, "Zu Grundlagen und Absicht prophetischer Sozialkritik," *KuD,* 18 (1972), 2-17; H. Wildberger, *Jesaja. BK,* X/1 (1972), 453; H. W. Wolff, *Die Stunde des Amos, Prophetie und Protest* (1969); *idem,* "Herren und Knechte, Anstösse zur Überwindung der Klassengegensätze im AT," *TrThZ,* 81 (1972), 129-139; cf. additional literature under → אֶבְיוֹן *'ebhyôn.*

[3] *AHw,* 153.
[4] *AHw,* 153, 175.
[5] *CAD,* III, 178.
[6] *AHw,* 154; *CAD,* III, 52.
[7] Deimel, *SL,* III/I, 80.
[8] Whitaker, 183; *UT,* 664; *WUS,* 744.
[9] G. H. Dalman, *Aramäisch-Neuhebräisches Handwörterbuch zu Targum, Talmud und Midrasch* (1938, 1967), 98f.
[10] *DISO,* 58.
[11] Dalman, *loc. cit.*

dallīl/dalīlā'/dᵉlīlā', "light, small," [12] Mandean *dalil* 1, "discomfort," *dulum* 1, "oppression." [13] In South Semitic this root is widespread: it appears in Arab. *ḏalla*, "to be small, despised, to be humble," *ḏalīl*, "lowly, despised, humble," *maḏalla*, "humility, submissiveness," [14] then Meḥri *he-delûl*, "be without help," Soq. *delel*, "humiliate," [15] and the isolated Old South Arab. *ḏll*, "to make low or of little worth." [16]

2. *Extrabiblical Occurrences*. a. In Akkadian, the earliest occurrences of the root for *dullum* go back into the Old Akkadian period. Here it means "trouble, oppression, distress," which penetrates to the heart, [17] causes grief, and makes the heart burn. [18] In Late Babylonian the root denotes the "misery" that comes upon the sick; [19] for sickness fills one with *dullu*. [20] In the Gilgamesh Epic, it is Enkidu for whom Gilgamesh makes the people of Uruk weep and mourn, and for whom he fills the people with *dullu*. [21] Even at an early period (Old Babylonian, Neo-Assyrian), the root takes on the concrete meaning of "work, hard work," which a person takes up, which he has to perform, [22] "forced labor." An Old Babylonian text from Elam tells how some people were set free from the forced labor (*dullu*) that the local citizens had to do. [23] Similarly a Neo-Babylonian boundary stone tells how the inhabitants of the capital were exempted from forced labor in the construction of the royal canal. [24] Nebuchadnezzar put the entire people under forced labor for the rebuilding of Etemenanki (*ina epēšu Etemenanki du-ul-lum*). [25] The expression *bēl dulli* is used for "taskmaster" only in Neo-Assyrian. [26] Much more often, from the Middle Babylonian period on, *dullu* means "work" without the intensive nuance of forced labor. It is used of the work of the artisan or the goldsmith, or of artistic work which requires the use of precious metal, fine gold, ivory, etc. [27]

In the following period (most of the examples appear in Neo-Assyrian and Neo-Babylonian), *dullu* is a general term for work of most varied types. It can be imposed as a duty (*dullu emēdu*, EnEl VI, 8), begun (*ṣabātu*), [28] done (*epēšu*), [29]

---

[12] Brockelmann, *LexSyr*, 72.

[13] *MdD*, 100, 104.

[14] Wehr, 311.

[15] Leslau, *Lexique soqotri* (1938), 128; *idem, Or*, 37 (1968), 352.

[16] ContiRossini, 129.

[17] *VAB*, VI, 89, 20.

[18] *RB*, 59 (1952), 242f.

[19] CT 38, 33, 17.

[20] A. Schollmeyer, *Sumerisch-babylonisch Hymnen und Gebete an Šamaš* (1912), 96, 18.14.

[21] A. Schott-W. von Soden, *Das Gilgamesch-Epos* (1958), 61.

[22] *MDP*, 24, 379, 8.

[23] *VAS*, 7, 67, 15.

[24] *MDP*, 2 pl 21, II.18.

[25] *VAB*, IV, 148, 3, 23.

[26] *ABL*, 885, r. 16.

[27] Cf. additional examples in *CAD*, III, 176.

[28] *VAB*, II, 4, 40, 45, 47.

[29] *Ibid.*, 20, 21f.

or neglected (*muššuru*); [30] one can run away from it [31] or finish it; [32] etc. The root is used for work in building houses and temples (*dullu ša bīt ili*; *dullu ša ᵈziqqur-rat*; *dullu ša Esagila*; *dullu ša akītu*) [33] and also for work on rivers (*dullu ša nāri*), canals (*dullu ša mušannītu*), and harbors (*dullu ša kāri*). Occasionally, the work is named after the material the worker uses: daubing work (*dullu ṭīdī*) or writing work (*dullu ṭupšarrūtu*). Metal is given to the blacksmith to work (*ana dullu*); [34] of the same type of work (*dullu qātēšu*) is that of the baker and the carpenter, which one person can teach to another. [35]

It is possible that the expression *dullu qātēšu* has an equivalent in the *dl ydyh'* of 1QGenAp 20:7f. This might be an example of the wisdom of Sarai, as van Selms assumes. [36] He renders it "ability in a trade, manual skill." [37] It seems preferable, however, to see here a connection with Aram. *dalīl*, "thin," [38] and to translate the expression "smallness, delicacy of her hands" as an example of the beauty of Sarai. [39] Moraldi reads *wdlydyh'* as one word, not two, "everything that is in her hand," "everything that she has," and understands *dl* as a crasis of *d+l*. [40]

dullu also appears in some Middle Babylonian literature as a medicinal treatment. In the sphere of secular service, the Neo-Assyrian *dullu* also means "service" for a king, a crown prince, or a country, and in the cultic sphere it denotes "temple service," the performance of sacrificial and magical rites; in this connection, sometimes *dullu* can also signify the "ritual" itself, or even the "cult." [41] Then, along with work as an obligation, in later texts *dullu* also denotes a finished piece of work, a manufactured article or product; cf., e.g., *dullu pesû*, "white (wool) product," [42] for which the customer will pay upon delivery. [43] The expression *bīt dulli* is found once in Neo-Babylonian with the meaning "place of work, workshop," then also "cultivated field." [44]

---

[30] *Ibid.*, 20.

[31] *ABL*, 49, r. 9.

[32] *ABL*, 467, r. 13.

[33] Otherwise *CAD*, III, 177.

[34] *ABL*, 1317, 4.

[35] *Texte und Materialien ... Hilprecht* (1932ff.), 2, 214, 6; etc.

[36] Van Selms, 51ff.; cf. also T. Muraoka, *RevQ*, 8 (1972), 41.

[37] Otherwise N. Avigad; Y. Yadin; H. Bardtke: "the tips of her fingers"; H. L. Ginsberg, *JNES*, 18 (1959), 147: "the work of her hands" (he appeals to the Talmud *dwyl ydyh*, "trade," *Pesaḥim* 28a).

[38] Cf. I.1.

[39] So A. Dupont-Sommer; Maier; E. Osswald, *ZAW*, 72 (1960), 13; cf. in Ugarit *CTA*, 23 [SS], 25.

[40] L. Moraldi, *I Manoscritti di Qumrān* (Turin, 1971), 622; cf. F. Rosenthal, *JNES*, 18 (1959), 84; G. Vermès, *Studia Postbiblica*, 4 (1961), 99, n. 3; J. A. Fitzmyer, *BietOr*, 18 (1966), 110f.; etc.

[41] *AHw*, 175; *CAD*, III, 177.

[42] *VAS*, VI, 71, 1; so *AHw;* otherwise *CAD:* "clean garments"; but cf. van Selms, 52, n. 4.

[43] *VAS*, VI, 12, 6.

[44] *CAD*, III, 177.

b. In addition to the scanty occurrences of the verb *dalālu*, "to be miserable," we find the adj. *dallu*, "miserable, needy" (of men in proper names), then also "inferior" (in antithesis to *damqu*, "good, of high quality"), of grain. [45] *Dullulu* appears only twice in the Late Babylonian Inscription of Esarhaddon, where it stands in parallelism with *maḫār katrê*, "bribery," [46] and means "oppression," which consists in the "suppressing of the weak" (*enšu iḫabbilu*) and their "surrendering to the strong." In a catalog of his social accomplishments, [47] Esarhaddon boasts that he had restored the *andurāru* (→ דרור *d^erôr*) of the "oppressed Babylonians" (*mārē Babili dul-lu-lu-te*), i.e., he had procured their freedom.

c. At Ugarit in particular the identification of this root poses great difficulties. According to Whitaker, the root *dll* is found in Ugaritic 18 times. [48] Of these, *PRU*, II, 46, 31; V, 117, 37; V, 72, 13; *CTA*, 119, III, 28 can be omitted from this discussion, because in these texts *dll* appears as a proper name, which according to *UT*, 665 and *PRU*, III, 258 is to be connected with the proper name *dá-li-li* (Heb. *delilah*, "Delilah") found in Ugaritic-Akkadian texts. One must assume that the root here is *dll* II. [49] In any case, the example in *CTA*, 4 [II AB], VII, 45 does not seem to belong to our root. Gordon, Virolleaud: *dll* II; Aistleitner, *WUS*, 744: *dll* III; and Driver, *CML*, 101, "send a guide for," connect it with Akk. *dayyālu*, "spy," [50] and postulate a root *dll*, "to be directed." [51] Sometimes the examples of *dl* seem to exhibit a crasis of *d + l* in the sense of *'šr lm'n*, "in order thereby to," [52] or *'šr l'*, "that (so as) not": [53] *CTA*, 3 [V AB], C, 23; cf. *CTA*, 1 [VI AB], IV, 7; 10 [IV AB], I, 3.

A group of seven examples in a ritual text reveals a formally similar structure: *CTA*, 32 [2], 8, 13, 22, 30; *CTA*, App. I, 1, 6, 16; 2, 24 (the latter is probably a duplicate of *CTA*, 32).

The difficult and controversial text *CTA*, 32, contains a corpus which is repeated four times but which is constant in its basic content. An introductory summons to the assembled citizens of Ugarit is followed by the main part of the corpus, in which a series of geographical-ethnic terms, some headed by *ꜣlp*, in interwoven parallel structure (syntactically dependent on *npy*), culminates in the list *ꜣlp. ḫbtkm. ꜣlp. mdllkm. ꜣlp. qrzbl* (?), which obviously contains verb forms. The latest research offers essentially three interpretations, each of which is based on a different explanation of the terms *npy* and *ꜣlp*.

(1) Dhorme, Aistleitner, Virolleaud, *et al.*, translate *npy* by "drive away!" and *ꜣlp* by "leader" (> Heb. *'alluph*). In the text as a whole they see a ritual in

---

45 *VAB*, VI, 155, 9.
46 R. Borger, *Die Inschriften Asarhaddons. BAfO*, 9 (1956), 12 c 9.
47 *Ibid.*, 25a.
48 Whitaker, 183.
49 Cf. *KBL*³, 213; Noth, *IPN*, 227.
50 *AHw*, 150.
51 With S. Rin, *et al.*; cf. J. C. de Moor, *AOAT*, 16 (1971), 168.
52 C. Virolleaud, *La déesse 'Anat* (Paris, 1938), 38.
53 M. Dahood, *Psalms*, II. *AB*, XVII (1968), 269; Driver, *CML*, 75.

which petitions to avert a political calamity were made to the gods, that they might drive away out of Ugarit the various territorial princes, the leaders of those "who plunder you (*ḫbtkm*), the leaders of those who despise/oppress you (*mdllkm*)."

(2) Gray explains *npy* in terms of Arab. *wfy*, and translates: "may atonement be made!"; and *ȝlp* he takes with A. Caquot as a crasis of the conjunctions *'u* and *lp* with the meaning "according to the measure of"; "vis-à-vis." [54] According to him, this text is a penitential ritual, in which atonement is to be made for different sins, thereby effecting a pacification of the nations and of those "who impoverish you (*mdllkm*)." In his view this ritual is bipartite: in the first part, atonement is made to avert a calamity brought about by external enemies and possibly consisting of exploitation and "oppression," but in the second it is made for transgression (anger, intolerance, crime).

(3) Van Selms translates *npy* by "weave, work," and *ȝlp* by "prince." [55] Viewing the entire text as a "promise of compensation," [56] or an "oracle of salvation," [57] he arrives at the interpretation that the territorial princes, like "the prince who plundered you, who inflicted hard work upon you (*mdllkm*)," will do weaving work (*npy*) for Ugarit and its inhabitants as a tribute, the type of work which is now exacted as a tribute from the citizens of Ugarit themselves.

That *dll* stands in parallelism with *ḫbt*, "to plunder, steal, rob," [58] would suggest that it has a similar meaning, perhaps "to make poor, oppress, enslave." Elsewhere also the noun *dl* means the "oppressed" whose possessions have become the spoil of others. According to *CTA*, 16 [II K], VI, 48, the oppressed will be "trampled down" (*tš*) under the feet of their enemies (cf. Am. 2:7). Yṣb sternly rebukes Keret because as king he does not prevent this oppression, dispense justice to the "needy" (*qṣr npš*, 47), or feed orphans (*ytm*, 49), but turns his back on the widow (a similar list of terms is found in Isa. 10:2; Ps. 82:3f.; Job 31:16f.; Sir. 35:13f.). In Ugarit, as everywhere in the ancient Near East, the regency of a king was essentially evaluated by his social attitude and actions in relation to the lowest stratum of the people. Thus we are told that Dan'il "sat in the opening of the gate among the nobles.... He defended the cause of the widow and procured justice for the orphan." [59] The orphan (*ytmt*) had to suffer under oppression and could thus be described also as the "oppressed." [60] At Ugarit, then, the root does not seem to be connected so much with the idea of

---

[54] J. Gray, "Social Aspects," 186-190; but otherwise in *Legacy*, 204ff.

[55] A. van Selms, *JNWSL*, 56ff.; idem, "CTA 32. A Prophetic Liturgy," *UF*, 3 (1971), 235-248; idem, "Mappam ... Poeni Sibi Vindicant," *Festschrift H. L. Gonin*, ed. D. M. Kriel (Pretoria, 1971), 191-99.

[56] Van Selms, *UF*, 3, 245.

[57] *Ibid.*, 247.

[58] *WUS*, 1002; *UT*, 927.

[59] *CTA*, 17 [II D], V, 4-8.

[60] *PRU*, II, 1, 22, 24; cf. M. Dahood, *Ugaritic-Hebrew Philology. BietOr*, 17 (1965), 25.

"poor, helpless, miserable" (→ אֶבְיוֹן *'ebhyôn*), as with that of "oppressed, enslaved, exploited." [61]

In two broken passages, scholars sometimes conjecture a *dl* form: thus, *CTA,*
23 [SS], 25 has preserved the text: *špš mǵprt dlthm,* which Aistleitner, *WUS,* 744
translates: "the sun caused her (i.e., Atrt's) tender members to become volup-
tuous" (cf. 1QGenAp 20:7f.); [62] similarly, *CTA,* 2 [III AB, A], IV, 5 is disputed:
l'rṣ ypl ǵlny wl 'pr, where Aistleitner reads *dlny*: "He who humbles me will fall
to the ground." [63]

d. The occurrences of *dl* in Phoenician-Punic are no less disputed. [64] Apparently *dl* appears with the meanings "little, small, etc.," "door," and "with,"
which has led to great confusion among the commentators. Three occurrences
of this root in Punic sacrificial tariffs [65] allow only a small margin of interpretation. In these instances, at the end of a list of decreasing tariffs, which regulates
the amount of tax given to the sacrificial priests according to the number of
sacrifices offered, it is specified that the *dl mqn'* and the *dl ṣpr* [66] do not have
to pay taxes to the high priests exceeding the value of the sacrifice itself. The
interpretations "owner of cattle, owner of poultry," [67] do not agree with the list
of decreasing tariffs and rates of taxes that are provided for this *dl.* Here, then,
dl means one who is "poor in cattle" and "poor in poultry." [68] The priesthood
does not require him to pay a tariff. It would seem that this was done in order that
the "poor" (*dl;* Phoen.-Pun. do not use *'ebhyon* or *'ani* to denote the "poor,
humble") might be able to offer a sin-offering (cf. Lev. 14:21). In *KAI,* 26 II.6;
80.1; 81.2f., *dl* could mean "faulty, damaged, damage," [69] but neither interpretation, nor the conjecture that *dl* here means "with," [70] does much to make the texts
intelligible. The interpretation of F. Rosenthal was the first to shed new light on
the difficult passage in the Karatepe Inscription. [71] Rosenthal connected *dl* with
Akk. *dullu* and translated: "work with spindles": [72] Azitawada has cleansed
the land of criminal elements, so that now a woman can peacefully do "work
with spindles" on the street, where earlier even a man was afraid to go.

---

[61] On social problems in Ugarit, cf. J. Gray, *Legacy,* 218-258; *idem,* "Social Aspects,"
172ff.

[62] But this phrase is translated differently by Virolleaud, *Syr,* 14 (1933), 133, 143, "lean
cows"; Gordon, Barton: *dlt,* "door"; Dussaud, Largement, Follet, Gaster, Driver (*CML,* 123),
and most recently L. R. Fisher, *Ras Shamra Parallels,* I. *AnOr,* 49 (1972), 407f.: *dlw,* "grapevine, tendril."

[63] In agreement with M. Montgomery, *JAOS,* 55 (1935), 274. This reading has correctly
been disputed by R. Dussaud, *Syr,* 16 (1935), 196f.; 17 (1936), 102; Gordon; Driver; *et al.*

[64] *DISO,* 58; cf. J. Friedrich, *Phön.-pun. Grammatik*[1]. *AnOr,* 32 (1951), § 308, 2, with
J. Friedrich-W. Röllig, *Phön.-pun. Grammatik*[2]. *AnOr,* 46 (1970), § 250.

[65] Marseille, *KAI,* 69.15; Carthage, *KAI,* 74.6 and *CIS,* I, 3915, 4.

[66] Only *KAI,* 69.15.

[67] *AOT,* 449; J. G. Fevrier; G. Levi della Vida; and the comm. on *CIS,* I, 3915, 4.

[68] *DISO; ANET*[3]*; KAI;* etc.

[69] *DISO* with Friedrich, *Phön.-pun. Grammatik*[1].

[70] *KAI* with Friedrich–Röllig, *Phön.-pun. Grammatik*[2].

[71] *KAI,* 26 II.6.

[72] *ANET*[3], 654, n. 4.

Van Selms thinks *dl* also means "work" (sometimes in the sense of "finished product") in *KAI,* 10.14; 13.4-6; 80.1; 81.2f.; 119.2; 145.9; 161.3; and 165.6. In some of these texts this obviously makes good sense, but it is totally unsatisfactory in *KAI,* 10.14; 145.9; and 165.6.

Thus the passages in which the root occurs with any degree of probability suggest the following nuances: poor=having little; work as performance; work as a finished product. This favors the idea that this Phoen.-Pun. word is a loan-word from the East Semitic region.

3. *zll.* A spiral form going back to the same root appears in Heb. *zll* ("to be thoughtless or inconsiderate, be despised"),[73] Syr. "contemptuous," Mandean "to be of little value, despise,"[74] but especially in the South Semitic region (Arab., Ethiop., Ge'ez, Tigr.).[75]

This verbal root, which appears in the OT particularly in forms of the qal participle, means something that is worthless either in itself (Jer. 15:19; Ps. 12:9 [Eng. v. 8]) or in the eyes of others, "despised" (Lam. 1:11). It is then used for willful behavior that "frivolously, extravagantly," intentionally diminishes true values and treats them "contemptuously" (Dt. 21:20; Prov. 23:20f.; 28:7; Sir. 18:33; Jer. 2:36—conjec.). In the hiphil, *zll* is used as an antonym of the piel of → כבד *kbd,* and means the refusal of *kabhodh* ("honor, glory"), the "disdain" that is shown for someone who is contaminated by sin (Lam. 1:8).

4. *Biblical Occurrences. dal* occurs 48 times in the OT, predominantly in poetic texts (39 times): Gen. 41:19 (E [J]); Ex. 23:3 (the Book of the Covenant), 3 times in P, 4 times in Judges-Samuel, 4 times in Amos, 5 times in Isaiah (twice in Isa. 25f.), twice in Jeremiah, once in Zephaniah, 5 times in Psalms, 15 times in Proverbs, 6 times in Job, and once in Ruth. In contrast to the more frequent → אביון *'ebhyôn* and → עני/ענו *'anî/'ānāv,* the sudden increase of frequency in the Wisdom Literature (Proverbs) of the early monarchical period (like that of *rash,* "poor") is striking, while to a large extent it goes out of use in the later poetic literature (Psalms). After the exile, the term disappears almost entirely and reappears again only in Ben Sirach (11 times).

dallah appears 5 times in the OT, exclusively in the tradition of the Babylonian exile: 2 K. 24f.; Jer. 40; 52.

dalal is found 7 times in the OT: once in Judges, and 3 times each in Isaiah and Psalms.

5. *Word Combinations.* The close synonymity of *dl* with other Hebrew terms used for "poor"[76] makes it natural that the root should be used frequently in

---

[73] *KBL³,* 261.

[74] *MdD,* 159, 168.

[75] Cf. Dillmann, *Lexicon Linguae Aethiopicae* (1865), 1033; *TigrWb,* 493b; Leslau, *Contributions,* 19; in Old South Arabic it occurs only in the causative IV stem, "to reject," and V stem, "submit," in the context of submission and subjugation: A. Jamme, *Sabaean Inscriptions from Maḥram Bilqîs* (1962), 669.21f.; 644.8.

[76] → אביון *'ebhyôn,* I.3.

synonymous parallelism with these terms (with *'ebhyon*: 1 S. 2:8; Isa. 14:30; 25:4; Am. 2:7; 4:1; 5:11; 8:6; Ps. 72:13; 82:4; 113:7; Job 5:15f.; 31:16; Prov. 14:31; with *'ani*: Isa. 10:2; 26:6; Zeph. 3:12; Ps. 72:13; 82:3; Job 34:28; Prov. 22:22; with *'anav*: Isa. 11:4; Am. 2:7; with *rash* only in Ps. 82:3). Nevertheless fixed combinations and stereotyped phrases are hard to prove with certainty. Thus *dal* occurs at Jgs. 6:15 in a formula for modesty which one encounters again in a similar form in Prov. 22:22 (in the 3rd person sing.). Its usage is governed by the situation and is thus variable: with *qaton*, "small," in Am. 7:2, 5; 1 S. 9:21; and with *na'ar qaton*, "a little child," in 1 K. 3:7b. In this formula, *dal* stands for the obviously more familiar *qaton*;[77] cf. also Ex. 23:3,6 with Dt. 1:17.[78] The expression *'ashaq dal*, "oppress the poor" (Am. 4:1; Prov. 14:31; 22:16; 28:3), and the combination *dal–'almanah–yathom*, "poor–widow–orphan," are common. Occasionally *ki dallothi me'odh*, "for I am brought very low" (Ps. 142:7[6]), and *ki dallonu me'odh*, "for we are brought very low" (79:8), are advanced as reasons for a favorable response. In a song of praise too, they explain a favorable response (116:6).

6. *In the LXX.* The LXX translates *dal* in different ways with no apparent criterion. It shows a preference for *ptōchós*, "beggarly, poor" (20 times [7 times in Sir.]), while it uses *pénēs*, "poor, needy," only 8 times (the situation is reversed in the case of *'ebhyon*). *tapeinós*, "poor, lowly," occurs 5 times, mainly in Isaiah (twice in Sir.), *adýnatos*, "powerless, impotent," 3 times (only in Job), *asthenḗs*, "weak, powerless," 3 times, *penichrós*, "poor, needy," twice, and *asebḗs*, "ungodly, impious" (in the moral explanation of Prov. 10:15), *hḗssōn*, "lesser, inferior, weaker," and *ponērós*, "sick, painful, poor," once each. It also uses forms of *pénesthai*, "to be made poor, become poor," twice; *hádros*, "strong, great, large," in Job 34:19 is a mistaken reading for *gadhol*, "great"; in Jer. 39:10 the LXX has no equivalent of *dal*. These statistics show that the LXX understood *dal* relatively often (as *'ani* 9 times, and *'anav* 6 times) in terms of being "humbly bowed down" (*tapeinós*)[79] or in terms of "physical weakness and poor health" (*asthenḗs*).[80]

In 2 Kings the LXX translates *dallah* by *ptōchós*, "beggarly, poor." It renders the verb *dalal* 3 times by *ekleípein*, "to fail, come to an end" (in Isaiah), and twice each by *tapeinoún*, "to humble, humiliate," and *ptōcheúein*, "to be poor." In Job 28:4 it links *dallu* with the root by using *asthenein*, "to be weak, sick, powerless" (although it may be conjectured with *BHK* that the correct reading here is *dalu* from the root *dalah*, "to hand, cling"). It renders the not undisputed *dlwt* in Sir. 10:31 by *ptōcheía*, "poverty."

---

[77] Cf. II.1 below.
[78] Cf. II.2 below.
[79] Cf. J. Coste, *Trois essais sur la Septante à partir du mot* ταπεινός (Lyon, 1953); S. Rehrl, *Das Problem der Demut in der profangriechischen Literatur im Vergleich zu Septuaginta und NT* (1961), 147-172; W. Grundmann, 6-10.
[80] Cf. G. Stählin, "ἀσθενής, etc.," *TDNT*, I, 490-93.

II. 1. *dal As a Term for a Psychosomatic Constitution of Men and Animals.*
dal, which appears only rarely in the ancient sources of the Pentateuch, still
reflects in one of its earliest occurrences in Gen. 41:19 (E [J]) the old valence
of the Semitic root, before it came to be restricted exclusively to men. Pharaoh
in his dream sees *paroth dalloth,* "poor cows," coming up out of the Nile, and
they eat up the seven cows that are described as *yephoth mar'eh ubheri'oth
basar,* "sleek and fat" (v. 2), *beri'oth basar viphoth to'ar,* "fat and sleek" (v. 18),
and summarily *tobhoth,* "good" (v. 26). In antithesis to these cows, the *paroth
dalloth* are characterized more precisely by expressions like "ugly in appearance
(gaunt)" (*ra'oth mar'eh*) and "lean in flesh" (thin) (*daqqoth basar*) (vv. 3f.,19,27;
read *rqwt* with *BHS*). In connection with these terms, the meaning "impoverished,
emaciated," is an apt one for *dal.* In this light the later development to "poor" is
not surprising (cf. the similar development of the meaning of *ṣ'p*). [81] While the
terms used to describe the cows and the ears in all three passages in this dream
narrative are sometimes composed of two members and sometimes of one (in the
case of the summary *tobhoth* in v. 26), three members appear only in the second
passage in the description of the lean cows and ears: *dalloth,* "poor," is added in
the allegory of the cows in v. 19, and *tsenumoth,* "withered," in the parallel allegory
of the ears in v. 23. These additional members do not have the force of an additional synonymous characterization, nor are they exaggerations, [82] but they represent attempts to explain the dreams allegorically, i.e., *dal* already suggests the years
of "emaciation" or "poverty," just as *tsenumoth* suggests the years of "drought."
The use of these terms further sharpens the contours of the picture. The instances
of *dal* in the Deuteronomistic history (except in Hannah's Song of Praise in 1 S.
2:1-10) move in the same conceptual sphere of somatic anomaly, only now transferred to man and his powers (2 S. 13:4), or to those of the tribe or clan (Jgs.
6:6,15; 2 S. 3:1). Thus *dal* is used to describe the psychosomatic weakness of
Amnon, who "is sick" (*hithchallah*) for love for his half-sister Tamar (2 S. 13:2),
and whose condition is perceived and designated by Jonadab as *dal,* here probably "miserable, weak, exhausted," as a consequence of the prior psychological
state of "almost morbid passion" (v. 4.). [83] In 2 S. 3:1 it is the *beth sha'ul,* "house
of Saul," that "becomes weaker and weaker" (*holekhim vedhallim*) as its internal
war with David becomes longer and longer, while David "grows stronger and
stronger" (*holekh vechazeq*) as a result of his military successes; both of these
expressions undoubtedly refer to military power. In Jgs. 6 warlike conflicts also
lead quickly to an "impoverishment" of the whole people, for the Midianite
attacks (vv. 3ff.) caused Israel to "become very weak" (*vayyiddal me'odh,* v. 6)
both militarily and agriculturally, especially as the Midianites, who are compared
with locusts because of their great numbers and insatiability, wasted the land
(v. 5). It is also because Israel had "become very weak" (*dalal*) (v. 6) that Gideon
uses this term in the formula of modesty when he meets the *mal'akh yhvh,* "angel
of Yahweh," at the terebinth of Ophrah (vv. 11ff.); in keeping with the situation

---

[81] L. Kopf, *VT,* 9 (1959), 254.
[82] Cf. D. B. Redford, *SVT,* 20 (1970), 79f., 87.
[83] H. W. Hertzberg, *I & II Samuel. OTL* (trans. 1964), 324.

qaton, "small," which is well known from Amos on, is replaced by *dal*, [84] in an attempt to avoid the divine commission to deliver Israel (v. 14). The precise nuance of meaning of *dal*, which occurs in synonymous parallelism to *tsaʿir*, "young, weak" (v. 15b), may be seen from its antonym in the statement of the divine messenger: "May Yahweh be with you, you mighty man of valor (*gibbor hechayil*)" (v. 12), and later (7:2ff.) in the statement that "the people are too many (*rabh*)" for the battle. This clearly shows that *dal* is related semantically to the description of a quality and not to numerical quantity. God makes use of the *dal* to achieve his great plans in the history of the chosen people, which gave the Wisdom Literature occasion for its distinctive understanding of *dal* (cf., e.g., 1 S. 2:8).

2. *dal As a Social Concept in the Book of the Covenant and the Priestly Code.* The Book of the Covenant already uses the term *dal* in a social context when in the so-called Mirror for Judges in Ex. 23:1-9 it juxtaposes the instructions not to be partial (*hadhar*) to the *dal* (MT) in his suit (v. 3), and not to pervert (hiphil of *natah*) justice due to the *'ebhyon* (v. 6). On the strength of Lev. 19:15 (P): "you shall not be partial to (*nasa' panim*) the *dal* or defer (*hadhar*) to the *gadhol*" (on the antithesis between *dal* and *gadhol*, cf. Jer. 5:4f.), and the Deuteronomic formula, "you shall hear the small and the great alike" in judgment (Dt. 1:17), *dal* in Ex. 23:3 has often been emended to *gadhol*, "great." [85] This emendation has the advantage of seeing a limit set on permissible latitude in legal decisions by prohibiting both partiality toward the great and prejudice against the poor.

In spite of the arguments of Cazelles and Koch, [86] the weight of the passages cited is so strong that this emendation must be adopted as the original text. To be sure, *dal* must have come into the MT relatively early (before the LXX). This insertion was hardly made deliberately as a rebuke against "class conflicts" [87] (it cannot be proved that there were class conflicts in the OT), [88] or even to meet the danger of attempts by mobs of the socially weak to intimidate the great (v. 2 already sees this danger). Rather, the insertion was made in an effort to find and preserve the proper degree of *tsedhaqah*, "righteousness," in the jurisdiction. This was done by emphasizing that too little righteousness and too much righteousness alike are in fact unrighteousness, as is set forth paradigmatically in vv. 3 and 6. This type of remodelling might have occurred at a time when the socially weak strata of society were regarded as the righteous ones of Yahweh and when these "poor" were granted juridical prerogatives for this reason. We occasionally encounter similar instances in the Egyptian literature too. [89] Lev. 19:15

---

84 Cf. I.5.

85 Since Knobel in 1857; cf. recently G. Wehmeier, *THAT*, I (1971), 471; → אביון *'ebhyôn*, II.2; von Waldow, 183; McKay, 316f.

86 H. Cazelles, *Études sur le Code de l'Alliance* (Paris, 1946), 87f.; and K. Koch, 247.

87 A. Menes, *BZAW*, 50 (1928), 34ff.; H. Schneider, *EB, in loc.*

88 Cf. van der Ploeg, 268; Wolff, *TrThZ*, 139.

89 Cf. Brunner, 340f.

prohibits any kind of partiality in making legal decisions and culminates with the exhortation to judge one's neighbor ('amith) "in righteousness" (betsedheq). The right conduct which God has ordained for the individual in the community is endangered when a legal decision must be made in extreme cases in which either a dal or a gadhol is arraigned. Hence the explicit selection of these two opposites should be understood as a special reference to the basic principles in far from everyday cases.

In the OT the dal is not seen fundamentally in relation to the regulations governing the Sabbatical Year, the Year of Jubilee, and letting the land lie fallow. Nor is he reckoned among the four types of dependents in the family ('ebhedh, "male slave," 'amah, "female slave," sakhir, "hired servant," and toshabh, "sojourner," Lev. 25:6). The formula also says that the dal, like the 'ashir, "rich," must pay a half-shekel as an inspection fee (Ex. 30:15). It may be concluded, then, that the dal was not numbered among dependents who have no property. This is further demonstrated by the rules laid down for the sacrificial tariff in Lev. 14:21. These show that the dal was obviously in a position to offer a lamb, a tenth (of an ephah) of fine flour, and a log of oil for a guilt-offering. [90] This is the third lowest tariff, for the OT provides two lower tariffs for those who cannot afford more (lo' thassigh yadho, Lev. 5:11), and for those who cannot afford anything (lo' thimtsa' yadhah, Lev. 12:8). Thus the dal is not adequately understood as a "proletarian who has no property," [91] or as "one who has no property." [92] Instead, the early passages in which the word appears picture him as a free and full citizen, whose "property is small," [93] who is perpetually caught up in the struggle to make a daily living by hard work, [94] who in this constant grind has to give up his independence to a large extent, and who is thus a "little man" [95] and "helpless," [96] particularly in court, where he needs special protection. Since these passages have to do with agricultural matters, it would seem that the dal was a small farmer.

3. *Form of the Tribal Ethos in the Wisdom Thought of the Early Monarchical Period.* The early wisdom thought of the early monarchical period takes over the ethos of the Book of the Covenant and of the ancient traditions that lie behind the collection in the Priestly Code, and applies it especially to the protection of the dal. The frequent occurrences of this root in collections II (15 times) and V (7 times) of the book of Proverbs, as well as its appearance in collection III (Prov. 22:22 [twice]), which is dependent on the Egyptian wisdom teaching of Amenemope, show the great importance of this question. [97] When the wisdom

---

[90] Cf. I.2.d above.
[91] R. Hentschke, *Satzung und Setzender. BWANT,* 5/3 (1963), 13.
[92] Van Oyen, 78.
[93] Koch, "Entstehung," 242.
[94] Cf. I.1 above.
[95] G. von Rad, *OT Theol,* II (trans. 1965), 135.
[96] Botterweck, → אביון *'ebhyôn.*
[97] For a study of the ideas of poverty and wealth in Proverbs, cf. → אביון *'ebhyôn,* III.

teachers use the word *dal,* they never mean people who have become poor by their own fault, e.g., through laziness (cf. Prov. 12:11,24; 13:4; 24:33f.), negligence (cf. 18:9; 19:15; etc.), or extravagance (cf. 13:18a). For this reason the "very cool and unemotional" style [98] which characterizes what is said about those who have become poor by their own fault gives place to concerned attention when the reference is to the *dal,* the *'ani,* and the *'ebhyon.* This indicates that these terms "already expressed a social responsibility," [99] as may be seen especially clearly in the emphatic reason given in Prov. 22:22 (cf. Amenemope 2, 4) for not robbing the poor, *ki dhal hu',* "because he is poor," using the vetitive. Various considerations cause the wisdom teachers to speak about the *dal:* (a) One is that his (at best few) possessions are withheld from him [100] (Prov. 14:31; 22:16; 28:8), or are even stolen from him (→ גזל *gāzal*) [101] by naked force (22:22). The wisdom teachers see in this an offense against the order of creation (14:31; cf. 22:2; 29:13), but they also (by way of comfort) see something positive for the *dal* himself, for as a result of the exploitation he receives certain advantages on the basis of Yahweh's compensatory justice (22:16). Yahweh will plead his *ribh* (cause) and take the life of those who despoil him (22:22f.). (b) It is generally recognized that a *dal* has no friends (10:15; 19:4; cf. 19:7 [*rash*]; particularly frequent in the Psalms: 41:10[9]; 116:11; 142:5[4]; etc.). This is later stated in an especially dramatic form by Ben Sirach: "When a rich man (*'ashir*) totters, he is steadied by friends, but when a humble man (*dal*) falls, he is even pushed away by friends" (Sir. 13:21). It may be asked whether such maxims belong only to a realm "where social aspects are not envisaged at all" [102] or whether they are to be understood as a call to eliminate such conditions. (c) Awareness of the connection between an action and its consequences leads to the conclusion that it is right to help the *dal,* for "he who is kind to the poor (*dal*) lends to Yahweh, and he will repay (*shillem*) him for his deed" (Prov. 19:17), and he who shares his bread with the poor (*dal*) "will be blessed" (*nibhrakh*; → ברך *bārakh*) (22:9). On the other hand, he who closes his ear to the "cry" (→ זעק *zā'aq,* used here as a legal term: the complaint of the one to whom injustice has been done) [103] of the poor (*dal*), and thus tolerates the injustice done to the *dal,* cannot expect Yahweh to hear his cry (21:13; cf. Job 34:28). (d) Belief that the compensatory justice of Yahweh operates in the world is the background for the statements in Prov. 22:16 and 28:8. (e) Wealth is no guarantee of wisdom. Self-conceit based on great possessions can only bring "contempt" (*ḥqr*) [104] from a poor man (*dal*) who has understanding (*mebhin*) (28:11). For this reason, too, the young Ruth thought it best not to choose the man who should redeem her on the basis of whether he was "poor"

---

98 Von Rad, *Wisdom,* 76.
99 Kuschke, 47.
100 For this meaning of *'ashaq,* cf. A. Phillips, *Ancient Israel's Criminal Law* (1970), 140.
101 On this term, cf. Phillips, *ibid.;* B. S. Jackson, *Theft in Early Jewish Law* (1972), 1-19.
102 So von Rad, *Wisdom,* 116.
103 Cf. W. Richter, *BBB,* 21 (1964), 18ff.
104 Cf. Kopf, *VT,* 9, 256f.

(*dal*) or "rich" (*'ashir*) (Ruth 3:10). (f) The wisdom teacher is greatly concerned to define the right behavior of the *tsaddiq* (righteous): he must not trust in riches (Prov. 11:28); he gives and does not hold back (21:26); and he has mercy on his beast (12:10). His conduct is blameless (20:7), and (knowing what it is to be deprived of justice, 18:5) he knows and "is concerned about" (*yadha'*) [105] the rights (*din*) of the poor (*dal*, 29:7a), while conversely the wicked man does "not understand such knowledge" (*lo' yabhin da'ath*, 29:7b; cf. Ps. 82:3ff.). (g) The king and ruler has an important responsibility toward the *dal*: collection V in the book of Proverbs (chaps. 28f.) deals with this point. Also intended for the king are the pronouncements of the Book of the Covenant on the duties of righteousness and incorruptibility in reaching legal decisions. All injustice, then, must be an abomination to the king (*melekh*, 16:12), and it is his glory (*kabhodh*) to search out a matter scrupulously (25:2), for on his impartial (*be'emeth*) judgment of the poor (29:14) depends the everlasting stability of his throne, which he establishes by *tsedhaqah*, "righteousness" (16:12; 25:5). Therefore one maxim given to Lemuel is that kings and princes should abstain from wine and strong drink in order that they might not pervert the rights of the *bene 'oni*, "afflicted" (31:5).

This royal ethic contains striking parallels to Ugaritic axioms. [106] Proverbs also uses "a large number of pre-Israelite, Canaanite concepts and linguistic elements," [107] and a corpus of ideas from Mesopotamian and Egyptian royal ideology. [108] Parallels to Mesopotamian law could be cited in great number, e.g., parallels to the Babylonian *mîšarum* statute, a "law for the protection of the poor, widows, and orphans." [109] The promise that one who defends the poor will have long life also appears in ancient Near Eastern literature outside the OT. [110]

While the *melekh*, "king," gives stability to the land by justice (*mishpat*) (29:4), a wicked ruler (*moshel*) brings destruction on the people and the land, and is like a rapacious beast of prey (a lion or a bear), for his subjects soon become a "lowly, poor people" (*'am dal*, 28:15; cf. Zeph. 3:3f.). A "ruler" (head, *ro'sh*) [111] who oppresses the poor (*dal*) is like a beating rain that erodes the fertile, lifegiving soil and therefore "leaves no food" (28:3).

Consequently, in the early wisdom teaching there is a growing recognition that Yahweh [112] appears as a lawyer for the lower classes, which include the *dal* now

---

[105] Cf. G. J. Botterweck, *Gott erkennen. BBB*, 2 (1951), 14.

[106] I.2.c.

[107] H. H. Schmid, *Wesen und Geschichte der Weisheit. BZAW*, 101 (1966), 169; J. Gray, "Social Aspects," *passim*.

[108] Cf. Gamper, 156ff.; Fensham, 129ff.; Brunner, *passim;* Donald, 30ff.

[109] Cf. P. Koschaker, *ZA*, 43 (1936), 220; A. Falkenstein, *Die neusumerischen Gerichtsurkunden*, I. *ABAW*, N.F. 39 (1956), 145; F. R. Kraus, *Ein Edikt des Königs Ammi-ṣaduqa* (Leiden, 1958).

[110] Cf. *SAHG*, 94; in Egypt: Instructions of Merikare, A. Volten, *Analecta Aegyptiaca*, 4 (1945), 22f.

[111] Following the emendation of B. Gemser, *HAT*, 16 (²1963), 98.

[112] In Egypt: Re; cf. The Wisdom of Amenemope, *ANET³*, 421-24; in Mesopotamia: Ninurta, cf. *BWL*, 86ff.; Shamash, cf. *BWL*, 132f.

that this word is coming to be used more and more as a synonym of ʿani and
ʾebhyon. Like these two groups, the dal enjoys great sympathy from the wisdom
teachers. [113] Even though it is quite clear that he has some personal possessions,
he still needs mercy (28:8), material help (22:9), and legal protection, especially
from the king, who is the executor of the divine will (29:14).

III. 1. *Intensification of Socio-Ethical Statements by Amos.* Amos is probably referring back to this ethos expressed in early wisdom teaching. Like the
wise men, Amos also uses dal (Am. 2:7; 4:1; 5:11; 8:6), ʾebhyon (2:6; 4:1; 5:12;
8:4,6), and ʿanav (2:7; 8:4) synonymously. He makes concrete the traditional
social ethos of the covenant law and wisdom when in his oracles he exposes
widespread sin and brings accusations against the moral decay in the time of
great economic prosperity under Jeroboam II. Undoubtedly dal in the time of
Amos still includes those who have possessions, for grain (5:11) and wine (4:1;
cf. Job 20:10) can be exacted from him. But more than ever in Amos the dal is
presented as a totally helpless person who has been handed over defenseless to
the hashshoʾaphim, "those that trample" (2:7), to the haʿosheqoth, "those who
oppress" (4:1), to the boshaskim, "those that trample" (5:11: reading contested),
and (like the ʾebhyon) to the slave-dealers (8:6). This exclusive riveting of the dal,
"small farmer," to the context of exploitation and enslavement for debt has led
many scholars to conjecture that the historical background was a reform of the
agricultural structure, the aim of which was to "bring to an end" the status of the
small farmer (8:4) and to benefit the large and lucrative landed estates. It cannot
be proved, however, that such a reform was undertaken in this period as an
"intentional action." [114] It seems more likely that the background was an anti-
social struggle by the owners of large landed estates, the stewards of the royal
domains, to expand the size of their property. [115] This struggle for expansion helps
to explain the systematic way in which the rich proceeded against the small
farmers: the exacting of exorbitant taxes (5:11), the blocking of lawsuits and
claims for compensation by bribing judges and legal maneuvering (2:6f.; Donner
even conjectures that the official upper class attempted "to subvert by administrative rulings the judicial system which had been laid down in the community
from time immemorial," [116] their aim being to exploit the law to satisfy their
own greed; cf. also Isa. 10:2)—and finally the buying up of their victims as slaves
for a paltry sum (8:6; cf. 2:6). The purpose of Amos, then, is not to maintain
the position of the small farmer. Instead, his intention is to brand the behavior
of the upper stratum of society toward the lower stratum as contrary to the will
of God. Exorbitant tax assessments are not founded on the law nor are they
necessary to finance the government; they are made because of the reprehensible
greed, gluttony, and drunkenness of the "cows of Bashan" (4:1)—an expression

---

[113] U. Skladny, *Die ältesten Spruchsammlungen in Israel* (1962), 61.
[114] K. Koch, "Entstehung," 249.
[115] Cf. Botterweck, *BiLe*, 218ff.; Kraus, "Botschaft," 123f.
[116] Donner, 236.

which probably does not refer to the women of the royal court in Samaria [117] but is an appropriate figure for rich upper class wives.[118] High taxes are also imposed because of the ostentation of the mighty, who build their vaunting palaces with wealth extorted from the poor (5:11). According to Amos, enslavement for debt, which the ancient law provides for (Ex. 21), is justified, but flagrant injustice is done when the 'ebhyon, "needy," is bought for a pair of sandals or the dal, "poor," for (an unstated amount of) silver (8:6; tsaddiq, 2:6). Since tsaddiq in 2:6 does not mean a "righteous" person, but one who is "innocent of an accusation," the phrase introduced by be ("for silver") emphasizes the paltriness of the debt, so that the selling of this man is attacked as without foundation or justification. On the other hand 8:6 (where dal is used for tsaddiq!) refers to the buying of debtors, and therefore to the purchase price, whose trifling nature betrays a culpable lack of respect for human worth. In 2:6 people owe little; in 8:6 they cost little. [119] In addition to unjustified enslavement for debt Amos sees in this whole system the evil that the "poor, weak, lowly, and innocent" are made the object of the mercantile calculations of the "early capitalistic" [120] upper class. In 2:7, too, the prophet is concerned about the lack of respect for human worth. He denounces here the turning aside of the way of the afflicted and "trampling on the head" [121] of the poor (both to be taken literally), [122] and he announces judgment as a result.

2. *Wrong Social Behavior As a Consequence of Human Hubris in Isaiah.* In the prophets after Amos statements about the dal are so rare that one can almost conclude that this social class had become extinct. Only two dal sayings can be attributed to Isaiah with any certainty (Isa. 10:2; 11:4); of these, the Woe Oracle in 10:2, from the first period of his prophetic career, is thought to be wholly in the style of Am. 2:7. In this oracle Isaiah does not primarily attack the wealthy upper stratum of society (as he does in 1:21-26; 3:14f.,16ff. [the last of these passages is directed against the wealthy wives of these men]). His target is the choqeqim, "those who decree decrees." These officials dated from the premonarchical period, when they had particular duties in connection with the holy war and the sacral act of apportioning the land.[123] In the time of Isaiah they were responsible for regulating property and inheritance laws, and perhaps also for collecting taxes and duties (Isa. 10:13f.). [124] In doing this, however, they deviated from the norm of mishpat, "justice" (the old nachalah [inheritance] law of Yah-

---

[117] W. Richter, *Recht und Ethos. StANT,* 15 (1966), 186.
[118] S. Speier, *VT,* 3 (1953), 306f.
[119] But cf. Wolff and Rudolph, comms., *in loc.,* who think these two verses mean essentially the same thing.
[120] Kraus, "Botschaft," 123.
[121] Cf. *CTA,* 16 [II K], VI, 48.
[122] Cf. the comms.
[123] Hentschke, 18f.
[124] But cf. Wildberger, *BK,* X, *in loc.*

weh) [125] in order to help the upper classes of society in their struggle to expand their holdings (Isa. 5:8: "those who join house to house, who add field to field"; cf. Mic. 2:1-5). With questionable zeal, they proclaimed (piel of *ktb*—RSV "keep writing") decrees (*chuqqim*) that were intended to legalize the unjust exaction of taxes (Isa. 10:1f.). Isaiah calls such modifications of the law *chiqeqe 'aven*, "iniquitous decrees," which no longer simply withhold justice from the *dallim* (RSV "needy") (5:23) by "turning aside" (hiphil of *natah*) their legal claims, but also make every legal claim of the *dal* a priori impossible, for they rob (*gazal*) the poor of their right. Job 20:19 also seems to allude to the same kind of activity when it describes the evildoer as one who crushes the arm of the *dallim* [126] and thus renders them defenseless. While Isaiah still defends a specific social stratum in the imperative of 1:17, he goes beyond the limits of this stratum by including the widows and the fatherless, and he directs his prophetic criticism against the authoritarian disregard for *mishpat*, "justice." His social demand is embedded in a sermon against pride (cf. 2:9-17) and the conceited self-sufficiency of man. [127]

The application of the righteous (*betsedheq*) administration of justice (*shaphat* and *hokhiach*) as a *munus regium* (gift of the king, cf. Isa. 9:6[7]) to the king of the age of salvation (Isa. 11:4; cf. the similar petition for the present king in Ps. 72) is based on Prov. 29:14. This future king will take special interest in the *dallim* (poor) and the *'aniyye 'arets* (meek of the earth), [128] who stand in antithesis to the *'arits*, [129] "violent person, ruler," and *rasha'*, "evildoer, ungodly." Here again as in Amos, *dal* undergoes a change of emphasis in the direction of weakness and godliness. [130]

3. a. *Israel As dallim in Post-Isaianic Traditions.* Post-Isaianic traditions interpret *dallim* and *'ebhyonim* collectively as the whole "people of Yahweh" (in the meantime, the upper stratum of society had been carried away into exile), [131] who feed in Yahweh's pasture (Zion) [132] in safety, while the enemy devastates neighboring Philistia (Isa. 14:30). The Song of Thanksgiving in Isa. 25:4 praises Yahweh because he has proved himself to be a stronghold to the *dal* and the *'ebhyon*. They are the remnant in the ruins of the *yoshebhe marom*, "the inhabitants of the height" (26:5), whom they trample with their feet (26:6; cf. Zeph. 2:9c), so that by God's help they are the real victors (on trampling with the feet as an ancient Near Eastern gesture of victory, cf. → הדם *ha dhōm*; → רגל *reghel*).

---

125 So Donner, 239; cf. also Koch, "Entstehung," 248.

126 So Fohrer with Beer.

127 Koch, "Entstehung," 247.

128 So with *BHS* and Wildberger, 453.

129 *BHS;* Wildberger.

130 On the characterization of the administration of justice by this king, cf. further D. N. Freedman, "Is Justice Blind? (Is 11,3f.)," *Bibl,* 52 (1971), 536.

131 Cf. IV.2.

132 Duhm.

b. *"The Remnant" in Zephaniah.* Zeph. 3:11 announces the destruction of the "proudly exultant ones," out of which only an *'am 'ani vadhal,* "a people humble and lowly," is left as the remnant of Israel (v. 12).[133] This *'am,* "people," alone has the right attitude of humility before God (*baqqeshu tsedheq baqqeshu 'anavah,* "seek righteousness, seek humility," 2:3b; *hasu beshem yhvh,* "they shall seek refuge in the name of Yahweh," 3:12b). It can therefore hope in his special protection, and will receive his help and an answer to its prayers. It is in the position of a *dal* (*dalal*), since it "calls on the name of Yahweh" (*qara' bheshem yhvh,* Ps. 116:4-6).

IV. 1. *dallim As the "Lower Stratum of the People" Detached from the Social Ethos in Jeremiah.* Apparently Jeremiah does not have a good opinion of the *dal;*[134] he does not see him socially as a victim of exploitation and legal manipulation (like the *'ebhyon* and the *'ani,* Jer. 5:27f.; 22:16). After searching for a man who does *mishpat,* "justice," Jeremiah is forced to state that the "common people" (RSV "poor")[135] on the streets of the city are characterized by false swearing, obstinacy, and an unwillingness to repent (5:1-3). Nevertheless, Jeremiah still seems to know of the high estimation of the *dal,* for he tries to excuse his failings on the basis of his ignorance of the "way" (*derekh*) and "judgment" (RSV "law," *mishpat*) of God—an ignorance caused by his environment, for he had to struggle for existence and had little opportunity for development (5:4). The prophet also has to condemn the upper stratum (*gedholim,* "the great") for ignorance (*lo' yadha'*), which in their case is inexcusable. Here *dallim* and *gedholim* stand for the whole people.

2. *dallim and dallah in the Post-Jeremian Exilic Tradition.* Jer. 39:10 is certainly secondary.[136] Here the *dallim* are defined as that part of the people (partitive *min*) "who own nothing" (*'asher 'en lahem me'umah*), an explanation that goes beyond the nuances of meaning attached to *dal* up to this time. Some of the "little people," who are called *dalloth ha'am,* "the poorest of the people," in Jer. 52:15 (the text here is uncertain), *dalloth ha'arets,* "the poorest of the land," in 52:16, *dallath 'am ha'arets,* "the poorest people of the land," collectively in 2 K. 24:14, and *dallath ha'arets,* "the poorest of the land," in 2 K. 25:12, were carried into captivity in the first deportation by Nebuchadnezzar II (597 B.C.), together with the princes, the mighty men of valor, the craftsmen, and the smiths, while only a part of the poorest of the land were left in Judah under Gedaliah (Jer. 40:7). The divergent statement in 2 K. 24:14 says that the *dallath 'am ha'arets,* "the poorest people of the land" (without defining them more explicitly; thus, this probably means all the poor people), were left in Judah, as in the second deportation under Nebuzaradan (587 B.C.). The cap-

---

[133] Cf. Ruppert, 23f.
[134] Bammel, 893.
[135] But cf. H. L. Ellison, *EvQ,* 33 (1961), 29: "poor in the knowledge of God."
[136] Rudolph, *HAT,* 12 (³1968), 245.

tain of the guard gave (*nathan*) the *dallim* vineyards and fields (Jer. 39:10), not as possessions, but as places of work. They were to work here as *yoghebhim* and *koremim* (Jer. 52:16 = 2 K. 25:12), i.e., as dependent "vintage servants" and "forced laborers," [137] thus providing subsistence for the occupied province.

Since the OT makes no statement about the number that were left behind in Judah, it is impossible to determine with certainty what portion of the people made up the *dallah* at this time. Bright, following Albright, estimates that about 125,000 were left behind and that 10,000-12,000 were carried into exile (cf. the statements made in 2 K. 24:14,16; Jer. 52:28ff.). [138] If these numbers are approximately correct, about 90 percent of the population must have belonged to the lowest social stratum called the *dallah*. This percentage understandably provoked prophetic criticism, even if it is assumed that it varied in different periods.

V. 1. *The dallim Under the Protection of Yahweh, the King, and His Fellow Men (Psalms).* The Psalms know the root *dll*, but they use it only 5 times (in contrast to 'ani—32 times; 'ebhyon—23 times; and 'anav—13 times): the verb *dalal* occurs 3 times, which shows here a strong semantic approximation to the noun.

a. In Ps. 82, which is probably preexilic, [139] the early wisdom motif, "Yahweh as attorney for the socially inferior," is presented in the mythical figure of Yahweh enthroned in the assembly of the 'elohim, "gods." He issues an ultimatum to the gods who are assembled around him. They are to be just when they judge, to judge (*shaphat*) the *dal* [140] and the fatherless (justly) (v. 3a), and to maintain the right of (*hitsdiq*) the afflicted ('ani) and the destitute (*rash*) (v. 3b). In these imperatives, which in the framework of the exposing of sin are to be understood as re-citations of the charges given at the installations of officials, [141] the failure of the divine judges is evident. In a third and fourth imperative, Yahweh charges them to remedy the abuses which their judicial failings have caused by rescuing (*pillet*) the *dal* and the 'ebhyon (v. 4a), and by delivering (*hitstsil*) them from the hand of the wicked, i.e., from those who instigated the false administration of justice and made a profit from it (v. 4b). These judges have forfeited their judgeship; [142] *tsedhaqah*, "righteousness," as a "foundation of the world" is shaken (v. 5). [143]

Scholars have interpreted Ps. 82 in the following ways: as a fictional account

---

137 H. Gese, *VT*, 12 (1962), 433.

138 J. Bright, *A History of Israel* (²1972), 344; cf. E. Janssen, *Juda in der Exilszeit. FRLANT*, 69 (1956).

139 So Schmidt, Oesterley, Kraus, *et al.*; but cf. Ackermann, Dahood: pre-monarchical; Eissfeldt: in the period of the Davidic kingdom; Deissler, Jüngling: in the period of the exilic renaissance; Gunkel-Begrich: postexilic.

140 Many scholars want to emend the text to *dakh*, "oppressor": *BHS*, Kraus, Kissane, Schlisske, *et al.* This emendation, however, must be rejected with Dahood, *Psalms*, II, 269.

141 H. W. Jüngling, *Der Tod der Götter. SBS*, 38 (1969), 86.

142 Cf. W. H. Schmidt, *Königtum Gottes in Ugarit und Israel. BZAW*, 80 (²1966), 40-43.

143 Cf. H.-J. Kraus, *in loc.*, and Ps. 58:2f. (1f.).

of Yahweh's victory over the agricultural gods to establish Israelite claims to mastery; [144] as a cult-prophetic debate with preexilic syncretism; [145] as a liturgical manifestation of the kingship of Yahweh at the Enthronement Festival; [146] as a literary echo of international political events in which "imperial powers" exploited smaller nations; [147] and as an admonition to the judges officiating in Israel. [148]

If we interpret this psalm against the historical background of the time of Amos and Isaiah, many difficulties are solved. Its prophetic-admonitory, visionary, and imperious style call to mind these prophets. This makes it likely that Ps. 82 also was directed against the official ruling class of that time, which was predominantly permeated by Canaanite ideals, [149] and which had been administratively reshaping the legal system and transferring it to its own jurisdiction. In the mythical figure of Yahweh, the divine judge, who strips the other gods of their power, the authority to administer justice in Yahweh's government is denied to them.

b. The description of the king according to ideal categories in Ps. 72:12f. is undoubtedly preexilic. [150] The king delivers (hitstsil) the 'ebhyon, the 'ani, and "him who has no helper" ('en 'ozer lo, v. 12), and has pity on (nicham) the dal and the 'ebhyon, and saves (hoshia') them from oppression and violence (vv. 13f.), aid that goes beyond help that may be given in a juridical forum (vv. 2,4,7). In these activities, the execution of the divine will through the king (cf. Isa. 11:4; Prov. 29:14; etc.) is especially clear. The king deserves the blessing for which the poor whom he has delivered pray on his behalf (Ps. 72:15ff.; cf. Prov. 22:9).

c. The great importance that the Psalms attach to right conduct toward the poor is evident in a striking way in Ps. 41:2(1), where, in a makarism or beatitude (→ אַשְׁרֵי 'ashrê), right conduct toward God (Ps. 1:1; 34:9[8]; 40:5[4]; etc.) is replaced by right conduct (hiskil, "considers") toward the dal (cf. Mt. 5:7). It is easy to see that the author of this Thanksgiving Song understood himself to be a dal, [151] who had been the victim of disease, malicious slander, greed, and suspicion. But he has now experienced deliverance by Yahweh (vv. 12ff.[11ff.]), since he is tsaddiq, "righteous," i.e., innocent of the accusations brought against

---

[144] O. Eissfeldt, "Jahwes Königsprädizierungen als Verklärung national-politischer Ansprüche Israels," Wort, Lied und Gottesspruch. Festschrift J. Ziegler, II (1972), 51-55, esp. 54; in slightly modified form, Fensham, 135.

[145] Kraus; H. D. Preuss, Verspottung fremder Religionen im AT. BWANT, 92 (1971), 112ff.; W. Schlisske, Gottessöhne und Gottessohn im AT. BWANT, 97 (1973), 44f.

[146] S. Mowinckel, E. Lipiński, W. H. Schmidt.

[147] F. Horst, "Naturrecht und AT," EvTh, 10 (1950/51), 253-273, esp. 261 = ThB, 12 (1961), 245.

[148] Kissane, Morgenstern, et al., by removing the mythological framework.

[149] Donner, 236; cf. III.1 above.

[150] Contra Kissane.

[151] A. Weiser, Psalms. OTL (trans. 1962), 343; K. Schwarzwäller, Die Feinde des Individuums in den Psalmen (1963), 94ff.

him by his enemies (vv. 6-8[5-7]). [152] This worshipper probably looks on his deliverance as a reward for his right relationship to the *dal*, a viewpoint which he expressed at the beginning of his prayer in the form of a beatitude.

d. A recurring motif in the Psalms is that Yahweh raises up the lowly and the poor. [153] According to Ps. 113:7; 1 S. 2:8 (cf. Sir. 11:1), the *dal* also shares in this blessing. The raising up of the *dal* from the dust (ʿaphar) and the ash heap (ʿashpoth) does not necessarily imply that *dal* means "sick" [154] on the ground that the sick were cast out of the community and spent their life on the dump outside the city. Instead the antithesis between these terms and the "seat of honor with princes" is meant to bring out by way of contrast the magnitude of divine power and grace. [155]

2. *The dallim Under the Protection of the Righteousness of God (Job).* God's compensatory justice is the theme in which the book of Job places the *dal*. The *dal* can have hope (Job 5:16), like the "lowly" and "those who mourn" (v. 11), the "prisoners" [156] and the "needy" (ʾebhyonim, v. 15), for God saves (hoshiaʿ) them from the power of the mighty (chazaq). Thus when Eliphaz, operating on the wisdom principle that there is an inseparable connection between one's deeds and one's lot in life, tries to answer Job's question as to the cause of his misfortune, it is clear that he understands the words *dal* and ʾebhyon as moral qualifications, for only in terms of conduct are they relevant to the inseparable connection between one's deeds and one's lot in life. The basis for this semantic enrichment was laid by Amos when he closely related *dal* and *tsaddiq*, "the righteous," the man "with whom no fault can be found judicially," [157] who is innocent of all accusations brought against him. Both terms (cf. also → עָנִי ʿanî) continued to be closely connected with *tsaddiq* and came to be identified with it more and more as *tsaddiq* semantically came to mean simply "a righteous person." The wicked (reshaʿim) do not endure and cannot spend the wealth they have accumulated. Instead, their children, trapped in a solidarity of guilt, must "restore to" (ratsah) the *dal* that which had been stolen from him (20:10), [158] which the wicked had taken away from him forcibly by oppressions (20:19; the text of this verse is very controversial). This argument of Zophar, too, remains in the sphere of traditional theology, which cannot answer Job's question, "Why?" In his oath of purification, Job absolves himself of any such conduct, for he emphasizes his right relationship to the *dal* (which here stands in parallelism with ʾalmanah, "widow," yathom, "fatherless," ʾobhedh, "one who perishes," and

---

[152] Cf. Ruppert, 30.

[153] Cf. C. Westermann, *The Praise of God in the Psalms* (trans. 1965), 118.

[154] Weiser, *in loc.*

[155] On the concept of "raising up," cf. also the Egyptian parallels in Brunner, 326f.

[156] Emended following F. Horst, *BK*, XVI, *in loc.*

[157] Donner, 238.

[158] So with Dhorme, Weiser, Hölscher, *et al.*, because of the parallel term *heshibh*, "to give back"; but cf. Fohrer, Guillaume, Gordis, *et al.*, who argue that the root is *ratsaʾ*, "to run."

'ebhyon, "poor," 31:16ff.; cf. the negative confessions in the Egyptian Book of the Dead for parallels). In response to Job's complaint that God was unjust because he had taken away his right (34:5), Elihu argues that God as creator is of necessity just and impartial: before him princes (sarim), nobles (shova'), and poor (dal) are equal, because they are all his creatures (34:19). This righteousness of God appears especially in the destruction of the mighty (kabbirim) (v. 24), who by estrangement from God and nonobservance of his ways err in the social realm as well and practice legal distortion, so that the "cry" of the dallim and the 'aniyyim reaches to heaven (v. 28).

3. *In Ben Sirach.* The term dal experiences a renaissance in the Wisdom of Ben Sirach (where it appears 11 times). Here the terms 'ebhyon, 'ani misken, and rash are used in antithesis to the rich ('ashir) and the wicked ('ish chamas). The statements in which these terms occur have to do with riches and poverty, wisdom and folly. True wisdom is independent of wealth, so that a wise dal can also be honored (Sir. 10:30f.; 11:1), and it is not right to despise him (10:23). Nevertheless, he has a hard time getting a hearing (13:22); instead, people say in contempt, "Who is this fellow?" (mi zeh), and cry out, "Shame" (ga' ga'), when he begins to speak (13:22f.). A rich man is favored everywhere but no one pays attention to the entreaties of a dal. Even his friends take advantage of his tottering to push him down completely (13:21,23). Ben Sirach pictures the poor as pasture for the rich to describe this continuous exploitation (13:19). In contrast Sirach advances a comprehensive, theologically grounded catalog of right social conduct (4:1-10).

VI. dalal. In all the passages where the verb dalal appears, it essentially reflects its original, etymological meaning, "to be/become lowly, small." In preexilic texts, this term remains in the psychosomatic sphere. According to Jgs. 6:6, Israel became "very weak."[159] But it can also be used in a transferred sense. The kabhodh, "glory," of Jacob "disappears" when God intervenes in judgment (Isa. 17:4). This can be compared metaphorically with the disappearance (niphal of razah) of the fat of the flesh. God's threatened judgment will have an impact on nature: the streams of Egypt "will diminish" (dalal), the canals will "dry up" (charabh), "be dried up" (nashath), and "be dry" (yabhesh), so that they "stink badly"[160] (Isa. 19:5f.). These natural catastrophes will cause Egypt to turn to God (vv. 21f.). Affliction, illness, and nearness to death cause the eyes to be "cast down" (dalal) (Isa. 38:14). This includes at the same time a confident turning of the eyes to Yahweh, as the added phrase lammarom, "upward," shows. The absence of a second action verb may be due to the cramped language Hezekiah uses in his lament. In any case, it is not necessary to turn to another root dll, "to be directed."[161] The prisoner asks Yahweh to hear his prayer because

---

159 II.1.
160 Read with 1QIsa, KBL³, 264, hiznichu.
161 S. Rin, "Ugaritic-OT Affinities," BZ, N.F. 7 (1963), 25; idem, Aliloth ha-elim (Jerusalem, 1968), 176; cf. also de Moor, AOAT, 16, 168.

he is "weak, exhausted" (RSV "brought very low," *ki dhallothi me'odh*, Ps. 142:7[6]); he is referring to the bodily exhaustion caused by imprisonment (v. 8 [7]). [162] The motif of hearing and trusting also appears in the (post)exilic passages, Ps. 79:8; 116:6 (where it is parallel to *'anithi me'odh*, "I am greatly afflicted," v.10). Here, however, it cannot be shown conclusively that *dalal* refers to somatic existence. Rather, there is assimilation to the meaning of the noun, in which the elements of helplessness and resignation to the will of God overlap bodily weakness. [163]

Fabry

---

[162] Kraus, *BK*.
[163] Cf. → עָנִי *'anî* with the Excursus on "Poverty."

דֶּלֶת deleth; דַּל dal

Contents: I. 1. Etymology, Occurrences in Ancient Near Eastern Literature; 2. Occurrences in the OT, Meaning, Synonyms. II. Literal Usage. III. Figurative Usage. IV. Special Problems.

I. 1. *Etymology, Occurrences in Ancient Near Eastern Literature.* The noun *deleth* occurs in most Semitic languages in a form appropriate to each (Akk. *daltu*, [1] Ugar., Phoen., Pun. *dlt*) [2] as a biliteral word with a feminine ending. The masculine form *dal* appears, but is rarer (it is found in Heb., Phoen., and Pun.). [3] Aram. *daš, daššā* and Ethiop. *dēdē* probably arose by assimilation (cf. also Arab. *darfe, daffe?*). There is no verb belonging to the same root (Akk. *edēlu* [4] [as well as the noun *e/idiltu*, cf. Syr. *'edḷāṭā*] is a secondary form). The original meaning throughout is "door." Attempts to find an original meaning "curtain" (of a tent), and thereby to trace this word back to the nomadic era, are not satisfactory in

---

deleth. G. Dalman, *AuS*, VII, 50-54, 67-70; L. Delekat, "Tür," *BHHW*, III, 2031f.; F. Ebert, "Thyra," *PW*, VI A, 737-742; K. Galling, "Tür," *BRL*, 525f.; J. Jeremias, "θύρα," *TDNT*, III, 173-180; S. Krauss, *Talmudische Archäologie*, I (1910=1966), 36-42; É. Masson, "Recherches sur les plus anciens emprunts sémitiques en grec," *Études et Commentaires*, 67 (Paris, 1967), 61-65; M. L. Mayer, "Gli imprestiti Semitici in Greco," *Rendiconti dell'Instituto Lombardo, Cl. Lettere*, 94 (1960), 311-351; Th. Nöldeke, *Neue Beiträge zur semitischen Sprachwissenschaft* (1910), 123f.; A. Salonen, *Die Türen des Alten Mesopotamien. Eine lexikalische und kulturgeschichtliche Untersuchung. AnAcScFen*, B, 124 (1961); H. Zimmern, *Akkadische Fremdwörter als Beweis für babylonischen Kultureinfluss* (²1917), 30.

[1] *AHw*, 154.
[2] *WUS*, 78; *DISO*, 58.
[3] *DISO*, 58.
[4] *AHw*, 185f.

view of this clear evidence. The word obviously arose in a settled society where there were immovable houses (in Mesopotamia?) and it has the concrete sense of a doorway that is closed by a single or double door made out of solid material (cf. Akk. *dalat bābi*, "wing of a gate," and the verb *edēlu*, "to close, shut"). Even the letter *daleth* probably meant originally a door that turned on a hinge.

The meaning "board," especially "slate," "board covered with writing" (whence the Gk. *déltos*), is also found in Ugaritic and Phoenician, but it is clearly derived from the original meaning. The common folded double boards, which scribes in the ancient Near East used for notebooks, [5] are very similar in appearance to a double door.

2. *Occurrences in the OT, Meaning, Synonyms.* *deleth* appears 87 times in the OT (*dal* only once): 22 times in the singular, 23 in the dual (including Isa. 26:20), and 42 in the plural. The feminine ending is treated as a part of the root by the vocalization.

Both the meanings found in the ancient Near East also occur in the OT. To be sure, the word means a "slate" only in the Lachish Ostraca, [6] but *delathoth*, which is used for the columns of a scroll in Jer. 36:23, is a derivative.

Elsewhere in the OT, *deleth* and *dal* mean a door or something comparable. Gen. 19 shows very clearly that a precise distinction was made between *deleth* and other Hebrew words that we translate "door": Lot goes out of the door (*pethach*) and shuts the door (*deleth*) after him (v. 6). The men of Sodom try to break the door (*deleth*) (v. 9). Then the angels that had come to destroy the city bring Lot into the house and shut the door (*deleth*) (v. 10), while outside the men of Sodom, whom the angels had stricken with blindness, seek in vain for the door (*pethach*) (v. 11). A sharp distinction is made here between the doorway (*pethach*) and the door (*deleth*). The word *deleth* refers primarily to the door. This literal meaning is retained in the later development of the Hebrew language and also by Josephus in Greek translation. [7] The LXX obliterates the distinction between *pethach* and *deleth* (even in Gen. 19) by translating both words *thýra*.

Thus the closest synonyms of *deleth* in the OT are not other words for "door" but *luach*, which can mean "board" (cf. Ex. 27:8; 38:7; 1 K. 7:36; Ezk. 27:5; Cant. 8:9) or "slate" (Isa. 30:8; Jer. 17:1; Hab. 2:2; Prov. 3:3; 7:3; esp. as a term for the tables of the law, Ex. 31:18; 32:15; Dt. 9:9; etc.). *luach* differs from *deleth* in that it denotes planks, boards, or slates in general, without connecting them with the opening of a door. The terms for openings in a building (*pethach*, "door," *'arubbah*, "window," *sha'ar*, "gate") are clearly used in a different sphere. Of these, *sha'ar* comes closest to the meaning of *deleth*, since "the gate" can be used as a shortened form of "the doors of the gate" (cf. 1 S. 21:14 [Eng. v. 13] with Josh. 2:5,7). Words for "curtain," such as *parokheth* and *masakh*,

---

[5] Cf. *BRL*, 464.
[6] *KAI*, II, 194.
[7] *TDNT*, III, 173, n. 4.

nowhere stand in parallelism with *deleth;* this also argues against an etymological connection. [8]

II. Literal Usage. That *deleth* is used for the lid on a chest (2 K. 12:10[9]) shows very clearly that this word means a swinging board firmly connected with an opening. The word is naturally used for doors in the description of the temple building (1 K. 6:31f.,34; 7:50; 1 Ch. 22:3; 2 Ch. 3:7; 4:9,22; Ezk. 41:23ff.). Prov. 26:14 also uses it in the figure of a door turning on its hinges. [9] Elsewhere *deleth* appears in contexts that speak of shutting doors: in this semantic field, the verb *saghar,* "to close, shut," is found most frequently (17 times) along with *pathach,* "to open," *na'al,* "to bar, bolt, lock," and *shabhar,* "to break down." The nouns that are used most frequently with *deleth* are *beriach* or *man'ul,* "bar, bolt," → שַׁעַר *sha'ar,* "gate," and → חומה *chômāh,* "wall."

The *deleth* primarily offers protection—from dangers, but also from disturbances. The gates (along with the *chomah,* "wall," and *beriach,* "bars") were essential parts of the fortifying of a city against siege (Dt. 3:5; 1 S. 23:7; 2 Ch. 8:5; 14:6[7]; cf. Job 38:10); their absence was an indication of unconcern (Jer. 49:31; Ezk. 38:11) or of serious danger (cf. Isa. 45:2; Ezk. 26:2; Jgs. 16:3). Thus the installation of the gates in the city gateways can signify the end of a program of building and fortification (Josh. 6:26; 1 K. 16:34; Neh. 3:1ff.; 6:1; 7:1; cf. Job 38:8,10). Doors are closed in the evening and opened in the morning (Neh. 7:3; 13:19—of the Sabbath), not only at the city gates, but also at the temple (1 S. 3:15) and at houses (Jgs. 19:27). By opening one's door to a stranger in the evening (Job 31:32; cf. Gen. 19; Jgs. 19), one shows hospitality. When the normal rhythm is disturbed, e.g., when the doors of the temple are closed at the wrong time, this denotes the interruption of sacrificial worship (2 K. 18:16; 2 Ch. 28:24; 29:7; cf. Mal. 1:10); when the doors are opened again, sacrificial worship is resumed (2 Ch. 29:3).

The *deleth* of a house promotes a feeling of security. He who goes out (*yatsa'*) of the door (Josh. 2:19; Jgs. 11:31; cf. Gen. 19:6; Jgs. 19:22) is exposed to danger. He who locks himself in his house or in a certain room by shutting the *deleth* does so out of fear of danger (2 K. 6:32; Neh. 6:10 [of the temple!]; Isa. 26:20), or in order not to be disturbed while working, either because he fears the light (Jgs. 3:23ff.; 2 S. 13:17; Isa. 57:8), or because the work of God must be done in secret (2 K. 4:4,33; 9:3,10).

To one standing outside the door, the *deleth* is in the first instance an obstacle that must be overcome. He must beat on the door (Jgs. 19:22; cf. 1 S. 21:14[13]), open it with some effort (*pathach* is used for opening a door from the outside: Jgs. 3:25; Isa. 45:1; Zec. 11:1; Ps. 78:23), or break it down (*shabhar*) by force (Gen. 19:9; Isa. 45:2; Ezk. 26:2; Ps. 107:16).

It is clear from this survey of the use of *deleth* that in the sense of "door" the reference is exclusively to the possibility of closing it. When the OT wishes to

---

[8] See above.

[9] For technical details, cf. *BRL, BHHW.*

suggest that a door is a passageway from one area to another, it has to use *deleth* in parallelism with *pethach* or *shaʿar* (cf. Prov. 8:34; Isa. 45:2).

III. Figurative Usage. The idea of an actual "door" is also clearly assumed in the figurative use of the word in the OT. The great predominance of the dual form shows that what are in view in the metaphor are the double doors of a city or a temple. In keeping with this *deleth* is used as a figure for shutting out. The expression "doors of the sea" in Job 38:8,10 is used to convey the thought that the sea is restrained, just as an enemy who comes to besiege a city is restrained by a city wall with gates and bars (*beriach*, "bars," are explicitly mentioned in v. 10). The meaning of the expression "doors of heaven" in Ps. 78:23 is not quite so clear. There seems to be no way to distinguish between this and the related expressions *shaʿar hashshamayim*, "gate of heaven" (Gen. 28:17), and *ʾarubboth hashshamayim*, "windows of heaven" (Gen. 7:11; 8:2; 2 K. 7:2,19; Isa. 24:18; Mal. 3:10), unless it be that behind this figure stands the idea of a "brass heaven" (Dt. 28:23) which must be opened in order that the manna may come forth. The "doors of the lips" (Ps. 141:3: *dal*) and the "doors of the crocodile's jaws" (Job 41:6[14]) show clearly what the background of the figure is, as do also the "doors of the womb" (= the vulva, Job 3:10; cf. the parallelism in Job 38:8) and the "gates of wisdom" (Prov. 8:34). In all these passages *deleth* is plainly used to suggest a possible obstacle, a shutting out. Finally, the same is true in the figure used for aging in Eccl. 12:4 and in Tyre's joyful shout at the breaking down of the "door (RSV gate) of the peoples," i.e., Jerusalem, in Ezk. 26:2. [10]

IV. Special Problems. When all this is taken into account one can hardly assume that there is a different usage in Cant. 8:9. It is unlikely, then, that the common conjecture is correct that in this passage *deleth* refers to the girl's "easy accessibility" or "indiscretion." Rudolph's appeal to *Ket.* 9aff. [11] does not support this conjecture, because this text uses not only *deleth* but also *pethach pathoach* to denote the woman who has already had sexual intercourse. Our point of departure, then, must be that the parallelism here is synthetic. [12] In this verse, too, *deleth* stands in synonymous parallelism with *chomah*, "wall," so that what the writer has in view is the strengthening of the girl's defenses.

When it is laid down that lifetime slaves are to be marked at the door or doorpost (*mezuzah*) (Ex. 21:6; Dt. 15:17), some scholars connect this with the household gods that were kept there (cf. Isa. 57:8?); but others see a reference, not to the house door, but to the door of the temple. [13]

Baumann

---

[10] Cf. Zimmerli, *BK, in loc.*

[11] W. Rudolph, *KAT, in loc.*

[12] With H. Ringgren, *ATD, in loc.*

[13] Cf. the comms. and O. Eissfeldt, *KlSchr,* I (1962), 266-273; O. Loretz, *Bibl,* 41 (1960), 167-175.

דָּם dām

Contents: I. 1. Etymology; 2. Occurrences. II. Concepts and Customs of the Nations:
1. In General; 2. In Mesopotamia; 3. In Egypt; 4. In Canaan; 5. In Arabia. III. In the
OT: 1. Physiology; 2. Ethics and Law; 3. Semantic Multivalence. IV. Theological Usage:
1. Magical Power; 2. Eating Blood; 3. Blood of Sacrifices; 4. Blood of the Covenant;
5. Yahweh As Avenger of Blood.

I. 1. *Etymology*. The word for "blood" is basically the same in all Semitic
languages: Akk. *dāmu*, Ugar. *dm*, Arab., Ethiop. *dam*, Aram. *dam, dᵉmā'* (Mandean *zᵉmā'*), *'admā'*, Phoen. *'dm* (?),[1] *edom*,[2] *'edmā'*.[3] It belongs to the very
limited category of biliteral nouns, which have been shown to belong conceptual-

---

dām. J. Behm, "αἷμα," *TDNT*, I, 172-77; A. Bertholet, "Zum Verständnis des alttestamentlichen Opfergedankens," *JBL*, 49 (1930), 218-233; E. Bischof, *Das Blut im jüdischen
Brauch* (1929); F. Blome, *Die Opfermaterie in Babylonien und Israel*, I (Rome, 1934), 167-
173; H. Bonnet, "Blut," *RÄR*, 121f.; T. Canaan, "Das Blut in den Sitten und im Aberglauben
der palästinischen Araber," *ZDPV*, 79 (1963), 8-23; A. Charbel, "Virtus sanguinis non ex-
piatoria in sacrificio *šelāmîm*," *Sacra Pagina*, I (1959), 366-376; J. Chelhod, *Le sacrifice chez
les Arabes* (Paris, 1955), 173ff.; S. R. Curtiss, *Ursemitische Religion im Volksleben des heu-
tigen Orient* (1903); L. Dewar, "The Biblical Use of the Term 'Blood'," *JTS*, N.S. 4 (1953),
204-208; E. Dhorme, "L'emploi metaphorique des noms de parties du corps ...," *RB*, 29
(1920), 472-506; R. Dussaud, *Les origines Cananéenes du sacrifice Israélite* (Paris, ²1941);
E. Ebeling, "Blut," *RLA*, II, 57f.; W. Eichrodt, *TheolOT* (trans. 1961), I, 141ff.; J. G. Frazer,
The Golden Bough (3 vols., ²1900), see Index, *s.v.* "Blood"; N. Füglister, *Die Heilsbedeutung
des Pascha. StANT*, 8 (1963), 77-105; K. Galling, "Blut im AT," *RGG³*, I (1957), 1328; H.
Gese, M. Höfner, K. Rudolph, *Die Religionen Altsyriens, Altarabiens und der Mandäer.
RdM*, 10/2 (1970); K. Goldammer, *Die Formenwelt des Religiösen* (1960), see Index, *s.v.*
"Blut"; J. Herrmann, *Die Idee der Sühne im AT* (1905); E. O. James, *Sacrifice and Sacra-
ment* (London, 1962); A. R. Johnson, *The Vitality of the Individual in the Thought of An-
cient Israel* (Cardiff, ²1964), 71-74; K. Koch, "Der Spruch 'Sein Blut bleibe auf seinem
Haupt' ...," *VT*, 12 (1962), 396-416; M. J. Lagrange, *Études sur les religions sémitiques*
(Paris, ²1905), 247-274; D. J. McCarthy, "The Symbolism of Blood and Sacrifice," *JBL*, 88
(1969), 166-176; *idem, JBL*, 92 (1973), 205-210; L. Morris, "The Biblical Use of the Term
'Blood'," *JTS*, N.S. 3 (1952), 216-227; N.S. 6 (1955), 77-82; J. Pedersen, *ILC*, I-II, III-IV
(1926, 1940); H. Graf Reventlow, "'Sein Blut ...'," *VT*, 10 (1960), 311-327; T. H. Robinson,
"My Blood of the Covenant," *Vom AT. Festschrift K. Marti. BZAW*, 41 (1925), 232-37; H.
H. Rowley, "The Meaning of Sacrifice in the OT," *BJRL*, 33 (1950), 74-110; F. Rüsche, *Blut,
Leben und Seele* (Paderborn, 1930); L. Sabourin, "Nefesch, sang et expiation," *Sciences
Ecclésiastiques*, 18 (1966), 25-45; R. Schmid, *Das Bundesopfer in Israel. StANT*, 9 (1964);
D. Schötz, *Schuld- und Sündopfer im AT* (1930); W. Robertson Smith, *Religion of the
Semites* (³1927), see Index, *s.v.* "Blood"; J. E. Steinmueller, "Sacrificial Blood in the Bible,"
Bibl, 40 (1959), 556-567; H. Strack, *Das Blut im Glauben und Aberglauben der Menschheit*
(²1900); R. J. Thompson, *Penitence and Sacrifice in Early Israel* ... (Leiden, 1963); J. H.
Waszink, "Blut," *RAC*, II, 459-473; J. Wellhausen, *Reste arabischen Heidentums* (³1961),
116ff.

[1] *KAI*, 43.11.
[2] Augustine *Enarratio in Ps. 136:18*.
[3] Brockelmann, *VG*, I, 217, 334; *KBL³*, 215.

ly to the oldest linguistic stratum. [4] The etymological opaqueness here is nothing unusual. *dam* is also isolated in the vocabulary of Biblical Hebrew: it cannot be derived from another known root nor has it produced derivatives. The attempts of scholars to connect it with the color *'adhom* (which is used of shades ranging from "bright red" to "reddish-brown") are understandable, but it is hard to determine in which direction dependence should be assumed. It is just as logical to argue that *dam* was derived from *'adhom,* [5] and to suppose that "red" was the original term for "blood," as to argue that the color *'adhom* was derived from *dam,* because it was the "color of blood." [6] If one connects *'adham* with *'adhom,* [7] then there is a linguistic relationship between the Hebrew words for "man" and "blood." Today, however, this relationship has been mostly abandoned. [8]

Although the origins are no longer accessible to linguistic research, it can still be stated that the Hebrews made linguistic connections between *dam, 'adhom,* and *'adham.* Alleged etymologies in the OT "were taken very seriously as a means of reaching certain important pieces of knowledge." [9] When the formula adopted from ancient sacral law speaks in Gen. 9:6 of the *dam ha'adham,* "blood of man," and when the prophet describes sins as being "red" (*ya'dimu,* Isa. 1:18), they are not just using alliteration or metaphor. Instead, a profound relationship is being clarified in the context of an ethico-religious saying. At a later time, the Talmud says: *'adham hari'shon damo shel 'olam.* [10]

There is a linguistic and conceptual parallel to this in the traditions of the Caras Indians (of South America). "They designate themselves with the word for 'red, colored' (*caro*), which also means 'blood' (*cara*). But it also means 'man'...." [11]

2. *Occurrences.* The word *dam* occurs about 360 times in the OT, including the pl. *damim* 70 times. (Variations in the textual tradition [e.g., at Ezk. 9:9] [12] make it impossible to know exactly how many times the word occurs.) The article or pronominal suffixes can be appended to both singular and plural forms, and both forms can be used in the construct as a *nomen regens* (governing noun) or a *nomen rectum* (governed noun). Some scholars have attempted to distinguish between these two forms semantically.

It should be noted that *dam* always appears in the plural when the reference is to the blood of another which has been shed violently and which presses heavily upon the murderer,

---

[4] S. Moscati, *An Introduction to the Comparative Grammar of the Semitic Languages* (²1969), 73.

[5] B. Davidson, *The Analytical Hebrew and Chaldee Lexicon* (repr. London, 1966), VII; cf. also Akk. *adammu, adamātu,* "(dark) blood," from the root *'dm, AHw,* 10a.

[6] *BLe,* § 466; H. Holma, *Die Namen der Körperteile*... (1911), 7.

[7] *VG,* II, 48; so already Josephus *Ant.* i.1.2.

[8] → אדם *'ādhām,* I.5.

[9] G. von Rad, *OT Theol,* II (trans. 1965), 83.

[10] Jer. *Sabb.* ii.5b.

[11] Goldammer, 294.

[12] Cf. *BHK, in loc.*

while the singular is used when the reference is to one's own blood. If blood is no longer part of a closed system but is dispersed in pools, spurts, or drops, then *damim* is used.[13]

But these definitions do not agree entirely with the evidence. In most cases, the two forms are used indiscriminately. Evildoers lie in wait for *damim* (Mic. 7:2) or for *dam* (Prov. 1:11); they shed *dam* (Ezk. 22:3) or *damim* (1 Ch. 28:3); they are guilty of *dam* (Nu. 35:27), or *damim* (Ex. 22:1 [Eng. v. 2]). A dead man lies wallowing in his *dam* (2 S. 20:12), but the blood of menstruation can also be called *damim* (Lev. 20:18). Consequently, the hypothesis of a strict logical and conceptual distinction between *dam* and *damim* cannot be maintained. Nevertheless, certain consistent usages are evident. The plural is never used for the blood of animals, but as a *nomen rectum* it is always used attributively in the sense of bloodguiltiness ('*ish damim*, "man of blood," 2 S. 16:17f.; etc.; '*ir haddamim*, "city of blood, bloody city," Ezk. 22:2; *beth haddamim*, "house of blood," 2 S. 21:1). Originally the plural seems to have been used to express the affective value attached to blood in certain situations. To some extent, then, its use remains optional, but it is never used in some expressions ("avenger of blood" is always *go'el haddam*, and never *go'el haddamim*).

Since style and dialect may have been more determinative than semantic influences, variations in the textual tradition are not surprising. The singular occurs in the *qere* of 2 S. 1:16 (the *kethibh* has the plural), the Samaritan Pentateuch of Lev. 20:9 (the MT has the plural), some Hebrew manuscripts of Ezk. 18:13[14] (the MT has the plural), and the MT of Jer. 2:34 and Ezk. 22:13 (the LXX has the plural). Later Midrashic exegesis found in the plural a point of departure, e.g., in the Mishnah *Sanh.* iv.5: "It is not written (Gen. 4:10), 'the *dam* of your brother,' but 'the *damim* of your brother,' i.e., his own blood and that of his descendants." In postbiblical Hebrew, there arose a homonym of *damim* derived from *damah*, "to be similar, equivalent" (→ דמה *dāmāh*); this was *damim*, "price, cost."[15] Again, the Targum of Ezk. 19:10 derives *bedhamekha*, "in your blood," which is hard to understand in this context, from *dmh/y*, and translates: "...is like (the grapevine)." Two Hebrew manuscripts read *krmk*: "...a grapevine in your vineyard." König reads, "at the time of your birth" immediately after '*immekha*, "your mother."[16] The LXX usually translates *damim* by *haíma* (but also *haímata*),[17] "blood," which can also mean "bloody deed, murder," "blood line, blood relationship," "vitality," etc. In isolated cases, a more sharply defined Greek word emphasizes the nuance contained in the Hebrew. Thus the LXX translates *dam* and *damim* by *énochos*, "guilty," in Ex. 22:2(3); Lev. 20:9; etc.; Nu. 35:27; *haímati énochos*, "guilty of blood," in Dt. 19:10; *phónos*, "murder," in Dt. 22:8; Prov. 1:18; etc.; and *dólios*, "fraud, cunning," in Prov. 12:6. The Vulgate almost always translates these words by

---

[13] Koch, 406; similarly already *GK,* § 124n.
[14] Cf. *BHK.*
[15] Levy, *WTM,* 411.
[16] E. König, *Hebr. und aram. Wörterbuch* (1910), 70.
[17] See Behm.

sanguis, "blood" (also *sanguines,* "bloods"). [18] The synonym *cruor,* which means "blood flowing out of a wound" in Classical Latin, and then by metonymy "murder," is used only for stylistic reasons, viz., when *dam* had already been translated by *sanguis* in the same verse (Ex. 7:19; Nu. 35:33; Dt. 21:9; etc.) A noteworthy example of a later understanding of *dam* is found in 2 Ch. 19:10, where the word is translated by *cognatio,* "relatives."

II. Concepts and Customs of the Nations.

1. *In General.* Blood plays a prominent role in popular beliefs, myths, and magical cultic acts. Along with sperm, mother's milk, spittle, urine, tears, and perspiration, blood is one of the fluids that originate in the body in a way inexplicable to ancient man and are thus regarded as bearing secret power. Of these, blood is identified to a special degree with vitality. On the one hand experience teaches that when it flows out of a living creature, life comes to an end; on the other hand the blood of menstruation, like the blood shed at birth, points to sexual intercourse, reproduction, and fertility, i.e., to the beginning of new life. Some scholars explain the idea of the indwelling power of blood animistically, [19] while others explain it dynamistically: [20] blood is thus understood as the essence of the personal powers that are at work in man and beast, or else as containing mana in a special way. Vestiges of animism and manaism appear in the customs and myths of the more highly developed religions, along with more advanced theological and speculative concepts which frequently overlap them. [21] In any case, the belief in the enormous power of blood results in a conflicting attitude: on the one hand, man treats blood with reverential awe and surrounds it with a series of taboos; on the other hand, he hopes to make use of these powers in appropriate rites. In the most widely divergent nations and cultural communities, then, one encounters a similar polarity in the legal regulations: bloodshed is to be avoided (even when killing is permitted: Socrates is given a cup of poison!) because it leads to death, but sacrifices are frequently offered on account of the blood of men or animals obtained thereby. Eating blood can be strictly forbidden [22] but it can also be commanded ritually. [23] Contact with blood must be avoided, but a baptism of blood (e.g., the taurobolium in the cult of Attis) can de demanded. The blood of menstruation makes a woman unclean, [24] and yet it can be recommended as a medicine. [25]

2. *In Mesopotamia.* In the Babylonian myth man is created from the blood of the slain god (EnEl VI, 33). [26] Blood is regarded as the true life substance, so

---

[18] See F. P. Kaulen, *Sprachliches Handbuch zur biblischen Vulgata* (²1904), 107.
[19] Smith, Frazer.
[20] Bertholet, Pedersen, Dussaud.
[21] See IV.2 below.
[22] Frazer, I, 353.
[23] *Ibid.,* 133.
[24] *Ibid.,* 361.
[25] Strack, 14, 55ff.
[26] *KAR,* 4, 26.

that *dāmu* and *balāṭu* can be used in parallelism (so a vocabulary from Assyria). Relatives have the same blood: "I am your brother, your flesh, your blood (*dāmuka*)." [27] Blood plays an important role in magical rites and medicine. In rites of renewal, the blood of the person being renewed is obtained by cutting the skin, or an animal is slaughtered as his substitute and its blood is used. In Assyrian legal documents, red wine as a penitential gift symbolically represents human blood. (Sometimes tapped juices of trees are called *dāmu*.) On the other hand, a libation of sacrificial blood is never mentioned, even though frequent references are made to the most widely divergent animal sacrifices. *da-me* also means "murder" and "atonement money" that must be paid for murder. [28] In the omen literature blood (like the color red in general) is regarded as a sign of threatening calamity.

Kedar-Kopfstein

3. *In Egypt.* In Egypt the idea that blood is a bearer of life can be deduced from certain myths which state that living creatures and objects originate from drops of divine blood, e.g., Hu and Sia from blood from the phallus of Re, [29] and Persea trees from drops of Bata's blood. [30] In the cult and the sacrificial rite blood plays scarcely any role at all, although deities, whose bloodthirsty character is emphasized, are summoned to drink the blood of sacrificial animals. [31] The beer which appeases the angry goddesses in the legend of the heavenly cow, and which is like human blood, points in the same direction. Bloodthirsty demons, who live on the blood of the dead, also appear in the Egyptian underworld. An amulet, the so-called Blood of Isis, [32] plays a role in chap. 156 of the Book of the Dead.

The figurative use of blood in Egyptian literature is limited: the fighting king has "bloody eyes," and in times of unrest the river will turn to blood. [33]

Bergman

4. *In Canaan.* The Amarna correspondence, which comes from Canaan, has the phrase "give us his blood" for "let us kill him" (EA 138, 14), and mentions blood revenge (EA 8, 29). In the Canaanite myths from Ugarit, shedding blood in battle is often extolled. The warlike goddess 'Anat wades in the blood of her enemies [34] and washes her hands in it. [35] The food offered to her by El is bread and *yn*, "wine," which is called *dm ʿṣm*, "blood of the grapevine," in the parallel line. [36] The OT attests to the extensive agreement between the types and materials

---

[27] *CAD*, III, 79.
[28] *Ibid.*
[29] F. Lexa, *La magie dans l'Égypte antique* (trans. 1925), II, 65, I.1.
[30] *RÄR*, 121f.
[31] *ZÄS*, 47 (1910), 73f.
[32] RÄR, 332f.
[33] H. Grapow, *Die bildlichen Ausdrücke des Ägyptischen* (1924), 124f.
[34] *CTA*, 7 [V AB, B], I, 9; 18 [III D], IV, 24, 35; 3 [V AB], II, 14, 27.
[35] *CTA*, 3 [V AB], II, 34.
[36] *CTA*, 4 [II AB], IV, 38.

of Canaanite sacrifices and those which were customary in Israel or commanded in the law. This is confirmed by Ugaritic and Phoenician texts. None of the texts, however, mentions the significance of the blood in the ceremony. [37] *šlm* (sing.! *sk šlm lkbd 'rṣ*) [38] has reference to a libation, but there is no reason to assume that the liquid used here was blood.

5. *In Arabia.* Interpretation of the material dealing with belief and cult among the pre-Islamic Arabs is beset with methodological difficulties. The oldest inscriptions are all brief and hence are not very instructive; later detailed accounts are not always reliable. The Koran mentions the creation of man from a clot of blood (96:2); this would seem to go back to an early understanding. Commonality of blood is regarded as a basis of close relationship. [39] Blood brotherhood can be achieved by a ceremony in which the partners mix their blood or drink one another's blood. When a person is murdered, the members of his tribe must avenge his blood by killing the murderer. Blood is regarded as the element of life and thus is called *nafs* ("the breath of life"). The sacrifice of domestic animals was already a widespread practice among the pre-Islamic Arabs; the blood of the victim was rubbed on a stone altar.

III. In the OT.

1. *Physiology.* In the OT *dam* is used of the blood of men (2 S. 20:12), mammals (Gen. 37:31), and birds (Lev. 14:6) (but never fish—whether accidentally or because the blood of fish is different must be left undecided). Twice in poetic texts wine is called *dam 'anabhim* or *'enabh*, "the blood of grapes or of the grape" (Gen. 49:11; Dt. 32:14). This was a weak metaphor at a later stage of the language (Sir. 39:26), but the hypothesis that the phrase is based on a magical concept of analogy in early religion cannot be dismissed out of hand. Juice was regarded as the blood of plants. Not only, then, could red wine be substituted symbolically for blood (Dt. 32:38; 1 Macc. 6:34) but the concepts could also arise of intoxicating blood and of war as a huge wine press (Dt. 32:42; Isa. 49:26; 63:2f.; Ezk. 39:19; Joel 4:13 [3:13]). [40]

Blood is prominent in connection with wounds and the dissection of sacrificial animals. In these contexts *dam* is often mentioned along with other components of the body ("flesh," Isa. 49:26; "fat," Ezk. 44:7; "skin," Nu. 19:5). In poetic texts *dam* and "flesh" can stand in synonymous parallelism in two parallel stichs (*basar*, Isa. 49:26; Ps. 79:2f.; *she'er*, Jer. 51:35; Zeph. 1:17, *lḥm*?), and by synecdoche they denote the whole person when death and destruction are anticipated. In the apocryphal literature (Sir. 14:18; 17:31), the NT (Mt. 16:17), and the Talmud (*Ber.* 33a), the expression *basar vadham*, "flesh and blood," is used to denote the frailty of man. In the canonical books this meaning is borne by → בשר

---

[37] Cf., e.g., the sacrificial ritual in the Keret Epic, *CTA*, 14.
[38] *CTA*, 3 [V AB], IV, 53.
[39] Smith, 40f., 312ff.; Wellhausen, 193.
[40] Dhorme, 474ff.

bāśār alone. When the Greek speaks of *haíma kaí sárx*, "blood and flesh," [41] this is a purely physiological description.

At an early period *dam* appears in parallelism with → חלב *chelebh*, "fat," as 2 S. 1:22; Isa. 34:6f.; etc., show. Here it is worth noting that both these components of the body are regarded as particularly important. This also comes to expression in the sacrificial ritual (Isa. 1:11; Ezk. 44:7,15; Ex. 23:18; Lev. 3:17; 7:25-27).

In the vision of the resuscitation of the dead bones (Ezk. 37:1-14), the prophet names the following components of the body that are fitted together before the spirit revives them: bones, sinews, flesh, and skin. Similarly, Job 10:9ff. mentions these components: sperm, skin, flesh, bones, and sinews; then life is given (cf. Gen. 2:21ff.). Blood, then, is not part of the framework of the body. [42] In contrast to internal organs like the heart, liver, kidneys, etc., as well as the *nephesh*, "soul," and *chelebh*, "fat" (which was regarded as the seat of self-confidence and arrogance, Job 15:27; Ps. 17:10; 119:70), blood has nothing to do with feelings. Relatives have the same "bone and flesh" (Gen. 29:14; Jgs. 9:2; 2 S. 19:13f. [12f.]; etc.), but not the same blood; [43] however, cf. later Jth. 9:4 (on the development of life in the womb as a coagulation of the maternal blood, cf. Wisd. 7:2, though cf. also Jn. 1:13).

Lifting out a concept which is exclusively connected with *dam*, we may say that it is the bearer of personally differentiated life, the vital element in the individual. [44] Thus the word is semantically close to *nephesh* to the extent that this can denote life as such (2 S. 23:17; Lam. 2:12). Since, however, *nephesh*, the breath of life, is present in a living person, but blood is found in one who is bleeding to death, the emphasis in the former is mainly positive, but in the latter negative: when a man's life is saved, it is called his *nephesh*, but when he loses it, it is called his *dam* (Ezk. 3:16ff.; 33:1ff.). Within the framework of later rationalization an attempt was made to bring these two life principles into a definable connection: "the life (*nephesh*) of every creature is the blood (*dam*) of it" (Lev. 17:14); "the blood (*dam*) is the life (*nephesh*)" (Dt. 12:23); but also, "the life (*nephesh*) . . . is in the blood (*dam*)" (Lev. 17:11). Important though these definitions have become for the theology of sacrifice, [45] they can hardly be the proper point of departure in a discussion of the meaning of *dam*: instead, they are the final result of speculation. (They appear in the relatively late Pentateuchal sources Pʰ and D and presuppose a weakening of the concept *nephesh*; [46] in their divergent formulations, they bear the stamp of artificiality.)

---

[41] Polyainos *Strat.* iii.11.1.

[42] On the role of *ruach*, "spirit, breath," in Ezk. 37:5ff., cf. Zimmerli, *BK*, XIII, 895f., 565f.

[43] Contra Pedersen, *ILC*, I-II, 50, 179, 267, etc.

[44] Similarly already Jerome, comm. on Zeph. 1:17: "sanguis igitur hominis *tó zōtikón aítios*, id est 'vitale', quo vegetatur et sustentatur et vivit, debet intelligi," "therefore the blood of man, the life-giving originator, i.e., 'life,' which is quickened and maintained and lives, is to be understood." *CChr*, LXXVIA, 675f.

[45] IV.2.

[46] Cf. J. Schwab, *Der Begriff der nefeš* . . . (diss., Munich, 1913), 23f.

The coincidence of *dam* and *nephesh* is not essential in passages where *nephesh* simply means "person": "a man who is burdened by the blood of a (murdered) person ..." (Prov. 28:17); " ... the blood of people, poor and innocent" (Jer. 2:34; *naphshoth 'ebhyonim* could also be a variant gloss on *dam neqiyim*, see the LXX). Gen. 9:5 should also be translated similarly: " ... your blood, of each individual, I will require." [47] At the same time, *lenaphshothekhem* can also be explained as indicating that bloodless homicide will be punished too, [48] or that the shedding of blood will be avenged only when it results in the destruction of a *nephesh*. [49]

2. *Ethics and Law.* As a result of the far-reaching complex of ideas connected with *dam*, the word experienced an important expansion of meaning. As a crucial factor in one's vitality, it could represent dialectically the ideas of "life" and "death." For reasons that have already been given, this is by far the most common use. *dam* is attested as a synonym of "life" in only a few verses, and not indisputably even in these. One passage that must be considered in this regard is Ps. 72:14: "From oppression and violence he redeems their life (*nephesh*), and precious is their blood (*dam*) in his sight." The parallelism between *nephesh* and *dam*, and the connection between "precious" (*yaqar*) and *dam* (cf. 1 S. 26:21; 2 K. 1:13, which speak of "precious," i.e., preserved life), favor the MT (against the LXX, which reads *shem*, "name," instead of *dam*) and this interpretation. Another passage is Ps. 94:21: "They band together against the life (*nephesh*) of the righteous, and condemn innocent blood (*dam*) (RSV, and condemn the innocent to death)." Since the expression "condemn blood" is unusual, some scholars have proposed a textual emendation here (to *'adham* [?], "man"). [50] But this destroys the parallelism. Thus it seems best to leave *dam* in the text but to interpret it as "living person" (if not as a prolepsis: "condemn one who is innocent to be executed"). A similar explanation is apposite in Dt. 27:25: " ... to slay the life (*nephesh*) of an innocent blood (*dam*)" (the LXX and Vulg. understand *nephesh* as a *nomen regens* [governing noun]). But this could also be an abbreviation for "to slay a life (*nephesh*) so that innocent blood (is shed)." *dam* means "death, destruction," in Ps. 30:10(9): "What profit is there in my blood (*dam*) ... ?" This psalm is not describing some sort of bloody action but is the Thanksgiving Song of one who had been saved from death (vv. 3f.[2f.]).

Since, however, *dam* denotes above all a violent death (1 K. 2:9), by metonymy it can convey the idea of "war": "pestilence and blood (*debher vadham*) shall pass through you" (Ezk. 5:17; cf. the connection of → דבר *debher* with "war" and "sword," Ezk. 6:11; Jer. 28:8; etc.). The expression *shaphakh dam*, "shed

---

[47] So already Ibn Ezra and many modern commentators.

[48] Rashi, *in loc.*; Jerome, comm. on Zeph. 1:17: "alii occiderunt homines veneno vel suspendio et tamen cum homo mortuus sit, non est sanguis effusus?" "Some men have been put to death by poison or hanging, and yet when a man is dead, is not blood shed?" *CChr*, LXXVIA, 675f.

[49] Ehrlich, *Mikra ki-Peshuto, in loc.*

[50] Cf. *BHK;* otherwise *BHS.*

blood," is synonymous with "destroy life, kill, murder" (Gen. 9:6; Ezk. 18:10; etc.), and hence also with "destroy *nephesh*" (Prov. 1:18; Gen. 37:21,22; Ezk. 22:27). The literal meaning, "to pour out blood," is retained in Lev. 4:30,34. To destroy a human life is the greatest evil, but the actual shedding of blood in murder imposes a special burden. Thus Joseph's brothers discuss together how they might destroy him without shedding blood (Gen. 37:18ff.). The same Joseph story gives semantic expression to a higher ethic by using the word *dam* for putting a person to death maliciously even when no blood is shed (Gen. 42:22). The crime of shedding blood could be expiated only with blood, primarily that of the murderer (Gen. 9:6; Nu. 35:31ff.). The law required that if the murderer could not be found, a ritual was to be held in which the blood of a slain animal was substituted for that of the murderer (Dt. 21:1ff.). This act of atonement, which originally was a sacrifice, [51] should be regarded as only one example of a very polymorphic assortment of rites that have to do with murder and its atonement. According to the general view, the power released when blood was shed brought about and demanded vengeance. On one view a victim's blood becomes a burden to the murderer (Prov. 28:17), clinging to his hands (Isa. 1:15; 59:3), to his clothing (1 K. 2:5; the LXX reads the 1st person and means David himself, while the 3rd person of the MT means Joab), to his head, or to an animal (Gen. 9:5; cf. Ex. 21:29) or object (Dt. 22:8) that has caused the death. In certain cases the possibility is suggested that one might be cleansed from this blood. [52] From another standpoint shed blood becomes a sphere of danger which moves with fearful power against the murderer and seeks to explode upon him (2 S. 16:8; 1 K. 2:33; Jer. 26:15; 51:35; Ezk. 35:6). This can be averted and directed toward another object (Jgs. 9:24; 2 S. 1:16; 3:28f.; 1 K. 2:37; Jonah 1:14). Here the question of guilt becomes the burning problem. [53] Finally, shed blood could be seen as clinging to the ground and polluting it (Nu. 35:33; Ps. 106:38). As long as it remains uncovered (Gen. 37:26; Ezk. 24:7; Job 16:18), it cries from the ground for vengeance (Gen. 4:10; cf. 4:12).

The responsibility of avenging the blood of a murder victim, i.e., of shedding the blood of the murderer, belongs to the *go'el haddam*, "avenger of blood" (Nu. 35:9ff.; Dt. 19:6; 2 S. 14:11). [54] Undoubtedly this has reference to one of the closest relatives, since this is the way the *go'el* is defined in the regulations concerning the redemption of alienated family property (Lev. 25:25ff.,48f.). It might be possible to pursue this analogy further and to see in the *go'el haddam* the one who makes possible "the return of the shed blood to the ancestral community." [55] It is sufficient, however, to view the *go'el* as one having a specific responsibility to his relatives (1 K. 16:11). In this case, this responsibility pertains to the *dam*, i.e., blood vengeance. [56] The blood is sought (*biqqesh,* 2 S. 4:11),

---

[51] Marti, *HSAT, in loc.;* different from von Rad, *Deuteronomy. OTL* (trans. 1966), 136: "magical procedure."

[52] See above on Dt. 21; Isa. 4:4.

[53] See below.

[54] → גאל *gā'al,* II.c.

[55] Koch, 410.

[56] Cf. M. Noth, *BK,* IX/1, 348.

required (*darash,* Ezk. 33:6), or redeemed (→ גאל *gā'al*). Through executing blood vengeance, the blood of the innocent victim is "removed": *ubhi'arta dham hannaqi* (Dt. 19:13). Here as elsewhere the legal regulations of the OT clearly limit the execution of this responsibility to willful murder (Ex. 21:12ff.; Nu. 35:11ff.). This is why the need to discuss the question of guilt arose (Josh. 20:1ff.).

It was in fact inevitable that different types of homicide should be assessed differently. The concern of the community to preserve itself demanded that the *go'el haddam,* "avenger of blood," should be viewed differently from the murderer, and the one who killed in combat from the one who killed in peace time. The accusation made against Joab is that " . . . he placed in time of peace *damim* (blood) which had been shed in war" (1 K. 2:5; perhaps this should be emended to read, "he avenged in time of peace *damim* [blood] which had been shed in war").[57] The language can denote this when it connects the attributive *naqi,* "innocent," with *dam,* "blood," and thus explicitly characterizes the crime as shedding the blood of *innocent* persons (2 K. 21:16; Isa. 59:7; Joel 4:19[3:19]; Ps. 106:38; Prov. 6:17; etc.). Of course the same is often meant even when the word *naqi* is not added (Ezk. 22:3,6,9,12).

The Masoretic vocalization has both the form *dām nāqî* (Isa. 59:7; etc.) and the form *dam nāqî* (Dt. 19:10; etc.). The latter is in the construct and the former in the absolute: "blood of an innocent person" (Dt.), and "innocent blood" (Isa.). The construct with the plural, *dam neqiyyim,* "blood of the innocents" (Jer. 19:4), and the use of the article with the *nomen rectum, dam hannaqi,* "blood of the innocent" (Dt. 19:13; 2 K. 24:4), show that the original expression was "blood of an innocent person." On the other hand, the expression "innocent blood" is not just derived artificially from the pointing, for Dt. 21:9 has *haddam hannaqi,* "the innocent blood" (variations in the textual tradition where this phrase occurs are not surprising).[58]

The examination of evidence to determine guilt is the task of the judicial system. According to Dt. 17:8, it is the task of the law courts to investigate individual cases of property claims, bodily injury (*ben din ledhin ubhen negha' lanegha',* "between one kind of legal right and another, or one kind of assault and another"), and especially murder (*ben dam ledham,* "between one kind of homicide and another"). The task of the law officers appointed by Jehoshaphat (2 Ch. 19:10) is described in a similar way: in each case brought before them, they are to give instructions as to whether it involves *ben dam ledham* or something else. Rashi already explains that this Hebrew expression is distinguishing between accidental homicide and deliberate murder. *dam* develops here from an object of primitive fear to an object of ethico-judicial decision.

This is quite clear in the casuistic legal regulations in Ex. 22:1f.(2f.). In both the cases cited here, the one who is killed, i.e., whose blood is shed, is a thief found breaking and entering. The difference is that only if the incident takes

---

[57] See *BHK.*
[58] Cf. *BHK* on Dt. 19:10; 27:26.

place in daylight is the owner of the house guilty of *damim,* "blood." If it occurs during the night, *'en lo damim,* "there shall be no bloodguilt for him." It is very plain here that *dam* does not mean a bloody *deed,* but blood*guilt.* [59] The priests entrusted with the responsibility of making sacral legal pronouncements express their decisions in a similar way (Lev. 20:11ff.; Ezk. 33:4f.). [60] Serious crimes, even if they do not involve shedding blood, are considered to incur bloodguilt (*dam*) (Lev. 20:18; 17:4 uses the expression *dam yechashebh la'ish hahu',* "bloodguilt shall be imputed to that man"). Frequently, too, *dam* is used in parallelism with → חמס *chāmās,* which means "violent deed," but also "legal injury." The phrase "his blood remain upon him, be upon his head," or the like (Josh. 2:19; 2 S. 1:16; 1 K. 2:37), apparently goes back to the primitive idea of an active sphere of blood; [61] in later usage (Ezk. 18:13; 33:4), however, it denotes no more than a guilty verdict. [62]

Since the determination of serious guilt also meant the proclamation of the sentence of death, the meaning of *dam* in some of the passages just cited hovers between bloodguilt and the death penalty. Thus even *hatstsileni middamim* in Ps. 51:16(14) has been expounded as a prayer for deliverance from a "bloody punishment." [63]

3. *Semantic Multivalence.* The word *dam* is used extensively by metonymy and synecdoche in the OT. Also in prophetic and poetic passages it is used in hyperbole: here less serious transgressions, or transgressions of at least a very different kind, are called *dam* or mentioned with it in the same breath. Thus *dam* is closely connected not only with *chamas,* "violence" (Ezk. 7:23; etc.; in 9:9 the textual tradition oscillates between *chamas* and *dam*), [64] but also with → גלולים *gillûlîm,* "idolatry" (RSV "idols") (Ezk. 22:3), n'p, "adultery" (Ezk. 23:37,45), *'kl dam,* "eating blood" (Ezk. 33:25), *'avon,* "iniquity" (Isa. 59:3), *ra',* "evil" (Isa. 33:15), *'avlah,* "wrong" (Mic. 3:10), *cherpah,* "shame" (RSV "reproaches") (Hos. 12:15[14]), *betsa',* "dishonest gain" (Ezk. 22:13), *sheqer,* "lie" (Isa. 59:3), and *mirmah,* "deceit, treachery" (Ps. 5:7[6]; 55:24[23]). Even though this usage is strong evidence for the ethical seriousness prevalent in the OT, one must not overlook that the extensive use of the word *dam* was destined to lead to its erosion and devaluation. In many texts the precise meaning of the word is hard to decide.

In individual cases the decision must be left to the commentaries. Here we can only illustrate the nature of the problem by giving a few examples. In Ps. 106:38 a glossator [65] has already connected *dam* with offering children as sacrifices to Molech (rather than with the execution of an innocent person). Most exegetes

---

[59] Pedersen, *ILC,* I-II, 420ff.
[60] See Reventlow, 311ff.
[61] Koch.
[62] Reventlow.
[63] H. Schmidt, *HAT,* 15, *in loc.;* but cf. 3 below.
[64] See *BHK.*
[65] Kraus, *BK,* XV/2, *in loc.*

understand *damim* in Isa. 1:15 as "bloodguilt," but Duhm [66] and Herntrich [67] think that in the context of the prophet's overall polemic it means "sacrificial blood." Speaking rhetorically, Prov. 12:6 says that the "words of the wicked" *'rb dam*, "lie in wait for blood." In this connection it must be asked whether *ne'erbhah ledham* in Prov. 1:11 means an actual ambush or deceitful intrigues and money transactions. [68] Delitzsch wants to interpret *dam* here as "young blood, young man" [69] (others emend the text to *tam*, "blameless"); cf. Jer. 22:3, 17; Ps. 26:9; 59:3(2). In Isa. 33:15 "listening to *damim*" is usually understood as planning murders, but Guthe expounds it as listening to "words that must be punished like bloodguilt, e.g., blasphemy or incitement to idolatry." [70] In Isa. 4:4 "the *dam* of Jerusalem" relates to "bloodguilt." And yet the word *dam* here appears in parallelism with the "filth (...of Zion)." The idea of uncleanness caused by menstruation probably lies behind this passage. The same is true of Ezk. 36:18, which seems to be an explanatory gloss on v. 17; [71] also cf. Ezk. 18:5 with 18:10. The statement in Ezk. 23:37, "and *dam* is upon their hands," belongs to a paragraph dealing with unchastity, not with murder. Accordingly, Rashi understands "blood" to refer to the unchaste act itself. (In *Meg.* 14b *mibbo' bhedhamim* in 1 S. 25:33 is explained ambiguously as murder and adultery.) In Ps. 51:16(14) *(hatstsileni) middamim* can mean "bloody punishment" [72] or "deadly peril" in general, but most commentators interpret it as "bloodguilt." [73] The LXX translates *velo' thasim damim bebhethekha* in Dt. 22:8, "so that no fatal accident may occur in your house," while the Targum renders it, "so that no death penalty will have to be imposed on the members of your house."

IV. Theological Usage.

1. *Magical Power.* Obviously in the blood rites described in the OT we are not dealing with a peculiarly Israelite invention. Primitive customs, whose origins and purposes can only be conjectured, were preserved and given a new interpretation. This new interpretation, however, is not always consciously formulated but often must be determined from the whole context. Here two points of crystallization are of crucial importance: the Israelite concept of God and the tendency to historicization. The OT is concerned to connect regulations and customs with Yahweh and to anchor their origin in a specific historical time.

According to the OT blood can defile (Isa. 59:3; Lam. 4:14) or cleanse (Lev. 14:14,49ff.). Blood that defiles includes particularly the blood of menstruation (Lev. 15:19ff.; 18:19; Isa. 64:5 [6]) and childbirth (Lev. 12:2ff.). It is the task

---

[66] Duhm, *GHK* (⁴1922), *in loc.*
[67] Herntrich, *ATD*, XVII (1950), *in loc.*
[68] G. Boström, *Proverbia-Studien. LUÅ*, 30/3 (1935), 59, 88.
[69] F. Delitzsch, *Das Salom. Spruchbuch* (1873), *in loc.*
[70] Guthe, *HSAT, in loc.*
[71] Rothstein, *HSAT, in loc.*
[72] See above.
[73] *GesB*, 164.

of the priests to supervise the cleansing rites commanded by Yahweh. In Ezekiel's allegory of Jerusalem as a foundling, Yahweh himself removes the traces of blood on the newborn child and later on the grown woman (Ezk. 16:6,9).

According to the accent, v.6: "I said to you in your blood: Remain alive...,"[74] should be read: "I said to you: In your blood you shall live (or remain alive)," i.e., the time has not yet come to wash you,[75] or, in spite of the blood that still defiles you, you shall live.

The OT ascribes apotropaic power to blood. The event narrated in Ex. 4:24ff. is obscure in its details. At all events, however, the blood of circumcision functions as a powerful and effective protection against the sinister threat posed by Yahweh. Furthermore, the etiological interest of the narrative is clear: a historical origin needs to be given to the phrase chathan (→ חתן chāthān) damim, "bridegroom of blood," which is familiar to the narrator only as an unintelligible archaic formula. It is impossible to determine with certainty who is meant by the chathan damim, "bridegroom of blood," in the context of the present narrative.[76] But the formula may be viewed as a saying originally in connection with circumcision,[77] and it shows that the blood shed in circumcision was regarded as an essential component of the ceremony.[78]

In the Passover story a protective blood rite is mentioned at an important point (Ex. 12:13,23): Yahweh will slay the firstborn of Egypt, but the houses of the Israelites, on whose doorposts and lintel the blood of the paschal lamb is smeared, are spared. Here an ancient nomadic custom, "which was intended to protect the herds from the influence of demons,"[79] is connected with the story of the exodus. A further spiritualization occurs when the Deuteronomic law is to be written symbolically on the doorposts and to represent the blood (Dt. 6:4ff.; 11:18ff.). In the same context, totaphoth, "commemorative symbols" on the forehead, are also mentioned. These, too, were originally apotropaic blood symbols, "drops."[80]

2. *Eating Blood.* Eating blood was strictly forbidden both to Israelites and to strangers in the OT (Lev. 17:10ff.; etc.). This prohibition, which goes back to a taboo that is also known elsewhere, is placed by the P source in the primeval history, and eating blood is put on the same plane as murder (Gen. 9:4ff.; cf. Ezk. 33:25). According to 1 S. 14:32ff. the aversion to eating blood in Israel seems to come from the earliest time. But one should not ignore the polemic contained in this narrative, a polemic that is continued in the repeated warnings against "eating blood" (Dt. 12:16) or "eating with the blood" (Lev. 19:26; cf. Ezk.).[81]

---

[74] So *HSAT*, etc.
[75] Ehrlich, *Mikra ki-Peshuto, in loc.*
[76] E. Meyer thinks it refers to God; Jer. *Ned.* iii.14, to Moses; Ibn Ezra, to the son.
[77] Kosmala, *VT*, 12 (1962), 14ff.
[78] See 4 below.
[79] Von Rad, *OT Theol*, I (trans. 1962), 253.
[80] Curtiss, 216f.
[81] See above.

'akhal 'eth haddam and 'akhal 'al haddam possibly mean the same thing ("over"=together with). The Talmud (Sanh. 63a) explains the difference thus: the flesh is not to be eaten "over" the blood, i.e., as long as the sacrificial blood is still in the sacrificial dish; or, a funeral meal is not to be eaten after a person had been condemned to death, etc. Pedersen explains the transgression of the people in 1 S. 14:32ff. as eating flesh over the blood shed on the earth, while Saul removed the blood with the help of the stone, which thus was not an altar. [82]

There must have been a long controversy on this question, either between Israel and the cult practices of the surrounding nations (Zec. 9:7; Ps. 16:4), or within Israel itself. [83] It is noteworthy that in poetic passages drinking the blood of the enemy is glorified (Nu. 23:24; Zec. 9:15—LXX). In ancient times everything that was slaughtered was a sacrifice and—perhaps according to a rite that was not generally binding—the blood belonged exclusively to the deity. It was poured out on a stone altar (Jgs. 6:20; 13:19; 1 S. 6:14; 14:33). The later Pentateuchal sources, D and H, which already allow for secular slaughter, ordain that when an animal is slain, the blood should be poured out on the ground like water (Dt. 12:23f.) and covered with dust (Lev. 17:12f.).

3. *Blood of Sacrifices.* The function of the blood remained the same in the sacrificial act (2 K. 16:13). The Priestly Code inserted in the Sinaitic legislation a system of blood manipulations that accompany the sacrifices or even are their climax. In the burnt-offering and peace-offering the blood of the victim must be sprinkled all around the altar (Lev. 1:11; 3:7,13), or, if the burnt-offering is a bird, the blood must be drained out on the side of the altar (1:15). In the sin-offering for the prince and the individual, some of the blood is put on the horns of the altar and the rest is poured out at the base of the altar (4:25ff.). In the sin-offering for the anointed priest and the whole community, the blood is brought into the tent of revelation and part of it is sprinkled seven times before Yahweh, before the veil in the sanctuary. Then some of the blood must be put on the horns of the altar of incense inside the tent of revelation, and the rest is to be poured out at the base of the altar of burnt-offering before the tent (4:6ff.). On the Day of Atonement the manipulation of blood attains its highest intensification: the sacrificial blood must be sprinkled on the *kapporeth*, "mercy seat," and seven times before it; the altar also is to be cleansed, as its horns are smeared with blood and seven times some blood is sprinkled upon it (16:14ff.). Ezk. 45:18ff. provides for a purification of the sanctuary twice a year. In this ceremony the blood of the sin-offering must be smeared on the altar and the doorposts of the temple.

Any attempt to determine the meaning of blood manipulation is subject to serious methodological questioning, for it originated in an early period impervious to our view, and later ideas connected with it do not seem to be at all homogeneous. [84] With this reservation, this much can be said: The primitive

---

[82] Pedersen, *ILC,* III-IV, 338f.
[83] Gressmann, *RGG,* III (1912), 2086; Dewar.
[84] Von Rad, *loc. cit.*

origin of blood manipulation in magical modes of thought is everywhere apparent. The sphere of magical thinking, however, is limited from the very first, because the meticulously graded blood manipulations of the OT are regulated by Yahweh himself, and thus their efficacy is wholly dependent on his sovereign will. The OT opposes and transcends the idea that the deity requires blood for food (Isa. 1:11; Ps. 50:13). On the contrary, man offers to God the blood that he is forbidden to eat. The closer it is brought, the holier it is, and the more significant the sacrifice. The element of atonement comes to the forefront (Lev. 6:23[30]), until finally this classic formulation is attained: "I have given it (the blood) ... upon the altar to make atonement for you (*'al naphshothekhem*), for it is the blood that makes atonement, by reason of the life (*ki haddam hu' bannephesh yekhapper*)" (17:11). He who offers a sacrifice puts back into the hands of God a life contained in the blood. Whether this life was regarded as a particularly valuable sacrifice, or was offered as a substitute for the life of the one making the sacrifice, does not have to be decided absolutely, but the idea of vicarious sacrifice is clear. [85] In the ordination of the priests, another application of blood is mentioned along with the familiar blood rite (Ex. 29:20; Lev. 8:23): the tip of the right ear lobe, the right thumb, and the great toe of the right foot must be smeared with sacrificial blood. That the intention of this was to bestow a "holy character on the organs of hearing, acting (especially in the cult!), and walking (in the holy place)" [86] must be called into question in view of the analogous ceremony used in connection with the cleansing of leprosy (Lev. 14:14). The intention of both ceremonies is to cleanse the people involved, who are represented by their bodily extremities *partes pro toto*.

In preparing the water of purification, a red heifer (→ פרה *pārāh*) must be burned to ashes (Nu. 19). This ceremony also has been interpreted as a sin-offering by the glosses in vv. 4,9. The original rite, however, seems to involve the transformation of the crimson color and of the blood to white ashes, and thus the efficacy of magical purification. [87]

4. *Blood of the Covenant.* Ex. 24:5ff. tells of a ceremony in which half the sacrificial blood is sprinkled on the altar and the other half on the people participating in the ceremony. What is described here is the concluding of a covenant, as it was done between human partners, [88] but doubtless also in the form of a sacral league between tribal groups and their God. [89] Many scholars think this was a type of oath rite according to which the blood of the covenant breaker was to be shed like the blood of the animal in the rite. [90] The Penta-

---

[85] Eichrodt, *TheolOT,* I, 165f. Cf. Philo *De specialibus legibus,* I, 205 (Cohn-Wendland): *psychḗs gár kyríōs eipeín apoleiphthḗnai psychikḗs spondḗs.* (The soul is libation, or more precisely, the blood.)

[86] Holzinger, *HSAT,* on Exodus.

[87] Cf. also Noth, *Numbers. OTL* (trans. 1968), 140.

[88] Wellhausen, 128.

[89] Smith, 312f.

[90] See → ברית *berîth* and the literature listed there; cf. also E. Kutsch, *Verheissung und Gesetz. Untersuchungen zum sogenannten "Bund" im AT. BZAW,* 131 (1973), 80-88.

teuchal narrative transforms a regular cultic celebration into a single historical event. By a complicated redactional process, [91] it comes to stand after the Decalog and the Book of the Covenant. In this way the redactor makes the content of the covenant ethico-judicial, and closely connects the *dam habberith,* "blood of the covenant" (v. 8), with the *sepher habberith,* "book of the covenant" (v. 7). Zec. 9:11, "because of the blood of my covenant with you (*bedham berithekh*), I will set your captives free," seems to have the Sinai covenant in mind, [92] though some exegetes have also connected this verse with circumcision. [93]

5. *Yahweh As Avenger of Blood.* The Israelite concept of Yahweh as the righteous judge (Jer. 11:20; Ps. 9:5[4]; etc.) lays its impress on the idea of murder and atonement. The blood of a murdered man, which previously had been depicted as wandering about and crying out to its avenger, can now lift up its voice to Yahweh (Gen. 4:10; Job 16:18f.). Yahweh is the *doresh damim,* "avenger of blood," who does not forget the cry of the afflicted (Ps. 9:13[12]; cf. 72:14). He intervenes when human justice proves to be powerless or irresolute in executing his commands. After Jezebel (?) murders the prophets, Elisha declares: "Thus says Yahweh ..., I will avenge on Jezebel the *damim* (blood) of my servants the prophets, and the *damim* (blood) of all the servants of Yahweh" (2 K. 9:7). After Ahab executes Naboth, Yahweh announces to him that the dogs will lick up his blood (1 K. 21:19). Ezekiel uses the figure of the watchman in wartime to describe the responsibility of the prophetic office. When watchman or prophet causes the death of those entrusted to him by not doing his duty, Yahweh will require their blood at his hand (Ezk. 3:18,20, *vedhamo miyyadhekha 'abhaqqesh;* 33:6, *vedhamo ... 'edhrosh;* cf. Lam. 4:13).

Above all, however, Yahweh is the one who reveals himself in history. The word *dam* occurs frequently in the theological interpretation of a historical process which may often look like a series of bloody wars. Just as Yahweh helps the righteous get blood revenge on the evildoer (Ps. 58:11[10]; cf. 68:24[23]), [94] he allows his people Israel to drink the blood of its enemies (Nu. 23:24). The people, of course, brings down *dam* upon itself by injustice and violence, so that it is itself threatened by *dam* as a punishment (Ezk. 5:17; 14:19; 22:3ff.; Zeph. 1:17). Nevertheless, the divine activity is directed especially against the arrogant enemies of Israel. The water of the Nile that had been turned to blood (Ex. 4:9; 7:15ff.) is already a sign of the terrible humiliation of Egypt, which is personified by the Nile. Israel's enemies pour out its blood like water; God must avenge it (Ps. 79:3,10). A bloody punishment is announced against the Egyptians (Jer. 46:10; Ezk. 32:6), the Babylonians (Jer. 51:35), the Sidonians (Ezk. 28:23), the Moabites (Jer. 48:10), the Ammonites (Ezk. 21:37[32]), and especially the Edomites (Ezk. 35:6; Isa. 34:3ff.; 63:1ff.). It is only a small step from this to eschatol-

---

[91] Noth, *OTL, in loc.*

[92] Rashi; Elliger, *ATD,* XXV, *in loc.*

[93] Cf. Ibn Ezra; Marti, *HSAT, in loc.*

[94] However, Albright, *HUCA,* 23 (1950/51), 28f., reads *lamah 'anath tirchatsi raghlekha bedham,* "Why did Anath wash your feet in blood?"

ogy; the war theophanies become End Time expectations. [95] In Isa. 34 the motifs of Edom and all the nations of the world have already been combined. In the End Time the blood of the Jews will be avenged by the blood of their enemies (Isa. 49:26; Ezk. 38:22; 39:17ff.), as by a sacrifice (Joel 4:19ff.[3:19ff.]).

Obviously, Judean national concepts play a major role here. And yet a universal perspective is evident: crimes committed in the history of mankind must be expiated before the kingdom of peace without bloodshed (cf. 1 Ch. 22:8f.) can become a reality.

Kedar-Kopfstein

---

95 Von Rad, *OT Theol*, II, 124f.

דָּמָה *dāmāh;* דְּמוּת *dᵉmûth*

Contents: I. Occurrences and Semantic Field of the Verb. II. Sphere of Use. III. The Noun *demuth*.

I. Occurrences and Semantic Field of the Verb. The verb *damah* I cannot always be clearly distinguished from *damah* II/*damam*. [1] A comparison of the concordances shows that scholars disagree as to which root lies behind the occurrences in 2 S. 21:5; Jer. 6:2; Ezk. 32:2; Ps. 49:13,21 (Eng. vv. 12,20). Since the only example in this group that can be assigned to *damah* I is that found in 2 S. 21:5, 27 occurrences of the root in Hebrew and two in Aramaic remain to be investigated.

damah appears 13 times in the qal (Heb.), where it is intransitive and should be rendered "to be like, look like" (Isa. 1:9; 46:5; Ezk. 31:2,8 [twice],18; Ps. 89:7[6]; 102:7[6]; 144:4; Cant. 2:9,17; 7:8[7]; 8:14). We may add to this two occurrences in the Aramaic peal in Dnl. 3:25; 7:5. The LXX usually translates the qal by *homoioún*, "to be like" (9 times), and rarely also by *hómoios*, "like,"

---

dāmāh. M. Dahood, "Accadian-Ugaritic *dmt* in Ezekiel 27,32," *Bibl*, 45 (1964), 83f.; E. Jenni, *THAT*, I, cols. 451-56; G. Johannes, *Unvergleichlichkeitsformulierungen im AT* (diss., Mainz, 1966); C. J. Labuschagne, *The Incomparability of Yahweh in the OT* (Leiden, 1966); O. Loretz, *Die Gottebenbildlichkeit des Menschen* (1967); T. Mettinger, "Abbild oder Urbild? 'Imago Dei' in traditionsgeschichtlicher Sicht," *ZAW*, 86 (1974), 403-424; J. M. Miller, "In the 'Image' and 'Likeness' of God," *JBL*, 91 (1972), 289-304; H. D. Preuss, *Verspottung fremder Religionen im AT. BWANT*, 92 (1971); W. H. Schmidt, *Die Schöpfungsgeschichte der Priesterschrift. WMANT*, 17 (³1973); C. Westermann, *BK*, I/1, 201ff.; H. W. Wolff, *Anthropology of the OT* (trans. 1974), 95, 159ff.

1 Cf. *KBL³*, 216b; J. Blau, *VT*, 6 (1956), 242f.; N. Lohfink, *VT*, 12 (1962), 275-77; L. Delekat, *VT*, 14 (1964), 23-25.

or *hómoios eínai,* "to be like." *damah* also occurs 13 times in the piel (Nu. 33:56; Jgs. 20:5; 2 S. 21:5; Isa. 10:7; 14:24; 40:18,25; 46:5; Ps. 48:10[9]; 50:21; Cant. 1:9; Lam. 2:13; Est. 4:13). It has in this case a "declarative-estimative" meaning (to declare or consider something or someone to be in the condition suggested by the verb),[2] i.e., the piel of *damah* should be translated "to compare, to consider suitable or appropriate," but also "to plan" and even "to think." It is true that the LXX mostly translates the piel too by *homoioún,* "to be like" (5 times), but it also uses *eipeín,* "to speak" (Est. 4:13; Isa. 14:24), *hypolambánein,* "to think" (Ps. 48:10[9]; 50:21), *diaginōskein,* "to decide, determine," *enthymeísthai,* "to consider, think," *ethélein,* "to wish, will," *paralogízesthai,* "to deceive," and *exolethreúsai,* "to destroy utterly." The only occurrence in the hithpael (Isa. 14:14) points to the meaning, "to make oneself like, put on the same level" (LXX: *hómoios eínai,* "to be like"). The examples in the niphal cited by some scholars (Ezk. 32:2; Ps. 49:13,21[12,20]) belong to the root *damah* II.[3]

The only other language in the ancient Near East in which the root *damah* I occurs is Aramaic.[4] In the OT the verbs → מָשַׁל *māshal,* "to be like," → עָמַם *ʽāmam,* "to be comprehensive, include," → עָרַךְ *ʽārakh,* "to compare," and → שָׁוָה *shāwāh,* "to be like, resemble," and the recurring comparative formulas with *ke,* "like, as,"[5] especially *ʼen ke,* "there is none like," and *mi khe,* "who is like?" belong to the same semantic field.

II. Sphere of Use. For the secular use of *damah,* attention must first be called to the examples in Canticles (4 times in the qal and once in the piel, always with *le*), where the verb (mainly in the so-called Descriptive Songs or waṣf Poems) is used for comparisons between the two lovers and their attributes on the one side, and on the other side things from the realm of nature, particularly from the animal world (cf. 8:14 with the comparisons using *ke* in 2:3; 4:5=7:4[3]),[6] as in the love poetry of other ancient peoples, especially the Egyptians. In 1:9-11, the young man, in a direct address, "compares" his beloved with a magnificently bridled mare drawing the chariot of Pharaoh (1:9, piel). In 2:9 (in the pericope 2:8-14; a "door lament" at the place of rendezvous[7]), the young woman declares: "My beloved is like (qal ptcp.; cf. 2:17, which has an impv.; so also 8:14 in a veiled invitation to make love) a gazelle or a young stag." In the "Song of Admiration" in 7:7-11(6-10),[8] which is very closely connected with the Descriptive Song, the young man says (7:8[7], using the qal): "Your stature is such that it is

---

[2] E. Jenni, *Das hebräische Piʽel* (Zurich, 1968), 40f.

[3] On the example in Hos. 12:11(10), which is not considered in the following discussion, cf. the remarks of I. Willi-Plein, *Vorformen der Schriftexegese innerhalb des AT. BZAW,* 123 (1971), 218; further, on Hos. 4:5, cf. Rudolph, *KAT,* XIII/1, 97; and on Ezk. 32:2, cf. Zimmerli, *BK,* XIII, 763.

[4] Cf. *KAI,* 276.10 and *DISO,* 58; also Dnl. 3:25; 7:5 in Aram.

[5] Cf. also Jenni, *THAT,* I, cols. 454-56; and Johannes, *loc. cit.*

[6] Cf. also Gerleman, *BK,* XVIII, 63-72.

[7] Gerleman, 123; cf. Rudolph, *KAT,* XVII/1-3, 133.

[8] Gerleman, 202; Rudolph, 175.

like a palm tree, and your breasts like grapes." [9] Extended comparisons (often with *ke*) occur in Descriptive Songs, as in 4:1,2,3,4,5; 7:5(4).

damah is also used in a secular context in Dnl. 3:25; 7:5 (Aram.), where it means "to look like." The latter passage, however, reflects already the imagery of apocalyptic. [10] *dimmah* (piel) is used in speaking of men "planning, intending, considering, or drawing comparisons" in Jgs. 20:5; 2 S. 21:5; and Est. 4:13. The texts in which the plaintive psalmist says that he is like a jackdaw (?) of the wilderness (Ps. 102:7[6]), etc., compose a group that is already more significant theologically. This comparison stands in the context of the description of distress in an Individual Lament (vv. 2-12[1-11]; cf. also the recurring *ke* in the context around v. 7[6]). Like the similar text in Ps. 144:4 (qal; line b again uses *ke*; the context in vv. 1-11 is a litany of a king?), it is intended to emphasize the weakness and distress of man in order to strengthen the expectation that the plaintive petitions will be answered.

Isa. 1:9 also belongs in this context. After (or in?) Isaiah's Woe (1:4-7), the inhabitants of Jerusalem, who are left in the city because of the forbearance of Yahweh Sebaoth, declare that if Yahweh had not spared a few survivors, they would have been like (*daminu*) Sodom and Gomorrah (cf. Am. 4:11; Zeph. 2:9; Isa. 13:19; Dt. 29:22[23]). Finally Lam. 2:13 (piel) belongs to this group of Laments; *shavah*, which belongs to the semantic field of *damah*, also appears in this passage (cf. Isa. 40:25). In this alphabetic Lament (Lam. 2) over Jerusalem and its misfortune, the section which constitutes a lament in the narrower sense poses the question: "What shall I cite you as an example (read the *qere*), to what shall I compare you, O daughter of Jerusalem?" (v. 13). The author wants to speak comforting words to Jerusalem by citing similar instances of suffering and distress and by showing that comfort can come only by turning to Yahweh (vv. 18f.) and following him (vv. 20ff.). [11] In this case (as in Ps. 48:10[9], which uses the piel), too much is asked of the verb *dimmah* if one tries to deduce from it that in Israel's worship the proclaimer of salvation was obviously seeking "figures" so as to pass on to the community a word of comfort, [12] especially as it is not at all clear to what extent the questions in this strophe have the form of prolegomena to a priestly or prophetic salvation oracle. [13]

Ps. 48:10(9) and 50:21 (both of which use the piel of *dmh*) also have a cultic setting. In the framework of a cultic-(48:10b[9b])-hymnic glorification of the city of God, the community worshipping in the temple says: "*dimminu* (We have thought), O God (should one read Yahweh, since this is in the Elohistic Psalter?), on your steadfast love in the temple." In interpretation it is impossible to demonstrate that vv. 5-8(4-7) have in mind a specific historical event (Sennacherib's invasion of Jerusalem in 701 B.C.?). But v. 9(8), which immediately precedes the passage under investigation in v. 10(9), undoubtedly refers to cultic

---

9 On the translation, see Gerleman, 201.
10 See III below.
11 So with Rudolph, *KAT*, XVII/1-3, 224.
12 So Kraus, *BK*, XX, 40f.
13 So Kraus, 34.

hearing and seeing, so that it is certainly too weak to translate *dimminu* by "con-sider."[14] The point is that God's (Yahweh's?) deeds were represented and im-parted in the word. This is what the community is gratefully confessing here. It "makes comparisons," "compares," "ponders"[15] what has been said and heard (experienced?) and its own reality (v. 12![11]). Whether "paradigmatic demon-strations" were performed with the intention of glorifying Yahweh and his city[16] cannot be demonstrated.[17]

Ps. 50 (which is to be dated later than the similar psalms, 81 and 95, and is dependent on Deutero-Isaiah), is the cult psalm of a (covenant-?) festival. As such it contains in vv. 16ff. a priestly (not cult-prophetic)[18] penitential oracle, which, as an oracle of Yahweh, reproaches the wicked (v. 16a; secondary?) of Israel for their sins, and admonishes them to live according to the statutes of Yahweh (vv. 7-22, in which vv. 8-15 compose a thematically definable unit). In the charge in v. 21 (does v. 21c belong with v. 7?),[19] Yahweh says: "These things you have done and I have been silent; you thought (*dimmitha*) that I was one like yourself," i.e., "you compared yourself with me."[20] By saying this, Yahweh consciously and emphatically lifts himself above any human analogy (this same thought appears in Isa. 31:3; Ezk. 28:2-9; Job 40:9). Except in Ps. 102:7[6]; 144:4; Job 40:9, the verb *dmh*, when it is used with Yahweh, mainly expresses his incomparability.[21]

In Isaiah's Woe Oracle against Assyria (Isa. 10:5-8,13-15), the prophet uses *dmh* in the piel in v. 7 in the same sense of "think, plan" (cf. → חשׁב *chāshabh*; → יעץ *yāʿats*, and Isa. 14:14, which uses *dmh* in the hithpael).[22] The oracle of judgment against Assyria (Isa. 14:24-27) corresponds to this. Here, according to 14:24, Yahweh's thoughts and plans (cf. 31:3) are against Assyria's, viz., as a fixed and self-fulfilling (*taqum*) resolution to destroy Assyria. Assyria no longer "plans" punishment in the sense that Yahweh does (10:5ff.), but in its arrogance intends to destroy and exterminate its enemy, Judah.

The same arrogance is also described in Isa. 14:14 (which uses *dmh* in the hithpael). This is part of the ancient and originally highly mythological core

---

[14] So Gunkel, comm. *in loc.*

[15] So Dahood, *Psalms*, I. *AB*, XVI (1965), *in loc.*

[16] So Kraus, *BK*, XV, 359; cf. H.-P. Müller, *Ursprünge und Strukturen alttestamentlicher Eschatologie. BZAW*, 109 (1969), 43; A. R. Johnson, *Sacral Kingship in Ancient Israel* (Cardiff, ²1967), 79. But what would this mean?

[17] Cf. the analogy to Lam. 2:13 above: frequently both passages are translated, "we acted out (mimed)."

[18] So with J. Jeremias, *Kultprophetie und Gerichtsverkündigung in der späten Königszeit Israels. WMANT*, 35 (1970), 125-27.

[19] So Gunkel, comm. *in loc.*

[20] On the difficult *heyoth*, cf. Kraus and Dahood; the latter translates (*AB*, XVI, *in loc.*), "You harbor (cf. *dmh* in 2 S. 21:5; Nu. 33:56) evil desires: Am I like you?" and appeals to Ps. 52:9(8).

[21] See below.

[22] On the wisdom terminology in Isaiah reflected here, cf. J. W. Whedbee, *Isaiah and Wisdom* (1971), who also discusses the present passage.

(vv. 12-15) of 14:1-23. In the course of the tradition, however, different elements have been combined with the core. The original reference of the pericope was to the gods Shahar and Shalim, Dawn and Dusk, manifestations of the evening star ʿAṭṭar, which were well known in Ugarit and South Arabia as sons of El [23] (on the content of this passage, cf. Ezk. 28:2,6,9,14; 31:2-10,18; 32:19; Isa. 47:10), and whose attempt to rebel against El and overthrow him was frustrated on Mt. Zaphon. They wanted to "become like" → עֶלְיוֹן ʿelyôn, to "make themselves like" him. This text prepares the way for the use of dmh in Deutero-Isaiah [24] inasmuch as it speaks of the forbidden and presumptuous attempt to make oneself like the highest deity (cf. also Ps. 89:7[6]), by which the present passage Isa. 14:1-23 naturally understands Yahweh (14:5!). Here, however, the piece is politically historicized as a mocking and triumphing funeral song which is first directed against a king of Assyria and then later (by adding the framework 14:1-2,3-4a, 22f.) against a king of Babylon. The use of dmh (cf. the qal in Isa. 1:9, and the piel in 10:7) in 14:24 (where it is closely connected with yaʿats) raises the question whether the Yahwicizing and initial historicizing of this mythical material (14:12-15) could conceivably have been accomplished by Isaiah himself (on Isa. 14:24, cf. also Ps. 48:10[9] in the context of the Zion tradition?).

On the other hand, when we turn to Nu. 33:56 (part of the pericope Nu. 33:50-56 [Pg], which contains Deuteronomistic additions to P that presuppose Deuteronomy and the Holiness Code), this verse, which bears the strong impress of the Deuteronomistic School, is speaking about a plan, a purpose, a consideration of Yahweh. "And I will do to you as I had planned (dimmithi) to do to them." According to this theory, Yahweh has commanded the expulsion of all Canaanites from the land, and he now states the consequences of disobeying this command (vv. 55f.). He intends to punish Israel through the peoples that they allow to remain in the land—a typical Deuteronomistic argument. [25]

The instances of dmh (in the qal) in Ezk. 31:2,8(twice),18 are to be found in similar contexts to that of Isa. 14. Within the oracles against Egypt, 31:1-18 describes "the pomp and ruin of the tree of life—a figure of the Pharaoh." [26] The question that introduces the first pericope, vv. 2b-9 [27] (was it placed before vv. 3-9 at a later time?), "is similar in content to a hymn of praise." [28] In a personal address, the prophet asks the pharaoh: "Whom are you like (damitha) in your greatness?" Verse 8 again takes up the key word damah [29] (cf. further v. 18 as

---

[23] Cf. the literature and examples, as well as a more detailed discussion of the text, in Preuss, Verspottung, 140; see also J. W. McKay, VT, 20 (1970), 451-56; U. Oldenburg, ZAW, 82 (1970), 187-208; F. Stolz, Strukturen und Figuren von Jerusalem. BZAW, 118 (1970), 210-12; M. Metzger, UF, 2 (1970), 146f.

[24] See below.

[25] Cf. also G. Schmitt, Du sollst keinen Frieden schliessen mit den Bewohnern des Landes. BWANT, 91 (1970), 42, 47, 98f.

[26] Zimmerli, BK, XIII, 746.

[27] On the original composition of this text, cf. Zimmerli, 751.

[28] Zimmerli, 755; on the LXX reading, see Zimmerli, 747.

[29] On this text, additions to it, and problems connected with it, see Zimmerli, 627 on 27:5; and 758.

a final pendant to v. 2). It speaks of the tree of life as a great cedar with whose boughs the (boughs of the?) fir trees cannot compare (*lo' dhamu*), and whose branches the (branches of the) plane trees cannot equal; no tree in the garden of God is like it in beauty. Verse 18 repeats and intensifies the question in v. 2 and states its implications. The framework of the section is thus completed. It has the form of a crescendo suggested by the key word *damah*. Within this the hymnic ring of v. 2 increasingly changes to that of the political lament [30] (on v. 18 cf., e.g., Isa. 14:1-23, esp. v. 14). [31] The frequent use of the allusive vocabulary of comparison in Ezk. 31 (cf. the analogous use of *demuth* in Ezk. 1 and 10) [32] points to a fact which can be substantiated elsewhere in the history of the tradition, namely, that there is a path from Ezekiel to early apocalyptic (later cf. Aram. *dameh* in Dnl. 3:25 and 7:5, and Heb. *demuth* in Dnl. 10:16).

Finally, the most pregnant use of *damah* (in the qal and piel) in the OT is found in affirmations of the incomparability of Yahweh. [33] Ps. 89 is in the first instance a hymn of praise to Yahweh for the manifestations of his steadfast love in creation and in the choice of the Davidic dynasty (vv. 2-19[1-18]; vv. 20-38[19-37] carry this thought further, while vv. 39-52[38-51] contain a lament over the downfall of the kingdom of David; the time is probably that of the exile rather than of Josiah, as is also suggested by the close similarity between Ps. 89:7[6] and Deutero-Isaiah, e.g., Isa. 55:3f.). Within the psalm vv. 6-19(5-18) constitute a kind of cosmic hymn. [34] Verses 7-9(6-8) give reasons why the heavens should praise Yahweh as they are summoned to do in the somewhat isolated v. 6 (5). Verse 7(6) is particularly important to the present discussion. It contains a rhetorical question which is typical in this connection. [35] The particle *ki* forms a link with v. 6—a reason is being given for this—and also leads on to the further consideration: "For who in the skies can be compared (*ya'arokh*) to Yahweh, who among the heavenly beings is like (*yidhmeh*) Yahweh?" The gods are stripped of power and degraded to a position in Yahweh's court. In contrast with them, Yahweh is incomparable in his majesty. In the pitiable situation this gives hope in spite of all appearances to the contrary (cf. Deutero-Isaiah).

In affirmations of Yahweh's incomparability it is especially Deutero-Isaiah who uses the verb *damah* (4 times; and also the noun *demuth*). [36] This verb appears in the piel first of all in Isa. 40:18,25, i.e., in the disputation oracle in 40:12-31, which is permeated with hymnic elements (cf. the similar genre in 46:1-7). [37] Hymnic affirmations emphasizing Yahweh's incomparability (cf. also Isa. 43:10-13; 44:7) are interspersed with questions that convey the same thought

---

[30] Cf. Zimmerli, 761.

[31] See above.

[32] See III below.

[33] See Johannes, Labuschagne, Preuss; but cf. also *TDOT*, I, 282-84, 474, 478.

[34] Cf. J.-B. Dumortier, *VT*, 22 (1972), 179.

[35] Cf. Preuss, *Verspottung*, Index *s.v.* "Fragen, rhetorische."

[36] See III below.

[37] For a more detailed discussion of 40:12-31, cf. Preuss, 193-203.

in this passage (cf. v. 18 after vv. 12-17, and v. 26 after v. 25). [38] These questions, which are not simply rhetorical, are characteristically used by Deutero-Isaiah as introductory questions (cf. perhaps 40:12f.,18,21,25,26,27; 41:4; 44:10; 48:14; 50:2; etc.). Among the exiles whom he addressed there were evidently some who made comparisons (similar to those suggested in the questions here) between Yahweh and the foreign gods who may have seemed to them to be victorious. In opposition to this, Deutero-Isaiah makes Yahweh's incomparability one of his central themes; and in order to make his audience aware of this emphasis and to develop it he uses the questions: "To whom then will you liken God ('el!)?" (40:18; cf. also 46:5), or more directly: "To whom then will you compare me, that I should be like him? says the Holy One" (40:25; with *shavah* in the context and the semantic field; cf. also 46:5 and Lam. 2:13). Here (and only here in Deutero-Isaiah) *damah* is for "comparison with something in the heathen world," although in relation to Yahweh this is clearly impossible (cf. also Lam. 2:13 in an analogous exilic situation(?); as regards foreign deities, cf. also Ps. 89:7[6]; Isa. 14:14). Isa. 40:25 intensifies v. 18 by having Yahweh speak directly. The context tells of Yahweh's incomparable glory as Creator, [39] but this has Israel in view and is extolled and attested on account of Israel. Finally Isa. 46:5 (cf. 40:18) in 46:1-7 (45:18–46:11 or 13?) [40] should be mentioned. The idols, which in a mocking polemic are identified with the foreign gods, will be carried out of the conquered city as booty by the victors, as was customary in those days. Deutero-Isaiah sees this event as a sign and part of the dawning era. Usually men carried these idols in solemn processions, but now animals will carry them out decidedly less ceremoniously as helpless booty being taken into captivity. Verses 3f., then, are conscious and flagrant antitheses to vv. 1f. The Yahweh hymn is (here also) a contrasting correlative to the ridicule of idols, its purpose being to show unmistakably the incomparability of Yahweh. This antithetical "comparison" (vv. 1f. with 3f.) was necessary because people evidently made such comparisons and thought that they could and should do so. [41] In v. 5, then, Yahweh finally asks a pointed (he uses *dmh* twice—in the piel and the qal; and he intensifies this by using the verbs *shavah* and *mashal*, which have a similar meaning) and direct question, and this question, which is typical in Deutero-Isaiah, has a doxological function. Verse 5 is clearly looking ahead to something else and it demands vv. 6f. as its continuation. Then again these verses take up many of the points in vv. 1-4 and are anticipated by them, so that they are not to be regarded as an insertion. Yahweh's uniqueness is displayed positively in striking contrast to the idols, which are now indeed "unable to compare" with him (cf. the end of v. 4 with the end of v. 7).

Thus the verb *damah* (as also the noun *demuth*) [42] makes very clear the polar-

---

[38] See also Labuschagne, 74, 123; and *TDOT*, I, 283.

[39] On the text, cf. also C. Stuhlmueller, *Creative Redemption in Deutero-Isaiah. AnBibl*, 43 (1970), 144-152.

[40] Cf. Preuss, 217-222.

[41] Cf. above on 40:18,25.

[42] See III below.

ity of God's relationship to Israel, because it declares both distance and also the intimate relationship between Yahweh and his world or human creatures, both the incomparability of Yahweh and also his solidarity (Gen. 1:26!). The concentrated use of the word in exilic texts (cf. also the use of *demuth*) suggests that the question whether Yahweh could be compared with anyone or anything was a special issue of the exilic period.

III. The Noun demuth. The verbal abstract *demuth*, which is derived from the verb *damah* I,[43] occurs 25 times in the OT: Gen. 1:26; 5:1,3; 2 K. 16:10; Isa. 40:18; Ezk. 1:5 (twice),10,16,22,26 (3 times),28; 8:2; 10:1,10,21,22; 23:15; Ps. 58:5(4); Dnl. 10:16; 2 Ch. 4:3 (in Isa. 13:4 read *hamoth*, "to be in commotion, be boisterous," and in Ezk. 1:13 *ubhenoth*, "and between, among"). The LXX usually renders *demuth* by *homoíōma*, "likeness, form, appearance" (14 times), but we also find *homoíōsis*, "likeness, resemblance" (5 times), *eikṓn*, "image, likeness" (once, Gen. 5:1), *idéa*, "appearance, aspect, form" (once, Gen. 5:3), and *hómoios*, "like" (once, Isa. 13:4), while the Vulgate predominantly translates it by *similitudo*, "likeness" (19 times). The thesis that *demuth* is an Aramaic loanword[44] has much in its favor, because this word is found in various Aramaic dialects[45] and in Middle Hebrew, while in the OT its use is limited mainly to exilic and postexilic texts (particularly texts with a priestly stamp).

demuth is used with *be*, "in," only in Gen. 5:1,3; it occurs with *ke*, "after, in," in Gen. 1:26; Ps. 58:5(4); and Dnl. 10:16.[46]

Probably the earliest example of *demuth* in the OT is found in 2 K. 16:10. Here the word still has the relatively concrete meaning of "image" or "copy, reproduction" (but cf. Ezk. 23:15). Its predominant usage in exilic texts, however, suggests the translation "form," "appearance," or more weakly "something like (similar to)."[47] It should be noted that the context of 2 K. 16 is full of words and expressions that are characteristic of P.

The word *demuth* occurs most frequently in the book of Ezekiel, where it is found both in texts going back to Ezekiel himself and also in texts that were added later in the course of redaction. A cluster of occurrences appears in Ezk. 1:5,10-28 and 10:1-22, i.e., in the great "visions," where it is made clear that *demuth* is a favorite word of Ezekiel and his "school." In 1:5, where *demuth* is used twice, the description of the glory of Yahweh's throne speaks of the "form (RSV likeness) of four living creatures" that carry the throne, and it is said of their appearance that they "were formed like men" (RSV, "they had the form of

---

[43] J. Barth, *Die Nominalbildung in den semitischen Sprachen* ([2]1894), § 260c; L. Delekat, *VT*, 14, 23-25.

[44] J. Wellhausen, *Prolegomena to the History of Ancient Israel* (trans. 1957), 389.

[45] Cf. *KBL*[3]; *DISO*, 58; Jenni, 451.

[46] On this use of the prepositions *be* and *ke* and their interchangeability (but cf. Gen. 1:26 with 5:1,3), see W. H. Schmidt, *Schöpfungsgeschichte*, 133 (cf. also 133f. for a general discussion of *demuth* with literature); O. Loretz, *Gottebenbildlichkeit*, 61, with literature (cf. also 56, 58-64 for a general discussion of *demuth*); Westermann, *BK*, I, 201.

[47] Cf. L. Köhler, *ThZ*, 4 (1948), 16-22, esp. 20.

men"). 1:26 (3 instances), which in the original text was connected with v. 22a, [48] speaks of "something like (RSV, the likeness of) a throne," and "what appeared to be like a man" (RSV, "a likeness as it were of a human form") ("And 'behold,' above the solid platform over their heads there was to be seen something like a sapphire stone [?]—something like a throne, [on which] was to be seen something that appeared to be like a man"). [49] In the final verse of chap. 1 (v. 28), the priestly-declaratory (cf. Gen. 1:26!) summation is: "Such was the appearance of the form (RSV likeness) of the glory (→ כבוד kābhôdh) of Yahweh." 1:10 (in 1:5-12) and 1:16 (in 1:15-21; read dhemuth 'achath: all the wheels had "the same form [RSV likeness]") belong to the later interpretation. Here the appearances of the living creatures and the wheels of the throne chariot are described in more detail.

Ezk. 8:2 allusively describes the "form" of the 'ish, "man," that brought Ezekiel to Jerusalem. [50] Then chap. 10 (see v. 1) describes the glory of Yahweh on his throne. In the later revision, which resembles Ezk. 1–3, it exhibits many contacts with chap. 1, especially the additions made there. [51] Hence it uses demuth frequently (cf. 1:26 with 10:1; 1:16 with 10:10; 1:10 with 10:22; and 1:8a with 10:21, where 10:21 has an extra demuth). The statement about the cherubim under whose wings was "something like human hands" (RSV, "the form of a human hand") (10:8) should be compared with Dnl. 10:16. [52] This passage shows that the language of apocalyptic (with its recurring "something like" or simply "like"; the MT of Isa. 13:4 uses demuth in the sense of ke; cf. Ps. 58:5[4]), which intentionally speaks often only in allusions, is in this respect, too, anticipated and influenced by Ezekiel, who, like his redactors, uses demuth when, especially in the accounts of visions, he can speak only in allusions and deliberately veiled statements, when his expressions and descriptions necessarily remain ambivalent and indistinct. When Oholibah saw men portrayed upon the wall (Ezk. 23:15, in the original text of 23:1-49), "a likeness (RSV picture) (cf. also 2 K. 16:10) of Babylonians whose native land was Chaldea," she sent an embassy to them. [53] But → צלם tselem, "image," also occurs (v. 14b) in this context (vv. 14b-17a). Here, then, the affinity of tselem and demuth (cf. Gen. 1:26) is already plain.

In Isa. 40:12-31 demuth is used in the sense of "comparison" (with the verb damah I, "to compare") in v. 18. This is set in a hymnic proclamation of the incomparability of Yahweh (vv. 12-17) which has been inserted into a disputation oracle, which shows that nothing and no one can be compared with Yahweh (vv. 18-24), and which reaches its goal in vv. 28-31. The context and flow of its statements are typical of Deutero-Isaiah (cf. also the semantic field represented

---

[48] Zimmerli, BK, XIII, 30: "something like a solid platform."
[49] Zimmerli's translation.
[50] Cf. also → בוא bô', VII; here read 'ish, "man," instead of 'esh, "fire," cf. Zimmerli, 191; cf. also 1:27 and on this point Zimmerli, 210.
[51] On the stratification of this chapter, cf. Zimmerli, 202ff.
[52] And Plöger, KAT, XVIII, 145.
[53] On this point, cf. Zimmerli, 545f.

here), so that there is no reason to cut off vv. 19f. from the surrounding material. [54]

In the original Priestly writing, also exilic, the use of *demuth* in the story of early man (Gen. 1:26; 5:1,3) has always been of particular interest. [55] *demuth* is used here with *tselem*, "image" (cf. Ezk. 23:14f.); it appears after *tselem* in Gen. 1:26 and before *tselem* in 5:3, while *tselem* occurs alone in 5:1. This interlacing and substitution suggest that very little distinction can be made between the two words. In 1:26 the terms are used with the prepositions *be*, "in," and *ke*, "after" (the latter with *demuth*), while in 5:1,3 *demuth* is used with *be* (in v. 3 *tselem* is used with *ke*). This dovetailing opposes too strong a differentiation between *demuth* and *tselem* (cf. further also 5:1 [56] and 9:6 [P], and again Ezk. 23:14f.). It also opposes an overemphasis on the use of the words with prepositions in contrast to their use alone. Instead, the juxtaposition of the two words in Gen. 1:26 suggests that the writer is making a statement about the dignity of man, which he intensifies by combining similar concepts. Thus *kidhmuthenu*, "after our likeness," in Gen. 1:26, [57] no matter how it may be elucidated by the otherwise predominant and characteristic use of *demuth*, can only correct a too direct understanding of *tselem*, which has a strongly concrete and plastic reference. This in turn paves the way in P (cf. Ezk.!) for the recognition that in respect of an analogy no identity of God and man can or should be asserted, but only a similarity ("something similar to us"). At the same time, what the author of Gen. 1:26 has concretely in view cannot be determined simply by investigating these related ideas. It emerges only from the broader context (v. 28) and is explained as a cooperative sharing in dominion. One cannot prove that because of its similarity to → דם *dam*, "blood," *demuth* was original in 9:6 and *tselem* was first substituted for it by P, [58] especially as v. 6b hardly formed an original unity with v. 6a.

Finally, the use of *demuth* in 2 Ch. 4:3 (in the secondary passage 4:2b-3aβ) [59] corresponds to this use. Here the writer has "something like oxen" (one should

---

[54] For a more detailed discussion, cf. Preuss, *Verspottung*, 193-203; but cf. also Elliger, *BK*, XI, *in loc.* and his discussion of *demuth* on p. 66. According to Elliger, the addition in 40:19f. must have misunderstood *demuth* in v. 18 as "image," but instead of viewing this as a misunderstanding, it should be regarded as a deliberate adoption and expansion; cf. also C. R. North, comm. *in loc.*, "What sort of *demuth* will you compare with God?" where, however, only man is the *demuth* of God; cf. Gen. 1:26. On statements about the incomparability of the deity in the OT and the ancient Near East, see the literature already cited under II above on Isa. 40:18; on the Hymn of Inanna, which is frequently mentioned in this connection (lines 10 and 40: "... does any, a god, measure up to me?" and elsewhere), see the revision by W. H. Ph. Römer, *Or*, 38 (1969), 97-114.

[55] On this problem, see W. H. Schmidt; O. Loretz; J. M. Miller; W. Eichrodt, *TheolOT* (trans. 1965), II, 122ff.; von Rad, *OT Theol*, I (trans. 1962), 144ff.; Westermann, *BK*, I, 201ff., all with literature; and the volume edited by L. Scheffczyk, *Der Mensch als Bild Gottes* (1969); cf. also the discussion under → אדם *'ādhām* in *TDOT*, I, 84f.

[56] Cf. P. Weimar, *BZ*, N.F. 18 (1974), 78.

[57] On the plural suffix, cf. Westermann, *BK*, I, 200f.

[58] Miller, 301f.

[59] Cf. Rudolph, *HAT*, 21, 205-207.

read the collective sing. *baqar* with Rudolph, and move the final *mem* of *beqarim* to the following *tachath* and interpret it as an assimilated *min*). This is his attempt to render the *peqa'im* of 1 K. 7:24, which is never used in Chronicles and which is virtually unintelligible (colocynths? RSV "gourds"). Once again, then, *demuth* means "as a type of." That is to say, it is "a mark of the hypothetical in the substitution." [60]

In the Qumran texts the verb *damah* has not yet been found and the noun *demuth* appears only in 4QSl 40. [61] This is surprising in view of the numerous texts in this material that are classified as apocalyptic or are closely related to it.

Preuss

---

[60] So Th. Willi, *Die Chronik als Auslegung. FRLANT,* 106 (1972), 139.
[61] Cf. *RevQ,* 4 (1963), 189.

דָּמָה *dāmāh* II; דמם *dmm;* דום *dwm;* דְּמִי *d°mî;*
דְּמָמָה *d°māmāh;* דֻּמָּה *dummāh;* דּוּמָם *dûmām;*
דּוּמִיָּה *dûmîyyāh;* דּוּמָה *dûmāh;* חָשָׁה *chāshāh;*
חָרַשׁ *chārash* II; חֵרֵשׁ *chērēsh;* חֶרֶשׁ *cheresh*

Contents: I. Etymology, Use in the Ancient Near East. II. *chāshāh.* III. *chārash.* IV. *dāmāh* II/*dmm*/*dwm*: 1. Occurrences, Semantic Field; 2. Usage in Legal Proclamations and Funeral Dirges; 3. Usage in Prayers for Favorable Hearing and in the Reception of Revelation.

I. Etymology, Use in the Ancient Near East.

The most common words in the semantic field meaning "to be silent" have (in spite of occasional overlapping) clearly discernible nuances of meaning and usage. *charash* means in the first instance "to be deaf, deaf and dumb," as in Aramaic and Arabic, and then in a

---

dāmāh II. J. B. Bauer, "Hes XXIV,17," *VT,* 7 (1957), 91f.; O. Betz, "φωνή," *TDNT,* IX, 284, n. 26; J. Blau, "Über homonyme und angeblich homonyme Wurzeln," *VT,* 6 (1956), 242f.; P. A. H. de Boer, "Notes on the Text and Meaning of Isaiah XXXVIII, 9-20," *OTS,* 9 (1951), 178f.; M. Dahood, "Textual Problems in Isaiah," *CBQ,* 22 (1960), 400-403; *idem,* "Hebrew-Ugaritic Lexicography II," *Bibl,* 45 (1964), 402f.; M. Delcor, "ḥrš schweigen," *THAT,* I, 639-641; L. Delekat, "Zum hebräischen Wörterbuch," *VT,* 14 (1964), 23-25; G. R. Driver, "Problems in the Hebrew Text of Job," *SVT,* 3 (1955), 86f.; K. Elliger, *Jesaja II. BK,* XI, on 41:1; A. Guillaume, "Hebrew and Arabic Lexicography," *Abr-Nahrain,* 1 (1959/60), 21f.; P. Haupt, "Some Assyrian Etymologies," *AJSL,* 26 (1909), 4f.; J. Jeremias, *Theophanie. WMANT,* 10 (1965), 112-15; N. Lohfink, "Enthielten die im AT bezeugten Klageriten eine Phase des Schweigens?" *VT,* 12 (1962), 260-277; T. F. McDaniel, "Philological Studies in Lamentations I," *Bibl,* 49 (1968), 27-53, esp. 38-40; W. Rudolph, *Hosea. KAT,* XIII/1, on 4:5; G. V. Schick, "The stems *dûm* und *damám* in Hebrew," *JBL,* 32 (1913), 219-243; W. A. Ward, "Some Egypto-Semitic Roots," *Or,* 31 (1962), 397-412, esp. 400-403; H. Wildberger, *Jesaja. BK,* X/1, on 6:5; W. Zimmerli, *Ezechiel. BK,* XIII/1, on 24:17.

wider sense it denotes the inability to communicate, which may be due to physical incapacity or to a specific and intentional decision. *chashah* has the very general meaning of silence in the sense of refraining from speaking, as in Aramaic (and Arabic?).

A special problem appears in connection with the roots *dmm*, *dwm*, and *dmh* II, and their derivatives, because it is difficult to differentiate them from one another or from → דמה *dāmāh* I. The words in other Semitic languages that are appealed to on the ground of relationship cover a wide range of meaning extending from "lament, groan" (Akk., Ugar.), by way of "murmur" (Arab., Aram.), to "be terrified, frightened" (Ethiop.), "destroy" (Arab.), and "be silent, regret" (Ugar., Aram., Arab.). It is not suggested, of course, that these meanings can with the same certainty be attached in the different languages to the roots *dmm*, *dmy*, or *dwm* (possibly other roots come into play). Similar overlappings of meaning also appear in Hebrew, as the many cross references in lexicons show. Since 'ayin vav/yodh and double 'ayin verbs are related to each other in other roots,[1] the textual tradition and vocalization of the words presently being considered reveal some uncertainty, and since the LXX does not render them consistently but obviously translates on the basis of what the context seems to require, Blau's opinion concerning these roots is probably correct: "Their meanings were rather closely related at first, and afterward they were felt to be cognate in linguistic consciousness; then they became contaminated in such a way that in most cases there can be no thought of separating them."[2] Whether the distribution of the three roots corresponds to special nuances of meaning has not yet been settled conclusively.[3] It is thus advisable to treat *dmy* II, *dmm*, and *dwm* with their derivatives as a unit, the primary meaning of which is silence in the face of an impending catastrophe or one that has already struck, or in preparation for a revelation.

II. chāshāh. *chashah* means in the first instance ceasing to speak or not speaking. It is thus used in antithesis to speaking in Eccl. 3:7. It occurs 16 times in the OT, predominantly in later texts. In its semantic field one finds *charash*, "to be still, deaf" (Isa. 42:14; Ps. 28:1), *'aphaq*, "to restrain oneself" (Isa. 42:14; 64:11 [Eng. v. 12]), *shaqat*, "to rest" (Isa. 62:1), *'lm + dumiyyah*, "to be dumb and silent" (Ps. 39:3[2]), *domi*, "rest" (Isa. 62:6), and *demamah*, "stillness" (Ps. 107:29). The hiphil imperative *hachashu*, "Hold your peace" (2 K. 2:3,5), comes near in function and meaning to *has*, "Silence! Hush! Sh-h-h!" (Jgs. 3:19; Am. 6:10; 8:3; Hab. 2:20; Zeph. 1:7; Zec. 2:17[13]), and *hasah*, "to still, quiet" (Nu. 13:30; Neh. 8:11).

The idea of ceasing to speak or not speaking seems to be so strong in *chashah* that for the purpose of clarification it is necessary to translate it this way in the majority of passages in which this is in view. In some passages indeed *chashah*

---

[1] Cf. Blau.

[2] Blau, 242.

[3] Cf. provisionally S. Moscati, ed., *An Introduction to the Comparative Grammar of the Semitic Languages* (²1969), 168f.

refers not to speaking, but to acting in general. In such cases *chashah* (appearing primarily as a hiphil ptcp.) means "to be idle, inactive" (cf. Jgs. 18:9; 1 K. 22:3; 2 K. 7:9; but also Isa. 65:6; Ps. 107:29), or "to summon to be idle, inactive" (Neh. 8:11, where the Levites urge the people to stop weeping, with *hassu*, "Be quiet!"). Therefore, *chashah* means "to be silent," with an emphasis on passivity. No special religious use of this word is discernible.

III. chārash. In contrast to *chashah*, *charash* emphasizes active, intentional silence. In the eight passages that refer to the physical impediment of a *cheresh*, "deaf person," who is usually connected with an *'ivver*, "blind person" (Lev. 19:14, and particularly in figurative language, Isa. 29:18; 35:5; 42:18f.; 43:8), or with an *'illem*, "dumb person" (Ps. 38:14[13]), or with both (Ex. 4:11), his impaired hearing condition is described in more detail (Isa. 29:18; 35:5; 43:8; Ps. 38:14[13]; 58:5[4]).

Of the 44 passages where *charash* occurs (to which may be added the hapax legomenon *cheresh* [RSV "secretly"] in Josh. 2:1), it is used in connection with hearing in Mic. 7:16. In this same passage, however, *charash*, "to be deaf," is connected with "laying the hand on the mouth" (cf. Jgs. 18:19). The expressions "close (*'atam*) the lips" (Prov. 17:28; cf. Ps. 58:5[4]) and "restrain oneself" (*'aphaq*) (Isa. 42:14) point in the same direction. The only passage where *charash* is used in connection with *damah* is Ps. 83:2(1). [4]

As an expression for the deliberate interruption of communication by someone who can and should speak for himself, the clearest rendering of *charash* would thus seem to be "to hold the tongue." This happens most frequently out of caution, embarrassment, or anxiety (cf. esp. Jer. 4:19, which describes anxiety that makes it impossible to hold the tongue, i.e., to keep the teeth from chattering and to check cries of fear; and Ps. 32:3, which describes the consequences of deliberately concealing one's sin). It can also be the result of wise discretion (cf. Gen. 24:21) and may be maintained only with difficulty in a dispute (cf. the passages in the book of Job); the speaker who cannot exercise this restraint proves himself to be unwise ("if you had been silent" [RSV, "Oh that you would keep silent"] . . . : Job 13:5; Prov. 11:12; 17:28). Since what is in mind here is refraining from giving one's own opinion, silence can be understood as consent (Nu. 30:5ff.[4ff.]). There is thus a strong element of urgency in the request not (no longer) to be silent (directed to Samuel in 1 S. 7:8; and to God in the language of prayer, Ps. 28:1; 35:22; 39:13[12]; 83:2[1]; cf. the expression of confidence in 50:3). Ex. 14:14 is also to be understood in this way: since Yahweh will fight for you, you can control yourselves; you do not even need to give the battle cry.

IV. dāmāh II/dmm/dwm.

1. *Occurrences, Semantic Field.* *damah* II/*dmm*/*dwm* and their derivatives appear 62 times in the OT (including Ezk. 24:17 and Isa. 38:10). [5] The distinc-

---

4 On the connection of *charash* with *chashah*, see above.

5 See also → דמה *dāmāh* I.

tion between the various words involved here is disputed in a number of cases. Like the search for a basic meaning, this need not be pursued here. Since it is impossible to determine whether several originally independent roots have been mixed together, or whether several similar roots were formed from one root, there is no basis on which to resolve the question. One must begin, then, with the usage.

In the semantic field of *damah* we find expressions for "fear": → פחד *pāchadh*, "dread"; → אימה *'êmāh*, "terror" (Ex. 15:16); → ערץ *'ārats*, "to fear"; → חתת *chāthath*, "to terrify" (Job 31:34); for "excitement": *rāthach*, "to seethe (RSV, be in turmoil)" (Job 30:27); for "destruction": → שדד *shādhadh*, "to lay waste, destroy" (Isa. 15:1; Jer. 47:4f.); → כרת *kārath*, "to cut off" (Zeph. 1:11); → שמד *shāmadh*, "to destroy" (Hos. 10:7f.); → נפל *nāphal*, "to fall" (Jer. 49:26; 50:30; 51:8); for "standing still": → עמד *'āmadh*, "to stand still" (Josh. 10:12f.; 1 S. 14:9); for "lamentation," "mourning": → ילל *yālal*, "to wail" (Isa. 23:1f.; Zeph. 1:11); *dim'ah*, "tears" (Jer. 14:17; Lam. 2:18; cf. 3:49); → אבל *'ābhal*, "to mourn" (Ezk. 24:16f.; cf. Lam. 2:10); but also for "waiting, hoping": → יחל *yāchal*, "to wait" (Lam. 3:26; cf. Ps. 37:7); → קוה *qāwāh*, "to hope" (Lam. 3:28f.); → שוה *shiwwāh*, "to calm" (Ps. 131:2). All these can hardly be reduced to a common denominator. Two areas stand out: legal proclamation and the address to God in prayer. It is remarkable how seldom words for "to be silent" appear in this semantic field. [6]

2. *Usage in Legal Proclamations and Funeral Dirges.* The words *damah* II/*dmm*/*dwm* and their derivatives occur particularly often in connection with legal proclamation, or with the divine epiphany interpreted as such. They appear both in announcements of future catastrophes (e.g., Isa. 23:2; Jer. 48:2; Hos. 4:5f.) and also in descriptions of reactions to them and of misfortunes that have already occurred (e.g., Ex. 15:16; Isa. 6:5). From the detailed description of the condition of the nations in Ex. 15:16, who had become "as a stone," one could characterize them as "numb with terror and grief, dismayed, overwhelmed." This meaning fits very well in the context of a whole series of passages (cf. Lev. 10:3; Isa. 23:2; Jer. 6:2; 47:5; 48:2; Ezk. 24:17; 27:32; 32:2). But this translation is not completely adequate. The first reaction of terror is so varied that it is not always clear in specific cases whether it makes the person speechless, rendering him dumb (cf. Lev. 10:3; Isa. 6:5; Hos. 4:5; Am. 5:13), or whether it makes him unable to move ("standing still as if nailed to the spot," cf. possibly also Josh. 10:12f.; 1 S. 14:9), whether it brings mortal fear upon him (Isa. 38:10; [7] Ps. 31:18[17]; cf. also 1 S. 2:9 and the LXX rendering of *dumah* in Ps. 94:17 and 115:17 by *hádēs*, "Hades"), or whether it even brings real death and destruction (Isa. 6:5; Jer. 8:14; 25:37; 47:5; 49:26; 50:30; 51:6; Hos. 10:7, 15; Ob. 5; Zeph. 1:11). In this light one can understand the great fluctuation in

---

[6] For *chashah* and *charash*, see above.
[7] De Boer.

suggested translations when the context offers no criteria by which to determine the precise meaning. In such cases the entire spectrum of possible renderings must be kept in mind.

Lohfink has shown that these reactions of terror occur not only directly on the announcement or beginning of catastrophes, but also later in the funeral lament. This explains the frequent reference to mourning customs in connection with *damah* II/*dmm*/*dwm*. Jer. 47:5 connects the announcement of coming disaster with the announcement of baldness (*qorchah*), which is a customary sign of grief. Some passages give almost a complete list of mourning customs (Ezk. 24:16f.; Job 30:27-31; Lam. 2:10; 3:28). Hence the word group also denotes what took place during mourning rites. In some passages (Isa. 23:2; 38:10; Jer. 47:5; Ps. 4:5[4]; Job 31:34), it can even be considered whether one might not translate the words by "lament, mourn." Yet the translation "remain (be) silent" is usually more natural (cf. the context in Lam. 2:10; 3:28).

3. *Usage in Prayers for Favorable Hearing and in the Reception of Revelation.* Lam. 3:28f. (cf. vv. 49f.) indicates a transition to another usage of *damah* II/*dmm*/*dwm*: As in other mourning customs,[8] so in the case of *damah* II/*dmm*/*dwm*, when the occasion is not actual death but general distress, the observance is later connected with a quiet expectation that a change of things is coming. It is described as an experience in Lam. 3:28f., and stated as the goal of weeping in 3:49f., that Yahweh might "look down" from heaven and "see." The use of words like *dumiyyah, dumam,* and *domi,* which occur predominantly in texts from the postexilic period, is characterized accordingly. *dumiyyah* can actually be translated by "quiet expectation" (Ps. 39:3[2]; 62:2[1]—cf. v. 6[5]; 65:2[1]); it is connected with *tiqvah,* "hope," and *yeshu'ah,* "salvation." In Ps. 22:3(2) it even has the sense of "favorable hearing." *domi* is used in a similar context (Isa. 62:6f.; Ps. 83:2[1]). Ps. 30:13(12) and Job 29:21 (where the expectation is not directed to God, but to Job, whose extraordinary trust is emphasized thereby) are to be understood along the same lines. (In certain other passages, viz., Jer. 14:17; Ps. 35:15; Job 30:27, the words in the negative have the colorless sense of "unceasing.")

dumam occurs only in Isa. 47:5; Hab. 2:19; and Lam. 3:26, and probably the clearest meaning that can be assigned to it is "to be silent," again in connection with rigidity and immobility. The idol which stands fixed and dumb (Hab. 2:19), the "daughter of Babylon" who sits and broods apathetically (Isa. 47:5), and the help of Yahweh which is anticipated with eager expectation (Lam. 3:26) again make clear the distinctiveness of the word group *damah* II/*dmm*/*dwm*. If silence is the basic meaning of the words, it is a silence caused by the powerful impress of an impending or actual calamity or by the expectation of coming salvation, and this is what gives it its specific nuance.

The word *demamah* has aroused particular interest because it is used in the unique Elijah theophany in 1 K. 19:12. The only other passages in which it oc-

---

8 Cf. → אבל *'ābhal,* III.1.

curs in the OT are Job 4:16 (is this dependent on the Elijah passage?) and Ps. 107:29. In Ps. 107:29 (as also in the Qumran writings), it is contrasted with the raging elemental forces (→ אֵשׁ 'ēsh) or with other loud and active phenomena; in fact, the *demamah* follows the tumult, when all the noise and commotion have died away. If *demamah* is used in a particular way in Job 4:16 and 1 K. 19:12 to describe the reception of a revelation, a theophany, this is to be understood as a deliberate attempt to separate the Israelite concept of theophany from the religious ideas of the ancient Near East. At the same time, that which is totally imperceptible, intangible, invisible, and inaudible in the theophany is characterized most clearly. Theophany occurs when all tangible manifestations of power are out of the question, and yet it is just as immediately and intensively near as an unsuspected breath of air (the LXX translates *demamah* by *aúra*).

Baumann

דִּמְעָה *dim'āh* → בכה *bākhāh*

דְּרוֹר *d^erôr*

Contents: I. 1. Occurrences in Hebrew; 2. Akkadian Parallels; 3. Arabic *drr/dwr*. II. Usage in the Prophets: 1. *áphesis*-Nuances; 2. Jeremiah: Of Persons, Parallel to *shemittah*; 3. Ezekiel: Of Property, Parallel to *yobhel*; 4. Deutero-Isaiah: Of Prisoners, Rescue. III. Late Usage: 1. Leviticus=*yobhel;* 2. In the Qumran Literature and the Talmud. IV. Conclusion.

I. 1. *Occurrences in Hebrew.* The writing prophets are the first to use *deror* (Jer. 34:8,15,17 [twice]; Ezk. 46:17; Isa. 61:1). In them it represents the spiritualizing of an "emancipation" originally regarded as economic. The original, literal meaning appears for the first time in Lev. 25:10. [1] (Two homonymous

---

d^erôr. R. Bultmann "ἄφίημι," *TDNT,* I, 509-512; M. David, "The Manumission of Slaves under Zedekiah," *OTS,* 5 (1948), 63-79; G. Driver and J. Miles, *The Babylonian Laws* (Oxford, 1952-55); P. Grelot, "Soixante-dix semaines d'années," *Bibl,* 50 (1969), 169-186; F. R. Kraus, "Ein mittelassyrischer Rechtsterminus," *Symbolae M. David* (Leiden, 1968), 2, 7-40; J. Lewy, "The Biblical Institution of *d^erôr* in the Light of Accadian Documents," *Eretz Israel,* 5 (1958), 21*-31*; E. Neufeld, "Socio-Economic Background of Yōbēl and Šmiṭṭâ," *RSO,* 33 (1958), 53-124; R. North, *Sociology of the Biblical Jubilee. AnBibl,* 4 (1954), 62-66; J. D. Smart, *History and Theology in Second Isaiah* (1965); M. Tsevat, "עניין שמיטה אצל הר סיני" (The Regulation pertaining to the Year of Jubilee in Connection with Sinai), *Sepher Šemu'el Yeivin* (Jerusalem, 1969/1970), 283-88; A. S. van der Woude, "Melchisedek als himmlische Erlösergestalt in den neugefundenen eschatologischen Midraschim aus Qumran Höhle XI," *OTS,* 14 (1965), 354-373; and *NTS,* 12 (1966), 301-326 (Eng. with M. de Jonge), on these, J. A. Fitzmyer, *JBL,* 86 (1967), 25-41; and M. P. Miller, *JBL,* 88 (1969), 467-69; R. de Vaux, *AncIsr,* 175; H. Wildberger, "Israel und sein Land," *EvTh,* 16 (1956), 404-422; W. Zimmerli, "Das 'Gnadenjahr des Herrn'," *Festschrift K. Galling* (1970), 321-332.

[1] Elliger: Ph[1].

words occur in Ex. 30:23, "myrrh"; and Ps. 84:4 [Eng. v. 3]; Prov. 26:2, a kind of bird ["swallow"?].)

2. *Akkadian Parallels.* The Akkadian cognate *andurāru* is amply attested from the oldest through the latest Babylonian (2200-600 B.C.) in the sense of "remission of (commercial) debts," "manumission (of private slaves)," [2] and also "the canceling of services illegally imposed on free persons." [3]

Most *andurāru*-texts happen to be negative and refer to cases in which the expected remission will not take place. [4] One also finds the paradoxical combination "even in the release will not be free" (*kaspum šū andurārum liššakinma ul iddarrar*). [5] Here a relation to the verb *darāru* is obvious. [6] Kraus proposes that *andurāru* is used mostly of persons (at least after 1700 B.C.), as *zakûtu* is used of things (*ca.* 1170 B.C.). [7] This seems to fit the Sumerian equivalent *ama.ar.gi₄,* "return someone to his mother," but the examples in Kraus show that *zakûtu* relates more to the preceding state of immunity (also of persons) than to the act of setting free. [8]

3. *Arabic drr/dwr.* From Alalakh 65, 6, *ina andurārim ul innandar,* it might be conjectured that the initial radical of the verb was originally *n.* What we have here, however, is an N-form of the root *drr,* [9] which is also attested in Arabic in the sense "to flow (freely), run." Most likely a biliteral root *dr* developed into *ndr* and *drr,* and also into → דור *dwr,* "to run *around,* to return to one's point of origin." [10]

nadarraru, "to move about freely," is construed by Lewy [11] as a niphal infinitive which is cognate with the noun *durāru,* and *durāru* is equal to *andurāru* as *dinānu/andunānu,* but is not related to *darāru,* "to be independent." [12] According to Lewy *andurāru* is restricted to Amorite enclaves and was brought from there to Canaan, yet in a primal form not requiring a royal proclamation [13] (which the only Egyptian parallel, Bocchoris, 720 B.C., demands). [14] Lewy's proposed primal form fits the texts better than Noth's conjectured "adaptation" to the biblical milieu. [15] Ugaritic has no *drr* (or *šmṭ* or *ybl*).

---

2 *CAD,* I/2, 115.

3 *Ibid.,* 117.

4 R. Harris, *JCS,* 9 (1955), 98 B VI, 8.

5 *ARM,* VIII, 33.14.

6 *CAD,* III, 109: "to become free (of a task), to move about freely, to run off," e.g., a woman will not be released, a debt will not be remitted.

7 Kraus, 39.

8 *Ibid.,* 32.

9 Von Soden, *Or,* 20 (1951), 259.

10 A. Klostermann, *ThStKr,* 53 (1880), 730; N. Snaith, *Leviticus* (1967), 163, prefers *dûr* in the sense of having no fixed abode, with Rabbi Judah.

11 Lewy, 21*.

12 Against *CAD, AHw,* 163.

13 Lewy, *HUCA,* 17 (1942), 71.

14 J. Pirenne, *AHDO,* 4 (1949), 12.

15 M. Noth, *Leviticus. OTL* (trans. 1965), 187.

II. Usage in the Prophets.

1. *áphesis-Nuances.* The theological and most common biblical sense of *deror* is found in all three major prophets. That they are citing Lev. 25:10 is presumed even by recent commentators who date P later. Though the P legislation preserves archaic usages and even formulas, its actual composition is dependent upon Ezekiel [16] and presupposes the text of Jeremiah and Isaiah. Furthermore, Lev. 25:10 is not cited in the similar passage in Neh. 5:5, presumably because it did not yet exist then. In all six prophetic occurrences (as well as 1 Macc. 10:34; cf. 13:34) *deror* is rendered in Greek by *áphesis,* "remission." The same term is also used for *shemittah:* four times in Dt. 15, as well as the hiphil of *šmṭ* in Dt. 15:3, and the qal of *šmṭ* in Ex. 23:11. Moreover, the LXX uses *áphesis* for *yobhel* throughout Lev. 25 after v. 13; but in vv. 10-13 the "proclamation of an *áphesis*" is used instead, while in v. 10 *áphesis* alone corresponds to *deror.* Elsewhere *deror* is translated by *eleuthería,* "freedom, liberty," or simply transliterated in some manuscripts. The LXX *áphesis* is used also to translate *chophshi,* "free" (Isa. 58:6); *hanachah,* "(holiday-)rest" (Est. 2:18), "freed" (of the goat for Azazel, Lev. 16:26), "watercourse" (*'aphiq,* 2 S. 22:16; Joel 1:20; *pelegh,* Lam. 3:48), *shilluchim,* "sending (away)" (Ex. 18:2); doubtfully *'ephes* (RSV "ankle-deep," Ezk. 47:3) and the piel of *naphats* (RSV "shattering," Dnl. 12:7).

2. *Jeremiah: Of Persons, Parallel to shemittah.* The earliest datable assured use of *deror,* "emancipation," is found in Jer. 34. This chapter is to be put after 597 B.C. because of vv. 1 and 8. It is thus under direct influence of Babylonian legislation. Zedekiah, who had been installed as king by Nebuchadnezzar, but was not minded to be a puppet of Babylon (2 K. 24:20), had proclaimed a *deror* on his own initiative (Jer. 34:8). According to v. 9, those who were freed were "Hebrew slaves, male and female, so that no one should enslave a Jew, his brother." This clearly echoes Ex. 21:2, but adds the freeing of women, in contrast to Ex. 21:7. Ex. 21:2,7 both form part of the legislation of Ex. 21-23, which is before E and has so much in common with Hammurabi. [17] Even more clearly the *shemittah* of Dt. 15:2 is echoed in the *deror* of Jer. 34:14. [18] Dt. 15:2 has links with Ex. 21:2 but also differs from it. Neither passage uses *yobhel* or *shemittah,* but Ex. 23:11 uses the verb *šmṭ* for releasing from crops (of the fallow land), like the cultic passage Lev. 25:4, but more in a humanitarian sense. [19] The verb that is used for the execution of the *deror* in Jer. 34:9ff. is not *šmṭ,* but *shillach,* which appears three times with *chophshim* to express the idea "to set free" (as in Ex. 21:5).

Jeremiah's great concern is with the insincerity or rather the unfaithfulness of these who submitted to the decreed *deror* (34:15) but as soon as the crisis was

---

[16] Similarly de Vaux, *AncIsr,* 176.
[17] Despite H. Cazelles (1946) and A. Jepsen (1927).
[18] J. Bright, *Jeremiah. AB,* XXI (1965), 223.
[19] North, 31.

over took their slaves back again. For such conduct there will be an ironic *deror* (v. 17), "freedom indeed," the free unimpeded opportunity for disaster to fall upon the whole land. In this way, the land will have its own sabbaths or years of jubilee, i.e., times when its fields will not be cultivated, as 2 Ch. 36:21 puts it (echoing Lev. 26:43; 25:4).

3. *Ezekiel: Of Property, Parallel to yobhel.* "Emancipation" (*deror*) in its earliest occurrences relates, then, to persons; less obviously, however, is there any reference to the regular repetition of manumission every seven years (Ex. and Dt., in contrast to Hammurabi, § 117, which has every four years). Yet even in this context *deror* could also mean "permission to be free," which is vague enough to be applied to the land or natural forces as well. Ezk. 46:17, a passage that is often regarded as inauthentic, deals with royal property which is inalienable to the extent that it must always be inherited by sons. It can be signed away, even as a gift, only until the year of *deror,* at which time the property is to revert to the king (*shabhath,* alluding to *shabbath,* "Sabbath," in Lev. 25:2-7, or a scribal error for *shabhah,* from *shubh,* "to return"?).

Fohrer categorically reduces this *deror* to the seven-year cycle of Jer. 34:14 [20] and calls it a "year of release" like Ex. 21:2; Dt. 15:12; Lev. 25:2. According to Zimmerli, however, Ezk. 46:17 "in no way" refers to the sabbath year; instead it has reference to the restitution of property (*yobhel*) in the fiftieth year. [21] Wildberger, too, thinks that the restitution of inherited property actually took place (cf. Lev. 25:10,13). [22] In itself the "release" (*deror/anduraru*) emphasizes the fact of recurrence rather than telling us how long after or from what burden it occurs. In any case, slavery and loss of property both mean bankruptcy. [23] Eichrodt thinks that seven years is a rather short term for the restoration of property and so he suggests the year of jubilee (in the fiftieth year); [24] the fifty-year period is preferred in this case by Rashi and Kimchi. A fifty-year period is also to be assumed in Lev. 25:10 (which is later than Ezekiel!). Thus the *deror* of the fiftieth year corresponds more to the *anduraru* than do, probably, the *shemittah* of Dt. 15:1 and the seven-year cycle of Lev. 25:4 correspond to the *šudutu* in Nuzi. [25]

4. *Deutero-Isaiah: Of Prisoners, Rescue.* The theological bearing of this economic usage is more prominent in Jeremiah than in Ezekiel, but it culminates in Isa. 61:1. Here *deror* is used not for land or slaves, but for prisoners. Though the captives in exile are presumably meant, their release is made parallel to an "opening (of the eyes! so the LXX) for the fettered." But then the phrase "proclaim a *deror*" is echoed more notably by "proclaim the year of Yahweh's

---

20 G. Fohrer, *HAT,* 13 (²1955), 255; with reservation, David, 75.
21 Zimmerli, *BK,* XIII/2, 1179.
22 Wildberger, 413-15.
23 North, 167; so rightly Josephus *Ant.* iii.12.3; cf. G. Lambert, *NRTh,* 72 (1950), 235.
24 W. Eichrodt, *Ezekiel. OTL* (trans. 1970), 578.
25 Neufeld, 56; L. Gordon, *RB,* 44 (1935), 39.

pleasure (ratson)." As a comfort to mourners, this day is then also described as "the day of God's vengeance," or rather "requital": [26] what betters the victims' lot inevitably works hardship on those who are greedy for profit. The LXX translates both deror in Isa. 61:1 and shillach chophshim in Isa. 58:6 by áphesis, "remission," which is cited in Lk. 4:18 (Jesus) and 1:77 (Zechariah).

III. Late Usage.

1. *Leviticus=yobhel*. The *deror* of Lev. 25:10 represents the end and not the beginning of this development, although Zimmerli rightly emphasizes that related and ancient economic customs were presupposed and spiritualized in Isa. 61:1. [27] "You shall hallow the fiftieth year, and proclaim *deror* (RSV liberty, as Isa. 61:1) on the land (as Ezk. 46:17) for all its inhabitants (cf. Jer. 34:8); it shall be a jubilee (→ יובל *yôbhēl*) for you." Here *deror* is equated with release of the land and it occurs in the fiftieth (or forty-ninth) year, yet not in any technical or exclusive sense like *yobhel*, whose meaning can be gleaned only from this chapter or even this verse. Our attempt to prove that *ybl* already in itself means *áphesis* has not met with acceptance.

2. *In the Qumran Literature and the Talmud*. The main example of *deror* in the Qumran texts (11QMelch 6) [28] is more closely related to Isa. 61:1 than to Lev. 25:10. Melchizedek proclaims a *deror* for captives in a year of *ratson*, but with an eschatological nuance and with the forgiveness of sins as in Isa. 52:7. In the rest of the Qumran literature, one catches only a general allegorizing echo of Lev. 25:8 in the framework of other festival seasons (1QS 10:8 refers to the *deror*, "release," at the *shebhu'im*, presumably 7×7, or 49 years).

The only addition in the Talmud is at *Meg.* 12a, which has a pun on *dar* in Est. 1:6: freedom for those in business.

IV. Conclusion. Lev. 25:10 arbitrarily resorted to a more urban economic arrangement to unify and sacralize ancient convictions as to the inalienability of the person and of family property. Postbiblical usage, however, returns to the sense of an interior release which *deror* had gradually taken on in the prophets.

North

---

[26] Smart, 261, following Torrey.
[27] Zimmerli, 327.
[28] Van der Woude, 359.

דֶּרֶךְ *derekh;* דָּרַךְ *dārakh;* שׁוּק *shûq;* חוּץ *chûts;*
מְסִלָּה *mesillāh;* הָלִיךְ *hālîkh;* הֲלִיכָה *halîkhāh;*
מַעְגָּל *maʿgāl;* נָתִיב *nāthîbh;* נְתִיבָה *nethîbhāh;*
שְׁבִיל *shebhîl;* אֹרַח *ʾōrach*

Contents: I. The Present Status of Research: 1. Inadequate Treatment of This Subject; 2. Literal and Figurative Usage; 3. Oneness of Life and Conduct. II. In the Ancient Near East: 1. In Egyptian Texts; 2. In Akkadian Texts. III. Survey of Pertinent Words: 1. *drk;* 2. *shuq;* 3. *chuts;* 4. *mesillah;* 5. *halikh/halikhah;* 6. *maʿgal;* 7. *nathibh/nethibhah;* 8. *shebhil;* 9. *ʾorach;* 10. *ṣʿd, ʾšr, pʿm, reghel.* IV. In Pre-Deuteronomic Narratives: 1. Literal Usage; 2. Direction of an Individual's Life; 3. Oracle and Prayer; 4. *derekh* As Salvation History; 5. The Divine *derekh.* V. In the Psalms: 1. Frequency of Occurrences; 2. The *derekh* of the Individual; 3. Divine Intervention. VI. In the Wisdom Literature. VII. In Prophecy of the Babylonian Period: 1. In Jeremiah; 2. In Ezekiel; 3. In Deutero- and Trito-Isaiah. VIII. In the Deuteronomic and Deuteronomistic Literature. IX. In Apocalyptic Literature. X. In the Qumran Literature.

I. The Present Status of Research.

1. *Inadequate Treatment of This Subject.* The diversified references to the human or divine way and conduct, which hold a central position in the religious statements of OT wisdom, prophetic, and apocalyptic books, have not yet been investigated scientifically. The changing terminology in the various periods and areas of life has not been sorted out, nor has the semantic field been fully surveyed. The unsystematic listing of the meanings of the most important noun in the word group (*derekh*) even in the most recent lexicon[1] is significant: (1) road; (2) stretch of road; (3) journey (venture, business, campaign, pilgrimage); (4) style, custom, conduct (as *darkhe maveth,* "the ways of death," etc.); (5) (pl.) theological: (a) God's behavior, measures; (b) the behavior required by God; (6) condition, situation; (7) (?) strength, might. As for other nouns in the field, exegetes are satisfied with the translation "path" without any more exact definition or differentiation, in the case of *nathibh/nethibhah*[2] or *shebhil.*[3] In view of the inadequate treatment of this theme, only a few significant features of Hebrew usage can be indicated at present.

derekh. B. Couroyer, "Le chemin de vie en Égypte et en Israël," *RB,* 56 (1949), 412-432; A. Gros, *Le thème de la Route dans la Bible. Études Religieuses* (1957); A. Kuschke, "Die Menschenwege und der Weg Gottes im AT," *StTh,* 5 (1951), 106-118; W. Michaelis, *TDNT,* V, 48-60; F. Nötscher, *Gotteswege und Menschenwege in der Bibel und in Qumran. BBB,* 15 (1958); G. Sauer, *THAT,* I, 456-460.

On the general background: *Um das Prinzip der Vergeltung in Religion und Recht des AT. Wege der Forschung,* 125, ed. K. Koch (1972).

1 *KBL³,* 222f.
2 *KBL²,* 641.
3 *KBL²,* 942.

2. *Literal and Figurative Usage.* The distinction between a literal or proper use of the nouns for a traversable stretch of country and a so-called figurative or transferred use presents a special problem. In some words connected with the concept of "way" the figurative use is so prominent that the literal meaning is not attested at all, e.g., in the case of *ma'gal* or *shebhil,* while in others the literal meaning is dominant, and in the case of *chuts* the figurative sense is completely missing. To some extent both usages are attested already in pre-Israelite literature (Ugar. *ntb/ntbt*), [4] and for 2000 years the figurative is connected so closely with the literal that it is very difficult to distinguish between them. [5] The latest treatment of the nouns attempts a distinction in relation to *derekh,* but it shows how uncertain such an endeavor is: Sauer argues that the original meaning of *derekh* was a "(travelled and therefore well-established) road," but in time this changed imperceptibly to "movement on the road" and also to "journey, venture, military campaign, or stretch of road." [6] The figurative use of *derekh* in the sense of "conduct, behavior," and to denote "certain fundamental facts in the life of man and nature," derived from this. But if "venture" is still a literal meaning of *derekh,* can "behavior" be differentiated from it as a fundamentally different figurative use? In Psalms and Proverbs, *derekh* hardly ever means a stretch of road, and yet these books nowhere give the impression that the substantive is used metaphorically for something that might be expressed differently and more precisely. One suspects, then, that the distinction between a literal and a figurative use of *derekh* is due to a prior judgment based on modern Western languages, in which we do not view life primarily as a coherent movement (toward a conscious goal). Moreover, this reduces the cultic, wisdom, and prophetic passages about *derekh,* 'orach, etc., to devotional and flowery jargon, and conceals the anthropological and historico-theological implications of the substantive for Hebrew self-understanding. [7] The label "figurative" also suggests an affinity with other linguistic areas and concepts which is hardly suitable in this form. As is well known, there is, of course, a road symbolism in many cultures (e.g., in Buddhism and Taoism), but if we consider the figurative use in modern language we see how little these associations can be involved. "The American way of life" does not mean the same thing at all as the German "Lebensweg," and in turn neither expression has much in common with the Heb. *derekh chayyim.* In the following discussion, then, the concepts "literal" and "figurative" will be avoided, and instead a distinction will be made between the foreground sense of a spatial stretch of road, and the background sense of behavior or condition. This is not to say that the Hebrew consciously differentiated between the foreground and the background meanings of the words in question. It is difficult for us, however, to achieve an understanding without some such distinction.

3. *Oneness of Life and Conduct.* With regard to the background use, all exegetes affirm that the Heb. *derekh* embraces both the course of life (as the ethic-

---

[4] *WUS,* No. 1870.
[5] Kuschke, 115.
[6] Sauer, *THAT,* I, 458.
[7] Cf. Kuschke.

ally neutral unity of the life-story in which one participates passively rather than actively) and also "conduct" (as responsible and ethically accountable actions in specific periods of life). Nötscher in particular has convincingly worked out the dual character of the "figurative" usage. It means "conduct and destiny, the living of life and the course of life in the sense of prosperity or adversity in a causal relationship.... The way of uprightness and the way of security and prosperity are the same (Prov. 3:23). They are not to be distinguished and thus they are often covered by the one term.... Evil behavior and an evil condition go together; they are as it were one and the same way to destruction; they cannot be distinguished from one another conceptually."[8] This duality of meaning applies not only to derekh but also to ma'gal and nethibhah.[9] 'orach includes the idea "both of moral behavior and ordained condition,"[10] as do also mesillah[11] and ṣ'd.[12] For Nötscher, the existence of this causal relationship is explained by divine recompense: "Recompense is the avowed end to which the eyes of God are directed on all the ways of man,"[13] although the divine activity of recompense on the way of man cannot be shown from the Hebrew texts themselves. Nötscher acknowledges that this interpretation is not completely satisfactory. "The unsolved problem remains of divine sovereignty and human freedom, of divine grace and human merit."[14] But is this problem really insoluble for the OT writers, or is it so only for the modern observer, who when he speaks of recompense and merit attributes popular Christian concepts to a Hebrew way of thinking which has an entirely different orientation?

Pedersen succeeds in working out a homogeneous interpretation of the complex use of derekh and all related words against the background of a primitive way of thinking completely different from that of all modern languages. An action and its consequences cannot be distinguished from a central concept of soul (man does not have a nephesh, he is nephesh). "The actions are not sent away from the soul, they are the outer manifestations of the whole of the soul, the traces of its movements; its 'ways'."[15] If Pedersen's observation of the inseparability of an action and its consequences is right, his idea of the soul is problematic. The words for "way" are hardly ever connected with nephesh, "soul," in the OT (one exception is to be found in Prov. 16:17). derekh is never presented as something that comes forth from nephesh. For this reason Koch has attempted to explain the unity of life and conduct in terms of a specifically Hebrew conception of a sphere of activity that effects destiny. On this view, a man's deeds cling to him as it were, wrapping themselves around him as an invisible domain, which

---

8 Nötscher, 60f.
9 *Ibid.*, 14f.
10 *Ibid.*, 17.
11 *Ibid.*, 13.
12 *Ibid.*, 11f.
13 *Ibid.*, 53.
14 *Ibid.*, 64.
15 Pedersen, *ILC,* I-II, 128; cf. 337, 361f.

one day is transformed into a corresponding condition or state, and then recoils on the doer. [16]

Koch

II. In the Ancient Near East.

1. *In Egyptian Texts*. a. The main Egyptian word for "road" is *w3.t*. [17] The words *mtn* [18] and *my.t* [19] should also be mentioned. All three of these words can mean roads and streets in an entirely specific sense. *W3.t* can also mean waterway, and Egyptians speak of the ways in the heavens: the sun and the stars have their prescribed "ways." [20] Expressions with *w3.t* are used half-figuratively to express the omnipresence of God, e.g., "no road is unoccupied by him" (Amon); [21] "every road is full of his sunbeams" (the sun-god). [22] Statements about the absolute guidance of God, such as "he leads men on every road," and "he reveals to everyone the road on which he should go," [23] are also to be connected with these.

The wolf-god Upuaut is regarded in various ways as the "opener of the way." [24] Thus he prepares the roads for the king in battle and as the foremost of the standard deities he opens royal processions. The "way of God" (*w3.t ntr*) can also mean concretely the way the procession goes.

b. Roads are often mentioned in a funeral context. From the time of the Pyramid Texts (822, 1153, 2062) on, Egyptian texts refer to the "beautiful roads" to the west. In the Mastabas of the Old Kingdom, we read of "the magnificent roads on which the venerable ones (the dead) go." [25] With the gradual shift of the world of the dead into the gloomy regions of the underworld, the ways of the dead play an increasingly greater role. [26] One must know these ways and their names. [27] They are often called "the dark ways" [28] and "the secret ways." [29] In order to further a knowledge of the ways, the oldest guide to the underworld, the so-called Book of the Two Ways, [30] was produced, complete with a kind

---

[16] Koch, *Prinzip der Vergeltung*, 164.
[17] *WbÄS*, I, 246ff.
[18] *WbÄS*, II, 176.
[19] *WbÄS*, II, 41.
[20] Cf. H. Grapow, *Die bildlichen Ausdrücke des Ägyptischen* (1924), 65.
[21] Greater Leiden Hymn, II, 18.
[22] Berlin Papyrus 3050, VI, 5.
[23] Greater Leiden Hymn, V, 20, and IV, 8 respectively; see J. Zandee, *De hymnen aan Amon* (1947), 31f.
[24] *RÄR*, 842ff.
[25] E.g., Junker, *Gîza* (1929ff.), II, 58; cf. *CT*, V, 166; VI, 135, 248.
[26] J. Zandee, *Death As an Enemy* (1960), 162ff.
[27] *CT*, VI, 390.
[28] *CT*, VI, 242, 386.
[29] *CT*, VI, 388, 411.
[30] *CT*, VII, 252-521.

of map or sketch. [31] But the two ways, the black land way and the blue water way, lead to the same place, to the rose dew, and thus do not represent mutually opposed alternatives, as, e.g., the west and the east way do in other Coffin Texts ("pleasant" or "miserable"). [32] The later books of the underworld and the Book of the Dead contain sayings for overcoming obstacles and dangers on the way of the sun-god and of the dead. Here also, Upuaut is sometimes called an "opener of the way."

c. The figurative use of *wȝ.t* is very widespread and varied. [33] The clever official "finds a way in connection with every difficult matter at court." [34] Pianchi "finds no way of fighting" against a city. [35] He offers his opponents an alternative: "You have two ways before you: choose how you wish. Open and you will live; keep yourselves shut in, and you will die." [36] From the Middle Kingdom on, frequently a series of expressions with *wȝ.t*, *mtn*, and especially *mw*, "water, waterway," are used to express loyalty (fidelity) or its antithesis: "to be or go on someone's water or way," "to violate or reject the way of someone." [37]

d. In the Egyptian Wisdom Literature the expressions "way of life" and "way of God" occur as key ideas. [38] "The Egyptian educates for life: he puts the young man on the 'way of life,' as is said time and time again." [39] The Teaching of Cheti for his son reads: "See, I put you on the way of life" (11:2). The Teaching of Amennacht begins with the words: "The beginning of instruction, of sayings for the way of life." The author of the Teaching of Anii prays to the god of wisdom: "Put Anii on your way" (10:11). Nachtef-Mut (22nd Dynasty) says, "How beautiful it is to walk on the way of God." The inscriptions in the tomb of Petosiris [40] are especially productive. "Father, Father, how beautiful it is to go on the way of God. Everyone who is on it passes before God. . . . God has guided your heart" (58:22). "For you walk on the way of your God, Thoth, because he has done magnificent things for you. He guides your heart to do that which is delightful to him" (58:31). Finally, Brunner observes: "The Egyptian hardly ever speaks in detail about the other way, the false way. He is kept from doing so by his hesitation to say anything negative or dangerous and thereby to invest it with reality." [41]

Bergman

---

[31] H. Kees, *Totenglauben* (1926), 425-449; *RÄR*, 882f.
[32] *Ibid.*, 290.
[33] See *WbÄS*, and Grapow, *Bildl. Ausdrücke*, 64f.
[34] *Urk.*, I, 84.
[35] *Urk.*, III, 31.
[36] *Urk.*, III, 26.
[37] E. Otto, *Gott und Mensch* (1964), 43ff.
[38] H. Brunner, *Altägyptische Erziehung* (1957), 117, 123ff.; cf. Couroyer.
[39] Brunner.
[40] Published by G. Lefèbvre (1924).
[41] Brunner, 125.

2. *In Akkadian Texts.* In Akkadian there are several words that mean "road." The most common is *alaktu* (pl. *alkakātu/ilkakātu*; root *hlk*), [42] "road, way, journey, advance, caravan, expedition, conduct." More or less synonymous with *alaktu* are *urhu(m)/arhu/uruḫḫu*; cf. *'orach*, "road, path," *usu(m)*, "road, path," *gerru*, [43] "road, (commercial) route, campaign, procession, way of life," *ḫarrānu*, [44] "road, street, (commercial) route, caravan," *ḫūlu*, [45] "road" (often "road and canal"), *ṭūdu*, "mountain road, path," *kibsu*, [46] "footprint, road, path, track, walk," *sūqu*, [47] "street," *padānu*, [48] "road, lane, path." The West Semitic word *drk* also appears as a loanword (*daraggu*) in various forms.

As can be seen from this survey, the conceptual complex "way" contains different nuances. The specific meaning "road, street," is also expanded to "journey, caravan, procession, campaign, etc." Several words are connected with *parāsu*, "to close, shut, lock." [49] Akkadian texts also speak of the ways of the stars. [50] Figuratively, "road, way" often means "behavior, conduct, way of life," etc., e.g.: "You know this man and his behavior" (*alaktu*, "the way he always acts"); [51] "their behavior was not good" (EnEl I, 28, of the gods against Tiamat); "whose behavior (actions, *alkakātu*) is especially pleasing to Ashur"; [52] "Fix my destiny, Make my way of life (*alaktu*) happy"; "Put me on the right way" (*kibsu*); [53] guardian spirits who keep "my royal way (*kibsu*) and make me happy." [54] A happy man complains: "My way (*alaktu*) will not be determined by the seer and the interpreter of omens," [55] i.e., he has not been able to explain the situation. The Sumerian loanword *ūsu* (Akk. *rīdu* and *kibsu*) means "way" in the sense of "prescribed way," usually in a figurative sense (Sum. *ús*, "to follow").

Some words for "road, way" are used of the way of the gods, especially with reference to the plan or the activity of the gods: "Who can understand the way (*alaktu*) of the gods?" [56] "Where did the beclouded ones (men) learn the way of the gods? He who was alive yesterday is dead today." [57]

Haldar-Ringgren

The so-called Babylonian Theodicy [58] speaks of a man who runs his way like a lion (XXIII, 247), of the ways of rich men that lead to condemnation (VI, 65),

---

[42] *AHw*, 31, 36, 371.
[43] *AHw*, 285.
[44] *AHw*, 326f.
[45] *AHw*, 354.
[46] *AHw*, 471f.
[47] *AHw*, 1061.
[48] *AHw*, 807f.
[49] *CAD*, I/1, 299; 5, 90, see *AHw*, 831 *s.v. parāsu*, G 6.
[50] *CAD*, I/1, 298.
[51] *CAD*, I/1, 297.
[52] *AOB*, I, 112, 8.
[53] Several examples appear in *CAD*, VIII, 338.
[54] R. Borger, *Die Inschriften Asarhaddons. BAfO*, 9 (1956), 64, VI, 63.
[55] *BWL*, 32, 52f.
[56] *AGH*, 72, 11.
[57] *BWL*, 40, 39; cf. also 76, 86; *Ludlul*, II, 38, *ANET*, 597.
[58] *AOT*, 287-291; *ANET*, 601-604; *BWL*, 70ff.

like the way of prosperity which the ungodly travel for a while (VII, 70). It also refers to the way a demon takes (XIII, 244). Since this complex of ideas is less prominent in Mesopotamian literature than in Egyptian, it may perhaps be assumed that it did not originate in a special wisdom vocabulary but in other areas of life or in everyday speech.

III. Survey of Pertinent Words.

1. *drk*. Hebrew has a proportionately extensive vocabulary for "road, way, street, etc." By far the most common word used to convey this idea is *derekh*, which occurs 706 [59] or 710 [60] times in the OT. In the majority of cases, this word is used, not in the foreground sense of a stretch of road or a movement across country, but figuratively for human activity in general. Adjectives used with *derekh* indicate that it can be understood as a feminine or a masculine noun. The noun *midhrakh*, "treading-place, footstep," occurs once (Dt. 2:5). [61] The cognate verb *darakh* appears about 48 times in the qal and 13 in the hiphil. In addition to the meaning analogous to that of the noun, viz., "to move, take steps," the verb has developed three special meanings: (a) to tread = to draw the warrior's bow that has been placed on the earth; (b) to tread the wine press (so the noun, 1 K. 18:27?); [62] (c) to trample down grain on the threshing floor. [63]

The root *drk* is attested as a verb and a noun in Phoenician [64] and later in Egyptian Aramaic, Jewish Aramaic, Mandean, and Syriac, also as a verb in Arabic (*daraǧa*, "to go") and possibly in Ethiopic (*daraka*, "to be hard"). Perhaps it was originally a (North-) West Semitic word. The rare Late Bab. *daraggu*, "way," [65] is a loanword and possibly also the Bab. adj. *darku/derku*, "following, subsequent, next," which in that case was adopted at a different time and derives from a doubtful verb *darāku*. [66] Whether *durgu*, "innermost part" (of a mountain range), [67] and *darīku*, "receptacle or container for dates," [68] belong to the present root is uncertain. It is surprising that the root is not found in Ugaritic except for a substantive *drkt*, "royal dominion," [69] which may perhaps occur again in the Hellenistic period in the name of the goddess Derketō of Ashkelon, the mother of Semiramis, the prototype of a goddess. [70] From the diffuse material it is impossible to obtain a convincing etymology for the root in Hebrew.

Nor can one arrive at a simple "basic meaning." To be sure, *derekh* is trans-

---

[59] *THAT.*
[60] *KBL³.*
[61] *KBL².*
[62] L. Hayman, *JNES,* 10 (1951), 57f.
[63] Nötscher, 34f.
[64] *KAI,* 26 A II.5; 27.7f.; *DISO,* 60.
[65] *AHw,* 163.
[66] *AHw,* 163f.
[67] *AHw,* 177.
[68] *AHw,* 163.
[69] *WUS,* No. 792; *UT,* No. 703; also *Ugaritica,* V (1968), 551, lines 6f.
[70] W. F. Albright, *Yahweh and the Gods of Canaan* (1968), 113; H. Gese, *Die Religionen Altsyriens . . .* (1970), 214.

lated by "way." If one wishes to render this Hebrew word by a single equivalent, there is no better alternative than this. The English word, however, has misleading associations. Thus the beginning of a *derekh* is strikingly called its "head" (Ezk. 16:25,31) and the parting of a *derekh* its "mother" (Ezk. 21:26 [Eng. v. 21]), while a clear indication of destination: the "way toward..." or "road to...," is rare. A genitive with *he*-locale is hardly ever added (Gen. 38:14; Ezk. 8:5). It is true that construct expressions using *derekh* as the *nomen regens* (governing noun) are common. The *derekh* of (RSV "to") the Red Sea (Nu. 21:4; Dt. 1:40) would seem to denote the destination, as does also the *derekh* of (RSV "to") the hill country of the Amorites (Dt. 1:19; cf. also 1 S. 13:17f.). In several passages, however, the construct expressions using *derekh* as the *nomen regens* are ambiguous. Is *derekh habbashan* in Dt. 3:1 the caravan road leading *through* Bashan, or the road *to* Bashan? Is *derekh hayyam* in Isa. 8:23(9:1) the highway leading *to* the sea or the road *alongside* the sea? The *derekh* of the tent-dwellers is the road *in* and not *to* the land of the nomads in Jgs. 8:11. Uncertainty as to the meaning of *derekh* in construct expressions applies not only to the foreground use but to the background use as well.

derekh does not refer to a stretch of road that has been levelled for the purpose of travel from one place to another. Rather, the concept is tridimensional. The OT speaks much more often of going *in* (*be*) a *derekh* (Ex. 4:24; etc.) than of going *on* (*ʿal*) a *derekh* (Gen. 38:21; etc.). Moreover, *derekh* is not a road or way that has come into existence without people moving on it, but is that on which and in which people move. It more frequently denotes the movement than the condition.

The German word "Gang" is an approximate equivalent of Heb. *derekh*. It denotes a specific stretch of road, but conceived tridimensionally (cf. "a subterranean Gang"), also the manner in which people move (e.g., "a swaying Gang"), and movement toward a destination (e.g., to the post office). The word is also used figuratively ("the course of things"). Nevertheless, versatile though it is, the German word has never become the subject of anthropological or even theological reflection in the same way as its Hebrew counterpart.

The much more frequent background (or transferred) use of *derekh* with man as the logical subject embraces in a single term that which breaks down into conduct and course of life in translation. When *derekh* is used with Yahweh in the construct or with a suffix, difficulty arises, for it can mean either God's own way or the way of man brought about by God. The background use of *derekh* will be discussed below on the basis of certain selected OT books. Here already, however, it may be pointed out that understanding of a central anthropological "concept" is blocked if it is supposed that one has here merely a "figurative" use of an intrinsically simple basic meaning.

2. *shuq*. In surveying words whose meaning is similar to that of *derekh*, it seems advisable to begin with those in which a basic "physical" connotation seems to be most prominent, and which are thus easier for us to grasp today. Although we will note the relationship of each of the terms to *derekh*, it will not be possible to investigate their relationships to one another.

The plainest Hebrew word in this respect is *shuq*, which occurs three times in the OT. This word denotes a *street in the city* which is shut off by gates (it has the same meaning in related languages: Arab. *sūq*, Akk., Jewish Aram., Syr.). [71] It comes from the root *šwq* I, "to be narrow." *shuq* is not a flat object, but tridimensional. One goes along (*be*) the *shuq* (Prov. 7:8). The relationship of *shuq* to *derekh* is discernible in Prov. 7:8: he who individually and intentionally takes the *derekh* to the strange woman turns aside from the *shuq*.

3. *chuts*. Usually the Israelite village had no designed street but narrow *lanes* covered with mire (2 S. 22:43; etc.). The OT uses the word *chuts* for a lane about 165 times. It has no corresponding verbal expression (other West Semitic languages have *ḥwṣ*, "to crowd together"). [72] The city (Jerusalem: Jer. 5:1; etc.) or its inhabitants (bakers: Jer. 37:21) can be named after *chuts* in the construct. Occasionally the overland road can also be called *chuts* (used symbolically of devastated Jerusalem, Isa. 51:23). According to *KBL*[3], *chuts* in the plural can even denote an open field, but this is uncertain (Ps. 144:13, paths in a field, lanes? Prov. 8:26, overland roads that existed from the creation?). *chuts* is not used figuratively, but the substantive often means "that which is outside or without" from the perspective of a community of people, especially in the expression *michuts*, "outside" (of the tent, Lev. 14:8; of the house, Ezk. 40:5; of the camp, Ex. 33:7; etc.), or in the phrase *hachutsah*, "toward the outside," often connected with "go out" (to become *hachutsah* = to marry into another tribe [RSV "family"], Dt. 25:5); cf. the adjective *chitson*, "located outside, outer, external." In contrast to the private sphere of the house, *chuts* is the public place (Isa. 42:2; Jer. 11:6). Like the German "Gasse" (alley, lane), sometimes *chuts* has a pejorative ring: the road or way on which one lives unprotected (Lev. 18:9; Dt. 32:25; Ezk. 7:15), or where the mutual tension of the spheres of clean and unclean is no longer significant (Lev. 14:3,8; Dt. 23:11[10]). The specific ideas associated with *chuts* are quite different from those connected with *derekh*. It is significant that the two words hardly ever appear together (an exception is Ezk. 47:2).

4. *mesillah*. A prepared road leading across country is called *mesillah* 27 times and *maslul* once (Isa. 35:8, road up to the temple? so Akk. *mušlālu*). [73] *mesillah* is cognate with the verb *sll*, "to carry out road work, cast up a highway." The substantive can be used in giving directions ("from . . . to," Isa. 19:23). One goes in (*be*) the *mesillah* (Joel 2:8), and hopes it will be straight and level (*yšr*) (Isa. 40:3). A street of this kind runs in front of the gates of Jerusalem on (to?) the Fuller's Field; here Isaiah meets with two kings of Judah (Isa. 7:3; 36:2). There are also *mesilloth* in heaven, i.e., permanent (though invisible) streets for locusts (Joel 2:8) and for stars (Jgs. 5:20). Deutero-Isaiah describes the great *mesillah* of Yahweh which is built miraculously from Babylon to Palestine (Isa.

[71] *KBL*[2], 957.
[72] *KBL*[3], 286.
[73] *AHw*, 684.

40:3; 49:11; cf. 11:16; 62:10). *mesillah* can stand in synonymous parallelism with *derekh* (Isa. 40:3; cf. 35:8), and occasionally *derekh* without a suffix appears in antithetic parallelism with *mesillah* with a suffix (Isa. 59:7f.).

In its background sense, which is rare, *mesillah* means a venture or enterprise which is connected with planning and the heart (as the seat of thought) (Isa. 59:7; Jer. 31:21; Ps. 84:6[5]; [74] Prov. 16:16f.). *derekh* appears in these passages as something that follows: *derekh* is possible as a movement on the *mesillah* as thus understood. There is, perhaps, a "street of death" (*msl mt*) in Ugaritic; [75] the Hebrew equivalent to this is *derekh* in the plural (Prov. 14:12).

5. *halikh/halikhah.* The masculine noun *halikh* (path? only in Job 29:6) and the feminine noun *halikhah* (6 times), which have parallels in Ugar. *hlk* and Akk. *alaktu, alkakātu,* and *ilkakātu,* [76] are derived from the widely used verb *halakh,* "to go." The feminine means the path that people take. This does not have to be a set road. The reference may be to caravans (Job 6:19), troops in fortifications (Nah. 2:6[5]), domestic activities (Prov. 31:27), the stars (Hab. 3:6), or the theophany of Yahweh from Sinai to the sanctuary (Ps. 68:25[24]). The cognate words in Akkadian also have the background sense of "course of life" and "conduct," like Heb. *derekh.*

6. *maʿgal.* *maʿgal* occurs 4 times in the singular, 3 times in the masculine plural, and 6 times in the feminine plural, in the OT. The lexicons usually render this word by "wheel- or wagon-track, track, path," and connect it with *ʿaghalah,* "cart, wagon." [77] On this basis, they claim that the word is "also used figuratively." [78] There is, however, no example of its foreground spatial use in the OT. If one wishes to infer this use, the most appropriate translation would seem to be "(double-tracked?) highway" (*maʿgal* stands in synonymous parallelism with *mesillah* in Isa. 59:7f.). The verb *pls* in the piel, "to prepare a way or road," is closely connected with *maʿgal* (*pls* occurs 6 times in the OT and it is used with *maʿgal* in Isa. 26:7; Prov. 4:26; 5:[6],21; there seems to be no good reason to divide *pls* into two roots). [79]

The background sense of *maʿgal* is a developed habit, good or bad, which will ultimately determine the fate of the person practicing it, whether that fate be salvation (*tsedheq,* RSV "righteousness," Ps. 23:3) or the spirits of the dead (Prov. 2:18). Yahweh also rides on his highway, either in a theophany (? Ps. 65:12[11]), or in his traditional instruction to man, which is directed to a specific goal (Ps. 17:5). When *maʿgal* and *derekh* are found together, the *derekh* of wisdom or prosperity appears as the initial factor to which man orients himself in order to find a salvific *maʿgal* (Isa. 59:8f.; Prov. 4:11; cf. 5:21).

---

[74] But cf., e.g., H. Schmidt, *HAT,* 15 (1934), *in loc.*
[75] *CTA,* 10 [IV AB], III, 29; *CML,* 119.
[76] See II.2 above.
[77] *KBL²,* 544; *THAT,* I, 459.
[78] *KBL².*
[79] So *KBL²,* 764.

7. *nathibh/nethibhah*. The masculine noun *nathibh* occurs five times in the Psalms and Job, and the feminine noun *nethibhah* appears 21 times in the poetic writings. No verbal cognate of these substantives is used in the OT. Neither one of the nouns is used much in the foreground sense for a stretch of road. The translation "path" [80] seems possible at Isa. 58:12 (*nethibhah* = an unfortified *derekh*?); however, the earliest example of either noun in Jgs. 5:6 uses *nethibhah* in synonymous parallelism with *'orach* as any type of caravan route. A *nathibh* can lead into a mine (Job 28:7) and Leviathan can leave a shining *nathibh* behind him in the sea (Job 41:24[32]).

In the background sense these substantives can denote the nexus of deeds and events when people are faithful to each other in a common bond of fellowship (Ps. 142:4[3]; 119:105). But they can also signify the conduct of people who are hostile to one another, who make their *nethibhah* crooked, and who thus subvert *shalom*, "peace" (Isa. 59:8). In Prov. 12:28, *derekh* as "individual conduct" is perhaps connected in the construct with *nethibhah* in the absolute as the way used by the great masses and leading them astray. The OT can also speak of Yahweh's *nathibh*, which he makes for his anger (Ps. 78:50), or of his *nethibhoth*, which go back to primitive times and open the future to the man who walks resolutely therein (Jer. 6:16; cf. Job 24:13; masc. Ps. 119:35).

Masculine and feminine nouns from a cognate root are found in Ugaritic. [81] The masculine is used only in the background sense: on the *ntb* of rebellion (*pš'*) or of pride (*g'n*), the goddess Anat encounters the sinful man and tramples him down under her feet. [82]

8. *shebhil*. In Jer. 18:15 and Ps. 77:20(19) *shebhil* seems to mean the same thing as *derekh*, though it is found in the plural in the former text and in the singular in the latter (the *qere* of Ps. 77:20[19] has the plural). *KBL²* conjectures that this noun is connected with a verb meaning "to hang down long," [83] but this is of no help in interpretation. The noun is perhaps attested in Phoenician. [84] In Hebrew it never has the foreground sense of a stretch of road, not even in Sir. 5:9 and 1QH 7:14f. If one wishes to infer such a usage, *shebhil* does not mean "path," but a prepared and well-known road; it stands in contrast to *nethibhah* in Jer. 18:15.

9. *'orach*. Next to *derekh*, *'orach* is the most important word for "way" in the OT: it occurs 57 times. The cognate verb *'rh* is used six times. The feminine active participle *'orechah* means "caravan," and the feminine passive participle *'aruchah*, "food carried on a journey." [85] It is also possible that the masculine

---

[80] *KBL²*, 641; *THAT*, I, 459.
[81] *WUS*, No. 1870; *UT*, No. 1715.
[82] *CTA*, 17 [II D], VI, 43-45.
[83] *KBL²*, 942.
[84] *DISO*, 288; otherwise, *KAI*, 1, 2.
[85] According to *KBL³*, 84, this word is from a different root.

active participle *'oreach* should be interpreted independently as "wanderer." [86] Akkadian uses *a/urḫu* for "road, way," and has a verb *arāḫu* meaning "to hasten, hurry." [87] In Phoenician only the piel masculine participle is attested as an epithet of the god Ešmun ("leader"?). [88] On the other hand, the substantive is widespread in Aramaic. [89] This root does not seem to be found in Canaanite, nor does it occur in Ugaritic.

BLe § 2n has seen in the juxtaposition of *'orach* and *derekh* an argument in favor of the thesis that Hebrew is a mixture of Aramaic and Canaanite. Nevertheless, in spite of the frequent occurrence of *'orach* and *derekh* as corresponding elements in synonymous parallelism, they are not simply synonymous. There are various indications of this. For one thing *'orach* occurs predominantly in the plural whereas more than 75 percent of the instances of *derekh* are in the singular. Again, the two words can stand in a construct relationship to each other, as in the expression *derekh 'orchothekha*, RSV, "the course of your paths," in Isa. 3:12. Evidently a *derekh* can be composed of several *'orachoth*. Furthermore the OT can speak of Yahweh's own *derekh*, while apparently it can speak of Yahweh's *'orach* only when it means an *'orach* which God has ordained for man (Ps. 44:19[18]). According to Isa. 41:3, an *'orach* is a path on the ground which the wonderful hero Cyrus does not need to travel with his feet. The antithesis to "going along" (*'rḥ*) is "lying down" (Ps. 139:3). The translation "path" [90] for *'orach*, which suggests an unconstructed "beaten path," leaves the wrong impression. *'orach* is "the route of travel and what one experiences on it." One passes by (*'br*) on an *'orach* (Ps. 8:9[8]; Isa. 33:8; Job 19:8). The noun also denotes the path of fish in the sea (Ps. 8:9[8]) and of the sun in the sky (Ps. 19:6[5]). *'orachoth* which are winding and overgrown are no longer real *'orachoth* at all (Jgs. 5:6).

When *'orach* is used in the background sense, the emphasis lies more on the state or condition of the man under consideration than on his action. This is true even though a supposed sphere of activity determines his destiny. Thus *'orach* is normally used for the way of life (good fortune?) (Prov. 2:19; 5:6; 15:24; Ps. 16:11; cf. Prov. 10:17; 12:28; only 6:23 has *derekh*). The conditions and spheres of life which, as it were, lie "before" the subsequent sphere of *chayyim* are also connected with the word *'orach*, e.g., *tsedhaqah*, "righteousness" (Prov. 12:28), or *mishpat*, "justice" (Prov. 17:23; cf. Isa. 40:14). To be sure, the OT also speaks of the *'orach* of the evildoer (Prov. 22:25); in the absolute, however, *'orach* denotes the way of the righteous (Prov. 15:10).

10. *ṣ'd, 'šr, p'm, reghel*. Words meaning "to step," "step or stride," and "foot" are also important in an analysis of the theme of the "way." Although the Hebrew is keenly aware of the role the hand plays in human actions, he still

---

[86] G. Lisowsky, *Konkordanz zum hebräischen AT* (²1966), 140.

[87] *AHw*, 63.

[88] *DISO*, 24.

[89] *DISO*, 24.

[90] E.g., Nötscher, 15 ("Pfad").

places more emphasis on the significance of the foot than do modern languages. Human action consists of spatial forward movement to a goal.

For this reason the nouns formed from the verb *ṣ'd*, "to move along, step, march (majestically and audibly)," viz., *tsaʿadh*, "step, pace" (14 times), *tseʿadhah*, "marching," and *mitsʿadh*, "step, pace," are important not only in Yahweh's theophany,[91] but also as terms describing behavior which has become a habit and which has thus set one on a course destined to lead to a specific state or condition (the *tseʿadhim* of the strange woman lead to Sheol, Prov. 5:5). This semantic field is related to *derekh*. The restricting of one's steps by actions hostile to the community is to be avoided (Job 18:7; Prov. 4:12); one should aspire to have "a wide place" for his feet (Ps. 18:37[36]) and to have his steps "firmly established" (Jer. 10:23?; Prov. 16:9; Ps. 37:23; Sir. 37:15). In several passages derivatives of *ṣ'd* stand in parallelism to *derekh* (Jer. 10:23; Job 31:4; 34:21; etc.).

The situation is similar in the case of *'ashur/'ashshur*, which derives from *'šr*, "to follow a track, march, go straight, go on, advance." In the foreground sense these nouns may mean "footstep" and "step,"[92] but in the nine certain examples appearing in the OT they are used only in the background sense, primarily to denote movement toward or away from Yahweh's ways and *torah*, "law" (Ps. 17:5; 37:31; 44:19[18]; Job 31:7?).

The use of the noun *paʿam*, which is related to the verb *p'm*, "to thrust, push forward, impel," is somewhat different. It means "foot," but also the foot's deliberate forward movement, a "step" (including the divine step), and finally a "constant" rhythmic movement in the sense of two or three or more times, etc. The use frequently moves on "from the concrete and the literal to the figurative,"[93] especially in passages where snares and nets are set for the feet, i.e., for a man's enterprises (Ps. 57:7[6]; 140:5f.[4f.]; Prov. 29:5), or where the righteous hopes that God will set his feet (*reghel, 'ashurim*) on a firm place (Ps. 40:3[2]; 119:133).

reghel, "leg, foot," is also used in connection with *derekh*. Through certain acts, the "legs" walk in the way of hostility to the community and therefore toward calamity (Prov. 1:15f.; 5:5), or else they lead to a secure condition or state (Prov. 4:26). Here also a direct action of Yahweh is expected on this part of the body and its movement (Ps. 18:34[33]; 25:15; 31:9[8]).

A diachronic description of the role of the words for "road, way," in the religious language of the OT is more important for the exegete than a summary lexicographical survey.

IV. In Pre-Deuteronomic Narratives.

1. *Literal Usage.* In the earlier strata of the books from Genesis through 2 Kings, *derekh* is used frequently in the literal or foreground sense of road, move-

---

91 Nötscher, 11f.
92 *KBL³*, 96.
93 Nötscher, 10f.

ment, and journey. It is indeed twice as common as, e.g., *chuts*, "lane, alley." The following verbs are often used with *derekh*: *halakh*, "to go, undertake," *natah min*, "to turn aside" (Nu. 22:23; cf. Gen. 38:16), *shubh be* (1 K. 13:9f.) or *shubh le* (1 K. 19:15), "to return," in the more abrupt form *haphakh*, "to turn away" (1 S. 25:12). These verbs are also important in a figurative sense in the later period.

derekh is used in a specific sense to mean "military expedition" (1 S. 15:20; 18:14; 2 S. 11:10), which is usually carried out in a sacred and ritual manner, and only by way of exception in a secular manner (*chol*, RSV "common," 1 S. 21:6[5]).

2. *Direction of an Individual's Life*. *derekh* is used in the early monarchical period for the direction of life which an individual takes for himself or which is set for him by others (1 S. 24:20[19]: no one will let his enemy go on a *derekh tobhah*, "good way"). At an early period the noun is also used for general "trends" in a person's destiny. Sexual intercourse between man and woman (Gen. 19:31) and the death of old people (1 K. 2:2) are part of the way of all the earth (*derekh kol ha'arets*). The "*derekh* of women" is menstruation (Gen. 31:35). *derekh* is not used, however, for the whole course of life, and only rarely do we find it in an ethical evaluation (*derekh tobhah*, the "good way," in 1 S. 24:20[19] means the way to prosperity, not the way of good deeds).

3. *Oracle and Prayer*. *derekh* acquires a special emphasis in the language of oracle and prayer, because it is presupposed that only the divine concursus will make one's way successful and prosperous (*tsalach* in the hiphil, "to make prosperous, successful," Gen. 24:21; Jgs. 18:5; *sakhal* in the hiphil, "to prosper, have success," 1 S. 18:14). The foreground and background meanings of *derekh* overlap when God is asked to keep (*shamar*) the *derekh* of a man (Gen. 28:20), his invisible guidance being received (*nachah*, Gen. 24:27,48) or his personal presence enjoyed (prep. *'im*, Gen. 35:3; 1 S. 18:14). God sends (*shalach*) man on a specific *derekh* (1 S. 15:18), or he sends his angel to keep or change the way man is going (Nu. 22:22f.).

4. *derekh As Salvation History*. Israel as a whole goes on a *derekh*, or has gone on it. To be sure, the extant examples of this use of *derekh* carry only a restricted reference to salvation history from the exodus out of Egypt to the conquest. The "*derekh* in which we went" is simply another way of saying what is expressed by the formula, "Yahweh brought us up" (*'alah* in the hiphil) (Josh. 24:17; Ex. 32:7f.; cf. 33:12f.; Josh. 5:4f.,7). In the exodus Yahweh himself led his people in a pillar of cloud (Ex. 13:21), and at the conquest he led them by his angel (Ex. 23:20). The course of the *derekh* of salvation history was interrupted by a severe test when Israel rebelliously turned aside (*sur*) from the *derekh* that Yahweh had commanded (*tsivvah*) by embracing the cult of the golden calf (Ex. 32:8; cf. Jgs. 2:17). Yahweh was thus forced into the position of having to "consume" his own people on the *derekh* (Ex. 33:3). To be sure, in some passages it is questionable whether *derekh* is used emphatically for salvation history. Later

the exodus event seems to have been summed up in the key phrase *bedherekh mitsrayim,* "in the way (after the manner) of Egypt" (Am. 4:10; Isa. 10:24,26), where the construct expression is hard to explain. Does it mean the "history of Israel in Egypt" or Yahweh's deeds in Egypt? It certainly does not mean the actions of the Egyptians themselves.

5. *The Divine derekh.* If we disregard 1 K. 18:27 (cf. Gen. 19:2), where it is assumed that an anthropomorphous deity sometimes goes on a journey, God's own *derekh* appears only in passages that are late from a traditio-historical point of view. The use of *derekh* in the prayer of Moses in Ex. 33:12-14 is more figurative. Moses asks Yahweh to show (*hodhiaʿ*) him his way in order that he might find favor in his sight to lead the people. Here the way of God includes not only the fixing of a route from Egypt to Canaan but also the successful following of the route through "the one whom thou sendest with me," God granting his own presence (*panim*). Gen. 18:19 (J?) says that Abraham shall charge his descendants to keep the *derekh* of Yahweh, which is identified with doing *tsedhaqah,* "righteousness," and *mishpat,* "justice," so that Yahweh can bring to realization his promise to Abraham. Here the divine *derekh* is extended further than it is in Ex. 33: it begins with the patriarchal period and ends perhaps with the rise of David's kingdom. As in Ex. 33, *derekh* denotes a historical development from a fundamental promise to its final accomplishment in external reality—a development which is brought about by God and which spans the centuries. It cannot be abstracted from the conduct of the group of people concerned. The human conduct required in Gen. 18:19 does not seem to be based on specific divine commands or laws, but on *tsedhaqah* ("righteousness") as "loyalty to the community" within the relationships established by the *derekh* of Yahweh, i.e., the divine covenant and the community of tribe or nation. [94] Along the same lines *mishpat* means the continuous determination to maintain and strengthen these institutions.

V. In the Psalms.

1. *Frequency of Occurrences.* In the Psalms the noun *derekh* occurs 66 times (16 in Ps. 119), the verb *drk* 10 times, *ʾorach* 14 times (5 times in Ps. 119), *maʿgal* 4 times, *nethibhah* twice, and *shebhil* once. Only rarely here do these words have the foreground sense of a traversable stretch of road or movement on such a road (80:13[12]; 89:42[41]; 110:7; of the *ʾorach* of the sun, 19:6[5]). It is significant that *derekh* and *ʾorach* appear especially in Individual Laments where we regularly find psalms with *derekh* as their theme (e.g., Pss. 1, 25, 37, 119), these being generally regarded as Wisdom Psalms. In agreement with this, the words for "way" are related in content to individual conduct or to divine guidance of an individual's life. In two psalms *derekh* is used of the deeds and conduct of the

---

[94] On *tsedhaqah* as "fidelity to the community and the resultant saving state or condition," see Koch, *ZEE,* 5 (1961), 72-90.

king (18:33[32]; 101:2f., cf. v. 6). In collective songs, the substantives for "way" occur only sporadically, and refer to a movement of the people on the divine way (44:19[18]; 81:14[13]; 95:10; 103:7), to Yahweh's "highway" (ma'gal in the plural) which brings fertility to the cultivated land (65:12[11]), or to his deed of *tsedheq*, "righteousness" or "salvation" (85:14[13]; 67:3[2]). The people is never the subject of its own *derekh*! There is an unmistakable shift of emphasis in the usage as compared to the narrative tradition.

2. *The derekh of the Individual*. The psalmist longs to keep his *derekh* (39:2[1]) and complains when his strength is broken on the *derekh* (102:24[23]). One's particular *derekh* is determined by systematic thinking about its objectives (36:5[4]) and is thus a kind of outward realization of self-awareness. When someone becomes important, successful (*ṣlḥ*, 37:7), or upright (*yšr*, 37:14; 107:7; with *'orach*, 27:11), there is always a danger that he will revert to the opposite, to a way of darkness (35:6), a *derekh* which the burden of arbitrary transgression (*pesha'*) turns into disaster (107:17). The ethical quality of the sum of human actions in a given section of life is crucial. In the preexilic period, this is evaluated, not on the basis of formulated laws, but according to one's general behavior toward the community which is fashioned by blood relationship or covenant relationship. Good and evil deeds done to a brother become for the doer a sphere which invisibly envelops him (especially if he habitually repeats them), which accompanies him on his *derekh,* which in the course of time ripens into a corresponding state or condition, and which either isolates him completely from the life-giving institutions of the community through sickness, persecution, and death, or leads him through well-being and prosperity to the harmonious experience of *shalom* ("peace") with his environment. Only on the basis of this concept of a sphere of action which determines one's fate [95] can we understand the effort to shape and experience one's life as a *derekh tamim*, "way that is blameless" (101:2,6; cf. 119:1). "Blamelessness" here means both a course of behavior that continually gives strength to the community and also a basically untroubled and happy state or condition. [96] Some psalms influenced by wisdom thinking speak of a conventional alternative which summons to decision. Over against the *derekh* of those who are faithful to the community (*tsaddiqim*, "the righteous") stands the *derekh* of sinners and of the wicked (1:1,6; 146:9; cf. 49:14[13]), which is a false *'orach* for others as well as a fateful one for the evildoers themselves (119:104,128).

3. *Divine Intervention*. The psalmists do not reflect on the functioning of a human *derekh* taken by itself. Rather, in both lament and praise, they express the longing for a prosperous *derekh* through Yahweh's help. They tell him of their ways (119:26), for he is always acquainted with every individual human *derekh* (139:3). Furthermore, he causes the individual to move forward (*hidhrikh*,

---

[95] For a discussion of this matter, see Koch, *Prinzip der Vergeltung*.
[96] Cf. Nötscher, 51.

107:7) on the good way, guards him (91:11), leads him (139:24), and makes him complete (*tmm*, 18:33[32]) by bringing him to the appropriate condition or state. Yahweh is also grieved about the *derekh* of these who are hostile to the community. He therefore diverts it (107:40) or brings it to ruin (146:9). It should be noted that divine intervention on the individual *derekh* is usually expressed in the same words as are used elsewhere to express the interest of the person concerned in the course of his own life (*šmr, tmm, t'h*). The psalmists, however, place less emphasis on the negative initiation and execution of a wickedly disposed way than on its positive consequences. The evildoer comes to the fatal end of his *derekh* with greater ineluctability than the one who is faithful to the community comes to happiness and prosperity. This antithesis is expressed in 1:6: "Yahweh knows the *derekh tsaddiqim*, 'way of the righteous,' but the *derekh resha'im*, 'way of the wicked', shall perish (of its own accord)."

In order to avoid an evil end, the righteous wisely commits his *derekh* to Yahweh, who in a happy lot reveals to man the relationship between deed and state (37:5f.).

VI. In the Wisdom Literature. The words for "way" play an important role in the Wisdom Literature of the OT, as may be seen in the oldest of these writings. *derekh* occurs 75 times in the book of Proverbs, more often than in the Psalms. One cannot fail to recognize an increase in its use from chaps. 25–27, which is usually considered to be the oldest part of the book, and in which *derekh* occurs only once, in the foreground sense, to the collection in chaps. 1–9, which is usually regarded as the latest part, and in which *derekh* appears about 30 times, *'orach* 12, and *ma'gal* 7.

The book of Proverbs speaks of the divine *derekh* only twice. According to 10:29 it is a refuge to the upright (*tom*) but destruction to evildoers. 8:22 describes personified Wisdom as the first-born and therefore the most powerful creature of the divine way, which thus begins with creation (cf. Job 40:19). These two passages in Proverbs are isolated and presumably come from another linguistic realm.

By way of contrast, the book of Proverbs says a great deal about the *derekh* of individuals, and this can be summed up under the following heads.

1. A *derekh* originates in the heart (*lebh*) as the center of rational planning (16:9; 23:19) and it leads to an action which in turn reacts upon the *lebh* (14:14).

2. Man is viewed as an active subject whose character manifests itself in the pursuit of a purposeful *derekh* directed toward a happy life. But the Hebrew man finds life only in connection with the community and by constantly maintaining a positive relationship to it (*tsedhaqah*, "righteousness," as salvation or well-being arising out of fidelity to the community). *derekh*, then, is identical with the totality of human work (21:8; cf. 8:22); in contrast an idler despises his *derekh* and consequently dies (19:15f.; cf. 15:19).

3. When thought develops into action, regard should be had to the course of one's *derekh* (8:32; 16:17), and one must make it firm and solid (21:29; cf. 4:26). It is most important to understand one's *derekh* (4:19; 5:6; 14:8; 20:24), for he who loses his way lands in the underworld (21:16).

4. The root *tmm,* "complete, blameless," is frequently connected with *derekh.* It denotes both an ethically perfect quality and also the resultant condition of unimpaired prosperity (10:9; 13:6; 28:6; cf. 28:18).

5. *yšr,* "righteousness, righteous," also occurs frequently with *derekh,* again in the twofold sense of action and resultant condition (29:27; 21:29; 14:12).

6. He who proves himself to be a man by setting out on a *derekh* does not pioneer his course. Two movements are presupposed which are above the individual: the *derekh* of those who are faithful to the community (*tsaddiqim,* "the righteous," 2:20; 4:18), and the *derekh* of evildoers (4:19; 15:9). The former is frequently defined by the general term *tsedhaqah,* "righteousness," which for the Hebrew is no abstract idea but a powerful field of force encompassing *derekh* understood in a tridimensional sense and consisting of the well-being of those who are faithful to the community. As the power of the *tamim,* "blameless," *tsedhaqah* smooths the *derekh* and keeps death at a distance (11:3-5).

7. The book of Proverbs only rarely mentions an objective for going on the *derekh* of human life (cf. 2:11-21; 3:23). At best it refers to a final stage (*'acharith,* 14:12; 16:25). It is possible that the expression "way of life" (*'orach chayyim,* 2:19; [4:18]; 5:6; 6:23; [8:32; cf. 8:35; 10:17; 12:28]; 15:24) is to be interpreted as an objective genitive: the way that leads to life. But it can also be taken as a subjective genitive: the way continually surrounded by "life." Apparently the wise man is satisfied with movement on his *derekh* as such if only it is supported and controlled by spheres of salvation. He is afraid of erring and stumbling, not of the endlessness of the journey.

8. The success of one's *derekh* requires the help of wisdom. This is incarnate in the mouth of the wisdom teacher. Wisdom herself walks in the *'orach tsedhaqah,* "way of righteousness" (8:20); he who walks on her way finds well-being (RSV "peace," 3:17).

9. Instruction (Torah) in wisdom on the way is indispensable for this life relationship. High esteem for Torah has its anthropological presupposition in the concept of the *derekh.* He who binds the Torah upon his *lebh,* "heart," and acts accordingly, experiences it as an illuminating revelation of the way of life (6:20-23; 4:10f.; 28:6-10; cf. 7:1-5). Thus the Torah of the wisdom teacher is not an authoritative commandment which cannot be questioned; rather it brings the instruction that a man needs and must understand if his *derekh* is to be successful.

10. God also intervenes on human *derakhim* both when man's way pleases him (16:7) and when it is an abomination to him (15:9). The ways of all men are before the eyes of Yahweh, and he makes them into the "highways" (*ma'gal* in the pl.) of the corresponding condition (cf. 5:21 with 4:26). God's reaction to

man's *derekh* is expressed by the same verbs that denote man's works on his own way (*yšr*, "make straight," cf. 3:6 with 9:15; *pls*, "prepare," RSV "watch," cf. 5:21 with 5:6 and 4:26; *kun*, "direct, establish," cf. 16:9 with 21:29; *šmr*, "guard, keep," cf. 2:8 with 8:32). This should dissuade us from interpreting the divine cooperation in this context as a "recompense" that comes from without or is even juridical. Instead, Yahweh cooperates in that which man fashions as his fate; on and around the *derekh* he sets in force the sphere of activity which brings the fate into effect.

11. As the author of wisdom (8:22) Yahweh has some share in the success of the movement of human life. There is a complex relationship between Yahweh's *chokhmah*, "wisdom," and human activity (2:6-15).

12. On the basis of the Ugaritic substantive *drkt*, *derekh* is sometimes taken to mean "sovereign power" in certain texts, especially in the Wisdom Literature. [97] Dahood goes even further when he assumes that the meaning of this word has changed from "sovereign power" to "sexual potency" in Prov. (19:16); 31:3; and Hos. 10:13. [98]

VII. In Prophecy of the Babylonian Period.

1. *In Jeremiah.* Around 600 B.C., the concept of way/movement connected with *derekh* begins to become a central point in prophetic thought. It does so first in Jeremiah. The main concern of Jeremiah is the past and future *derekh* of his people. He thinks that the ruling classes in Jerusalem should know the *derekh* of Yahweh as his *mishpat*, "justice," and observe it in their practical conduct. He obviously has in mind an understanding of the history that Yahweh had brought about and the institutions that have developed out of it. These ought to be the source of an endeavor constantly to preserve good relationships in the community (5:4f.). The *derakhim* that come from primeval times mean the same thing: He who walks thereon is on the good *derekh* and attains to the rest of salvation (6:16). Other nations have another *derekh* in their cultic practices (and in their history?), and this has less power for salvation (10:2; cf. Am. 8:14). (Completed) salvation history can also be called a *derekh* on which Yahweh has led (*molikh*) his people (2:17; cf. 2:6). Prophetic criticism begins with the insight that Israel has raised the cultic question about the history which God has wrought and has decided to "go after" (*halakh 'achare*) unprofitable or worthless idols (2:5-8). In this way, as Yahweh's wife, Israel has prepared for herself a *derekh* on which she brings evil upon herself or Yahweh causes evil to come upon her (2:33; 4:18;

---

97 W. F. Albright, *SVT*, 3 (1955), 7; *idem, Mélanges... A. Robert* (Paris, 1957), 23f.; P. Nober, *VD*, 26 (1948), 351-53; J. B. Bauer, *VT*, 8 (1958), 91f.

98 M. Dahood, *TS*, 13 (1952), 593f.; 15 (1954), 627-631; *Proverbs and Northwest Semitic Philology* (1963), 40; *Ugaritic-Hebrew Philology* (1965), 55. The problem with this sort of interpretation has been discussed by H. Zirker, *BZ*, N.F. 2 (1958), 291-94.

cf. 3:13), for Yahweh's eyes are upon all the movements of human life, and he is able to see them in the *lebh*, "heart, mind," before they are executed, and to prepare the appropriate fate (16:17; 17:10). Jeremiah, however, does not believe that all hope is lost. He appeals to his hearers to return (*shubh*) to Yahweh, and this appeal is significant in light of his concept of the *derekh*. He has in mind a genuine return from a historically perverted way to a fundamentally positive way laid down by God (3:21f.; 31:21; etc.). The demand for a concrete individual decision is crucial in view of the siege of Jerusalem: Yahweh sets before the people the way to life by surrendering to the Babylonians, and the way of death by remaining in the city that is doomed to death (21:8). The school of Jeremiah drew further inferences and expected that in the future a new covenant for the people would bring one *lebh*, "heart," and one saving *derekh* (32:39). At that time even the nations would learn and confess Israel's *derekh* (12:16).

2. *In Ezekiel*. Shortly after Jeremiah comes Ezekiel, who is more closely wedded to the vocabulary of the Jerusalemite cult, and who adopts the *derekh* of the individual as one of his prophetic themes. In no other OT book is the noun *derekh* used so often (107 times). Ezk. 18, which has incorrectly been called a chapter on "individual retribution,"[99] concludes with a discussion of the question whose *derekh* is reliable, the divine or the human (vv. 25ff.; 33:17-20). Part of the divine *derekh* is that it guarantees the functioning of the sphere of act and condition within the movement of human life. Yet the preeminence of the *derekh* of Yahweh may be seen in that it does not bring about a mechanical functioning of this sphere but makes possible the return (*shubh*) from a false *derekh* and thus allows the evildoer to avoid stumbling. This return is again based on the concept of the *derekh*.

Ezekiel, however, can also speak of ways/movements of the entire people. It is in this context that for the first time expressions denoting cultic impurity come to the forefront to characterize the predominant history of disaster. Remarkably formal language is used. The future catastrophe will strike because Yahweh lets loose his anger and "judges Israel according to its movements or ways" (*kidhrakhav špṭ*), which means that he will "requite their way (RSV deeds) upon their head" (*ntn darkam bero'sham*) (7:3-9; 36:17-19; 9:10; 11:21; 16:43; 22:31), so that abominations done in the midst of the people will bring about the disaster (7:3f.). After the collapse, however, there will come a time when the Israelites will consider their ways and be released from their power (36:31f.).

3. *In Deutero- and Trito-Isaiah*. The theme of the *derekh* plays an important role in Deutero-Isaiah too. Yahweh's power is apparent when he opens a *derekh* for historical movements, as he does in Israel's case in the exodus from Egypt (43:16,19; 51:10) and the sending of the messiah, Cyrus (45:13; 48:15). In particular, Yahweh will soon prepare a wonderful highway through the wilderness from Babylon to Palestine. This will become his own *derekh* at the time of the

---

[99] On this, see *Prinzip der Vergeltung*, 148.

return from exile. The Israelites will follow him on this road (40:3; 42:16) and he will expand it in all directions for the return of the dispersed Israelites (49:9-11). The *derekh* on which Yahweh will lead Israel means much more, of course, than the actual road on which the exiles will return to Palestine. It includes divine commandments (*mitsvoth*) which come from afar and into which salvation comes to be integrated (48:17-19). In this light it is easy to understand how disciples of Deutero-Isaiah could reinterpret the concept of Yahweh's eschatological high-way as a historical movement designed to prepare and mold Israel with the help of a *ruach*, "spirit," fashioned by Yahweh (57:14-21; 62:10-12; this concept is "spiritualized" even more in 1QS 8:14f.).

The famous passage in 55:9 must be interpreted in terms of the use of *derekh* in Deutero-Isaiah:
"For as the heavens are higher than the earth,
   so are my ways higher than your ways
   and my thoughts than your thoughts."
"Height" here does not denote distance and incomprehensibility, as is usually assumed, but as in other passages "high" is a predicate indicating secure author-ity to which one looks with confidence (e.g., in 52:13). At all events the context in 55:6-13 has on this view a compelling logic. Because Yahweh brings about a great transformation by his *derekh*, the wicked is to forsake his own disastrous *derekh* and return (*shubh*) to the majestic *derekh* of Yahweh which the prophetic word prepares. In this way the possibility of returning from exile is held out to Israel.

The relevant passages in Trito-Isaiah stand at the beginning of a transition to postexilic usage, where man's own ways are given a negative emphasis and become the way of error and aberration from God (53:6; 56:11; 57:17).

VIII. In the Deuteronomic and Deuteronomistic Literature. The divine and human *derekh* are also a basic concept in the Deuteronomic/Deuteronomistic writings. In the first instance *derekh* is salvation history from the exodus to the conquest. In the foreground sense it is the route through the wilderness and in the background sense it is the historical "runway" for the history of the people (Dt. 1:31,33; 8:2; 24:9; 25:17). Israel is not to return this way again by active dealings with Egypt (17:16). But Yahweh's way includes even more, especially directions for the future conduct of his people. In this regard Deuteronomy does not connect *derekh* with Torah (as in the Psalms), but with *mitsvah* and the verb *tsivvah*. These do not just mean "commandment" and "to command." They denote statutes which are not made known in every case to the human covenant partner. These statutes are not intended to define human conduct alone, but also the resultant state or condition which the good or evil sphere of act/condition produces. The *derekh-mitsvah* combination, which has hardly been noticed by exegetes, establishes for Deuteronomy the unity of law and history, and shows that laws were a functional necessity in the course of Israel's history. As long as Israel walks in the way laid down by Yahweh at Horeb, she will live, it will go well with her, and she will live long in the promised land (5:32f.; 8:6f.; 11:22-24;

19:8f.). With the covenant relationship, the possibility of walking in God's own *derakhim* has begun for Israel (26:17f.; 28:9). In this connection the anthropological relationship between *lebh*, "heart," and *derekh* continues. In order to direct the human mind to the divine ways and statutes, the fear (*yir'ah*) of Yahweh must be present as the framework for practical conduct.

Nevertheless, the divine history as the *derekh* from which Israel comes, and whose legal implications open up a future of salvation, is not an irrevocable entity. Just as Israel fell away from the *derekh* that Yahweh commanded on the occasion of the golden calf (9:12-16), it is possible at any time for a false prophet to divert the people from this *derekh* and from following Yahweh (13:5f.[4f.]; cf. 11:28). If the awful thing should happen that Israel forsakes this *derekh* permanently and thus becomes unfaithful to the history that God has wrought, evil will certainly come upon her at the end of the days (31:29).

In the Deuteronomistic portions of the books of Kings, the *derekh* of the Israelite kings is decisive for the fate of the people. Thus the fate of the northern kingdom is set by the *derekh* of the first king, Jeroboam I, which moves in a sphere of specific sins and which his successors also follow (1 K. 15:26,34; etc.). Total collapse comes because the whole people refuses to heed the prophetic call to return from its evil ways (2 K. 17:13). The development is not quite so clear in the case of the southern kingdom. The evil way of Manasseh was followed by only one generation, and the *derekh* of Yahweh was totally rejected (2 K. 21:21f.). Only David and Josiah walked completely in the way of Yahweh (2 K. 22:2).

IX. In Apocalyptic Literature. The apocalypses of the new age again make thematic use of the words for "way," although these words do not play any particular role in the Apocrypha in the narrower sense. [100] In the search for understanding of "universal history," the background sense of Heb. *derekh* and of Biblical Aram. *'arach*/*'orchāh* (masc. or fem.?) [101] can be used to denote the history both of a king (Dnl. 5:23) and also of an ordinary person (Syriac Apocalypse of Bar. 77:6) in the unity of act and experience. The course of human life is here subsumed in the great historical way of Yahweh (Dnl. 4:34[37]; cf. with 5:23; 3:27 [LXX]). In 2 Esdras in particular the history of Israel and the nations is understood as the way of the Most High which runs from creation through the ages and whose inscrutability inspires the apocalyptists (2 Esd. 3:31; 4:2f.,10f.; 12:4; cf. Syriac Apocalypse of Bar. 14:5; 20:4; 44:6). The divine way also embraces the origin of the evil heart in human history, cosmological phenomena on the bottom of the ocean and in the orbit of the stars, and eschatological perfection through the ways into paradise (2 Esd. 4:2-10). To recognize the direction of God's way in history is to understand the meaning of one's own national and individual existence and thus to find the way to life. Ezra writes down the canon, and thus passes on reliable accounts of all that has happened since the

---

[100] Nötscher, 69.
[101] *BLA*, 230, w'-x'.

beginning of the world, in order that men may assuredly find "the way" (Syr. *shebhil,* used absolutely) to life (14:22), for in God-governed history the saving propensity of the Creator will be victorious in the end, in spite of appearances to the contrary.

In addition to God's single and consistent historical way, the apocalyptists also speak of his ways in the plural, ways in the life of Israel, the nations, and individuals which he has laid down as tracks and directions (*ṣwh*), as Torah that must be heeded (2 Esd. 7:23f.,79,88; 8:56; 9:9; 14:31; Syriac Apocalypse of Bar. 14:5; 44:3) if he who is faithful to Yahweh may on his individual way, which now is understood as a continuous battle, attain at last to the life of the age to come (2 Esd. 7:129).

In later books closely connected with Apocalyptic (2 En. 30:15; Testament of Asher 1:3-5; only incidentally in 1 En. 91:18f.), the idea of the two ways appears. These are the way of uprightness and the way of corruption. They are both open to man from his creation and he has to choose between them. This concept is important for early Christianity. It has antecedents in Greek literature, but not in the OT. [102]

X. In the Qumran Literature. The Qumran literature again reflects a distinct use of *derekh,* especially for the life history of an individual, whose perfection (*tom*) is the supreme goal of human activity (1QS 11:2,10; etc.). The old idea of a determinative sphere of activity which surrounds and accompanies a *derekh* and causes it to be to salvation or destruction, may be seen in, e.g., CD A 3:15f.: at the making of the covenant God revealed the ways of his *'emeth,* "truth," while man actualizes them (*'asah*) and enters into life thereby. A negative life history is seen from the standpoint of the sphere of impurity (1QS 4:10; cf. 9:9; 1QH 6:20f.; cf. Ezk.), from which one can be liberated by atonement (1QS 3:6).

A saving *derekh* is possible only when man walks in the divine *derakhim.* The ancient belief that a *derekh* originates in the heart (=the intellect) is also upheld and is even applied to God (1QH 6:20f.). It interacts, however, with a newly arisen *ruach* (spirit) anthropology. Every human *derekh,* with its related nexus of deed and circumstance, originates in the *ruach,* to which God has given the power to create and act (1QH 15:22; 4:30,32). Does this mean that God is the author of corrupt ways? 1QS 3:13-4:8 solves the problem with its doctrine of the two Spirits of light and darkness which God created. "Upon these he (God) has founded every work, ... and on their ways every work takes place" (3:25f.). The Spirit of light enlightens the *lebhabh,* "heart," and thus brings the doer to the *darkhe tsedheq,* "ways of righteousness" (4:2).

It is understandable, then, that man prepares the *derekh* of God by studying and fulfilling the law (so Isa. 40:3 reinterpreted in 1QS 8:13-15). The eternal and inscrutable ways of God, however, are by no means exhausted in that which men do (1QH 7:31f.). Furthermore, the divine way, as instruction and law, is

---

102 *TDNT,* V, 57f. [42-46, 53ff.]; against St.-B., I, 460f.

always a prerequisite for the actualized way of man (1QS 1:12f.; CD A 1:11; 3:15f.; CD B 2:18).

In this connection the Qumran literature also speaks in the absolute of the *derekh* which one chooses or from which one departs (1QS 9:17f.; CD A 1:13). Repo defines *derekh* here as "true religion,"[103] and contends that this lies behind the use of "Way" in the book of Acts.[104] It should be noted, however, that Isa. 30:11,21; Job 31:7 already use *derekh* in an absolute sense.

Surprisingly the emphatic usage of the divine and human way in Apocalyptic and the Qumran writings is not continued in the Rabbinic literature.[105]

Koch

---

[103] E. Repo, *Der 'Weg' als Selbstbezeichnung des Urchristentums. AnAcScFen*, B, 132 (1964).

[104] So also V. McCasland, *JBL*, 77 (1958), 224-26.

[105] *TDNT*, V, 58, and n. 48.

דָּרַשׁ *dārash;* מִדְרָשׁ *midhrāsh*

Contents: I. The Root: 1. Etymology; 2. Occurrences; 3. Meaning. II. General Use: 1. Seeking and Asking in the Literal Sense; 2. Seeking and Asking in the Figurative Sense; 3. *darash* in Legal Terminology. III. Theological Use: 1. The Anthropological Aspect; 2. The Specifically Theological Aspect. IV. The Derivative *midhrash*. V. In the Qumran Literature.

I. The Root.

1. *Etymology*. The root *drš* is found in several Semitic languages: Aramaic, Arabic, Ethiopic, Syriac, and Mandean, and is attested in Ugaritic (as yet only once, according to Bauer's reconstruction).[1] It is debatable whether Akk. *darāšu* has anything to do with the same root.[2] The original meaning of *drš* is hard to

dārash. G. Gerleman-E. Ruprecht, *THAT*, I, 460-67; H. Greeven, "ζητέω, etc.," *TDNT*, II, 892-96; H. Madl, *Literarkritische und formanalytische Untersuchungen zu 1 Sam 14* (diss., Bonn, 1973), 217-257; M. Mannati, "Le désir de Dieu dans les Psaumes," *Carmel*, 4 (1971), 287-298; W. Richter, *Die sogenannten vorprophetischen Berufungsberichte. FRLANT*, 101 (1970); M. Sabbe, "Het bijbelse zoeken van Jahweh," *CollBG*, 8 (1962), 145-170; W. H. Schmidt, "'Suchet den Herrn, so werdet ihr leben'. Exegetische Notizen zum Thema 'Gott suchen' in der Prophetie," *Ex Orbe Religionum. Studia Geo. Widengren*, I (1972), 127-140 (=*SNumen*, 21); C. Westermann, "Die Begriffe für Fragen und Suchen im AT," *KuD*, 6 (1960), 2-30; R. R. Wilson, "An Interpretation of Ezekiel's Dumbness," *VT*, 22 (1972), 91-104.

---

[1] *WUS* (³1967), No. 795.

[2] Cf. *KBL*³ with the literary evidence given there.

determine. It is probably correct to translate it by the English words "seek," "ask," "inquire (of)" (Ugar. "interrogate, question"?). The root must have undergone a change of meaning in the course of its use. In late Semitic languages such as Middle Hebrew, Jewish Aramaic, and Syriac one encounters meanings like "interpret," but also "tread," "trample."

2. *Occurrences*. *darash* in its various forms appears around 165 times in the OT. In the overwhelming majority of cases it occurs as a verb in the qal, eight times in the niphal, and twice as a noun *midhrash* meaning "exposition, interpretation." In the Qumran texts, one encounters about 40 verbal and a few nominal forms of the root. *darash* is also found in Sir. 46:20; 51:23. The distribution of *darash* in the OT is not nearly as extensive as that of the parallel root → בקשׁ *bqš*. *darash* does not occur at all in 14 OT books (Nu., Josh., Joel, Ob., Jonah, Nah., Hab., Hag., Zec., Mal., Ruth, Cant., Neh., Dnl.), and only once or twice in several others (e.g., Gen.–2; Ex.–1; Lev.–1; Jgs.–1; 1 S.–2; 2 S.–1; Deutero-Isa.–1; Hos.–1; Mic.–1; Zeph.–1; Prov.–2; Eccl.–1; Lam.–1; Est.–1). On the other hand, it appears very often in 1 and 2 Ch. and Pss., and relatively often in Dt., Ezk., Jer., and 1 and 2 K. With full awareness of the problem of statistics, it still would seem valid to conclude from this analysis that *darash* is dominant in relatively late OT literary contexts, viz., in the Deuteronomic-Deuteronomistic traditions, in prophetic texts of the seventh and sixth centuries B.C. (if individual passages in these books are not to be regarded as even later), in the Chronicler's Historical Work, and in songs used in worship. Obviously *darash* is not a wisdom term.

3. *Meaning*. The meaning of *darash* is hard to fix when it is so difficult to pin down the original sense. To be sure, in the case of both *darash* and *biqqesh* one can always go back to the basic meaning "seek" or "ask." Yet the meaning of these words varies in each specific instance. The precise sense is given by the context. If one insists nonetheless on trying to find a general definition, then "go to see" and "search for," or "go" and "inquire about (of)," are about as close as one can come (cf. Dt. 12:5). The element of movement as a presupposition for the process of seeking and asking seems to be more or less inherent in all OT examples, even when it is not explicitly mentioned but is clearly indicated by the context (e.g., in Isa. 11:10). Frequently this movement is indicated by verbs of motion (*halakh*, "to go," *bo'*, "to come," *shalach*, "to send," 2 K. 8:8; Ezk. 20:1; Jer. 37:7) or by imperative constructions (Am. 5:4-6). The proper response to "asking" is *'anah*, "answering" (Ps. 34:5 [Eng. v. 4]), and to "seeking," *matsa'*, "finding" (Dt. 4:29; Jer. 29:13). There are many nuances of meaning in the word *darash*, ranging from "demanding," "avenging," "creating," "investigating," "searching," to "being concerned about" and "striving for." But weaker meanings like "pay attention to," "question," "consider," "inquire about," "seek information," and religious meanings like "ask for, entreat," "turn to God," "seek God," are also covered by *darash*. These various nuances are expressed by *darash* + prepositional constructions (as with *le, be, 'al, 'el, be'adh, me'im,*

me'otho, miyyadh, and *'achar*).[3] Worthy of note is the overwhelmingly theological use of *darash* in the OT in contrast to the smaller general or secular use. Obviously *darash* means "to seek" in a literal sense and yet the number of passages in which it is used in a figurative sense is disproportionately greater. In this regard one should especially take into account the communicative and consultative or advisory element in the meaning of *darash*. In the few OT examples of the niphal, the verb has the passive meaning of the qal (Gen. 42:22), "to be sought, asked, required, avenged," or in a more developed sense it has a tolerative connotation, "to let oneself be sought," or "not to let oneself be sought," "to let oneself be inquired of," or "not to let oneself be inquired of" (Ezk. 14:3; 20:31).

II. General Use.

1. *Seeking and Asking in the Literal Sense. drš* takes a material object much less frequently than the parallel root *bqš*. In the oldest example of this use in the OT (Jgs. 6:29), it is clear that the object of *drš* is a person, but this is unexpressed. The juxtaposition of *drš* and *bqš* here can denote the urgency of the action, but it can also mean that "seeking" is connected with "asking." The niphal of *drš* is used in 1 Ch. 26:31 of persons "being sought." In Ps. 109:10 *drš* must be understood as a corruption of *grš,* "to be driven out,"[4] unless one takes it passively, "to be sought (for)," in the sense of Jer. 50:20; Ezk. 26:21. It would also be conceivable to translate the 3rd person plural by the indefinite "one." In both cases the context would then suggest, of course, that what is sought cannot be found. The transition from actual seeking to inquiring after always involves personal objects in the accusative, e.g., in 2 S. 11:3 (with *le*); Jer. 30:14,17. Two passages speak of seeking animals (Dt. 22:2 and Lev. 10:16 [the animal of the sin-offering]). One says that the good housewife seeks wool and flax so that they will always be in the home (Prov. 31:13). It is easy to see how the meaning "to take care that" could arise from this. Hezekiah's "seeking after" the taxes that the people brought for the priests and Levites is already in fact an "inquiry, investigation" (2 Ch. 31:9, "*among* the priests and the Levites *because of* the taxes that had accumulated"; both times *drš* is construed with *'al* here). The meaning of *drš* is similar when we are told that the Babylonian envoys "sought after" the miraculous sign (either the sundial or the recovery from illness) which was given to Hezekiah (2 Ch. 32:31). Here again the meaning of *darash* tends toward the figurative sense of "ascertaining, gaining information." Another instance of the literal use of *darash* is in Job 39:8: the wild ass searches after food.

2. *Seeking and Asking in the Figurative Sense.* When the root *drš* is used in a figurative sense, it takes abstract objects. One of the oldest examples of this

---

[3] Cf. *KBL*[3].
[4] Cf. Kraus, *BK,* XV/2, 745.

use is found in Isa. 1:17 (impv. *dirshu mishpat*, "seek justice," in a prophetic torah). [5] The activity of "seeking" implies the implementation of what is sought, as the context impressively suggests. To "seek justice" here means to "do justice, practice justice" (cf. Isa. 16:5). The same is true of *drš 'eth shalom* (Jer. 29:7; 38:4), "seek welfare or peace," and of the expressions "seek good" and "seek evil" (Dt. 23:7[6], *shalom*, "peace," and *tobhah*, "good" [RSV "prosperity"]; so also Ezr. 9:12; Est. 10:3, where only *darash tobh le* occurs; Ps. 38:13[12], *doreshe ra'athi*, "those who seek my hurt," in synonymous parallelism with *mebhaqeshe naphshi*, "those who seek my life"; Prov. 11:27). All these examples suggest that "seeking" contains an element of activity, action, and energy. The act of *darash*, "seeking," is completed only with the practicing of what is "sought." *drš* is also used figuratively in the sense of "care for, pay attention to," as in Ps. 142:5(4) (with *lenaphshi*, "for my soul" [RSV "for me"]), a passage in which *drš* has a positive meaning, in contrast to *biqqesh* ("there is none who takes notice of me; ... no man cares for me"). Just as in English the expression "no one asks about me" means "no one cares about me," so Heb. *drš* can convey a similar thought (1 Ch. 13:3, "to care about the ark of God"). 2 Ch. 24:6 (where an inf. const. is dependent on *darash*) shows that an anticipated deed can be the object of "seeking." Here *darash* can mean "pay attention to," "take care that." Eccl. 1:13, *drš... 'al kol 'asher*, "to seek... all that...," also belongs to this category of figurative meanings. The precise meaning of *kol* is clarified by a relative clause, which is thus part of the object of *drš*. "All that is done under heaven" is the object of the search. Here the verb *tur*, "search out," functions as a parallel, so that *darash* can mean properly "investigate, study, inquire into." This nuance of meaning is further emphasized by the addition of the instrumental *bachokhmah*, "by wisdom." Other possible meanings of *drš* in the figurative sense will be discussed below under the theological [6] and legal instances. [7]

3. *darash in Legal Terminology*. One encounters a specific form of the figurative use of the root *drš* in the legal and sacral-legal texts of the OT. In that portion of the book of Deuteronomy in which laws and precepts have been collected (chaps. 12–26), it is assumed in several cases that an investigation will have to be made before a decision can be rendered. Along with other verbs *darash* is also used for this process of investigation and inquiry on the basis of given legal regulations, e.g., in Dt. 13:15(14) in connection with incitement to forsake Yahweh. Here *chaqar*, "make search," and *sha'al*, "ask," are used alongside *darash*. These are verbs whose meanings suggest an official procedure. The expected exactness and accuracy of the investigation is indicated by the ensuing infinitive absolute, *hetebh*, "diligently" (cf. Dt. 17:4, which does not have the parallel verbs, but does have the ensuing *hetebh*). These two examples belong in the sphere of sacral law, while the regulations in Dt. 17:9 take us into the realm

---

[5] Cf. H. Wildberger, *BK*, X, 36, 47.

[6] See III below.

[7] See II.3 below.

of criminal law, especially, it would seem, in matters pertaining to capital crimes. If the handling of such cases seems to be too difficult for the local court (v. 8), then a judicial inquiry (darash) is possible at a central authority. The decision reached there is binding and must be carried out by the local judiciary. According to the text the central court, which can be sought in "the place which Yahweh your God will choose," consists of the Levitical priests and the judge who is in office at the time. In this context it does not matter whether this combination is original or not. The wording suggests in any case an official court and an official procedure. Both show that darash is a part of the legal vocabulary. The binding (applicative) proclamation of the legal decision is expressed by higgidh + le, "declare to" (v. 10). If the statements of witnesses conflict with one another in a legal case, again it is the responsibility of the central court (where one actually stands "before Yahweh") to investigate the matter diligently until the false witness is convicted (Dt. 19:17f., vedhareshu hashshophetim hetebh, "and the judges shall inquire diligently") and a verdict is reached. In this passage "priests" and "judges" are mentioned first in relation to the investigation, and then only "judges" (in the pl.). But again this need not detain us. Clearly enough, darash is a legal term. The same is true in the realm of civil law (Ezr. 10:16), where darash again means "to investigate." [8] It is expressly stated that those designated to hear a case "sat down" (yšb) to "examine" the matter, while dabhar is used for the "case" under investigation. darash is also used as a legal term in covenant or contract law. Insistence on observing the terms of the agreement and the obligating of the other are both expressed by the root, e.g., in Dt. 18:19. In the so-called prophetic law there is a responsibility to hear the prophet that God sends, and here, of course, "hearing" means doing what is heard. As for him who does not meet this obligation, 'anokhi 'edhrosh me'immo, "I will require it of him." The same applies to paying a vow (Dt. 23:22[21]). In this passage darash with the suffixed me'im is a technical term, and is intensified here by the infinitive absolute preceding the finite verb.

The priestly tradition of God's covenant with Noah has preserved ancient legal ideas (esp. in Gen. 29:6, cf. vv. 4f.) In v. 5 darash is used three times in the sense of "requiring" or "avenging." God himself assumes the role of the blood-avenger or recompenser (cf. Ps. 9:13[12]; 2 Ch. 24:22, where the expression is shortened). Here the objects of the darash process are dam, "blood," and nephesh, "soul, life." miyyadh, "from the hand of," is used to express the relationship to the evildoer who is called to account (even the beast which kills a man is not excluded); cf. also Ezk. 33:6 (the prophet is indirectly guilty if in his office as a watchman he fails to warn those entrusted to him of approaching disaster). The legal use of drš may be found, too, in the Joseph story, where Reuben tells his brothers that Joseph's blood will be required of them (vegham damo hinneh nidhrash, Gen. 42:22). In Ezk. 34:10 the same legal idea lies behind the figure of the shepherd and the sheep entrusted to him. darash is used once in connection with sacrifice (Ezk. 20:40): Yahweh demands what belongs to him in the

---

[8] Read lidhrosh with BHK instead of ledharyosh; see Rudolph, HAT, 20, in loc.

holy place. [9] *darash mishpat*, "to seek justice," is the responsibility of all Israelite society, its individual members, its notables (Isa. 1:17), and especially of its official judges (Isa. 16:5). As has already been emphasized, [10] "seeking justice" implies practicing it. To this extent, too, *darash* is part of the legal terminology of the OT. The meaning of Ex. 18:15 is uncertain. The statement falls in the section on the new method of administering justice. [11] The verses before and after v. 15 speak of cases up for decision and v. 15 contains a stylized statement of Moses: "The people come to me *lidhrosh 'elohim* (RSV, to inquire of God)." It is undoubtedly difficult to distinguish between sacral and secular law here, because the two were related to each other.

The examples adduced show that the use of *darash* has been extended to juridical and sacral-juridical contexts, and in this process the stereotyped language of fixed formulations is still recognizable. Nothing certain can be said about the antiquity of these ideas and their formal fixation. Most of the literary strata in which *darash* has been handed down as a legal term are late (Deuteronomic-Deuteronomistic, Priestly, Chronicistic), but naturally this does not rule out the possibility that later sources used earlier material.

III. Theological Use.

1. *The Anthropological Aspect.* It is striking that the theological use of *drš* is far more predominant in the OT than its general use. Within the theological realm itself the examples of the root that use man as the subject of *darash* are in the majority. When man is the subject, the object of *darash* may be God (Yahweh), or a place or text (law, command) belonging to God, or an abstract idea (justice, peace, good) connected with man's relationship to God. The cultic funeral is intended in Dt. 12:5 (*darash* and *bo'*, "go," with reference to the *maqom*, "place," that Yahweh will choose) and 2 Ch. 1:5 (*darash* with the *mizbach hannechosheth*, "bronze altar"). It is also assumed in the dispute of Amos (Am. 5:4-6): *ve'al tidhreshu beth'el*, "but do not seek Bethel," where *darash* is used in parallelism with *bo'*, "enter," and *'abhadh*, "serve" (MT has *'abhar*, "cross over"). Amos contrasts this cultic act, which he rejects, with the divine oracle, *dirshuni vichyu*, "Seek me and live," i.e., seeking God is important and necessary if one is to live (v. 4; in the later interpretation in v. 6 we read, *dirshu 'eth yhvh vichyu*, "Seek Yahweh and live"). [12] Verse 14 seems to explain how this is to be done concretely (*dirshu tobh ve'al ra'*, "Seek good and not evil," cf. Mic. 6:8), viz., by doing good, hating evil, and establishing justice in the gate (v. 15). Modern exegetes, however, think that v. 14 too belongs to the later interpretative sections of the book of Amos, and that it comes from disciples of Amos who had been influenced by wisdom teachers. [13] Thus, Wester-

---

[9] Otherwise Zimmerli, *BK*, XIII/1, 457f.
[10] II.2.
[11] M. Noth, *Exodus. OTL* (trans. 1962), 150.
[12] Cf. Wolff, *BK*, XIV/2, *in loc.*
[13] *Ibid., in loc.*

mann wants to interpret the passage in the light of Jeremiah, Ezekiel, and 1 and 2 Kings. The reference as he sees it is to a turning to Yahweh brought about by a prophet. [14] Trito-Isaiah is describing acts of worship when he represents Yahweh as saying, *'othi yom yom yidhroshun*, "they seek me daily" (Isa. 58:2; note the context!). [15] When *darash* is used in connection with the ark (1 Ch. 13:3), it is clear that it can be understood only in a cultic-ceremonial sense. In late texts the personal relationship is sacrificed to the written Torah (Ezr. 7:10) and its common parallels *piqqudhim*, "precepts" (Ps. 119:45,94), and *mitsvoth*, "commandments" (1 Ch. 28:8), which now become the objects of *darash*. Here again "seeking" obviously implies doing what one is seeking. This is expressed in 1 Ch. 28:8 by the additional verb *shamar*, "observe" (see also Ps. 119:44), and in Ps. 119:45 by *'ethhallekhah*, "I shall walk," which is used in the preceding parallel stich. Ethical obligation follows from occupation with the law of God (Ezr. 7:10, *la'asoth*, "to do [it]"). The *ma'ase yhvh*, "works of Yahweh," like the law, are the object of investigation, of occupation (*derushim*, "open to investigation," "worthy of inquiry") (Ps. 111:2). The English equivalent, "to be occupied with," denotes the theoretical element of "research, investigation, study," which is everywhere present in the texts. The urgency and intensity of doing is expressed— and not only here—by *hekhin lebhabho lidhrosh*, "he set his heart to seek" (Ezr. 7:10; 2 Ch. 30:19; etc.). In this doing lies the way of salvation. Anyone who does not strive for the law of God disqualifies himself as one of the *resha'im*, "wicked," from whom *yeshu'ah* is far away (Ps. 119:155). What is meant by the *sepher yhvh*, "book of Yahweh," from which (*me'al*) those addressed in Isa. 34:16 (a late passage) are to "seek" the confirmation of the prophetic message, is not certain. The passage undoubtedly presupposes occupation (*darash*) with a fixed text. The same thing cannot be said of *dabhar* ("word") passages. In 1 K. 14:5; 22:5 (=2 Ch. 18:4), however, "seeking after a word (of God)" refers to an immediately expected oracle (of God) which, it is hoped, will give direction and help in an acute emergency. It is thus one of the many instances in which we have a direct formula for "seeking Yahweh" through the mediation of a prophet.

As in the case of *biqqesh*, there are cases in which the qal active participle of *darash* (with a suffix, or referring directly to Yahweh in the construct) can be understood as a technical term in the history of piety, as, e.g., in Ps. 24:6, *dor doreshav* (*qere*), "the generation of those who seek him" (which stands in parallelism with *mebhaqeshe phanekha*, "those who seek thy face"); 22:27(26); 9:11(10); 34:11(10); 69:33(32). With the exception of Ps. 24:6, these passages are probably late. Kraus thinks this expression refers to pilgrims at the sanctuary, to members of the "true cultic community." [16] Ps. 34:11(10), at least, presupposes situations at a holy place (cf. v. 5[4]: "I sought Yahweh, and he answered me"). The same is true, in fact, of 22:27(26), another psalm of Individual Thanks-

---

[14] *Ibid.*, 22; and see below.
[15] Cf. Westermann, *Isaiah 40–66. OTL* (trans. 1969), 334f.
[16] Kraus, *BK*, XV/1, 197, 268f.

giving (cf. 69:33[32]). Ps. 24 is a Liturgy of the Gate or an Entrance Liturgy (Entrance Hymn, Entrance Torah). In Ps. 9:11(10), "those who seek thee" is in synonymous parallelism with *yodhe'e shemekha,* "those who know thy name." This passage could also refer to the devout gathered for worship. The only question is whether the *doreshim,* "those who seek," are essentially the Israelites in general as members of the ancient covenant people, or whether there is concealed behind the term a more restricted group of cultic participants, or temple visitors, who consciously profess their allegiance to Yahweh. On the basis of the small number of texts bearing on this issue, it is not possible to do more than simply raise the question. The same problem exists in connection with the use of → בקשׁ *bqš.*

The use of *darash* in Chronicles for membership in a community is much more broad and general than that which seems to be reflected in the above-mentioned passages from the Psalms. The fundamental attitude of a member of the people of God experiences a theological definition and evaluation by the use of the expression *darash yhvh,* "seek Yahweh" (or *lo' dharash yhvh,* "not seek Yahweh"; *drš* is also used with *'eth, be,* and *le* to convey this idea). Thus a loyal, positive, devoted commitment to Yahweh is expressed very generally by the expression "seeking Yahweh." The phrase qualifies an Israelite as a true one, just as "not seeking Yahweh" disqualifies him. It is applied in the first instance to the basic stance of the various kings with whom the Chronicler's Historical Work is concerned. Thus the Chronicler attributes Saul's downfall to his not having sought Yahweh (1 Ch. 10:14 and context). The parallel failings define this as unfaithfulness, disobedience to the word of Yahweh (*lo' shamar,* "he did not keep" the command of Yahweh), and inquiring of the spirit of the dead (*sha'al,* "consult," and *darash,* v. 13). David admonishes Solomon to "seek Yahweh" (1 Ch. 28:9). God's faithfulness to those who seek him is manifested in his letting himself be found by them (*yimmatse' lekha,* "he will be found by you," 1 Ch. 28:9; 2 Ch. 15:2; Jer. 29:12-14; etc.), or his being good (*tobh*) to them (Lam. 3:25). The expressions which 1 Ch. 28:9 use in parallelism with "seeking Yahweh," and which thus help to define this phrase, are "knowing (*yadha'*) God" and "serving (*'abhadh*) him with a whole heart." This involves an act of will (*hekhin libbo lidhrosh,* "he set his heart to seek" Yahweh), for which Rehoboam, e.g., was not ready (2 Ch. 12:14). On the other hand, the Chronicler states that Jehoshaphat (2 Ch. 19:3; 22:9) and Uzziah (2 Ch. 26:5) set their hearts to seek Yahweh, and in the latter case "seeking Yahweh" is connected with being instructed in the fear of God. [17] "Seeking God" and "being successful" also go hand in hand in Chronicles. As has already been suggested, this basic disposition is expected not only of the king but also of the people (2 Ch. 30:19). Hence they can be commanded to "seek Yahweh" (2 Ch. 14:3[4]). They can also place themselves under an oath to "seek" him (*vayyabho'u bhabberith lidhrosh . . . ,* "and they entered into the covenant to seek" Yahweh, 2 Ch. 15:12). One encounters the same view in Trito-Isaiah (Isa. 65:10; cf. with v. 11): the chosen people (*'ammi,* "my people") proves

---

[17] See *BHK³.*

itself to be such by "seeking Yahweh" (*darash 'eth yhvh*). This concept is so complex that very important consequences are causally connected with it according to the Chronicler's theology: success (2 Ch. 17:5); possession of the land and peace (2 Ch. 14:6[7]; 15:15); and life (1 Ch. 10:13f.; 2 Ch. 15:13). That the Chronicler understands "seeking Yahweh" in a broad sense is also indicated by the fact that in parallel expressions very different activities help to define its material content. In 2 Ch. 17:4 he equates it with walking in the commandments of God (*bemitsvothav halakh*, cf. 1 Ch. 28:8f.). It is also keeping the *torah*, "law," and the *mitsvah*, "commandment" (2 Ch. 14:3[4]; cf. Ps. 119:2,10; and Isa. 58:2 [Trito-Isaiah]). In other passages it involves the destruction of idolatry, which puts allegiance to Yahweh to the test (2 Ch. 19:3), keeping the *debhar yhvh*, "word (RSV commandment) of Yahweh" (1 Ch. 10:13f.), and turning away from impurity and establishing cultic purity (Ezr. 6:21). If 1 Ch. 28:9 already has possible cultic ramifications, the building of the temple and the establishment of the cult are themselves an expression of *lidhrosh leyhvh*, "seeking Yahweh," in 1 Ch. 22:19 (cf. Ezr. 4:2). 1 Ch. 15:13 shows that the fundamental cultically ordained (*kammishpat*) attitude toward Yahweh was well known to the Chronicler (cf. 1 Ch. 16:11, as well as Ps. 105:3f.). 1 Ch. 21:30 undoubtedly has reference to a cultic ceremony when it alludes to David's connection with a sanctuary of burnt-offering in Gibeon. Finally Ezr. 4:2 (with the *qere*) also links seeking God and sacrificing to him very closely together. The idea of "seeking God" is so complex and so general in the Chronicler's Historical Work that one must consider the possibility that when all is said and done it denotes nothing other than the Chonicler's typical ideal of piety. For this reason these passages in Chronicles might be set in association with the participial forms of *darash* in the Psalms, which can be interpreted as technical terms in the history of piety.

The observation that *darash ('eth) yhvh*, "seeking Yahweh," seems to have had a place in prophetic appeals for repentance is worthy of note. "Seek me and live" in Am. 5:4-6 is equivalent to a summons to repentance. The situation is no different in Hos. 10:12, where "seeking God" is associated with the social duties of "sowing righteousness" (*tsedhaqah*) and "reaping steadfast love" (*chesedh*). Again, the purpose of the words in Jer. 29:13 (12-14) is to bring the hearers to repentance, and the same idea is fairly clear in Isa. 9:12(13). The former passage implies that turning to Yahweh (*qara'*, "call upon," *hithpallel*, "pray to," *biqqesh*, "seek," *darash*, "seek") results not only in his willingness to hear and to be found (*venimtse'thi*), but also in his changing one's unhappy fate (*veshabhti*, RSV, "restore your fortunes") (the same thought is clear in Isa. 55:6f. [Deutero-Isaiah]). The Deuteronomic/Deuteronomistic summons to repentance also uses the same term (Dt. 4:29). The idea that "seeking God" means repentance or conversion must have been deeply rooted in the general consciousness of Israel, for the lyrical-poetic-cultic literature also uses it in this sense (Ps. 78:34; 14:2 = 53:3[2], where it is represented as a significant, intelligent action corresponding to the divine expectation). In an Individual Lament it denotes turning to God and is accompanied by verbs meaning to "call out," "cry out," and "pray" (Ps. 77:3 [2], see the context). Finally, it is possible to understand Job 5:8 in the same way, viz., as the return to God of someone who is in despair of self. If one wishes to place the book of Lamentations in a setting of penitential worship where the call to repentance was uttered, Lam. 3:25 can be understood as an expression of confidence that Yahweh will bless the penitent. The opposite of this aspect of prophetic preaching lends support. This consists of an announcement that calamity will come upon those who are not converted to Yahweh, who do not seek him or inquire of him (Zeph. 1:6; Jer. 10:21), which is an act of stupidity (Jer. 10:21; cf. Ps. 14:2 = 53:3[2]). In this connection, *darash* has something directly to do with trust and reliance (Isa. 31:1; see also v. 2).

In a whole series of passages, mainly in the books of Kings, Chronicles, Jeremiah, and Ezekiel, *darash* must be translated "inquire of God," "consult Yahweh." In the large majority of these passages a mediator or prophet plays an important role, so that one is tempted to assume that a prophet acts as mediator even when there is no specific mention (e.g., in Gen. 25:22 [J]; 2 Ch. 16:12). The situation is different in Isa. 11:10, which describes the eschatological endeavor of the nations to seek (*darash 'el*) the root of Jesse "in that day." There is no idea of mediation here. Usually these passages have a verb of motion (*halakh*, "go"; *bo'*, "come"; *shalach*, "send") before *darash*. This shows that a willingness to inquire must first bring one to the place where it is possible to do so. In Gen. 25:22; Ps. 34:5(4); and possibly Job 5:8 it must be assumed that the "inquiring" took place in a cultic center. But this is not so sure in 1 S. 9:9; 1 K. 14:5; 2 K. 1:16; 3:11; 8:8; 22:13,18; 2 Ch. 34:21,26. The important thing in these passages is that a prophet is present who mediates the question put to Yahweh and Yahweh's answer. In the light of 2 K. 22:14 (and par.), which makes some very detailed statements about the "private dwelling" of Huldah the prophetess, to whom Josiah sent some of his officials (cf. also 1 K. 14:5), it must be assumed that the cultic center is not the only one where inquiry can be made of God. As long as a prophet or man of God is present, Yahweh may be consulted. Nevertheless, in the story of Micaiah ben Imlah (1 K. 22:7f.; 2 Ch. 16:6f.) the use of *darash* as a term meaning "to seek an oracle" (in connection with the war of Yahweh) is hard to explain apart from cultic integration. It has been suggested that *darash* here assumes the function of *sha'al*, "ask," which is really a technical term for seeking an oracle before entering into a war of Yahweh. [18] In the context of 2 Ch. 20 Jehoshaphat's seeking or inquiring of Yahweh (v. 3, *darash*, "to seek"; v. 4, *biqqesh*, "to seek"; in vv. 14ff. note the man of God figure) cannot be understood in any other way than cultically. 2 Ch. 34:3 defines Josiah's "seeking God" in terms of purifying the cult. Unfortunately the way in which one inquired of God through a prophet (cultically or noncultically) cannot be determined conclusively from Jeremiah and Ezekiel. A noteworthy factor, however, is that people came to both these prophets where they lived to make inquiry of Yahweh, and that they prayed to Yahweh for an answer on behalf of those who came (Jer. 21:2; 37:7; Ezk. 14:7,10; 20:1,3). This is expressed and construed in different ways syntactically, but the differences yield no nuances of meaning which are significant for the present discussion. In addition to the

---

[18] On this whole issue, cf. Westermann, 17ff., esp. 19f.; Madl, 248-252; Richter, 178.

traditional formula *darash ('eth) yhvh*, "seek (inquire of) Yahweh" (Ezk. 20:1), we also find *darash + be'adh* with a suffix before (Jer. 21:2) or after (2 Ch. 34:21) the object. *darash + me'otho* after the object is a peculiar usage denoting mediation ("to inquire by someone"). The apparatus in *BHK*[3] suggests that one should understand this as a form of the preposition *'eth*, adducing various manuscripts and versions in support (2 K. 3:11; 1 K. 22:7). The occasion of an inquiry is introduced by *'al* (=concerning) (2 K. 22:13). The constructions *darash le* or *be* are also used frequently to mean "inquire of." It is always in a situation of need that one seeks an explanation by inquiring of Yahweh. Relief is expected (if possible) as a result of the inquiry. Some passages have to do with personal calamities such as illness (Gen. 25:22; 1 K. 14:1ff.; 2 K. 1:2,16; 8:8; 2 Ch. 16:12), and others with group calamities (1 K. 22:7f.; 2 K. 3:11; 22:13,18; 2 Ch. 20:3; and the texts in Jeremiah and Ezekiel). For the first group of passages Westermann has worked out a fixed sequence of individual features in the process of inquiry, but the sequence for the second group can only be conjectured. Most of the examples come from the monarchical period (in Gen. 25:22, J perhaps projects this usage from the monarchical period back into the patriarchal history), suggesting that in this period the Israelites inquired of (consulted) God through the prophets. Many details of this thesis are obscure, especially in relation to the way in which the inquiry was made. [19]

Many passages in the OT attack the abuse of *darash*. The hopeful appeal to an authority can be made to other gods, the dead, and the spirits of the dead. This abuse is also expressed by *darash* in the familiar constructions indicated above. Well known are the Deuteronomistic warnings against turning to foreign gods (Dt. 12:30, naturally with the intention of worshipping ['*abhadh*, "serve"] them, even if it is "only" an inquiry, as here), and inquiring of the dead (Dt. 18:11, *doresh 'el hammethim*, RSV "necromancer," which appears in parallelism with *sha'al 'obh veyidde'oni*, RSV, "a medium, or a wizard"). Here also reference is made to a mediator (1 S. 28:7, *'esheth ba'alath 'obh*, RSV, "a woman who is a medium" [twice]), through whom those who inquire (*darash be*) come in contact with the spirit of the dead. Here and in 2 K. 1 the movement (*halakh*, "go") prior to "inquiring" may be clearly seen. It is necessary to go to the place where inquiry can be made. If the book of Deuteronomy refers very generally to the gods of the nations around Israel as the objects of such inquiry, 2 K. 1:2,3,6,16 specifically names Baal-zebub, the god of Ekron, of whom Ahaziah inquired (*lekhu dhirshu be*, "Go, inquire of") about his sickness by sending messengers to Ekron. In both instances this kind of "inquiring" is cause for death, according to the Deuteronomic/Deuteronomistic theology (cf. 1 Ch. 10:13f.; 2 Ch. 16:12). It is also possible that this abuse of "inquiring of God" is denounced as early as in Proto-Isaiah (Isa. 8:19), though the passage is fragmentary. The reference to "the spirits of the dead (RSV, the mediums and wizards) who chirp and mutter" does not furnish any precise information as to the way

---

[19] Cf. Westermann, *KuD*, 6, 2-30; on inquiring of Yahweh by means of the lot oracle, cf. Richter, 177f.; Madl.

in which such illegitimate inquiries were made. Once again the passage simply uses well-known expressions for "inquiring" of a higher power (*darash be'adh hachayyim 'el hammethim*, RSV, "Should they consult the dead on behalf of the living?"). The nations may inquire of their gods in this manner (Isa. 19:3) and they constantly do so, although from the standpoint of the Israelites there is an element of Yahweh's judgment in this (in this case against Egypt). Jer. 8:2 is something of a *locus classicus* in this respect, since it places *darash* in a whole series of activities which mutually interpret one another. The sun and moon and all the host of heaven are objects of *darash, 'ahabh*, "love," *'abhadh*, "serve," *halakh 'achare*, "go after," and *hishtachavah*, "worship." It is difficult not to see behind these verbs specific cultic-ceremonial acts, directed not to Yahweh but to the celestial deities. The Chronicler's Historical Work also recognizes the dangerous consequences of turning away from Yahweh. It praises Jehoshaphat because *lo' dharash labbe'alim*, "he did not seek the Baals" (2 Ch. 17:3), but censures Amaziah for bringing back the gods of the Edomites, and setting them up as his gods, when he returned from his victorious campaign against Edom (2 Ch. 25:14). Amaziah established a cult for these gods which is described as *darash 'elohe ha'am*, "resorting to (seeking) the gods of a people" (v. 15). This abuse of *darash* brought about the overthrow of Amaziah in a battle with Israel (v. 20). Basically the whole time that Israel was in the land of Canaan there was a constant danger that it would fall away from Yahweh and turn to other deities, magic, and sorcery. This danger repeatedly became a reality and circles that were faithful to Yahweh continually had to contend with it, according to the witness of the OT. *darash* is used along with other verbs to describe this apostasy. The examples again span the entire monarchical period. It is worth noting that this illegitimate "seeking" or "inquiring" was obviously done in the same forms and methods as the legitimate. Not without interest is the list of objects of the abuse of *darash*, "seeking, inquiring," although the number of examples is not large: *be'alim*, "the Baals," *'elohe haggoyim*, "the gods of the nations," *'elohe bene se'ir*, "the gods of the sons (men) of Seir," *ba'al zebhubh 'elohe 'eqron*, "Baal-zebub, the god of Ekron," *methim*, "the dead," *'obh(oth)*, "medium(s)," *repha'im*, "the shades," *'elohe 'edhom*, "the gods of Edom," *'elilim*, "the idols," *yidde'onim*, "the wizards," *'ittim*, "the sorcerers," *shemesh*, "the sun," *yareach*, "the moon," and *kol tsebha' hashshamayim*, "all the host of heaven."

2. *The Specifically Theological Aspect.* The specifically theological aspect of the use of *darash*, in which God (Yahweh) is the subject of the verb, is relatively less well attested in the OT than the anthropological aspect. It has been introduced already in connection with passages in which *darash* is used as a legal term, [20] especially in certain juridical ideas in the law of debt, revenge, and contracts. These passages, which have already been discussed, are Gen. 9:4-6; Dt. 18:19; 23:22(21); Ezk. 20:40; 33:6; 34:10; Ps. 9:13(12); 2 Ch. 24:22. The specifically theological use of *darash* is also apparent in the correlative ideas of

---

[20] See II.2 above.

"being found" (or "not being found") and "answering" (Isa. 55:6; Ps. 34:5[4]). Furthermore, attention should be called to some passages that use the niphal of *darash* in the sense "to be sought (out)," "to let oneself be sought, inquired of" (Isa. 65:1; Ezk. 36:37), or "not to let oneself be sought, inquired of" (Ezk. 14:3; 20:3,31), i.e., with reference to Yahweh's offer of salvation, which has been constantly rejected (Trito-Isaiah), or with reference to God's future act of salvation for his people (Ezekiel, where *darash* slides over to the meaning "ask": "I will let myself be asked"), or as an expression of divine judgment: "I will not let myself be sought, asked, consulted." The thirty-fourth chapter of Ezekiel, which contains the treatise on true and false shepherds, is also well known. Here Yahweh, the true and faithful shepherd who searches for (*darash*) his sheep and seeks them out (*biqqer*) (v. 11), is contrasted with the notables of God's people, who, as unfaithful and selfish shepherds, neither search (*darash*) nor seek (*biqqesh*) for the sheep that have gone astray from the flock (v. 6, cf. v. 8). In this passage *darash* means "caring," the concern of the one responsible for those who are committed to his charge (cf. Job 3:4). In this sense, Trito-Isaiah (Isa. 62:12) can call the city of Jerusalem *derushah*, "Sought out"; Yahweh cares for it and searches it out to save. The Deuteronomic note, in which Yahweh is described as one who continually cares for (*doresh*) the land allotted to his people (Dt. 11:12), is to be understood in a similar way. 2 Ch. 14:6(7) describes very vividly the antecedent grace which motivates the covenant people to seek God in response to his prior action (following the reading of the LXX and other ancient versions): "he has sought us, and has given us peace on every side."

Another realm of the specific theological use of *darash* is that of God's expectations of men, particularly of members of the covenant people (Mic. 6:8). Man is shown what Yahweh "seeks," expects, wants him to do (*doresh mimmekha*). In one passage (Job 10:6) in this realm *darash* means "to investigate, search for"; God investigates *chatta'th*, "sin" (this stands in parallelism with *biqqesh le'avon*, "seek out iniquity"). Finally the three examples in Ps. 10 (vv. 4,13,15) must be mentioned. These ascribe to God the power to avenge (*darash*) wicked behavior, especially when the wicked challenge and deny God. The godly man prays that God will break the malice of the evildoer and actively requite him for mocking Yahweh (v. 15), which vexes the righteous (v. 13). Thus the relatively small number of examples of the specifically theological use of the root *dršr* give evidence of a lively and vivid use. God turns to his own to save them, he expects certain things of them, he cares for them, he requires certain things of those that belong to him, he can requite men for their deeds, he graciously allows himself to be sought of men, and he turns himself aside from them in judgment by "not allowing himself to be sought of them." The instances may be few but *darash* presents us with a dramatic and exciting view of God.

IV. **The Derivative midhrash.** The derivative *midhrash*, which is to be defined grammatically as an Aramaic infinitive of the qal, is used as a noun in the construct in the two passages in which it appears in the OT (2 Ch. 13:22; 24:27). In the LXX this term is translated *epí biblíō*, "in the book of," in the former passage, and *epí tēn graphēn*, "in the writing of," in the latter, while the Vulgate has *in libro,* "in the book of," in both places. Rudolph reads "work" in both verses, but in a note differentiates "investigation," "composition," "study." [21] Galling translates by "exposition" in both passages, puts the untranslated "midrash" in brackets, and renders 2 Ch. 24:27 literally: "Exposition (Midrash) of the Book of Kings." [22] Exegetically both passages refer to a historical source, 13:22 to a work attributed to the prophet Iddo, and 24:27 possibly to the historical work on (RSV, "the Book of the Chronicles of") the kings of Judah mentioned in 2 K. 12:20(19). Since "midrash" in postbiblical Judaism means approximately the same thing as "exposition," "explanation," "commentary" (of [or on] a scriptural passage), [23] the reference might already be to the cited interpretation of a source in these very late biblical texts in Chronicles. Galling leaves this question open. [24] The Qumran literature could function as a connecting link. Here *midhrash* has the general sense of "exposition" (4QFlor 1:14), "exposition and study of the law" (*midhrash hattorah,* CD 20:6; 1QS 8:15; cf. v. 24), while in 1QS 6:24; 8:26, it is to be understood as the term for an official court of investigation and exposition in the Qumran community. This understanding would not be at variance with the thought of commentary in the above mentioned texts in Chronicles and later writings.

V. In the Qumran Literature. In the Qumran literature most of the passages using *darash* occur in the Manual of Discipline, the Damascus Document, and the Hodayoth or Thanksgiving Psalms. The use of *darash* varies in all three documents. A familiar expression is *doreshe chalaqoth,* "those who seek smooth expositions (things)" (1QH 2:15,32; 4QpIsᶜ 10; 4QpNah 2:7; CD A 1:18), probably a term used at Qumran for the Pharisees. "Those that look for deceit" (*remiyyah*) (1QH 2:34) means the same thing. The worshipper in 1QH 4:6 realizes that because he has sought the Lord (*'adhoreshekhah,* "I have sought thee"), he is set apart from the majority of the people, who are defined and disqualified by their activities and attitudes. They do not seek God with the whole heart, but *belebh valebh,* "with a double heart" (1QH 4:14; the positive anthithesis of this is *belebh shalem,* "with a perfect heart," CD A 1:10); in fact, they even seek him among *gillulim,* "idols" (1QH 4:15; the verb used in synonymous parallelism with *darash* here is *tur,* "seek"), and their attitude to God is according to the preaching of the prophets of falsehood (*mippi nebhi'e khazabh*) (1QH 4:16). But this worshipper was evidently one of those of whom it is said in CD A 6:6 that they sought God, i.e., held fast to him. The Rule of the Community (*sepher serekh hayyachadh*) accomplishes its purpose when it motivates a man to "seek God," which involves doing what is good and right, as God commanded through Moses and the prophets (1QS 1:1-3). God's laws and commandments are to be investigated (1QS 5:11;

21 Rudolph, *HAT,* 21, 238, 276.
22 Galling, *ATD,* XII, 108, 138.
23 Cf. H. L. Strack, *Einl. in Talmud und Midrasch* (⁵1921/1930, repr. 1967); Ch. Albeck, *Einführung in die Mischna* (1971).
24 Galling, *loc. cit.*

6:6: *darash* and *biqqesh*); he who does not do this is not counted in "his covenant." The covenant also belongs to those who seek it (1QH 5:9). The *shomere habberith,* "those who keep the covenant," and the *doreshe retsono,* "those who seek his will," are the sons of Zadok the priests, but also all the men of the covenant (1QS 5:9; cf. 4QFlor 1:17). The study of the law (*darash battorah*) is to take place day and night and to serve as the investigation of *mishpat,* "justice" (1QS 6:6,7). In CD A 6:7, it is not entirely clear who the "rod" is that is identified with the *doresh hattorah,* "seeker of the law." He may be the teacher of the law, or the "star out of Jacob" mentioned in CD A 7:18, who is also called *doresh hattorah,* a salvation figure (cf. 4QFlor 1:11), possibly the Teacher of Righteousness, perhaps the same figure who stands behind 1QH 4:24, and who speaks of those who let themselves be sought by him as members of the covenant community (*hannidhrashim; darash* is used here as a missionary concept).

The rigorous legal piety of the Qumran community included a system of examinations which were administered by specially ordained officers to the unstable, the deviant, and those ready for admission (1QS 5:20f.; 6:14,17; CD A 15:11). The technical term for this examination is *darash.* One of the mutual ethical responsibilities of members of the community was *lidhrosh 'ish 'eth shelom 'achihu,* "to seek each man the well-being of his brother" (CD A 6:21). In 1QS 8:24, *vedhareshu hammishpat* can mean "to seek a decision," [25] or "to explain the law," [26] or "to investigate a case." [27] On the whole, in the Qumran texts *darash* should be understood essentially as one of the terms used to express strict legal piety, its investigation and exposition of the law, and the relationship manifested thereby both to God and also to the covenant and the true community.

Wagner

---

[25] J. Maier.
[26] E. Lohse.
[27] H. Bardtke.

דֶּשֶׁא *deshe'*

Contents: I. Etymology, Occurrences in Ancient Near Eastern Literature. II. Occurrences in the OT. III. Meaning.

I. Etymology, Occurrences in Ancient Near Eastern Literature. The Hebrew noun *deshe',* "vegetation, young fresh grass," has cognates in most Semitic

---

deshe'. S. Talmon, "The Gezer Calendar and the Seasonal Cycle of Ancient Canaan," *JAOS,* 83 (1963), 177-187; C. Westermann, *Genesis. BK,* I/1, 170-75.

languages: Jewish Aram. and Bab. Aram. *dit'ā* (Syr. *tēdā* or *tad'ā*, with meta-thesis), Akk. *daš'u*, "spring," *dīšu*, "grass, spring," Old South Arab. *dt'*, "spring,"[1] Arab. *data'ī*, "spring rain" (cf. *ta'ad*, "moisture, dampness"). Verb forms of the root are found in Akk. *dešû*, "to sprout," Jewish Aram. *d't* in the haphel, "to cause to sprout," and Heb. *dš'*.[2] The meaning of Akk. *daš'u*, *dīšu* is particularly instructive, e.g., "Adad causes the rain to fall, and the spring grass sprouts (*ellâmma dīšum*)";[3] Old Assyr. *ištu daš'ē adi ḫarpē*, "from spring to harvest."[4]

In a Sabean inscription *dt'n* denotes abundant spring rain (in the month *'l'lt*); in both Sabean and Minean there is a *wrḥ d-dt'*, "month of spring rain".[5] Among the South Arabic Kabyles, *ditā'* denotes the early harvest time.[6]

II. Occurrences in the OT. The substantive *deshe'* occurs 14 times in the OT, almost exclusively in poetic texts (Moses' Farewell Song, David's Farewell Song, Isaiah, Jeremiah, Psalms, Job, Proverbs; the statement in Gen. 1:11f. has a certain poetic diction). The verb *dasha'* (which is probably a denominative) is found only twice, viz., in Gen. 1:11 (in the hiphil), and in Joel 2:22 (in the qal).

III. Meaning. In the P account of creation the noun *deshe'* and the verb *dasha'* appear together in an etymological figure: on the third day of creation God brings forth vegetation, saying *tadhshe' ha'arets deshe'*, "Let the earth bring forth vegetation." Then in what follows *deshe'* is divided into *'esebh*, "plants," and *'ets peri*, "fruit trees" (this passage hardly has in mind three different types of plants). It is worth noting that on the third day of creation, unlike the first two, the word of God does not do its creative work directly, but through the mediation of the earth, which has already been created and which receives the command to bring forth vegetation. The execution of this command is described by the statement, *vattotse' ha'arets deshe'*, "and the earth brought forth vegetation" (v. 12). Here the verb cognate to *deshe'* is replaced by *yatsa'* in the hiphil: "caused to go forth, brought forth." The vegetation is thus present, as it were, in the earth, and now it sprouts up.

Vegetation, then, is a part of God's good creation. This is also emphasized in Job 38:26f.: it is God who sends rain on the desert, "to satisfy the waste and desolate land, and to make the thirsty ground put forth *deshe'*, grass." For this reason the wild ass is satisfied when he has grass (*deshe'*), just as the ox is with his fodder (Job 6:5). Prov. 27:25 depicts grass (*chatsir*) and herbage (*deshe'*) as basic necessities of life for the intelligent sheepherder.

In the Last Words of David the just ruler is compared with the morning sun, "which after the rain causes vegetation (*deshe'*, RSV grass) to sprout from the

1 ContiRossini, 127.
2 See below.
3 H. Zimmern, *Beiträge zur Kenntnis der babylonischen Religion* (1901), No. 100, 7.
4 *JSOR*, 11 (1927), 117, No. 11, 11; Talmon, 184f.
5 Talmon, 185.
6 Glaser, *SAW*, 91 (1885), 89f.

earth" (2 S. 23:4). Similarly the Farewell Song of Moses compares the speech of Moses with life-giving dew and rain "on the young vegetation (RSV tender grass)" (deshe᾽, Dt. 32:2). Thus the deshe᾽ becomes the symbol of sprouting life and of fertility as a blessing of God. Dwelling in ne᾽oth deshe᾽, "green pastures," in Ps. 23:2 expresses God's shepherd care.

Negatively the withering of deshe᾽ is regarded as a sign of destruction. Thus we read in the description of the drought in Jer. 14:5 that the hind leaves her young in the lurch because there is no vegetation. The oracle concerning Moab in Isa. 15:6 (genuine?) [7] says that the waters of Nimrim are a desolation, "for the grass (chatsir) is withered (yabhesh), the vegetation (RSV new growth) fails (kalah deshe᾽), there is no herb (RSV, the verdure is no more)" (yereq) (the last statement is perhaps a [materially correct] gloss). [8] In Isa. 37:27 (=2 K. 19:26) the prophet describes the devastation brought about by the Assyrian king, and he compares the inhabitants of the conquered lands with "plants of the field (᾽esebh sadheh) and young vegetation (RSV tender grass, yeraq deshe᾽)," which are dried up like grass on the housetops. Similar ideas lie behind the statement in Ps. 37:2 that the wicked and wrongdoers "will soon fade (yimmalu from mll) like the grass and wither (nbl) like the green of the herb (RSV green herb, yereq deshe᾽)." They have no staying power.

On the other hand the word appears twice in promises of restoration. Isa. 66:14 predicts the revival of Jerusalem, and compares it with the sprouting up of vegetation: "your heart shall rejoice; your bones shall sprout (RSV flourish, parach) like the vegetation (RSV grass, deshe᾽)." The promise corresponds to the lament: "In anguish the bones waste away (Ps. 31:11 [Eng. v. 10]). Similarly, in joy they become green." [9] Finally, Joel 2:22 describes the time of salvation as a time when the pastures of the wilderness are green (dashe᾽u ne᾽oth midhbar) and the trees bear their fruit.

Ringgren

---

[7] Cf. O. Kaiser, *Isaiah 13–39. OTL* (trans. 1974), 60-62.

[8] Cf. *ibid.*, 57, n. j.

[9] C. Westermann, *Isaiah 40–66. OTL* (trans. 1969), 420f.

> ## דָּשַׁן dāshan; דֶּשֶׁן deshen; דָּשֵׁן dāshēn

Contents: I. Etymology, Occurrences. II. Ideas Connected with the Root. III. Fat Ashes.

I. Etymology, Occurrences. Arab. *dasima*, "to be fat," Akk. *duššumu*, "very fat,"[1] and possibly Akk. *dašnu* as a synonym of *dannu*, "huge, big,"[2] are related etymologically to the Heb. root *dšn*.

The root *dšn* occurs only 30 times in the OT, probably because the idea "fat" is expressed by other words also, especially → חלב *helebh* and the root → שׁמן *šmn*.

The root *dšn* is found in both verb and noun forms. The verb appears once in the qal, "to become (grow) fat," Dt. 31:20; six times in the piel: (1) "to make fat," to anoint in order to honor and gladden (Ps. 23:5); "to refresh," in synonymous parallelism with *simmach*, "to gladden" (Prov. 15:30; similarly Sir. 26:13); (2) "to regard as fat," "to accept" (a burnt-offering, *'olah*) (Ps. 20:4 [Eng. v. 3]); (3) "to cleanse, purge (the altar) of the fat ashes" (privative)[3] (Ex. 27:3; Nu. 4:13); four times in the pual with the meaning "to be made fat" (Isa. 34:7, of the earth or land that is soaked with blood and fat; Prov. 11:25; 13:4; 28:25, of the abundant provisions given to men); and once in the hothpaal, "to fatten oneself" (RSV, "to be gorged with fat") (Isa. 34:6, of a sword that is smeared with blood and fat). Some late occurrences of the niphal with the meaning "to enjoy, treat oneself well" (Sir. 14:11, where it is used in synonymous parallelism with *hetibh,* and several passages in the Qumran literature) may be added to these instances.

The noun *deshen* occurs seven times in the OT with the meaning "fat" (of the "fatness" of the olive tree, Jgs. 9:9; with reference to food and drink, Isa. 55:2; Jer. 31:14; Ps. 36:9[8]; 63:6[5]; 65:12[11]; Job 36:16; also Sir. 38:11 of a fat sacrifice). In seven other texts it refers to the fat ashes on the altar.[4] The adjective *dashen*, "fat," is found three times in the OT: Isa. 30:23 (of bread); Ps. 92:15 (14) (of men who "flourish" and become strong); and Ps. 22:30 (29) (where it could refer to strong and powerful people).[5]

II. Ideas Connected with the Root. The beginning of the development of the meaning of *dšn* is the basic concept "to be fat," which is to be taken quite literally in some cases. Thus Isa. 34:6 speaks of Yahweh's sword, which drips (RSV "is sated") with blood and fat; in the next verse, the figure passes

---

dāshan. E. Kutsch, *Salbung als Rechtsakt. BZAW,* 87 (1963), 11ff.

[1] *AHw,* 179.
[2] *AHw,* 165.
[3] *GK,* § 52h; but cf. Kutsch, 11: "to make fat" > "to make shiny, glittering" > "to cleanse, purify."
[4] See below.
[5] But see below.

over into a description of the blood and fat of sacrificial animals. Both passages refer to the terrible destruction of Edom. The "fatness" of the olive tree (Jgs. 9:9) is at one and the same time its oil and the characteristic feature of the tree which causes men and gods to honor it. [6] Then the idea is expanded to fat, nourishing food: Isa. 30:23: luscious (dashen, RSV "rich") and fat (shamen, RSV "plenteous") bread as a gift of God in the time of salvation; Isa. 55:2: to delight oneself in fatness (fat food, in synonymous parallelism to "eat the best" [tobh]); Job 36:16, "what was set on your table was full of fatness." Sir. 38:11 apparently has in mind a fat-offering; the same could be true of Ps. 36:9(8): "the fatness (RSV abundance) of thy house," which stands in synonymous parallelism with "the river of thy delights." [7] On the other hand Ps. 63:6(5) speaks figuratively of fat(ness) and marrow which satisfy the soul. Ps. 65:12(11) refers to the fertility and produce of the earth: "thou hast crowned the year with thy good (tobh, RSV bounty), thy tracks drip with fatness."

A special use of dšn is found in Ps. 20:4(3), "May he remember all your offerings, and pronounce your burnt-sacrifices fat," i.e., accept them. According to Schottroff there is an allusion here to a cultic declaration formula by which the sacrifice was acknowledged. [8] Kutsch, however, rejects any special formula. [9]

Since the fat was regarded as particularly nourishing food, dšn is connected with the idea of satisfaction, of being pleased, of abundance. Thus we find the pual form in Prov. 11:25; 13:4; 28:25 with reference to the abundant provisions given to the liberal, the diligent, and one who trusts in God; and in Ps. 92:15(14) the adjective dashen is used of the righteous, who "still brings forth fruit in old age, and is 'fat' (fresh, RSV full of sap) and green (ra'anan)." Occasionally the piel means "to rejoice, refresh," as in Prov. 15:30 (where it stands in synonymous parallelism with → שׂמח śimmah, "gladden"); Sir. 26:13; [10] and Ps. 23:5, where the anointing (dishshen) with oil both indicates an honoring of the guest and also echoes the idea of abundance (kosi revayah, "my cup overflows"). Dt. 31:20 also contains a description of abundance: "I will bring them (the people) into the land flowing with milk and honey, which I swore to give to their fathers, and they will eat their fill and become (grow) fat" (dšn in the qal), but this abundance will lead to arrogance and apostasy: "they will turn to other gods and serve them, and despise me and break my covenant" (cf. Dt. 32:15, where, however, šmn is used). Here also belongs Ps. 22:30(29) if one follows the MT: all dishne 'erets (RSV, "the proud of the earth") shall fall down before Yahweh, this being usually understood as "all the fat ones," i.e., the mighty or "the important ones." [11] Often, however, instead of dishne scholars read yeshene, i.e., "all who sleep in the earth," which fits better in the context. [12]

---

[6] But cf. Kutsch, 14: "with which one honors men and gods."

[7] H. Ringgren, Faith of the Psalmists (1963), 4f.

[8] W. Schottroff, "Gedenken" im Alten Orient und im AT. WMANT, 15 (²1967), 227f., 393.

[9] Kutsch, 11f.

[10] According to the text published in Tarbiz, 29 (1959/60), 133.

[11] Kutsch, 13.

[12] Cf. BHS.

III. Fat Ashes. It might seem curious, then, that *deshen* also means "ashes" (for which *'epher* is ordinarily used). *deshen,* however, refers to the fat ashes which are produced when the fat of the sacrifice is burned on the altar (Lev. 1:16; 4:12; 6:3f.[10f.]; 1 K. 13:3,5; Jer. 31:40). As is well known, in sacrifices that were not entirely burned, the blood was sprinkled on (RSV "thrown against [or on]") the altar and the fat (*chelebh*) was burned (Lev. 3:1-7; 4:8f.; 7:1-27). One can thus say that the blood and the fat belong to God. In the case of the blood, this is supported by the fact that the life is in the blood (Lev. 17:14; Dt. 12:23). There is no explicit support for the idea that "all fat is Yahweh's," but the prohibition against eating fat (even of animals that are fit for sacrifice) (Lev. 3:16f.; 7:23ff.) implies that it had a special significance; many support this on the ground that the fat (*chelebh*) was regarded as the seat of the emotions. [13] In this generalization Lev. 3:16f. is relatively late, as 1 S. 9:24; Gen. 4:4 (Abel sacrifices "some of" the fat); Dt. 32:14; Ps. 63:6(5) show. [14] On the other hand, according to Lev. 7:24 the fat of an animal that dies of itself or is torn by beasts is released for economic purposes. There is no clear instruction in the OT concerning what to do with the blood and fat of an animal slaughtered in a secular setting. [15]

There seems to have been a special place beside the altar of burnt-offering where the fat ashes were kept (Lev. 1:16; 6:3[10]). From there, after a certain time, they were carried to a clean place outside the city (Lev. 4:12; 6:4[11]). A gloss in Jer. 31:40 speaks of "dead bodies and ashes" in the Valley of Hinnom, but here the glossator probably has in mind the sacrifices in the Valley of Topheth: the unclean places shall become sacred in the future.

deshen ("fat")-ashes have nothing to do, then, with ashes as a symbol of nothingness and of grief ("dust and ashes"; → עפר *'āphār*).

Negoită-Ringgren

---

[13] Van den Born, "Fett," *BL,* 478.
[14] Cf. Elliger, *HAT,* 4, 53.
[15] *Ibid.,* 101f.

הֶבֶל hebhel; הָבַל hābhal

Contents: I. 1. Occurrences; 2. Etymology. II. 1. Semantic Field, Syntax; 2. In the LXX; 3. Meaning. III. Areas of Usage in the OT: 1. In Gen. 4 (Abel); 2. In Statements Expressing Worthlessness; 3. In Laments; 4. In Polemics Against the Worship of Foreign Gods; 5. In Ecclesiastes; 6. In the Qumran Literature.

I. 1. *Occurrences.* hebhel, which occurs 73 times in the MT, and the denominative verb *habhal,* which occurs 5 times, are found more frequently in the later strata of OT Hebrew. The earliest example of the root which can be dated with certainty is at Isa. 30:7 (or Dt. 32:21; the dates of the *hebhel*-Abel passages in Gen. 4:2,4,8,9,25 [J] are open to question). Then follow Jeremiah with 10 occurrences (including the verb form twice); Kings, 3 (verb once); Deutero-Isaiah, Trito-Isaiah, Lamentations, Zechariah, once each; Proverbs, 3; Psalms, 11 (with Jonah 2:9 [Eng. v. 8]) (verb once); Job, 6 (verb once); and finally Ecclesiastes, with over half the occurrences of the noun in the OT: 38! *hbl* continued to be used in post-OT Hebrew (Middle Hebrew, Modern Hebrew).

In West Semitic the root has thus far been attested elsewhere only in the later Aramaic dialects that were influenced partly by the OT: Jewish Aramaic (Babylonian), "warm breath or breeze, vapor"; Jewish Aramaic (the Targumim), "breath, vanity" (haphel, "to do vainly"); Syr. *heblā,* "dust, vanity," *habāla,* "vapor"; Mandean *habla, hbila,* "breath, vapor";[1] Nabatean *hblw,* a divine name.[2] In South Semitic the root is authenticated as a loanword in Late Egyptian: *hblʿ* (not *hblʾ*),[3] "breath, wind"; so also in Ethiopic;[4] in Old Arabic one encounters the name of a pre-Islamic (rain-?) deity called *Hubal* that was worshipped in Mecca (coming originally from Moab?),[5] then the noun *hibāl,* "wind," in a poem from the sixth century A.D.[6] Arabic also has *habalat,* "vapor."[7] The verb

---

hebhel. R. Albertz, *THAT,* I, 467-69; O. Bauernfeind, "μάταιος, etc.," *TDNT,* IV, 519-524; G. Bertram, "Hebräischer und griechischer Qohelet," *ZAW,* 64 (1952), 26-49; R. Braun, *Kohelet und die frühhellenistische Popularphilosophie. BZAW,* 130 (1973), 45f.; O. Eissfeldt, "Gott und Götzen im AT," *ThStKr,* 103 (1931), 151-160=*KlSchr,* I (1962), 266-273; F. Ellermeier, *Qohelet,* I (1967), 36ff.; J. Hehn, "Zum Problem des Geistes im Alten Orient und im AT," *ZAW,* 43 (1925), 210-225; O. Loretz, *Qohelet und der Alte Orient* (1964), 218ff.; W. E. Staples, "The 'Vanity' of Ecclesiastes," *JNES,* 2 (1943), 95-104; M. Zer-Kabod, " עַל בְּעָיַת הַשֵּׁם 'הבל' בסְפֶר קהלת," *Bar-Ilan,* 4s (1967), 50-59.

[1] *MdD,* 115a, 129b.
[2] *CIS,* 198; *AH,* I/1, 49, No. 11, 8; I/2, 44.
[3] *KBL³,* 227; W. Erichsen, *Demotisches Glossar* (1954), 273.
[4] Leslau, *Contributions,* 17; *habbala,* "to babble, chatter," is to be understood differently: *TigrWb,* 15b.
[5] Staples, 96.
[6] W. Spiegelberg, *OLZ,* 14 (1911), 193-95.
[7] According to *KBL³;* however, *habila,* "to be foolish," and derivatives (according to G. R. Driver, *ZAW,* 50 [1932], 144, *habila*), *ḥabila,* "to be pregnant," and derivatives, and *habila,* "to be deprived of the son" (?), probably do not belong here; on the latter, see A. Guillaume, *JSS,* 9 (1964), 282f., on Gen. 4:24.

habb(a), etc., "to blow (of wind)," which is widespread in Modern High Arabic, and its different derivatives (*habba*, "gust of wind"; *habāb*, "fine dust"; *hibāb*, "soot"; *habūb*, "violent wind"; *mahabb*, "place where wind blows"; *habhāb*, "mirage"; etc.), [8] also seem to be comparable. An Akkadian equivalent of the root has not yet been found. In this area the word *šāru*, "wind, breath," performs corresponding functions. [9]

2. *Etymology*. Like corresponding terms in other languages (Gk. *atmís, atmós;* German "Atem, Odem"), *hebhel* is in all probability a special onomatopoeic word formation of Hebrew. [10] This is indicated not only by its constellation of consonants and weak vowels, but also especially by its regular triliteral qaṭl structure, and by the absence of a common Semitic primary verbal root. The Aramaic examples, and to some extent also the Arabic, are probably of secondary origin (loanwords). The analogous Arab. *habb(a)* word group is probably to be explained as an independent onomatopoeic parallel formation (cf. Tigr. *habbala*, "to babble, chatter"), and not to be traced back to an original biliteral Semitic root *hb* > *hbb* or *hbl*. It cannot be demonstrated with complete certainty that there is a connection between this root and the name "Abel," which appears only in Gen. 4. [11] It is even more difficult to demonstrate a relationship between *hbl* and the god *hblw* (to be identified with the Moabitic-Meccan rain deity *Hubal?*), who is mentioned on a Nabatean tomb inscription from the first century B.C. or A.D. [12]

II. 1. *Semantic Field, Syntax. hebhel*, which is common in both the singular and the plural, generally appears in the absolute, and less frequently as a *nomen regens* (governing noun). That it appears as a comparative with *min* and *le* (Ps. 62:10[9]; Prov. 13:11; Ps. 144:4) indicates that the term expresses an evaluation of people or things; in the same way, its use with the particle *be* (Ps. 78:33; Eccl. 6:4) and as an adverb (Isa. 49:4; Zec. 10:2; Job 9:29; 21:34; 27:12; 35:16) shows that it accomplishes a (negative) qualification. The primary syntactical position in which *hebhel* occurs is as the predicate of a nominal sentence (thus expressing a value judgment). Qoheleth offers the most independent constructions, along with the special religious use: in paronomasias (Eccl. 1:2; 12:8), with the singular suffix (6:12; 7:15; 9:9), and in various formulas of evaluation. [13] The verb *habhal* appears in the qal and hiphil.

Several words and expressions appear in the semantic field of *hebhel: riq*, "empty" (Isa. 30:7), *tohu*, "emptiness, vanity (RSV nothing)" (Isa. 49:4), *sheqer*, "deceit, falsehood" (Jer. 10:14; Zec. 10:2; Prov. 31:30), '*aven*, "deceit," or *shav'*,

---

[8] Wehr, 1016f.
[9] Hehn, 210ff.; Loretz, 126ff.
[10] Bertram, 30.
[11] As S. Mowinckel, *ANVAO* (1937), 30; and C. Westermann, *BK*, I/1, 398, think. See Guillaume, 282f.; *KBL³*.
[12] Cf. Staples, 96.
[13] III.5.

"deceit, falsehood" (Zec. 10:2), *lo' ho'il*, "to have no value, be good for nothing, be of no profit" (Isa. 30:6; 57:12; Jer. 16:19; cf. Lam. 4:17), and in parallelism especially *ruach*, "wind" (Isa. 57:13; Jer. 10:14; Eccl. 1:14; etc.). *hebhel*, however, covers only the first two of the many meanings of *ruach*: (1) "wind, breath, storm," (2) "breath of life" (cf. *neshamah*), (3) "spirit, *animus* (mind, heart)," (4) "Spirit of God." Thus *ruach* has an equivalent or similar meaning to *hebhel* in relatively few instances (e.g., in Ps. 135:17; Job 7:7; Isa. 26:18; 41:29; Mic. 2:11; Job 20:3; 15:2; 16:3; Jer. 5:13; Eccl. 5:15[16]). It also lacks the emotional force which is proper to *hebhel*.

2. *In the LXX.* The LXX renders *hebhel* concretely only in a few passages (in distinction from Aquila, Symmachus, and Theodotion) [14] (Gen. 4: Abel): Eccl. 9:9: *atmós* or *atmís*, "breath, vapor, mist, smoke" (which is preferred by the Hexaplaric translations especially in Eccl.); Isa. 57:13: *kataigís*, "storm"; then Dt. 32:21; Jer. 14:22; 16:19: *eídōlon*, "idol." In almost all the other passages it uses either *kenós*, "empty, vain" (Job 7:16; 21:34; 27:12), or forms of the root *mat*, especially *mataiótēs*, "emptiness," so as to emphasize that the abstract is the essential meaning of the word. [15]

3. *Meaning.* In virtue of its supposed onomatopoeic origin, *hebhel* consistently retains the meanings "breath" and, especially with reference to the visible aspect, although possibly delimited by the stronger *ruach*, "vapor, mist, smoke." It cannot be demonstrated that *hebhel* has a primary relationship to the rites of nature cults. [16] Ideas of transitoriness and fleetingness are associated with the word when it means "breath," and these tend to point toward an abstract connotation (cf. the LXX). This tendency is aided by the capability and openness of onomatopoeic words for new meanings. Moreover, since *hebhel* is one of a group of words meaning "vanity" (*tohu, riq, sheqer, shav', 'aven*), it is used in condensed expressions in the style of emotional embellishment (the synonymous words *ruach*, "wind," and *neshamah*, "breath," are quite different; the word order in Eccl. 1:14: *hakkol hebhel ure'uth ruach*, "all is vanity and a striving after wind" [and not the reverse!], is characteristic; cf. 5:15[16]). Consequently, the range of meaning of *hebhel* is open. It has a broad emotion-laden stratum with strong evocative possibilities, and it is especially suited therefore to be a keyword or catchword.

III. Areas of Usage in the OT.

1. *In Gen. 4 (Abel).* *hebhel* appears in Gen. 4 as the name of the second male child of Adam and Eve (LXX: *Abél*). Since this is the only instance of the name, since it is not explained etymologically (in contrast to the name *Qayin*,

---

[14] Cf. Bertram, 26ff.
[15] Cf. Bauernfeind, 521, n. 4.
[16] Staples, 95f.; the deity *Hubal*, I.2.

"Cain"), and especially since it is attached to a "'novellistic' figure,"[17] everything favors the view that the name is intended to signify the breath character of the fleeting life of the victim and, in general, "the transitoriness or vanity of man even [as] a possibility of our common human existence."[18] In this case Gen. 4 (J) contains the earliest occurrence of the word hebhel and its meaning as a name does not have to be explained, since it is phonetically motivated and is thus directly present. Another possibility is that hebhel is a distortion of the name yabhal, "Jabal," in Gen. 4:20.

2. *In Statements Expressing Worthlessness.* hebhel has a strictly concrete meaning only in a few passages. Sometimes this is made clear by the parallel ruach, "wind," or by the context: "A wind will carry them (i.e., idols) off, a breath will take them away (yiqqach; possibly a play on hebhel in the sense of "idol")[19] (Isa. 57:13). In the balances men go up; they are "together lighter than a breath" (Ps. 62:10![9]). "The getting of treasures by a lying tongue is a fleeting vapor" (hebhel niddaph, Prov. 21:6; a play on the idea of "breath, vapor"; cf. Prov. 13:11).[20] But the terms with which hebhel is associated in different contexts reveal already that it means more than the act of breathing and that the figurative use passes over into abstract evaluation: "Man is like a breath, his days are like a passing shadow" (Ps. 144:4). The adverbial use of hebhel reflects the same process in an advanced stage. Always, however, it is locutive actions (twice with nhm in the piel, "to comfort": Job 21:34; Zec. 10:2; twice with yagha‘, "to labor": Isa. 49:4; Job 9:29—related to speaking, as in Job 27:12; 35:16) whose character is to be exposed as breath and vanity, as spoken into the wind. The context also indicates that the word is supposed to remedy a rising excitement. The same emotionally related evaluation, together with the meaning "breath, vanity," may be found again in passages that use the denominative verb habhal (in a paronomasia: Jer. 2:5; 2 K. 17:15; Job 27:12; also in Ps. 62:11[10]; comparable with Jer. 23:16 [using the hiphil]; the subject, and in the latter case the object of the verb is affected; Prov. 13:11 [possibly hbl here is to be emended to the pual]: "Wealth fraudulently acquired dissolves," fits into this framework). Finally the special trend toward negative judgment may be seen in connection with the predicative-metaphorical use of the noun. The following are said to be "vain, worthless": the help of Egypt (Isa. 30:7) or of other countries (Lam. 4:17), a woman's beauty (Prov. 31:30), and youth (Eccl. 11:10);[21] i.e., things which in general are highly esteemed. The OT attacks them by breathing upon them the negating hebhel and thus emphatically rejecting them.

---

[17] Mowinckel, 30.

[18] Westermann, *BK,* I, 398.

[19] III.4.

[20] G. R. Driver, 144, conjectures that the text here should be emended to a pual form of the verb habhal.

[21] III.5.

3. *In Laments.* Since everyday language is reflected in this usage, it is especially striking that in a special function *hebhel* shows an affinity with the situation of the lamenter: Ps. 39:6,7,12(5,6,11); 62:10,11(9,10); 144:4; then Isa. 49:4; Job 7:16; 9:29; 21:34; 27:12; as a scattered motif in Ps. 78:33; 94:11 (although not in Ps. 31:7[6]; Jonah 2:9[8]); [22] and in Eccl. 6:12; 7:15; 9:9. The distinctive thing here is that only two (very broad) subjects are said to be *hebhel:* all men, the sons of men (*bene 'adham*), man (Pss. 39, 62, 94, 144), and the days of a man's life (Job; Ps. 78; Eccl.). Here again one sees a development of meaning from "breath, vapor," to the vague and very abstract notion of "fleetingness, transitoriness"—everything that breathes is destined to die, cf. Eccl. 3:19—which is intended to suggest a general pessimistic assessment of human life. [23] Again this context is also fed by emotional strata (cf. *'ekh,* "how," which is a motif of the lament) and *hebhel* obviously has a liberating effect.

4. *In Polemics Against the Worship of Foreign Gods.* *hebhel* is used in a special sense in the Deuteronomistic polemic against foreign gods. It occurs here in a group of OT terms for "idols" "which deny the existence of these beings": [24] → שֶׁקֶר *sheqer,* "falsehood, deception," → שָׁוְא *shāw',* "emptiness, vanity," → אֱלִיל *'elîl,* "vanity, worthlessness," and *lo' 'el* or *lo' 'elohim,* "no god" (cf. → אלהים *'elōhîm*). That the name of the deity *Hubal* (or *hblw*) is connected with this usage, and that *hebhel* "originally" meant something like a "cult mystery" in the Canaanite nature rite, [25] is wholly undemonstrable, and is not supported by assuming that this word was onomatopoeic in origin nor especially by the non-theocentric usage with its particular nuances. Rather, the reason the meaning of this word became more restricted is that the figurative use (occasionally in Gen. 4) solidified into a logogram which in the emotionally tense field of religious polemic came into common use on analogy with other terms for idols. The context of Isa. 57:13 and Jer. 10:14f. (51:18) shows that the concrete meaning still stands in the background. The latter passage, with its alternation of *ruach* (v. 14) and *hebhel* (v. 15), is especially illuminating: "for his images are false, and there is no breath in them. They are worthless, a work of delusion. . . . " A certain indefiniteness in the transitional stage to the common use of *hebhel* must be inferred from the passages that define this word more precisely: *habhle nekhar,* "foreign idols" (Jer. 8:19), *habhle haggoyim,* "false gods of the nations" (Jer. 14:22). On the other hand the addition of *shav',* "vain," in Ps. 31:7(6) and Jonah 2:9(8) probably serves rather to intensify the negative emphasis in the emotional evaluation with the intention of defaming foreign idols. Even the pericope in Jer. 10:1-16, which develops the *hebhel* motif and uses it for polemical purposes, still presupposes the whole range of possible nuances. In v. 3 *hebhel* functions syntactically as a predicate nominative (the text is uncertain) [26]

[22] III.4.
[23] Cf. "Abel," III.1.
[24] Eissfeldt, *KlSchr,* I, 271.
[25] Staples, 95f.
[26] Cf. W. Rudolph, *HAT,* 12, 64; A. Weiser, *ATD,* XX, 85.

to describe idols made by human hands (it might also be interpreted as an ana-coluthon here: "the statutes of the nations—[that which they prescribe] is an idol"); v. 8, however, uses it as a catchword in a parallel construction: "the instruction of idols—it is wood (like itself)"; then v. 15 returns to the predicate use and calls attention to the lifelessness of idols: "They are breath (as out of a human mouth)." The remaining examples reflect a certain formality (parono-mastic construction: Jer. 2:5; 2 K. 17:15 [with *halakh 'achare,* "to go after"]; with *k's,* "to provoke": Dt. 32:21; Jer. 8:19; 1 K. 16:13,26), which is to be traced back to a specific repertoire of religious polemic in which *hebhel* too found a place. [27]

5. *In Ecclesiastes.* Qoheleth makes the most individual use of *hebhel.* The 38 occurrences of the word in Ecclesiastes indicate the leitmotiv character that it has in this book. [28] A comparison with its use elsewhere makes it clear that Qoheleth knows and uses all its nuances. Its connection with *ruach,* "wind," in Eccl. 1:14; etc., brings out its original figurative-concrete meaning; its relationship to creaturely existence (3:19; cf. v. 21) connects this idea with the breath of life. Obviously Qoheleth has taken over the word as an expression of worthlessness (11:10). It is characteristic of the position of Qoheleth that the evaluation of man which is first found in the lament becomes a constitutive element in his reflections (e.g., in 2:17). It is striking, then, that Qoheleth evidently does not know or does not consider the restricted meaning that had become common in religious polemic, so that he can even dare to create a new logogram with suffix forms in 6:12; 7:15; 9:9 (cf. also 5:6[7]; 6:4,11f.; 4:7; 8:14). On the other hand the emotional dimension seems to be exploited to the full in Qoheleth, as the evaluative emphasis shows; cf. the intensified form in 1:2; 12:8. In general Qoheleth seems to have thought—influenced perhaps by the Mesopotamian tradition of the *topos* [29]—that this word, which was not as yet overworked, and whose onomatopoeic basis gave it a certain attractiveness, was especially well suited for radical polemic and the definition of new insights. The various relapses of Qoheleth into conventional uses prohibit a restriction of his use of the term to the meaning "incomprehensible, unintelligible." This is very tenuously based on a connection with the cult mysteries, nor can it always be supported by the context, the meaning of the word, [30] or by the figurative connotation "puff of wind." [31]

Some scattered passages in Qoheleth show a conventional usage. Thus 11:10, like Prov. 31:30 (which occasionally is considered to be redactional), [32] says that "youth and dark hair (RSV, the dawn of life)" are vanity. 6:3ff. rates an untimely

---

[27] Cf. H. D. Preuss, *Verspottung fremder Religionen im AT. BWANT,* 92 (1971), 160, 164.
[28] Cf. Loretz, 169ff.
[29] *Ibid.,* 126ff.
[30] Against Staples, 96ff.; in addition, Zimmerli.
[31] Loretz; in addition, Ellermeier; Galling, *HAT,* 18, 79.
[32] Cf. Galling.

birth higher than an unfulfilled life, for it "comes into vanity and goes into darkness." From the symmetry of this sentence it must be inferred that *hebhel* is analogous to *choshekh*, "darkness," that it corresponds to this atmospheric phenomenon, and that it is thus intended to denote the concealing sphere of vapor. In 5:6(7) *habhalim* probably has reference to "many words" (not to "dreams"), so that the verse is similar in meaning to 6:11. As elsewhere, [33] the association between "word" and "breath" is basic here.

The distinctive role of *hebhel* in Qoheleth occurs in the various statements about "vanity." [34] Relevant here is the connection of *hebhel* with Qoheleth's characteristic formula *re'uth ruach* or *ra'ayon ruach* (1:14), which is to be rendered "feeding on wind" (Heb.) or "striving (straining) after wind" (Aram.). For in this combination *hebhel* has its basic figurative meaning in central passages, as in the royal statement in 1:12ff. with which the book originally opened. Prominence is thus given to the more intensive thought of breathing or striving for air, which symbolically undergirds statements about "vanity."

Among the words used in antithesis to *hebhel*, *yithron*, "profit, advantage, gain," plays a dominant role as a term meaning "that which counts or matters," "that which results or issues from all our work." It forces upon *hebhel* the special sense of "that which does not count or matter," "null," "vain," "that which yields no results." [35] Along the same lines we find other antithetical terms such as → חלק *chēleq*, "part, portion" (RSV "reward," 2:10), → טוב *ṭôbh*, "good" (2:3; 6:9), and → יתר *yether*, "profit, advantage" (6:11). On the other side, the parallel words *tsel*, "shadow" (6:12), and *ruach*, "wind" (5:15[16]), emphasize the aspect of fleetingness or transitoriness, while the additional terms *choli*, "affliction" (6:2), and *ra'ah*, "evil" (2:12), make the meaning of *hebhel* even clearer.

The dominant use of *hebhel* in a nominal statement shows that for Qoheleth too the word serves the purpose of evaluation, or, more accurately, devaluation, with a critico-polemic intention. The total equalization of all earthly, human activity in 1:14 runs contrary to a sapiential value system; such a radical disqualification is directed against the norm of *yithron* thinking which underlies this system. *hakkol*, "all," is the subject of *hebhel* in the predicate nominative in several passages. In 1:13f. and 2:17 it denotes the totality of human activity, in 2:11 the speaker's own work as "king over Israel in Jerusalem," in 3:19 all living things, and in 11:8 the future. In 1:2 and 12:8 it is used in a universal sense. The reference, then, is to creaturely, breathing, working life. Based on this are the special *hebhel* statements introduced by *gam zeh*, "this also," or *vehinneh gham hu'*, "and (but) behold, this also," which describe particular earthly possessions and values as *hebhel*, "vanity": 2:15(1:17), striving after wisdom; 2:2, laughter and pleasure; 2:19,21,23,26, the life work of the wise; 4:4, energy ex-

---

[33] III.2.

[34] Cf. W. Zimmerli, *Die Weisheit des Predigers Salomo* (1936), 13f.; M. A. Klopfenstein, "Die Skepsis des Qohelet," *ThZ*, 28 (1972), 97ff.

[35] Galling.

erted by the skillful; 4:8 and 5:9(10), wealth; 4:16, the career of the wise; 6:9, zeal; 7:6, criticism of the wise; 8:10, decisions of the mighty; 8:14, confidence in the law of just retribution—particularly ways and goals of life that wisdom holds in high esteem. Thus *hebhel* serves as "destructive judgment," [36] a devaluation of the system of norms established by traditional wisdom, a polemic against its sensible value regulations, a defamation of the wisdom ideal of life. It proves to be an effective catchword to the extent that it extends those values into the grotesque (cf. the mental figure "breath," exaggeration, contrast, and monotonous repetition).

The result is that occasionally Qoheleth can omit the vanity formula, and replace it by *hebhel* alone, which has become a catchword. This occurs in 4:7; 8:14 (cf. 6:11); and in the passages where *hebhel* appears with suffix forms (6:12; 7:15; 9:9), which reflect Qoheleth's own usage. Furthermore the peculiar formula in 1:2 and 12:8 is a result of this use, inasmuch as it shows that the negative *hebhel* judgment is a basic theme in Qoheleth's teaching. As is shown by the intensive form with a negative, the repetition after the interjection: "says Qoheleth!" (1:2), and the explanatory *hakkol hebhel*, "all is vanity," the phrase *habhel habhalim*, "vanity of vanities," [37] is due to the frequency of usage and the large number of subjects and circumstances which Qoheleth covers with this word ("iterative" significance). [38] To judge from the maxims, it is a "specification of the reflections" of Qoheleth, [39] for this is the mental image which affects his thinking. The framework verses, 1:2 and 12:8, display indeed an expansion into the universal and a heightening of emotional interest that cannot be demonstrated in the maxims. In this way the catchword and battle cry of Qoheleth is elevated to a summary ideological conclusion, the expression of a nihilistic judgment on the world and its values.

6. *In the Qumran Literature.* The spectrum of possible uses of *hebhel* in the OT is for the most part maintained in postcanonical writings, as is attested, e.g., in the Qumran literature. In 1QS 5:17ff. the scriptural understanding of man as him "in whose nostrils is breath" (Isa. 2:22), and whose work is thus to be regarded as *ma'ase hebhel*, "a work of vanity," is connected with the religious polemic, "for they are all *hebhel* (vanity) who know not his covenant." The defamatory term *goy hebhel* ("the nation(s) of vanity") in 1QM 4:12; 6:6; 9:9; 11:9 (14:12?) is directed against the enemy *goyim*, "nations." The relating of breath to speaking in the context of a negative judgment clarifies the harlot fragment, 4Q184 1:1: [40] הזונ[ה] תוציא הבל ובל]א, "The har]lot utters vanities and [...] errors. She seeks continually [to] sharpen [her] words." [41]

Seybold

---

36 Albertz.

37 Cf. *BLe*, § 573x; possibly Aramaic, cf. Wagner, *BZAW*, 96 (1966), 134.

38 Ellermeier, 99.

39 Galling, *HAT*, 18, 84.

40 *DJD*, V, 82ff.; *PEQ*, 96 (1964), 53ff.

41 On the LXX, cf. Bertram; on the NT, Bauernfeind; and on the Targum, M. Jastrow, *Dictionary of the Targumim* (1903, repr. 1950), I, 329f.

הָגָה hāghāh; הֶגֶה hegheh; הָגוּת hāghûth;
הִגָּיוֹן higgāyôn

Contents: I. Etymology. II. Occurrences and Meaning. III. Meditation in the OT. IV. In the Qumran Literature.

I. Etymology. The root *hgy* is also found in other Semitic languages. Aram. *hagha* means "to think or meditate, murmur, speak,"[1] the noun *heghyona*, "reading, thinking or meditating," Syr. *hᵉgā*, "to meditate" (cf. *hᵉgāyā, hegyānā, hugyā*, "meditation, study," *haggānā*, "reading"), while Arab. *haǧā* means above all "to mock, deride, ridicule" (the *hiǧāʾ* poetry!), but occasionally "to express, state." In Tigré, *te-haga*, "to speak," appears.[2] In Ugaritic, *hg*, "to count, reckon," is used in synonymous parallelism with *spr*.[3]

There is also in Hebrew another root *hgh*, "to separate, remove," which is probably connected with *ygh*.[4]

II. Occurrences and Meaning. *haghah* appears 22 times in the OT as a verb in the qal (including 6 times in Isaiah, and 10 times in the Psalms). In addition the hiphil occurs in Isa. 8:19, and the curious form *vehogho* ("and they will say") in Isa. 59:13. The nouns *hegheh* (3 times), *haghuth* (once), and *higgayon* (4 times) are derived from this root.

The verb has the following meanings:

(a) To utter inarticulate sounds, as the roaring of the lion or the cooing of the dove: Isa. 31:4, "as the lion 'roars' (the LXX translates this by *boáō*, "to call, shout, cry out"), and the young lion, over his prey..."; Isa. 38:14, "like a swallow (a thrush) I chirp (*tsiphtseph*), I 'coo' (LXX *meletáō*, "to think about, meditate upon") like a dove"; Isa. 59:11, "we all growl (*hamah*) like bears, we 'coo' (LXX *poreúō*, "to go") like doves." The noun *hegheh* is also used of the rumbling of thunder (Job 37:2) and of sighing (Ps. 90:9, "we end our years like a sigh"). To be noted too is the noun *higgayon* in the sense of "playing, music" (Ps. 92:4 [Eng. v. 3]).

(b) "To mutter" or "to whisper," as in Isa. 8:19 (in the hiphil), of those who consult the dead, who "chirp (*tsiphtseph*) and whisper (RSV mutter)."

---

hāghāh. H. J. Franken, *The Mystical Communion with JHWH in the Book of Psalms* (Leiden, 1954), 18-22; W. Schottroff, *"Gedenken" im Alten Orient und im AT. WMANT*, 15 (²1967), 130-32, 180, 390.

[1] Dalman.
[2] Leslau, *Contributions,* 17.
[3] *WUS,* No. 813.
[4] *KBL³,* 228.

(c) "To speak," etc. This meaning is clear from the occurrences of *haghah* in synonymous parallelism with verbs of speaking, or in connection with "lips," "tongue," etc.: Ps. 37:30, "the mouth of the righteous 'utters' wisdom, his tongue speaks what is right"; 38:13(12), "those who seek my life ... 'speak' of corruption (*havvoth*, → הוה *hawwāh*), and speak (or meditate, LXX *meletáō*) treachery all the time"; 71:24, "my tongue will 'talk' of thy righteousness"; Job 27:4, "my lips will not speak injustice (RSV falsehood, *'avlah*), my tongue will not 'utter' (LXX *meletáō*, "to meditate") deceit" (*remiyyah*); Prov. 8:7, "my mouth 'speaks' truth, and wickedness is an abomination to my lips"; Ps. 115:7, idols "do not 'speak' with their throat"; Isa. 59:3, "your lips speak lies, and your tongue 'mutters' wickedness" (cf. *haghuth*, "meditation," in Ps. 49:4[3]). Some passages may contain a contrast between *haghah* in the sense of "thinking," and speaking: Prov. 15:28, "the heart of the righteous 'ponders' what to answer, but the mouth of the wicked bubbles over (*hibbia'*) with evil"; 24:2, "their heart 'plans' violence, and their lips speak calamity" (cf. *higgayon*, "meditation," in Ps. 19:15[14]; Lam. 3:62).

(d) Particular kinds of speaking, e.g., praising or lamenting: Isa. 16:7 (=Jer. 48:31), "therefore let Moab wail (*helil*) over Moab ..., 'let them moan' as they are destroyed" (cf. *hegheh* in Ezk. 2:10, "lamentation [*qinah*], 'sighing,' and woe" [*hi=hoy*, or read *nehi*?]); Ps. 35:28, "my tongue will 'announce' (praise) thy righteousness, thy praise all the day long."

(e) "To reflect," "think," "meditate" (LXX *meletáō*).

Negoiṭă

The last group of examples is especially hard to evaluate. → זכר *zākhar*, "to remember, call to mind," and → שׂיח *śîach*, "to consider, ponder," are often used in synonymous parallelism with *haghah*. Ps. 143:5 contains a confidence motif: "I remember (*zakharti*) the days of old, I meditate on (*haghithi*) all that thou hast done; I muse (*'asocheach*) on what thy hands have wrought." "The recollection of God's saving deeds shows the psalmist where he can find help in his distress." [5] Schottroff discusses the possibility of understanding "remembering" here as "pondering faith formulas that are recited in a murmur." He comes to the conclusion, however, that the emphasis here is not on speaking, but on confidence-producing recollection of God's historical deeds. Similarly the lament in Ps. 77:12f.(11f.) says: "I will call to mind (*'ezkor*, qere) the deeds of Yah, yea, I will remember (*'ezkerah*) thy wonders of old. I will meditate on (*vehaghithi*) all they work, I will muse (*'asichah*) on thy deeds." In vv. 6f.(5f.), the verbs *chishshebh*, "to calculate, consider," and *chippes*, "to seek thoroughly, investigate," also occur in a similar context. Here the recollection of Yahweh's earlier deeds shows the difference between the past and the present, but also the reason for hope in the distress. [6] In this psalm, then, the lament opens out into praise.

---

[5] Schottroff, 130.
[6] *Ibid.*, 131f.

Ps. 63:6f.(5f.) also contains a confidence motif: "my mouth praises (*yehallel*) thee with joyful lips (*siphthe renanoth*), when I think of thee (*zekhartikha*) upon my bed, and meditate on (*'ehgeh*) thee in the watches of the night." The next verse speaks of God helping (*'ezrah*) the psalmist, and of the psalmist rejoicing (*'arannen*). The use of verbs like *hillel* and *rinnen* here may cause one to think of something audible: meditation is expressed in a song of praise.

Audible murmuring is even more likely when the object of *haghah* is the law (*torah*), as in Josh. 1:8, "this book of the *torah* shall not depart out of your mouth, but you shall 'meditate' on it day and night, that you may be careful to do according to all that is written in it." This could have reference to softly spoken oral recitation in connection with the study of the law; so we find in Ps. 1:2, "his delight is in the law of Yahweh, and on his law he 'meditates' day and night." In any case, *haghah* means the zealous study of the law, which results in being filled with the will of Yahweh and the doing of his commandments.

Ps. 2:1 is usually translated, "Why do the peoples rage (*ragheshu*), and the nations meditate (*yehgu*) what is vain?" Along these lines it is natural to construe *haghah* as an expression of rebellious muttering. But sometimes the root *rgš* expresses the idea of association or conspiracy (*reghesh* or *righshah* stands in synonymous parallelism with *sodh*, "counsel," in Ps. 55:15[14]; 64:3[2]).[7] If this is so, it is possible that *haghah* means "to devise, plan," in this verse.

Ringgren

III. Meditation in the OT. It follows from the examples cited above that *haghah* is not a common word for speaking. Hebrew has other words for this, like → אמר *'āmar,* → דבר *dibber,* or → קרא *qārā'*. On the other hand, *haghah* is sometimes used to express the feelings of the human soul. With *siach* in particular, *haghah* means that a man "is lost in his religion,"[8] that he is filled with thoughts of God's deeds or his will.

In the earlier psalms *haghah* is used primarily in connection with Yahweh's historical deeds, which give confidence or joy to the psalmist. In later psalms (Pss. 1, 119), the teaching or "law" (*torah*) of God is the object of meditation. "Oh, how I love thy law! It is my meditation (*sichah*) all the day" (Ps. 119:97). Many passages in this same psalm speak of the joy that comes from studying the law, e.g., v. 72, "The law of thy mouth is better to me than thousands of gold and silver pieces"; v. 103, "How sweet are thy words to my taste, sweeter than honey to my mouth!"; v. 164, "Seven times a day I praise thee for thy righteous ordinances"; vv. 147f., "I rise before dawn and cry for help; I hope in thy words (*kethibh*). My eyes are awake before the watches of the night, that I may meditate upon (*siach*) thy promise"; v. 62, "At midnight I rise to praise thee, because of thy righteous ordinances."

[7] See Briggs, *Psalms,* I. *ICC,* 18.
[8] Franken, 21.

This praise of the study of the law reaches a high point in Sir. 38:24–39:11. Here the author first states that the peasant and the workman cannot devote themselves wholly to "wisdom." "It is different with one who gives his soul over to the fear of God (so the Syriac) and meditates (*dianoéomai*) on the law of the Most High, who seeks out the wisdom of the ancients, and is concerned with prophecies. He preserves the discourse of notable men, and penetrates the subtleties of parables; he seeks out the hidden meanings of proverbs, and is at home with the obscurities of parables.... He sets his heart... to seek the Lord..., and makes supplication before the Most High..." (39:1-3,5).

The Manual of Discipline from Qumran contains this precept: "Let the 'many' (full members) watch in common a third of all the nights of the year, to read out of the book, to investigate justice, and to praise in common" (1QS 6:7f.).

Philo tells of the assembly in the synagogue on the Sabbath day, in which the holy books were read, and explained in a symbolic way.

IV. In the Qumran Literature. The occurrences of *haghah* in the Qumran literature appear in fragmentary passages and are less conclusive. The clearest is in 1QH 11:21f., which says that man's reflection on his guilt leads to the muttering of grievous muttering (*lahaghoth haghi yaghon*), to groaning and lamentation. In 1QH 11:2, *bhgy lby* seems to mean "in the thought of my heart." The verb may occur again in 1QH 17:28, but the context here is disturbed (an accompanying verb is *'ahabh*, "to love").

The "Book of *hgv* (*haghu* or *haghi*, *hgy*?), in which the priestly leaders of the community are supposed to be learned," is mentioned twice in the Damascus Document (CD A 10:6; 13:2) and it deserves special consideration. [9] According to 1QSa 1:7 all the fully accepted members of the Qumran community are supposed to be instructed in this book (here we find clearly *hgy*=*haghi*). It cannot be determined whether this is a proper name or a word for "meditation."

Negoiță

----

[9] Cf. J. Maier, *Die Texte vom Toten Meer*, II (1960), 54f.

הֲדֹם *hᵃdhōm*

Contents: I. Etymology. II. 1. The "Stool" in Mesopotamia; 2. In Egypt; 3. In Ugarit; 4. In Greece. III. 1. An Analysis of the Term in the Bible; 2. In the LXX; 3. Related Ideas; 4. God's Stool; 5. The King's Stool.

I. Etymology. The word *hadhom* occurs in the Hebrew OT only as a construct in the expression *hadhom raghlayim*, "the footstool of the feet." The absolute is found only in Ugaritic.

The earliest examples of the root *hdm*, which are found only in Hebrew, Ugaritic, and Egyptian (*hadmu*),[1] date in the eighteenth dynasty (1580-1350 B.C.) in Egypt, and at approximately the same time in Ugaritic literature. Whether the Egyptians borrowed this term as a loanword from Northwest Semitic dialects,[2] or vice versa,[3] can no longer be decided with certainty.[4]

If it was not originally a noun,[5] *hadhom* is perhaps a nominal form of the root *dwm* I with the hiphil prefix *h*.[6] In this case the verb means "to lie quietly, motionless,"[7] "to stand, stay,"[8] and may be related to Ugar. *dm* II, "to remain, abide,"[9] and Heb., Aram. *dmm*, "to be quiet, still."[10] One would thus assume that the original meaning of *hdm* was "a place which gives rest." Ugar. *hdm*

---

hᵃdhōm. W. F. Albright, "The Furniture of El in Canaanite Mythology," *BASOR,* 91 (1943), 39-44; P. Artzi, "הדם רגלי, *Gištappu ša šēpēka,*" *Sepher Šᵉmuʾel Yeivin* (Jerusalem, 1970), 331-37; S. Baker, *Furniture in the Ancient World* (1966); K.-H. Bernhardt, "Schemel," *BHHW,* III (1966); G. H. Davies, "Footstool," *IDB,* II, 309; T. H. Gaster, "The Furniture of El in Canaanite Mythology," *BASOR,* 93 (1944); 20ff.; F. Gössmann, "Scabellum Pedum Tuorum," *Divinitas,* 11 (1967), 31-53; F. Hintze, "Hdm rdwj," *ZÄS,* 79 (1954), 77; H. Kyrieleis, *Throne und Klinen* (1969); S. Laser, "Hausrat," *Archaeologia Homerica,* ed. F. Matz and H. G. Buchholz, II (Paris, 1968), 44-56; M. Metzger, "Himmlische und irdische Wohnstatt Jahwes," *UF,* 2 (1970), 139-158; G. Rühlmann, "'Deine Feinde fallen unter deine Sohlen'. Bemerkungen zu einem orientalischen Machtsymbol," *WZ* Halle-Wittenberg, 20 (1971), 61-84; A. Salonen, *Die Möbel des Alten Mesopotamien. AnAcScFen,* B, 127 (Helsinki, 1963); R. de Vaux, "Les chérubins et l'arche d'alliance," *MUSJ,* 37 (1960/61), 93-124 = *Bible et Orient* (1967), 231-259.

[1] Cf. W. F. Albright, *Vocalization of the Egyptian Syllabic Orthography* (1934), 52.

[2] So Nötscher, *Biblische Altertumskunde* (1940), 32; *WbÄS,* II, 505; *BRL,* 521; Albright, *BASOR,* 91, 42; A. Gardiner, *Ancient Egyptian Onomastica,* I (1947), 68; Dahood, *Psalms,* II. *AB,* XVII (1968), 369.

[3] J. de Savignac, *OTS,* 9 (1951), 115; de Vaux, 118; Gössmann, 36, n. 12.

[4] But cf. II.3.

[5] Cf. Gordon, *UT,* Glossary, No. 751.

[6] Cf. *BLe,* § 486.

[7] *KBL³,* 208.

[8] P. Haupt, *AJSL,* 26 (1909/10), 22.

[9] *WUS,* 755.

[10] *KBL³,* 217.

appears in this sense as a place of rest and relaxation for the feet.[11] It is to be observed that in the OT *hdm* stands in synonymous parallelism with *menuchah*, "rest" (Ps.132:7f.; Isa. 66:1). Thus, when the term *hadhom* means "footstool" it is really denoting a function, whereas its only (not undisputed) synonym, *kebhesh*, "footstool," in 2 Ch. 9:18,[12] Aram. *kibhsha'*, Syr., Targum, Christian Palestinian *kebhash*,[13] which occurs in the midrash for *hadhom*, does not denote the function of resting but understands the footstool phenomenologically as the object on which one "props" his feet. *kebhesh* is derived from the Hebrew, Aramaic, Arabic, and Mandean verb *kbš*, "to trample upon," figuratively, "to subjugate,"[14] Akk. *kabāsu*, "to tread,"[15] El Amarna, *kab/pāšu*, "to tread."[16] Then in the Targum *kebhesh* can also mean "staircase, flight of stairs, platform, or ramp."[17]

II. 1. *The "Stool" in Mesopotamia.* While the literary examples of *hadhom* go back into the middle of the second century B.C., the object called *hadhom* is much older, and occurs archeologically at least as early as the Jemdet-naṣr period (*ca.* 3000 B.C.) in Mesopotamia. The representation on the fresco from Teleilāt Ghassūl possibly goes back into the fourth century B.C.[18]

Originally the stool seems to have been a hump, a primitive low seat made out of bundles of reed that had been tied together.[19] A footstool is depicted on the early dynastic consecration plate from Khafāge,[20] and there is evidence that footstools were made of wood at an early period. Sometimes Hittite footstools are blocklike or boxlike.[21] Like the legs of a throne, the legs of a stool are also formed theriomorphically; in early Mesopotamia (Sumer) the legs of a bull are preferred, and in Egypt the legs of a lion.[22] Even if the significance of the animal feet is no longer evident, the animal as a symbol of strength has the function of supporting gods and rulers.[23] In the Urartian region, leafy garland ornamentation is dominant. The finest timbers (*ušû*, ebony, acacia) were preferred. Sometimes these were plated with gold and adorned with costly intarsia.[24] As such a valuable item, the stool becomes a popular object of exchange, a part of the bridal

---

[11] *CTA,* 17 [II D], II, 10f.; cf. *nḫt,* "rest," along with *hdm* in *CTA,* 4 [II AB], I, 34f.; cf. also EA 84, 4, 13.

[12] Cf. the cautious discussion of this passage in F.Lanziana-G.Pettinato, "Salomos Thron, philologische und archäologische Erwägungen," *ZDPV,* 81 (1965), 88-108.

[13] Levy, *WTM,* II, 290ff., 393.

[14] *GesB,* 334; *BDB,* 461; *MdD,* 202f.

[15] *AHw,* 415.

[16] EA 213, 5; 241, 6; etc.

[17] Levy, *WTM.*

[18] L. Pirot, *DBS,* 8 (1970), 427, 445f.; but cf. Gössmann, 45 (6th century); figs. in *Teleilāt Ghassūl,* I (Rome, 1934), Plate 56, 1; 66.

[19] Falkenstein, *Archaische Texte aus Uruk* (1936), No. 502.

[20] Salonen, Plate VIII 1.

[21] See III.4 below, and H. T. Bossert, *Altanatolien* (1942), figs. 761, 765, 957.

[22] Kyrieleis, 74-81.

[23] Cf. H. Demircioğlu, *Der Gott auf dem Stier* (1939); M. Weippert, "Gott und Stier," *ZDPV,* 77 (1961), 93-117.

[24] *RA,* 43 (1949), 142, 49; *ARM,* X, 82.21.

price, [25] of the booty taken in war, [26] or of the dowry. [27] As a rule the footstool is part of the throne (→ כסא *kissē'*), its purpose being to support the feet of the one sitting on the throne. The footstool also has a function beside a high bed. [28] It enables one to climb upon the bed or to eat comfortably in bed. It is also used as a place to deposit shoes and other footwear. [29] Frequently it has the same ornamentation as the throne. [30] Along with its practical usefulness as a support for the feet, the footstool gives the one sitting on the throne a hieratic solemnity, and therefore it finds abundant usage especially in the royal court. The throne and the footstool serve to raise the one sitting on the throne out of the general, human sphere. Another expression of this elevation motif is the *báthron*, the "base or pedestal" which was built like a podium under the throne and which extended out so far in front that there was room to support one's feet. [31] Sometimes the *báthron* was finished with steps. In some cases the stool was built as one solid piece with the throne, like a step extending out before it. But the most common type is the footstool which is separate from the throne. In the early period glyptic symbolism depicts fish (→ דג *dāgh*) as footstools of the deity. [32]

The elevation motif occurs primarily in representations of reigning deities and sacrificial scenes. [33] But it is then transferred to depictions of the king in order to express his divine origin, power, and superiority over his enemies. This paved the way for the use of conquered (or, magically, yet to be conquered) enemies as support figures (caryatid, atlantes) in the architectonic structure of a throne. [34] Even if the combination of enemies and footstool [35] did not find its way into the plastic art of Mesopotamia, [36] it does appear in Mesopotamian literature. The most familiar term for footstool here is Sum. *GIŠ.GIR.GUB (GIR,* "foot" + *GUB,* "to set, put"), "that on which one puts or sets his feet" (as a loanword in Akk.: *girbubbu,* "pedal, footboard"). [37] In addition to this logogram, one encounters various Akkadian words, *ke/irṣappu, kilṣ/tappu* (Qatna), *gištappu* (Mari, EA), meaning "footstool, base, pedestal," and in three passages "threshing-sledge." [38] Some inscriptions show that the footstool was a pedestal for a divine statue, [39] or in Late Babylonian a cult stand for the (holy) sandals in the temple

---

[25] EA 5, 28, 30.

[26] The Gardiner Ostracon, 44.

[27] Meissner, *BuA,* I, 406.

[28] Wiseman, *The Alalakh Tablets* (1953), No. 227, 14; *PRU,* III, 184, 14.

[29] E.g., in the Hittite text *KBo,* V, 2, verso II, 49-51.

[30] *ANEP,* 460, 463.

[31] Cf. the *Kudurru* tablets of Meli-Šipak from Susa, 12th century B.C., *ANEP,* 529; this is very clear also on the scroll seal representations of the Ur III period, Salonen, Plate XXVIII/XXIX.

[32] Cf. E. D. van Buren, *Iraq,* 10 (1948), 110f.

[33] Cf. perhaps the stela of Hammurapi, and *Syr,* 18 (1937), Plate XVII; cf. Gössmann, 46.

[34] Kyrieleis, *loc. cit.*

[35] Cf. Ps. 110 below.

[36] II.2.

[37] *AHw,* 286; *CAD,* VIII, 361ff.; Salonen, 24ff.

[38] Salonen, 27, n. 1.

[39] Cf. examples in Salonen, 27.

É.NIR; [40] cf. also its use in the cultic context of the *kalû* ritual, [41] and as a golden base for a falcon statue. [42] The building of a throne and its footstool in a city is equivalent to establishing residence and confirming permanent sovereignty. [43] The enthronement of a king on his seat and stool is a symbolic representation of the peaceful rest that prevails in the sphere of his kingdom, so that a loyal vassal is regarded as a "resting-place" (*tarbaṣi*) of the sovereign. [44] It is a sign and testimony of his humble "vassalage" when he "prostrates himself seven times seven," [45] and when in so doing he speaks of himself as the sovereign's "servant" (*ardu*), "the dust of his feet," the "clay" and "ground" (*qaqqaru*) on which the Pharaoh walks, and the "seat" (*kussû*) on which he sits. In such relationships vassals are called *gištabbu ša šēpēka*, "the footstool of thy feet." [46] When the vassal refers to himself metaphorically as the "footstool of the king's feet," he not only expresses an attitude of humility and vassalage, but perhaps also promises to be a helpful support to the king, in order to emphasize to the king that he will supply the requested (military) help.

In contrast to the Tell El-Amarna tablets, the motif of oppression is expressed more strongly in Assyria. Thus Tukulti-Ninurta I (*ca.* 1230 B.C.) describes his military victory over Kastiliash IV of Babylon with the words, "I trampled on his lordly neck with my feet, as on a stool." [47] The phrase "trample on the neck" is very common in the ancient Near East (cf. Josh. 10:24). Similarly, on the base of the throne of Shalmaneser III (*ca.* 850 B.C.) it is stated that he "placed his feet on the neck of his enemies," and with the help of the god Ashur "trampled all lands under his feet like a footstool." [48] Oppression as a result of military conflict extended not only to the conquered king as the representative of the land, but also to the land itself. The designation of the conquered land as a footstool simply means that the conqueror rules over it completely, suppresses it with the full weight of his power, and makes it serviceable to himself as part of his possessions. A little later Shamshi-Adad V writes that his enemies were subjected "under my feet like a stool." [49] In all cases it is the king under whose feet a land and a people lie like a footstool.

2. *In Egypt*. Representations of the footstool in Egypt go back to the third millennium B.C. if one can call the *báthron*-like stand of the *sedia gestatoria* of Ipi of Sakkara (sixth dynasty) a footstool. [50]

---

[40] *AO,* 6460, recto 6f.
[41] *RA,* 41 (1947), 33; cf. *AOT,* 303ff.
[42] *RA,* 43 (1949); 142f., line 49.
[43] Cf. R. Borger, *Die Inschriften Asarhaddons* (1956), § 84 r 39.
[44] EA 84, 13.
[45] Familiar devotional testimony, EA 84, 4ff.; 176, 5ff.; 213, 4ff.; 282, 5; etc.
[46] Rib-Addi of Gubla: EA 84, 4; 106, 6; Ammunira of Berut: EA 141, 40; Namiawaza (of Mitanni?): EA 195, 9; and Ruṣmania of Šarūna: EA 241, 7; cf. Artzi, 333ff.
[47] E. Weidner, *Inschr. Tukulti-Ninurtas,* No. 5, 62.
[48] *Iraq,* 25 (1963), 52, line 10.
[49] *AfO,* 9 (1933/34), 91.
[50] Baker, 52, fig. 49.

In Egyptian literature no term has yet been found for a footstool. The official title *ʒtw ḫr tb.t.wy* in the inscription of Uni, lines 32, 34, does not mean "master of a footstool," [51] but indicates that Uni was a personal servant "under the sandals" of the pharaoh (a "sandal bearer"). [52]

In Egyptian mythology the throne was almost deified as the mother goddess Isis, and the footstool was integrated into it, as the adornment on the head of Isis shows. Behind this lies the old idea that the throne brought forth the pharaoh. [53] The stool came to be regularly connected with representations of the throne for the first time in the eighteenth dynasty. It was often preserved as a possession of the pharaonic house. In keeping with the wealth of Pharaoh it was elaborately embellished and sometimes it was provided with a cushion to make it more comfortable. [54] In order to indicate the pharaoh's ruling position even in the hereafter, and to serve his comfort there, his throne and stool were included among the items placed in his tomb. As a symbol of exaltation, sometimes the footstool also seems to indicate distinctions of rank in depictions of festive meals. [55] The combination of footstool with enemies is familiar in the New Kingdom. Amenophis II is represented as the one who, ruling on the bosom of his "great foster-mother" (a deification of the throne), [56] sets his feet on the heads of nine bound captives. [57] The one who painted this scene was probably looking at real objects, such as are represented very clearly approximately 100 years later on the three footstools of Tutankhamen. [58] The nine bow signs, which already appear in the Middle Kingdom, and which from the eighteenth dynasty on are frequently depicted under the feet of the ruling pharaoh, symbolize in a similar way the whole of the foreign world, whose ruler Pharaoh claims to be. [59]

Footstools were made with the right and left sides open, and the front and back sides extending all the way to the ground the entire breadth of the stool as supports for the surface. On the stool of the famous "golden throne" are depicted human figures linked three by two, while on the stool of the "ceremonial chair" are incrusted five and four captives with different faces representing different nations. The appended inscription explains the representation: "All lands, all foreign soils, the capital of the entire retinue is also under his sandals, and also under Re for ever." Another stool of Tutankhamen contains the representation of two enemies, and two enemies are depicted on the footstool of Amenophis III, but here the nine traditional enemies, bound together from neck to neck, are

---

[51] So Breasted, *Ancient Records of Egypt*, I (1906), 147.
[52] Rühlmann, 76.
[53] *WbMyth*, I/1, 367.
[54] *ANEP*, 409, 411.
[55] Cf. the scene on the tomb of Nebamun, in Baker, color photograph XI.
[56] See above.
[57] *AOB*, 59; *BL*, 1536.
[58] Baker, figs. 91, 93, 94; *ANEP*, 417; *BHHW*, III (1966), 1978.
[59] Cf. *Urk.*, IV, 282, 284, etc., "the nine nations of the bow are linked together under thy feet"; cf. Rühlmann, 70ff.

depicted on the *báthron,* "base, pedestal, foundation." [60] The conquest of enemies by Pharaoh is depicted in realistic symbolism by figures on footstools; on the treading down of enemies, cf. the Victory Song of Thutmose III; [61] the enemies are under the feet of Pharaoh [62] and serve him. [63] The footstool, then, was a fitting realistic symbol for the victorious rule of Pharaoh over men and nations; in the list of the defeated, his program of military government is presented.

It is in parallelism with these representations that one encounters the term *hdmw* for the first time. [64] It occurs occasionally in the expression *hdmw rd.wy,* "stool of the feet," [65] which is also familiar in Hebrew. In the Legend of "Truth and Falsehood," the offering of the footstool occurs in the context of a Re investiture. At a later time the term takes on the meaning "throne." [66]

3. *In Ugarit.* Of the eleven occurrences of *hdm* in Ugaritic, the absolute is predominant (9 times) in contrast to one example of *hdm ʒl* in *CTA,* 4 [II AB], I, 35. In Ugaritic the form *hdm rglm* (*rd.wy*), "the stool of the feet," which occurs in Egyptian and Hebrew, has not yet been found. This would seem to suggest that the term *hdm(w)* was first expanded to *hdm rd.wy* in Egypt, and then came into Hebrew literature in this expanded form. In Ugaritic the meaning "footstool" is also certain without any additional explanatory phrase. A footstool is included along with a *báthron,* "base, pedestal, foundation" (*kt*), a throne (*kht*), a bed (*n'l*), and a table (*tlhn*) among the "divine" (*ʒl*), i.e., expensive, gifts that Baal prepares for Asherah in order to persuade her to intercede in his behalf to El. [67] It was furnished with a leather (?) cushion (*d-prš' b-br*). [68] Along with tables and stools (*ks't*), footstools (*hdmm*) are a part of the furniture of 'Anat, which she used once as missiles, [69] and then immediately afterward rearranged into a festive table. [70] The throne of El has a *hdm.* When El learned that Ba'al Aliyan was dead, he came down off his throne (*ksʒ*) and sat down on his stool (*lhdm*), so that from here he might come down to the earth and sit in the dust. [71] Thus, while the footstool plays a role as a place of abasement in the mourning rite, it is conversely a sign of the highest joy (*yshq*) when El comfortably places his feet on the stool (*p'nh. lhdm. ytpd*) in order to rest after mourning and agita-

---

[60] Cf. R. Giveon, *Les Bédouins Shosou des Documents Égyptiens. Documenta et Monumenta Orientis Antiqui,* 18 (Leiden, 1971), 29f., fig. I.

[61] Erman, *Literature of the Ancient Egyptians* (trans. 1927), 254ff.

[62] *Ibid.,* 269f.

[63] On the promise of victory over enemies at the Sed Festival, the throne jubilee of the pharaoh, cf. *RÄR,* 158ff.; Kraus, *BK,* XV/2, 883.

[64] *Urk.,* IV, 666.

[65] Truth and Falsehood 6:3f.; the Gardiner Ostracon, 44; *RT,* 19 (1897), 95, B.3f.; Abydos, III, 54, 8; etc.

[66] Edfu, II, 40, Edfu, Mammisi, 77; 92.

[67] *CTA,* 4 [II AB], I, 35.

[68] Albright, 41; Gaster, 21, and *BASOR,* 101 (1946), 26, 29.

[69] *CTA,* 3 [V AB], B, 22; 7 [V AB, B], I, 6 (the reading is disputed).

[70] *CTA,* 7 [V AB, B], I, 37.

[71] *CTA,* 5 [I* AB], VI, 13; cf. Ezk. 26:16 and N. Lohfink, *VT,* 12 (1962), 269ff.

tion, [72] and to play with his fingers (*krkr*). [73] The size and furnishings of a throne and footstool indicate the stature and power of its occupant. When it is said that ʿAṭṭar's feet do not reach to the stool (*pʿnh. ltmǵyn. hdm*), and that his head does not reach to the back of Baʿal's throne, this is a humiliating sign that he is incapable of replacing Baʿal and of attaining his rank. [74]

4. *In Greece.* In the realm of Greek culture the footstool (*thrĕnus* < *thráomai*, "to sit"; *sphélas*) is attested archeologically from the thirteenth century B.C. on (the footstool from the palace of Nestor). [75] It appears as an accessory to the *thrónos*, "throne," and *klismós*, "couch," and sometimes is rigidly connected with them, but it can also be used as a missile, as at Ugarit. [76]

III. 1. *An Analysis of the Term in the Bible.* *hadhom raghlayim* occurs six times in the OT. In contrast to Egyptian and Ugaritic literature it is used only figuratively for the ark, Zion, and the earth as the "footstool of God," and for enemies as the "footstool of the king." The term appears in the beginning of the monarchical period (Ps. 99:5; 110:1; 132:7). All the other passages (Lam. 2:1: exilic; Isa. 66:1; 1 Ch. 28:2: postexilic) are closely connected with the David-ark-Zion tradition.

2. *In the LXX.* The exclusively figurative use of *hadhom* in the OT has caused the LXX to choose the expression *hypopódion tōn podṓn*, "footstool of the feet" (which is unusual elsewhere in Greek), to translate *hadhom raghlayim*. When the LXX translates *hadhom raghlayim* by *stásis podṓn*, "standing (placing) of feet," in 1 Ch. 28:2, and by *tópos hoú éstēsan hoí pódes*, "place where the feet stood," in Ps. 132:7, it excludes limiting the footstool to a literal piece of furniture, and understands by the term the incomprehensible power of God.

3. *Related Ideas.* The only real synonym of *hadhom raghlayim* is *kebhesh*, "footstool," which is used to denote the golden footstool of the Solomonic throne (2 Ch. 9:18). This term is not used figuratively in the OT.

a. God's footstool is also called *meqom kisʾi*, "the place of my throne," and *meqom kappoth raghlai*, "the place of the soles of my feet" (Ezk. 43:7). This is what Yahweh calls his sanctuary on Zion, where he "will dwell in the midst of the people of Israel for ever," in the temple vision in the book of Ezekiel (v. 7aβ). In Trito-Isaiah God's footstool is called *meqom raghlai*, "the place of my feet,"

---

[72] *CTA*, 6 [I AB], III-IV, 15; this also applies to men, *CTA*, 17 [II D], II, 11.

[73] *CTA*, 4 [II AB], IV-V, 29.

[74] *CTA*, 6 [I AB], I, 604; cf. J. Gray, *The Legacy of Canaan. SVT*, 5 (²1965), 65ff.; J. C. de Moor, *AOAT*, 16 (1971), 202-206.

[75] Baker, 248f.

[76] Homer *Odyssey* xvii.231, 409, 462, 504; xviii.394; Laser, 44f.; C. H. Gordon, *HUCA*, 26 (1955), 62.

in synonymous parallelism with *meqom miqdashi*, "the place of my sanctuary" (Isa.60:13; cf. Ps.24:3; Jer.17:12; Ezr.9:8). Here Yahweh's power and *kabhodh*, "glory," is manifested, and to it the subjected enemies of Israel go in procession to show their respect to the "city of Yahweh." A secondary textual tradition [77] inserts the explanation that the enemies shall bow down *'al kappoth raghlayikh*, "at the soles of your feet" (RSV, "at your feet") (v.14aβ). This terminology is also closely connected with terms like *mishkan*, "dwelling place," and *meqom menuchathi*, "the place of my rest" (Ps 132:7f.; Isa.66:1), expressions in a theology of the divine presence originally connected with the ark. [78]

b. In the figure in which the footstool is used of enemies, the foot (→ רגל *reghel*) of the victorious oppressor represents his power [79] in an allegorically compressed description of subjection and servitude (2 K.19:24 = Isa.37:25; Ps. 89:11[10]). In a symbolic act the conqueror puts his foot on the neck (*'al tsavva'r*) of the conquered (Josh.10:24) as a sign of total humiliation. In order to show subjection and respect, the vassal falls at the feet of his lord, embraces them, and kisses them [80] (2 K.4:27; Ps.2:12). Yahweh puts Israel's enemies under the feet of his chosen people (1 K.5:17[3]; Ps.47:4[3]; cf. also Ps.18:39 [38]; Mal.3:21[4:3]). They "lick the dust of (Israel's) feet" (Isa.49:23). The back of those who are subjugated is compared with the ground (*'erets*) and the street (*chuts*) for those who pass over (Isa.51:23), but the conqueror walks over his back (RSV, "tread upon their high places," *darakh 'al bamoth;* Dt. 33:29).

Another indication of the importance of the foot is expressed in the custom of depositing covenantal documents "at the feet of the deity" or "under the feet of the deity." [81]

4. *God's Stool.* In the early monarchy the footstool of "his (Yahweh's) feet" is a term for the ark (→ ארון *'ᵃrôn*), the entrance of which into Jerusalem (2 S. 6) was represented cultically in the form of a solemn ark procession. The bringing of the ark into the temple was accompanied by a summons to pay homage: "Let us go to his dwelling place; let us fall down (RSV worship, *nishtachaveh,* → חוה *hāwāh*) before (RSV at) his footstool!" (Ps. 132:7). In this context the ark certainly was not understood as an empty throne seat. [82] Its similarity with the box-like footstools of the Hittites [83] and of Tutankhamen [84] is more natural. Falling

[77] Westermann, *OTL, in loc.*; K. Pauritsch, *Die neue Gemeinde. AnBibl,* 47 (1971), 125.

[78] Cf. von Rad, *OT Theol,* I (trans. 1962), 234ff.; Metzger, 156; Zimmerli, *ThB,* 51 (1974), 249.

[79] Weiss, *TDNT,* VI, 626f.; E. Dhorme, *L'emploi métaphorique des noms de parties du corps* (Paris, 1963), 157ff.

[80] P. C. A. Jensen, *Texte zur assyrisch-babylonischen Religion,* I. *KB,* VI/2 (1915, repr. 1970), 108f.; Erman, 269.

[81] Cf. R. de Vaux, *MUSJ,* 37, 120ff.; G. J. Botterweck, *BBB,* 1 (1950), 26-32.

[82] So Kraus, *BK,* XV/2, 683, 757, 885, etc.

[83] II.1.

[84] II.2.

down before the ark as the valid embodiment of Yahweh's presence [85] is an expression of reverence and appreciation for the one God and also of subjection under his rule over Israel (cf. Ps. 95:6). In this connection the ark, as the footstool of the one sitting on the throne, is regarded as the place where Yahweh visibly comes into contact with the human world, but at the same time is also in a characteristic manner "exalted" above it (elevation motif). There is no historical connection between the motif of the ark and that of the high sanctuary, [86] nor is the ark as God's footstool seen as a representation of the holy mountain. [87] The summons to worship is also found in a modified form in Ps. 99 on Yahweh as King. The psalmist says in v. 5: "Extol Yahweh our God; worship at his footstool! Holy is he!"—a summons in the form of a refrain, in which *lahadhom raghlav*, "at his footstool," is interchangeable with *lehar qodhsho*, "at his holy mountain" (v. 9). This suggests that *hadhom* here does not necessarily mean the ark, [88] but the city that Yahweh chose to be his royal residence, Zion. [89] Here he summons men to pay homage to him as king in the form of the ancient Near Eastern homage ritual at the royal court. In this connection the expansion of *hadhom* from the ark to Zion is a confession of the greatness of Yahweh. This concept is also attested in the exilic period in the complaint that "the Lord has not remembered his footstool in the day of his anger" (Lam. 2:1; here *hadhom* occurs in synonymous parallelism with "the daughter of Zion" and "the splendor of Israel"). In this verse the author is not mourning the loss of the ark, as Weiser, [90] Kraus, [91] and others think. Rather, it is to be assumed that the growing detachment from the idea of Yahweh's materialistic presence is expressed here too (cf. already Isa. 6), so that *hadhom* can mean the temple [92] on Zion or even the "entire holy land." [93] A complete shattering of materialistic bounds may be seen in the emphasis on divine transcendence in Isa. 66:1: the heaven as the throne (*kisse'*) of God (cf. Ps. 11:4; 103:19; Isa. 40:22) is contrasted with the earth (*'erets*) as his footstool. For Trito-Isaiah this theme is the basis of the suggestion that literal concern for the rebuilding of the Jerusalem temple expresses a false confidence in the temple and a "depersonalization of the religious sphere." [94]

Later the Chronicler [95] takes up again the old idea of the ark as Yahweh's footstool in David's speech about the planned building of the temple (1 Ch. 28:2). The additive parallelism *'aron*, "ark," and *hadhom*, "footstool," would

---

[85] Eissfeldt, *KlSchr*, III, 526f.

[86] W. Reimpell, *OLZ*, 19 (1916), 326ff.; W. B. Kristensen, *MKAW*, Afd. Letterkunde 76, Ser. B, 5, 136-171; → במה *bāmāh*.

[87] *Ibid.*

[88] It probably does not mean the "Holy Rock" either, as H. Schmidt, *HAT*, 15, 182, and *Eucharisterion H. Gunkel. FRLANT*, 19 (1923), I, 132, n. 1, supposes.

[89] Kissane, Kraus, Dahood, J. Maier, *BZAW*, 93 (1965), 68; etc.

[90] A. Weiser, *Psalms. OTL* (trans. 1962), 642.

[91] H.-J. Kraus, *BK, in loc.*

[92] Plöger, *HAT, in loc.*; Rudolph, *KAT, in loc.*; J. Maier, 69.

[93] Rudolph.

[94] Pauritsch, 211.

[95] Galling, *ATD*, XII (1954).

seem to call synonymity in question, so that *hadhom* here may be another term for *kapporeth* (RSV "mercy seat") (from P on, a shorthand term for the lid of the ark). [96]

5. *The King's Stool.* In the context of the Enthronement Ritual the promise is given to the king that Yahweh will make his "enemies his footstool" (Ps. 110:1). When this is coupled with the affirmation that Yahweh will "send forth the king's mighty scepter" (v. 2), [97] it is clear that the speaker here is promising the king powerful assistance from God in the battle "in the midst of his foes." Yahweh himself wages war for his king and gives him the conquered as a gift. This psalm (which a large majority of scholars date in the early period of the Davidic dynasty, 10th century B.C.) probably goes back linguistically to Canaanite origins, [98] while the ritual behind the text has abundant prototypes in the Egyptian court ceremonial of the eighteenth dynasty. [99] The final subjugation of the enemies and the completion of the conquest are moved into the future by the statement *'adh 'ashith,* "till I make." Dahood understands *'adh* differently as "throne" = Ugar. *'d,* "throne room": [100] "Sit enthroned at my right hand. A seat have I made your foes, a stool for your feet." [101] At a later time this promise was referred to the messianic king (pre-Christian Judaism). When Primitive Christianity applied it to Jesus Christ, the Rabbis of the time turned aside from the messianic interpretation. [102]

Fabry

[96] Cf. Curtis, *ICC, in loc.;* Briggs, *Psalms,* II, 379; J. Maier, *BZAW,* 93, 60; Davies.

[97] Cf. J. Schreiner, *Sion-Jerusalem, Jahwes Königssitz. StANT,* 7 (1963), 113.

[98] H. G. Jefferson, *JBL,* 73 (1954), 152-56; J. Schreiner, 121.

[99] L. Dürr, *Ps 110 im Lichte der neueren altorientalischen Forschung* (1929); G. von Rad, "The Royal Ritual in Judah," *The Problem of the Hexateuch and Other Essays* (trans. 1966), 222-231; S. Herrmann, "Die Königsnovelle in Ägypten und Israel," *WZ* Leipzig, 3 (1953/54), 37.

[100] *UT,* 1814.

[101] *Psalms,* III. *AB,* XVIIA (1970), 112ff.

[102] Cf. "Der 110. Psalm in der altrabbinischen Literatur," St.-B., IV/I, 452-465; on the use of Ps. 110:1 in the NT, cf. S. Kistemaker, *The Psalm Citations in the Epistle to the Hebrews* (Amsterdam, 1961), 27ff., 80f.; F. Schröger, "Der Verfasser des Hebräerbriefes als Schriftausleger," *Bibl. Untersuchungen,* 4 (1968), 201ff.; A. Vanhoye, *Situation du Christ; Hébreux 1-2. LD,* 58 (Paris, 1969), 102ff., 208ff.

הָדַר hādhār

Contents: I. 1. Etymology; 2. Occurrences; 3. Parallel Expressions; 4. Usage. II. 1. *hadhar* in Relation to God; 2. In Relation to the King; 3. In Relation to Man; 4. Other Occurrences in the OT. III. The Feminine Noun *hadharah*. IV. The Verb *hadhar*.

I. 1. *Etymology.* The original meaning of *hadhar* must remain uncertain, because a connection of *hadhar* with words from the same root can be demonstrated with certainty only in Aramaic. In Old South Arabic *hdr* possibly meant "ornament." [1] The original meaning of *hadhar* has been sought in Arab. *hadara*, "to rave, babble,'" and *hadara*, "to roar, swell." [2] It has also been connected with Heb. *'dr*, → אַדִּיר *'addîr*, [3] and with Assyr. *adāru*, "to fear," [4] which is questionable. *hdr*, "glory," and *hdyr*, "glorious," occur in Official Aramaic (Ahikar, lines 108 and 207), [5] as well as in Aramaic dialects, [6] and Syr. *hedrā'*, "ornament, splendor, glory." [7] Moreover, this is to be compared with Egyp. *h3dr.t*, probably part of a necklace. [8]

2. *Occurrences.* The word appears in the absolute *hādhār*, in the more common construct *hᵃdhar*, and in the construct *hedher* in Dnl. 11:20. [9] The feminine noun **hadharah* is found only in the construct. Emphatic and suffixed forms of the root occur in Biblical Aramaic. *hadhar* appears 31 times in the OT (including

---

hādhār. P. R. Ackroyd, "Some Notes on the Psalms. The Interpretation of הדרת קדש," *JTS,* 17 (1966), 392-99; A. Caquot, "In splendoribus sanctorum (Ps. 92,2; 96,9; 1 Chr. 16,29)," *Syr,* 33 (1956), 36-41; F. M. Cross, "Notes on a Canaanite Psalm in the OT," *BASOR,* 117 (1950), 19-21; H. Donner, "Ugaritismen in der Psalmenforschung," *ZAW,* 79 (1967), 322-350, esp. 331-33; G. R. Driver, "Psalm CX: Its Form, Meaning and Purpose," *Festschrift M. H. Segal* (Jerusalem, 1964), 17*-31*, esp. 22*f.; H. Gross, "Die Gottebenbildlichkeit des Menschen," *Lex tua veritas. Festschrift H. Junker* (1961), 89-100; S. Mowinckel, *Psalmenstudien,* II (1922), 158; Pedersen, *ILC,* I-II, 237f.; H. J. Stoebe, "Erwägungen zu Psalm 110 auf dem Hintergrund von 1. Sam. 21," *Festschrift F. Baumgärtel* (1959), 175-191, esp. 187; G. Wehmeier-D. Vetter, *THAT,* I, 469-472; H. Wildberger, "Das Abbild Gottes, Gen 1,26-30," *ThZ,* 21 (1965), 481-501, esp. 481f.

[1] Cf. ContiRossini, 131b.
[2] *GesB,* 175; J. Gray, *The Krt Text in the Literature of Ras Shamra* (²1964), 55; *WUS* (³1967), No. 817; Driver, *CML,* 32f.; *KBL³,* 230a calls attention to another meaning of *hadara*: (blood) "is poured out with impunity, (trouble) is brought about to no purpose," *hadr,* "worthless"; cf. the survey of the Arabic meanings in Wehr, 1022.
[3] W. J. Gerber, *Die hebräischen Verba denominativa* (1896), 164; Brockelmann, *LexSyr,* 172a; cf. also H. Cazelles, *VT,* 20 (1970), 124.
[4] *GesB,* 175.
[5] *DISO,* 63.
[6] *KBL²,* 226a.
[7] Brockelmann, *LexSyr,* 172.
[8] Cf. Donner, 331, n. 57; and Brockelmann, *LexSyr,* 172a.
[9] Cf. *BLe,* § 552; *KBL³,* 230a.

Dnl. 11:20), and *hadharah* 5 times. In spite of textual difficulties, the following passages are to be included in this group: Ps. 110:3 (several Heb. mss., the Syr., and the Vulg. read *harere*, "mountains," instead of *hadhre*, "array," and many exegetes concur);[10] 45:5 (Eng. v. 4) (the repeated *hadharekha*, "in your majesty," at the end of v. 4[3] and the beginning of v. 5[4] presumably arose through dittography; the second *vahadharekha* is missing in two Heb. mss., the Vulgate, and some mss. of the Syr.; the LXX translation would suggest Heb. *vehadhrekh*, "and span the bow, conquer completely"); and 145:5. The verb *hadhar* occurs six times in the OT.

3. *Parallel Expressions*. Parallel ideas can contribute to a more precise definition of *hadhar: kabhodh*, "glory" (Ps. 21:6[5]; Isa. 35:2); *pachadh*, "terror" (Isa. 2:10,19,21); *koach*, "power" (Ps. 29:4); *po'al*, "work" (Ps. 90:16; 111:3); *niphla'oth*, "wondrous works" (Ps. 145:5); *gebhuroth*, "mighty deeds" (Ps. 145: 12); *tiph'ereth*, "beauty" (Ps. 96:6; Prov. 20:29); *to'ar*, "form" (Isa. 53:2); *'oz*, "strength" (Ps. 96:6; 1 Ch. 16:27); *chedhvah*, "joy" (1 Ch. 16:27); *ga'on*, "majesty," and *gobhah*, "dignity" (Job 40:10). Again, the meaning of *hadhar* hardly differs from that of words with which it is closely connected in conjunctive expressions. The stereotyped phrase → הוד *hôdh vehadhar*, "glory (honor) and majesty," appears often in the OT (Ps. 45:4[3]; 96:6; 104:1; 111:3; Job 40:10; 1 Ch. 16:27); *kabhodh vehadhar*, "glory and honor" (Ps. 8:6[5]), and *'oz vehadhar*, "strength and dignity" (Prov. 31:25), also occur. In construct expressions *hadhar* functions as a *nomen rectum* (governed noun) in: *hadhar zeqenim*, "the beauty of old men" (Prov. 20:29); *hadhar ge'ono*, "the glory of his majesty" (Isa. 2:10, 19,21); *hadhar hakkarmel*, "the majesty of Carmel," *hadhar 'elohenu*, "the majesty of our God" (Isa. 35:2); and *hadhar kebhodh hodhekha*, "the glorious splendor of thy majesty" (Ps. 145:5); as a *nomen regens* (governing noun) in *peri 'ets hadhar*, "the fruit of goodly trees" (Lev. 23:40); and as a second word in construct in *kebhodh hadhar malkhutho*, "the glorious splendor of his kingdom" (Ps. 145:12).

Scholars disagree as to whether the meaning of the feminine *hadharah* in Ps. 29:2; 96:9; 1 Ch. 16:29 should be deduced from that of *hadhar* and its cognates in the OT,[11] or with the help of the Ugaritic hapax legomenon *hdrt*.[12] The latter stands in synonymous parallelism with *hlm*, "dream," which would indicate that *hdrt* means "vision, appearance."[13] But primarily *hadharah* is to be connected with *hadhar*. In order to account for both derivations, Gordon assumes a development: "(divine) majesty—theophany—dream";[14] but this remains conjectural.[15]

---

[10] Cf. H.-J. Kraus, *BK*, XV/2 (⁴1972), 753.
[11] So Donner; Caquot; E. Vogt, *Bibl*, 41 (1960), 24; Wehmeier, *THAT*, I, 471; etc.
[12] *CTA*, 14 [I K], III, 155.
[13] Cross, 19-21; H.-J. Kraus, *BK*, XV/1, 233.
[14] *UT*, 752; cf. Ackroyd, 393-96.
[15] Cf. *OLZ*, 62 (1967), 538; and see III above.

4. *Usage.* *hadhar* is used in relation to God (Ps. 21:6[5]; 45:4,5[3,4]; 145:5, 12; etc.) and the king (Ps. 21:6[5]; etc.). Man can be endowed with *hadhar* (Isa. 53:2; Ps. 8:6[5]; etc.). Nature (Lev. 23:40; Isa. 35:2a), a city (Ezk. 27:10; Lam. 1:6; Isa. 5:14), or a bull (Dt. 33:17) can also be distinguished by it.

II. 1. *hadhar in Relation to God.* God's *hadhar* is a sign of the royal dignity [16] of the universal ruler. *hadhar* is the garment which he puts on (Ps. 104:1; cf. Job 40:10: God's "royal robes" are *ga'on vaghobhah*, "majesty and dignity," *hodh vehadhar*, "glory and splendor"). This can be seen not only in light (Ps. 104:2), but the whole of his marvelous creation in heaven and earth attests to his *hadhar* (vv. 2ff.). In a storm his voice thunders in *hadhar* ("full majesty") as an expression of his power, which brings tumult and destruction upon nature (Ps. 29:4,5; cf. v. 10; Yahweh as king). [17]

If the working of God in nature can demonstrate his *hadhar*, then "majesty" is particularly appropriate to the rule of the heavenly king and judge. Ps. 96:6 (1 Ch. 16:27) personifies the attributes of *hodh vehadhar*, "honor and majesty," before God's face [18] (cf. also v. 5: The creator of the heavens is above the gods). They are the Lord's attendants, whose creative works and especially his righteous rule are emphasized (vv. 10,13). If Job was to take over God's dominion (Job 40:10) (this is what God means when he challenges Job to deck himself with *hodh*, "glory," and *hadhar*, "splendor," which here stand in synonymous parallelism with *ga'on vaghobhah*, "majesty and dignity"), [19] he had to prove his power by doing creative deeds and especially deeds of judgment (abasing or bringing low the proud, and treading down or destroying the wicked). Thus *hadhar* is also active in the judgment of God: When Yahweh rises up to establish justice, men will be afraid of the "glory of his majesty" (here *mippene pachadh yhvh*, "from before the terror of Yahweh," is parallel to *mehadhar ge'ono*, "from the glory of his majesty") (Isa. 2:10,19,21).

This *hadhar* which is claimed for God is reason to praise him (Ps. 104:1) and to summon the nations to give him honor and worship (Ps. 96:6ff.).

In Songs of Praise the term *hadhar* is used especially for God's mighty and glorious deeds in Israel's history (Ps. 111:3). The grandeur and splendor of the royal majesty evident in God's actions stand in the background here. "The singer sees salvation history in the light of the royal glory of God." [20] When one generation tells the coming generation of Yahweh's works and might, it extols the "glorious splendor of his majesty" (*hadhar kebhodh hodhekha*, Ps. 145:5), his wonders, his terrible acts, and his greatness. *hadhar* also belongs to the group of terms denoting Yahweh's works in history (*ma'aseykha*, "thy works," and

---

[16] Gross, 96; W. H. Schmidt, *Die Schöpfungsgeschichte der Priesterschrift. WMANT*, 17 ([31]1973), 132ff., esp. 140f.; also Wildberger, 481f.

[17] On this psalm, cf., e.g., B. Margulis, *Bibl*, 51 (1970), 332-348; H. Strauss, *ZAW*, 82 (1970), 91-102; P. C. Craigie, *VT*, 22 (1972), 143-151; → הוד *hôdh*.

[18] Cf. Kraus, *BK*, XV/2, 667.

[19] Cf. above.

[20] Kraus, 768.

gebhurotheykha, "thy mighty acts," Ps. 145:4; *niphle'otheykha,* "thy wondrous works," v. 5; and *nore'otheykha,* "thy terrible acts," and *gedholotheykha,* "thy good things"). Thus the "glorious splendor of his kingdom" (*kebhodh hadhar malkhutho*) reigns in God's everlasting kingdom (v. 12). It "consists of the faithfulness and grace, care and righteousness of the ruler: an ideal government!" [21] A prayer for compassion and help (Ps. 90:15) precedes the wish that God let his "glory" (RSV "glorious power," *hadhar*) be manifest (v. 16).

In Mic. 2:9 *hadhar* has a social aspect. In the battle against social oppression free life on the inherited land can be called "splendor" (RSV "glory"). If the land is seized, the debtor and his wife must leave, "and their children, who are now deprived of the 'glory' of Yahweh for ever, of the honor of being his free farmers on his land." [22] According to Weiser, "the right to a portion in Yahweh's inheritance, to the family possession," is to be understood under "Yahweh's glory." [23]

2. *In Relation to the King. hadhar,* usually with → הוד *hôdh,* is also used to describe the glory of the earthly king. In view of this, it is impossible to decide whether *hadhar* was used "first to praise the human king or the divine king." [24] Even if *hadhar* was attributed first to the earthly king, his majesty was a divine gift (Ps. 21:6[5]; 45:3-5[2-4]). So, according to Ps. 21:6(5), the *hodh vehadhar* ("splendor and majesty") of the king are bestowed by Yahweh, which is a cause of thanksgiving for the psalmist. This God-given *hadhar* is manifested in the glory, blessings, and good fortune that the king enjoys (vv. 4,5,7[3,4,6]). The terms *hodh vehadhar* also depict the "glory and majesty" of the king as a brilliant warrior (Ps. 45:4,5[3,4]), but these terms are used not only to call upon the king to go into battle victoriously, but also to call upon him to help and protect the oppressed (v. 5[4]; cf. v. 8[7]). *behadhre qodhesh,* "in holy majesty (or array)," in Ps. 110:3 is textually difficult; among other things, this is the only passage in the OT where *hdr* appears in the plural. Perhaps the text here should be emended to *beharere qodhesh,* "upon the holy mountains" (so the RSV). [25] The MT *hadhre qodhesh* probably means the royal regalia (pl. because the author is thinking of the various pieces of such a regalia?). [26] But it is also translated abstractly "in the splendor of holiness," or something similar. On the recurring expression *hodh vehadhar,* see → הוד *hôdh.*

3. *In Relation to Man.* Like the *hadhar* of the king, all the *hadhar,* "honor," of man is a divine gift (Ps. 8:6[5]). God gives man a portion of his lordship, he crowns him whom he makes little less than '*elohim* with *kabhodh vehadhar,*

---

21 H. Gunkel, *Die Psalmen* (⁵1968), 610.

22 T. H. Robinson-F. Horst, *HAT,* 14 (³1964), 135.

23 A. Weiser, *ATD,* XXIV (⁴1963), 251.

24 So Wildberger, 482; cf. also the idea of the close relationship between the deity and the king in the ancient Near East.

25 Cf. above, and Kraus, 753, 759.

26 Cf. G. Widengren, *Sakrales Königtum im AT und im Judentum* (1955), 103, n. 22.

"glory and honor." This statement stands in the tradition that the characteristics of the royal majesty were democratized. Hence vv. 6f.(5f.) describe man as being "in a royal position." [27] In this connection the psalmist emphasizes the surpassing majesty and dominant position of man in creation (vv. 7,9[6,8]). At the same time the *hadhar* of man is an indication of God's greatness (vv. 5,6[4,5]) and cause to praise him (v. 10[9]). Perhaps it is as a royal task that the righteous are given the "honor" (RSV "glory," *hadhar*) of executing judgment on heathen nations and kings amidst songs of praise to God (Ps. 149:9). They are "agents of the rule and judgment of Yahweh." [28]

The clothing of the efficient housewife is *hadhar* (Prov. 31:25). Clothing can be used symbolically for inner characteristics. According to the context *hadhar* denotes her external appearance, perhaps "her friendly, radiant appearance" [29] or form. Its connection with *'oz*, "strength," and the emphasis on diligence raise the question, however, as to whether *hadhar* does not emphasize chiefly her hard-earned prosperity. [30]

hadhar is the glory, the beauty, the special quality of a man. The "beauty" of old men is their gray hair (Prov. 20:29). The Servant of God lacks all "comeliness" (Isa. 53:2) (cf. the parallel expressions: he also has no *to'ar*, "[beautiful] form," or *mar'eh*, "pleasant appearance" [RSV "beauty"]). A man's *hadhar* is a reason for looking at him (v. 2).

4. *Other Occurrences in the OT*. *hadhar* is used to describe the fruit of goodly trees which is gathered at the Feast of Booths (Lev. 23:40). The majesty, glory, and beauty of wooded mountains and fruited plains are called the *hadhar*, "majesty," of nature in comparison with the dry steppe and the desolate wilderness (Isa. 35:2). This is a gift, and God can bestow it even on the wilderness. The *hadhar* bestowed upon the wilderness indicates the "glory" of Yahweh. When the wilderness is given the "majesty" of Carmel and Sharon, God's "glory" is manifest (cf. v. 2a with 2b: here *hadhar 'elohenu*, "the majesty of our God," is parallel to *hadhar hakkarmel vehashsharon*, "the majesty of Carmel and Sharon"). Jerusalem's beauty, her renown among the nations, is due entirely to the *hadhar*, "splendor," which Yahweh bestowed upon her. He helped her, clothed her with silk and variegated materials, decked her with silver and gold, gave her abundance, and even crowned her (Ezk. 16:6-13,14). But she lavished this *hadhar* on her idols (vv. 15ff.). Thus *hadhar* can be used in a critical context. The prophet sees the *hadhar*, "nobility," of Jerusalem go down into Sheol with her tumult (*hamon*) and uproar (*sha'on*) (?) (Isa. 5:14). [31] And Jerusalem lost her *hadhar*. After the captives were led away and the princes lost their position and became powerless, the lament went forth: From the daughter of Zion has departed all her magnificent "splendor" (Lam. 1:6).

---

[27] Schmidt, 141, n. 6; cf. also *idem*, "Gott und Mensch in Psalm 8," *ThZ*, 25 (1969), 12.
[28] Kraus, 967.
[29] B. Gemser, *HAT*, 16 (²1963), 109.
[30] Cf. W. Frankenberg, *Die Sprüche* (1898), 168.
[31] Cf. H. Wildberger, *BK*, X/1, 177, 190.

According to Dt. 33:17 *hadhar* can be used of a bull as a symbol for the tribe of Joseph. The word emphasizes this animal's majestic appearance and strength (cf. v. 17b, which describes his warlike successes).

The application of *hadhar* in Dnl. 11:20 is not clear. Does it emphasize Jerusalem or Judah or Palestine as the "glory of the kingdom" (perhaps "royal dignity" or "royal majesty" is to be understood)? [32] An army of mercenaries can bring a city *hadhar*, "honor and might," and thus make its beauty perfect (Ezk. 27:10f.).

III. The Feminine Noun hadharah. The feminine noun *hadharah* occurs five times in the OT: four times in the expression *behadhrath qodhesh*, "in holy array" (Ps. 29:2; 96:9; 1 Ch. 16:29; 2 Ch. 20:21), and once in the expression *hadhrath melekh*, "the glory of a king" (Prov. 14:28). The translation in the last instance is certain. The contrast with *mechittah* (destruction, ruin) and the relationship of *hadharah* with *hadhar* suggest the meaning "majesty, glory, splendor, grandeur" (thus in Prov. 14:28: the king's "glory" depends on a multitude of people). The only intelligible translation of *behadhrath qodhesh* in 2 Ch. 20:21 is "in holy adornment (or ornaments)." This interpretation alone fits the description of the singers who go before.

It has been suggested that *hadharah* in Ps. 29:2; 96:9; and 1 Ch. 16:29 should be translated "vision, apparition," or "theophany, appearance," on the basis of the parallelism between *hdrt* and *ḥlm* (dream) in *CTA*, 14, 155. [33] Since this change of meaning is conjectural, however, and since the meanings "vision, apparition," do not improve the context, in these three passages preference should be given to the translation "adornment, ornaments, array," which appears in the other two; [34] and yet final certainty on the point cannot be attained. [35]

IV. The Verb hadhar. The verb *hadhar* is a denominative from the substantive *hadhar*. [36] On the basis of this assumption and of the contexts in which it appears, it follows that the meaning of this verb in the qal is "to adorn, distinguish, honor someone." If gray hair (*sebhah*) is said to be the "glory, honor" (*hadhar*) of old men in Prov. 20:29, [37] then the verb *hadhar* in a similar context (Lev. 19:32) means: to act in a way that is in keeping with *hadhar*, i.e., to distinguish by respect, to show respect: "honor old age." The parallel statement (which has become a familiar saying): "You shall rise up before the hoary head," offers an example of respect. In Isa. 63:1 the passive participle is defined more

---

[32] Cf. J. A. Montgomery, *The Book of Daniel. ICC* ([3]1959), 444f.; N. W. Porteous, *Daniel. OTL* (1965), 165.

[33] See I.3 above.

[34] However, cf. D. N. Freedman-C. F. Hyland, *HThR*, 66 (1973), 243f.

[35] Cf. Donner, 331-33; W. H. Schmidt, *Königtum Gottes in Ugarit und Israel. BZAW*, 80 ([2]1966), 56; E. Vogt, "Der Afbau von Ps 29," *Bibl*, 41 (1960), 24; Caquot, 37-41; B. Margulis, *Bibl*, 51 (1970), 337; W. Schlisske, *BWANT*, 97 (1973), 50f.; etc.

[36] Gerber, 163f.

[37] Cf. above.

precisely by *be*: *hadhur bilebhusho,* "glorious, glittering in his apparel." In the judicial realm the qal of *hadhar* means "to be partial to someone," etc. (Lev. 19:15): "You shall not be partial to the poor or defer to the great" (*lo' thissa' phene dhal velo' thehdar pene ghadhol*). *hadhar* is to be translated in the same way in Ex. 23:3. In the above-mentioned passages (Lev. 19:15,32; Ex. 23:3) *hadhar* takes the accusative (usually with *pene*). Accordingly the hithpael means: "to honor oneself, boast, be presumptuous" (Prov. 25:6: "do not boast [RSV, put yourself forward] in the king's presence," which appears in parallelism with "do not stand in the place of the great"); and the niphal, "to be honored" (Lam. 5:12). Here again *hdr* is used in reference to *zeqenim,* "the aged" (cf. Prov. 20:29; Lev. 19:32). They are not given proper consideration and respect. Their fate is servitude and death (cf. Lam. 5:12a,14).

In Aramaic, *hdr* in the pael (Dnl. 4:31,34[34,37]; 5:23) means "to honor" God (it appears in parallelism with *brk* in the pael, "to bless," in 4:31[34], with *rum* in the polel, "to extol," in 4:34[37]; and with *šbḥ* in the pael, "to praise," in 4:31,34[34,37]; 5:23).

Warmuth

הוּא *hû';* אֲנִי *'ᵃnî;* אָנֹכִי *'ānōkhî*

Contents: I. 1. Use of the Personal Pronoun, Especially the Third Person; 2. Special Expressions with *hu'*; 3. In the Qumran Literature. II. "I" Statements: 1. General Observations; 2. In Egyptian Literature; 3. In Mesopotamian Literature; 4. In West Semitic Literature. III. "I" Statements in the OT: 1. In Self-Representation Formulas: a. In the Stories of the Patriarchs and Moses; b. As a Pronouncement of the Decalog, the Holiness Code; c. In the Early Prophets; d. In Deutero-Isaiah; 2. In Statements of Proof.

I. 1. *Use of the Personal Pronoun, Especially the Third Person.* Since the various forms of the Hebrew verb contain within themselves the personal subject, personal pronouns are used as subjects of a verb only when the writer wants

---

hû'. Y. Bakr, "Le pronom '*anā*' dans les langues sémitiques," *Mélanges Ṭaha Hussein,* I (Cairo, 1962), 397-407; H. Bardtke, "Das Ich des Meisters in den Hodajot von Qumran," *WZ* Leipzig, 6 (1956/57), 93-104; J. Bergman, *Ich bin Isis* (Uppsala, 1968), 219-233; H.-M. Dion, "Le genre littéraire sumérien de l' 'hymne à soi-même' et quelques passages du Deutéro-Isaïe," *RB,* 74 (1967), 215-234; K. Elliger, "Ich bin der Herr—euer Gott," *Festschrift K. Heim* (1954), 9-34=*KlSchr. ThB,* 32 (1966), 211-231; K. Günther, *THAT,* I (1971), 216-220; E. Katz, *Die Bedeutung des hapax legomenon der Qumraner Handschriften HUAHA* (Bratislava, 1967); E. Norden, *Agnostos Theos* (1913=⁴1956), esp. 207-220; A. Poebel, *Das appositionell bestimmte Pronomen der 1. Pers. Sing. in den westsemitischen Inschriften und im AT.* Chicago Oriental Institute, Assyriological Studies, 3 (1932); G. von Rad, "Die Anrechnung des Glaubens zur Gerechtigkeit," *ThLZ,* 76 (1951), 129-132=*GSAT. ThB,* 8 (⁴1971), 130-35; M. Reisel, *Observations on* הואהא, אהיה אשר אהיה *and* שם המפורש (Assen, 1957); R.

to place special emphasis on the pronoun.[1] Obviously the personal pronoun is also used as a subject in a nominal clause. It can also be used to emphasize a suffix, e.g., *hatsom tsamtuni 'ani,* "was it for *me* that you fasted" (Zec. 7:5); *'eth damekha gam 'attah,* "*your own* blood also" (1 K. 21:19).

The OT uses the 3rd person pronoun (*hu'*; fem. *hi'*; pl. *hem[mah], hennah*) in certain special ways: it is used as a demonstrative: *hammaqom hahu',* "that place" (Gen. 22:14); *ba'eth hahi',* "at that time" (Nu. 22:4); cf. also *ballaylah hu',* "that night" (Gen. 19:33).[2] *hu'* is also used in apposition to the subject in order to emphasize it,[3] e.g., *yitten 'adhonai hu' lakhem 'oth,* "Yahweh himself will give you a sign" (Isa. 7:14); *yhvh hu' hattobh be'enav ya'aseh,* "Yahweh will do what seems good to him" (1 S. 3:18); cf. Ps. 48:15 (Eng. v. 14). It also functions as a connecting link (copula) in a nominal sentence,[4] e.g., *yoseph hu' hashshallit,* "Joseph is the ruler" (Gen. 42:6); *tsaddiq hu' yhvh,* "Yahweh is just" (Lam. 1:18); *'attah hu' ha'elohim,* "thou art (the) God" (2 S. 7:28); *'ani hu' hamedhabber,* "it is I who speak" (Isa. 52:6); *halo' 'att hi' hammochetseth* (so 1QIs^a) *rahabh,* "is it not thou that didst crush Rahab?" (Isa. 51:9).

2. *Special Expressions with hu'.* The following expressions using *hu'* are especially significant.

a. The so-called Declaratory Formulas,[5] i.e., short nominal clauses with *hu'* (or *hi'* or *hem*) as the postpositive subject, which "usually makes a brief concluding statement about the respective subject."[6] Such formulas appear with special frequency in connection with various types of sacrifice: *'olah hu',* "it is a burnt-offering" (Ex. 29:18; Lev. 1:13,17; 8:21); *minchah hi',* "it is a cereal-offering" (Lev. 2:6,15); *chatta'th hu',* "it is a sin-offering" (Ex. 29:14; Lev. 4:24; 5:9,12; Nu. 19:9); *'asham hu',* "it is a guilt-offering" (Lev. 5:19; 7:5); *'ishsheh hu',* "it is an offering by fire" (Ex. 29:25; Lev. 8:28); *pesach hu',* "it is a passover sacrifice" (Ex. 12:11). Occasionally this formula is expanded, e.g., *chatta'th haqqahal hi',* "it is the sin-offering for the assembly" (Lev. 4:21); *'ishsheh hu' leyhvh,* "it is an offering by fire to Yahweh" (Lev. 8:21,28); *'olah hu' lereach*

Rendtorff, *Die Gesetze in der Priesterschrift. FRLANT,* 44 (1954); H. P. Rüger, "הואהא—Er. Zur Deutung von 1 QS 8,13-14," *ZNW,* 60 (1969), 142ff.; E. Schweizer, *Ego eimi. FRLANT,* 38 (1939, ²1965); N. Walker, "Concerning *hû'* and *'anî hû',*" *ZAW,* 74 (1962), 205f.; W. Zimmerli, "Ich bin Jahwe," *Festschrift A. Alt* (1953), 179-209=*Gottes Offenbarung. ThB,* 19 (1963), 11-40; idem, *Erkenntnis Gottes nach dem Buche Ezechiel. AThANT,* 27 (1954)= *ThB,* 19 (1963), 41-119; idem, "Das Wort des göttlichen Selbsterweises (Erweiswort), eine prophetische Gattung," *Mélanges . . . A. Robert* (Paris, 1957), 154-164=*ThB,* 19 (1963), 120-132; H. Zimmermann, "Das absolute ἐγώ εἰμι als die neutestamentliche Offenbarungsformel," *BZ,* N.F. 4 (1960), 54-69, 266-276.

[1] Brockelmann, *Synt.,* § 34b; *GK,* § 135a.
[2] *Synt.,* § 23d.
[3] *Ibid.,* § 67b.
[4] *Ibid.,* § 30a.
[5] Von Rad.
[6] Rendtorff, 74.

nichoach, "it is a whole burnt-offering, a pleasing odor" (Lev. 8:21); etc. By using such formulas the priest was obviously issuing a final official statement as to the nature of a sacrifice.

Other examples are related to cultic cleanness or uncleanness: *tahor hu'*, "he is clean" (Lev. 13:13,17,37,39,40,41); *tame' hu'*, "he is unclean" (Lev. 11:35; 13:15, 36,44,46,55; 14:44; 25:2,25; Nu. 19:15,20); *qodhesh hu'*, "it is holy," or *qodhesh qodhashim hu'*, "it is most holy (Lev. 6:18,22 [25,29]; 7:1,6; 14:13); *sheqets hu' (hem),* "it is (they are) an abomination" (Lev. 11:13,41). Here also expanded forms occur (with *leyhvh, lekha,* and *lakhem*). [7] Further, the priestly judgment concerning leprosy is expressed in such formulas: *tsara'ath hu'*, "it is leprosy" (Lev. 13:3,8,11,15; etc.; cf. other types of skin eruptions in Lev. 13:6,23,28; etc.). Here, then, we have, so to speak, the official diagnosis of the priest in cases of cleanness and uncleanness, or of leprosy.

A third example of a declaratory formula occurs in Ezk. 18:9, [8] where the final judgment concerning the righteous is expressed in the phrase, *tsaddiq hu'*, "he is righteous." Since Ezekiel uses the terminology of priestly law in chap. 18 and elsewhere (e.g., in chap. 14), it would seem valid to conclude that declaratory formulas were also used in this terminology.

The declaratory formula, then, is a judgment which is uttered with divine authority and which expresses the final decision in a case.

b. In Jer. 5:11f. the following statement appears in an accusation against Judah and Israel: "they have been utterly faithless to me (*baghodh baghedhu bi*); ... they have spoken falsely of (*kichashu*) Yahweh and have said, *lo' hu'*, he will do nothing; no evil will come upon us." If the text is correct, it can hardly represent a theoretical denial of the existence of God (this would in any case require *'enennu,* and not *'en hu'*, as Duhm thinks), [9] but rather expresses a disposition that does not consider Yahweh to be the almighty, much like the thought conveyed in Zeph. 1:12: "he will not do good, nor will he do ill" (cf. Ps. 10:4; 14:1, where even *'en 'elohim,* "there is no God," appears without representing a theoretical atheism). This also fits the context: *kichesh,* "speak falsely," and "no evil will come (*bo'*, i.e., happen)." [10] Weiser's translation: "it is nothing to him," [11] expresses the thought very well. [12]

Some Canaanite proper names may perhaps support a stronger emphasis on the existence of God. Thus one finds *hy 'dt,* which can be translated "the lady exists," [13] and *hy 'bn,* "the rock exists." [14] This translation is supported by a note

---

[7] Cf. *ibid.,* 74f.

[8] Cf. Zimmerli, *BK,* XIII/1, 398f.

[9] B. Duhm, *KHC, in loc.*

[10] → בוא *bô',* V.

[11] A. Weiser, *ATD,* XX-XXI, *in loc.*

[12] Similarly Rudolph, *HAT,* 12, *in loc.*

[13] F. M. Cross, *Canaanite Myth and Hebrew Epic* (1973), 64, n. 73; but cf. Gröndahl, *PNU,* 45: "it is the lady."

[14] Gröndahl: "it is our father"!

in a quadrilingual vocabulary list from Ugarit where *ú-wu* (= *huwa*, "he") is connected with Hurrian *manni*, "he is." [15] The Hebrew proper name Jehu could therefore be explained in this way: *yahu-hu'*, "Yahweh exists" > *yahwu* > *yohu* > *yehu* (dissimilation). [16]

The expression *'ani hu'* (Isa. 41:4; 43:10,13; 48:12) or *'attah hu'* (Ps. 102:28 [27]) presents a special problem. First of all, the former expression must be distinguished from other "I" statements in Deutero-Isaiah, where *hu'* is used as a copula between *'ani* and a participle, as in Isa. 43:25, "I, I am he who blots out your transgressions" (*'anokhi 'anokhi hu' mocheh* ...); 51:12, "I, I am he that comforts you" (*'anokhi 'anokhi hu' menachemkhem*); 52:6, "it is I who speak: here am I" (*'ani hu' hamedhabber hinneni*).

The literal translation of *'ani hu'* would be "I am he," which could be understood either as simply "It is I (with whom one always and only has to reckon)," or as "I am (always) he, i.e., the same." Ps. 102:27f.(26f.) in particular favors the latter interpretation: heaven and earth will perish (*'abhadh*), but God will endure (*'amadh*); they will wear out (*balah*) like a garment, but "thou art the same (*'attah hu'*), and thy years have no end (*lo' yittammu*)." Thus, the creator is the one who endures and is the same for ever, who outlives his creation. Similar ideas appear in Isa. 41:4 and 48:12: Yahweh is "the first and the last," the one who abides and acts perpetually; he is *hu'*, "he, that one." But in Isa. 43:10, the main emphasis is placed on Yahweh as the one God: "before me no god was formed, nor shall there be any after me." 43:13 is not entirely clear: before *'ani hu'* one finds the phrase *'ani 'el*, "I am God," and after it there is a reference to the mighty and irresistible work of Yahweh. But what is meant by *gam miyyom 'ani hu'*? Is *miyyom* a scribal error for an original *hayyom*, "today," or does it somehow mean "since time immemorial"? In either case, the translation "I am the same" is conceivable. Job 3:19 might also favor this interpretation: "the small and the great are *hu'* (i.e., possibly, the same, alike) there (in Sheol)." In fact the formula *'ani hu'* (like *'attah hu'*) is found in contexts that have to do with Yahweh as the only God, [17] the creator, or the God who acts in history. Whether there is also here an allusion to the revelation of the divine name Yahweh in Ex. 3:14 with the words *'ehyeh 'asher 'ehyeh* (RSV, "I am who I am"), [18] is uncertain. This much at least is true, that there too Yahweh shows himself to be God by his presence or by his being who he is, i.e., by his deeds for Israel.

Dt. 32:39 occupies a special place in that *'ani* is repeated here: *'ani 'ani hu'*. Albright interprets *hu'* as a postpositive copula and translates the phrase "I am

---

[15] *Ugaritica,* V (1968), 244.

[16] See Cross, *loc. cit.;* and cf. W. F. Albright, *Yahweh and the Gods of Canaan* (1968), 228, n. 155. In this connection cf. the Hebrew names *'abhihu*, Noth, *IPN*, 143f.; *KBL*³: "he is father"—or "my father exists"; and *'elihu'*, "he is my God" (*BDB;* Zorell, *Lex. Hebr.* [1966]), "it is God" (Noth, 143f.)—or "my God exists."

[17] Cf. K. Elliger, *BK*, XI, 125: "a monotheistic formula"; likewise C. R. North, *The Second Isaiah* (1964), 94.

[18] Walker, who considers the possibility of a ptcp. *hoveh*, "the existing one"; P. E. Bonnard, *Le second Isaïe* (Paris, 1972), 109.

I."[19] But it is more likely that the repeated *'ani* is intended as an intensification and the translation "It is I," or "I am the same," is preferable. As in Deutero-Isaiah, the point in this verse is that Yahweh alone is God, and that he alone acts in human history.

Ringgren

3. *In the Qumran Literature.* The aversion to mentioning the name of Yahweh, which is to be observed in late texts of the OT and in the LXX, led to a prohibition against speaking the word "Yahweh" in the Rabbinic period (see *Sanh.* vii.5). Now to a great extent it becomes the function of *'ani* and *hu'* to act as a substitute for the divine name (*'ani: Sukka* iv.5; 53a; *hu'*: see *Schab.* 104a; *PesiqR* 104a on Isa. 42:8; *Sukka* iv.5).[20] This tendency is taken over in the Qumran literature only to the extent that in the scrolls the Tetragrammaton (*yhvh*) is either written in hieratic ancient Hebrew letters or replaced by 4 dots (1QS 8:14; 1QIsᵃ 40:7; 42:6; 4QTest 1:19), while the personal pronoun appears only rarely as a substitution for the Tetragrammaton. Thus *'ani* in particular (46 times in 1QH out of a total of 51), and *hu'(ah)* (50 times in the legal literature out of a total of 92), function instead as ordinary pronouns. In 1QH *'ani* denotes much less the "articulated individual I" of a specific worshipper (the Teacher of Righteousness?), and much more (as in the OT Psalms) a "typical I." It thus refers to a formulated community self-understanding in the texts characterized thereby.[21] Probably only *hu'* in CD A 9:5 (for *yhvh*, in a quotation from Nah. 1:2b), and the hapax legomenon *hw'h* in 1QS 8:13, which is usually interpreted as a lengthened form of the 3rd person masculine singular pronoun (*hw'h + aleph* otiosum),[22] and understood as an "emphatic He,"[23] are used as a substitution for the Tetragrammaton in the Qumran literature. It is possible, however, that the latter represents a scribal error, since 4QSᵉ reads here *ha'emeth*, "the truth." Others think that *hw'h* is an abbreviation for *hw' h'(lhym)*, "He is God,"[24] or for the introduction of the Shemaʿ: *yhvh 'elohenu yhvh 'echadh*, "Yahweh our God, Yahweh is one."[25] Still others think *hw'h* is a proper noun derived from the personal pronoun,[26] but without sufficient philological support. Finally, Reisel tried to show that *hw'h* was a dialectical alternative for **yhw'h* (= a cult-musical extension of the Tetragrammaton).[27] Not aversion to uttering the divine name, but liturgical interests led to the creation of this form.[28]

Fabry

---

[19] W. F. Albright, *VT,* 9 (1959), 342f.

[20] Zimmermann, 268ff.

[21] Cf. O. Eissfeldt, *The OT* (trans. 1965), 656; Bardtke, *passim;* J. Maier, *Die Texte vom Toten Meer,* II (1960), 64.

[22] Rüger.

[23] W. Baumgartner, *ThR,* 19 (1951), 134.

[24] Brownlee, Bardtke, etc.

[25] Katz.

[26] Yalon, Habermann, Morag.

[27] Reisel, 41.

[28] Cf. also G. W. Nebe, *ZNW,* 63 (1972), 283-89.

II. "I" Statements.

1. *General Observations.* The last-mentioned group of *hu'* statements [29] belong to the *'ani* statements, which are especially numerous in Deutero-Isaiah. It is advisable, therefore, to investigate more closely the different forms and functions of these "I" statements in the ancient Near East and in the OT. In doing this, one can disregard the commonplace secular use of "I" in statements like *'ani yoseph,* "I am Joseph" (Gen. 45:3); or *'anokhi ruth,* "I am Ruth" (Ruth 3:9; in answer to the question, "Who are you?"; cf. further Gen. 24:34; 2 S. 14:5). Such expressions are quite self-explanatory and have no formulaic function.

Following Bultmann, [30] scholars usually distinguish between four different types of "I am" formulas: 1. the presentation formula (in answer to the question, "Who are you?"); 2. the qualification formula (in answer to the question, "What are you?"), e.g., in Isa. 44:6,24; cf. Ezk. 28:2,9 (the king of Tyre says: "I am a god"); 3. the identification formula, in which the speaker casts himself in the role of another person or of a deity; and 4. the recognition formula (in answer to the question, "Who is the one expected, inquired of, being discussed?"), e.g., in Isa. 41:4; 43:10f.; 52:6.

2. *In Egyptian Literature.* In Egyptian literature, "I" formulas occur especially in the following instances: [31]

a. As a self-representation of gods who appear in a dream or otherwise; so, e.g., on the sphinx stela of Thutmose IV:[32] "I am your father Harmachis-Khepre-Re-Atum, I am giving you my kingdom on earth..."; on the so-called famine stela:[33] "I am Khnum, who formed you" (line 18). For the deity to represent himself thus is rare according to Morenz,[34] but Bergman cites a series of examples with reference to Isis.[35]

b. Of the king as representative of the deity, e.g., Ramses II on a stela in Abu Simbel: "I am Re, the lord of heaven, who is on the earth. I treat you excellently, like a father";[36] "I am Horus, etc."[37]

c. Of the priest, who plays the role of a god, e.g., in the house where children were born at Edfu: "I am Thoth, oldest son of Re.... I have descended on the earth with the mysteries of the one of the horizon."[38]

---

[29] I.2.

[30] R. Bultmann, *Das Evangelium des Johannes. MeyerK* ([18]1964), 167.

[31] Cf. J. Assmann, "Aretalogie," *LexÄg,* 425-434.

[32] *Urk.,* IV, 153, 9ff.

[33] *Bibl. d'études,* 24 (1953); G. Roeder, *Urkunden zur Religion des alten Ägypten* (1923), 177ff.

[34] S. Morenz, *Egyptian Religion* (trans. 1973), 33.

[35] Bergman, 224f.

[36] Morenz, 41; Bergman, 226.

[37] See Bergman, 224, n. 3.

[38] E. Chassinat, *Mammisi d'Edfou,* Plate 116; Morenz, 33; cf. Bergman, 222f.

d. Of the dead who identifies himself with a god by a magical saying in order to acquire his might and to be able to carry out his functions. [39] This formula often stands at the end of the text, e.g., "I am the one whom the one Lord created, before two things originated in this land.... I am the 'sorcerer' (Hike)." [40] This usage has to do primarily with primeval and creator-gods, and gods who give life and provision. [41]

e. As a self-representation of the worshipper in prayers, etc., e.g., "I am your son Horus. I have come after I have defeated your enemies"; "I am a servant of your Ka." [42]

3. *In Mesopotamian Literature.* In Sumerian and Akkadian literature "I" formulas occur in the following instances:

a. The self-praise of the deity in hymns, etc., [43] e.g., "I (am) Ningirsu, who holds back the turbulent waters, the great hero beside Enlil, the lord who has no adversary..." (Gudea); [44] "Am I not the queen, the lady of Uruk..., the queen, the great lady of the lands, the queen, the lady of Babylon?" [45] The oldest example comes from the time of Gudea, and the latest dates only a little later than the first Babylonian kingdom; only one example [46] is written in Akkadian. [47] Of the 11 examples cited by Dion, 5 are concerned with Inanna-Ishtar. The self-representation is done by mentioning the names and titles of the deities, defining their position in the world of the gods, and describing their good deeds and awesome characteristics.

b. Salvation oracles, e.g., "I am Ishtar of Arbela. Do not be afraid! Glorify me!" or "I am Ishtar of Arbela, who will destroy your enemies before your feet"; [48] and in the form of a question, "Am I not Adad of Kallassu, who brought him up...?" (from Mari). [49]

c. In royal inscriptions, e.g., "Hammurabi, the shepherd, the one called by Enlil, am I, who stores up wealth and superfluity.... The royal shoot from eter-

[39] Morenz, 285f., n. 79; Bergman, 222; S. Schott, *Mythe und Mythenbildung im alten Ägypten* (1945), 131; Assmann, *LexÄg,* 426.

[40] *CT,* III, 382ff.; H. Kees, *Ägypten. Rel.-gesch. Lesebuch,* ed. A. Bertholet, 10/2 (1928).

[41] Assmann.

[42] A. Barucq, *L'expression de la louange divine et de la prière dans la Bible et en Egypte* (Cairo, 1962), 364ff.

[43] Dion, 222, n. 36, gives a list of 11 examples which "could easily be multiplied"; cf. also W. G. Lambert, "The Gula Hymn of Bullutṣarabi," *Or,* 36 (1967), 105-132; Å. Sjöberg, "Nungal in the Ekur," *AfO,* 24 (1973), 19-46.

[44] *SAHG,* 147.

[45] *SAHG,* 228f.

[46] *SAHG,* 239f.

[47] Dion, 223.

[48] IV R, 61; *AOT,* 281; *ANET,* 449f.

[49] See F. Ellermeier, *Prophetie in Mari und Israel* (1968), 50f.

nity, the mighty king, the sun of Babylon, ... the darling of Inanna am I" (the beginning and end of the prologue to the law); [50] "I am the king, the lord, ... I am the invincible weapon, which overcomes the land of its enemies; I am the king, strong in the battle ... " (Ashurnasirpal). [51]

d. In magical texts, where the exorcising priest proves his legitimacy by a self-representation formula: "I am the man of Ea; I am the man of Damkina; I am the messenger of Marduk. My incantation is the word of Ea; my exorcism is the exorcism of Marduk." [52]

e. As a self-representation of the worshipper, e.g., "Hear my prayer. However, I am the king, who gives liberally and gladdens your heart ... " (Nebuchadnezzar speaking to Marduk). [53]

4. *In West Semitic Literature.* In West Semitic inscriptions, an introductory *'nk*, or *'nh*, "I (am)," appears in the Mesha Inscription: [54] "I am Mesha, son of *Kmš* [. . .], king of Moab" (then follows the historical recital); in the Inscription of Panammuwa: [55] "I am Panammuwa the son of *Qrl*, the king of Ya'udi, it is I who have erected this statue ... " (then follows the historical recital); and in two inscriptions of Barrakib. [56] There are no examples in Ugaritic literature.

Beginning with Sumerian material, Poebel rejects the translation, "I am So-and-so," and understands the "I" as the appositional subject of the sentence: "I, So-and-so, who ... has done this and this." Nevertheless, the character of a self-representation cannot be wholly denied. Poebel's translation does not fit the OT material, as Zimmerli has shown. [57]

III. "I" Statements in the OT. Two main expressions containing the pronoun *'ani/'anokhi* are of theological significance in the OT. The one is the self-representation formula, "I am Yahweh" (or some other divine name or title), while the other is the so-called statement of proof, "You will know that I am Yahweh."

1. *In Self-Representation Formulas.*

a. *In the Stories of the Patriarchs and Moses.* Real self-representation appears almost exclusively in the stories of the patriarchs and Moses. Yahweh

---

[50] *AOT*, 381ff.; *ANET*, 164f.

[51] Cf. Norden, 212; Dion, 228f.; and cf. S. Mowinckel, "Die vorderasiatischen Königs-und Fürsteninschriften," *Eucharisterion H. Gunkel. FRLANT*, 19 (1923), I, 278-322.

[52] Meissner, *BuA*, II, 219; cf. also Norden, 214; R. Largement in *Histoire des religions*, ed. M. Brillant and R. Aigrain, 4 (Paris, n.d.), 146.

[53] *SAHG*, 283.

[54] *KAI*, 181.1f.

[55] *KAI*, 214.1.

[56] *KAI*, 216.1f.; 217.1f.; other examples are given by Poebel.

[57] W. Zimmerli, "Ich bin Jahwe"; but cf. A. Jepsen, *ZAW*, 79 (1967), 285f., with a reference to the Decalog.

appears to Abraham and says: "I am Yahweh, who brought you from Ur" (Gen. 15:7 [J]; cf. P, Gen. 17:1, "I am El Shaddai"). He represents himself to Isaac as "the God of Abraham your father" (Gen. 26:24 [J]). He says to Jacob: "I am Yahweh, the God of Abraham your father, and the God of Isaac" (Gen. 28:13 [J]); or, "I am God, the God of your father; do not be afraid..." (Gen. 46:3 [E]). Further, the *mal'akh yhvh*, "angel of Yahweh," speaks to Jacob and says: "I am the God whom you saw in Bethel" (Gen. 31:13 [E]). Finally, Yahweh reveals himself to Moses: "I am the God of your father, the God of Abraham, the God of Isaac, and the God of Jacob" (Ex. 3:6 [E]; then follows the promise of the deliverance from Egypt). Except in Gen. 31:11ff. the self-representation of God introduces the real revelatory utterance. In E, i.e., in Gen. 31:11f.; 46:3; and Ex. 3:6, an introductory call by God stands first, and then the man (Jacob or Moses) declares his readiness to hear by replying, *hinneni*, "Here am I." Twice the expression "Do not be afraid" occurs (Gen. 26:24; 46:3). God represents himself as the one who is already known, and refers to earlier associations with the fathers. Usually the divine utterance contains a promise of imminent help and guidance. [58]

In form these I statements call to mind the Assyrian salvation oracles. [59] Zimmerli conjectures that in Israel these were given the form of a promise of divine hearing along with the self-representation formula. [60]

Yahweh's revelation to Moses is also related by P (Ex. 6). But here the self-revelation formula becomes the making known of the name Yahweh. Earlier he had made himself known to the fathers only as El Shaddai (vv. 2f.). Here also the promise of deliverance from bondage and of the making of the covenant follows, and then the recognition statement: "you shall know that I am Yahweh your God..." (v. 7). Ezk. 20:5-7 refers to this event, using the formula, "I am Yahweh your God." It is strange that no allusion to the fathers is made here. Only the deliverance from bondage and the gift of the land are mentioned. A piece of legislation is also woven in: "Cast away the detestable things..., and do not defile yourselves with the idols of Egypt; I am Yahweh your God" (v. 7). [61] In both instances, the purpose of the revelation is the communication of the name Yahweh, and ultimately the recognition that Yahweh is God (cf. Ezk. 20:44, "You shall know that I am Yahweh, when I deal with you for my name's sake" [*lema'an shemi*, cf. also vv. 9,14,22]).

b. *As a Pronouncement of the Decalog, the Holiness Code.* The self-representation of Yahweh stands at the beginning of the Decalog (Ex. 20:2; Dt. 5:6). It thus serves in some way as a basis for the commandments. This thought is further developed in the frequent use of the formula, "I am Yahweh (your God)," in the Holiness Code. According to Elliger, two different formulas are represented here, which are to be assigned to different strata of H: one is the simple self-representation, which he calls the holiness or majesty formula, and which is

---

[58] Zimmerli, "Ich bin Jahwe," 193=25f.
[59] See II.3 above.
[60] Zimmerli, "Ich bin Jahwe," 195=27.
[61] Cf. below on Ex. 20.

designed to inspire obedience to the holy God (Lev. 18:5,6,21; 19:12,14,16,18, 28,30,32,37; 21:12; 22:2,3,8,30,31,33; 26:2,45; also 11:45; Ex. 6:2,6,8,29; 12:12); the other is the expanded formula, "I am Yahweh your God," which he characterizes as a salvation-history or grace formula, and which points "to the duty of gratitude for blessings received as a motive for keeping the commandments" (Lev. 18:2,4,30; 19:3,4,10,25,31,34,36; 20:24; 23:22,43; 25:38,55; 26:13; also Ex. 29:46; Nu. 10:10; 15:41). [62] A broader form of the first formula, *’ani yhvh meqaddesham* or *meqaddeshkhem,* "I am Yahweh who sanctify them/you," occurs especially in commandments that have to do with the preservation of holiness (Lev. 20:8; 21:8,15,23; 22:9,16,32). [63] Zimmerli, however, thinks it is possible to demonstrate that these two formulas are used interchangeably. [64]

In two psalms, viz., 50 and 81, the self-representation of God appears in such a context that it can be assumed that a liturgical proclamation of the Decalog somehow occurred. Thus Ps. 50:7 says: "Hear, O my people, and I will speak, O Israel, I will testify against you. God, your God, am I" (*’elohim ’eloheykha ’anokhi*—note the word order). [65] In vv. 16ff. the commandments of the Decalog are presupposed. Ps. 81:9-11 (8-10) says: "Hear, O my people, while I admonish you! O Israel, if you would but listen to me! There shall be no strange god among you; ... I am Yahweh your God (*’anokhi yhvh ’eloheykha*), who brought you up out of the land of Egypt." It can probably be concluded from this that the reading of the Decalog, at least in part, had a cultic setting, and that the self-representation formula played an important role in it. [66] Jgs. 6:10 also refers to this. The formulas in H probably have their root here.

c. *In the Early Prophets.* The self-representation of God does not occupy a special position in the early prophets (it does not appear at all in Isa., Am., or Mic.). [67] The only exception is Hosea, who used it twice, viz., in 12:10(9), "I am Yahweh your God from the land of Egypt," and in 13:4, "I am Yahweh your God from the land of Egypt; you know no God but me, and besides me there is no savior." Even though there seems to be an allusion to the first commandment in the latter passage, these formulas are rather to be regarded as confession formulas. [68]

d. *In Deutero-Isaiah.* It is different in Deutero-Isaiah and Ezekiel. A great number of I statements occur in Deutero-Isaiah, both self-representation formulas and other statements in which Yahweh speaks of himself with an emphatic *’ani* (or *’anokhi,* or even both, Isa. 43:11). The phrase, "I am Yahweh," occurs

---

[62] Elliger, "Ich bin der Herr—euer Gott," 16=216.
[63] Cf. Elliger, *HAT,* 4, 274.
[64] Zimmerli, "Ich bin Jahwe," 181=13; cf. "Selbsterweis," 158=125, where he admits that "Yahweh's gift to Israel is expressed more fully" in the grace formula.
[65] Zimmerli, "Ich bin Jahwe," 203f.=36.
[66] *Ibid.,* 202ff.=34ff.
[67] See *ibid.,* 195=28.
[68] *Ibid.,* 195f.=28.

independently (45:6,7,18), partly in statements of proof (45:3; 49:23), and once as a question, "Am I not Yahweh?"[69] Usually this formula is expanded in different ways: "I am Yahweh your God" (41:13; 48:17); "I am Yahweh your God, the Holy One of Israel, your Savior" (43:3); "I am Yahweh, who creates (*'asah*) all things" (44:24; or should this be translated, "I, Yahweh, make all this"? cf. 45:7,9); "I am Yahweh, your Holy One, the Creator of Israel, your King" (43:15); "I am Yahweh, that is my name" (42:8); "I am Yahweh, and there is no other (*ve'en 'odh*), besides me there is no God" (45:5,6,18; cf. "I am God [*'el*], and there is no other," 45:22; 46:9).

This self-representation formula appears in Deutero-Isaiah both in judgment and disputation oracles, where the formula introduces the divine self-affirmation with which Yahweh answers the questions of the community (41:4; 43:11,12,13; 45:18,21; 48:12), and also in salvation oracles, or in oracles of favorable divine response as a motivation for consolatory statements (with *ki,* "for," 41:13; 43:3; further 43:15; at the beginning, 41:17; 48:17), or in the conclusive statement of proof as a statement of purpose (49:23,26). To these should be added a couple of examples in call oracles (42:6,8 [call of the Servant of Yahweh]; 45:2f.,5f.,7 [call of Cyrus]).

This twofold usage goes hand in hand with a twofold content in the I statements of Deutero-Isaiah. On the one hand these statements contain God's self-glorification, which calls to mind the self-praise of the gods in Sumerian hymns, and according to Dion perhaps has been mediated through the royal inscriptions. Yahweh is the Only One and the Incomparable One, who can be compared with nothing. Here also belongs the statement, "I, Yahweh, am the first, and with the last am I" (*'ani* [*hu'*], 41:4; 44:6)[70]—thus, he is independent of time and unchangeable, always the same.

On the other hand the self-representation formula serves as a motive for consolation: Yahweh is the only savior and helper (43:11; 45:21; 49:23; cf. "your God" in 41:13; 43:3). By way of contrast, the deliverance from Egypt, which is prominent in Hosea, is not mentioned here.[71]

I statements that call to mind those in Deutero-Isaiah occur also in Isa. 60:16, 22; Zec. 10:6; Joel 2:27; Dt. 32:39;[72] cf. also Isa. 61:8; Jer. 17:10.

2. *In Statements of Proof.* *'ani yhvh,* "I am Yahweh," occurs frequently in Ezekiel as an element in statements of proof or recognition. This formula is found 54 times in the simple form,[73] and 18 times with expansions.[74] An original situation for a recognition statement may be found in passages like 1 K. 20:13,28, where Yahweh, through a prophet, promises Ahab victory over the Arameans

---

[69] Cf. "Am I not Adad?" in the Mari letter mentioned above; Zimmerli, "Ich bin Jahwe," 195=27f.

[70] Cf. I.2 above.

[71] Zimmerli, "Ich bin Jahwe," 200=33.

[72] See above.

[73] Zimmerli, *Erkenntnis,* 5=43, n. 5.

[74] *Ibid.,* nn. 6-9.

(Syrians). Thus the real concern here is a sign (→ אות 'ôth), which is intended to prove the authority of the word of Yahweh given by the prophet. One could also call to mind Ex. 6:7; 7:5; 14:4,18 (P), or 7:17; 8:6 (10); 10:2 (J),[75] where the sign consists in the deliverance from Egypt. This formula occurs four times in Deutero-Isaiah (Isa. 45:3,6; 49:23,26),[76] in Joel 2:27; Mal. 3:6; Jer. 24:7; and with the imperative, "know that...," in Ps. 46:11(10) (here only 'anokhi).

The point at issue here is the recognition that Yahweh is God (cf. Dt. 4:35; 7:9; 1 K. 8:60; 2 K. 19:19). One encounters the execution of an announced punishment (Ezk. 6:7; 13:14; 7:4,27; 11:10,12), or the reassembling of dispersed Israel (Ezk. 36:11,23,38; 37:6,13), as signs by which Yahweh may be known.

Ringgren

---

[75] *Ibid.*, 23f.=62f.
[76] Cf. above.

הוד *hôdh*

Contents: I. 1. Etymology; 2. Parallel Terms; 3. Occurrences. II. 1. *hodh* in Relation to God; 2. In Relation to the King; 3. In Relation to Moses/Joshua; 4. Other Occurrences; 5. In Proper Names.

I. 1. *Etymology.* The etymological derivation of *hodh* is disputed. Attempts have been made to establish connections between *hodh* and **neḥôdh* or Arab. *nahuda*, "to be beautiful, strong,"[1] Arab. *'awada*, "to be hard, difficult,"[2] West Semitic *ydh* in the hiphil (cf. also the proper names),[3] and Akk. *addu*, "thunder."[4]

2. *Parallel Terms.* Similar concepts connected with *hodh* illuminate its semantic field: → הדר *hādhār*, "majesty," in Ps. 21:6 (Eng. v. 5); 45:4(3); 96:6; 104:1; 111:3; Job 40:10; 1 Ch. 16:27 (in the Psalms, *hodh* is found almost exclusively in the phrase *hodh vehadhar*, "glory [splendor, honor] and majesty"). In 1 Ch. 29:11 *hodh* is associated with *gedhullah*, "greatness," *gebhurah*, "power," *tiph'ereth*, "glory," and *netsach*, "victory." In Ps. 145:5, the construct expression *hadhar*

---

hôdh. G. Boström, *Proverbia-Studien. LUA*, 30/3 (1935), 139; H. Gross, "Die Gottebenbildlichkeit des Menschen," *Lex tua veritas. Festschrift H. Junker* (1961), 89-100, esp. 96ff.; S. Mowinckel, *Psalmenstudien*, II (1922), 158; Pedersen, *ILC*, I-II, 237f.; D. Vetter, *THAT*, I, 472ff.

[1] Cf. F. Zorell, *Lexicon Hebraicum et Aramaicum Veteris Testamenti* (1966), 186a with additional references; E. König, *Hebr. and Aram. Wörterbuch zum AT* (1910), 76b.
[2] Cf. J. Barth, *Wurzeluntersuchungen zum hebr. and aram. Lexicon* (1902), 11.
[3] *GesB*, 176b.
[4] *CAD*, I/1, 111; cf. H. Cazelles, *VT*, 20 (1970), 124; however, *addu*=Adad/Hadad.

kebhodh hodhekha, "the glorious splendor of thy majesty," describes Yahweh's majesty. The following terms appear in synonymous parallelism with *hodh: tehillah,* "praise" (Hab. 3:3); *'oz,* "strength," and *tiph'ereth,* "beauty" (Ps. 96:6), or *chedhvah,* "joy" (1 Ch. 16:27); *niphla'oth,* "wondrous works" (Ps. 145:5); *kabhodh,* "glory" (Ps. 21:6[5]); *ga'on,* "majesty," and *gobhah,* "dignity" (Job 40:10); and *shenoth,* "years" (Prov. 5:9).

3. *Occurrences. hodh* is ascribed to God (Ps. 8:2[1]; 96:6; 111:3; 145:5; 148:13; Hab. 3:3; Job 37:22; 1 Ch. 16:27; 29:11), the king (Jer. 22:18; Ps. 21:6 [5]; etc.), individuals (Nu. 27:20; Prov. 5:9; etc.), the people (Hos. 14:7[6]), animals (Zec. 10:3; etc.), and plants (Hos. 14:7[6]). *hodh* can also be used to describe a person's complexion (Dnl. 10:8).

hodh occurs 24 times in the OT (8 times in Pss., 3 times each in Job and 1 Ch., twice each in Zec. and Dnl., and once each in Nu., Isa., Jer., Hos., Hab., and Prov.).

II. 1. *hodh in Relation to God.* God's *hodh* is manifest in his lordship in creation and history: the description of Yahweh's majesty in Ps. 104:1b,2a (he is clothed with *hodh vehadhar,* "honor and majesty," and with a garment of light)[5] is continued in affirmations concerning creation. His creating and maintaining the universe are part of his "honor and majesty" (v. 1) (→ הדר *hādhār*). Because of this majesty, the psalmist praises him (v. 1). Thus the praise of God's "glory above earth and heaven" acknowledges his manifest power (Ps. 148:13; cf. v. 5; 8:2[1]; cf. v. 4[3]; if *tenah* in 8:2[1] is to be read as *nathattah,* "set," it is particularly emphasized how evident God's "glory" is). The response to his "glory" is the exaltation of his name (Ps. 148:13).[6] Since it is the *hodh* of the Omnipotent One, such praise must embrace the whole earth, even ignorant children, the old and the young, and all peoples with their kings (Ps. 148:11-13; 8:2,3[1,2]).

hodh vehadhar, "honor and majesty," stand as servants before God, who is distinguished from the nothingness of heathen gods by his creation of the heavens (Ps. 96:6; 1 Ch. 16:27). They are attributes of his universal dominion, of his being king and judge (Ps. 96:10). His creation and right judgment of the peoples belong here (vv. 10ff.). Thus David pays homage to God in 1 Ch. 29:11 when he says: "Thine is the... majesty" (*hodh,* which appears in parallelism with *gedhullah,* "greatness," *gebhurah,* "power," *tiph'ereth,* "beauty," and *netsach,* "victory"). For all that is in the heavens and in the earth is God's, and he is head and ruler over all, and all things come from him (cf. vv. 12ff.). *hodh* is God's royal attribute.

If Job could have put on God's royal robes (Job 40:10), he would also have had to perform his sovereign tasks of abasing the proud and haughty and destroying the wicked (→ הדר *hādhār*). *hodh* is also an attribute of the royal judge (cf.

---

[5] Cf. R. Eisler, *Weltenmantel und Himmelszelt* (1910), I, 51ff.

[6] On 8:2,3(1,2), cf. also R. Tournay, "Le psaume VIII et la doctrine biblique du Nom," *RB,* 78 (1971), 18-30: the name of God itself represents the revelation of majesty.

Ps. 96:6). *hodh* and *hadhar* are so much an expression of the greatness of God's sovereign dominion that the ironic invitation to Job to put them on demonstrates human weakness (Job 40:10). Thus *hodh* reflects Israel's astonishment and joy at Yahweh's power, and it is a reason for calling the whole earth again and again to praise God, to give Yahweh the glory (Ps. 96:7ff.; cf. Job 40:9).

Israel especially praises the splendor of the heavenly ruler, since it has experienced his *hodh* in the mighty demonstrations in its history. Generation after generation lauds and declares his wonderful works. They speak of the *hadhar kebhodh hodh*, "the glorious splendor of (his) majesty" (Ps. 145:5), when they refer to Yahweh's helping acts (cf. the parallel ideas denoting his historical activity). God's rule is "honor and majesty" (*hodh vehadhar*, Ps. 111:3). His help is unforgettable and full of wonders. For Israel the salvation and preservation of the people becomes God's *hodh* (vv. 3f.). It is again a reason to praise him (vv. 1f.). The psalmist summons all creatures to praise God for his exalted name, praises him because his "glory" is above earth and heaven, and sings of the help he has given to his people (Ps. 148:13f.). Yahweh's *hodh* is also active in his coming: brightness and rays surround him. To his glory that covers the heavens there again corresponds his praise that fills the earth (Hab. 3:3b). This verse is a result of the reflection that, "in conjunction with the appearance of brightness in the following verse, desires to praise in hymnic style Yahweh's majesty, which is exalted over all the world."[7] Yahweh's appearance is accompanied by pestilence and by the shaking and splitting of the earth (Hab. 3:3ff.). The "majesty" that surrounds God at his appearing is terrible (Job 37:22), it is an expression of God's incomprehensibility by man (v. 23), who cannot bear the shining glory of his light. When God approaches in the storm he causes the power of his voice (RSV, "his majestic voice," *hodh qolo*) to be heard (Isa. 30:30). This brings destructive judgment upon the nations.[8]

2. *In Relation to the King.* *hodh* also serves as a royal attribute of the earthly ruler (Jer. 22:18). From the "external splendour of the power and pomp displayed by the court for the purpose of representation" to the "hidden religious motives on which the king's power to command, his dignity, and his authority to order the material and spiritual life of the nation are ultimately based," this term embraces "the special position which the king occupies among the people of the OT as the viceregent of God."[9] Like *hadhar*, *hodh* is a technical term for royal majesty.

The king's "glory and majesty" are especially evident in courageous military ventures (Ps. 45:4[3]); but the king is also obliged to seek truth and right (v. 5 [4]). Thus his acts are extolled by the concepts *hodh vehadhar*. In contrast to the lament for a man, "Ah my brother!" the lament for a dead king, "Ah lord! Ah

---

[7] J. Jeremias, *Theophanie* (1965), 45.

[8] On the relationship between thunder and *hodh*, cf. Cazelles, *loc. cit.;* cf. p. 123: Akk. *melammu* corresponds to Heb. *hodh vehadhar*, "honor and majesty," rather than to *kabhodh*, "glory"; cf. Élena Cassin, *La Splendeur divine. Introduction à l'étude de la mentalité mésopotamienne* (Paris, 1968).

[9] A. Weiser, *Psalms. OTL* (trans. 1962), 214.

his majesty!" (Jer. 22:18), shows clearly how closely the concept *hodh* is related to the office of king.

The phrase *hodh malkhuth*, "royal majesty," occurs in 1 Ch. 29:25 and Dnl. 11:21: the "majesty" of Solomon's kingdom was grounded in his reputation in all Israel and in the obedience of all Israel to him (1 Ch. 29:25). But royal majesty should not be given to a contemptible person (Dnl. 11:21). The lord of the time of salvation will win royal honor (Zec. 6:13: *hu' yissa' hodh*), i.e., he will become king and ruler (cf. v. 13a,b).

As with *hadhar,* it is hard to determine whether *hodh* was used first with reference to the earthly or the heavenly king. Some scholars are of the opinion that the word *hodh* was "frequently attributed to a king and then, metaphorically, also to God," [10] while others think it was "applied first of all to God," and that it is God "who gives the king a share in his own majesty, glory, and might." [11] The ratio of passages in which *hodh* occurs favors the latter view: it refers to God 11 times; it is applied to the king in Ps. 21:6(5) and 45:4(3) together with *hadhar;* it occurs in the dirge in Jer. 22:18, in the phrase *hodh malkhuth* in 1 Ch. 29:25 and Dnl. 11:21, [12] and in Zec. 6:13 with reference to the lord of the time of salvation.

3. *In Relation to Moses/Joshua.* In the appointment of Joshua (Nu. 27:20) Moses secures the obedience of the community to Joshua by transferring his *hodh* to him. [13] The form of this transfer is uncertain. It is, however, a prerequisite if Joshua is to take over Moses' office. But just as Moses gave only a portion of his *hodh* to Joshua, so also the relationship of Joshua to the priest Eleazar is one of dependence. [14] It is best to translate *hodh* here by "glory, majesty, authority." [15]

4. *Other Occurrences.* Independence and autonomy belong to the "honor" (*hodh*) of man, so that the threatening and loss of wealth can mean the loss of honor (Prov. 5:9). In Dnl. 10:8 *hodh* means "complexion, appearance, countenance," which reflects knowledge, feeling, and experience. It is an expression of human independence. Israel's "beauty," which Yahweh promises him (Hos. 14:7 [6]), is compared with the "beauty" of the olive tree, which is that this tree brings forth fruit even in old age. Its trunk is strong, and it is surrounded with an abundance of tender twigs with unwithering leaves. [16]

In the battle of liberation Yahweh will make his people victorious heroes, so that they are like the "splendid" (RSV "proud") steed of the fighting God (Zec. 10:3).

---

[10] M. Noth, *Numbers. OTL* (trans. 1968), 215.

[11] Weiser, *loc. cit.*

[12] Cf. above.

[13] Noth, *loc. cit.*

[14] *Ibid.*

[15] Noth translates "vitality," but mentions the uncertainty of the meaning. *hodh* denotes something active, not something visible (*ibid.*).

[16] Dalman, *AuS,* IV, 164.

In Job 39:20 the *hodh* of the terrifying snorting of the horse is a figure for the magnificence of this proud animal. This is an indication of the majesty of the Creator (cf. the questions in v. 19).

5. *In Proper Names*. Names composed of *hodh* and a form of *Yahweh* signify an acknowledgment and glorification of Yahweh (*hodhiyyah*, "Hodiah," 1 Ch. 4:19; Neh. 8:7; 9:5; 10:11,14,19[10,13,18]; *hodheyah*, "Hodeyah," Neh. 7:43 [*qere*]). Other combinations also occur ('*achihudh*, "Ahihud," 1 Ch. 8:7; '*abhihudh*, "Abihud," 1 Ch. 8:3 '*ammihudh*, "Ammihud," Nu. 1:20; 2:18; 7:48, 53; etc.), which originally no doubt ascribed *hodh* to tribal members. [17]

Warmuth

---

[17] Noth, *IPN*, 146; J. J. Stamm, "Hebräische Ersatznamen," *Festschrift B. Landsberger* (1965), 413-424, esp. 416, 418.

הַוָּה *havvāh;* הֹוָה *hōvāh*

Contents: I. Etymology, Occurrences. II. Semantic Field and Ideology. III. In the LXX.

I. Etymology, Occurrences. *havvah* is to be derived from the root *hvy*. But there seem to be several roots *hvy* in the Semitic languages. On the one hand, Hebrew knows *hvh* as a secondary form of *hyh* (*hayah*), "to be," where a connection with Akk. *ewû/emû* is probably to be assumed;[1] *h^avāh* is the normal form of the verb in Aramaic.[2] Von Soden also connects *ewû* with Arab. *hawā*, "to fall, die"; cf. Syr. *h^ewā*, "to fall."[3] Furthermore, there is an Arab. *hawiya*, "to love" (cf. *hawan*, "inordinate desire, caprice"), which is also to be connected with Ugar. *hwy*,[4] if it means "to desire."[5] *KBL*[3] connects *havvah* with these last words, and gives it the meaning "caprice, inordinate desire."

Ugar. *hwt* seems to be related to Akk. *awātu/amātu*, "word"; Guillaume[6] connects Heb. *havvah* with this, and gives it the meaning "command, curse."[7]

---

havvāh. G. R. Driver, "Witchcraft in the OT הוה," *JRAS* (1943), 6-16; A. Guillaume, "Magical Terms in the OT," *JRAS* (1942), 111-131.

[1] With von Soden, *AHw*, 266.
[2] M. Wagner, *Aramaismen. BZAW*, 96 (1966), 45; *DISO*, 63f.
[3] Cf. J. L. Palache, *Semantic Notes on the Hebrew Lexicon* (Leiden, 1959), 22f.
[4] *CTA*, 5 [I* AB], I, 15; *Ugaritica*, V (1968), 559: RS 24.293, line 5.
[5] *WUS*, No. 820; *CML;* but according to *UT*, 754a, "to be"; on this latter meaning, however, cf. C. Virolleaud, *GLECS*, 8 (1957-59), 65f.
[6] Guillaume, 113f.
[7] See below.

The word *havvah* occurs 16 times in the OT: ten times it occurs in the plural, and twice it is written as *hayyah* (Job 6:2; 30:13). These occurrences stand exclusively in poetic texts. *hovah* appears twice (Isa. 47:11; Ezk. 7:26).

II. Semantic Field and Ideology. The word *havvah* is usually connected with men who are unfaithful and rebellious against God, who are not willing to adapt themselves to the good ordinances of God, but pervert the right according to their evil desires. Mic. 7:3 speaks of *havvath nephesh*, i.e., the inner desire of man which leads to an evil and perverted action. *havvah* is thus connected with the *resha'im*, "wicked" (Prov. 10:3), and the *boghedhim*, "treacherous" (Prov. 11:6). Ideologically the point is that man must hearken to the voice of God and adapt himself to the ordinance of God in order to be able to act righteously. When man breaks free from God and does not get his wisdom from him, he deprives himself of the good life. He then becomes a *rasha'*, "wicked person," or *boghedh*, "treacherous person," who follows the impulses and inordinate desires of his evil heart, which leads to malice, lying, perversity, oppression, etc. It is typical for the word *havvah* or more frequently *havvoth* to appear in contexts that speak of *'aven*, "wickedness," *sheqer*, "lie, falsehood," *mera'*, "evildoer" (Prov. 17:4), *resha'*, "wickedness," *holelim*, "the boastful," *po'ale 'aven*, "evildoers," *dobhere khazabh*, "those who speak lies," *'ish damim umirmah*, "bloodthirsty and deceitful men" (Ps. 5:5-7 [Eng. vv. 4-6]), etc.

It is often emphasized in the OT that the perverted and evil act has its root in the innermost part of man (e.g., Gen. 6:5; 8:21). He who does evil walks in the stubbornness of his heart and follows his deceitful heart instead of hearkening to the voice of God (Jer. 7:24ff.; 11:7f.; 14:14; 23:17). Therefore it is natural for *havvah* to mean both the inner root of evil, "the inordinate desire," and its consequences, falsehood, perversity, deception, and misfortune. The plural *havvoth* in particular is used with reference to the fruits of evil desire. Prov. 17:4 has to do above all with deceitful and lying speech: *leshon havvoth*, "a mischievous tongue," and *sephath 'aven*, "wicked lips," mean a tongue and lips that speak what is rooted in evil desire. In Ps. 5:10(9) (*qirbam havvoth*, RSV, "their heart is destruction") and 55:12(11) (*havvoth beqirbah*, RSV, "ruin is in its midst"), emphasis is placed on the inner root of evil which leads to outward evil (*'aven*, "mischief," *'amal*, "trouble") in the form of falsehood (*dobhere khazabh*, "those who speak lies," *mirmah*, "fraud") and oppression (*'ish damim*, "bloodthirsty men," *tokh*, "oppression"). In Ps. 38:13(12) *dibberu havvoth*, "they speak of ruin," stands in parallelism with *yehgu mirmoth*, "they meditate treachery"; and Ps. 52:4f.(2f.) says that those who desire *havvoth* (RSV, "plot destruction") work treachery (*'asah remiyyah*) and love evil (*ra'*) and lying (*sheqer*). The main point at issue here is evil and deceitful speaking. Verse 9(7) of the same psalm says that he who does not trust in God, but in his wealth, is strong in his *havvah*, "destruction." Job 6:30 speaks of unjust speech.

When he who follows his own thoughts and desires sits on the judgment seat, the result is unjust judgment, oppression, and the shedding of innocent blood. Ps. 94 speaks of this, and significantly calls the judgment seat a *kisse' havvoth*, "seat of destruction" (v. 20), i.e., the seat where men sit who are called *resha'im*, "wicked" (v. 3), *mere'im*, "wicked," and *po'ale 'aven*, "evildoers" (v. 16). It is a seat where one uses violence in the name of right (*yotser 'amal 'ale choq*, "who frame mischief by statute," v. 20).

When Prov. 19:13 says that a foolish son (*ben kesil*) is *havvoth le'abhiv* (RSV, "ruin to his father"), *havvoth* seems to mean above all "ruin." The same is true of *debher havvoth*, "ruin-bringing pestilence," in Ps. 91:3. "Evil desire" does not fit the context of Job 6:2 or 30:13 (the reading here is *hayyah*) either, but only the consequences of evil desire, viz., "ruin, calamity." In two passages, Isa. 47:11 and Ezk. 7:26, the word *hovah* means "ruin, disaster," as punishment for the pride and apostasy of men. In the former passage *hovah* appears in synonymous parallelism with *ra'ah*, "evil," and *sho'ah*, "ruin." It is uncertain whether *hovah* here can be derived from Arab. *hawā*, "to blow, storm, be stormy."

III. In the LXX. The LXX does not translate words derived from the root *hwy* consistently, as the following list shows: *adikía*, "unrighteousness, wickedness, wrongdoing" (Ps. 52:4[2]; 55:12[11]); *anomía*, "lawlessness" (Ps. 57:2[1]; 94:20); *apóleia*, "destruction" (Prov. 11:6); *mátaios*, "idle, empty," *mataiótēs*, "emptiness" (Ps. 5:10[9]; 38:13[12]; 52:9[7]); *odýnes*, "pains, woes" (Job 6:2); *talaipōría*, "wretchedness, distress, trouble, misery" (Isa. 47:11); *ouaí*, "woe, alas" (Ezk. 7:26); *aischýnē*, "shame, disgrace, ignominy" (Prov. 19:13); etc.

KBL³ reckons with two roots: I "caprice, inordinate desire" (Mic. 7:3; Prov. 10:3; 11:6), and II "ruin" (the other occurrences in the OT). Guillaume thinks all the occurrences in the OT come from one root meaning "to speak," and he understands *havvah* as a "magical word, exorcism." [8] In fact, in eight passages *havvah* is either connected with organs of speech or stands beside a word that denotes speaking. As an analogue, he cites Akk. *amātu/awātu*, "word," "word of command or decree," "exorcism." Driver, however, objects that *amātu* means "word" in general and not a magical word in particular. Instead, he connects *havvah* with the Arabic root *hawā*, "to blow," and translates in all passages "evil wind," which at the same time can also mean "ruin or distress."

Erlandsson

---

8 Guillaume, 111ff.

הוֹי *hôy*

Contents: I. Occurrences. II. Grammatical Construction of *hôy* and *'ôy*. III. Basic Meaning of *hôy* and *'ôy*. IV. Form Criticism. V. The *hôy* Oracles of the Prophets.

I. Occurrences. The interjection *hôy* is found in both Biblical and Middle Hebrew. The interjection *hô*, attested only in Am. 5:16, is derived from it.[1] The latter word is represented in the LXX by *ouaí*, as is the former in most cases (32 times). *hôy* is also represented by *ó* (12 times) and *oímmoi* (once). The interjection *'ôy* is similarly represented in the LXX by *ouaí* (14 times), *oímmoi* (4 times), and *ó* (3 times). The form *'ôyāh* is also represented by *oímmoi*.

The words *hôy* and *'ôy* may be related to the Ugar. interjections *'u*,[2] *w*,[3] and possibly *my*,[4] all meaning "alas," but the nature of the relationship is obscure. Cf. also Akk. *ū'a*, *u'ai*, and *ai*, "alas."[5]

II. Grammatical Construction of *hôy* and *'ôy*. The use of the same words in the LXX to render both *hôy* and *'ôy* might suggest that there is no essential difference between the two interjections. Such an assumption is contradicted, however, by the different syntax of the two words, pointed out with emphasis by Wanke. His statistical survey, rechecked by C. Hardmeier,[6] shows that the 51 occurrences of *hôy* include 6 where it is used as an exclamation lamenting a death (1 K. 13:30; Jer. 22:18 [4 times]; 34:5)[7] and 8 where it is an independent

---

hôy. R. J. Clifford, "The Use of HÔY in the Prophets," *CBQ*, 28 (1966), 458-464; J. L. Crenshaw, "The Influence of the Wise upon Amos," *ZAW*, 79 (1967), 42-52; G. Fohrer, "Prophetie und Magie," in his *Studien zur alttestamentlichen Prophetie, 1949-1965. BZAW*, 99 (1967), 242-264, esp. 254f.; E. Gerstenberger, "The Woe-Oracles of the Prophets," *JBL*, 81 (1962), 249-263; J. Hempel, *Die althebräische Literatur* (1930), 60f., 66; H. J. Hermisson, *Studien zur israelitische Spruchweisheit. WMANT*, 28 (1968), 88f.; W. Janzen, "'*Ašrê* and *Hôi* in the OT," *HThR*, 62 (1970), 432f.; idem, *Mourning Cry and Woe Oracle. BZAW*, 125 (1972); H.-J. Krause (*sic*), "*hôj* als profetische Leichenklage über das eigene Volk im 8. Jahrhundert," *ZAW*, 85 (1973), 15-46; J. Scharbert, *Der Schmerz im AT. BBB*, 8 (1955), 70f.; G. Wanke, "אוֹי und הוֹי," *ZAW*, 78 (1966), 215-18; W. W. Weir, *The Nature and Origin of the Woe-Speeches of the Prophets* (diss., Southern California, 1971); cf. *DissAbsInt*, 32 (1971/72), 1069-A; C. Westermann, *Basic Forms of Prophetic Speech* (trans. 1967), 190-98; H. Wildberger, "Weherufe über Rücksichtslosigkeit und Leichtsinn," *BK*, X (1972), 175-202; J. G. Williams, "The Alas-Oracles of the Eighth Century Prophets," *HUCA*, 38 (1967), 75-91; H. W. Wolff, *Amos, the Prophet* (trans. 1973), 17-34; idem, *Joel und Amos. BK*, XIV/2 (1969), 284-87.

1 *KBL³*.
2 *CTA* [2], 32, 11,20,23,31; cf. Egyp. *i*, "O!"
3 *CTA*, 32, 4,10,11, etc.
4 *CTA*, 5 [I* AB], VI, 23; 6 [I AB], I, 6.
5 *AHw*, 23.
6 In Wolff, *BK*, XIV/2, 285, n. 1.
7 Cf. *hô hô* in Am. 5:16, a lament for the dead.

interjection (Isa. 1:24; 17:12; 55:1; Jer. 30:7; 47:6; Zec. 2:10 [twice], 11 [Eng. vv. 6,7]), thus indicating that *hôy* is fundamentally a pure interjection, which is always linked with a substantive in laments for the dead. [8] Among the other 37 occurrences of *hôy*, there are only 4 instances when it is followed by a preposition (*'el*: Jer. 48:1; *'al*: Jer. 50:27; Ezk. 13:3; *le*: Ezk. 13:18). A participle follows in 23 instances (Isa. 5:8,11,18,20; 10:1; 29:15; 31:1; 33:1; 45:9,10; Jer. 22:13; 23:1; Ezk. 34:2; Am. 5:18; Mic. 2:1; Hab. 2:6,9,12,15,19; Zeph. 2:5; 3:1; Zec. 11:17; also the conjectural passages Am. 5:7; Hab. 2:5), a substantive or proper noun in 7 instances (Isa. 1:4; 10:5; 18:1; 28:1; 29:1; 30:1; Nah. 3:1), and an adjective in 3 instances (Isa. 5:21,22; Am. 6:1). Like the participles, the substantives and adjectives describe the conduct of the person or country to which the *hôy* is addressed.

In contrast, the word *'ôy*, which occurs 23 times, appears as an independent interjection only in Nu. 24:23, a late passage; in Prov. 23:29 it is used as a substantive. In the majority of cases (19 times, or 20 counting *'ôyāh*), it is followed by *le* + suff. (in Isa. 3:9 *lenaphshām*). [9] In 6 cases the suffix is 1st person singular (Isa. 6:5; 24:16; Jer. 4:31; 10:19; 15:10; 45:3; also Ps. 120:5 [*'ôyāh*]), in five cases 2nd singular (Nu. 21:29; Jer. 13:27; 48:46; Ezk. 16:23 [twice]), in five cases 1st plural (1 S. 4:7,8; Jer. 4:13; 6:4; Lam. 5:16), and twice 3rd plural (Hos. 7:13; 9:12; also Isa. 3:9). Ezk. 24:6,9 can also be included here (*'ôy* followed by the object addressed, the "bloody city"). Last but not least, we may note that most of these 21 occurrences of *'ôy* are followed by a motivating clause. In 12 instances this clause is introduced by *kî* (also in Jer. 48:46 conj.), in 3 it is an independent main clause, once it is a question, and once an infinitive construction. In other words, *'ôy* acquires its specific meaning in each case from the clause that follows it, without which it would be meaningless.

In certain respects this situation resembles the use of Ugar. *ỉ* (*'u*), which is always followed by *l* + the 2nd person suffix, together with a motivating clause introduced by *d*, "because."

III. Basic Meaning of hôy and 'ôy.
The difference in the grammatical construction of *hôy* and *'ôy* reveals the difference in their basic meanings. The construction with *le* + suff. always restricts *'ôy* to specific persons, groups, or well-defined collectives. The motivating clause that is usually added makes it clear that the person concerned is undone (→ אבד *'ābhadh*, Nu. 21:29; Jer. 48:46), can no longer live (→ חיה *chāyāh*, Nu. 24:23), will die at the hands of murderers (*hāragh*, Jer. 4:31), is lost (→ דמה *dāmāh*, Isa. 6:5) or ruined (*šdd*, Jer. 4:13; cf. *shōdh*, Hos. 7:13)—in short, faces death and destruction. As a further detail we may note that in combination with *le* + suff. in the 1st singular or plural *'ôy* expresses fear or dread on the part of the speaker (→ ירא *yārē'*, 1 S. 4:7,8); in combination with *le* + suff. in the 2nd person or 3rd plural, it expresses a threat. [10]

---

[8] Williams.

[9] Cf. Brockelmann, *Synt.*, § 11c.

[10] Wanke, 217.

No motivating clause, however, is needed to determine the meaning of *hôy*. Its meaning is defined by its use as an interjection in laments for the dead. In combination with *'ādhôn* (Jer. 22:18; 34:5), *'āch* (1 K. 13:30; Jer. 22:18), *'āchôth* (Jer. 22:18), and *hōdhōh* (Jer. 22:18), *hôy* constitutes the lament "Alas, lord," etc. All the other occurrences of *hôy* appear without exception in the prophetic literature, where our word takes on the meaning of a threat (cf. V).

IV. Form Criticism. The fundamental difference we have just observed between *'ôy* and *hôy* can be traced also in form and genre criticism.[11] The typical use of *'ôy* in the expressions "woe is me" and "woe to us" is rightly termed a "cry of anguish or despair."[12] It is also used by the Philistines when the ark arrives in the Israelite camp (1 S. 4:7,8) and by the foes attacking Jerusalem when night begins to fall (Jer. 6:4). But Isaiah can cry out the same when confronted with the glory of Yahweh (Isa. 6:5), as can Jeremiah in one of his confessions (Jer. 15:10), or the people of Israel (Jer. 4:13; 10:19). This cry of anguish is therefore not something peculiar to Israel. Neither is it possible to determine a particular genre to which this cry belongs. It is found in narrative genres (1 S. 4; Isa. 6), in laments of the community (Lam. 5:16) or of the individual (Ps. 120:5; cf. Jer. 15:10), in threats pronounced by the prophets (Jer. 4:13,31; 6:4; etc.), and in an apocalyptic text (Isa. 24:16). The situation is not much different with occurrences of the phrase "woe to you/him/them" used as a threat. Apart from the threat against Moab inserted into the song summoning the people to build up Heshbon (Nu. 21:29),[13] we find this cry in the prophets' threats (Isa. 3:9,11;[14] Jer. 13:27; Ezk. 24:9;[15] Hos. 7:13; 9:12) and invectives (Ezk. 16:23; 24:6).

Fundamentally, *hôy* forms part of laments for the dead; in the prophetic literature it occurs as an element of prophetic invective. There is a formal similarity between the use of *hôy* in laments for the dead and its use in invective: in both contexts it is followed by a nominal construction. In invective, however, these nominal forms do not define the relationship of the mourner to the subject of his lament as they do in laments for the dead. They describe instead the reprehensible conduct of men toward Yahweh, thus motivating the threat that follows (Isa. 1:4; 5:8,11; 18:1; 28:1; 45:9,10; Am. 6:1; Mic. 2:1; Nah. 3:1; Zeph. 2:5; 3:1). But we also find prophetic invective introduced by *hôy* without any associated threat (Isa. 5:18,20,21,22; 29:15; Am. 5:7 conj., 18; Hab. 2:5 conj., 6, 9,12,15,19); the exclamation subjects human misconduct to harsh criticism. The fact that it is a human being who formulates and pronounces the *hôy* cry in both laments for the dead and invective also provides a common bond between the

---

[11] Cf. Weir.

[12] Wolff, *BK*, XIV/2, 284f.

[13] Cf. M. Noth, *Numbers* (trans. 1968), 165; Noth terms the passage a "lament."

[14] G. Fohrer, *Das Buch Jesaja*, I (²1966), 62f. (p. 65 in 1960 ed.); Fohrer terms the passage a "wisdom aphorism."

[15] Cf. W. Zimmerli, *BK*, XIII/2 (1969), *in loc.*

two. It is therefore reasonable to suppose that the OT prophets drew on laments for the dead to shape their message of judgment and lend it emphasis. This theory seems the more plausible when one considers that such pointed criticism presupposes the kind of conscious reflection that likewise leads to the borrowing of the lament for the dead.[16] When prophetic invective using this cry occurs independently,[17] even though the unspoken threat of judgment is unmistakable, the hôy oracles of the prophets closely resemble laments for the dead even in content.

In other words, we are suggesting that in the hôy oracles the prophets were seeking to make the point that judgment is inescapable. The subsequent development of this genre confirms this theory. The most striking change is the incorporation of the invective motivating God's judgment into the words spoken by God, obliterating the prevalent distinction between invective, spoken by the prophet, and threat, spoken by God. Because both ultimately go back to Yahweh, the prophet has put both into the mouth of Yahweh speaking in the 1st person (Isa. 10:1,5; 29:1; 30:1; 31:1; Jer. 22:13; 23:1; Ezk. 13:3,18; 34:2; cf. also Isa. 33:1; Zec. 11:17).

With respect to the question of the secular background of the prophetic hôy oracles, we thus conclude that the most likely answer is adaptation of a cry found in laments for the dead;[18] Westermann's proposed connection with curse formulas appears incorrect. But there is still the question whether the prophets adopted the cry of lament directly, to lend emphasis to their message, or whether we should assume that there was an intermediate stage consisting of hôy clauses used by early pedagogical clan wisdom to warn men against the evil way that leads to death.[19] The nouns "brother" and "sister" show that the cry of lament for the dead is associated with the clan, but this observation does not prove anything for the hôy oracles of the prophets. And Amos' use of hô hô (5:16) in lament for the dead rather than the hôy used in the hôy oracles does not necessarily imply stereotyped hôy oracles; dialectal differences are an equally good explanation.[20] Since there is also no attestation for such pedagogical hôy sayings, there is no need to accept this hypothesis. Nonetheless, many 'ôy sayings undoubtedly belong to the realm of proverbial wisdom (Isa. 3:11; Prov. 23:29; Eccl. 10:16 conj.). It must also be observed that the differences between 'ôy and hôy emphasized above (II, III) became blurred in the course of time. On the one hand, minatory 'ôy makes its appearance in prophetic invective and threat; on the other, some hôy oracles come to use the prepositional construction of 'ôy oracles and are understood as threats. This shows that the influence of wisdom did not come at the beginning of the development of these oracles but rather made itself felt after the passage of time.[21]

---

[16] Cf. Wanke, 218.

[17] Cf. Hempel, 60f.; W. Zimmerli, *BK*, XIII/1 (1969), 286.

[18] This is the view of Hempel, 66; Wanke; Clifford; and H. W. Wolff, *BK*, XIV/2.

[19] Wolff, *op. cit.*, with bibliography; cf. Janzen and, most recently, Cazelles, *TDOT*, I, 445.

[20] Cf. Wolff, *op. cit.*, 286.

[21] Cf. Westermann, *Isaiah 40–66. OTL* (trans. 1969), 166.

V. The hôy Oracles of the Prophets.

When we come to examine the prophetic hôy oracles, the first thing we observe is a certain tendency for them to occur in series. In Isa. 5, six hôy oracles are linked together (vv. 8,11,18,20,21, 22) and in Hab. 2, five are found (vv. 6,9,12,15,19; textual emendation yields a sixth in v. 5). The only two hôy oracles in Amos are found in close proximity (5:18 and 6:1; 5:7 conj. should possibly be included), and the only two in Deutero-Isaiah occur side by side (Isa. 45:9,10).

The themes developed in the hôy oracles correspond to those observed elsewhere in the preaching of the prophets. Disdain for righteousness and justice is condemned in Jer. 22:13 and Am. 5:7 (conj.); Isa. 10:1 speaks in similar terms of those who make iniquitous decrees, and Mic. 2:1 castigates the greed of the rich. In all of these oracles, the misconduct in question lies in the social sphere. Thematically similar but couched in more general terms are the oracles in Isa. 5 directed against large landowners (v. 8), drunkards (vv. 11,22), and godless sophists (v. 20). Self-confidence combined with mockery of God or criticism of his governance is attacked in Am. 5:18; 6:1; Isa. 5:18,21; 28:1; 45:9,10. Here should be classed also the oracle against those who worship wood and stone (Hab. 2:19), because it, too, like the hôy oracles just mentioned, concerns the cultic sphere. In the political realm, the despotism of those in power (Isa. 29:15), their misguided policy of forming alliances (Isa. 30:1; 31:1), their greed, ruthlessness, and excesses (Hab. 2:5 conj., 6,9,12,15) are stigmatized. The leaders of the people, spiritual and temporal, are called worthless shepherds (Jer. 23:1; Ezk. 34:2; Zec. 11:17), foolish prophets or deluded prophetesses (Ezk. 13:3,18). The hôy oracles are addressed to all realms of life and all classes of people, and thus even to Jerusalem (Isa. 29:1; Zeph. 3:1) or Israel as a whole (Isa. 1:4). Last but not least, this observation that the hôy oracles reflect the entire range of the prophetic message is further strengthened by the fact that such sayings, in the context of oracles against foreign nations, are directed against Assyria (Isa. 10:5), Ethiopia (Isa. 18:1), Nineveh (Nah. 3:1), and Moab (Jer. 48:1), as well as the Cretans (Zeph. 2:5) and the "destroyer" (Isa. 33:1). These oracles indirectly promise salvation for Israel.

When we come to examine the content of the prophetic hôy oracles, we must first remember that most of these oracles are in the form of invective, formulated by the prophet himself. In them the prophet displays the sinful behavior and wrong conduct of men. He is able to do this by judging the actions of men from the perspective of Yahwism, observing his contemporaries through the eyes of Yahweh. As in the case of laments for the dead, we are therefore dealing here, too, with a definition of the relationship between the speaker and those he is addressing. The continued influence of laments for the dead on the prophetic hôy oracles can be seen further in the earlier hôy oracles of Amos and Isaiah, where there are frequently overtones of lament. The prophet does not simply stand on the side of Yahweh; he remains throughout a member of his own people. Because of his solidarity with them, he suffers under the message of judgment that he is commissioned to proclaim.

One final consideration must be mentioned in this context. If the hôy oracles of the prophets go back to the cry of lament for the dead, to cry hôy is tanta-

mount to a prediction of death, a proclamation of the judgment of Yahweh.[22]
Those to whom the *hôy* is addressed have separated themselves from Yahweh
through their godless actions or conduct, or at least have distanced themselves
from him. But separation or distance from Yahweh ultimately means death. One
might object that the *hôy* oracles are invective, not threats, and that in association with a threat their only function is to motivate the predicted judgment of
Yahweh. Ultimately, however, this position is untenable. The real distinction is
that in invective the prophet speaks, whereas in threats it is Yahweh who speaks
through the prophet. If, however, this prophet discloses sin, he does so with the
firm conviction that if the sin does not cease, Yahweh's response will be judgment. Thus the *hôy* oracles, as invective, remain the words of the prophets; but
the very use of *hôy* makes these words point with all possible emphasis and certainty to the deadly consequences entailed by such actions and conduct on the
part of men.

Zobel

---

[22] *Ibid.*

הוֹן *hôn*

Contents: I. 1. The Root *hwn*; 2. Etymology; 3. Meaning; 4. Occurrences; 5. Semantic
Field; 6. LXX. II. Use in the OT. III. Qumran.

I. 1. *The Root hwn.* The noun *hôn* is derived from the root *hwn*, which
is found in Hebrew, in Palestinian Jewish Aramaic (*havnā*, "wealth; ability,
strength"), and in Palestinian Christian Aramaic (*hôn*, "understanding"), as well
as in Syriac (*havnā*, "understanding"). Grelot claims to find in Ahikar 103 a
verb *hwn* meaning "put on (an article of clothing)."[1] In Ugaritic the name *hyn*
is found for the god ktr whss ("skillful and clever"). Gordon[2] leaves the name

---

hôn. E. Bammel, "πτωχός," *TDNT*, VI, 885-915; H. Cazelles, *Le Deutéronome. La Sainte
Bible* ([3]1966); L. de Dieu, *Animadversiones in Veteris Testamenti libros omnes* (1648); T.
Donald, "The Semantic Field of Rich and Poor in the Wisdom Literature of Hebrew and
Accadian," *OrAnt*, 3 (1964), 27-41; A. B. Ehrlich, *Randglossen zur hebräischen Bibel*, II
(1909, [2]1968); P. Grelot, "La racine HWN en Dt. I 41," *VT*, 12 (1962), 198-201; F. Hauck and
W. Kasch, "πλοῦτος. B. Riches and the Rich in the OT," *TDNT*, VI, 323-25; F. Horst,
"Zwei Begriffe für Eigentum (Besitz): *naḥᵃlāh* und *'ᵃhuzzāh*," *Verbannung und Heimkehr.
Festschrift W. Rudolph* (1961), 135-156; F. de Hummelauer, *Commentarius in Deuterono-
mium* (1901); A. Jamme, *Cahiers de Byrsa*, 8 (1958/59), 172 (cf. *Bibl*, 42 [1961], 146*, no.
2017); H. Junker, *Das Buch Job*. EB (1959); A. Kuschke, "Arm und Reich im AT mit
besonderer Berücksichtigung der nachexilischen Zeit," *ZAW*, 57 (1939), 31-57; J. D. Michaelis,
Supplementa ad lexica Hebraica, II (1785); N. Peters, *Das Buch Job. EHAT*, 21 (1928); A.
Schultens, *Opera minora* (1769); A. D. Singer, "Philological Notes," *JPOS*, 21 (1948), 104-109;
R. de Vaux, *AncIsr*, 72-74.

[1] See below.
[2] *UT*, No. 761.

untranslated, but Aistleitner [3] connects it with Heb. *hôn* and renders it "the skill-ful one" (cf. *hôn* in Palestinian Jewish Aram.). In Arabic, the verb *hāna* from the root *hwn* means "be or become light, of minor importance"; IV "treat care-lessly or scornfully, despise." Nouns from the same root include *haun*, "facility, ease," and *havān*, "shame, disgrace." The adjective *hayyin* means "easy, insignif-icant."

2. *Etymology*. The etymology of *hôn* can be traced through the verb *hwn*, which is attested only once in Hebrew: the hiphil *vattāhînû* occurs in Dt. 1:41bβ. The versions appear to diverge in their translations: LXX *synathroisthéntes;* Aquila *homonoḗsantes;* Targum *shar͏ᵉthûn*, "you began"; Syr. *'etgaragtûn*, "you incited yourselves"; Vulg. *pergeretis* (*in montem*). At a later date, the Aldine edition (*espeúsate*), the Arabic translation of Saadia, and the London polyglott render the verb as "you hastened (to go up)" (*badara* III); an Arabic manuscript published by Erpenius renders "you began" (*bada'a*). [4] Today [5] the Hebrew hiphil of *hwn* is almost universally associated with Arab. *hāna* and translated "treat casually, consider easy," or with the Arab. idiom *'ahāna* (*nafsahū*), "de-spise one's soul, risk one's life." [6] Others seek to interpret the hiphil of *hwn* as a term for putting on clothing, corresponding to the preceding verb *chāghar*, "gird." [7] Still others try emendation. [8] The meaning derived from the Arabic is unlikely because none of the ancient versions understood *hwn* in this sense; the Arabic translations in particular do not use the root *hāna*. Above all, however, it is impossible to derive some such meaning as "wealth" for the substantive *hôn* from a root *hwn* with the meaning "be light, easy." [9] The Hebrew mentality does not associate wealth with lightness or ease but rather with *kābhôdh*, "heaviness, weightiness," as witnessed by the juxtaposition of *'ōsher*, "riches," and *kābhôdh* in 1 K. 3:13 and eight other passages, and of both with *hôn* in Prov. 8:18, as well as the phrase *k͏ᵉbhôdh 'oshrô* in Est. 5:11. On the other hand, no one has sug-gested that in the verb *hwn* and the substantive *hôn* we are dealing with two different homophonic roots.

For a correct understanding of *hwn*, Rashi is of help. The context of Dt. 1:41bβ is Dt. 1:24-44, a passage that draws upon the original tradition of the Israelites' reaction to the report delivered by the men sent to spy out the land of Canaan (Nu. 13:22-24,27-31; 14:1b,4,11a,23b-25,39-45). The phrase *vattāhînû la'᷅lôth hāhārāh* in Dt. 1:41bβ corresponds in meaning not to Nu. 14:44a (cf. Dt. 1:43bβ) but to the statement in Nu. 14:40b: *hinnennû v͏ᵉ'ālînû 'el-hammāqôm 'ᵃsher-*

---

[3] *WUS,* No. 825.

[4] Michaelis, 516.

[5] Following de Dieu, 103; Schultens, 154; and Michaelis, 515f., no. 543.

[6] Singer, 106ff.; *KBL*[3].

[7] De Hummelauer, 190; Cazelles, 27f. Grelot (199) cites לתהן (from Ahikar 103), an explanation of "obscurum per obscurius."

[8] Ehrlich, 251: ותהיו.

[9] See above. The attempt on the part of H. L. Fleischer in Levy, *TW*, I, 423f. merely underscores the problem rather than solving it.

'āmar yhvh, "See, we are here, we will go up to the place which Yahweh has promised." Following rabbinic tradition, Rashi equates the meaning of vattāhînû la'ªlôth with that of hinnennû ve'ālînû and explains both as meaning nizdᵉmantem, "you were ready, made yourself ready." Now in Middle Heb. and Jewish Aram. the root zmn has a rather broad range of meanings. Rashi's use of zmn in the nithpael corresponds to the Jewish Aram. zᵉmîn, "ready" (Targ. Ex. 19:11,15; 34:2; = MT nākhôn, LXX hétoimos). Other meanings—if Dt. 1:41bβ had the nithpael of zmn instead of the hiphil of hwn—would agree with the way the versions interpret Dt. 1:41bβ: for the meaning "meet, encounter" (Heb. nithpael, Jewish Aram. ithpael[10]), cf. LXX (cf. Nu. 16:11, where MT y'd niphal = Targ. zmn ithpael = LXX synathroízomai); for the meaning "agree" (Dnl. 2:9; zmn ithpael), cf. Aquila; for the meaning "set about" (Jewish Aram. ithpael[11]), cf. the Targum on Dt. 1:41bβ and the versions. If we are not to assume that the versions —and Rashi—were merely guessing in their interpretation of hwn hiphil, we can only conclude that the root hwn found in Dt. 1:41bβ corresponds in meaning to the Heb. and Jewish Aram. root zmn. If so, the versions with their various renderings have grasped different portions of the range of meanings represented by hwn. Like zmn, then, hwn means "be ready"; the hiphil means "be ready, make oneself ready, set about."[12] This gives rise to the meaning "incite each other" (Syr.), "hasten (to do something)" (Saadia and others).

If we do not have to consider such meanings as "be easy, be light" for the root hwn, the emendations suggested for Job 30:24[13] and Hab. 2:5[14] are likewise unnecessary.

3. Meaning. The noun hôn, derived from the root hwn, "be ready," means "what stands ready," i.e., "property, possessions" = LXX tá hypárchonta (Prov. 6:31; 11:4 [Cod. A]), hē hýparxis (Prov. 13:11; 19:14). If a thief is caught, "he will pay sevenfold; he will give kol-hôn bêthô (all the goods of his house)." "House and wealth are inherited from fathers, but a prudent wife is from Yahweh" (Prov. 19:14). In these passages there is not yet any emphasis on the greatness of the wealth or possessions; but elsewhere hôn does develop the meaning "great wealth, riches":[15] "hôn-vā'ōsher (wealth and riches) are in his house" (Ps. 112:3, of the man who fears Yahweh). Finally, from the meaning "ready" (cf. LXX hikanós in Prov. 30:15, which usually represents dai, "enough" [Ex. 36:7, etc.]) or "wealth" (cf. rabh, "much, enough," 1 K. 19:4, etc.) hôn takes on the sense "enough" (Prov. 30:15,16).

---

[10] Levy, WTM, I, 542a; TW, I, 224a.

[11] Levy, TW, I, 224.

[12] On the hiphil, cf. GK, § 53d; BLe, § 294b‴; but the hiphil of hwn is no more denominative than is zyd hiphil in Dt. 1:43bβ.

[13] Peters, 322f.; Junker, 383; cf. KBL³.

[14] Horst, HAT, 14 (³1964), 176.

[15] Cf. the shift of meaning from 'āthîdh, "prepared" (Job 3:8; 15:24; Est. 3:14; 8:13 Q), to 'ªthîdhôth, "treasures" (Isa. 10:13 K).

4. *Occurrences*. *hôn* appears 26 times in the OT: Ezk. 27:12,18,27,33 (MT plural); Ps. 44:13 [Eng. v. 12]; 112:3; 119:14; Prov. 1:13, 3:9; 6:31; 8:18; 10:15; 11:4; 12:27; 13:7,11; 18:11; 19:4,14; 24:4; 28:8,22; 29:3; Cant. 8:7; also Prov. 30:15,16 in the sense "enough."

5. *Semantic Field*. The semantic field of *hôn* includes several terms. Corresponding to the meaning "possessions" we find the words *nachᵃlāh* and *'ᵃchuz-zāh*.[16] Corresponding to the meaning "riches, wealth" we find not only *'ōsher*, "wealth" (Gen. 31:16 and 36 other occurrences), and *nᵉkhāsîm/nikhᵉsîn*, "treasures" (Josh. 22:8 and 5 other occurrences), but also various words meaning primarily "strength, power" or the like: *'ôn* (Hos. 12:9[8]; Job 20:10), *chayil* (Gen. 34:29, etc.), *kābhôdh* (Gen. 31:1, etc.), *kabbîr* (Job 31:25), *kōach* (Prov. 24:10), and *hāmôn* (Ezk. 29:19 and 4 other occurrences). The words *hôn* and *'athîdhôth* take on the meaning "wealth" or the like from "be ready"; *'ōsher* (usually plural) derives its meaning from "stores" (cf. also *chōshen*, "reserves, treasure," and *maṭmôn*, "hidden treasure"). For a discussion of the semantic field of "poverty" cf. → אביון *'ebhyôn*.

6. *LXX*. The translation of the LXX reflects both the original and the derived meaning of *hôn*, as well as the specific shades of meaning conveyed by other words for "riches": *hypárchonta* and *hýparxis* (see above), *ktễma* (Prov. 12:27) and *ktễsis* (3 times), *ploútos* (6 times, plus *plouteín* in Prov. 28:22), and *plễthos* (Ezk. 27:33), but also *dýnamis* (Ezk. 27:18,27), *ischýs* (Ezk. 27:12), *dóxa* (Ps. 112:3), and *timễ* (Ps. 44:13[12]). In Cant. 8:7, LXX heightens the statement by translating *hôn* as *bíos:* in Prov. 3:9, "honor Yahweh with your substance," it introduces an ethical distinction by translating *díkaioi pónoi*. For *hôn* in the sense "enough," it uses *hikanón* or *arkeí* (Prov. 30:15,16).

II. Use in the OT. Social problems, the distinction between rich and poor, were not considered in Israel until the time of the monarchy. The early traditions accordingly do not use the most important word for "wealth," → עָשַׁר *'ōsher*, or *hôn*. In general, *hôn* refers to the property or wealth of an individual. Only once do we hear of the *hôn* of a city: according to Ezk. 27, it was the basis for the commercial dominance of Tyre.

Unlike *'ōsher*, *hôn* is a term found primarily in the language of wisdom, where it occurs 19 times (including Ps. 112:3) as opposed to 7 occurrences elsewhere (4 in Ezk. 27). This impression is reinforced by its 3 occurrences in Sirach (6:14; 8:2; 34[31]:3). The word *hôn* appears in all the major collections in Proverbs except chaps. 25–27, which does not touch at all on the theme "wealth/poverty." Wisdom places a high estimate on the value of wealth and property. For its possessor, *hôn* provides—in fact (Prov. 10:15, in contrast to *rêsh*, "poverty") or in his imagination (Prov. 18:11)—security and protection. It means power (Sir. 8:2) and brings friends (Prov. 19:4). Wealth is the fruit of diligence (Prov. 12:27);

---

[16] See Horst.

a more profound comprehension, however, traces it back to wisdom and knowledge, and a theological statement understands *hôn*, *'ōsher,* and *tsedhāqāh* as the reward for fear of Yahweh (Ps. 112:3). Ultimately a man owes his *hôn* to his creator; he can therefore be exhorted to honor his creator with his substance (Prov. 3:9). Anyone who seeks to acquire wealth hastily (Prov. 13:11; 28:22) or by taking advantage of another's need (28:8) will lose whatever he gains. The company of harlots will waste a man's substance (29:3). Thieves endanger the property of others (1:13) but also their own (6:31). In other words, *hôn* is worth striving for, but it is not the highest goal. A prudent wife is more to be esteemed than house and *hôn* (Prov. 19:14). The psalmist prefers a life according to the will of Yahweh above all riches (Ps. 119:14); for riches offer no protection against the wrath of Yahweh, but only righteousness, *tsedhāqāh* (Prov. 11:4).

III. Qumran. While there appears to be no mention of *'ōsher* at Qumran, *hôn* became an important term there. It occurs more than 50 times in the documents published to date. The word is used primarily in its basic meaning of "possessions." The Qumran community holds property in its own name (1QS 6:17; 7:6 [*hôn hayyachadh*]; 9:8; cf. 1QpHab 12:10). A novice remains independent with respect to his possessions for a year (1QS 6:17); in his second year he transfers his *hôn* to the overseer (6:19), and not until his third year does he share in the property of the community (6:22). Anyone who falsifies his possessions is punished (6:24f.). Any damage to the property of the community caused by a member must be made good (7:6f.); this regulation obviously presupposes that the members were authorized to dispose of their own property. In CD 8:5; 19:17 the apostate priests in Jerusalem are charged with proficiency in profit and property; their property is described as *hôn* (*hā*)*rish'āh,* "wicked possessions." This accusation, however, does not imply that all property is considered reprehensible, especially since CD 20:7 deals with property (of the individual? cf. 1QS 7:24f.; 8:23).

Kutsch

הָיָה *hāyāh*

Contents: I. 1. Related Terms in the Ancient Near East; 2. Occurrences in the OT.
II. 1. Meaning in General Use: a. Exist, Be Present; b. Come into Being, Happen; 2. Auxil-
iary Uses: a. Indication of Time; b. Verbification; c. Use with Participles; 3. Niphal.
III. Meaning in Theological Use: 1. General Use in Theological Discourse: a. Blessing and
Cursing; b. Covenant Formula; 2. Use in Describing Creation (P); 3. Use with the Pro-
phetic Word; 4. Ex. 3:14. IV. The Controversy between Boman and Barr.

I. 1. *Related Terms in the Ancient Near East.* a. To date the verb *hyh* is
attested only in the OT. There is a corresponding Aram. root *hwh*, used in the
Old Aramaic inscriptions in about the same way that *hyh* is used in the OT.[1] We
must therefore assume that the root is peculiar to the Aramaic-Hebrew branch
of Semitic.

Amorite personal names exhibit an element *ya-aḫ-wi*, alternating with *ya-wi*,
which might suggest a verb *hawā*, although the first form could also derive from
ḥayā, "to live."[2] The interpretation as "to be" may be supported by the occurrence of such Akkadian personal names as *Ibašši-ilu*, "God is (i.e., proves to be)
a helper."[3]

A problematic occurrence in Ugaritic[4] as the equivalent of Akk. *ú-wa* most
likely indicates the 3rd person singular masculine pronoun.[5] Historically, there
may be a relationship with Akk. *ewû*.[6] This Akk. root, which appears in Neo-

hāyāh. B. Albrektson, "On the Syntax of אהיה אשר אהיה in Exodus 3:14," *Words and
Meanings. Festschrift D. Winton Thomas* (1968), 15-28; A. Alt, "Ein ägyptisches Gegenstück
zu Ex. 3,14," *ZAW,* 58 (1940-41), 159f.; S. Amsler, *THAT,* I (1971), 477-486; J. Barr, *The
Semantics of Biblical Language* (1961), 58-72; G. Benveniste, *Problèmes de linguistique générale* (1966), 187-207; K. Beyer, *Semitische Syntax im NT,* I (1962), 29-65; T. Boman, *Hebrew
Thought Compared with Greek* (trans. 1960), 38-49; O. Eissfeldt, "Jahwe, der Gott der
Väter," *ThLZ,* 88 (1963), 481-490=*KlSchr,* IV (1968), 79-91; *idem,* "'Äḥeyäh 'ašär 'äḥeyäh
und 'Ēl 'ôlām," *FuF,* 39 (1965), 298-300=*KlSchr,* IV, 193-98; D. N. Freedman, "The Name
of the God of Moses," *JBL,* 79 (1960), 151-56; M. Johannessohn, "Das biblische καὶ ἐγένετο
und seine Geschichte," *Zeitschrift für vergleichende Sprachforschung,* 53 (1926), 161-212;
idem, "Die biblische Einführungsformel καὶ ἔσται," *ZAW,* 59 (1942/43), 129-184; L. Koehler,
"Syntactica IV: Hypertropher Gebrauch von *uajeḥī*," *VT,* 3 (1953), 299-305; J. Lindblom,
"Noch einmal die Deutung des Jahwe-Namens in Ex 3,14," *ASTI,* 3 (1964), 4-15; C. H. Ratschow, *Werden und Wirken; eine Untersuchung des Wortes* hajah *als Beitrag zur Wirklich-
keitserfassung des AT. BZAW,* 70 (1941); E. Schild, "On Exodus III 14—'I Am That I Am,'"
VT, 4 (1954), 296-302; W. von Soden, "Jahwe 'Er ist, Er erweist sich,'" *WO,* 3 (1964/66), 177-
187; T. W. Thacker, "Compound Tenses Containing the Verb 'be' in Semitic and Egyptian,"
Hebrew and Semitic Studies Presented to G. R. Driver (1963), 156-171; T. C. Vriezen, "''Ehje
'ašer 'ehje," *Festschrift A. Bertholet* (1950), 498-512.

[1] *DISO,* 63f.
[2] *APNM,* 71f., 191.
[3] Von Soden, 179.
[4] C. F. A. Schaeffer, *Ugaritica,* V (1968), 245, 28.
[5] F. M. Cross, "Yahweh and the God of the Patriarchs," *HThR,* 55 (1962), 254.
[6] *AHw,* 266f.

Babylonian texts as *emû*, has the meaning "become," in the causative "change, transform"; [7] it is therefore semantically much narrower than *hyh* and *hwh*. Whether there is a connection with Arab. *hawā*, "fall," remains unclear.

B. Jacob [8] has suggested the meaning "moan, cry out" for a few occurrences: *hāyînû* in Isa. 26:17; *'ehyeh* in Ps. 102:8 (Eng. v. 7); Job 3:16. In all these passages, however, the common meaning "to be" is possible, and there are no grounds for hypothesizing a homonymic root. J. Barth [9] assumes a root *hāyāh* with the meaning "be weak, fragile" (Arab. *wahā*) at Mic. 2:1; Dnl. 2:1; 8:27, but this assumption is hardly necessary. [10]

b. There is no verb in the other ancient Semitic languages that adequately represents the meaning of the Aram.-Heb. root. Akk. *bašû*, which has been suggested in this context, has "exist" as one of its meanings in the G stem. [11] It coincides, however, with only a portion of the semantic range of *hyh*, and above all is not used as an auxiliary verb. The same applies to Ugar. and Phoen. *kûn*. [12] There is a greater similarity to Sum. *me(n)*, especially with respect to the latter's use in place of the separate personal pronoun: Sum. *ᵈana lugal-la-a-meš* = Akk. *ᵈAnim šarri šunu*, "they are king Anu's."   *Bernhardt*

c. The Egyptian language normally uses a nominal clause to express the meaning "to be." There are, however, verbs and particles that serve particularly to express existence: *iw*, [13] *wn* or *wnn*, [14] and *ḫpr*. [15] The word *iw*, which has been compared to *hāyāh*, can function as an independent word in conjunction with prepositions (e.g., *iw m*, "be something"), as an auxiliary verb, and as a particle. But it appears only in certain forms and compounds, with *wn/wnn* supplying the lacking forms. [16] The derivation of *iw* and *wnn* from verbs of motion (*iw*, "come"; *wny*, "hasten") is uncertain. The meaning "there is/was" in the sense of existence is expressed by a combination of both words: *iw wn*, negated *nn wn* or *n wn.t*.

The word *ḫpr*, "become, happen," not rarely conveys the meaning "be, exist," as in the idioms *ḫpr m ḥȝ.t*, "to have been earlier" (used of the primal gods, ancestors, etc.), *ḫpr.ty.fy*, "one who will be," and *rdy ḫpr*, "cause to exist, call into being." The various forms of existence are expressed by means of the corresponding substantive *ḫprw*, while nouns with the meaning "being, existence" deriving from the other words just mentioned are hardly ever found.

The most important word for "be present, exist" is *wn(n)*. Here a few significant idioms may be mentioned: [17] *nty (nt.t) wn*, "he who (that which) is present";

---

[7] *CAD*, IV, 413ff.

[8] *ZAW*, 18 (1898), 293.

[9] *Wurzeluntersuchungen zum hebräischen und aramäischen Lexicon* (1902), 12.

[10] See below, V.1.

[11] *CAD*, II, 144ff.

[12] *WUS*, 151; *DISO*, 117; cf. also Arab. *kāna*, Ethiop. *kôna* (→ כוּן *kûn*).

[13] *WbÄS*, I, 42f.

[14] *WbÄS*, I, 308ff.

[15] *WbÄS*, III, 260ff.

[16] See E. Edel, *Altägyptische Grammatik* (1955), §§ 880-900; A. Gardiner, *Egyptian Grammar* (³1957), §§ 461-475.

[17] For citations see *WbÄS*.

wn dy, "be here, exist"; *wn im,* "be there." Nonexistence is expressed by *nn wn* or *n wn.t,* while *tm wn* means "nonexisting" and *iry m tm wn* means "annihilate someone." The word *wnn.t* can mean "that which exists," just as *wnny.w* can mean "those who are," i.e., human beings. The word *wnn,* which can also be used to express the future tense, often emphasizes enduring existence. This is probably the case with *wnn-nfrw,* Onnophris, the common epithet for Osiris. This function is especially clear in some late temple hymns. At the great pylon at Philae, for instance, sevenfold repetition of *wnn* guarantees that the festivity of the birth-house will endure as long as the heaven remains on its pillars; reference is also made to the permanence of the earth, the day, the moon, Orion, Sothis (Sirius), the mountains, and the Nile. [18] The enthronement decree for the new-born Horus at Philae [19] uses 19 repetitions of *wnn n.k,* "to you belongs (and shall belong)..." to express his legitimate ownership of the world. In late temple scenes, the lines surrounding both gods and the king often begin with *wnn,* probably as a sign of the pharaoh's divine permanence: "As long as the god endures, the pharaoh will remain in office."

"That which is present" can also be expressed by *wnn.t* or *nt.t wn.* If the writer's purpose is to emphasize the totality, he uses the phrase *nt.t nb.t;* [20] this phrase is used especially of the creator-god, who made "everything that is." Parallel to this expression we also find the typical polar expression *nt.t iw.t.t,* "that which is and is not." [21] In hymns this formula frequently refers to Osiris: "To him comes everything that is and is not"; [22] he is "overlord of that which is and is not" [23] and "lord of those who exist and ruler of those who do not exist." [24] This formula is typical of the entire Egyptian world view: alongside the cosmos, comprising everything that exists, there is the chaos of that which does not exist. [25] But the expression can also be interpreted in dynamic terms, so that "what does not exist" can be understood as meaning "what does not yet exist" or "what no longer exists." Thus there arises an important parallelism between the formula *nt.t iw.t.t* and the divine name Atum (Itmw), which can mean both "the perfect one, the all-encompassing one" and "he who does not exist (any more)."

Alt has sought to find an Egyptian counterpart to the difficult theologoumenon Ex. 3:14 in lines 94f. of the Instruction for Merikare, which reads *wnn.y* (or *wn.y*) *wn.kwy,* translated by Alt as "I am by being myself."

Bergman

2. *Occurrences in the OT.* The verb *hyh* occurs 3632 times in the OT. Of these, 21 are niphal, 5 are aramaizing *hwh* (Gen. 27:29; Isa. 16:4; Eccl. 2:22; 11:3; Neh. 6:6), and 71 in the Aramaic portions are *hwh.*

---

[18] H. Junker, *Der grosse Pylon des Tempels der Isis in Philä* (1958), 279.
[19] *Idem, Das Geburtshaus des Tempels der Isis in Philä* (1965), 20f.
[20] *WbÄS,* II, 354, 6.
[21] *WbÄS,* I, 47, 2.
[22] *BM,* No. 580.
[23] *Urk.,* IV, 545, 7.
[24] *RT,* 33 (1911), 34.
[25] E. Hornung.

The verb is found especially often in the narrative books of the OT. Genesis alone, which comprises 6.4 % of the words in the OT, accounts for 8.6 % of the occurrences of *hyh*. But the distribution of occurrences in the historical books is itself uneven. It is used sparingly, for example, in 2 Kings, which, with 4 % of the words of the OT, contains 3.3 % of the occurrences of *hyh*. In 1 Kings, by contrast, the figures are 4.2 % and 5.4 %. The reason for this difference probably lies in the style of the various sources used. For example, the infrequent occurrence of *hyh* between 2 K. 9 and 16 stands in contrast to the comparatively large number of occurrences in passages of Deuteronomistic origin such as 1 K. 8 and 2 K. 17. Whether we can conclude that *hyh* came to be used with increasing frequency in the later period is doubtful. In any case, a preference for use of this verb is one of the stylistic marks of Deuteronomistic redaction. As one would expect, the frequency of occurrence is below average in the books containing extensive lists (Numbers, Chronicles) and in poetic texts. Psalms, Job, Proverbs, and the Song of Solomon together comprise 12.5 % of the words of the OT, but contain just 5.2 % of the occurrences of *hyh*. The greatest number of occurrences, both absolutely and relatively, is found in Ezekiel: with 6.1 % of the words of the OT, it contains 9.3 % of the occurrences of *hyh*. For the rest, the frequency of usage in the prophetic writings corresponds roughly to that of the historical books. Only Amos, Nahum, and Habakkuk are substantially below average.

The rare niphal is found primarily in exilic and postexilic texts (62 %).

II. 1. *Meaning in General Use*. In general, *hāyāh* can be translated with the English verbs "be" and "become," although stylistic considerations often suggest other renderings. Its semantic range, however, is wider than that of these corresponding English verbs. It includes, for example, the meaning "happen"; in combination with *le* it is used as a periphrastic idiom for "have," for which Hebrew does not have a corresponding verb. [26] See, for example, Gen. 13:5: "Lot . . . had (*lelôt . . . hāyāh*) flocks and herds and tents." In combination with various prepositions the verb can in fact express many very specific kinds of "being" or "becoming" that can be rendered in English only through periphrastic constructions. This is particularly true of its use with *'aharê* in the sense of "follow someone" and with *min* in the sense of "come, derive from." Instances of these two idioms are few, however (1 S. 12:14; 2 S. 2:10; 15:13; 1 K. 12:20 for the former, Gen. 35:11; Ex. 9:24; Josh. 11:20; Eccl. 3:20 for the latter).

It is no longer possible to determine with assurance an original, narrower meaning of *hāyāh*. Its occasional appearance in poetic parallelism with other verbs [27] does not provide sufficient evidence. It appears, however, that from the very outset *hāyāh* was used to refer to "being" in the sense of "exist, be present" (=what has come into being) and of "come into being, happen" (=what is coming into being).

---

[26] See Benveniste.

[27] *qûm*, Isa. 7:7; 14:24; *'āmadh*, Dnl. 11:71; Ps. 33:9; *lō' tēchath*, Isa. 51:6; cf. Ratschow, 5f.; Boman, 38f.

a. *Exist, Be Present*. Characteristic examples illustrating the meaning "exist, be present" frequently involve the infinitive construct (146 times). It refers predominantly to an enduring state or process lying in the future and therefore expected or announced (92 times). In particular, *lihyôth* can take on the specialized meaning "that which lies in the future."[28] Less frequent is its use to designate enduring existence in the present (24 times) or the past (30 times). Specifically, the infinitive construct can express, for example, the extended stay of a person at a specific place ("*bihyôth* of Joshua by Jericho...," Josh. 5:13), a person's belonging to a profession (*hᵉyôth kōhēn*, Jgs. 18:19), and the entire lifetime of a man (*bihyôthô chai*, 2 Ch. 10:6). It can also serve to indicate the continuation of an action ("And the war continued...," 1 S. 19:8) or a condition ("... that my covenant with Levi may hold [*lihyôth*]," Mal. 2:4). Occasionally the infinitive construct expresses existence in general: "... a time of trouble such as never has been since there was a nation (*mihyôth gôy*)" (Dnl. 12:1). An important mark or characteristic of existence can be stressed by its use *(bihyôthô thāmîm*, Ezk. 15:5). The verbal force of the root is especially clear in such idioms as Eccl. 3:15: "What has been (*mah-shshehāyāh*) already had been and what will be (*va'ᵃsher lihyôth*) already has been (*kᵉbhār hāyāh*)."

b. *Come into Being, Happen*. The meaning "come into being, happen," always expressed by finite forms of *hāyāh*, is not found very often (e.g., Ps. 64:8 [Eng. v.7]: "Their wounds came about [*hāyû*] suddenly"). We find it primarily in the context of creation and the prophets' reception of God's word (see III.2 below). The meaning "happen," however, is found quite frequently with an introductory or transitional imperfect or perfect consecutive. In most of these cases we are dealing with formal introductory idioms, especially when the verb is followed by *kᵉ, kî, ka'ᵃsher, 'achᵃrê haddᵉbhārîm hā'ēlleh*, or a temporal phrase ("And it happened the next morning that..."). In narrative texts such expressions account for a significant portion of the occurrences (in Genesis, for example, 59, or 18%).

2. *Auxiliary Uses*. The major use of *hāyāh* in its finite forms is as an auxiliary verb. These forms serve primarily to fix the temporal sphere of the clause more precisely and to define its logical structure unambiguously. Nevertheless, its use as an auxiliary verb in combination with a participle or infinitive as a periphrastic expression of modal or temporal circumstances[29] is much less frequent than in the Indo-European languages, since in Semitic aspect, mood, and tense can be indicated satisfactorily through conjugation and the use of various stems (e.g., *gādhal* = "he has become large"). But when the predicate is nominal, *hāyāh* or some other auxiliary verb is used to define mood or tense more precisely. If the clause is intended merely to indicate the simple presence of something, Hebrew—like all Semitic languages—can use a nominal clause without

---

[28] *GK*, § 114i.
[29] Cf. Thacker.

any auxiliary verb. Contrary to expectation, therefore, the use of *hāyāh* as a copula with the function of merely linking subject and predicate has not been convincingly attested.

In particular, the auxiliary use of finite forms of *hāyāh* in the qal may be illustrated by the following typical examples:

a. *Indication of Time.* The statement "The earth was without form and void" (Gen.1:2) can be expressed in Hebrew by the nominal clause *hā'ārets tōhû vābhōhû*. Since the temporal dimension is left open in a nominal clause, and since in this particular case the context does not provide an unambiguous temporal framework, the perf. *hāyᵉthāh* was used to make it clear that we are dealing with a state belonging to the past. In such cases *hāyāh* conveys no particular meaning of its own.

The impf. is used correspondingly to indicate that an action or condition will or should occur in the future. In 2 K. 2:21, for example, a syntactically quite superfluous *yihyeh* is inserted to make it unambiguous that in the future "neither death nor miscarriage shall come from it (*lō' yihyeh mishshām 'ōdh...*)." The consecutive tenses are often used merely to establish a logical connection or indicate the temporal framework. [30] The form *vᵉhāyāh* can actually take on the meaning "if," as in 1 K.18:12: *vᵉhāyāh 'ᵃnî 'ēlēkh mē'ittākh...* = "If I go away from you...."

b. *Verbification.* (1) In particular, *hāyāh* is used to take nouns that derive from a verbal root no longer productive or do not derive from any verbal root and turn them into verbs. For example, the statement "I have been young, and now am old" in Ps. 37:25 is rendered by *na'ar hāyîthî gam zāqantî*. A verbal root was available to express "be or become old," but there is no corresponding verb for "be young." In this case a nominal clause with *'ānî* might have been used, but then the temporal framework would have been obscured. It was therefore appropriate to use the perf. of *hāyāh*. Similar circumstances obtained in such expressions as "become a byword" (Ps. 69:12[11]), "be night" (Ps.104:20), and in many other cases.

(2) We find a similar situation when a root appears in a limited number of stems. For example, → חרף *chāraph* is used only in the qal and piel. To render the passive sense ("to be made a reproach") it was therefore necessary to use a nominal derivative (*cherpāh*) plus an auxiliary verb, a use for which *hāyāh* was available (Jer. 42:18; 44:8,12; 49:13; Ezk. 5:15; Ps. 31:12[11]; 69:11[10]; 79:4; 89:42 [41]; 109:25; Neh. 2:17).

The jussive, cohortative, and imperative are used especially often to incorporate a noun into a verbal phrase, since there is no way to express these moods by means of a nominal clause. In such combinations *hāyāh* is used to set the noun in motion. This helps explain the frequently emphasized "dynamic" character of

---

[30] See Johannessohn and Koehler.

the verb. The proportion of such hortatory expressions varies from 25 % (Psalms) to 7 % (Genesis) of the total number.

(3) There is an unmistakable preference for nominal expressions "verbified" with the help of hāyāh in certain cases where verbal expressions would have been possible. In Gen. 44:9, for example, the statement "we also will be my lord's slaves" is rendered by means of the noun 'ebhed in the plural preceded by nihyeh (impf. indicative with cohort. meaning). The same usage occurs again in Gen. 47:19. The use of hāyāh to paraphrase the desired verbal expression is unnecessary. Much more common is the use of the 1st person plural cohortative of the root 'bd (Ex. 14:12 and six other occurrences) or the corresponding form of the indicative (Jgs. 9:28 and seven other occurrences). There is no recognizable nuance conveyed by the periphrastic use of hāyāh. It is thus merely a stylistic peculiarity associated with the author's feeling for Hebrew. The preference for a noun plus an auxiliary verb illustrates the tendency that can be observed in many languages to reduce the active verbal vocabulary.

c. *Use with Participles.* The use of hāyāh in conjunction with a participle is especially interesting. Here the auxiliary function of the verb emerges clearly. A participle furnishes information about voice only: active or passive. The subject of the action is expressed either by a noun or by a pronoun (or pronominal suffix). If, however, the temporal framework is important for the meaning of the statement, an appropriate form of hāyāh often precedes or follows. Nu. 14:33, for example, reads: "Your children will be shepherding (yihyû rō'îm) in the wilderness forty years." The impf. of hāyāh in this passage makes it clear that we are dealing with something that will happen in the future. In Gen. 30:36, by contrast, the expression veya'aqōbh rō'eh 'eth-tsōn suffices; for the temporal framework is established unambiguously by the context. For the same reason, there is no need for hāyāh in Gen. 37:16: "Tell me where they are pasturing ('êphōh hēm rō'îm)." In association with a participle, hāyāh has no effect on voice. If such combinations indicate a continuous action or state, this statement is made by the use of the participle alone. [31] Besides determining the temporal framework, hāyāh can also define the mood of the participle. This is true above all when the jussive, cohortative, or imperative are employed to indicate that a certain continuous action or state may, should, or must happen in the future (II.2.c.; III.1.a). [32]

In the Aramaic portions of the OT, the use of havāh to clarify the temporal situation is especially developed (43 occurrences). [33]

Bernhardt

3. *Niphal.* The niphal is not used in Modern Hebrew. At Qumran, however, several examples are found. Most important are those that refer to God's pre-

---

[31] Contrary to Boman, 43f.
[32] For a discussion of hāyāh plus participle, see Ratschow, 23; Thacker.
[33] *BLA,* §§ 81, 82q, 98x.

destination of all that takes place. In the concluding hymn of the Manual of Discipline, for example, we read: "In [or: through] his knowledge (*bedha'tô*) everything has come to pass (*nihyāh*); and everything that comes to pass (*kôl hôveh*) he establishes by his thoughts" (1QS 11:11), and "everything that comes to pass (*kôl hannihyeh*) has come to pass (*hāyāh*) through thy will (*rātsôn*)" (1QS 11:18). In the didactic passage 1QS 3:15 we read: "From the God of knowledge (comes) everything *hôveh venihyeh*, and before it takes place (*liphnê heyôthām*) he has established it by his plan (*machshebheth*)." These passages raise two questions. First: what is the difference between the qal and the niphal? Everything *nihyeh* (niphal) *hāyāh* (qal) through God's will or according to his plan. Does *nihyeh* refer to predestination, i.e., the fact that it comes from God (cf. 1 K. 1:27; 12:24), or does it refer to the future, as in Sirach ("all that is yet to be")? The sequence *hôveh venihyeh* might argue for the latter. The same sequence also occurs in the War Scroll (1QM 17:5: Israel is ignorant of *kôl hôveh venihyeh*) and in the Damascus Document (CD 2:10: *kōl hōvê 'ōlāmîm venihyôth 'adh* comes to pass through God's foreknowledge of all ages and periods). But the opposite sequence is also found, namely in 1QS 11:4: *berāz nihyeh vehôvê' 'ôlām,* "the secret of what has come to pass(?) and what will come to pass(?) of the age." All that can be said with assurance is that the combination is meant to designate the totality of everything that comes to pass. It does seem clear, however, that here *hāyāh* does not refer to mere being or existence, but rather becoming or happening.

The phrase *rāz nihyeh* just mentioned also occurs twice in the so-called Book of Secrets (1Q27 1:3,4). In the first passage *rāz nihyeh* occurs with *qadhmōniy-yôth*; in the second, the context (*yābhô' 'alêhem*) suggests future reference. It is therefore likely that in the first passage *qadhmōniyyôth* does not mean the opposite of *nihyeh,* but is meant to be more or less synonymous.

The other occurrences at Qumran are less relevant. The phrase *lō' nihyethāh kāmôhā,* already found in the Bible, occurs at 1QM 1:12; 18:10. The expression *nihyê 'ōlāmîm* (1QM 17:5) or *nihyôth 'ôlām* (1QH 18:27; CD 13:8) refers to everything that takes place in this eon; *qēts nihyeh* (1QS 10:5; 11:9) designates the age or period that is "coming." In 1QH 3:33 *hahavvāh hannihyāh* means "the destruction that has come to pass." The expression *lehithchaddēsh 'im kōl nihyeh* in 1QH 11:14 is obscure; it may mean something like "to renew itself with all that has come to pass." The context refers to the eschatological (or incipient) age of salvation, but does not provide any clue to help interpret *nihyeh.*

Ringgren

III. **Meaning in Theological Use.** General usage would hardly lead us to expect that *hāyāh* would have a specialized theological meaning in precisely definable form. For the most part there is little more to say than that each of the semantic realms of *hāyāh* can apply not only to earthly entities and actions but also to God and his activity or conduct. This is self-evident with respect to the auxiliary function of the verb. We must accordingly distinguish between the general use of *hāyāh* as it occurs in theological contexts (III.1) and the specifically theological meaning that the root itself can take on in specific instances (III.2-4).

1. *General Use in Theological Discourse.* The general use of *hāyāh* in theological discourse is particularly clear in those more or less fixed literary forms that have a specific *Sitz im Leben* in the cult or at least serve to express a religious experience considered characteristic in Israel.

a. *Blessing and Cursing.* In the formulas of blessing and cursing,[34] we find *hāyāh* primarily in the description of the consequences. In Gen. 12:2, for example, the first half of the blessing given Abram is followed by the command: *vehyēh* (impv.) *berākhāh.* A corresponding function is performed by *hāyāh* in the account of the consequences of the curse upon Cain (Gen. 4:12) and in the specifics of the blessing upon Noah (Gen. 9:2f.). This use is sometimes even clearer in lengthy series of curses and blessings. Especially striking is the sevenfold *vehāyîthāh* in Dt. 28:25-37. Here *hāyāh* uniformly plays the verbal role in the expressions describing the consequences—especially upon the spirit—of the punishments threatened if the curse takes effect. Characteristic of this usage is the combination of the perfect consecutive with the participle, graphically expressing the inescapable fulfilment and lasting effect of the consequences of the curse. This combination can also be observed elsewhere in such formulas (Gen. 4:12; Dt. 7:14).

On the other hand, there is no lack of examples illustrating the combination of *hāyāh* with a noun in passages depicting the consequences of a blessing or curse (Gen. 9:25f.; Dt. 33:24; Job 3:4,7) or of *hāyāh* followed by *ke* to introduce the description of the condition that will result (Jer. 17:6,8; 20:16). Neither can those cases be overlooked in which *hāyāh* is not used at all and some other verb fulfils the function of *hāyāh* plus participle or noun ("It shall not cease...," Josh. 9:23; also Gen. 3:4f.,17f.; 49:7; 1 S. 26:25).

This observation shows that *hāyāh* is not a necessary element in the construction of such formulas. This holds true generally for the appearance of this verb in the various expressions with a religious aspect that contain a blessing, a promise, or a threat. Nevertheless, in these passages, especially in the prophetic oracles, *hāyāh* does take on a special force to the extent that the authority of Yahweh stands behind what is expected.

When, for example, Zeph. 2:4a threatens: "Gaza shall be deserted" (*azûbhāh thihyeh*), the combination of *hāyāh* plus the passive participle appears to have been chosen in order to lend adequate expression to the special quality of the expected event, the inexorability with which it will take place in the context of Yahweh's judgment. More likely, however, the reason for not choosing the readily available finite form of *'zb* in the pual was merely that it was less familiar (being found only in Isa. 32:14; Jer. 49:25). Significantly, *yeghāreshûhā* and *tē'āqēr* appear as parallels in Zeph. 2:4b. Therefore the "coming to pass" ex-

---

[34] Ratschow, 54ff.

pressed by the combination *'ªzûbhāh thihyeh* probably does not differ from the "coming to pass" already implicit in the two forms using the preformative conjugation without the addition of *hāyāh*.

b. *Covenant Formula*. The verb *hāyāh* appears to be firmly rooted in the covenant formulary characterizing the relationship between Yahweh and Israel. In Dt. 26:17f., where the formula occurs in its extended form, the infinitive *lihyôth* introduces each of the notes of the future covenant relationship. As is often the case, the use of the infinitive with *lª* lends the statement the force of a final clause. The purpose of the covenant obligation is a lasting, all-embracing, vital relationship between the parties, from which concrete details of their conduct follow. We frequently meet the abbreviated formula "I will be (*vªhāyîthî* or *'ehyeh*) your God and you shall be (*tihyû*) my people." It appears primarily in the Deuteronomistic sections of the prophetic books (Jer. 7:23; 11:4; 24:7; 31:33; 32:38; Ezk. 36:28; 37:27; similar statements in Jer. 30:22; Ezk. 11:20; 14:11; 37:23; Zec. 8:8; also Lev. 26:12). It is true that not infrequently the covenant formula also appears without the addition of *hāyāh: vª'āmartî 'ammî hû' vªhû' yō'mar yhvh 'ªlōhāi* (Zec. 13:9; likewise Hos. 2:25[23]; Ps. 100:3; cf. also Isa. 51:16; 63:8; Ps. 79:13; 95:7). This usage is found when the accent does not lie on the future nature of the covenant relationship as an assurance and promise or when the introduction to the formula makes it clear that we are dealing with a promise that will not be realized until some time in the future. The same holds true for other abbreviated forms of the formula, e.g., "I will be your/their God" (Gen. 17:8; Ex. 6:7; 29:45; Ezk. 34:24). Here, too, *'ehyeh* serves to define the mood and tense of God's promise unmistakably. By contrast, it is superfluous in the frequent formula "I am Yahweh your God" (Ex. 16:12; 20:2,5), which refers to the present. In this case a nominal clause with *'ªnî* or *'ānōkhî* (→ הוּא *hû'*) suffices.

An examination of other, similar phrases leads to the same conclusion. The simple statement "God is with you" is expressed by the nominal clause *'ªlōhîm 'immākh* (Gen. 21:22). When a distinction of mood or tense must be expressed, a verbal clause using *hāyāh* or some other verbal root is needed: "As I was (*hāyîthî*) with Moses, so I will be (*'ehyeh*) with you" (Josh. 1:5; 3:7).

2. *Use in Describing Creation (P)*. Various statements about God's work of creation, especially in the Priestly account of creation (Gen. 1:1–2:4b), exhibit a theologically motivated use of *hāyāh*. Here the verb (four times in the jussive, Gen. 1:3,5f., and twice in the perfect consecutive, Gen. 1:14f.) serves to express a theory of the process of creation that sees God's commanding word as the critical mark of his creative activity and accordingly interprets the earlier account of what God did by means of an account of what God said. [35] In this passage *hāyāh* is best translated "come to be." The execution formula *vayªhî khēn*, repeated seven times, is best rendered as "it happened" or "it came to pass." The

---

[35] W. H. Schmidt, *Die Schöpfungsgeschichte der Priesterschrift. WMANT,* 17 (³1973).

same is true of Ps. 33:9: "He speaks, and it already comes to pass." The use of *hāyāh* does not give any special quality of existence to whatever comes into being solely through God's word. The account of the creation of living creatures, which is the focal point of God's creative action, makes use of other verbs (Gen. 1:20,24). The use of the common word *hāyāh* to construct a verbal clause representing a command in 1:3,5f. is probably intended to obviate any anthropomorphic elaboration of the process of creation. This purpose is also expressed unmistakably in the laconic execution formula *vayᵉhî khēn*. For the same reason the indirect form of the jussive was employed: "Let there come into being.... "

3. *Use with the Prophetic Word.* Similar considerations may account for the periphrastic description of how the prophet receives Yahweh's word: "And the word of Yahweh came (*hāyāh*) to.... " In this form, usually with an introductory *vayᵉhî*, rarely with *hāyāh* later in the clause, the expression occurs 107 times.

The majority of occurrences are found in Ezekiel (47) and Jeremiah (36). The expression occurs frequently in the Elijah stories (8) and Zechariah (7). Except in 1 K. 6:11 (Solomon) and 1 Ch. 22:8 (David), the recipient of God's word is always a prophet. When the prophet is speaking, the recipient is designated by the word *'ēlai,* "to me." This usage is limited to Jer. 1:4–25:5; 32:6 (12 times), Ezk. (46 times), and Zec. (3 times). The expansion of the formula by the addition of *bᵉyadh* in Hag. 1:1,3; 2:1 is unique. Strangely enough, the use of *hāyāh* to describe the reception of God's word is not attested in the earlier prophets, with the exception of Isa. 28:13. It only occurs secondarily at the beginning of Hosea, Joel, and Micah, altered into the form of a superscription: *dᵉbhar yhvh 'ᵃsher hāyāh.* This use of *hāyāh* may well also derive from Deuteronomistic theology (cf. I.2).

There are few instances where the reception of God's word is described by means of a nominal clause without the use of *hāyāh* or some other verb (Jgs. 3:20; 1 K. 13:17; 19:9). Occasionally *hāyāh* is used to describe human communication (1 S. 4:1; 2 S. 3:17; 1 K. 1:7).

The use of *hāyāh* in the formula for reception of the word derives from the earlier use of the imperfect consecutive as an introducing and linking tense in narrative texts (II.2.b). This also accounts for the dynamic nuance of the verb: God's word "comes to pass." It is more than mere words spoken to the prophet. It is a word that "comes to pass," not only in the work of creation (III.2), but also in God's actions in history. Therefore the agreement between announcement and fulfilment is the criterion for the genuineness of prophetic speech. A prophetic word cannot come from God if what is announced does not come to pass (*lō' yihyeh,* parallel *lō' yābhô',* Dt. 18:22). A true word of God, on the contrary, will "surely come to pass" (1 K. 13:32, with inf. abs.).

4. *Ex. 3:14.* Special importance attaches to the theological use of *hāyāh* in connection with the revelation of the name Yahweh in Ex. 3:14. But the meaning of the expression *'ehyeh 'ᵃsher 'ehyeh,* found only in this passage, is unclear and disputed.

The very position of Ex. 3:14 in its context poses complications. Moses' question as to God's name in v. 13 is followed by two different answers. Verse 14 cites the *'ehyeh* formula, which does not really deal with the question, since it does not mention the name of God. In v. 15, however, the expected answer is given. The name of Yahweh is revealed and he is identified with the gods of the patriarchs. In this context v. 14 gives the impression of being an addition, the more so because it is unusual to provide an explanation of a name before the name itself is given.

Interpretation of the expression has varied since early days.

a. The LXX renders it as "I am the being one, I am he who is" (*Egṓ eimi ho ṓn*). According to this interpretation, Yahweh characterizes himself more precisely as the only one who is "real" (for Israel), the only one among the gods who "exists." Attempts have been made to resolve the syntactic problems of this translation by appealing to the rule of congruence in syndetic relative clauses, according to which Hebrew relative clauses dependent on antecedents in the 1st or 2nd person must have their verbal forms in the same person. Thus in such cases *'ehyeh* has the same meaning as *yihyeh*. [36]

b. A more literal rendering is "I am who I am." This translation suggests on the one hand that we see in God's answer a rejection of Moses' question on the grounds that Yahweh is ineffable and incomprehensible. This explanation would also account for the function of v. 14 in its context. On the other hand, Yahweh's answer "proclaims his boundless reality." [37] This interpretation is supported by similar expressions in Ex. 33:19 ("I will be gracious to whom I will be gracious, and will show mercy on whom I will show mercy") and Ezk. 12:25 ("I, Yahweh, will speak the word which I will speak"). [38]

c. Aside from Ex. 3:14, the 1st person singular imperfect of *hāyāh* occurs 64 times in the OT. If we ignore the 22 instances of its use with the *vav*-consecutive and the uncertain passages Job 3:16; 12:4, the form is always future in meaning, or at least optative (Ps. 50:21). Only in Ruth 2:13 is *'ehyeh* used in a context that would suggest translation as a present.

When the consecutive forms are eliminated, only 29 of the remaining occurrences belong to statements made by God concerning himself. The majority of these (22) are found in uses of the "covenant formula" (III.3) or similar statements. These fall into two distinct groups. In the first group, the verb is followed by *le* (something like "I will be God for you"); this construction is limited to Jeremiah, Ezekiel, Hosea, and Zechariah. [39] In the second group we find the preposition *'im* (something like "I will be with you"); this construction occurs exclusively in Genesis–Ruth.

---

[36] Most recently Lindblom.

[37] Eissfeldt, "'Ăheyäh," 299 = 195.

[38] Cf. Freedman.

[39] The singular statement "I will be your father" (2 S. 7:14; 1 Ch. 17:13; 28:6) may also be included.

This situation suggests that the correct translation of Ex. 3:14 should be "I will be who I will be." The ancient versions of Aquila and Theodotion understood the Hebrew text in this sense (*ésomai hós ésomai*). Such an interpretation is also supported by the appearance of the expression "I will be with you" in Ex. 3:12. This *'ehyeh 'im,* the fundamental promise in the election relationship between God and his people, would then be taken up in v. 14 to explain the name and nature of Yahweh. It is not possible, however, to be really certain of what the formula means. All that is sure is that the author of Ex. 3:14 sought to derive the name Yahweh from the root *hāyāh.*

Many scholars [40] have suggested vocalizing *'hyh* in Ex. 3:14 as a hiphil instead of the qal found in the MT. This would give the formula causative meaning, in the sense of "I call into being, I create." But there is no evidence that *hāyāh* was used in the hiphil.

IV. The Controversy between Boman and Barr. The controversy between Boman and Barr has contributed to our understanding of the semantic problems raised by *hāyāh.* In Boman's view, Hebrew "being" is "a dynamic, powerful, effective being," [41] in contrast to Greek thought, which understands being as something immutable. In Hebrew, too, "being" refers to existence; but in the Hebrew view existence expresses itself effectually. Therefore "existence is identical with effectiveness." [42] In the full sense of the word, then, being is, in its formal nature, personal being, which finds its highest development in the *hāyāh* of God. It is from this perspective that Hebrew thought interprets objective, substantial reality ("inner activity").

Barr [43] does not dispute in principle the presence of a "dynamic mode of thought" among the Hebrews; he does question, however, whether observations about the Hebrew verbal system are sufficient to reveal a static or dynamic mode of thought. In particular Barr singles out for special criticism Boman's procedure of paraphrasing the meaning of *hāyāh* more or less freely in the passages he cites and then using these paraphrases to demonstrate that the root means "effect." Barr's criticism is largely accurate.

Bernhardt

---

[40] Most recently Freedman, 152f.
[41] Boman, 188.
[42] *Ibid.,* 48.
[43] Esp. 74-77.

הֵיכָל *hêkhāl*

Contents: I. The Word: 1. Akkadian Origin; 2. Use in the OT. II. Description of the Temple: 1. General; 2. Furnishings. III. Interpretation of the Temple: 1. Central Sanctuary, Dwelling Place of God; 2. Cosmic Symbolism.

I. The Word.

1. *Akkadian Origin.* The word *hekhal* is a loanword from Sum. *é-gal,* "large house," "palace," "temple," which occurs in several temple names.[1] Oberhuber[2] conjectures pre-Sumerian origin. Akk. *ekallu* means "palace" and, much less often, "temple" (for which the usual term is *bîtu* or *ekurru*); it can also have such special meanings as "royal court," "office," "revenue department," and

---

hêkhāl. Y. Aharoni, "Arad: Its Inscriptions and Temple," *BA,* 31 (1968), 2-32; *idem,* "The Solomonic Temple, the Tabernacle and the Arad Sanctuary," *Orient and Occident. Festschrift C. H. Gordon. AOAT,* 22 (1973), 1-8; G. W. Ahlström, "Heaven on Earth—at Hazor and Arad," in *Religious Syncretism in Antiquity,* ed. B. Pearson (1975); T. A. Busink, *Der Tempel von Jerusalem von Salomo bis Herodes.* I. *Der Tempel Salomos* (1970); J. N. Carreira, *O plano e a arquitectura do templo de Salomão à luz dos paralelos orientais* (Porto, 1969); G. Cornfeld, *The Mystery of the Temple Mount* (Tel Aviv, 1972); *idem, Pictorial Biblical Encyclopedia* (1964), 680-87; German ed. (1969), 1411-1421; B. Diebner, "Die Orientierung des Jerusalemer Tempels und die 'Sacred Direction' der frühchristlichen Kirchen," *ZDPV,* 87 (1971), 153-166; K. Galling, "Serubbabel und der Hohepriester beim Wiederaufbau des Tempels," in his *Studien zur Geschichte Israels im persischen Zeitalter* (1964), 127-148; D. W. Gooding, "Temple Specifications: A Dispute in Logical Arrangement between the MT and the LXX," *VT,* 17 (1967), 143-172; J. Hofer, *Zur Phänomenologie des Sakralraumes und sein Symbolismus im Alten Orient* (diss., Vienna, 1970); A. S. Kapelrud, "Temple Building, a Task for Gods and Kings," *Or,* 32 (1963), 56-62; E. E. Knudsen, review of A. Ungnad and L. Matouš, *Grammatik des Akkadischen* (⁴1964), in *DLZ,* 87 (1966), 685f.; A. Kuschke, "Der Tempel Salomos und der 'syrische Tempeltypus,'" in *Das ferne und nahe Wort. Festschrift L. Rost. BZAW,* 105 (1967), 124-132; S. Landersdorfer, *Sumerisches Sprachgut im AT. BWAT,* 21 (1916), 42; R. de Langhe, "L'autel d'or du temple de Jérusalem," *Bibl,* 40 (1959), 476-494; K. Möhlenbrink, *Der Tempel Salomos. BWANT,* 4/7 [59] (1932); T. Oestreicher, *Reichstempel und Ortsheiligtümer in Israel. BFChTh,* 33/3 (1930); J. Ouelette, "Le vestibule du temple de Salomon était-il un *bit ḫilâni*?" *RB,* 76 (1969), 365-378; R. Patai, *Man and Temple in Ancient Jewish Myth and Ritual* (1947); H. Ringgren, *Israelite Religion* (trans. 1966), 158-166; K. Rupprecht, "Nachrichten von Erweiterung und Renovierung des Tempels in 1 Könige 6," *ZDPV,* 88 (1972), 38-52; H. Schmid, "Der Tempelbau Salomos in religionsgeschichtlicher Sicht," in *Archäologie und AT. Festschrift K. Galling* (1970), 241-250; K.-D. Schunck, "Zentralheiligtum, Grenzheiligtum und 'Höhenheiligtum' in Israel," *Numen,* 18 (1971), 132-140; R. de Vaux, *AncIsr,* 312-330; L. H. Vincent, "L'autel des holocaustes et le caractère du temple d'Ézéchiel," *Analecta Bollandiana,* 67 (1949), 7-20; P. Welten, "Kulthöhe und Jahwetempel," *ZDPV,* 88 (1972), 19-37; G. R. H. Wright, "Pre-Israelite Temples in the Land of Canaan," *PEQ,* 103 (1971), 17-32; Y. Yadin, *Hazor. Schweich Lectures, 1970* (1972), 75-95; S. Yeivin, "Was There a High Portal in the First Temple?" *VT,* 14 (1964), 331-343.

---

[1] *RLA,* II, 227f.
[2] K. Oberhuber, *BiOr,* 21 (1964), 315.

"bureau of standards." Large rooms in private houses and royal palaces can also be called *ekallu;* the phrase *ekal tapšuḫti,* "palace of repose," is used for a king's tomb. Finally, it can refer to a portion of the liver. [3]

The word appears early in the West Semitic languages: Ugar. *hkl,* [4] "palace," usually the dwelling place of a god and thus "temple," [5] often constructed with *bqrb;* [6] Aram. *hêkhal,* "palace" (e.g., Dnl. 4:1,26 [Eng. vv. 4,29]; 5:5; 6:19; Ezr. 4:14), "temple" (e.g., Dnl. 5:2f.; Ezr. 5:14f.; 6:5); Syr. *haykhᵉlāʾ,* "palace," "temple"; Arab. *haikal,* "large building," "altar," "temple," "skeleton," "framework." [7] In the Aramaic inscription *KAI,* 237.2 we find the word *ʾrdklʾ,* "architect," [8] probably derived from Akk. *arad ekalli,* "palace slave," "master builder." [9]

2. *Use in the OT.* In the OT, *hekhal* has three meanings: "palace," "temple," and the "middle area" in the temple of Solomon, also called the "holy place."

The word *hekhal* is often used interchangeably with → בַּיִת *bayith;* it refers primarily to royal palaces, e.g., the palace of Ahab (1 K. 21:1), the palace of the king of Babylon (2 K. 20:18; 2 Ch. 36:7; Isa. 39:7), and the palace of Nineveh (Nah. 2:7). Other passages also clearly refer to the royal residence: Am. 8:3; Dnl. 1:4; Ps. 45:16(15); 144:12; plural Hos. 8:14; Joel 4:5(3:5); Isa. 13:22; Ps. 45:9 (8); Prov. 30:28. For occurrences in Biblical Aramaic, see I.1 above.

Since a temple is often considered a god's dwelling place, the distinction between palace and temple is only minor. In the OT, *hekhal* in the sense of "temple" refers to the temple of Yahweh. The only exception seems to be Ezr. 5:14, which refers to the temple in Babylon. The phrase *hekhal yhvh* (21 x) alternates with *beth yhvh,* but never occurs in parallel construction. [10] Several temples are referred to as the temple of Yahweh: the temple at Shiloh (1 S. 1:9; 3:3), the temple of Solomon (2 K. 18:16; 23:4; 24:13; Jer. 7:4; 24:1), and the temple of Zerubbabel (Ezr. 3:10; Hag. 2:18). [11]

In the accounts of the building of the temple during Solomon's reign (1 K. 6–7; 2 Ch. 3–4), the word *hekhal* never refers to the temple as a whole, but to the area that is also called the "holy place" (*qōdhesh*). The same is true in Ezekiel's temple vision (Ezk. 41). In these texts, the word *bayith* is always used for the temple (cf. Dnl. 5:2). Two verbs are used for the "constructing" of the *hekhal: yasadh* (→ יסד *yāsadh*), "lay foundations" (niphal: Isa. 44:28; piel: Ezr. 3:10; pual: Hag. 2:18; Zec. 8:9; Ezr. 3:6), and *banah* (→ בנה *bānāh*), "build" (Hos. 8:14 [palaces]; Zec. 6:12f.,15; Ezr. 4:1).

---

[3] *AHw,* 191f.

[4] 53 x; Whitaker, 214.

[5] *WUS,* 827; *UT,* 763.

[6] See *WUS* and *Ugaritica,* V (1968), 545ff. (the temple of El); cf. Ps. 48:10 (Eng. v. 9). For a discussion, see F. C. Fensham, "The First Ugaritic Texts in Ugaritica V and the OT," *VT,* 22 (1972), 297f.

[7] For a discussion of the linguistic evolution of *é-gal* in the West Semitic languages, see Knudsen, 685.

[8] Cf. Jewish Aram. *ʾrdykl, AP,* 14, 2.

[9] Cf. A. L. Oppenheim, *ArOr,* 17 (1949), 227, 235.

[10] Cf. Fensham, 297.

[11] Cf. Galling, 127ff.

II. Description of the Temple.

1. *General*. The OT contains three descriptions of the Jerusalem temple: 1 K. 6:1–7:51; 2 Ch. 2:1–5:14 (temple of Solomon); and Ezk. 40–43 (Ezekiel's temple vision).

The central portion of Solomon's temple consisted of three rooms along an east-west axis, with the entrance at the narrow end ("long room" plan).[12] The vestibule (*'ûlām*) at the east end was 20 cubits wide and 10 cubits deep (1 K. 6:3; cf. Ezk. 40:49, where the depth is given as 11 cubits). Next came the temple chamber proper, the *hekhal* or *qodhesh,* the "holy place" or "nave," 40 cubits long (1 K. 6:17), 20 cubits wide, and 30 cubits high (1 K. 6:2). The innermost room, called the *dᵉbhîr* or *qōdhesh qᵒdhāshîm,* "holy of holies" or "most holy place" (RSV: "inner sanctuary"), was a cubical chamber 20 cubits on a side (1 K. 6:20). Thus the temple was 70 cubits long and 20 cubits wide, including the vestibule.[13] The length given in 1 K. 6:2, 60 cubits, probably refers to the two inner chambers, as is certainly the case in 2 Ch. 3:3. All of these measurements represent internal dimensions (1 K. 6:16). The vestibule and *hekhal* were separated by a wall with doors. From the vestibule a double door made of olivewood led into the nave, with four doorposts (1 K. 6:33ff.; Ezk. 41:21ff.—the precise arrangement is somewhat obscure). The sockets for the hinges holding the leaves were made of gold (1 K. 7:50).[14] The inner sanctuary was separated from the *hekhal* by a wooden wall.[15] Busink[16] suggests that the *debhir* had a small vestibule (איל by haplography from אילם). The *hekhal* and *debhir* were surrounded by galleries three stories high containing chambers (1 K. 6:5f.).[17] The windows of the temple (1 K. 6:4; cf. the temple of Baal described in *CTA,* 4 [II AB], V, 124; VII, 17) were therefore probably located in the upper half of the walls. For a reconstruction of the ceiling, see Busink, pp. 182ff.

The temple stood in the middle of the so-called inner court (→ חצר *chātsēr*), 1 K. 6:36, which was surrounded by the outer court, 1 K. 7:12. Solomon's palace was connected directly with the temple precincts (1 K. 7:8; cf. Ezk. 43:7f.).[18]

2. *Furnishings*. With the exception of the luxurious decorations on the floor and walls (1 K. 6:29ff.), little is said about the furnishings of the temple proper. The *debhir* contained two cherubim made of olivewood overlaid with gold (1 K. 6:23ff.), under whose wings rested the ark of the covenant. According to 2 Ch. 3:14, a veil decorated with cherubim hung before the holy of holies (cf. Ex. 26:33); 1 K. 6:21 and 2 Ch. 3:16 speak of chains of gold in front of the *debhir,* and 1 K. 7:50 speaks of doors. In temples 2 and 1A at Hazor, there was a wall at this point.[19]

---

[12] Cf. Diebner.
[13] Cf. Rupprecht, 40ff.
[14] Possibly not original; see M. Noth, *BK,* IX, *in loc.*; Busink, 234.
[15] Cf. Ezk. 41:3; de Vaux, 314.
[16] Busink, 206ff.
[17] De Vaux, 315.
[18] See also de Vaux, 316f.
[19] Yadin, 79, 87.

Within the *hekhal* stood an altar of cedar; it was used for incense offerings and was located on the main axis of the temple, immediately in front of the *debhir*. The other furnishings of the temple included the table for the bread of the Presence (→ לחם *lechem*) and the ten lampstands, which also stood in front of the *debhir*. These furnishings, described in 1 K. 7:48f., are increased in the Chronistic parallel (2 Ch. 4:7f.) to ten golden lampstands and ten tables, plus a hundred basins of gold. The tables are intended to hold the bread of the Presence (2 Ch. 4:19; cf. 1 K. 7:48). Ezekiel mentions only an "altar of wood" (41:22), of which it is said: "This is the table that stands before (*liphnê*) Yahweh." The Zadokite priests were allowed to approach this table (Ezk. 44:16). The altar mentioned by Ezekiel is probably to be identified with the altar of cedar mentioned in 1 K. 6:20; it is also called the *mizbach hazzāhābh*, "golden altar" (1 K. 7:48; 2 Ch. 4:19; cf. Ex. 39:38; 40:5,26; Nu. 4:11). On the basis of a South Arabic etymology, de Langhe prefers the translation "altar of incense." The temple excavated at Arad illustrates the use of an incense altar in front of the *debhir*. [20]

The concentration of cultic furnishings in the *hekhal* and the *debhir* shows that these areas constituted the central portion of the temple (cf. 1 K. 6:2). In the temple at Arad, there were three steps leading up to the *debhir;* this was probably also the case in the Jerusalem temple. [21] The terminology for the furnishings in the temple of El (*CTA*, 4 [II AB], I, 33-44) shows that the furnishings of the Jerusalem temple were traditional. The furnishings of the temple of El included a table (*tlḥn*). Some Canaanite temples had two tables (*tlḥnm; CTA*, 3 [V AB], II, 30) or several tables (*tlḥnt; CTA*, 4 [II AB], IV, 36) on which loaves of bread and libation vessels were placed. [22]

The great altar for burnt-offerings stood in the outer court (2 Ch. 4:1; 6:12; Ezk. 43:13ff.) in front of the temple (2 K. 16:14), together with the bronze sea (*hayyām*, 1 K. 7:39; 2 Ch. 4:9f.). [23]

A detailed description of the two pillars Jachin and Boaz is given in 1 K. 7:15-22. According to v. 21, they were set up *le'ulām hahêkhāl*, which must be understood as meaning "in front of the entrance to the vestibule." The same location is referred to in 2 Ch. 3:15 by the phrase *liphnê habbayith*. The phrase *'al pᵉnê hahêkhāl* (v. 17) is somewhat obscure; the translation "in front of the holy place" is not out of the question, and finds support in archeological discoveries at Arad[24] (cf. temple 1A at Hazor[25]). [26]

---

[20] Aharoni, 31.

[21] De Vaux, 314.

[22] M. Haran, "The Complex of Ritual Acts Performed Inside the Tabernacle," *ScrHier*, 8 (1961), 294, n. 25.

[23] Cf. Busink, 326.

[24] Aharoni, 2ff.

[25] Yadin, 89.

[26] For a discussion of the significance and function of the pillars, see Ringgren, 159f.; de Vaux, 314f.; for a reconstruction, see Busink, 299ff.; M. Noth, *BK*, IX, 149ff.

III. Interpretation of the Temple.

1. *Central Sanctuary, Dwelling Place of God.* In the OT, the word *hekhal* refers to the central sanctuary of Israel. [27] The temple at Shiloh (1 S. 1:9; 3:3) is undoubtedly so referred to because the ark of the covenant was kept there. In the ancient Near East, it was a function of the king to build a central sanctuary and organize its cult. A temple would be built under the direction of a king at the behest of a deity. [28] Similar motifs appear in the account of the construction and dedication of the Jerusalem temple. [29] The texts describing the making of the tabernacle (Ex. 24:12–40:33) and the temple (1 K. 3:4–9:9 [and Ezk. 40–48]) also contain many motifs of this sort. [30]

When the temple was completed, Yahweh took up residence there (1 K. 8:10f.; 2 Ch. 5:13f.; Ezk. 43:4ff.). [31] In the course of time, the ideological significance of the temple increased in Israel. [32] Although Yahweh was so great that "heaven and the highest heaven" could not contain him (1 K. 8:27), he took up residence in Zion (Ps. 132:13f.). The presence of Yahweh in the temple was depicted in the priestly tradition by the statement that his glory (→ כבוד *kābhôdh*) filled the temple (Isa. 6:1; Ps. 63:3[2]; depicted as a cloud in 1 K. 8:10f.; 2 Ch. 5:13f.). Deuteronomistic circles preferred to say that Yahweh's name (→ שׁם *shēm*) dwelt in the temple (Dt. 12:5, etc.; 1 K. 8:17,29). A name represents the person who bears it; where God's name is, there he himself is present (Ps. 18:7[6]; 2 S. 22:7).

The presence of Yahweh makes the temple holy. It is called "the temple of his/thy holiness" (Ps. 5:8[7]; 11:4; 65:5[4]; 79:1; 138:2; Jonah 2:5,8[4,7]; Mic. 1:2; Hab. 2:20; *hêkhal qodhshô/qodhshêkhā*). From it his voice is heard (Isa. 66:6).

In the opinion of some scholars, the word *hekhal* refers to the heavenly palace of Yahweh (2 S. 22:7; Ps. 11:4; 18:7[6]; Mic. 1:2; Hab. 2:20), but the evidence is hardly convincing. The texts tend more to support the impression that the reference is to the earthly temple, interpreted according to the theology expressed in the prayer of Solomon at the dedication of the temple (1 K. 8:27). When God appears in a theophany, the heavens and the earth tremble; but for the Israelite, the experience of God's appearance takes place in the earthly temple (cf. Isa. 6:1ff.).

Yahweh had chosen Jerusalem and its temple to be his dwelling place (Dt. 12:5, etc.), and this conception is intimately associated with the Davidic dynasty (1 K. 8:16; 11:13,32; 2 Ch. 6:5f.). This led to the conviction that Yahweh's presence guaranteed the security of Israel and that his temple would stand unscathed for-

---

[27] Schunk.

[28] R. Labat, *Le caractère religieux de la royauté assyro-babylonienne* (1939), 177-201; H. Frankfort, *Kingship and the Gods* (1948), 267-274; A. Moret, *Du caractère religieux de la royauté pharaonique* (1902), 115-145; S. Herrmann, "Die Königsnovelle in Ägypten und in Israel," *WZ* Leipzig, 3 (1953/54), 57ff.

[29] Cf. Herrmann, *loc. cit.*

[30] Kapelrud, 56ff.

[31] Cf. Ex. 40:34; Busink, 637ff.

[32] De Vaux, 321ff.

ever (2 K. 19:34; Isa. 37:35). This conviction is echoed in the preaching of Isaiah, which bears the stamp of the Zion tradition (Isa. 7); it was reinforced in 701, when Sennacherib raised his siege of Jerusalem following a series of miraculous events (2 K. 19). Jeremiah, however, has harsh words for those who thoughtlessly rely on the temple and say: "The temple (hekhal) of Yahweh, the temple of Yahweh, the temple of Yahweh" (Jer. 7:4). He points to the destruction of the temple at Shiloh, "where I made my name dwell at first" (Jer. 7:12). Although the temple was totally destroyed in 587, there was no dearth of hopeful prophecies. Yahweh sought to take "vengeance for his temple" (niqmath hêkhālô) (Jer. 50:28; 51:11). He established his dwelling place in Jerusalem once more (Zec. 1:17; 2:10[6]; 3:2). A new temple was built (Hag. 2:1ff.; Zec. 6:12-15; 8:9; Ezr. 3:6ff.; Neh. 6:10f.).

2. *Cosmic Symbolism.* In ancient Near Eastern temple ideology we encounter the idea that the temple came down from heaven or is a copy of a divine dwelling place in heaven.[33] There is no definite textual evidence for this notion in the OT; but cf. Ex. 25:40; 1 Ch. 28:11-19.

There is, however, a kind of cosmic symbolism associated with the temple, at least in intimation. Jerusalem is considered the "navel of the earth" (Ezk. 38:12; cf. → הר har, with somewhat different conclusions), and thus the focal point of the cosmos. This is possible only because Yahweh dwells in Jerusalem, where he has laid a cornerstone (Isa. 28:16).[34] This complex of ideas probably also includes Ezekiel's vision of the temple spring (Ezk. 47; → גיחון gîchôn). Similarly, all the nations shall one day flow to Jerusalem to learn of Yahweh (Isa. 2:1ff.; Mic. 4:1ff.).[35]

Several lists of the temple's furnishings appear to reflect notions of a cosmic symbolism.[36] The bronze sea may have symbolized the fresh-water ocean. According to Ezk. 43:14, the altar of burnt-offering rests on a slab called chêq hā'ārets, "bosom of the earth." Together with the word kiyyôr, which refers to the podium in front of the altar (2 Ch. 6:13; deriving from Sum. ki-ur, "foundation of the earth"), this term evokes certain cosmic associations. Similar notions, clearly expressed, were current in the contemporary environment.[37] Widengren[38] has distinguished two strands of myth and ritual in the symbolism of the temple: an earlier strand, comprising paradisal elements, and a cosmic strand. Both strands, in his view, were well known in Mesopotamia and in Palestine during the Israelite period. In later Judaism, these notions evolved into a luxuriant flora of legends.[39]

---

[33] Ahlström.

[34] See O. Kaiser, *Isaiah 13–39. OTL* (trans. 1974), *in loc.*, with bibliography.

[35] See H. Wildberger, "Die Völkerwallfahrt zum Zion," *VT*, 7 (1957), 62-81; cf. F. Stolz, *Strukturen und Figuren im Kult von Jerusalem. BZAW*, 118 (1970), 94f.

[36] Ringgren, 161.

[37] Cf. E. Burrows, "Some Cosmological Patterns in Babylonian Religion," *The Labyrinth*, ed. S. H. Hooke (1935), 45-70.

[38] C. Widengren, "Aspetti simbolici dei templi e luoghi di culto del Vicino Oriente antico," *Numen*, 7 (1960), 1-25.

[39] Patai, 57ff.

Certain mythological conceptions were borrowed from the Canaanite cult. These include the notion of Mt. Zion as the mountain of the gods in the far north (Ps. 48:3[2]; cf. also the association of paradise with the mountain of the gods in Ezk. 28:13f. [→ הר *har*]). The association of *'ºri'êl* in Ezk. 43:15f. [40] with Akk. *arallû,* "underworld," is still problematic. [41]

Ottosson

[40] Cf. Zimmerli, *BK, in loc.*
[41] W. F. Albright, *Archaeology and the Religion of Israel* ([4]1956), 151, 218.

הָלַךְ *hālakh*

הֲלִיכָה *hºlîkhāh* → דרך *derekh*

Contents: I. 1. Semitic Cognates; 2. LXX Equivalents; 3. Survey. II. Secular Use: 1. Concrete Meaning; 2. Metaphorical Meaning. III. Theological Use: 1. Walking before Yahweh; 2. Walking with God; 3. Following after Yahweh or Other Gods; 4. Going from Yahweh; 5. Walking in the Way(s) of Yahweh; 6. Messengers; 7. God's Going; 8. Conclusions.

I. 1. *Semitic Cognates.* Akk. *alāku,* cognate with Heb. *hālakh,* has both concrete spatial meaning and a metaphorical meaning in the sense "live, behave,

---

hālakh. G. W. Ahlström, *Psalm 89; eine Liturgie aus dem Ritual des leidenden Königs* (1959); G. J. Botterweck, "Ideal und Wirklichkeit der Jerusalemer Priester; Auslegung von Mal 1,6-10; 2,1-9," *BiLe,* 1 (1960), 100-109; H. A. Brongers, "Die Wendung *bešem jhwh* im AT," *ZAW,* 77 (1965), 1-20; M. Flashar, "Exegetische Studien zum Septuagintapsalter," *ZAW,* 32 (1912), 81-116; H. Fredriksson, *Jahwe als Krieger* (1945); K. Gouders, *Die prophetischen Berufungsberichte Moses, Isaias, Jeremias und Ezechiel* (inaug. diss., Bonn, 1971); A. Gros, *Je suis la Route; le Thème de la Route dans la Bible* (1961); E. Haag, *Der Mensch am Anfang; die alttestamentliche Paradiesvorstellung nach Gn 2-3. TrThSt,* 24 (1970); F. J. Helfmeyer, *Die Nachfolge Gottes im AT. BBB,* 29 (1968); H. Holzinger, "Nachprüfung von B. D. Eerdmans, 'Die Komposition der Genesis,'" *ZAW,* 30 (1910), 245-258; F. Horst, "Die Anfänge des Propheten Jeremia," *ZAW,* 41 (1923), 94-153; R. Kilian, *Literarkritische und formgeschichtliche Untersuchung des Heiligkeitsgesetzes. BBB,* 19 (1963); S. R. Külling, *Zur Datierung der "Genesis-P-Stücke" namentlich des Kapitels Genesis XVII* (1964); A. Kuschke, "Die Menschenwege und der Weg Gottes im AT," *StTh,* 5 (1951), 106-118; T. Lescow, *Mich 6,6-8; Studien zu Sprache, Form und Auslegung. ArbT,* 1/25 (1966); V. Maag, "Der Hirte Israels (Eine Skizze von Wesen und Bedeutung der Väterreligion)," *SchThU,* 28 (1958), 2-28; F. Nötscher, *Gotteswege und Menschenwege in der Bibel und in Qumran. BBB,* 15 (1958); G. von Rad, *Wisdom in Israel* (trans. 1972); J. Reindl, *Das Angesicht Gottes im Sprachgebrauch des AT. ErfThSt,* 25 (1970); H. Graf Reventlow, *Das Heiligkeitsgesetz formgeschichtlich untersucht. WMANT,* 6 (1961); idem, *Liturgie und prophetisches Ich bei Jeremia* (1963); C. Schedl, "Aus dem Bache am Wege; textkritische Bemerkungen zu Ps 110 (109), 7," *ZAW,* 73 (1961), 290-97; F. Schnutenhaus, "Das Kommen und Erscheinen Gottes im AT," *ZAW,* 76 (1964), 1-22; E. A. Speiser, "'Coming' and 'Going' at the City-Gate," *BASOR,* 144 (1956), 20-23; E. Testa, "De foedere Patriarcharum," *Studii Biblici Franciscani,* L.A. 15 (1964/65), 5-73; W. Zimmerli, "Zur Sprache Tritojesajas," *SchThU,* 20 (1950), 110-122 = *ThB,* 19 (1963), 217-233.

act."[1] To go with someone (*alāku itti*) means to accompany him: said of a god, it means divine protection;[2] said of a man, it can mean "do service."[3] The frequentative *atalluku/italluku*, "go repeatedly," refers to life and continual presence; the daughter of Sin, for example, is called *muttallikat māti*, i.e., "omnipresent in the land."[4]

In Ugaritic texts, *hlk* is used most often for the "going" of the gods.[5] Troops march,[6] stars "go,"[7] gray hair "flows" with blood,[8] wadis "flow" with honey.[9] In *CTA*, 19 [I D], 194f., *hlk* may be equivalent to "live" ("bless me, that I may go blessed; protect me, that I may go protected"). The word appears in a religious context in *CTA*, 23 [SS], 27: *hlkm bdbḥ nʿmt*, "going with a goodly sacrifice." In *CTA*, 16 [II K], 43 and perhaps also *CTA*, 18 [III D], II, 17, *hlk* serves as a hortatory particle ("Up! Go to it!"). In the Akkadian texts from Ugarit, *alāku* means "go"[10] and "perform a service."[11] The phrase *ālik pāni* refers to the leader of "a group of merchants."[12]

2. *LXX Equivalents*. In the LXX, *hālakh* is usually rendered by *poreúesthai* (some 947 times); *érchesthai* usually represents *bôʾ*, being used only 26 times for *hālakh*. The compound *apérchesthai* serves to render *hālakh* in 136 cases; other common equivalents are *badízein* (47 times) and *peripateín* (24 times). Besides these Greek equivalents and their compounds, some 48 other verbs are used in the LXX to render *hālakh*; some of these correctly interpret the Hebrew original, e.g., the representation of *hālakh* by *gígnesthai* in Gen. 26:13; 2 S. 18:25 (Cod. A).[13]

3. *Survey*. For nomadic groups it is not surprising that *hālakh* should represent the focus of activity. They live "on the move"; their life is mostly spent wandering. This experience may lead to an understanding of human life as a way or a pilgrimage. After his many "goings," a man finally "goes away": he dies. Beforehand, however, nomadic groups know by experience, and their settled neighbors know by memory, that their wanderings have a purpose, that they follow this or that leader, that the success of their journey depends on their conduct. Thus the word *hālakh*—above and beyond its concrete spatial mean-

---

[1] Cf. *CAD*, I, 309, 325f.
[2] Cf. *CAD*, I, 320f.
[3] Cf. *CAD*, I, 309.
[4] Cf. *CAD*, I, 325.
[5] Cf. *CTA*, 6 [I AB], II, 15: Mot; 4 [II AB], II, 13; 12 [BH], I, 34: Baal; 4 [II AB], II, 14; 5 [I* AB], VI, 26; 10 [IV AB], II, 28f.: Anat; 27:5: the sun-god; 17 [II D], V, 10; 1 [VI AB], IV, 7; 20 [IV D], II, 5; 23 [SS], 67: other gods.
[6] *CTA*, 14 [I K], 92, 94, 106, 182, 194, 207.
[7] *CTA*, 19 [I D], 52, 56, 200.
[8] *CTA*, 18 [III D], I, 11; 3 [V AB], V, 32.
[9] *CTA*, 6 [I AB], III, 7:13.
[10] Cf. *PRU*, V, 149; No. 1, 3; No. 60, 16, 22.
[11] Cf. *PRU*, III, 215, 226; No. 16.188, 7; 15.114, 17.
[12] *PRU*, IV, 259; No. 17.319, 29.
[13] Cf. Flashar, 96, 99, 101.

ing—takes on the meanings "conform to a norm, follow someone, behave." Since it is impossible to think of a journey undertaken without a specific goal, *hālakh* also means "plan, set about."

Whenever "going" is mentioned in Israel, there are echoes—more or less distinct—of the period of transhumance or transmigration, and any undertaking can be described with the word *hālakh*.

These "secular" experiences or memories lay the groundwork for a corresponding theological transposition. The tribal leader may lead (*hôlîkh*), but he, too, must rely on divine assistance or inspiration.[14] And so in the final analysis it is God who leads. Just as migratory groups follow the instructions of their leaders, so, too, do they and their descendants follow the instructions of God. The transposition to the theological realm can be localized and understood most directly in the case of nomadic groups, especially those engaged in transmigration, since here the tribal ancestor, probably divinized, plays an important role as leader of his group.

II. Secular Use.

1. *Concrete Meaning.* The spatial movement expressed by *hālakh* depends on specific fixed points that define the starting point or destination of the journey. These fixed points determine movement in space. A specific locality, person, or action can constitute the starting point of a journey (Gen. 12:1; 13:3; 26:16,31) or its destination (places: Canaan, Gen. 11:31; 12:5; 22:2; Sodom, Gen. 18:22; Beer-sheba, Gen. 22:19; Paddan-aram, Gen. 28:2; Egypt, Ex. 4:19,21; Gilead, Nu. 32:39; a man's house, Dt. 20:5-8; a high hill, Jer. 3:6; a sanctuary, Dt. 14:25; 26:2; Ps. 55:15 [Eng. v. 14]; 122:1; Eccl. 4:17[5:1]; persons: Gen. 24:5; 26:1,26; 32:7[6]; 41:55; Ex. 4:18,27; actions: Gen. 31:19; 37:12; Jgs. 1:3,10,11,17; 3:13; 1 S. 17:13). Here we also find texts in which, to our sense of language, *hālakh* appears superfluous. The existence of a spatial element cannot be denied, but it is of decidedly secondary importance. When, for example, Jacob says, "I will go and see him [Joseph] before I die" (Gen. 45:28), the emphasis in his statement lies on his intention of seeing Joseph (cf. similarly Gen. 22:13; 35:22; Ex. 4:21; 19:24; Nu. 24:25; etc.). What we see in these cases is not the prolixity of the Hebrew but his preference for detail that does more justice to the way men act than does our abbreviated form of expression. As the Hebrew views things, a man must make an approach before arriving at his central action. Before he undertakes something, he goes, he wishes, he plans. Thus his action appears as the goal of a journey; it does not appear suddenly and unprepared—a remarkable anthropological description that bears witness to a profound insight into the way human actions develop.

It is not just the starting point and destination of a journey that are defined in terms of a place, person, or action; the path between them is also so defined (Gen. 12:4; 13:5; 14:24; 33:12; Ex. 14:29; Josh. 14:10; 24:3; Jgs. 11:16,18).

---

[14] Cf. Maag, 14f.

The Hebrew mind can conceive of spatial going only as determined by specific places, persons, or actions. This observation is not contradicted by the expression *hālakh lᵉdharkô* (Gen. 32:2[1]; 1 S. 1:18; Jer. 28:11). In this context it is by no means "a passive neutral expression meaning nothing more than 'keep on going,'"[15] since it does not exclude a specific destination but rather implies a path to a specific goal.

Alongside → עלה *'ālāh* and → בוא *bô'*, *hālakh* seems to be used to describe the visit to a sanctuary. As in the case of the other two words, here, too, there is a fundamental local meaning, albeit with added sacral overtones occasioned by the purpose and goal of the pilgrimage or journey (Gen. 22:5; 25:22; Ex. 3:19; Jgs. 19:18; 1 S. 9:9; 1 K. 3:4; 1 Ch. 21:30; Isa. 2:3; 30:29; Jer. 3:6; Mic. 4:2; Ps. 55:15[14]; 122:1; Eccl. 4:17[5:1]; etc.). Even when the goal or destination is not mentioned explicitly (Ex. 10:8,11; Isa. 60:3,14; Jer. 29:12; Zec. 8:21), the context indicates that *hālakh* has more than merely spatial meaning.

In comparison with the passages where men are said to "go," the number of passages that speak of the "going" of objects or animals is insignificant. The verb is used of water in the sense of "flow" (cf. Gen. 2:14; 8:3,5; Ex. 14:21),[16] of boundaries (Josh. 16:8; 17:7), and of animals (cf. Gen. 3:14; Lev. 11:20,21,27, 42).

When someone goes, he does not set forth without any starting point or goal; neither does he go alone. Destination and companionship on a journey are the two points of departure for the metaphorical use of *hālakh,* in which the spatial element retreats into the background, although it does not vanish completely. Even when used metaphorically, *hālakh* preserves echoes of its original spatial meaning.

2. *Metaphorical Meaning.* Human life is a journey or way (→ דרך *derekh*). This understanding implies the metaphorical use of *hālakh,* in which the spatial element recedes into the background, albeit not its dynamic, purposeful character. The goals may be different; what they have in common is that they are reached by certain ways, i.e., by certain courses,[17] while certain criteria are taken into account.

When Moses is to show the judges the way in which they must walk and the works they must do (Ex. 18:20), we are dealing with instructions about what they are to do and how they are to do it. In both cases, which are clearly set in parallel, we are dealing with the actions of the judges. When someone "goes," when he undertakes something, when he acts, he follows certain criteria. In his choice of these criteria he can go astray—therefore the warning to Israel not to follow the customs of the Egyptians and Canaanites, not to act according to them (Lev. 18:3; 20:23; cf. Isa. 8:11; 57:17; Jer. 23:17; Ezk. 13:3; 16:47; 20:18; Mic. 6:16; Ps. 1:1; Job 31:5,7; Prov. 6:12; etc.). When someone "goes" he under-

---

[15] Nötscher, 42.
[16] Cf. also the Siloam inscription, *KAI*, 189.4f.
[17] Cf. Nötscher, 18.

takes something (Gen. 28:15; Josh. 1:7,9; Jgs. 18:5; 2 S. 7:9; 8:6,14; etc.), he has a purpose (Dt. 10:11; 17:3; Josh. 23:16; Jgs. 8:1; etc.). His going has a goal. Viewed in this light, all human life is a journey (1 S. 12:2), including the life of the sojourner who lives or dwells in the midst of Israel (Josh. 8:35).

The dynamic aspect of *hālakh* appears clearly in the metaphorical meaning "grow, increase, progress" (Gen. 26:13; Ex. 19:19; Jgs. 4:24; 1 S. 2:26; 14:16,19; 19:23; 2 S. 3:1; 5:10; 15:12; Jonah 1:11,13; Est. 9:4; Prov. 4:18). All human undertakings finally come to an end when a man departs, when he dies (Gen. 15:2; 25:32; Hos. 6:4; 13:3; Ps. 39:7[6],14[13]; 58:9[8]; 109:23; Eccl. 3:20; Job 7:9; etc.), when he goes the way of all the earth (Josh. 23:14; 1 K. 2:2). Here we are dealing not with "an euphemistic substitute for dying,"[18] but with the representation of human life as a journey.

III. Theological Use.

1. *Walking before Yahweh.* The expression "walk before (*hālakh/hithhallēkh liphnê*) God (or Yahweh)" is used by J (Gen. 24:40), E (48:15), and P (17:1), albeit in different senses, as its appearance in different genres suggests. In Gen. 48:15, the expression occurs in the introduction to a blessing, in 24:40 in a promise (a form related to the blessing), but in 17:1 in a command. In the context of blessing and promise, the expression represents an historical retrospect intended to confirm what is said: just as Israel's fathers walked before God, i.e., experienced his nearness and aid (Gen. 48:15, "the God who has been my shepherd"; v. 16, "the angel who redeemed me from all evil"), so shall it be with their descendants. The fact that the fathers can look back upon a life before God's gracious countenance guarantees the future described in blessing and promise.[19]

A different sense is found in Gen. 17:1. Past experience is replaced by the obligation *hithhallēkh liphnê*, accurately glossed by the addition of *vehyēh thāmîm* (→ תמם *tāmam*), i.e., "be devout . . ., the fundamental condition of the covenant" in the sense of P,[20] or more precisely "with complete, unqualified surrender."[21] For Gen. 17:1 the interpretation of the idiom as meaning "to deserve"[22] is accurate, but not for Gen. 24:40; 48:15, which presuppose an understanding of the expression in the sense of "to enjoy his approval and favor."[23]

---

[18] M. Pope, *Job. AB,* XV (1965), 105.

[19] H. Gunkel, *Genesis. GHK,* I/1 (⁷1966), 257, 473 translates: "Yahweh/God, who walked before me/my fathers," accurately reproducing the sense, although this textual emendation is not necessary and the present text can hardly go back to an emendation based on religious scruples.

[20] *Ibid.,* 267; similarly O. Procksch, *KAT,* I (²,³1924), 517. Cf. Testa, 22; Külling, 242f.

[21] Cf. G. von Rad, *Genesis. OTL* (trans. 1961), 193.

[22] S. R. Driver, *Genesis. Westminster Comms.,* I (¹⁵1948), 185.

[23] *Ibid.* Most commentators assume instead that the texts in question exhibit a uniform understanding, e.g., E. König, *Die Genesis* (²,³1925), 312; J. Skinner, *Genesis. ICC,* I (²1930), 291, 345, 507; E. A. Speiser, *Genesis. AB,* I (1964), 122, 176, 355.

The interpretation of the expression in Gen. 17:1 is connected with its use in the Deuteronomistic history, which places it in the mouth of Solomon in expansive prayers (1 K. 2:4; 3:6; 8:23,25; 9:4; 2 Ch. 6:16; 7:17). In this context Solomon refers back to the dynastic oracle (2 S. 7:11-16). A comparison of this oracle with the way it is quoted reveals the purpose of the Deuteronomistic historian. The unconditional validity of the oracle is here made conditional, primarily through the use of *hālakh liphnê*. Solomon's sons are to walk before Yahweh *bekhōl lēbhābh ûbhekhōl nephesh* (1 K. 2:4; 8:23), in faithfulness, in righteousness, and in uprightness (1 K. 3:6), and with integrity of heart (*bethom-lēbhābh;* 1 K. 9:4). This attitude finds expression in observance of the divine commandments (1 K. 9:4; cf. 2:3). In this manner David walked before Yahweh as his servant (1 K 3:6; 8:25; 9:4) and experienced the first fulfilment of the dynastic oracle in the succession of his son to the throne.

By itself *hālakh/hithhallēkh* means "live"; in conjunction with *liphnê yhvh* and the interpretative expressions just cited, it refers to the way of life God requires. [24] On his sickbed Hezekiah recalls this way of life in his prayer to God (2 K. 20:3 = Isa. 38:3). Since he has lived in faithfulness and with a whole heart before Yahweh, doing only what is good in Yahweh's sight, he can count on Yahweh's help.

While Gen. 17:1 (P) and the pertinent texts in the Deuteronomistic history agree in their understanding of the expression, Ps. 56:14(13); 116:9 follow the sense of the expression in Gen. 24:40 (J) and 48:15 (E), albeit with a difference. To the short form *hithhallēkh liphnê yhvh*, which suffices for J and E, they add the explanatory phrases "in the land of the living" (Ps. 116:9) and "in the light of the living" (Ps. 56:14[13]). In J and E, the expression without any further explication means a happy life, not just "life on earth" in contrast to dwelling in Sheol; [25] whoever walks before Yahweh lives *eo ipso* in the land or light of the living (→ חיה *chāyāh*). Ps. 56:14[13]; 116:9 emphasize this fact explicitly because the expression, probably because of its use in the Deuteronomistic history and P, no longer had just this one meaning, and possibly also because of the preceding context (cf. Ps. 56:2f.,7,14a[1f.,6,13a]; 116:3f.,8). Here, too, *hithhallēkh* by itself means "live, dwell"; in conjunction with *liphnê yhvh* it means "life in the full sense of the word—life that understands itself as God's gift and remains constantly hidden in God." [26]

The man who walks before Yahweh is the man to whom Yahweh turns his gracious countenance (J and E), then the man who need not fear the countenance and gaze of Yahweh in whatever he does (his "walking") (P). In this context Driver's interpretation is appropriate: "To 'walk before' anyone is to live and move openly before him." [27]

2. *Walking with God.* In Gen. 5:22,24; 6:9, P alone speaks of walking with God (*hithhallēkh 'ēth hā'elōhîm*) and limits this expression to Enoch (Gen. 5:22,

---

[24] Cf. König, 312: "order one's way of life in a manner pleasing to someone."
[25] Contra A. B. Ehrlich, *Randglossen zur hebräischen Bibel,* I (1908, ²1968), 27.
[26] H.-J. Kraus, *Psalmen. BK,* XV (⁴1972), 795.
[27] *WC,* I, 185.

24) and Noah (6:9). Against the background of P's understanding of what it means to walk before Yahweh in the ethical and religious sense, we might expect the same meaning for *hithhallēkh 'ēth hā'elōhîm*. This is true for Gen. 6:9, where Noah is described as *'îsh tsaddîq tāmîm*. [28] Noah is "culticly and ethically fault-less" (*tāmîm*); [29] he is a man "who stands upright before the bar of justice" (*tsaddîq*). [30] This description culminates in the statement that Noah walked with God—either a summation of the detailed characterization, or a new element going beyond what has already been said about Noah. If the expression means no more than "lead a life pleasing to God" [31] or wishes to state merely "that his manner of life was such as God approved," [32] we are dealing with a summary. Gunkel [33] sees in the expression a reference to Noah's intimate relationship with the Deity, illustrated by God's revelations to him in the Deluge story. This attractive interpretation may possibly be confirmed by Enoch's walking with God (Gen. 5:22,24), if Enoch is correctly associated with En-me-dur-an-ki, one of the primeval Babylonian kings and father of soothsayers. [34] The biblical text, of course, knows nothing of all this, and in connection with Enoch's walking with God merely says that God "took" him (Gen. 5:24). Since the prophet Elijah is also "taken" (→ לָקַח *lāqach;* 2 K. 2:3; etc.), it is at least reasonable to suggest that in Enoch we have to do with a similar figure (a prophet?). If so, however, *hithhallēkh 'ēth hā'elōhîm* means more than "live a life pleasing to God"; it means "intimate companionship" with God, [35] like that expressed in the divine revelations to Noah and perhaps also to Enoch. It certainly means more than simply "Enoch lived." [36] Neither can God's "taking" Enoch be accounted for by reference to his virtuous way of life. [37]

Levi's walking with *(hālakh 'ēth)* Yahweh (Mal. 2:6) presupposes the covenant between Yahweh and Levi (2:4f.), in which Yahweh offers life and peace, Levi the fear of Yahweh (2:5). In contrast to the present priesthood (cf. 1:6ff.; 2:8f.), Levi fulfilled his covenant obligations, in part by "walking in peace and upright-ness with Yahweh" (*beshālôm ûbhemîshôr hālakh 'ittî*, 2:6). The interpretation of P seems to have made no distinction between *hālakh 'ēth yhvh* and *hālakh liphnê yhvh*, [38] but the context suggests a different interpretation. If the reference to Levi's turning men from iniquity (2:6) does not refer clearly to "absolution after contamination" [39] but rather to "the precautionary function of the priestly

---

[28] Correctly noted by Holzinger, 257.
[29] Gunkel, *GHK*, I/1, 141.
[30] Procksch, *KAT*, I, 469.
[31] Ehrlich, I, 27.
[32] Driver, *WC*, I, 77.
[33] *GHK*, I/1, 141.
[34] Cf. Gunkel, *GHK*, I/1, 132, 136; Speiser, *AB*, I, 42; Skinner, *ICC*, I, 132; also Sir. 44:16.
[35] Skinner, *ICC*, I, 131; a similar interpretation is given by Driver, *WC*, I, 77.
[36] Contra Ehrlich, I, 27; U. Cassuto, *Genesis*, I (trans. 1961), 282.
[37] Contra Holzinger, 256; Cassuto, *Genesis*, I, 283.
[38] Cf. the translation "walk before" by K. Elliger, *ATD*, XXV (⁶1967), 194.
[39] *Ibid.*, 197.

office" exercised through instruction concerning cultic law, [40] Levi becomes the mediator of the Torah (cf. also 2:6f.). [41] It is questionable, however, whether Levi turns men from iniquity simply by instructing them in the cultic law. If he turns many from iniquity (*rabbîm hēshîbh mēʿāvōn*), iniquity is clearly already present. In this case, however, Levi is functioning as the prophets did later, the more so because, like them, he is Yahweh's messenger (v. 7: *kî malʾakh yhvh tsᵉbhāʾôth hûʾ*; usually considered a secondary addition). However this may be, both cultic instruction and prophetic summons to return to Yahweh presuppose knowledge of the will of God, in other words intimate companionship with God (*hālakh ʾēth*). This presupposition implies consequently corresponding conduct in the conscientious exercise of office, namely walking with Yahweh in peace and uprightness. [42] Smith [43] merely recognizes this conclusion when he states: "To 'walk with God' is to worship God."

Mic. 6:8 speaks of walking with God (*hālakh ʿim*) along with "doing justice" and "loving kindness." Nothing is said about a particular individual; the passage is a sententious [44] rule of life for all. Whoever would walk with God must do so "humbly." [45] Walking humbly with God goes beyond the summons to do justice and love kindness; it means setting God at the center of human life, and thus takes on something like the stamp of "eschatological existence." [46] Although there may be echoes of a torah liturgy, [47] no ordinances of God's law are cited. [48] The similarity of the language to wisdom usage [49] suggests a proverbial maxim, possibly having the preaching of the prophets as its locus. [50]

3. *Following after Yahweh or Other Gods.* "To follow after Yahweh or other gods" means cultic worship when it applies to other gods; when it applies to Yahweh, it means fulfilment of God's law, especially the commandment to accept Yahweh exclusively (→ אחרי *aḥᵃrê*).

4. *Going from Yahweh.* When Israel turns its back upon Yahweh, when it goes backward (*ʾāchôr tēlᵉkhî*, Jer. 15:6), this means it rejects Yahweh (*nāṭasht ʾōthî*, Jer. 15:6). Whoever goes with his back turned to someone else intends to act in secret; he doesn't want the other person to see what he is doing. The image likewise expresses Israel's lack of concern for Yahweh and his will: when someone turns his back on another person or—to use a modern idiom—gives him a cold shoulder, he is saying that he wants nothing to do with him. The specific

---

[40] *Ibid.*
[41] Botterweck, 109.
[42] *Ibid.,* 108f.
[43] J. M. P. Smith, *ICC,* XXV (1912), 39.
[44] Lescow, 54.
[45] Cf. *ibid.,* 46, 56.
[46] *Ibid.,* 60; cf. 56.
[47] T. H. Robinson, *HAT,* 14 (³1964), 146.
[48] Lescow, 19.
[49] Cf. *ibid.,* 56.
[50] Cf. *ibid.,* 22.

conduct involved is not described, but merely judged theologically. What is meant is probably worship of other gods (cf. Jer. 15:5 [51]), which is the reason for the catastrophe that has befallen Jerusalem (Jer. 15:7-9). Worship of other gods is probably also the "way" from which the people refused to turn (*middarkhêhem lō' shābhû*, Jer. 15:7b).

When Israel sacrifices to the Baals and burns incense to idols, the Israelites "go from Yahweh" (Hos. 11:2: *hāl^ekhû mippānai hēm* following LXX *ek prosōpou mou*, rather than MT *hāl^ekhû mipp^enêhem*. This conduct, described in an historico-theological indictment, [52] expresses the ingratitude of the people. [53]

In both cases (Jer. 15:6; Hos. 11:2), *hālakh* is used for actions or conduct in which men avoid the countenance or gaze of Yahweh. Israel acts with its back to Yahweh, and engages in conduct ill befitting his gaze.

5. *Walking in the Way(s) of Yahweh.* The importance assigned by Deuteronomy to the divine commandments, especially in the campaign against religious syncretism, is generally recognized. [54] Deuteronomy's concern is with the way of life that will effect and guarantee salvation for Israel, the chosen people (cf. Dt. 5:33; 30:16). Deuteronomy understands this life as a journey. But not all ways lead to the desired goal, only the ways Yahweh has shown his people, namely, his commandments (→ דרך *derekh*). Whoever follows God's commandments in his actions and conduct is going on the paths of Yahweh. [55] To go on the paths of Yahweh means to do (→ עשׂה *'aśāh;* on Dt. 5:33, cf. 6:1; 19:9) his commandments or to keep (→ שמר *shāmar*, Dt. 8:6; 19:9; 26:17; 28:9; 30:16) them; it means to fear Yahweh (→ ירא *yārē*, 8:6), to love him (→ אהב *'āhabh*, 10:12; 19:9; 30:16), to obey his voice (*shāma' b^eqôl*, 26:17), and to serve him only (*'ābhadh*, 10:12). In the last analysis, what we are concerned with here is adherence to Yahweh alone and exclusive fidelity to him. Therefore a false prophet makes Israel leave the way commanded by Yahweh (Dt. 13:6[5]) when he calls on men to go after other gods and serve them (13:3[2]). He, too, speaks of "going"; not, however, a going on the paths of Yahweh but rather a life in association with other gods.

The meaning of this idiom is also illuminated by the locus of its use, which can still be determined in Dt. 26:17; 28:9 and perhaps also 8:6. Dt. 26:17-19 stands out from its context: "its form looks like the draft of a contract." [56] Like 26:18f., 28:9 speaks of the election of Israel to be a people holy to Yahweh, and 8:5f. may represent the so-called general clause of the covenant formulary (8:2-4 = historical prologue; 8:10-17 = description of the land; 8:19f. = curse). In Deuteronomic usage, then, the expression serves to designate Israel's covenant obligation as the holy people of Yahweh.

---

[51] W. Rudolph, *HAT*, 12 (³1968), 95 assigns this passage to the Deuteronomistic school rather than to Jeremiah.

[52] H. W. Wolff, *Hosea* (trans. 1974), 193.

[53] Cf. A. Weiser, *ATD*, XXIV (⁵1967), 85.

[54] G. von Rad, *Deuteronomy. OTL* (trans. 1966), 26ff.

[55] Cf. Nötscher, 28-30; Gros, 26-28.

[56] Von Rad, *Deuteronomy*, 161.

The Deuteronomistic meaning of the term corresponds to the meaning in Deuteronomy. In the Deuteronomistic conclusion to the narrative of the entrance into Canaan (Josh. 21:43f.; 22:1-6; 23:1-16 [57]), walking in the ways of Yahweh (22:5) means observing his commandment. Here, too, the expression occurs in the context of the Deuteronomic terminology already mentioned (+ *dābhaq be*; → דבק *dābhaq*). The same interpretation may be assumed for Jgs. 2:22; 1 K. 2:3; 3:14; 11:33,38; 2 K. 21:22. The origin of the expression in the Deuteronomistic history should probably be looked for in prophetic circles (cf. 1 K. 11:33,38, where the prophet Ahijah is speaking), if the Deuteronomistic historian did not in fact place it in the mouth of the prophet. The Deuteronomistic examples have in common with Deuteronomic usage the fact that the expression refers to worship of Yahweh alone, to the exclusion of other gods (cf. 2 K. 21:22). Deuteronomy and the Deuteronomistic history agree likewise in using the term to designate the human side of the relationship between Israel and Yahweh, albeit the Deuteronomistic history refers not to the covenant but to the similar notion of the fulfilment of God's promises (on 1 K. 2:3, cf. v. 4; 1 K. 11:38).

This accounts for the association of the expression with the covenant formula (Jer. 7:23); the covenant relationship between Israel and Yahweh works to Israel's benefit only when Israel walks in the ways of Yahweh and obeys his voice. Israel can do so because Yahweh leads it in these ways (*madhrîkhakhā bedherekh tēlēkh*, Isa. 48:17) and teaches it (*melammedhkhā*). The upright (*tsaddîqîm*) walk in the ways of Yahweh (Hos. 14:10[9]), that is, those Israelites who conform to the communion with Yahweh established by the covenant, while the transgressors (*pōshe'îm*), those who fall away, who "drop out" of the covenant relationship, stumble in these ways. It is not Israel alone that is called on to walk in the ways of Yahweh, i.e., to heed and obey his instructions (cf. Isa. 42:24): the other nations, too, come to him to learn his ways (Mic. 4:2).

In the prophetic literature, too, the expression refers to the human side of the covenant (cf. Jer. 7:23; Hos. 14:10[9]) [58] or the condition on which fulfilment of a divine promise depends (cf. Zec. 3:7).

The use of the expression in the prophetic literature might suggest that it originated in these circles. Most of the relevant texts, however, are considered secondary. Jer. 7:23 is part of a collection of Jeremiah's oracles in a Deuteronomistic redaction; [59] Isa. 42:24 is probably a later interpolation [60] that recalls Deuteronomistic style and diction; [61] Isa. 48:17-19 derives from a glossator; [62] the terminology of Hos. 14:10(9) resembles that of the Deuteronomistic history [63] and "was appended to the book by a later hand"; [64] and Mic. 4:1-5 is considered an

---

[57] M. Noth, *HAT,* 7 ([2]1953), 133.

[58] Kuschke, 114.

[59] Rudolph, *HAT,* 12, 47, 50.

[60] C. Westermann, *Isaiah 40–66. OTL* (trans. 1969), 113.

[61] B. Duhm, *Das Buch Jesaja. GHK,* III/1 ([4]1922), 320.

[62] *Ibid.,* 365.

[63] Wolff, *Hosea,* 239.

[64] Weiser, *ATD,* XXIV, 104.

"interpolation by another hand." [65] And so we must conclude that the expression is first met with in Deuteronomy.

Furthermore, Hos. 14:10(9) and Isa. 48:17 may presuppose a different understanding of the expression, interpreting the way of Yahweh as his historical governance. [66] But the reference to commandments of Yahweh in Isa. 48:18 makes it possible to understand the expression as suggested above. [67]

Ps. 81:14(-17) (13[-16]) also exhibits a relationship to the preaching of history and judgment found in Deuteronomy and the Deuteronomistic history. [68] Whoever walks in the ways of Yahweh obeys above all the first commandment of the Decalog (cf. Ps. 81:10[9]). In Ps. 119:3; 128:1 the expression appears in a formula of greeting or good wishes; [69] it is one of the "notes of the *tsaddîq*" [70] who frames his life according to the instructions of Yahweh. The prayer of the petitioner pursued by his enemies, "Teach me the way I should go" (Ps. 143:8), may be asking what he should do or what will befall him in the future; in other words it may be a request for an oracle from God. [71] In the light of v. 10, however, it may also be a prayer that God will guide him along the path that will be pleasing to him. [72]

The image of the way is retained in passages that speak of walking in the good, upright, blameless way or in the paths of righteousness (1 K. 8:36; Isa. 57:2; Jer. 6:16; Ps. 101:6; Prov. 8:20). Although these passages do not speak explicitly of walking in the ways of Yahweh, their context shows clearly that what is meant is conduct according to the will of God. Solomon prays for this for the people (1 K. 8:36); those who are righteous and faithful walk in this way (Isa. 57:2; Ps. 101:6) in contrast to those who worship idols (on Isa. 57:2, cf. vv. 3-5,10); Yahweh invites the people to walk in this way, but they refuse (Jer. 6:16), although they might know from the ways of the past, from history, "that they prospered only when they remained faithful to Yahweh." [73]

The image of the way is still in the background, but of lesser importance, in those texts that speak of walking in Yahweh's law, etc. Here *hālakh bᵉ* is equivalent to "act according to, follow." In Ex. 16:4, [74] the reference to God's testing the people recalls Dt. 8:2-5,15f. and may indicate Deuteronomic influence, although this formulation is not attested in Deuteronomy. Deuteronomic origin is also suggested by Jer. 9:12(13); 26:4; 32:23; 44:10,23. [75] The use of the expression in Ezekiel (5:6,7; 11:12,20; 18:17; 20:13,19,21; 33:15; 36:27; 37:24) derives

---

65 *Ibid.*, 363.

66 For Hos. 14:10, see Weiser, *ibid.*, 104; the contrary opinion is held by Wolff, *Hosea*, 240. For Isa. 48:17, see Westermann, *Isaiah*, 202.

67 Duhm, *GHK*, III/1, 365f. considers 48:17-19 a unit.

68 Kraus, *BK*, XV, 563.

69 *Ibid.*, 823, 863.

70 *Ibid.*, 863.

71 *Ibid.*, 938.

72 H. Gunkel, *Die Psalmen. GHK*, II/2 (⁵1968), 603.

73 Rudolph, *HAT*, 12, 43.

74 Bracketed by M. Noth, *Exodus. OTL* (trans. 1962), 130.

75 Following Rudolph, *HAT*, 12, *in loc.*; cf. also Horst, 150.

in part from another hand (Ezk. 5:6,7; 11:12,20). [76] It is therefore hardly possible to say that the original locus of the expression was the preaching of the prophets. Here, too, it is most likely that the expression originated in Deuteronomic and Deuteronomistic literature (cf. 1 K. 6:12; 8:58,61; 2 K. 10:31) and in the circle of writers associated with this literature.

Since Lev. 26:3 belongs to the parenetic stratum of H, [77] which is not secondary in the sense of being a later parenetic redaction of H, [78] the idiom may possibly have its locus in levitical preaching. This is also suggested by the similarity between the conclusions of H and D (Dt. 28). [79]

It appears to be characteristic of later documents that, despite the continued use of *hālakh*, the notion of walking in a specific path recedes into the background. When Neh. 5:9 speaks of walking in the fear of God (*hālakh beyir'ath 'elōhênû*), it means the same as "fear God." Walking in integrity (*hālakh bethōm*) or uprightness (*hālakh beyōsher*), found exclusively in Psalms and Proverbs (Ps. 26:1,11; 84:12[11]; 101:2; cf. 15:2; Prov. 10:9; 14:2; 19:1; 20:7; 28:6; cf. 2:7), means no more than "act or live with integrity and uprightness." The process of abstraction that overtakes the original image seems to go hand in hand with a process of generalization or secularization. Walking in uprightness still is equivalent to "fearing Yahweh" (Prov. 14:2), and whoever does not do so despises Yahweh (14:2); but in general Yahweh and his commandments, especially the first commandment of the Decalog, retreat into the background; there is at least a suggestion that the important thing is a "proper" life. It is improper to take a bribe (on Ps. 26:11, cf. v. 10); it is in bad taste to lie (Prov. 19:1) or to go by devious ways (Prov. 14:2; 28:6). The blameless man (*hôlēkh tāmîm*) does not do such things, but speaks truth from his heart (Ps. 15:2). Theology is gradually displaced by an early form of humanism; [80] instead of walking in the ways of Yahweh, men now walk in their own integrity and uprightness (cf. Ps. 26:1,11; 101:2; Prov. 14:2; 19:1; 20:7; 28:6). [81]

In Ps. 26:3 and 86:11, walking in the faithfulness or truth (*'emeth;* → אמן *'āman*) of Yahweh stands in a context that suggests identification of the *'emeth* of Yahweh with the divine law. [82] The possibility of this interpretation cannot be excluded, the more so because the context speaks of such things as walking in integrity (Ps. 26:1,11) and fearing God (Ps. 86:11). Since, however, *'emeth* means "the faithful stability that Yahweh guarantees and gives in the covenantal relationship of community," [83] since the petitioner has the steadfast (covenant) love (→ חסד *chesedh*) of Yahweh before his eyes (Ps. 26:3), i.e., remembrance of God's

---

[76] Cf. W. Zimmerli, *Ezekiel* (trans. 1976), *in loc.;* W. Eichrodt, *Ezekiel. OTL* (trans. 1970), *in loc.*

[77] Reventlow, *Heiligkeitsgesetz,* 146.

[78] Kilian, 163; cf. 159.

[79] Cf. M. Noth, *Leviticus. OTL* (trans. 1965), 195.

[80] Cf. von Rad, *Wisdom,* 63, and *passim.*

[81] Cf. Kuschke, 107-109.

[82] Gunkel, *GHK,* II/2, 109, 377.

[83] Kraus, *BK,* XV, 598.

saving acts, since he is praying that his life will be preserved (Ps. 86:2) and that he may have a happy life (86:4), since he cites the incomparability of God and his works (86:8,10), another interpretation is also conceivable. Whoever walks in the faithfulness of Yahweh (ʾᵉmeth yhvh) lives under the protection of Yahweh, which Yahweh vouchsafes to those associated with him in the covenant (chāsîdh; cf. Ps. 86:2).

Mic. 4:5 does not belong with the preceding promise (4:1-4);[84] it is a statement of the present situation, possibly a "liturgical response of the assembled community,"[85] from which we learn that at that time each nation was still walking in the name of its own god, whereas Israel was walking in the name of its God Yahweh. Thus Israel confesses its relationship to Yahweh,[86] whose name is pronounced over Israel. This relationship implies divine protection, and thus the expression means the life of the community under the protection of Yahweh, to whom the community belongs. Thus hālakh bᵉshēm can be understood as "equivalent... to serving or worshipping a god"[87] to the extent that worship is a way of expressing this relationship. The interpretation of Mic. 4:5 in the sense of walking (living) in the strength of God (drawing on Zec. 10:12)[88] is accurate in the sense that God's help is a consequence of Israel's relationship to him.

Zec. 10:12 is probably based on the exodus tradition of the → מלאך malʾākh in whom is Yahweh's name (Ex. 23:20f.), especially since the exodus tradition plays a special role in the context of Zec. 10:12.[89] This makes unnecessary Elliger's suggestion, following the LXX, to emend ythlkw to ythllw.[90] In comparison to Mic. 4:5, there is more emphasis here on the protective relationship between Yahweh and Israel. Yahweh is the strength of those who return; they travel and live under his protection.

In a hymn to the chasdhê yhvh, which praises God's work of creation and his election of the Davidic dynasty (Ps. 89:2-19[1-18]), there is a gratulation[91] or blessing[92] in which those people are acclaimed blessed who know the "festal shout" (tᵉrûʿāh [→ רוע rûaʿ]) because they walk in the light of Yahweh's countenance (Ps. 89:16[15]), i.e., because "the mercy of Yahweh shines upon them."[93] Whoever walks in the light (→ אור ʾôr) of the divine countenance lives in God's grace and favor, and experiences good (Ps. 4:7[6]). To walk in God's light (Job 29:3) is to live under God's protection (shāmar, Job 29:2). Whether this expression contains "a reminiscence of the ancient theophany idea of the covenant

---

84 Weiser, ATD, XXIV, 265; cf. Robinson, HAT, 14, 140f.
85 Weiser, ibid.
86 Ibid., 266; similarly Robinson, HAT, 14, 141, with reference to election.
87 Brongers, 5; Robinson, HAT, 14, 141.
88 Cf. Brongers, 6.
89 Elliger, ATD, XXV, 157, with reference to Zec. 10:11; cf. F. Horst in Robinson, HAT, 14, 250.
90 ATD, XXV, 155.
91 Kraus, BK, XV, 621.
92 Gunkel, GHK, II/2, 389.
93 Ibid.

cult" [94] is questionable, [95] since it is more likely that the association with *hālakh* preserves a reminiscence of the journeyings of transhumant or migratory groups. [96] Here, of course, both *hālakh* and *'ôr* are being used metaphorically. It is therefore impossible to speak of a cultic meaning attaching to the expression "walk in the light of Yahweh's countenance." [97]

The summons in Isa. 2:5, "O house of Jacob, come, let us walk in the light of Yahweh," which is secondary in its present context, [98] means—on the basis of v. 3 and the nature of the summons—to live according to the Torah, [99] which results in a life in the salutary presence of Yahweh. [100]

6. *Messengers*. The messenger commission "Go and say . . ." is "the typical form of every prophetic commission to preach the word." [101] It is used primarily in prophetic oracles of judgment against individuals. Even though it is "almost always formulated by the narrator" and can therefore "scarcely belong to the original prophetic speech," [102] it does manifest the notion of the prophet's mission and legitimation and characterizes him as a messenger. The job of a messenger is to set out with a message. This accounts for the frequent use of the messenger commission to introduce prophetic oracles, with the imperative *lēkh/lᵉkhāh* (or the inf. abs. *hālôkh*) often being used as a stereotyped hortatory particle ("Up!"). The imperative *lēkh* takes its theological import from its context and becomes a divine "imperative of sending." [103] "Going" seems to be meant in the concrete sense when the destination of the journey is mentioned (Ex. 7:15f.; Jer. 35:2; Ezk. 3:4); elsewhere the imperative or infinitive of *hālakh* in this context serves merely to intensify the following command to speak (*lēkh/hālôkh vᵉ'āmartā*: Isa. 6:9; Jer. 28:13; 34:2; 35:13; 39:16; *lēkh/hālôkh vᵉqārā'thā*: Jer. 2:2; 3:12; *lēkh dabbēr*: Ezk. 3:1; *lēkh hinnābhē'*: Am. 7:15) or to perform a specific symbolic action (Hos. 1:2; 3:1; Isa. 20:2; Jer. 13:1; 19:1). Behind this usage stands originally the command to the messenger to set out on his journey and transmit a message (2 S. 18:21). Thus the imperative also appears in connection with sending outside the corpus of written prophecy (Gen. 37:14; 2 S. 18:21; 2 K. 5:5), as well as in the context of a divine commission (Ex. 3:16; 4:12; 1 Ch. 17:4; 21:10), especially to prophets (1 K. 18:1; 19:15; 1 Ch. 17:4; 21:10), of transmission of a message (Ex. 3:16; 1 K. 14:7; 2 K. 18:10; 1 Ch. 17:4; 21:10), of seeking an oracle (2 K. 1:2; 22:13), and of receiving a divine message (in Yahweh wars: Jgs. 4:6; 6:14; 1 S. 15:3,18; 17:37; 23:2; etc.; in other contexts: 1 K.

---

[94] A. Weiser, *ATD*, XIII (⁵1968), 205.
[95] A view also espoused by Reindl, 140.
[96] *Ibid.*, 142.
[97] Contra Ahlström, 88: "to participate in proper worship, worship of Yahweh."
[98] Cf., e.g., H. Wildberger, *BK*, X (1965), 77.
[99] Cf. O. Kaiser, *Isaiah 1–12*. OTL (trans. 1972), 27.
[100] Wildberger, *BK*, X, 88 proposes the opposite interpretation: "The gift of grace involves the imperative to live in grace."
[101] Reventlow, *Liturgie*, 50.
[102] C. Westermann, *Basic Forms of Prophetic Speech* (trans. 1967), 142.
[103] Gouders, 143; cf. also *TDNT*, VI (trans. 1968), 571.

20:22; 2 K. 8:10; cf. *KAI,* 181.14). Here, too, besides the concrete spatial meaning of *hālakh* we find its special use in the particular contexts just listed. Once again, in many cases the imperative *hālakh* serves only as a hortatory particle in the sense of "Up!" or "Be ready!" (cf. Gen. 37:13; 2 K. 5:5).[104]

7. *God's Going.* "A childish picture" of God, which is "impressive" nonetheless,[105] is betrayed by the account of Yahweh's brief sojourn in the garden (*mithhallēkh,* Gen. 3:8 [J]). Yahweh "goes for a stroll,"[106] he takes "his daily walk"[107] in the garden when the wind blows through the treetops (cf. 2 S. 5:24)—perhaps an answer (etiological?) to the question of the origin and nature of the cooling breeze, but more likely (for J) an expression of the intimate relationship between Yahweh and mankind,[108] for the presentation of which "everything is transposed into human terms."[109]

After the Fall, this intimacy is restricted to a few elect individuals, e.g., Abraham, who negotiates with Yahweh over the fate of Sodom and Gomorrah and from whom Yahweh then "goes his way" (Gen. 18:33 [J]), and the tribes departing from Egypt, who depend on God's leadership (Ex. 13:21, *hālakh liphnê;* 33:16, *hālakh 'im;* 34:9, *hālakh beqerebh*). Here, however, God no longer "goes" without substratum, but in the pillar of clouds and fire (Ex. 13:21; Nu. 14:14b, a "literal quotation" from Ex. 13:21;[110] on Nu. 12:9, cf. v. 5), in his *pānîm* (on Ex. 33:16, cf. vv. 14f.), or in his "abode" (on Lev. 26:12, cf. v. 11; 2 S. 7:6f.). To this notion is added that of being led by the → מלאך *mal'akh yhvh/'elōhîm* (Ex. 14:19; 23:23; 32:34). When Yahweh goes before, with, or in the midst of Israel, it means that he is present to lead them in both the first and the second exodus (Isa. 52:12). It can also mean help in battle,[111] especially in Deuteronomy (Dt. 1:30,33; 20:4; 31:6,8), where the expression appears primarily in the so-called "war speeches."[112] This idea is taken up by the Cyrus oracle in Isa. 45:2, which has a striking parallel in the Cyrus Cylinder:[113] "He [Marduk] made him [Cyrus] set out ... going at his side like a real friend." Even if the word *hālakh* is not used to represent an epiphany, the pillar of cloud and fire, as well as the *mal'ākh* and *pānîm,* associate it with epiphanic motifs.[114]

It spells disaster, by contrast, when Yahweh returns to his place (*'ēlēkh 'āshûbhāh,* Hos. 5:15), perhaps as a lion retreats into its den with its prey (5:14).[115] Nothing is said about the place Yahweh returns to, whether the

---

[104] Cf. *KAI,* 165.1; on *deúte* in the LXX, cf. Flashar, 99.

[105] Procksch, *KAT,* I, 33; similarly Gunkel, *GHK,* I/1, 18.

[106] Gunkel, *GHK,* I/1, 18.

[107] Ehrlich, *Randglossen,* I, 14.

[108] Von Rad, *Genesis,* 73; Driver, *WC,* I, 46: "God and man were wont to meet and to discourse together"; likewise Haag, 62.

[109] Speiser, *AB,* I, 25; similarly Cassuto, *Genesis,* I, 150.

[110] M. Noth, *Numbers. OTL* (trans. 1968), 112.

[111] Cf. Fredriksson, 11f.

[112] Cf. Von Rad, *Deuteronomy,* 41, 131.

[113] *ANET*³, 315.

[114] For a different opinion, see Schnutenhaus, 19.

[115] Cf. Wolff, *Hosea,* 116.

heavens or Sinai.[116] Job 22:14 uses the image of God walking on the vault of heaven to express his distance,[117] with more stress on his "living" or "dwelling" far off than on his "walking."

The notion of Yahweh's "going" or "walking" seems to have originated with J (Gen. 3:8; 18:33; Ex. 13:21); it is in line with J's anthropomorphic representation of Yahweh and his action, found in other passages as well. Initially, Yahweh's passage is manifest in the movement of the wind (Gen. 3:8) and in the pillar of cloud and fire (Ex. 13:21; cf. also the J material in Nu. 12:9; 14:14); later the expression serves to represent God's presence, his leadership, his help in battle. In a later period, which finds talk of Yahweh's "going" too anthropomorphic or out of date, the "righteousness" and "glory" of Yahweh take the place of Yahweh himself (Isa. 58:8b; cf. 52:12b).[118] Righteousness can go not only before Israel but before Yahweh himself (Ps. 85:14[13]). Whether the idea of the royal herald is still behind this manner of expression is dubious;[119] it seems more likely that we are dealing with the metaphorical use of hālakh in the sense "spread out" (2 Ch. 26:8; Ps. 91:6).

Not only does Yahweh go himself, he also causes others to go (hôlîkh), i.e., he leads, especially through the desert (cf. such passages as Isa. 48:21; Jer. 2:6; Hos. 2:16[14]; Am. 2:10; Ps. 136:16) and through water (Isa. 63:13; Ps. 106:9). "God's leading Israel through the Sea of Reeds and the desert is conceived both spatially as guidance and morally as help,"[120] but also as punishment (Hos. 2:16[14]; Lam. 3:2; Dt. 28:36).

8. *Conclusions.* Deuteronomy and the Deuteronomistic history have a propensity for using the general term "way" (→ דרך *derekh*) in a theological sense.[121] It is in these circles, most likely, that we should localize the theological use of hālakh, which takes the ways of Yahweh as his commandments and the walking of men in these ways as life according to these commandments. This interpretation is taken up by P, who expresses walking before Yahweh as an imperative (Gen. 17:1) and interprets Noah's walking with God (6:9) as referring to his ethical and religious integrity. This is in line with the use of the expression "walking in the ordinances of Yahweh" in preaching, probably levitical.

Another tradition, represented initially by J and E, understands "walking before Yahweh" as the experience of God's benevolent presence (Gen. 24:40 [J]; 48:15 [E]; cf. Ps. 56:14[13]; 116:9). Both interpretations meet in the description of a happy human life exclusively in the presence of God. Both share the view of human life as a journey, a heritage from the days "when Israel was a child" (Hos. 11:1).

Helfmeyer

---

[116] Cf. Weiser, *ATD,* XXIV, 56.
[117] Cf. the context and the translation of Weiser, *ATD,* XIII, 170.
[118] Zimmerli, 221.
[119] Gunkel, *GHK,* II/2, 374; Kraus, *BK,* XV, 593f.
[120] Nötscher, 33.
[121] Cf. Schedl, 294.

הלל hll I and II; הִלּוּלִים hillûlîm; תְּהִלָּה tᵉhillāh

Contents: I. 1. Etymology; 2. Ancient Near Eastern Parallels. II. Occurrences; LXX.
III. Piel: 1. Secular Use; 2. Praise of God. IV. Pual. V. Hithpael. VI. tᵉhillāh.

I. 1. Etymology. There are three different roots hll in Hebrew. The root hll
I is cognate with Arab. halla, "appear on the horizon," V "shine," hilāl, "new
moon"; Ugar. hll, "new moon." [1] From this root derive the hiphil, "shine, cause
to shine" (Isa. 13:10; Job 29:3; 31:26) and the impf. form yhlyl, "make shining"
(Sir. 36/33:27). Here also belongs hêlêl (hēlāl?) ben shachar as a term for the
morning star in Isa. 14:12. [2]

The root hll II means "praise, extol." It is associated etymologically with Ugar.
hll, "shout"; [3] Syr. hallel, "praise"; and Akk. alālu, a laborers' shout or song,
elēlu, "jubilation," [4] alālu (verb), "sing a song of joy," III "rejoice, shout." [5]
In Arabic, halla IV means "sing joyfully to someone"; tahallala means "shout
with joy." Cf. also Amharic ilīl, Tigr. ʿēlēl, "jubilation." [6] We are probably dealing with an onomatopoetic word. In this context, too, belongs the shout of jubilation hillûlîm (Jgs. 9:27) at the vintage or harvest festival (Lev. 19:24).

On hll III, see the article following.

2. Ancient Near Eastern Parallels. Other Akkadian words for "praise" include dalālu, "pay homage to, praise," [7] nâdu or naʾādu, "extol, praise" [8] (both
primarily with gods as their object, but sometimes with attributes), as well as
karābu, "salute with respect" (a god or the king), [9] zakāru, "speak well of," [10]
and elû, II "praise, exalt" (a god or attributes), [11] and finally šurruḫu, "extol,"
and šurbû, "magnify, praise." [12]

Egyptian possesses a wealth of words that express various aspects of praising.

---

hll. F. Crüsemann, *Studien zur Formgeschichte von Hymnus und Danklied in Israel.*
WMANT, 32 (1969); J. W. McKay, "Helel and the Dawn-Goddess; a Re-examination of the
Myth in Isaiah XIV 12-25," *VT,* 20 (1970), 451-464; T. Nöldeke, "Halleluja," in W. Franken-
berg, ed., *Abhandlungen zur semitischen Religionskunde und Sprachwissenschaft. Festschrift
G. von Baudissin. BZAW,* 33 (1918), 375-380; C. Westermann, *The Praise of God in the
Psalms* (trans. 1965); idem, *THAT,* I (1971), 493-502.

[1] *WUS,* No. 832.
[2] See comms.
[3] *UT,* No. 769.
[4] *AHw,* 197; cf. *CAD,* IV, 80.
[5] *AHw,* 34; cf. *CAD,* I, 331f.
[6] Nöldeke, 375f.
[7] *AHw,* 153.
[8] *AHw,* 705.
[9] *AHw,* 208.
[10] *CAD,* XXI, 19.
[11] *AHw,* 208.
[12] *AHw,* 940.

Among the most common is *dwꜣ*, "honor, praise" (perhaps originally: "sing the morning hymn"), which very often serves to introduce hymns [13] and indicates worship of the gods in pictorial representations. From the Old Kingdom onward biographical and funerary texts speak of worshipping a god for the benefit of a third party (*dwꜣ* + DN + *n* + noun or proper name).[14] Other general verbs are *ḥkn*, "praise" (a god), and *snsy/snsn*, "worship." Particular aspects of praise are brought out in *rnn*, "rejoice, extol," *wts nfrw*, "exalt the beauty of," *sꜣḥ*, "spiritualize, glorify," *sꜥꜣ*, "make great, magnify," *swꜣš*, "honor," and *ḏsr*, "make splendid."

II. Occurrences; LXX. The verb occurs in Hebrew in the piel, pual, and hithpael. Of the 113 occurrences in the piel, 9 that refer to persons or things are scattered throughout the OT; the majority of the other passages, which refer to God, his name, or his word, occur in the Psalms or in the psalms quoted in Chronicles. The pual occurs 10 times, the hithpael 19 times. In addition we find the nouns *tᵉhillāh*, "praise, hymn of praise" (57 times), and *hillûlîm*, "jubilation" (twice).

The LXX usually translates the piel of *hll* by means of *ainein*, but sometimes uses *hýmnein* or *exomologeísthai*. The hithpael is rendered with *enkaucḥástai*, *epainein*, and *endoxázesthai*. For *tᵉhillāh* we find *aínesis* and *hýmnos*. The phrase *halᵉlû-yāh* is transliterated *allēlouiá*.

III. Piel.

1. *Secular Use.* The range of meanings of the verb can be determined more or less accurately with the aid of its "secular" occurrences. The princes of Pharaoh "praise" Sarah for her beauty (Gen. 12:15). The people praise Absalom, likewise for his beauty (2 S. 14:25). According to Ezekiel, Tyre is a city renowned or praised (pual) for its wealth, for which, however, a lamentation (*qînāh*) is now to be raised (Ezk. 26:17). According to Prov. 12:8, a man is commended or praised (pual) for his good sense; the foolish man, by contrast, is despised (*yihyeh lābhûz* [→ בזה *bāzāh*]). Prov. 27:2 states that no one should "praise" himself, but should leave his praise to others—in other words, if a man is wise and acts rightly, others will in fact praise him. The wicked, however, are "praised" only by those who forsake the law (Prov. 28:4). We read that a good wife is "praised" by her works (Prov. 31:31), and it is stated as a general rule that a woman who fears Yahweh is to be praised (hithpael, v. 30). We also learn that the children of a good wife call her blessed (*'ishshēr*) and her husband "praises" her (v. 28). The same parallelism occurs in Cant. 6:9: the maidens call the beloved woman happy, while the queens and concubines "praise" her. The term *'ishshēr* obviously refers to salutation with the *'ashrê* formula (→ אשרי *'ashrê*); *hll* appears accordingly to refer

---

[13] S. Hassan, *Hymnes religieux du Moyen Empire* (Cairo, 1928), 6f.
[14] J. Sainte-Fare Garnot, *L'hommage aux dieu ... d'après les textes des pyramides* (1954), 10.

to public praise. This last passage might suggest a ceremonial praising of the bride, which may also be meant in Ps. 78:63: when God punished Israel, its maidens "were not praised" (pual), i.e., their praises were not sung in a marriage song. Public acclamation is quite clearly meant in 2 Ch. 23:12f.: the young king Jehoiada is "praised" as an act of homage by the people at his accession. Ps. 10:3 is obscure: the wicked man "praises" the desires of his heart (ta'ᵃvath naphshô)— but here *hillēl* is constructed with 'al and the text is clearly corrupt.

The self-praise expressed by the hithpael also contributes to our definition of the term. [15]

2. *Praise of God.* a. In the majority of passages, God is the object of the verb. In one single instance the verb is used of non-Israelites: the Philistines praise their god on account of their victory over Samson (Jgs. 16:24). Everywhere else we are always dealing with Yahweh (or *yāh*), although formally the object is often the name (→ שם *shēm*) of Yahweh. The verb takes either the accusative or the preposition *lᵉ*.

b. The locus of the praise is the temple (*bêth qodhshēnû*, Isa. 64:10 [Eng. v. 11]; "thy house," Ps. 85:5[4]; *chatsrôth qodhshî*, Isa 62:9) or the congregation (*bᵉthôkh qāhāl*, Ps. 22:23[22]; *bᵉqāhāl rābh*, *bᵉ'am 'ātsûm*, Ps. 35:18; *biqhal 'am ûbhᵉmôshabh zᵉqēnîm*, Ps. 107:32; *bᵉthôkh rabbîm*, Ps. 109:30). Correspondingly, the summons to praise is usually in the plural (*hallᵉlû*).

c. The nature of the praise is suggested by various parallel verbs: "sing" (*shîr*, Jer. 20:13), "sing praises, make melody" (*zimmēr*, Ps. 146:2; 149:3), "tell" (*sippēr*, Ps. 22:23[22]). Other passages state the manner of praising explicitly: "with a song" (*bᵉshîr*, Ps. 69:31[30]), "with dancing" (Ps. 149:3), "with music" (Ps. 150:1-5). The content of the term can be determined from parallel verbs belonging to the same semantic field: "thank" (*hôdhāh* [→ ידה *ydh*], Isa. 38:18; Ps. 35:18; 44:9[8]; 109:30; and the lists of the Chronicler[16]), "glorify" (*kibbēdh*, Ps. 22:24[23]), "magnify" (*rômēm*, Ps. 69:31[30]; 107:32), "extol" (*shibbach*, Ps. 117:1; 147:12), "bless" (*bērēkh* [→ ברך *brk*], Ps. 115:17f.; 145:2; cf. 1 Ch. 16:36), "invoke" (*hizkîr* [→ זכר *zākhar*], 1 Ch. 16:4; 2 Ch. 31:2), "rejoice" (*rinnēn, tsāchal,* Jer. 31:7).

d. In one group of occurrences in the Chronicler's history we learn more details about the cultic praise of Yahweh as conceived in the period of the Chronicler. The singing is performed by the Levites—as David himself had ordained: he appointed them as ministers (*mᵉsharᵉthîm*) before the ark *ûlᵉhazkîr ûlᵉhôdhôth ûlᵉhallēl lᵉyhvh*, "to invoke, to thank, and to praise Yahweh, the God of Israel" (1 Ch. 16:4; the praise is to be accompanied with music). When the Levites have finished singing their hymn (Pss. 105, 96, etc. are cited), concluding with *bārûkh*

---

[15] See below, V.
[16] See below.

yhvh, the people reply "Amen" and praise Yahweh (*v^ehallēl l^eyhvh*, 1 Ch. 16:36; similarly Neh. 5:13). In 1 Ch. 23 the organization of the Levites is established: 4000 of them are to praise Yahweh (*m^ehall^elîm l^eyhvh*) on the instruments made by David for praise (*l^ehallēl*) (v. 5). We also read that they stand (*'āmadh*) every morning and evening to thank and praise Yahweh (*l^ehōdhôth ûl^ehallēl l^eyhvh*) (v. 30). In 1 Ch. 25:3 it is decreed that the sons of Jeduthun under his leadership are to thank and praise Yahweh on the *kinnôr*. After completion of the temple, Solomon confirms these arrangements: the Levites are to praise and minister (*l^ehallēl ûl^eshārēth*) before the priests (2 Ch. 8:14, with *hillēl* constructed absolutely; cf. also 2 Ch. 31:2, *l^ehōdhôth ûl^ehallēl* under Hezekiah). When the ark was brought into the temple, the singers and musicians had already praised and thanked Yahweh in unison (*l^ehashmia' qôl 'echādh l^ehallēl ûl^ehōdhôth l^eyhvh*), "for he is good, for his steadfast love endures forever" (2 Ch. 5:13). [17] Thanking and praising with music as ordered by David is also mentioned at the dedication of the temple (2 Ch. 7:6). After the victory of Jehoshaphat over Israel's neighbors, the Kohathites and Korahites praised Yahweh "with a very loud voice" (*b^eqôl gādhôl l^emā'elāh*, 2 Ch. 20:19), and at a thanksgiving celebration the next day people are appointed to sing to Yahweh and praise him in holy array (*m^eshōr^erîm l^eyhvh ûm^ehal^elîm b^ehadhrath qōdhesh* [→ הדר *hādhar*], 2 Ch. 20:21). On the occasion of Hezekiah's reform of worship we are told once more how the Levites "praised Yahweh with the words of David" and how they sang praises (*hallēl* used absolutely) with gladness (*śimchāh*) and bowed down (*qdd*) and worshipped (*hishtach^avāh* [→ חוה *ḥvh*], 2 Ch. 29:30). Under Hezekiah the *matstsôth* festival was celebrated with great gladness (*śimchāh*), while "the priests and Levites praised Yahweh with instruments of might" (2 Ch. 30:21). Finally Ezr. 3:10f. tells how, when the cornerstone for the new temple was laid, the priests and Levites praised Yahweh according to the directions of David, and sang, praising and giving thanks (*b^ehallēl ûbh^ehôdhôth*) for his goodness and steadfast love (quotation as above).

These passages make it clear that the postexilic period felt the praise of God to be an institution inaugurated by David. It was entrusted to the priests and above all to the Levites; the people joined in by saying "Amen," but also were clearly able to praise Yahweh themselves (1 Ch. 16:36). Most frequently *hillēl* is combined with *hôdhāh; hizkîr* and *shôrēr* also occur, but *shērēth* is used differently. It is emphasized, furthermore, that the institutional praise of God is associated with gladness (*śimchāh*) and rejoicing (*t^erû'āh*, Ezr. 3:12). If we disregard the institutionalization, the picture agrees with what we can deduce from the Psalms.

e. In the passages from the Chronicler's history, those who praise God are usually the Levites; twice it is "the people" (1 Ch. 16:36; Ezr. 3:11). But the Levites praise God on behalf of the congregation. In the Psalms, as has already been mentioned, the summons to praise is almost always in the plural; in other

---

[17] On the quotation from Psalms, see below, g.

words, it is addressed to the community. The only exception (since Ps. 147:12 addresses Zion as a collective noun) is Ps. 146:1: "Praise Yahweh, O my soul." This form of address is usually used with *hôdhāh,* "thank," just as the summons to individuals to praise Yahweh is usually associated with *hôdhāh.* [18] In the singular we find instead the voluntative form "I will praise": at the beginning of a psalm of praise (145:2; 146:2), in the middle of a psalm (56:5,11[4,10]; 119:171), or as a vow of praise at the end of a lament (22:23[22]; 35:18; 69:31[30]; 109:30), but often with the addition of "in the congregation." Moreover, all creation can be called on to praise God (Ps. 148: angels, sun, moon, heavens, everything on earth; Ps. 150:6: "everything that breathes"; cf. Ps. 69:35[34]), as well as "all peoples" (Ps. 117:1; cf. 148:11).

f. As we have already stated, the praise is addressed to God, usually as Yahweh or the short form *yāh* (Ps. 102:19[18]; 115:17; 150:6; and 24 times in the formula *halelû-yāh*), only rarely as *'elōhîm* (Ps. 44:9[8]), or to his name (Joel 2:26; Ps. 69:31[30]; 74:21; 113:1; 145:2; 148:5,13; 149:3; 1 Ch. 29:13). In one single instance God's word is praised (Ps. 56:5,11[4,10]—possibly with reference to a favorable oracle).

g. The reason for praising God is indicated three times by the Chronicler by means of the formula *kî ṭôbh kî le'ôlām chasdô,* "for he is good, for his steadfast love endures forever"—a quotation from the Psalms (106:1; 107:1; 118:1,2,3,4, 29 [thanksgiving psalms]; 100:5; 136:1-26 [hymns]). God's *chesedh* is cited as a reason to praise him in Ps. 107:31f. (along with his *niphlā'ôth*); 117:1 (along with his *'emeth*). As concrete reasons for praise Isa. 62:9 cites harvest and food (cf. *hillûlîm* at the vintage, Jgs. 9:27; cf. Lev. 19:24); Joel 2:26 cites eating one's fill (along with God's wondrous acts [*haphlî'*]). Ps. 147:2 links praise with Yahweh's help, protection, and *shālôm.* Ps. 107 is a thanksgiving psalm for various categories of deliverance, introduced by "O give thanks to Yahweh, for he is good, for his *chesedh* endures forever." Verse 31 speaks of thanksgiving (*hôdhāh*); v. 32 uses the verbs *rômēm* and *hillēl.* The preceding verses speak of deliverance from peril at sea, the following verses of streams in the desert and fertility. Ps. 147 speaks in general terms of Yahweh's goodness, greatness, and compassion for the humble, but also more specifically of the building of Jerusalem and of protection and *shālôm* for the holy city, for which Zion is to bless (*brk*) and praise (*hll*) him (v. 12). In Ps. 149, Yahweh is praised as king of Israel, who is creator and gives his people victory over their enemies: they are therefore to sing him a new song, to be joyful and praise him. Here the motifs of an accession hymn stand out clearly. Ps. 148, which calls on all creation to praise Yahweh, justifies the praise in part on the grounds that "he commanded and they were created" (v. 5), in part quite generally by reference to his exalted name and his glory (v. 13). In conclusion it states that he has raised up a horn for his people that is a *tehillāh* for all his saints.

---

[18] Westerman, *THAT.*

Praise can also be presented as a fitting duty (Ps. 33:1; 147:1; and, with a minor emendation, 65:2).

In vows of praise deliverance of the petitioner is often cited as the reason (Ps. 22:23,24,27[22,23,26]; 35:18; 102:19[18]). Here we find with particular frequency a reference to deliverance of the poor (Ps. 69:35[34]; cf. vv. 30f.[29f.]; 74:21; 109:30f.; cf. 146:7 ["justice for the oppressed, food for the hungry"] and Jer. 20:13). Ps. 102 is a lament that turns into a thanksgiving, introduced by v. 14 (13): "Thou wilt arise and have pity on Zion"; this act of compassion will evoke praise in the future.

In Ps. 22:27(26), praise is associated with life. One might follow Westermann[19] and say that praise of God is, so to speak, a necessary condition for life. In any case, praise of God ceases with death (Isa. 38:18; Ps. 115:17—the latter passage states that the dead do not praise Yahweh, "but we [the living] will bless [brk]" him [v. 18]).

IV. Pual. Apart from the three occurrences mentioned in III.1 above, the only pual form found is the participle $m^e hull\bar{a}l$. It is applied to Yahweh four times in the Psalms, three of them in the formula "Great is Yahweh and $m^e hull\bar{a}l$ ('praised' or 'praiseworthy')" (Ps. 48:2[1]; 96:4 [cited in 1 Ch. 16:25]; 145:3). In Ps. 96 he is said in the same verse to be "feared" ($n\hat{o}r\bar{a}$'); in Ps. 145 his greatness is emphasized. Ps. 18:4(3) (= 2 S. 22:4), "I call upon Yahweh $m^e hull\bar{a}l$," is difficult; perhaps the meaning is "declaring him praiseworthy." In any case the participle refers to God.

According to Ps. 113:3, Yahweh's name is "to be praised" ($m^e hull\bar{a}l$). Verse 1 calls on men to praise Yahweh, and v. 2 contains the sentence "$b\bar{a}r\hat{u}kh$ be the name of Yahweh." The praise is addressed to the exalted God who delivers and raises up the poor and downtrodden.

V. Hithpael. In the hithpael, hll means "pride oneself," often with overtones of "brag, boast." A man can boast of his courage or peaceableness (1 K. 20:11) or of his generosity (Prov. 25:14). Ammon boasts of its fertile valleys (Jer. 49:4), the tyrant (gibbôr) of his evil (Ps. 52:3), the rich man of his wealth, in which he trusts (→ בטח‎ $b\bar{a}tach$) (Ps. 49:7[6]). According to Jer. 9:22(23), no one should boast of his wisdom, his might, or his riches; the only justified ground for boasting is knowledge of Yahweh. It is also wrong to boast about the morrow, because no one knows what it will bring (Prov. 27:1). The hithpael is used absolutely in Prov. 20:14: the buyer declares that the merchandise is inferior, but when he goes away "he boasts," i.e., he knows that he got a good buy.

But it is also possible to boast or glory in God, often in the context of rejoicing. The righteous will rejoice in Yahweh, the upright glory (in him), says Ps. 64:11 (10). The king will rejoice in God, and all who swear by him will glory (Ps. 63:1? [11]). "You shall rejoice in Yahweh; in the Holy One of Israel you shall glory," says Deutero-Isaiah (Isa. 41:17); the reason is triumph over enemies. Ps. 105:3

---

[19] *Ibid.*

summons the congregation to glory in the name of Yahweh and to rejoice (cited in 1 Ch. 16:10). According to Ps. 106:5, the nation rejoices in God's help, and glories. Thankful glorying in Yahweh is also mentioned in Isa. 45:25; the enemies of Israel are humbled and Israel has triumphed. The same is true in Ps. 34:3(2), where praise of God is coupled with boasting in him and the psalmist's deliverance is cited as the reason.

In one passage (Jer. 4:2), *hithhallēl* stands side by side with "bless oneself in Yahweh" (*hithbārēkh* [→ ברך *brk*]); the subject is "the nations," who will bless themselves in Yahweh and glory in him as a consequence of Israel's return to Yahweh. Finally, *hithhallēl bā'elîlîm* is used of those who worship idols in Ps. 97:7.

VI. teḥillāh. The noun *teḥillāh* scarcely adds anything new to the discussion. In a totally secular sense, it is used of the "renown" of Moab and Babylon (Jer. 48:2; 51:41), which is destroyed by Yahweh; Damascus is a *'îr teḥillāh*, a "famous" city (Jer. 49:25); cf. also Isa. 60:18; 61:3; 62:7. Occasionally *teḥillāh* stands side by side with *shēm* (Zeph. 3:19f.) or *shēm* and *tiph'ereth* (Dt. 26:19; Jer. 13:11). In the two latter cases we are dealing with the glory and praise that Israel will receive among the nations or from Yahweh as the God of Israel; in Zephaniah we are dealing with the praise that will follow upon Israel's restoration. In like fashion, Jer. 33:9 speaks of Jerusalem as an object of joy, praise, and glory for all the nations.

Close to this meaning are the Psalms passages that speak or proclaim the *teḥillāh* of Yahweh (*sippēr*: Ps. 9:15[14]; 78:4; 79:13; 102:22[21]; *hishmîa'*: Ps. 106:2; cf. 66:8 with *qôl*; *hāghāh*: Ps. 35:28; other verbs used with *teḥillāh* are *shîr* [Isa. 42:10; Ps. 106:12; 149:1], *higgîdh* [Isa. 42:12; Ps. 51:17(15)], *biśśēr* [Isa. 60:6], *hizkîr* [Isa. 63:7], *hibbîa'* [Ps. 119:171], and *dibbēr* [Ps. 145:21]). This seems to indicate that the "praise of God" is an entity that exists and need only be expressed. In concrete form this "praise" is a song of praise (e.g., Ps. 40:4; 145:1) or audible singing (Ps. 22:26[25]; 34:2[1]; 48:11[10]; 71:8,14; 100:4; cf. also Hab. 3:3).

God is the object of this praise; his deeds are the reason for it. He is therefore "the God of my *teḥillāh*" (Ps. 109:1) or even "my *teḥillāh*" (Jer. 17:14, as motivation for the prayer requesting healing and deliverance). Thus we read in Dt. 10:21: "He [Yahweh your God] is your praise; he is your God, who has done for you these great and terrible things (*gedhōlôth, nôrā'ôth*)." Here it is also possible for *teḥillāh* to refer to the object of praise. Ex. 15:11 describes the incomparable God as *nôrā' thehillōth, 'ōśēh phele'*, "terrible in glorious deeds, doing wonders"; as recipient of Israel's praise, he is referred to as *yôshēbh teḥillôth yiśrā'ēl*, "enthroned on the praises of Israel" (Ps. 22:4[3]). According to Isa. 42:8, Yahweh is jealous that his praise not be given to idols.

Ringgren

הלל hll III; הֹולֵל hôlēl; הֹולֵלֹות hôlēlôth;
הֹולֵלוּת hôlēlûth; תָּהֳלָה toholāh

I. Occurrences and Translation. II. Etymology. III. Use.

I. Occurrences and Translation. The root *hll* III occurs 19 (or 20) times in the Hebrew OT, 14 times as a verb (qal, poel, poal, hithpael), 5 times as a noun (*hôlēlôth, hôlēlûth*). In addition, Rashi, Ibn Ezra, and Dhorme[1] include the word *toholāh* in Job 4:18. Sirach also uses the word, as does the Hymn Scroll from Qumran. The noun is also attested, albeit rarely, in Rabbinic literature.

The verbal form is therefore primary. It occurs as follows: (a) qal ptcp. in the Psalms (5:6 [Eng. v. 5]; 73:3; 75:5[4]) and perhaps also poal ptcp. (Ps. 102:9 [8]); (b) poel or polel in Isa. 44:25; Job 12:17; Eccl. 2:2; 7:7; poal ptcp. in Ps. 102:9(8) MT; (c) hithpael in the earliest texts, 1 S. 21:14(13); Nah. 2:5(4); Jer. 25:16; 46:9; 50:38; 51:7. This form appears again in Sir. 3:27 and the Qumran hymns (1QH 2:36; 3:33; 4:8,12,17,20f.; 10:33).

The meaning is undoubtedly pejorative, except perhaps in Jeremiah and Nahum. In the Psalms, *hôlēl* is translated *"Tor"* (Ringgren, Galling), *"über-mütig"* or *"Prahler"* (Kraus), "boaster" (Briggs, Dahood), *"insensé"* (Caquot, Manatti). The verb refers to irrational behavior, but of what sort? The prophetic texts have suggested such translations as *"rasen," "sinnlos auf etwas trotzen,"* "drive madly," and *"foncer."* Even the LXX had difficulty with the word. Apart from the cases where it does not venture a translation at all (Isa. 44:25;[2] Eccl. 1:17; Ps. 102:9[8]), it renders the term by means of *parephéreto* (1 S. 21:14[13]), *synchythēsontai* (Nah. 2:5[9]), *manēsontai* (Jer. 25:16 [LXX 32:2]), *paraskeuá-sate* (Jer. 46:9 [LXX 26:9]), *esaleúthēsan* (Jer. 51:7 [LXX 28:7]), and *exéstēsen* (Job 12:17). In the Psalms we are dealing with those who transgress the law (cf. *anómois* in Ps. 73:3), which can be explained as being due to the influence of the Hebrew parallels (*reshā'îm, pô'alê 'āven*). The translator of Ecclesiastes chooses forms deriving from *periphérein*, "turn, overturn" (cf. Prov. 10:24, without Heb. equivalent). The grandson of Ben Sira was inspired by the Psalms (*ho hamartōlós prosthēsei*).

II. Etymology. As Podechard already stated,[3] the origin of the word is obscure. The following possibilities should be noted:

---

hll. T. Donald, "The Semantic Field of 'Folly,'" *VT*, 13 (1963), 285-292; F. Ellermeier, *Qohelet*, I (1967), 169; P. Joüon, "Notes de lexicographie hébraïque," *MUSJ*, 5/2 (1912), 415-446, esp. 422-24; O. Loretz, *Qohelet und der alte Orient* (1964), 241; M. Mansoor, "Studies in the New Hodayoth," *RevQ*, 3 (1961/62), 259-266, 387-394, esp. 263f.

[1] E. Dhorme, *Job* (1967), 53.
[2] Cf. M. Goshen-Gottstein, "Theory and Practice of Textual Criticism," *Textus*, 3 (1963), 153.
[3] E. Podechard, *L'Ecclésiaste. Études Bibliques* (1912), 255.

a. On the basis of Syr. and Aram. *hyll* (from the root *yll* [→ ילל *yll* II]), "wail, lament" (Ahikar 41), an echoic word like Heb. *hll* II, "praise, rejoice" (→ הלל *hll* I & II) has been suggested; cf. Akk. *alālu*, "shout, sing, rejoice, boast"; [4] Tigré *tĕ-hawläla*, "be praised"; Tigr. *ĕlĕll*, "shouts of joy." [5]

b. Joüon thinks in terms of *hll* I, "shine" (*hll* actually means "new moon" in Ugaritic, [6] as does *hilāl* in Arabic). In Nah. 2:5(4), the chariots that *yithhôlᵉlû* are compared to blazing torches. By this etymology the *hôlᵉlîm* would be "moon-struck."

c. M. Lambert [7] cites Arab. *hāla*, "startle," and finds in Job 12:17 a good parallel to *šll* from Arab. *šwl*, "confuse."

d. Mansoor has determined that the meaning "mad" is not appropriate in the Hodayoth; the translation should be "deceive," a meaning that fits the Psalms passages and Eccl. 7:3. Mansoor's observations are to the point. The root *yll* is out of the question. A better parallel is Akk. *ul, ullû, ullānu*, which is found as early as Old Akkadian [8] and means "negation, absence, distance" (Mari). (Akk. *ul* is usually connected with Heb. *'al*; cf. also *ulālu*, "weakling.") Originally, then, the *hôlēl* is closely related to the *'elîl* (→ אליל *'elîl*); both terms signify nothingness, powerlessness. [9]

III. Use. The meaning arrived at above fits the earliest citation, 1 S. 21:14(13), which contains very concrete images expressed in a difficult vocabulary. In the presence of the Philistines David changes his appearance (*vayshannô 'eth taʿmô*) before their eyes (*bᵉʿênêhem*), makes himself worthless (*vayyithhōlēl*) in their hands (*bᵉyādhām*), and feigns senility and mental breakdown; Achish treats him like a madman (the terms *hishtaggēaʿ* and *mᵉshuggāʿ* occur in the context).

Originally, then, the expression does not belong to the realm of wisdom (it never occurs in Proverbs), but to the military realm. This is still its context in Nahum and Jeremiah. In Nah. 2:5(4) we read that the chariots "plunge about" (*yithhôlᵉlû*; par. *šqq*; cf. Prov. 28:15; Isa. 29:8; and even Joel 2:9, of locusts overrunning the walls of the city). In Jer. 25:16, the nations "stagger and fall" (*vᵉhithgōʿᵃshû vᵉhithholᵉlû*) before the sword that Yahweh sends among them. Jer. 46:9 remains difficult. Here *hithhôlēl* seems exceptionally to have a positive meaning: the horses and chariots "charge." But in the prophet's vision, Egypt, mobilizing for war, will be destroyed. In Jer. 50:38, *hithhôlēl* refers to the idol worship of the Babylonians; in Jer. 51:7, it describes the consequences of drinking the cup of Yahweh's wrath (cf. 25:16).

---

[4] *AHw*, 34; *CAD*, I, 331f.
[5] Leslau, *Contributions*, 18.
[6] *WUS*, No. 832.
[7] *Revue des Études Juives*, 63 (1912), 310.
[8] I. J. Gelb, *Old Akkadian Writing and Grammar* (²1961).
[9] *TDOT*, I, 285.

In Isa. 44:25, the powerlessness of the magicians and diviners replaces military impotence. The word is used similarly in Ps. 5:6(5), in parallelism with *pô'ªlê 'āven*. According to Mowinckel, these latter were originally magicians: they may not appear before Yahweh and are hated by him. The other Psalms, following quite naturally in the footsteps of Deuteronomy's opposition to magic, think of the *hôlªlîm* as transgressors of the law. In Ps. 73:3 they are identified with the *rªshā'îm*, who arouse the envy of the psalmist. In Ps. 75:5(4), too, the *hôlªlîm* appear in parallel with the *rªshā'îm*; but *'al tāhōllû*, "do not practice *hll*, do not be *hôlªlîm*," stands in parallel with "do not lift up your horn." In Ps. 102:9(8), the *mªhôlālai* are the psalmist's enemies (→ איב *'āyabh*), who taunt and deride him.

From the vocabulary of the Psalms the word enters the wisdom books with Job 12:17, which states that God is able to render judges and kings powerless;[10] he likewise charges his angels with "weakness, worthlessness" *(tohºlāh)* (Job 4:18). The word was admirably suited to Ecclesiastes for describing the utter ineffectiveness of political wisdom. The author introduced the noun *hôlēlôth*, which he links with *ś/sikhlûth*, "folly," into the vocabulary of the Bible (1:17; 2:12; etc.). He sees in it "worthless actions" (fem. pl.); by analogy to *sikhlûth*, this form gives rise to an abstract noun in *-ûth* (Eccl. 10:13).[11] Like *chokhmôth*, *hôlēlôth* is not a real plural.

In Sirach and Rabbinic literature the word becomes vestigial. The uncertainty of the LXX robbed it of any influence in the NT. Its theological career was brief.

Cazelles

---

10 Dhorme, 176: "mad."
11 M. Dahood, "Qoheleth and Northwest Semitic Philology," *Bibl,* 43 (1962), 350.

הָמָה hāmāh; הָמוֹן hāmôn; הֶמְיָה hemyāh;
הַמוּלָה hᵃmûllāh

I. 1. Etymology; Related Roots; Semitic Cognates; 2. Occurrences. II. Secular Use:
1. Jumble of Noise and Movement; 2. Tumult. 3. Inward Agitation, Groaning; 4. Multitude, Wealth. III. Religious Use: 1. Yahweh's Mastery over the Sea and Forces of Nature;
2. Yahweh's Mastery over the Nations; 3. Yahweh's Mercy; 4. "Abraham." IV. Qumran.

I. 1. *Etymology; Related Roots; Semitic Cognates.* The root *hāmāh* and the
closely related roots *nhm,* → המם *hmm,* and *hvm* may go back to a biliteral onomatopoeic root *hm,* used to describe an unarticulated confusion of acoustical
and optical effects. The root *hāmāh* and its derivatives remained closest to this
nonspecific use and therefore have a wide semantic range, whereas the related
roots—possibly originating in the biblical period—seem to represent individual
aspects of the general meaning by virtue of specialization or intensification. The
onomatopoeic nature of the root was obviously felt at all times; this may explain
such otherwise unusual formulations as *hᵃmônîm hᵃmônîm* (Joel 4:14) or *lō'
mēhem vᵉlō' mēhᵃmônām vᵉlō' mēhᵉmēhem vᵉlō' nōaḥ bāhem* (Ezk. 7:11).[1]

Both *hāmāh* and *hāmôn* (whose derivation from *hvm*[2] has with good reason
not been accepted) are attested in Aramaic and Middle Hebrew in the sense "be
noisy, excited." The verb—in the reduplicated form *hmhm*—also appears in
Ethiopic, Coptic, and Arabic, with the meaning "mutter, growl, roar, say 'hm'";
cf. also Arab. *hamā,* "wander to and fro." Whether Ugar. *hmlt*[3] is connected
with *hᵃmullāh* is not entirely certain.

2. *Occurrences.* In the MT *hāmāh* occurs 34 times, always in the qal; 11 of
these occurrences are in the Psalms. Including *hᵃmônāh* (Ezk. 39:16), *hāmôn*
occurs 85 times in the MT (although 2 K. 25:11 should read *hā'āmôn*); the word
appears 27 times in Ezekiel (16 times in chaps. 29–32), 14 times in Isaiah, 10 times

hāmāh. G. Delling, "πλῆθος," *TDNT,* VI, 274-79; P. Derchain, "A propos de deux racines sémitiques **hm* et **zm*," *ChrÉg,* 42 (1967), 306-310; R. Frankena, *Kanttekeningen van
een assyrioloog bij Ezechiel* (1965); G. Gerleman, *Ruth/Das Hohelied. BK,* XVIII (1965) [on
Cant. 5:4]; *idem,* "Die lärmende Menge; der Sinn des Wortes *hamon*," *Wort und Geschichte.
Festschrift K. Elliger. AOAT,* 18 (1973), 71-75; A. M. Habermann, *BethM,* 14/3 [38] (1969),
86 (in Hebrew); P. Haupt, "The Book of Nahum," *JBL,* 26 (1907), 1-53, esp. 44; R. Hentschke,
Die Stellung der vorexilischen Schriftpropheten zum Kultus. BZAW, 75 (1957), 78; L. Kopf,
"Arabische Etymologien und Parallelen zum Bibelwörterbuch," *VT,* 9 (1959), 247-287, esp.
254; H.-M. Lutz, *Jahwe, Jerusalem und die Völker; zur Vorgeschichte von Sach. 12,1-8 und
14,1-5. WMANT,* 27 (1968), 48f., 60f.; W. Rudolph, *KAT,* XIII/2 (1971) [on Am. 5:23]; J.
Spiegel, "Der 'Ruf' des Königs," *WZKM,* 54 (1957), 191-203, esp. 193; F. Stolz, *THAT,* I,
502-504; H. Wildberger, *BK,* X/1 (1972) [on Isa. 5:13f.]; W. Zimmerli, *BK,* XIII (1969) [on
Ezk. 7:11ff.; 30:10].

[1] See IV.
[2] Haupt.
[3] *UT,* No. 777; *WUS,* No. 845.

in 1–2 Chronicles, but only 3 times in the Psalms. We find *hemyāh* once, *hᵃmullāh* twice.

II. Secular Use.

1. *Jumble of Noise and Movement.* The verb *hāmāh* and its derivatives cannot be dissociated from the concrete representation of a confused mixture of noise and movement. This can be seen in the frequent association of *hāmāh* (and *hᵃmullāh*) with *qôl*, and of *hāmôn* with *shā'ôn*. More specifically, the verb is often compared to the sound of musical instruments (flute, Jer. 48:36; stringed instruments, Isa. 14:11; 16:11) or the noises made by animals (bear, Isa. 59:11; dog, Ps. 59:7,15 [Eng. vv. 6,14]; dove, Ezk. 7:16); the object of the comparison is usually in the plural, possibly to suggest confusion.

That the word includes optical effects as well is shown by the comparison of a *hāmôn* to whirling dust or chaff (Isa. 29:5; cf. 17:12f.), but above all by its frequent comparison to the raging sea or waves (Isa. 17:12; 51:15; Jer. 5:22; 6:23 [=50:42]; 31:35; 51:42,55; Ezk. 1:24; Ps. 46:4[3]; 65:8[7]). In the context of this comparison we find verbs like *gā'ar* (→ גער *gā'ar*), *rāgha'*, and *gā'ash*, which underscore the elemental violence of the raging sea.

2. *Tumult.* In many passages, therefore, it is possible to speak simply of "tumult." The combination of visual and auditory effects is especially clear in the approaching thundershower (1 K. 18:41) and the rumbling chariot-wheels (Jer. 47:3), as well as the general confusion of a military camp, especially at the moment of attack and panic (1 S. 14:16,19; 2 S. 18:29; cf. Isa. 31:4; Ezk. 1:24) (→ המם *hmm*).

But there can also be tumult when a king is anointed (1 K. 1:41), when news is brought of a disaster (1 S. 4:14), when there is a cultic assembly (Jer. 3:23; 11:16; Am. 5:23 [=Ezk. 26:13]; Ezk. 5:7[?]; Ps. 42:5[4])—the choice of words does not necessarily imply criticism. But tumult is also a general characteristic of the city (1 K. 1:41; Isa. 5:14; 14:11; 22:2; 32:14; Ezk. 23:42; Job 39:7; Prov. 1:21). Here there is often an undertone of disapproval: tumult and exultant bravado often go together ('ālaz, Isa. 5:14; 22:2). The disapproval is even more pronounced when the verb is used directly to describe human behavior: men go about in turmoil but for nought (Ps. 39:7[6]), they prowl after the devout like a pack of dogs (Ps. 59:7,15[6,14]), "walk the streets" (Prov. 7:11; 9:13), turn into arrogant brawlers with too much wine (Prov. 20:1 [LXX = *hybristikós*]; cf. Zec. 9:15, if the text is correct). Here the emphasis is on unsteadiness and restlessness, to the wise man signs of inward disorder, of arrogance.

3. *Inward Agitation, Groaning.* The meaning develops in a totally different direction when the verb *hāmāh* serves to express inward agitation. This usage always occurs in the mouth of the person concerned (only the very late Isa. 63:15 speaks of *hᵃmôn mē'eykhā* with reference to Yahweh [4]): someone overwhelmed

---

[4] See III.3.

by emotion registers his agitation within his own body (usually *mēʿai,* but sometimes *libbî, qerābhai*); his agitation may be accompanied by groaning (→ נהם *nāham*). Such phenomena appear in moments of anguish (Jer. 4:19), mourning (Isa. 16:11; 59:11; Jer. 48:36—always in comparison to instruments or animals), apprehensive uncertainty in the face of peril (Ps. 42:6,12[5,11]; 43:5; 55:18[17]; 77:4[3]—always in combination with → שׂיח *śîach*), and sympathy (love: Cant. 5:4; mercy: see III.3).

4. *Multitude, Wealth.* The original meaning is most eroded where the noun *hāmôn* is used in the sense "multitude" or "wealth." Even so, in passages like Isa. 60:5; Jer. 49:32; and possibly also 2 K. 7:13 there still appears the notion of a multitude of various animals, and in Eccl. 5:9(10); 1 Ch. 29:16; and possibly Ps. 37:16 the notion of a multitude of coins. The word can refer to any large aggregate whose individual components are discernible (2 S. 6:19; Isa. 5:13; 16:14; Job 31:34; 2 Ch. 11:23; 31:10). As the passages cited suggest, this meaning probably did not come into being until the postexilic period.

III. Religious Use.

1. *Yahweh's Mastery over the Sea and Forces of Nature.* In descriptions of Yahweh's omnipotence, we find the statement that he stirs up the sea so that its waves "roar" (Jer. 31:35; Isa. 51:15) or creates the tumult of the thunderstorm (Jer. 10:13 [=51:16]; cf. 1 K. 18:41 and perhaps also Ezk. 1:24; Dnl. 10:6). In other passages it is not so obvious that the sea is obedient to Yahweh; it appears rather as a rebellious power that must be kept within its bounds by Yahweh (Jer. 5:22; Ps. 46:4[3]; 65:8[7]). Here we find echoes of ancient mythological conceptions of the sea as the forces of chaos [→ ים *yām*; → תהום *tehôm*). It is characteristic of *hāmāh/hāmôn* to be employed to designate both the raging of the sea and the raging of hostile nations; it even serves in many instances to link both manifestations of the forces of chaos (Ps. 46:4,7[3,6]; 65:8[7]) or to introduce a vivid comparison of an enemy attack to the raging of the sea (Isa. 17:12; Jer. 6:23 [=50:42]; 51:42,55). The confusion of acoustic and visual impressions referred to by the root *hāmāh* makes it appear particularly suited for representing everything chaotic.

2. *Yahweh's Mastery over the Nations.* When Yahweh appears as master over the nations, they, too, can be represented as either obedient instruments or rebellious powers; they can rage both against Yahweh's own people and against other nations. A few characteristic contexts can be distinguished:

The root *hāmāh* is occasionally used to depict the irresistible attack of the "foe from the north" (→ צפון *tsāphôn*) (Jer. 6:23 [=50:42]; 47:3). This holds true even more for the general attack by all the nations (→ גוי *gôy*); this is demonstrated not only by the classic passages Isa. 17:12; 29:5-8; Ps. 46:4,7(3,6); 65:8(7), but also by other passages belonging in this context (Isa. 13:4; 33:3; Ps. 83:3[2]), where *hāmāh* is frequently connected with → מוג *mûgh* (cf. 1 S. 14:16) or → מוט *môṭ*. The root also turns up in announcements of the day of Yahweh

(→ יוֹם yôm), where it can develop its full onomatopoeic force (Ezk. 7:11-14; Joel 4:14[3:14];[5] cf. Isa. 13:4).

This mythologically exaggerated language also lies behind the passages that speak of military events involving specific nations. Examples—apart from passages already cited—may be found in the oracles against the nations contained in the prophetic books (Jer. 49:32; 51:42,55). In historical narratives, too, *hāmôn* in the late period carries overtones of the assault of the nations: the particular attacker represents in concrete historical form the assault of all the nations (Jgs. 4:7; 1 K. 20:13,28; Dnl. 11:11-13; 2 Ch. 13:8; 14:10[11]; 20:2,12,15,24; 32:7).

This background also helps us understand the expression "king/general and his *hāmôn*" that crops up in the postexilic period (Jgs. 4:7; 16 times in Ezk. 29–32; Ezk. 39:11,15f.; 2 Ch. 32:7). Initially it refers to the army. Since, however, this army represents the powers of chaos in rebellion against God, *hāmôn* becomes increasingly a term for hubris, for revolt against Yahweh.

3. *Yahweh's Mercy.* Although the root *hāmāh* in the late period has overtones that are primarily negative, it can also be used in reference to Yahweh to indicate that he is inwardly agitated and shows mercy (Jer. 31:20; Isa. 63:15).[6] This, too, is probably a development of the later period, echoes of which can be heard in Isa. 51:15; Jer. 31:35.[7]

4. *"Abraham."* The popular etymology of the name "Abraham" (→ אברהם *'abhrāhām* I, III.4) in Gen. 17:4f. (P) is based on this positive sense of *hāmôn*: the name is a sign of God's favor and contains the promise of descendants beyond number. The expression conjures up the picture of a gigantic, tumultuous mob, and thus illustrates once more how the basic concrete meaning is preserved in almost all the semantic developments of the root.

IV. **Qumran.** The biblical usage of *hāmāh* underwent an interesting development in the Qumran documents. The theologoumenon of the incalculable multitude of God's mercies (*hᵃmôn rachᵃmeykhāh*) became a stereotyped formula in the hymns (1QH 4:36,37; 5:2; 6:9; 7:30,35; 9:8,34; 10:21; 15:16; cf. 11:29), usually in conjunction with *chesedh* and *sᵉlîchāh*. A contrary image appears once in the *hᵃmôn kôchô* with which Yahweh's judgment against his enemies blazes forth (1QH 3:34).

Above all, however, we encounter *hāmāh/hāmôn* in the context of the assault of the nations. In some sections various forms of the root appear repeatedly (1QH 2:12,16,27; 3:13-16,31-34; 6:23f.). It is interesting that the word for "abyss, chaos" (→ תהום *tᵉhôm*) also appears in this context (five times, with ten occurrences in all)—the acoustic similarity between *hāmāh* and *tᵉhôm* was obviously strongly felt (cf. 1QH 3:32: *vᵉyehᵉmû machshᵉbhê thᵉhôm bᵉhāmôn*, or

---

[5] See I.1.
[6] See II.3.
[7] See IV.

6:24: *vayyāhom tᵉhôm*). As the frequent comparison to the raging of the sea indicates, [8] this was probably also true for the OT: the Qumran texts provide the evidence. Probably, to be sure, we are dealing with a kind of popular etymology of the word *tᵉhôm*. In the context of the assault of the nations (characteristically transformed), *hāmāh/hāmôn* can refer to the attack of the hostile powers (1QH 2:12,16,27; 3:32; 5:29; 6:7), the enemy army (CD 2:1; 1QM 15:11; 18:3,12; 19:10), the clash of battle (1QM 1:11), as well as panic in the midst of the tumult (1QH 3:13-16; 5:31; 6:23f.; 7:5), which is frequently pictured as panic at sea.

That *hāmôn* can also refer to the multitude of cattle that will be part of the future time of peace (1QM 12:12; 19:4[?]) carries little weight in the face of all this evidence. The Qumran documents obviously continued and amplified the semantic development of the late OT period.

In his study of the word *hāmôn*, Gerleman comes to a conclusion largely similar to that presented here, defining the range of meanings as describing a double phenomenon of noise combined with movement. But his derivation of this "combination of the acoustic and the visual" [9] solely from the image of the sea is not convincing. It is hardly conceivable how this background could give rise to applications as diverse as the rumbling of wheels (Jer. 47:3), the growling of bears (Isa. 59:11), panic in camp (1 S. 14:16,19), and a city in tumult (1 K. 1:41). The meaning of the root in cognate languages also argues against this derivation.

Admittedly, however, especially in texts of more religious content, [10] the comparison to the sea plays an important role: the wildly surging sea was well adapted to be a vivid image for chaos and hybris. But an army or a tumultuous city could give the same impression of chaotic confusion.

Baumann

---

[8] See II.1 and III.1.

[9] "Die lärmende Menge," 75.

[10] See III.

הֲמַם *hmm;* **הוּם** *hwm;* **מְהוּמָה** *mᵉhûmāh*

I. Etymological Context. II. Qal: 1. With Yahweh as Subject; 2. With Human Subjects. III. Derived Stems.

I. Etymological Context. The Semitic languages and Egyptian make use of roots derived from the biliteral base **hm.* These can be divided into two groups. (1) The first group is onomatopoeic, imitating loud, inarticulate sounds, especially when they are repetitive. The Arab. durative *hamhama,* "mutter, growl" (used also of gods and those inspired by them[1]), is typical, as is Egyp. *hmhmt,* "shouting, roaring," and Demotic/Copt. *hmhm,* "roar." Here belong Heb. → המה *hāmāh,* "roar, be boisterous," and Heb., Aram., and Arab. *nhm,* "growl, (Arab.) be greedy" (cf. Egyp. *nhm,* "shout, dance for joy"). It may be noted that other verbs with initial *nun* also create onomatopoeic effects with their second and third consonants. (2) The other group, represented in both Hebrew and Arabic by the forms *hmm* and *hwm/hym,* comprises words meaning "confuse, discomfit" and (in Arabic) words indicating a state of confusion (*hamma,* "be apprehensive"; *hâma,* "be crazy [with love]").

The relationship between the two semantic clusters is clear: the words in the first group designate sounds evoked by or expressive of the unrest designated by words in the second.

II. Qal.

1. *With Yahweh as Subject.* The qal of *hmm* is used ten times in the OT (including Sirach) with Yahweh as its subject; *hwm* is used in the same way in Dt. 7:23.

In this usage, nine of the occurrences employ these verbs as technical terms for evoking panic, "holy terror." They are found accordingly in accounts of Yahweh wars (Ex. 14:24; Josh. 10:10; Jgs. 4:15; 1 S. 7:10; cf. also the retrospective Sir. 48:21) and in generalizing predictions of victory (Ex. 23:27; Dt. 7:23). The objects are the enemies of Yahweh and Israel, specifically the enemy camp (Ex. 14:24; Jgs. 4:15; Sir. 48:21); according to Dt. 2:15, however, the "hand of Yahweh" in the wilderness could also be against Israel itself, "to drive them in panic from the camp until they had perished." In Ex. 14:24 it is Yahweh's looking down from the pillar of fire and cloud that evokes panic; in 1 S. 7:10 it is his thundering, and in Sir. 48:21 his "blow" (*maggēphāh*). In Josh. 10:10 he throws the enemy into panic directly; in v. 11, which may represent an earlier stage of

---

hmm. P. Derchain, "A propos de deux racines sémitiques **hm* et **zm*," *ChrÉg,* 42 (1967), 306-310; H. Fredriksson, *Jahwe als Krieger* (1945), esp. 16f.; G. von Rad, *Der Heilige Krieg im alten Israel* (1951; ⁵1969), esp. 12f.; F. Stolz, *THAT,* I, 502-504; *idem, Jahwes und Israels Kriege. AThANT,* 60 (1972), esp. 20, 191.

[1] Cf. T. Fahd, *La divination arabe* (1966), 171-73.

tradition, Yahweh throws hailstones from heaven, which slay the enemy. The term *hmm* appears outside its military context in 2 Ch. 15:6, where a prophetic speaker describes the course of history as God's continual terrorizing of the nations, by means of "every sort of distress."

Dt. 7:23 adds the noun phrase *mehûmāh ghedhōlāh*, "great confusion," to *hwm* as a paronomastic second object. The result of this confusion, according to 1 S. 14:10, is that the enemy turn upon each other. As parallels to *mehûmāh*, the curse in Dt. 28:20 uses the nouns *me'ērāh* (→ ארר *'rr*), "curses," and *migh'ereth* (→ גער *gā'ar*), "rebukes." The verb to which the latter is related frequently refers to the rebuking of the chaotic sea (Isa. 17:13; Nah. 1:4; Ps. 106:9), of Satan (Zec. 3:2), or of the hostile nations (Ps. 9:6 [Eng. v. 5]) on the part of a militant Yahweh. A future "day (of battle) of confusion" is mentioned in Isa. 22:5 and Ezk. 7:7; according to Zec. 14:13f., at the eschaton men will fight against each other (even Judah will fight against Jerusalem, as a glossator adds) because "on that day" there will be a *mehûmath-yhvh rabbāh bāhem*. On the *mehûmāh* of an eschatological battle, cf. also 1QM 1:5; 4:7; 11:18.

The original notion has undergone modification in 1 S. 5:9, where the *mehûmāh* evoked by the arrival of the ark at Ashdod produces disease ("tumors"); v. 11, speaking of Ekron, the next city to be struck, speaks of a *mehûmath-māveth*, "deathly panic," among a portion of the population, while according to v. 12 the rest are stricken with tumors. Corresponding to the generalized use of the verb *hmm* in 2 Ch. 15:6, v. 5 contains the nominal expression *mehûmôth rabbôth 'al kol-yôshebhê hā'arātsôth*, which, as the introductory clause shows, means merely absence of peace (*'ên shālôm*).

According to the theophany depicted in 2 S. 22:15 (= Ps. 18:15[14]), it is not the enemies of the petitioner but the lightning bolts accompanying the coming of Yahweh and serving as the instruments of his intervention that are "agitated" by the deity. The meaning of *vayhummēm* is indicated by the parallel form *vayphîtsēm*, "he scattered them," referring to the arrows sent forth by Yahweh: in like manner he "drives" his lightning bolts before him. The immediate context makes it quite clear that the suffix -*ēm* cannot refer to the enemies of the petitioner. The same argument applies in Ps. 144, a hybrid psalm deriving from 2 S. 22 (= Ps. 18).[2] No "enemies" are mentioned as a possible object of *ûthehummēm* in v. 6. Verse 5 prays for Yahweh to come down and deliver the petitioner; in the following verse, the hiphil of → פוץ *pûts*, "scatter," refers to his lightning bolts, the qal of *hmm* to the arrows he sends forth. Of course in both 2 S. 22 (= Ps. 18) and Ps. 144 the lightning bolts and arrows suggest the terror of God that overcomes the enemies of the petitioner.

When we come to consider the religious or theological significance of the idioms using the qal of *hmm*, we must conclude that there is nothing specifically biblical in the notion of military intervention on the part of the deity or in the motif of an ensuing panic.[3] The *mysterium tremendum* of the power sublimated

---

[2] Cf. H. Gunkel, *Die Psalmen. GHK,* II/2 (⁵1968), 70, 606; for a different view, see *KBL²* and *KBL³ s.v. hmm.*

[3] M. Weippert, "'Heiliger Krieg' in Israel und Assyrien," *ZAW,* 84 (1972), 460-493.

in the deity everywhere evinces its destructive nature in battle, at the same time inspiring those fighting on the side of the deity with demonic frenzy. [4] In Israel the saving intervention of Yahweh in battle, and especially his creation of $m^eh\hat{u}m\bar{a}h$, becomes a prototype for his every action. Here we find an instance of the "demonic element in Yahweh" [5] that always characterized the God of the OT and indeed constitutes his perilous and consuming vitality. In the late pre-monarchical period, this conception appears to have been associated with the ark (1 S. 4:5; 5:9,11); the $m^eh\hat{u}m\bar{a}h$ may have been conceived as issuing from the "hand of Yahweh" (1 S. 5:9,11; 7:13; Dt. 2:15), which can intervene at any time to afflict or inspire. The frequent appearance of the terms hmm, hwm, and $m^eh\hat{u}m\bar{a}h$ in Deuteronomy and Deuteronomistic passages (Dt. 2:15; 7:23; 28:20; Ex. 23:27) is due to a theoretical schematization of military ideology introduced anachronistically in Deuteronomic and Deuteronomistic circles. On the other hand, the "day (of Yahweh)" (→ יום $y\hat{o}m$) with its $m^eh\hat{u}m\bar{a}h$ (Isa. 22:5; Ezk. 7:7; cf. Zec. 14:13f.) is a day of battle projected into the eschatological future. Because it participates in the perspective of hope, it is no longer subject to the limitations of the past. [6]

2. *With Human Subjects.* Significantly less often the qal of hmm is used non-technically with human subjects.

Just as Yahweh uses $m^eh\hat{u}m\bar{a}h$ to destroy his enemies, so in Est. 9:24 Haman's intention with respect to the Jews is $l^ehumm\bar{a}m$, "to crush them," intensified by the following infinitive $l^e{}'abb^edh\bar{a}m$, "and to destroy them." In Jer. 51:34, $h^am\bar{a}man\hat{i}$ is similarly used synonymously with ${}'^akh\bar{a}lan\hat{i}$ (→ אכל ${}'\bar{a}khal$), "devour," with reference to Nebuchadnezzar's attack on Jerusalem in 587. In both passages the word hmm is used metonymically with respect to its basic meaning. In other words, there is no need to postulate another root hmm II; neither does the Arabic parallel term $hamma$, "consume," cited by Rudolph [7] require a separate lemma. [8]

Like Yahweh "driving" his lightning bolts and arrows (2 S. 22:15; Ps. 144:6), the peasant, instructed by God and therefore expert, "drives his cart wheel" over the grain he is threshing (Isa. 28:28). In line with the way hmm is used as a verb with human subjects, the noun $m^eh\hat{u}m\bar{a}h$ (Prov. 15:16) can be used for the "trouble" men bring upon themselves with their foolish striving after wealth: that "little" that a man earns "with the fear of Yahweh" is better than "great treasure" associated with such $m^eh\hat{u}m\bar{a}h$. In Amos' attack on the palaces of Samaria (Am. 3:9), the expression $m^eh\hat{u}m\bar{o}th$ $rabb\hat{o}th$ stands in parallel to ${}'^ash\hat{u}q\hat{i}m$, "(social) oppressions"; v. 10 underlines the violence and robbery that they treasure up in these palaces. Less specific is the reference to Jerusalem as "infamous"

---

[4] F. Schwally, *Semitische Kriegsaltertümer* (1901), 99-105.

[5] P. Volz, *Das Dämonische in Jahwe. SgV,* 110 (1924).

[6] H.-P. Müller, *Ursprünge und Strukturen alttestamentlicher Eschatologie. BZAW,* 109 (1969), 72-85.

[7] W. Rudolph, *HAT,* 12 (³1968), 312.

[8] Contra *KBL³.*

and "full of *mᵉhûmāh*" in Ezekiel's indictment (Ezk. 22:5): vv. 3f. speak of bloodshed and idolatry.

The eschatological psalm of lament 1QH 3 speaks in line 25 of *mᵉhûmôth rabbāh*(!) parallel to *havvath madhhēbhāh,* "overwhelming destruction," and in line 38 of *havvôth mᵉhûmāh;* both expressions refer to the fateful consequences brought about by the acts of the wicked. At the eschaton, these overtake even the devout man, so that he cannot carry the day by his own efforts.

III. Derived Stems. The niphal of *hmm* or *hwm* refers to the panic brought about by human uproar or by dismaying news. Since forms like *yēhōm* with the root vowel "o" in the imperfect are found in both reduplicating verbs and biliteral verbs with a long vowel,[9] it is impossible to determine which of the two forms of the root the niphal forms derive from.

The niphal in 1 S. 4:5 comes closest to the technical use of the qal: the earth is "terrified" (*vattēhōm hā'ārets*) during the Philistine wars when the ark of Yahweh comes into the camp of the Israelites and the troops give a mighty shout. Jerusalem is put into an uproar (*vattēhōm haqqiryāh*), as Jonathan reports (1 K. 1:45), by the jubilant shouts of Solomon's partisans when he is anointed. In v. 41, the qal participle of → המה *hāmāh* is used to describe the same commotion (*maddûaʿ qôl haqqiryāh hômāh*). If we follow Gunkel[10] in reading *vᵉʾēhômāh miqqôl ʾôyēbh* in Ps. 55:3f.(3), an individual lament, the niphal here refers to the panic the "noise of the enemy" arouses in the speaker. In Ruth 1:19, finally, the niphal is used for the uproar provoked in Bethlehem by the arrival of Naomi and Ruth.

The phrase *tᵉhîmenāh mēʾādhām* in Mic. 2:12 is obscure. The form has been analyzed as a Samaritan qal imperfect of *hāmāh* (a *ypyʿl* form),[11] but more likely represents an original qal imperfect *tehᵉmeynāh* with the vowel letter erroneously metathesized.[12] The expression as a whole would then be a final or consecutive clause (with *vᵉ*- taken from the impossible *hdbrv*) whose subject is anticipated by the two preceding nouns *(bats)tsirāh* (following Targ. and Vulg.) and *haddōbher* (following Symmachus, Theodotion, Targ., and Vulg.): "I will set them [the remnant of Israel] together like sheep in a fold, like a flock in its pasture, that they [fold and pasture] may be filled with the uproar of men." In this case the passage would not serve as evidence for a conjectured hiphil of *hwm,* which would be awkward both here and in Ps. 55:3 because there is no grammatical object in the context and the hiphil is transitive in meaning. Since the basic meaning of the verb is itself passive, a so-called inner hiphil is out of the question.

H.-P. Müller

---

[9] Cf. R. Meyer, *Hebräische Grammatik,* II (³1969), § 79.3a and § 80.4a.

[10] *Psalmen,* 239.

[11] P. Wernberg-Møller, "Two Notes," *VT,* 8 (1958), 306; but cf. R. Macuch, *Grammatik des samaritanischen Hebräisch. Studia Samaritana,* 1 (1969), § 84aβ.

[12] Following J. Wellhausen, *Die kleinen Propheten* (⁴1963), 139.

הָפַךְ ḥāphakh; **הֲפֵכָה** hᵃphēkhāh; **מַהְפֵּכָה** mahpēkhāh

---

I. Occurrences and Meaning. II. General Use: 1. Idioms; 2. Technical Terms; 3. Special Meanings. III. Theological Uses: 1. Topoi; 2. Sodom and Gomorrah Tradition; 3. Specific Theological Statements.

I. Occurrences and Meaning. The root *hpk* is found in all the Semitic languages: Akk. *abāku* II, "turn upside down, upset," and the derivative *abiktu*, "defeat, carnage";[1] Ugar., Phoen. *hpk*, "overturn";[2] Aram. (Old Aram., Egyp. Aram., Palm., Jewish Aram., Christian Palestinian Aram., Syr., Mand.) *'/hpk*, "overturn, destroy," also "wander about";[3] Arab. *'afaka*, "pervert, lie."[4] Besides the verb, the following nominal forms occur in Hebrew: segholate *hēphekh*, "opposite, perversity"; with feminine suffix *hᵃphēkhāh*, "overthrow"; reduplicating *hᵃphakhpakh*, "crooked"; with *mem*-preformative *mahpēkhāh*, "overthrow," and segholate *mahpekheth*, "stocks"; and finally, found only in the plural, *tahpukhôth*, "perversities."

The verb occurs in qal, niphal, and hithpael (Job 30:15 may use the hophal). It can usually be translated "turn, overturn, overthrow," hence "change, transform." It can refer to an action that brings about a sudden change or to a process that suddenly and abruptly upsets a chain of events or a condition, often changing it into its opposite (frequently expressed by *lᵉ*-). The closest synonyms are *sbb*, "turn about, go around, surround" (qal), and *pānāh*, "turn." There are points of contact with the niphal of the former and the qal of the latter on the one hand and with the qal of the former and piel of the latter on the other, as well as in technical usage. But *sbb* focuses more on the action of "surrounding" as such, whereas *hāphakh* focuses on the effecting of an "overthrow." The verb *pānāh* is more general; cf. also the hiphil of *shûbh*. The nominal derivatives can be defined more precisely with reference to their dependence on the notion of being "bent" or "distorted" (ant. → יָשַׁר *yšr*; syn. → עָקַשׁ *'qš* and *lvz*) and their tendency toward ideas of "revolution," "perversion," and "opposite."

The LXX does not translate uniformly, but usually uses compounds of the verb *stréphein*.[5]

II. General Use.

1. *Idioms.* Characteristic of *hāphakh* is its use in more or less fixed phrases and idioms. Flat bread is turned when being baked (Hos. 7:8), bowls are turned

---

hāphakh. G. Bertram, "στρέφω," *TDNT*, VII, 714-729; T. Collins, "The Physiology of Tears in the OT," *CBQ*, 33 (1971), 30-31; G. R. Driver, "Some Hebrew Words," *JTS*, 29 (1927/28), 390; F. Prätorius, "הלך und ילך," *ZAW*, 2 (1882), 310-12.

[1] *CAD*, I, 8ff., 52; *AHw*, 2, 6; cf. Driver, 390.
[2] *WUS*, No. 855.
[3] *DISO, MdD*.
[4] Wehr; cf. *TigrWb*, 29b.
[5] Cf. esp. καταστροφή; Bertram, 715ff.

upside down (2 K. 21:13), chariots are overthrown (Hag. 2:22); sometimes the word is used of a throne (Hag. 2:22; *CTA,* 6 [I AB], VI, 28; *KAI,* 1.2), more frequently of a city (Gen. 19:21,25,29; Dt. 29:22 [Eng. v. 23]; 2 S. 10:3 [par., see below]; Jer. 20:16; Jonah 3:4; Lam. 4:6). In combination with *yādh,* "hand," it is an idiom for changing the direction of a chariot "by twisting the hand that holds the reins" [6] (1 K. 22:34 par.; 2 K. 9:23); as a repeated action (with *shûbh*) it is a gesture of rejection (Lam. 3:3). Used absolutely, it usually means "turn around" (Jgs. 20:39,41; 2 K. 5:26; etc.; cf. Josh. 7:8); occasionally, as in Aramaic, it can mean "wander about" (in a place), [7] the probable meaning in 1 Ch. 19:3 (2 S. 10:3?). In the context of archery, it can refer to the twisting of the bow (Ps. 78:57; cf. v. 9 conj.). The infinitive absolute serves to indicate the reversal of an action ("vice versa"; Est. 9:1; cf. Ex. 10:19 [8]).

2. *Technical Terms.* In Lev. 13, in the context of the sacral and medical diagnosis of leprosy, *hāphakh* becomes a technical term for the "turning (white)" of hair, etc. (vv. 3f.,10,13,16f.,20,25,55; cf. Jer. 30:6). The word *mahpekheth* refers to the "stocks" in which a prisoner's hands and feet are held while he is bent over (Jer. 20:2,3; cf. Acts 16:4). [9]

3. *Special Meanings.* In certain contexts, *hāphakh* and its derivatives can be used for specialized abstract concepts. In association with *tsîrîm,* "pangs," it seems to express the particular notion of wave upon wave of pain; with *lēbh/lēbhābh,* it appears to express a surge of emotion and sudden change of heart (Ex. 14:5; Lam. 1:20). [10] The use of the niphal in particular exhibits the tendency to represent the abstract idea of transformation into the opposite, a sense that evolves from the basic meaning but at the same time formalizes it (Job 20:14; Isa. 34:9; Jonah 3:4; etc.). [11]

The same polar tension in the meaning of the verb accounts for the derivatives *hēphekh* and *tahpukhôth.* In the case of *hēphekh,* the meaning "conversion" is combined with the notion of the opposite or contrary, so that it becomes a formal term; in its various occurrences, the general frame of reference (conversion = perversion) or the context (Ezk. 16:34: *hēphekh min hannāshîm,* "opposite of what is normal for women"; Isa. 29:16 used absolutely of perverting the creator/creature relationship) clearly indicates the word's negative qualification. Wisdom literature is especially fond of the plural form *tahpukhôth* (outside of Proverbs it occurs only in Dt. 32:20 in the sense of *hēphekh:* "generation of perversities," i.e., "perverse generation"). Here, in line with the tendency of wisdom to think in terms of what is straight (Prov. 21:8 contrasts the "crooked" [*haphakhpakh*]

---

[6] *KBL3.*

[7] *DISO,* 68.

[8] Bibliography in *KBL3.*

[9] On these and similar instruments see G. Hölscher, *HAT,* 17 (²1952), 35.

[10] Collins (30f.) takes a slightly different view, thinking of a change "in the physical composition of the heart"; on Hos. 11:8, see III.3 below.

[11] Cf. *KAI,* 222 C.19, 21. On the topoi of blessing/cursing and joy/sorrow, cf. III.1.

way of the guilty with the "straight" [yāshār] conduct of the pure; cf. 2:15), the word serves in the sense "crooked, perverted" as a general term of opprobrium for thoughts and words (thoughts: 6:14; 16:30; 23:33, "the heart of the drunkard utters perverse things"; mouth or tongue: 8:13; 10:31; cf. 17:20; speech: 2:12; cf. also 16:28 and Jer. 23:36). In this usage ʿqš (2:15; 6:12), "twist," and lûz (2:15), "turn aside," function as synonyms.

The passages using the hithpael exhibit a special development in the sense of backward and forward motion: Jgs. 7:13, describing a tumbling cake of barley bread; Gen. 3:24, "the flame of the jagged sword" (a dagger with a zigzag blade, forked lightning, or trident); [12] and Job 38:14, the lovely image of the earth's surface changing at dawn like clay beneath a cylinder seal.

Amos uses the verb deliberately in his metaphorical description of perverting justice (5:7; 6:12), turning it "to poison, to wormwood."

Ps. 32:4 is difficult because the subject of the change cannot be identified clearly (MT leshaddî).

III. Theological Uses.

1. *Topoi.* When used theologically (with God as the subject), the term is likewise characterized by preferential appearance in certain thematic realms; thanks to its own range of meanings and the notions associated with them, it dominates certain topoi and motifs to the point of becoming a catchword for them. In the case of the Balaam references in Dt. 23:6 and Nah. 13:2 ("Yahweh turned the curse into a blessing") we may consider direct dependence; but the motif of a miraculous transformation (water into blood, sea into land, etc.) in the context of the exodus, heard in Ex. 7:17,20 (niphal; cf. 10:19); Ps. 66:6; 78:44; 105:29; 114:8, appears to have been a fixed topos using *hpk* in the sense of "change (into the opposite)." The same can be said of the use of *hpk* in prayers and hymns (Ps. 30:12[11]; 41:4[3]; also 32:4; 114:8; Am. 5:8; Job 9:5): Yahweh's miraculously transforming intervention in both the life of the individual and nature is extolled, with the verb functioning to characterize the way Yahweh acts. This function appears likewise in the most common OT topos based on the polarity implicit in *hpk,* the motif of reversed emotions: "Yahweh has changed sadness to joy" (or the contrary, and with variations). A characteristic experience seems to have produced an idiom ascribing the sudden transformation (always defined in a construction using *le-*) to the working of Yahweh. The dynamic and transforming sense of the verb is underlined in each case by special means: by causative or factitive verbs in the immediate context (Am. 8:10; Jer. 31:13; Ps. 30:12[11]; Lam. 5:15), or by a preposition indicating the point of departure (*min*), with the goal indicated by *le-* (Est. 9:22).

2. *Sodom and Gomorrah Tradition.* The use of hāphakh, haphēkhāh, and mahpēkhāh is particularly striking as a fixed idiom in the tradition of Sodom and

---

[12] Cf. H. Gese, "Der bewachte Lebensbaum und die Heroen," *Wort und Geschichte. Festschrift K. Elliger. AOAT,* 18 (1973), 80f. = *Von Sinai zum Zion. Beitr. EvTh,* 64 (1974), 104f.; *ANEP,* No. 651; cf. Job 37:12.

Gomorrah. Not only does *hāphakh* appear in Gen. 19:21,25 (J) and 19:29 (P), whereby P, perhaps influenced by Akk. *abiktu*,[13] is obviously coining *hᵃphēkhāh*, "overthrow, catastrophe," as a new term for the action described by *hpk* and the piel of *šht;* Hosea, thinking of the same tradition, contrives an audacious new use of *hpk* (11:8).[14] Reflexes of this association are found in Lam. 4:6, and probably Isa. 34:9; Jer. 20:16 (cf. Jonah 3:4), in the gloss in Isa. 1:7 suggested by v. 9, and last but not least in the stereotyped formula *kᵉmahpēkhath* + obj. (Dt. 29:22[23]; Isa. 1:7; Jer. 49:18) or subjective gen. (Am. 4:11; Isa. 13:19; Jer. 50:40, in each instance with the formulaic addition of *'elōhîm*[15]). This tradition appears to have become the locus of *hpk* in a special way, in the sense that we can observe a conscientious effort to use this group of terms to conceptualize an event long felt to be paradigmatic.[16] This was made possible because on the one hand the basic sense of *hpk*, "overthrow," was able to cover the various vague ideas concerning the legendary catastrophe, and on the other Israel took this notion as typifying the judgment of Yahweh ("overthrow" par excellence). This means, however, thanks to the progressive process of abstraction, that we can no longer attach concrete meanings to the terms per se.[17] The tradition here visible of continuous theological reflection on a given motif shows how the concepts that could develop out of the verb *hāphakh* in particular situations must have appeared especially suitable as interpretative tools.

3. *Specific Theological Statements.* In the same conceptually theological environment, the context turns the verb in Am. 4:11 (*hāphakhtî bhākhem*, literally "I overthrew among you") into a term for God's judgment, a meaning it also bears elsewhere when used absolutely (Job 34:25; Prov. 12:7). Another specifically theological use is found when the verb applies directly to the human *lēbh*, expressing God's intervention to transform an individual's life, resulting in a "change of heart" (1 S. 10:9; cf. v. 6; Ps. 105:25; cf. Ex. 14:5 [niphal]; "purity of lips" is the result in Zeph. 3:9). The same line of thought appears in the niphal statement in 1 S. 10:6, which summarizes the prediction that Yahweh's spirit will come upon Saul so that he will behave like a prophet by saying: "You shall be turned into another man." With reference to the ecstasy described in vv. 9ff., *hpk* in the niphal (like the qal in v. 9) is meant to represent the resulting change as a perversion of what is normal.[18]

The most daring use of *hpk* to express a violent change of heart in Yahweh himself appears in Hos. 11:8b: "My heart recoils against me, my remorse is kindled." Note the characteristic Sodom motif borrowed from v. 8a, which gives the verb connotations of judgment and at the same time displaces these to the

---

[13] See I.1 above.

[14] See III.3 below.

[15] See R. Kraetzschmar, "Der Mythus von Sodoms Ende," *ZAW,* 17 (1897), 87f.

[16] H. Gunkel, *Genesis. GHK,* I/1 (⁷1966), 215f.; G. von Rad, *Genesis. OTL* (rev. trans. 1972), 221.

[17] Cf. the controversy between Wolff and Rudolph in their comms. on Am. 4:11.

[18] → אִישׁ *'îsh, TDOT,* I, 233.

person of Yahweh. Note also the strongly emotional parallel statement, echoed in the phrase *nehpakh libbî*,[19] and the unique construction with *'al,* "against," which demands the notion of "revolt" from *hpk*: *lēbh,* the will of the heart, against *'aph,* the will of a holy wrath (cf. Lam. 1:20). Taken together, these factors lend *hpk* in this passage a uniquely agitated and moving sense.

Finally, Isa. 63:10 (speaking for Israel) and Job 30:21 (speaking for the individual) lament that Yahweh (or the *"mal'ākh* of his presence," Isa. 63:9) has turned into an enemy, for good reason (Isa. 63:10) or without apparent cause (Job 30:21); *hpk* once again stands for sudden change and reversal.

Seybold

---

[19] Collins, 31.

הַר *har;* גִּבְעָה *gibh'āh*

I. Etymology. II. Meaning. III. Synonyms and Occurrences: 1. *har*; 2. *gibh'āh*; 3. Other Synonyms; 4. Parts. IV. Range of Usage: 1. Geography of Palestine; 2. *har* as a Topographical Term: a. For Mountains; b. For Mountain Settlements; 3. Mountains as Boundaries; 4. Use and Influence of Mountains. V. Religious Notions: 1. General; 2. World Mountain; 3. Omphalos; 4. World Axis; 5. Cosmogonic References; 6. Cosmic Mountains. VI. Israel's "Mountain-God": 1. Sources; 2. Israel's God in its Early History; 3. Identification of "Mountain" with "Sanctuary" in the Election of Jerusalem; 4. Mountains in OT Eschatology: a. The Place of Bliss; b. The Place of Judgment.

I. **Etymology.** We must consider *har* a primary noun whose etymology is unknown. Derivation from one of the roots *hwr* or *hrr,* which has occasionally been suggested, is questionable. In any case such an etymology contributes nothing to explaining the meaning of the word, which appears to be specifically Hebrew and is attested only rarely in other Semitic languages: as a Canaanite gloss *ḫa-ar-ri* on the Sum. *ḫur-sag* at Amarna,[1] in Phoenician,[2] in Punic,[3] and in a pseudo-hieroglyphic tablet from Byblos.[4] There is a single occurrence of *hr* in Ugaritic:

---

har. Y. Aharoni, *The Land of the Bible; a Historical Geography* (trans. ²1968); W. F. Albright, "Baal-Zaphon," *Festschrift Alfred Bertholet* (1950), 1-14; B. Alfrink, "Der Versammlungsberg im äussersten Norden (Is. 14)," *Bibl,* 14 (1933), 41-67; A. Alt, "Neues über die Zeitrechnung der Inschriften des Hermongebietes," *ZDPV,* 70 (1954), 142-46; R. Beer, *Heilige Höhen der alten Griechen und Römer* (1891); F. Böhl, "Über das Verhältnis von Shetija-Stein und Nabel der Welt in der Kosmogonie der Rabbinen," *ZDMG,* 124 (1974), 253-270; J. Boehmer, "Der Gottesberg Tabor," *BZ,* 23 (1935/36), 333-341; S. Bülow, "Der

(continued on p. 428)

---

[1] EA 74, 20.
[2] Eshmunazar (*KAI,* 14.17): *'n ydll bhr.*
[3] *KAI,* 81.4: *km(') šḫgr šmrt lhr.*
[4] *hr tbl;* Dhorme, 13, 15, 22.

hr ʾl,[5] which can be compared to *kᵉharᵉrê-ʾēl* (Ps. 36:7 [Eng. v. 6]) and perhaps also to *hahar'ēl*, *ʾᵃrî'ēl* (Ezk. 43:15; Isa. 29:1f.,7),[6] and *ġr ll*.[7]

The regular word for "mountain" in Ugaritic is *ġr* (=Akk. *ḫuršānu*), corresponding to Amor. *ṣr*, Aram. *ṭûr(āʾ)* (the usual translation of *hār* in the Targumim and Ahikar 62), Heb. *ṣûr*,[8] and Gk. *taúros*. Although no etymological connection can be made between Ugar. *ġr* and Heb. *har*, a common basis may be assumed.[9] The Akkadian word for "mountain" is *šadû*, probably equivalent to Heb. → שׂדה *śādheh*. Arab. *ǧabal* corresponds to Heb. → גבול *gᵉbhûl;* Ethiop. *dabra* can be compared to Heb. → מדבר *midhbār* and Ugar. *dbr*.[10] The distribu-

---

Berg des Fluches," *ZDPV*, 73 (1957), 100-108; M. du Buit, *Géographie de la Terre Sainte* (1958); W. Caspari, "ṭabur (Nabel)," *ZDMG*, 86 (1932), 49-65; E. Cassirer, *The Philosophy of Symbolic Forms*. II. *Mythical Thought* (trans. 1955), 83ff.; B. Childs, *Myth and Reality in the OT. SBT*, 27 (1960); R. E. Clements, *God and Temple* (1965); R. J. Clifford, *The Cosmic Mountain in Canaan and the OT. Harvard Semitic Monographs*, 4 (1972); P. C. Craigie, "A Note on 'Fixed Pairs' in Ugaritic and Early Hebrew Poetry," *JTS*, N.S. 22 (1971), 140-43; M. Dahood, *Psalms*, I. *AB*, XVI (1966); E. P. Dhorme, "Déchiffrement des inscriptions pseudo-hiéroglyphes de Byblos," *Syr*, 25 (1946/48), 1-35; D. Eichhorn, *Gott als Fels, Burg und Zuflucht. Europäische Hochschulschriften*, 23/4 (1972); O. Eissfeldt, *Baal-Zaphon, Zeus Kassios und der Durchgang der Israeliten durchs Meer. BRA*, 1 (1932); *idem*, "Der Gott Tabor und seine Verbreitung," *KlSchr*, II (1963), 19-54; *idem*, "Himmel und Erde als Bezeichnung phönizischer Landschaften," in his *Ras Schamra und Sanchunjaton. BRA*, 4 (1939), 109-127 = *KlSchr*, II, 227-240; *idem*, "Die Wohnsitze der Götter von Ras Schamra," *FuF*, 20 (1944), 25-27 = *KlSchr*, II, 502-506; S. Feigin, "The Meaning of Ariel," *JBL*, 39 (1920), 131-37; L. R. Fisher, "The Temple Quarter," *JSS*, 8 (1963), 34-41; *idem*, *Ras Shamra Parallels*, I. *AnOr*, 49 (1972); W. Foerster, "ὄρος," *TDNT*, V, 475-487; R. Frieling, *Der heilige Berg. Theologie und Kultus*, 4 (1930); J. Gray, *The Legacy of Canaan. SVT*, 5 (²1965); H. Gressmann, *Der Ursprung der israelitisch-jüdischen Eschatologie. FRLANT*, 6 (1905), 113-18; E. J. Hamlin, "The Meaning of 'Mountains and Hills' in Isa. 41, 14-16," *JNES*, 13 (1954), 185-190; W. Harrelson, B. Anderson, and G. E. Wright, "Shechem, the 'Navel of the Land,'" *BA*, 20 (1957), 2-32; J. Hehn, "Heilige Berge," *Theologie und Glaube*, 8 (1916), 130-141; A. Heidel, "A Special Usage of the Akkadian Term *šadū*," *JNES*, 8 (1949), 233-35; H. V. Herrmann, *Omphalos. Orbis Antiquus*, 13 (1959); R. Hillmann, *Wasser und Berg. Kosmische Verbindungslinien zwischen dem kanaanäischen Wettergott und Jahwe* (diss., Halle, 1965); S. Hooke, ed., *The Labyrinth* (1935), 45-70; P. C. A. Jensen, *Assyrisch-babylonische Mythen und Epen. KB*, VI/1 (1900); *idem*, *Die Kosmologie der Babylonier* (1890, repr. 1974); J. Jeremias, *Der Gottesberg* (1919); Y. Kaufmann, *The Religion of Israel* (trans. 1960); E. C. Kingsbury, "The Theophany *Topos* and the Mountain of God," *JBL*, 86 (1967), 205-210; S. N. Kramer, *Sumerian Mythology* (²1961), 40f., 72, 76, 81; H.-J. Kraus, "Die Kulttraditionen des Berges Thabor," *Basileia. Festschrift W. Freytag* (1959), 177ff.; Y. Kutscher, *Lešonenu*, 32 (1967/68), 346 (in Hebrew); B. Landsberger and J. V. Kinnier Wilson, "The Fifth Tablet of Enūma eliš," *JNES*, 20 (1961), 154-179; A. Lauha, *Zaphon; der Norden und die Nordvölker im AT. AnAcScFen*, B, 49 (1943); K. Marti, "Das Thal Zeboim, I Sam 13,18," *ZDPV*, 7 (1884), 125-130; B. Meissner, *BuA*, II, 110ff.; R. Meringer, "Omphalos, Nabel, Nebel,"

(continued on p. 429)

---

[5] *CTA*, 4 [II AB], 36.

[6] Cf. Mesha Inscription 12.

[7] Read *ġr ʾl; CTA*, 2 [III AB], I, 20; Clifford, 42, 43 n. 14.

[8] H.-P. Müller, 234; Michaud, 299f.

[9] *WUS*, No. 2166; *UT*, 1953; cf. L. R. Fisher and F. B. Knutson, "An Enthronement Ritual at Ugarit," *JNES*, 28 (1969), 157-167, esp. 158.

[10] *WUS*, No. 274.

tion of this group of words that mean "mountain" in some Semitic languages but "stony ground," "desert," "territory," or "border" in Hebrew may have its counterpart in the partial synonymy of Gk. óros (also hóros)—the usual LXX translation of har—and horos, "territory, boundary," which translates Heb. gᵉbhûl. The coalescence of these meanings may have been brought about by the widespread notion of mountains as territorial or political boundaries. [11]

II. Meaning. Like its Semitic and Greek counterparts, har in singular and plural can refer to both individual mountain peaks and mountain ranges. It can be used as a term of geological morphology as a geographical term for specific heights. Its synonym gibh'āh is used similarly, except that it usually refers to individual geomorphological elevations that are smaller or lower than those referred to by har. The singular gibh'āh, however, never refers to a whole range.

The words har and gibh'āh also serve as elements in place names, referring to places consisting of a temenos or having a temenos within their territory. The

Wörter und Sachen, 5 (1913), 41-91; M. Metzger, "Himmlische und irdische Wohnstatt Jahwes," UF, 2 (1970), 139-158; H. Michaud, "Un passage difficile dans l'inscription de Siloé," VT, 8 (1958), 297-301; J. C. de Moor, "Studies in the New Alphabetic Texts from Ras Shamra," UF, 2 (1970), 309ff.; O. Mowan, "Quatuor Montes Sacri in Ps. 89:13," VD, 41 (1963), 11-20; H.-P. Müller, "Notizen zu althebr. Inschriften, I," UF, 2 (1970), 229-242; W. Müller, Die heilige Stadt: Roma quadrata, himmlisches Jerusalem und die Mythe vom Weltnabel (1961); A. de Nicola, "L'Hermon, monte sacro," BeO, 15 (1973), 239-251; R. Patai, Man and Temple (1947), 85, 132; Pedersen, ILC, III-IV, 198ff.; M. H. Pope, El in the Ugaritic Texts. SVT, 2 (1955), 92-104; G. von Rad, "The City on the Hill," The Problem of the Hexateuch and Other Essays (trans. 1966), 232-242; H. Ringgren, Religions of the Ancient Near East (trans. 1973); A. Robinson, "Zion and Ṣāphôn in Ps XLVIII 3," VT, 24 (1974), 118-123; W. H. Roscher, Omphalos. ASAW, 29/9 (1913); idem, Neue Omphalosstudien. ASAW, 31/1 (1915); idem, Der Omphalosgedanke bei verschiedenen Völkern, besonders den semitischen. BSAW, 70/2 (1918); H. Schmidt, Der Heilige Fels in Jerusalem (1933); K. L. Schmidt, "Jerusalem als Urbild und Abbild," ErJb, 18 (1950), 207-248; K.-D. Schunck, "Zentralheiligtum, Grenzheiligtum und 'Höhenheiligtum' in Israel," Numen, 18 (1971), 132-140; A. W. Schwarzenbach, Die geographische Terminologie im Hebräischen des AT (1954); I. L. Seeligmann, Judah and Jerusalem (1957), 192-208 (in Hebrew); J. Z. Smith, "Earth and Gods," JR, 49 (1969), 103ff.; J. A. Soggin, "Der offiziell geförderte Synkretismus in Israel während des 10.Jahrhunderts," ZAW, 78 (1966), 179-204; idem, "Bemerkungen zur alttestamentlichen Topographie Sichems mit besonderem Bezug auf Jud 9," ZDPV, 83 (1967), 183-198; S. Talmon, "Typen der Messiaserwartung um die Zeitwende," Probleme biblischer Theologie. Festschrift G. von Rad (1971), 571-588; S. Terrien, "The Omphalos Myth and Hebrew Religion," VT, 20 (1970), 315-338; G. J. Thiery, "Remarks on Various Passages of the Psalms," OTS, 13 (1963), 77-97; D. Winton Thomas, "Mount Tabor, the Meaning of the Name," VT, 1 (1951), 229f.; M. Tsevat, "God and the Gods in Assembly," HUCA, 40/41 (1969/70), 123-137; idem, "Sun Mountains at Ugarit," JNWSL, 3 (1974), 71-75; N. H. Tur-Sinai, "טבור ובמה",הלשון והספר, III (1955), 233f.; C. Virolleaud, "La montagne du Nord dans les poèmes de Ras Shamra," Babyloniaca, 17 (1937), 145-155; H. G. Q. Wales, The Mountain of God. A Study in Early Kingship (1953); A. J. Wensinck, The Ideas of the Western Semites Concerning the Navel of the Earth. VAWA, N.R. 17/1 (1916); G. Westphal, Jahwes Wohnstätten nach den Anschauungen der alten Hebräer. BZAW, 15 (1908), 98-118; J. M. Wilkie, "The Peshitta Translation of ṭabbur ha'areṣ in Jud. IX 37," VT, 1 (1951), 144; G. R. H. Wright, "The Mythology of Pre-Israelite Shechem," VT, 20 (1970), 75-82.

[11] Cf. IV below.

use of *har* or *gibh'āh* as an abbreviation for such a site lends the words a dimension of indwelling sanctity. In such contexts, *har* and *gibh'āh* are used in parallel with → במה *bāmāh* (2 S. 1:19,25; cf. v. 21; on Ezk. 36:1, see below). The suggestion of holiness is enhanced by the recurrent location of theophanies on mountains and through the borrowing of mythological expressions and images from the Mesopotamian and Canaanite notion of sacred mountains. The terms *har* and, to some degree, *gibh'āh* express the inherent mythical qualities of mountains: they are older than creation or were among the first to be created (Prov. 8:25; Job 15:7) and will last forever (Gen. 49:26; Hab. 3:6). All these closely related aspects culminate in the terminology of the "holy mountain," which refers to Jerusalem and the temple mount.

III. Synonyms and Occurrences.

1. *har*. The word *har* occurs about 550 times in the OT, albeit not in Ruth, Ecclesiastes, Esther, or Ezra. It is found in the absolute singular (Josh. 17:18; Ps. 78:54; Job 14:18) and plural (*hārîm*, Dt. 11:11; Mic. 6:2), in the construct singular (*har gabhnunnîm*, Ps. 68:16[15]) and plural (*hārê n^echōsheth*, Zec. 6:1), in place names in both singular (*har bāshān*, Ps. 68:16[15]) and plural (*hārê 'ªrārāṭ*, Gen. 8:4), with the definite article in the singular (*hāhār haṭṭôbh hazzeh*, Dt. 3:25) and plural (*ra'shê hehārîm*, Hos. 4:13), and with prepositions (*mēhar*, Jer. 50:6; Ps. 42:7[6]; *bāhār*, Gen. 19:30; *b^ehārê*, Nu. 33:47; Ezk. 34:14). The construct form in the plural is either *hārê* (Gen. 8:4; Ezk. 19:9) or, poetically, *harªrê* (Nu. 23:7; Dt. 33:15; Hab. 3:6; Ps. 87:1). The two instances of the singular with a possessive suffix are textually insecure: Gen. 14:6 (*b^eharrām;* Versions *b^eharrê*) and Ps. 11:1 (*nûdhî harkhem tsippôr;* LXX, Syr., Targ. *har k^emô*). There are eight instances of the plural with the 1st person suffix (*harai*): Isa. 14:25; 49:11 (where the LXX reads *óros* = *har*); 65:9; Ezk. 38:21; Zec. 14:5 are textually uncertain. In two occurrences an old case ending has been preserved: Jer. 17:3 (*hªrārî baśśādheh*) and Ps. 30:8(7) (*harrî 'ōz*), if the reading should not in fact be *har^erê* (or, following the LXX, *hªdhārî*).

The proposed derivation of *hārîth / hāriyyôth* (2 K. 8:12; Hos. 14:1[13:16]; Am. 1:13) from *har*[12] is etymologically and semantically untenable. The passages clearly are speaking of "pregnant women" and the root is → הרה *hārāh*.

2. *gibh'āh*. The most frequently used synonym for *har* is *gibh'āh* (= Ugar. *gb'*; cf. Palestinian Aram. *gb'*, "swell up"). It occurs 60 times. In 31 cases *gibh'āh* is used in apposition or parallel to *har*, e.g., Isa. 40:4 (*v^ekhōl har v^eghibh'āh yishpālû*); Isa. 42:15 (*'achªrîbh hārîm ûgh^ebhā'ôth*); Isa. 30:25 (*'al kol har gabhōah ... v^e'al kol gibh'āh niśśā'āh*); cf. also 2 S. 21:6,9. The LXX normally uses *boúnos* to render *gibh'āh*, but sometimes *óros* (Isa. 31:4; Ezk. 34:26) or *thís* (Gen. 49:26; Dt. 12:2; Job 15:7). The usual Aramaic translation is *rāmā'* or *rûmā'*, occasionally *galm^ethā'* (Ps. 65:13[12]; 72:3) or *gibh'ªthā'*

---

[12] Proposed by Jacob of Serug and by Kimchi; similarly J. Valeton, *Amos en Hosea* (1894).

(Josh. 5:3; Jer. 31:39; Zeph. 1:10); cf. Syr. *rāmᵉthā'*. Both *gibh'āh* and *har* are used in the same expressions and images: *har gābhōah* / *gibh'āh gᵉbhōhāh* (Ezk. 40:2; Jer. 2:20); *har niśśā'* / *gibh'āh niśśā'āh* (Isa. 57:7; 2:14); *mᵉrôm hārîm* / *gibh'āh* (Isa. 37:24; [13] Jer. 49:16); *rō'sh har* / *gibh'āh* (Ex. 19:20; 17:9; etc.). It is likely that *gabh*, "back" (Ps. 129:3), and *gabhnunnîm* (Ps. 68:16f.[15f.]) are connected with *gibh'āh*.

3. *Other Synonyms.* Other words for "mountain" occurring in related languages but usually bearing a different meaning in Hebrew [14] are sometimes used as synonyms of *har*. For example, צור *tsûr* normally means "rock"; but its use in parallel with or as a synonym of *gibh'āh* (Nu. 23:9) and *har* (Isa. 30:29; Job 14:18; 18:4) suggests that in these instances it has the meaning "mountain." The expression *tsûr ye'taq* (Job 14:18) interchanges with *he'tîq hārîm* (Job 9:5). In the third line of the Siloam inscription (*ky hyt zdh bṣr*), H.-P. Müller translates "inside of the mountain" (cf. Job 28:9f.). [15]

Similarly, Heb. *śādheh*, which normally means "field" or "arable land," in several cases reflects the meaning "mountain" that attaches to Akk. *šadû*. [16] Thus the expression *mᵉrômê śādheh* (Jgs. 5:18) obviously means the same as *mᵉrôm har* / *gibh'āh*. In Ob. 19, *śᵉdhēh 'ephrayim* and *śᵉdhēh shōmᵉrôn* in conjunction with *gil'ādh* are synonymous with *har 'ephrayim* and *har shōmᵉrôn*. The expression *śᵉdhēh tsōphîm*, too, which in Nu. 23:14 stands in parallel with *rō'sh happisgāh* and in immediate proximity to the doublet *rō'sh tsûrim* / *gᵉbhā'ôth* (v. 9) and *rō'sh happᵉ'ôr hannishqāph 'al pᵉnê hayᵉshîmōn* (v. 28), appears to mean "lookout mountain," "watchtower." In the doublet *śādheh* / *ya'ar* (Ps. 80:14[13]; 96:12), the meaning is decided by the parallelism of both with *hārîm* in Ps. 50:10f. Possibly we should include here *śᵉdhēh 'ᵉdhôm* (Gen. 32:4[3]; Jgs. 5:4), *śᵉdhēh ya'ar* (Ps. 132:6; cf. *har yᵉ'ārîm*, Josh. 15:10), and *śᵉdhēh hā'ᵃmālēqî* (Gen. 14:7; cf. the parallel use of *har* in Jgs. 12:15).

The identification of Heb. גבול *gᵉbhûl*, usually "boundary, territory," with Arab. *ǧabal*, "mountain," is suggested by several passages. When 1 S. 13:18 *haggᵉbhûl hannishqāph 'al gê hatstsᵉbhō'îm*, where the LXX transliterates as *Gabee* (= *gebha'*), is compared to Nu. 23:28 *rō'sh happᵉ'ôr hannishqāph*, the best translation appears to be: "the hill that overlooks the Valley of Hyenas." [17] In Ezk. 11:10f., the *gᵉbhûl yiśrā'ēl* where God will judge his people is obviously identical with the *hārê yiśrā'ēl* (Ezk. 39:4) where Israel's adversaries Gog and Magog will be judged. The expression "*har nachᵃlāh* of Esau," which is separated in Mal. 1:3 (cf. Ex. 15:17), is rendered in v. 4 as the *gᵉbhûl rish'āh* that will be struck by the anger of Yahweh. In contrast to it stands the *gᵉbhûl yiśrā'ēl* (v. 5), over which his greatness and glory will appear. In Isa. 54:12, too, where Israel is promised a glorious future for *kol gᵉbhûlēkh*, the allusion to *nachᵃlāthᵉkhā* or *har yiśrā'ēl*

---

[13] Cf. Ugar. *mrym ṣpn* (*CTA*, 3 [V AB], IV, 45; 5 [I* AB], 11).
[14] See I above.
[15] *UF*, 2, 234.
[16] For an opposing view, see Schwarzenbach, 85-87.
[17] Wellhausen, Driver, Smith, Segal; for a different view, see Marti, 125ff.

is made more explicit by the use of images referring to Eden, the garden of God located on the mythical mountain of God (Ezk. 28:12ff.). Some scholars think the association of Eden and the mountain of God is late. [18] The same distribution of a single concept between two parallel members is found in Ps. 78:54, where *gebhûl qodhshô* in the first hemistich (LXX *óros*) is identified with *har zeh qanethāh yemînô* (cf. Isa. 11:9, *har qodhshô*) in the second hemistich. The choice of terms distinctly reflects the vocabulary of Ex. 15:17. Considered together, these two passages make it possible to reconstruct the expression *gebhûl nachalāh*, which is divided up into its components in Ps. 78:54f. and corresponds to the expression *har nachalāh* (Ex. 15:17). [19] From this we can conclude that the burial of Joshua *bighebhûl nachalāthô* (Josh. 24:30 = Jgs. 2:9) refers to a "high place" that had been assigned to his family in *har 'ephrayim*, comparable to the *gibh'ath pînechās* in the same region, where Eleazar was buried (Josh. 24:33).

The etymologically obscure word *shephî*, which occurs six times in Jeremiah (3:2,21; 4:11; 7:29; 12:12; 14:16), is frequently rendered "high place, mountain." This meaning is clearly applicable to Isa. 13:2, *'al har nishpeh śe'û nēs* (cf. vv. 3f.), and to the analogous *hārê nesheph* of Jer. 13:16, and is probably the correct reading in Isa. 41:18 (*'ephtach 'al shephāyîm nehārôth*), where the LXX uses *óros* to translate the noun (Syr. *ṭwr'*; on the image, cf. Job 28:10). In Jer. 3:3,21, the mention of sacral prostitution suggests cultic high places (cf. also Jer. 14:6). In Nu. 23:3, Ibn Ezra interprets (*vayyēlekh*) *shephî* as *'al har nishpeh* (cf. Isa. 13:2).

The suggestion of Y. Kutscher, [20] that *hēlebh* in parallel with *tsûr* be translated "hill" (Ps. 81:17[16]), is confirmed by comparison with Dt. 32:13 and the Ugar. doublet *ġr || ḥlb*. [21]

4. *Parts.* The literature of the OT frequently uses the terminology of the human body to refer to the various parts of a mountain: *rō'sh*, "top, peak" (Ex. 19:18-20; Nu. 20:28; Josh. 15:8f.; Isa. 42:11), for which *qātseh* can also be used (Ex. 19:12; Isa. 37:24 = 2 K. 19:23; cf. Josh. 18:16; 1 S. 14:2; *kāthēph*, "shoulder, slope," especially in defining boundaries (Josh. 15:8-11; Nu. 34:11; Isa. 11:14; Ezk. 25:9; metaphorically Dt. 33:12); *tsēlā'*, "side" (2 S. 16:13); *yarkethayim* (only plural), "recesses" (Jgs. 19:1,18; 2 K. 19:23 = Isa. 37:24; cf. Ugar. *ṣrrt* [22]); *tachtîth*, "foot" (Ex. 19:17; 24:4; 32:19; Dt. 4:11; cf. Ugar. *št ġr* par. *b'mq* [23]). Some of these terms (*kāthēph, tsēlā', yarkethayim*) are also used as architectural terms, especially with reference to the tent of meeting or the temple. This nomenclature may be an illustration of Cassirer's theory that the biblical authors—like mythical thinking in general—conceived the physical world after analogy with the human body. [24]

---

[18] Clifford, 159.

[19] Cf. Ugar. *ġr nḥlty* (*CTA,* 3 [V AB], III, 27; IV, 64), referring to the mountain of Baal.

[20] *Lešonenu,* 32, 346.

[21] *CTA,* 4 [II AB], VIII, 5-6; 5 [I* AB], V, 13-14; etc.

[22] Dahood, 289f.

[23] *CTA,* 3 [V AB], II, 5f.

[24] *Philosophy of Symbolic Forms,* II, 83ff.

IV. Range of Usage.

1. *Geography of Palestine.* The comparatively large number of occurrences of *har, gibh'āh,* and other synonyms in the literature of the OT reflects the geographical reality of the Syro-Palestinian landscape. Two great mountain ranges cross the region from north to south, the one to the west and the other to the east of the rift valley formed by the lowlands of the *'ᵃrābhāh,* the Jordan Valley, and, further north, the Biqa' Valley in Lebanon. These ranges parallel the low, comparatively narrow coast of the Mediterranean. The great difference in altitude between the low coastal region and the even lower rift valley, almost 400 meters below sea level at its lowest point, reinforces the impression of majestic size associated with mountains in the OT literature, which does not correspond to their actual altitude.

The geography of the Israelite heartland is reflected in the stereotyped description in Josh. 12:8, where the future territory of Judah is described as consisting of six parts: *hāhār, hanneghebh, hammidhbār, hā'ᵃshēdhôth, hā'ᵃrābhāh,* and *hashshᵉphēlāh.* The formula could be abbreviated, so that only the three most important regions had to be mentioned: *hāhār hanneghebh vᵉhashshᵉphēlāh* (Jgs. 1:9; cf. Dt. 1:7,19f.), with *neghebh* the southern (Nu. 13:17) and *shᵉphēlāh* the western gateway to the central highlands. The extraordinary significance of the highlands is shown by later usage, where the totality of Israelite territory could be referred to as *hārê yiśrā'ēl* (Ezk. 36:1-4; cf. *'artsî,* "my [i.e., God's] own land," in v. 5) and was further divided into *hārê yᵉhûdhāh* (Josh. 20:7; 21:11) and *har yiśrā'ēl* (Josh. 11:16,21) or *har 'ephrayim* (Josh. 19:50; Jgs. 2:9; 1 S. 9:4).

The ranges exhibit a variety of formations. While in some cases the slopes are smooth, in other cases a terracing gives the impression of a stairway (*madhrēghāh,* Ezk. 38:20; Cant. 2:14). Only a few mountains, like Tabor, stand out clearly from their surroundings (Jer. 46:18). The description of Jerusalem as a city upon a mountain surrounded by other mountains (Ps. 125:2) suggests quite accurately the nature of the Syro-Palestinian landscape. This fact appears to have decisively influenced the meaning and semantic content of the word "mountain" as well as its metaphorical use.

2. *har as a Topographical Term.* As a topographical term, *har* refers to:

(a) specific mountains or mountain ranges, which can be further defined by a descriptive element (*har haqqedhem,* Gen. 10:30; usually an adjective, e.g., *hāhār hechālāq ha'ôleh śē'îr[āh],* Josh. 11:17; 12:7; *hāhār hattôbh hazzeh,* Dt. 3:25) or a construct phrase (*har śē'îr,* Dt. 2:5; 2 Ch. 20:20-29; *har 'ēśāv,* Ob. 19, 21; *har haggil'ādh,* Gen. 31:21-25; *har naphtālî,* Josh. 20:7). The latter form of expression is the predominant way of designating individual mountains, such as *har sînai* (Ex. 19:11; Neh. 9:13), *har chōrēbh* (Ex. 33:6), *har hāhōr* (Nu. 20:22-28; Dt. 32:50), *har nᵉbhô* (Dt. 32:49f.; 34:1), *har tsiyyôn* (Isa. 4:5; Joel 3:5[2:32]; Lam. 5:18), *har hammôriyyāh* (2 Ch. 3:1; cf. Gen. 22:2ff.), *har hazzêthîm* (2 K. 23:13; Zec. 14:4), the twin peaks *'ēbhāl* and *gᵉrizîm* (Dt. 11:29; Josh. 8:33), *har shōmᵉrôn* (1 K. 16:24; Am. 4:1; 6:1), *har hakkarmel* (2 K. 2:25; 4:25-

27), *har tābhôr* (Jgs. 4:12), *har śî'ôn = har chermôn* (Dt. 3:8; 4:48), *har lebhānôn* (Jgs. 3:3; cf. Cant. 3:9; 7:5[4]).

(b) inhabited sites on hills and mountainsides (Josh. 11:21; 15:33,48; Am. 4:1). Such settlements are repeatedly mentioned as a class: *'ārê hāhār* (Dt. 2:37; Josh. 15:9 alongside *'ārê hashshephēlāh,* Jer. 32:44; 33:13). The names of some cities contain the element *har,* e.g., *har ye'ārîm* = Chesalon (Josh. 15:10), so that *har* can alternate with *'îr* in parallel passages: Jgs. 1:35 *har cheres* = Josh. 19:41 *'îr shemesh* (cf. Isa. 19:18 *'îr hacheres*); Mal. 1:3 *ve'āśîm 'eth hārāv shemāmāh* alongside Ezk. 35:7 *'āreykhā chorbāh 'āśîm.* This interchangeableness is also apparent in variant readings: LXX reads *óros* for MT *'îr* in 2 K. 17:6 (= 18:11); 23:16; 2 Ch. 21:11 (=MT mss.); the Targum reads *karkhā'* for MT *har* in 1 K. 16:24; 2 K. 19:23 (=Isa. 37:24); Isa. 13:2; Jer. 51:25; Am. 6:1; Ob. 8,9,19,21.

The Israelites' predilection for establishing their settlements on high ground is explained by the following considerations:

(a) The superior equipment and military organization of the indigenous population of Canaan in the period of the occupation enabled them to keep the Israelites from gaining a foothold in the lowlands. Israel was therefore compelled to settle in the hill country, often establishing new cities at previously unoccupied sites. During subsequent periods, once the monarchy had been established and Israel exercised sovereignty over the entire land, these sites remained settled.

(b) Military considerations also led the Israelites to maintain their settlements in the hill country even after they had occupied the lowlands. Heights had defensive potential and slopes could be used as the basis for fortifications.

(c) In order to preserve arable land in the valleys for farming, the settlements were located on the less fertile hilltops and terraces, a procedure still practiced in Palestine.

(d) Alongside these historical, strategic, and economic reasons for settling the hilly and mountainous regions, cultic and mythico-theological motives also play a role. The tendency to locate holy places on hills and mountains [25] arose from the endeavor to reduce the distance between earth and heaven. [26]

(e) The combination of the cultic and mythic holiness of the heights and their limited economic potential led to their being considered especially suitable as burial places. Biblical tradition records that Aaron (Nu. 20:28), Moses (Dt. 34:1-6), Joshua (Josh. 24:29f. [=Jgs. 2:8f.]), and Eleazar (Josh. 24:33) were buried atop hills or mountains. Several beloved prophets were buried *bāhār* near Bethel (2 K. 23:16); and Shebna, the Judahite court steward, had a tomb hewn out for himself on a hillside in the vicinity of Jerusalem (Isa. 22:15-19).

---

[25] Wensinck, 11f.
[26] See below.

3. *Mountains as Boundaries.* A similar combination of geographical characteristics and mythic and cultic notions caused mountains, like rivers and lakes,
to be thought of as territorial boundaries and thus sites for boundary shrines. The
impregnable massifs of the Lebanon and Antilebanon, together with Hermon, [27]
and likewise the mountains of Gilead, Moab, and Edom, define the northern and
eastern boundaries of the territory that Israel considered the ideal extent of its
land, as realized historically in the Davidic empire. To the west, the Mediterranean
constituted the boundary, and to the south the great desert. Within the land, too,
mountains were considered boundaries. [28] The hill country of Benjamin separated
the northern kingdom from the southern; the precise boundary ran in the vicinity
of Bethel and its mountain shrine (Jgs. 17–18; 19:1; Dt. 33:12). The boundaries
of the tribal territories coincide with mountain ranges where the landscape offers
the opportunity (Josh. 15ff.).

4. *Use and Influence of Mountains.* The differing morphology of mountains
accounts for their varying assessment and utilization. The various rock strata—
granite (in the extreme south), limestone, sandstone, flint, and basalt—were
quarried for stone, the most important building material (1 K. 5:15; 2 Ch. 1:18
[2:2]; 2:17[18]). In the south metal was produced, especially copper. [29] The comparatively copious rainfall on the mountains (*mashqeh hārîm mēʿaliyyôthāv*, Ps.
104:13; cf. Dt. 11:11) promotes the growth of trees (Josh. 17:18; Jgs. 6:2; Ezk.
17:23), used for their wood (2 K. 19:23 [=Isa. 37:24]; Hag. 1:8). On the other
hand, the sometimes torrential rains can erode the topsoil on the ledges and
slopes, which are not arable until careful terracing makes it possible to grow
grapes (Isa. 5:1f.; Ezk. 17:22f.; Am. 9:13; Joel 4:18[3:18]; Hag. 1:11; Ps. 80:9ff.
[8ff.]; 104:13-15) and plant fruit trees (Ezk. 36:8; Neh. 8:15), or for the thick-
leaved shade trees to flourish that played a role in the fertility cults. [30] A thin
layer of fertile soil together with rain and groundwater (Dt. 8:7; Isa. 30:25) are
sufficient for a luxuriant grass cover that provides pasture for both domestic
stock and wildlife (Ezk. 34:14; Ps. 72:16; 104:14,18; 147:8).

Mountainous terrain is not easy to cross. Before the introduction of the horse-
shoe, probably by the Assyrians, mountains were for all practical purposes inaccessible to horses (Isa. 5:28; Isa. 37:24 [=2 K. 19:23]) and were thus relatively
secure against invading armies (Ob. 3; Jer. 49:16). Hilltops served as lookout
posts from which the approach of friend or foe could be announced by pre-
determinal signals (Isa. 18:3; 40:9; 42:11; Lachish Letter IV, 10). On the other
hand, the thickly forested hill country often became a battlefield for footsoldiers
(2 S. 18:6ff.). Armies could camp with relative security in the mountains to prepare
for battle, which would be fought in the valleys (Jgs. 4:6,10-14; 2 S. 2:24f.). The
lack of roads and sparseness of settlements made the mountain area a desolate

---

[27] Alt.
[28] Cf. Y. Aharoni, "Mount Carmel as Border," *Archäologie und AT. Festschrift K. Galling*
(1970), 1-7.
[29] Cf. B. Rothenberg, *Timna. Valley of the Biblical Copper Mines* (1972).
[30] See IV.1 below.

place (Ezk. 7:16; Neh. 8:15), inhabited by birds of prey (Isa. 18:6) and wild beasts that threatened the lives of men and stray animals (Jer. 50:6). Insufficient rain (Hag. 1:11) could change the cultivated terraces back into an almost un-inhabitable desert (2 S. 1:21; Isa. 5:6; 42:15; Ezk. 35:1-7; Mal. 1:3).

Difficult access and scant population made mountaintops and remote ranges of hill typical hiding places (Jer. 16:16; Am. 9:3) and ideal places of asylum for fugitives (Josh. 2:16,22; 1 S. 13:6; 14:22; 23:14; Ezk. 7:16; cf. also Gen. 14:10; 19:17,19). All these concrete phenomena are reflected in biblical motifs deriving from the semantic field of *har* and *gibh'āh,* especially in the realm of belief and cult.

V. Religious Notions.

1. *General.* The mythological and theological values associated with *har* and some of its synonyms must be discussed within the framework of the Hebrew conception of space. Mythological thought assigned a special significance to both ordinary and unusual places, a significance that can be traced back to the mean-ing of spatial phenomena in accounts of primeval history and above all in cos-mogonies. In the biblical notion of space such mythological concepts played a formative role, but were effectively transformed and finally superseded by his-torico-theological and cultic notions that continued to evolve during the biblical period. The biblical thinkers rejected the mythological notion of space as being unalterably holy. With respect to the theological implications of *har,* the tension between the two modes of thought is illustrated on the one hand by the idea of a mountain as the chosen dwelling place of a god and on the other by the distinctly different statement that "the whole earth is full of his glory" (Isa. 6:3; Ps. 138). There is no place, not even a mountain, that is sacred in and of itself. Only an association with the God of Israel makes a region or space holy. This confluence of mythological thought with strictly biblical notions and expressions must be regarded when the theological dimensions of *har* in the OT are being examined.

2. *World Mountain.* The geomorphological and territorial nature of the Syro-Palestinian landscape resulted in mountains taking on two apparently opposite but in reality complementary significations. On the one hand, their imposing height, especially in the case of isolated peaks, led men to think of them as the focal point of the surrounding lowlands; on the other, as in Mesopotamia or Egypt, [31] mountains or ranges delimit the extent of a specific ethnic, political, [32] or cultic territory. In the OT, as a result, mountains are viewed as both focal points and perimeters. This notion finds its most striking expression in the description of Jerusalem and its holy Mt. Zion as being surrounded by a series of concentric mountain ranges, from the nearby hill of Judah (Ps. 125:1f.) to the surrounding nations (Ezk. 5:5) and the ends of the earth (Ps. 42), which

---

[31] Clifford, 10.
[32] IV.3.

apparently was conceived as a disk (Isa. 40:22; Job 22:14; 26:10; Prov. 8:27) or quadrangle (Isa. 11:12; Ezk. 7:2; Job 37:3; 38:13).

The latter image, however, cannot be associated with the reputed Mesopotamian interpretation of the world as a mountain (ḫursag, kur), consisting of four quarters (kibrāt irbitti) representing the four major lands of Akkad, Elam, Subartu, and Amurru. [33] The notion of the world mountain developed by several scholars since the beginning of this century [34] has meanwhile proved to be a false interpretation of the material in question [35] and is certainly not found in the OT. [36] Mesopotamian speculations about a "mountain" as the center of the cosmos are likewise incompatible with OT thought. This fact is indicated by the exclusive or almost exclusive use of the plural "mountains" rather than the singular "mountain" in references with cosmic significance.

3. *Omphalos.* According to several scholars, the representation of the world as a disk or quadrangle in which a mountain figured prominently points to the notion of a mountain as the indicator of the midpoint of the world, its *ómphalos* or navel. As W. H. Roscher has shown, with special reference to Greek mythology, this notion is found in the mythologies of several cultures. Homer referred to the geographical midpoint of the sea as its navel. [37] Roscher accordingly posited an early parallel concept for the earth, although there is no support for this view in Greek literature before Epimenides. [38] He went on to show that certain major Greek oracle sanctuaries like Didyma, Miletus, and especially Delphi were considered the navel or midpoint of the known world. Roscher's suggestion that this omphalos idea forms part of the conception of mountains shared by the ancient Near East, including Israel, [39] was further developed for the West Semites by Wensinck, with special reference to Hebrew thought. Most of his evidence, however, is drawn from Rabbinic literature and is therefore of limited value with respect to the significance of mountains in the OT. Wensinck isolated five aspects of the navel concept: (1) the navel is the midpoint of the world; (2) it is higher than the surrounding territory; (3) it is the point of contact between the lower and upper worlds; (4) it is the origin of the world; (5) it is the means whereby nourishment is distributed over the earth. Only the first three aspects appear to be applicable to the biblical notion of mountains. But even these, as we shall see, are not necessarily connected with the omphalos idea.

The frequently proposed identification of a mountain/navel/midpoint notion in the OT is based on a tendentious interpretation of a few passages that speak of the land of Israel or Jerusalem as lying "in the midst" of the surrounding territories, especially Ezk. 5:5 zō'th yᵉrûshālayim bᵉthôkh haggôyim śamtîhā

---

[33] Meissner, *BuA*, II, 107-111.
[34] Jensen, 195-201; Kramer; Clements.
[35] Clifford, 10ff.
[36] Alfrink, 64.
[37] *Odyssey* i.50.
[38] Plutarch *Moralia* 409 E.
[39] *Omphalos*, 23-31; *Omphalosstudien*, 12-18.

ûseʰbhîbhôtheyhā 'ᵃrātsôth. It must be stressed, however, that this passage refers to the city and its sanctuary, not to the mountain per se, and that expressions like beʰthôkh, beʰqerebh (Ps. 74:12), and be- simply indicate the position of an object within a certain perimeter (Ps. 46:6[5]; 55:12[11])[40] without necessarily referring to a geometrical or cosmic center. It would seem, therefore, that the point of the image here is more to indicate security than central geometric position, and that familiar metaphors for protection are being used (cf. Job 1:9-11; Ps. 125:1f.; 121:1-3).

Even more influential was the translation of ṭabbûr hā'ārets in Jgs. 9:37 and Ezk. 38:12 as "navel of the earth," which was adopted by several commentators on the basis of the LXX translation ómphalos tḗs gḗs/chṓras. From this translation was derived the theory propounded by Wensinck and accepted by many others[41] that Mt. Gerizim, identified with the ṭabbûr hā'ārets of Jgs. 9:37, was considered the "navel of the land." Caspari[42] rejected this theory on many grounds, but nevertheless interpreted ṭabbûr hā'ārets in Ezk. 38:12 as a reference to Jerusalem as the "center of the earth" or of "mankind," i.e., as a kind of cosmic midpoint.

But even the interpretation of ṭabbûr hā'ārets as "navel (midpoint) of the earth" appears untenable. The word ṭabbûr, which is attested only in Hebrew and Aramaic, is etymologically obscure. In mishnaic and later Hebrew it does mean "navel," but this meaning cannot be confirmed for Biblical Hebrew, which usually uses shōr as the term for "navel" or "umbilical cord" (Ezk. 16:4; Cant. 7:3[2]; Prov. 3:8). The context suggests that ṭabbûr hā'ārets in Ezk. 38:12 originally referred to a plateau whose height offered some security. In v. 11 the expression stands in parallel with 'erets peʰrāzôth, and both expressions refer to peaceful settlements that are protected by God and are secure without external fortifications. Almost the same terminology—with the exception of ṭabbûr hā'ārets—is used under similar circumstances in Ezk. 28:25f.; 34:25-29; 36:8-12; and especially Jer. 49:31f.; Jgs. 18:10 (cf. also vv. 7,27); 1 Ch. 4:40. In the last two examples 'erets rachᵃbhath yādhayim appears to replace the expressions 'erets peʰrāzôth and ṭabbûr hā'ārets in Ezekiel, which indirectly supports the translation "plateau" for ṭabbûr. This meaning also well befits Jgs. 9:36f., where the armies of Abimelech that are attacking Shechem come down from the ridge (mērā'shê hehārîm) and advance along the plateau (ṭabbûr), where they divide up into four companies. The notion of height associated here with ṭabbûr receives expression in the translation of the Targum (tuqpā' deʰ'ar'ā').[43]

The proposed translation of ṭabbûr as "navel" thus appears not to have any basis within the conceptual framework of the OT; it is rather an inference based on later Greek and Jewish ideas that merged with the literal and symbolic significance of mountains as heights.[44]

---

[40] Cf. Dahood, 290.

[41] Terrien, 317.

[42] ZDMG, 86, 58f.

[43] Cf. Rashi, "the highest mountain of all."

[44] Seeligmann, 209f.; cf. also E. A. S. Butterworth, *The Tree at the Navel of the Earth* (1970), esp. 1-17, 53ff.

4. *World Axis*. Impressed by the imposing height of the mountains, the OT writers speculated that these landforms extended invisibly beyond what could be seen of them into the heights and into the depths. Indeed, even the visible portions of the mountains had been submerged under the primal sea before creation, until the Creator commanded the sea to recede and the mountains stood forth: "The waters stood above the mountains. At thy rebuke they fled; at the sound of thy thunder they took to flight. The mountains rose, the valleys sank down to the place which thou didst appoint for them" (Ps. 104:6-8; cf. also 18:16[15] [= 2 S. 22:16]). This mythological notion may be observable in the inundation of the mountains by the waters of the Deluge (Gen. 7:19) and their reappearance after the waters above and the waters beneath began to recede (Gen. 8:2f.); here the theme of renewed creation is addressed (Gen. 9:1-17). This same notion is found in the Egyptian myth that describes the act of creation as the rising of the primal hill out of the depths of the primal ocean (Nun).

In the OT we also find the notion common among other Semitic and non-Semitic cultures that mountains constitute the world axis, the vertical link joining the three components of the cosmos (Gen. 1; Ex. 20:4; Prov. 8:28f.), i.e., the earth, the heavens, and the underworld. [45] At the same time, the foundations of the mountains (*qetsê hārîm* or *môsedhê hārîm*) are rooted in the depths of the abyss (Dt. 32:22; Jonah 2:7[6]), in Sheol, the land of Mot, [46] and serve as pillars supporting the earth (1 S. 2:8; Ps. 104:5; Mic. 6:2; Job 9:5f.; 38:4-6) and the heavens (Job 26:11). The mountain peaks (*merôm hārîm*, Isa. 37:24 [=2 K. 19:23]; Ezk. 17:23; 20:40; 34:14), on the other hand, are thought of as reaching up into the heavenly spheres that are God's dwelling place, and are also termed *mārôm* (Isa. 24:21; 33:5; 40:26; 57:15; Jer. 17:12; Ps. 7:8[7]; 68:19[18]; 93:4; 144:7; Job 25:2), so that they share in the glory of heaven. Metaphorical usage reflects Mesopotamian and Canaanite mythological ideas that are also associated with temples and other cultic buildings which plastically represent the notion of mountains as the dwelling places of the gods. The dwelling place of Baal is upon *mrym spn*. [47] The top of the temple tower belonging to the E-kur ("mountain house") at Nippur reaches to the heavens, while its foundations rest in the *apsû*, "abyss." [48] The temple of Marduk at Babylon, which is located on level ground rather than on a mountain, is the half-way house of the gods as they go between heaven and *apsû*, and the ideal place to meet them. [49] This shows that the idea of a world axis is not necessarily associated with a mountain, but only under certain geographical circumstances, as in Hittite, Hurrian, and Canaanite mythology. The proximity of mountaintops to heaven makes them the ideal site for statements that are ascribed explicitly or implicitly to a deity (Dt. 27; Josh. 8:30-35). Although the erroneous idea that a height provides better audibility

---

[45] Wensinck, 6; M. Eliade, *Images and Symbols* (trans. 1961), 27-56.
[46] His *'rṣ nḥlt* (*CTA*, 4 [II AB], VIII, 14; 5 [I* AB], II, 13-16).
[47] *CTA*, 3 [V AB], III, 43ff.; IV, 81f.; 4 [II AB], V, 84; 5 [I* AB], I, 10f.
[48] IV R, 27, No. 2, 15ff.; Jensen, 21; Alfrink, 51.
[49] Landsberger and Kinnier Wilson.

and visibility can be observed in the literature as a factor in the choice of mountaintops for such addresses (Jgs. 9:7; 2 Ch. 13:4; Isa. 13:2; 40:9; Nah. 2:1[1:15];
cf. Mt. 28:16), these considerations were most probably secondary to the preceding idea that they were being delivered from a holy space. The notion of a
mountain as a symbol for strength appears to be rooted in the actual existence
of mountain fortresses, which were considered practically impregnable (Jer. 49:16
[=Ob. 3]; Nu. 24:21; Hab. 2:9; Ezk. 17:23; 34:14), and also in the mythico-
poetic idea that mountains are the foundations of the universe, and are sacred
areas (Jer. 3:22f.; Ezk. 20:40; Ps. 125:1). On this basis, mountains and expressions associated with mountains become metaphors for the hybris of power (Zec.
4:7; Jer. 51:25). The fall of a powerful man can accordingly be described as his
being thrown down from his mountain seat (Nu. 24:21; Jer. 49:21; Ezk. 28:16f.);
the mountains are depicted as trembling and tottering before the Creator (Job
14:18; Jgs. 5:4f.; Ps. 68:9[8]; 18:7-10[6-9] [=2 S. 22:7-10]; Hab. 3:3-10; Nah.
1:3; Isa. 7:25; 63:20[64:1]; Mic. 1:4f.; Jer. 4:22-26), for his power surpasses even
their proverbial strength (Jer. 3:22f.; Ps. 89:27[26]; cf. Dt. 32:20,37; Ps. 125:1f.).

5. *Cosmogonic References.* The mythological notion of mountains as the
world axis must be distinguished from their interpretation as the umbilical cord
of the cosmos, which is connected with the omphalos idea. Despite the apparent
identity of function (bonding the universe together), the two motifs are fundamentally different. The language of the OT never adopted the mythological image
of a mountain fastness as the very site of cosmogony. In contrast to the Mesopotamian cosmogonies, the mountains play no cosmogonic role in the OT and
are not even mentioned in its account of creation (Gen. 1–4). But in the mythological substrate that appears in the prophets, Psalms, and Wisdom Literature,
we find definite references to creation myths in which mountains are mentioned
alongside the usual elements (earth, heavens, and sea) (Isa. 40:12; Ps. 90:2; Prov.
8:24-29). Some instances are reminiscent of Mesopotamian and/or Canaanite
cosmogonies, where the act of creation involves the victory of the creator-god
over the opposing primordial powers (Am. 4:13; 5:8f.; 9:5f.). Thus the mountains go back to the dawn of time, like the earth (*'erets*), the sea (*yām*), and the
abyss (*tᵉhôm*). The antithetic or parallel combination of these elements serves
as an appropriate image for the inhabited world, especially in the description
of cosmic upheavals that represent the wrath of the Creator and disintegration
of creation: "Though the earth should change, though the mountains shake in
the heart of the sea" (Ps. 46:3[2]); "He who removes mountains and they know
it not . . . , who shakes the earth out of its place" (Job 9:5f.); and especially Dt.
32:22, where God's anger is described as a fire that devours *shᵉ'ôl tachtîth*,
'erets, and *môsᵉdhê hārîm* (cf. Am. 7:4). In combination with *'erets*, *hārîm* can
replace *shāmayim*, as in Job 26:7: "He stretched out [the mountain of] the north
(*tsāphôn*) over the void, and hung the earth upon nothing." This is especially
the case when these pairs, which are synonymous with the "universe," appear
as witnesses in God's controversy (*rîbh*) with his faithless people Israel (Mic.
1:1f.; → ברית *bᵉrîth* IX.1).

6. *Cosmic Mountains.* The OT contains clear allusions to the ancient Near Eastern notion of mountains as the dwelling places of deities or the place where the gods assemble. [50] In the first place, we find references to "cosmic mountains," i.e., mountains on which cosmically important matters are decided. The fact that all these mountains are conceived as being located north or northeast of Israel demonstrates convincingly that they originated in Northwest Semitic (Ugaritic) and Mesopotamian mythology. There the metaphor of the world mountain was associated with specific mountains in a specific geographical region; they were viewed as earthly counterparts to heavenly phenomena. Irrespective of their size, they were even identified as the actual dwelling place of a deity. Mt. Casius in Syria is the *ġr* or *gbʿ spn* of Ugaritic myth; it also appears in non-Ugaritic texts. There Baal built his house after conquering his enemy Mot, the ruler of the underworld, with the aid of his sister and consort Anat, who is also associated with *spn*. [51] Mot dwells at the foot of a subterranean mountain, sometimes called *ġr trġzz*, [52] sometimes *ġr trmg*, [53] sometimes *ġr knkny*; [54] its peak may perhaps be considered the dwelling place of El (*ġr ʾl*). The mountain of El was the place where the council of the gods assembled (*pḫr mʿd*), a precise parallel to the Akk. *puḫur ilāni* (=*pḫr ʾlm*). [55] There, too, was located the source of the two rivers of the underworld at the *mbk nhrm...ʾpq thmtm*, where a variant of the myth also locates the dwelling place of El. [56] M. Pope has identified this spot with Aphaca, modern Khirbet Afqa, in Syria. [57]

A portion of this terminology was incorporated into the language of the OT by a process of "translation," [58] which looks like a direct borrowing from the Ugaritic epics. In the process, the polytheistic notions that were irreconcilable with the monotheistic faith of Israel lost much of their original vividness. They were used in the OT as literary stereotypes, sometimes in order to lend local color to statements and oracles concerning foreign peoples from whose cultural heritage the terms had been derived. [59] This applies particularly to passages describing the punishment of foreign kings who in their arrogance have attempted to assume the status of divinity by ascending the cosmic mountain, the dwelling place of the gods. In Isaiah's oracle against the king of Babylon, the cosmic mountain manifestly is viewed as heavenly, not earthly: "You said in your heart, 'I will ascend to heaven; above the stars of God I will set my throne on high; I will sit on the mount of assembly in the far north'" (Isa. 14:13). The same is true for Ezekiel's lament over the king of Tyre, who had arrogated to himself the

[50] Cf. E. D. van Buren, "Mountain Gods," *Or,* 12 (1943), 76-84.
[51] *Ugaritica,* V, 592: RS 24.253, lines 13f.; other citations in Whitaker, 542.
[52] *CTA,* 4 [II AB], VIII, 2-3.
[53] *Ibid.,* 3.
[54] *CTA,* 5 [I* AB], V, 12-13.
[55] *CTA,* 29, verso 7; *Ugaritica,* V, 45: RS 20.24, line 28.
[56] *CTA,* 3 [V AB], V, 13-16; 4 [II AB], IV, 20-24; 6 [I AB], I, 32-36; *Ugaritica,* V, 564: RS 24.244, line 3.
[57] Pope, 92-104.
[58] Clifford, 131f. and *passim.*
[59] Alfrink, 57.

role of an angelic being on the holy mountain of God (*bᵉhar qōdhesh 'elōhîm*) (Ezk. 28:14f.). It remains uncertain whether the preceding oracle (v. 13) means that the garden of God was located on this mountain or whether we have here a fusion of two independent traditions. [60] The two usurpers of divine status are punished by being hurled from the heights of heaven into the depths of the underworld (*'el shᵉ'ôl tûrādh / 'el yarkᵉthê bôr* [Isa. 14:15,19]) or "to earth" (*'al 'erets hishlakhtîkhā* [Ezk. 28:17]); in the last phrase, *'erets* may refer to the underworld, as it often does in the Ugaritic epic.

The mythological motif of the human king who claims divinity and ascends a cosmic mountain appears also to lie behind the attack on Sennacherib ascribed to Isaiah. The king's boast: "I have gone up the heights of the mountains [*mᵉrôm hārîm*], to the far recesses of Lebanon; ... I came to its remotest height, its densest forest" (Isa. 37:24), echoes the mythological terminology of the Ugaritic epic. In *PRU*, II, 3, 8-10, the struggle between Anat and the dragon is located upon Lebanon (rather than the more usual Zaphon). When she has conquered her opponent, she binds the dragon unmuzzled [61] to the heights of Lebanon (*tnn 'n lšbm tšt trks lmrym lbnn*). [62] In like fashion God muzzles the arrogant king of Assyria ("I will put my hook in your nose and my bit in your mouth," Isa. 37:29) to take him back where he came from.

A different tradition in Ezekiel's oracles against Tyre charges its king with having laid claim to divinity (*ya'an tittᵉkhā 'eth lᵉbhābhᵉkhā kᵉlēbh 'elōhîm*) and thus having as it were usurped the throne of the gods in the midst of the seas (*môshabh 'elōhîm yāshabhtî bᵉlēbh yammîm*) (Ezk. 28:1-6; cf. *mbk nhrm qrb 'pq thmtm*, [63] probably the underground mountain atop which El dwells). As punishment the king will be cast down to the base of the mountain, the domain of Mot (*lashshachath yôridhûkhā vāmattāh mᵉmôthê chālāl bᵉlēbh yammîm*, Ezk. 28:8). A similar idea lies behind the tradition of the Tower of Babel (Gen. 11:1-9), where the tower serves as a man-made substitute for a mountain. To build a tower whose top reaches to the heavens (11:4) is equivalent to the attempt to attain the sphere of the gods by ascending a cosmic mountain.

VI. Israel's "Mountain-God."

1. *Sources.* In the Israelite predeliction for locating "sacred space" on mountains or identifying it with mountains we can recognize a fusion of various motifs. These will merely be listed here, without any attempt to rank their importance in the formation of the notion of the "holy mountain."

(a) The influence of mythological ideas, Mesopotamian in origin, which Israel borrowed directly through contact with the Mesopotamian cultures or indirectly

---

60 Clifford, 103, 105.
61 Following Clifford, 60 (and others); disputed by J. Barr, "Ugaritic and Hebrew šbm?" *JSS*, 18 (1973), 17-39.
62 *PRU*, II, 3 [V MF], 8-10.
63 Cf. *mbk nhrm qrb 'pq thmtm* (cf. Whitaker, 410f.).

through the mediation of other Syro-Palestinian peoples, [64] appears in the cultic vocabulary of the OT, as well as in various images and motifs. These give evidence of the heavy penetration of mythological concepts and cultic practices into Israelite religion, both popular and official. Readiness to adopt such notions does not necessarily demonstrate any "officially promoted syncretism"; [65] on the other hand, it does contradict the view that Hebrew monotheism was not influenced in any essential area by the mythological world view of the "heathen." [66] The realm of mythological notions obviously represented a substrate of the Hebrew intellectual milieu that exercised varying influence on different strata of Israelite society. This substrate could never be fully escaped in the biblical period; it was incorporated into the civilization of Israel through various processes of sublimation, transformation, and reinterpretation, without, it would seem, changing decisively the code of beliefs and concepts of OT monotheism [67] as conceived or propagated most notably by the pentateuchal and prophetic writers.

(b) The major principles of OT monotheism find expression in official or authoritative statements in legal and prophetic literature, in historiography, and in historiographical reworking of other literary genres. These sources certainly display accurately the genuine achievements of Hebrew monotheism, irrespective of whether they were adopted by a majority or only a minority of biblical Israel.

(c) The form and content of this monotheistic faith were shaped by the geographical and geophysical realities experienced by the Hebrews in the initial stages of their contact with the land of Canaan, and were reinforced by economic and military considerations. [68]

2. *Israel's God in its Early History.* In depicting the period between the exodus and the occupation of Canaan, an early poetically framed tradition describes how the God of Israel went from south to north with or before his people, from mountain to mountain, with or without a man-made temenos. Some scholars think that the multiplicity of sacred sites appearing in biblical historiography is the result of a coalescence of various independent local traditions. [69] There are references to Mt. Seir (Jgs. 5:4; cf. Ps. 68:8[7]; 18:8[7]; 77:19[18]), Teman (Hab. 3:3; cf. Ps. 89:13[12]), Paran (Hab. 3:3), Sinai/Horeb (Ex. 3:1; 18:5; 20; 24:13; Jgs. 5:5; 1 K. 19:8ff.; Ps. 68:9[8]), Ebal and Gerizim (Dt. 11:26-29; 27:11-14; Josh. 8:30-35). Other references include Bashan (Nah. 1:4; Ps. 68:16[15]); the *har* where the Gibeonites executed Saul's sons in a cultic ceremony "before God" (2 S. 21:6-9), which is certainly to be identified with the nearby Gibeah of Saul, [70] his birthplace and official residence; and the mountain of Bethel (Gen. 28:10-22; 1 S.

---

[64] Gressmann, 114-18.
[65] Soggin.
[66] Kaufmann.
[67] Cf. V.1-6 above.
[68] IV.1-4.
[69] Clifford, 114-120.
[70] On *har* = *gibh'āh,* cf. Isa. 10:32.

13:2; etc.). Finally, Mt. Moriah must be mentioned, where Isaac was to have been sacrificed by his father (Gen. 22:1-19); tradition identified this mountain with the future site of the temple.

In consequence of this association of the God of Israel with a series of mountains (Hab. 3:10; Gen. 31:54; etc.) that had an aura of sanctity about them or came to be viewed as "holy mountains" on account of this association, Yahweh appeared to the non-Israelites to be a typical "mountain-god" (1 K. 20:23-28). These basic notions from an early stage in the development of Israelite religion are reflected later in the idea that the dynamic mobility of the nomadic deity represented a normative aspect of Hebrew monotheism. This notion became linked with an antagonistic attitude toward any permanent establishment of God's sanctuary at a fixed site. This attitude probably arose in prophetic circles; it finds its most powerful expression in Nathan's initial outright rejection of David's plan to build a temple (2 S. 7:4-7).

When the Israelite tribes settled in Canaan, they first occupied the central mountain range. There they took over the existing pagan temene, sometimes, as at Gibeon, complete with cultic institutions and personnel (1 K. 3:4ff., cf. v. 2; 2 S. 21:1-14; Josh. 9). These holy places were adapted syncretistically and later permeated with specifically Israelite religious traditions. The standard expression for idolatry and erotic cult practices, "on every high hill and under every green tree," [71] proves that these sites, sanctified by pre-Israelite mythological and cultic traditions, continued to flourish throughout the entire period of the first temple (1 K. 11:7; 2 K. 23:13) and perhaps to a lesser extent into the postexilic period, [72] although monotheistic theology disapproved strongly (Dt. 12:2; Isa. 57:7; Jer. 2:20; 3:2,6; etc.).

In OT tradition, then, mountains appear as the preferred sites for theophanies (Gen. 22:14; Ex. 3:1; 4:27; 18:5; 19–20; 32; 34; Dt. 4:11; 5:4; 9:15; 1 K. 19:11-14; Mic. 1:3; Ps. 18:7ff.[6ff.]; 97:4f.; etc.) and as places where God establishes his covenant with individuals (e.g., Gen. 31:54) as well as with his people. [73]

3. *Identification of "Mountain" with "Sanctuary" in the Election of Jerusalem.* In consequence of this development, "sanctuary" and "mountain" became conceptually identical, as is illustrated by the location of the earliest Israelite sanctuaries upon mountains: Gilgal, Bethel, the twin peaks Ebal and Gerizim, Shiloh, and finally the election of Zion (→ צִיּוֹן *tsiyyôn*) and Jerusalem (→ ירושלם *yerûshālayim*). These places represent the stage in the development of Israelite religion in which the permanence of the divine dwelling place had already been accepted. After all previously chosen places had been rejected (Ps. 78:67; 68:16-18[15-17]), God's presence finally and definitely came to rest upon Zion (Ps. 68:16f.[15f.]; 78:67f.; 132:13f.), "his holy mountain" (*har qodhshô*, Isa. 11:9;

---

[71] Cf. W. L. Holladay, "'On Every High Hill and Under Every Green Tree,'" *VT*, 11 (1961), 170-76.

[72] Smith, 82ff.

[73] See above.

27:13; 66:20; Jer. 31:23; Joel 2:1; 4:17[3:17]; Zec. 8:3; Ps. 3:5[4]; 43:3; 48:2; Dnl. 9:16,20), "his own mountain" (Ex. 15:17), which he had created for himself (*gᵉbhûl qodhshô har zeh qānᵉthāh yᵉmînô,* Ps. 78:54). The formative influence of historical fact on the cultic, ideological, and mythological appreciation of mountains becomes fully apparent in the traditions of Zion and Jerusalem. Kaufmann's assertion that the notion of Jerusalem's political election preceded that of its cultic election is well founded, [74] and reflects the essence of the OT view of Jerusalem. But it must be emphasized at the same time that the site where Solomon built his temple had undoubtedly had a long pre-Israelite cultic history. The name "Jerusalem" (from Canaanite *Ursalimmu*) suggests that the site was associated with the god Shalim or Shulmanu, probably of Mesopotamian origin, who was worshipped there. The tradition associated with the threshing floor of Araunah, which later became the site of the temple, suggests that it served as the temenos of the local deity (2 S. 24:18-25; 1 Ch. 21:13-26 [→ גרן *gōren*]).

When one considers Israel's constant contact with the ancient Near East and with Canaanite civilization in particular, it is only natural that originally pagan terminology should have been borrowed increasingly for the cultic vocabulary of Hebrew. Ugaritic mythological epithets and images are used to extol Yahweh and his sanctuary on Zion (Ps. 89:12f.[11f.]; Job 26:7; etc.). Specific expressions like *ṣrrt ġr ṣpn* (the dwelling place of Baal in Ugaritic mythology) were freed from their geographical and mythological context and applied to Jerusalem as Yahweh's dwelling place. Mt. Zion becomes Mt. Zaphon (*har tsiyyôn yarkᵉthê tsāphôn qiryath melekh rābh,* Ps. 48:2f.[1f.]), in its majestic height—if not geographically, at least in the minds of the devout—towering above all the other mountains of Canaan and the lands around it (Isa. 2:2 [=Mic. 4:1]; 10:32; Ezk. 17:22f.; 20:40; 40:2; 43:12).

At this point the new notion of the sanctity of Zion meant that the idea of the "holy mountain" had to be freed from the traces of the pagan sexual cults that had heretofore been associated with it. Kings of Judah who were faithful to the law, like Jehoshaphat (2 Ch. 17:6), Hezekiah (2 K. 18:4; 2 Ch. 29–31), and especially Josiah (2 K. 22–23; 2 Ch. 34), and even the Ephraimite Jehu (2 K. 10:18-27), periodically strove to destroy the *bāmôth* (→ במה *bāmāh*), i.e., the pagan high places such as were found also in other Semitic cults (e.g., in Moab). [75] Despite some subsequent temporary reverses, Josiah's reform put an end to the *bāmôth.* The *bāmāh* was usually, though not always, an artificial elevation outside a town; it can be considered a man-made representation of the holy mountain. This identification is demonstrated linguistically by the use of *har / gibh'āh* as synonyms for *bāmāh* (Ezk. 20:28; 1 K. 14:23; 2 K. 16:4; 2 Ch. 28:4). Lawgivers and prophets are concerned to purify the widespread popular cult of the *bāmôth,* a program that also affected the "high hills and green trees" associated with Canaanite erotic cult practices (Dt. 12:2; 1 K. 3:2-4; 11:7ff.; Isa. 57:7; Jer. 2:20; 3:2ff.; 17:2). It is significant that *bāmāh* is never used with reference to the temple at Jerusalem.

---

[74] Kaufmann, 267f.; cf. Seeligmann, 193.
[75] *KAI,* 181.3, 27.

4. *Mountains in OT Eschatology.* The complex ideas associated with "mountains" in the history of Israel, which culminated in the Zion traditions, were drawn upon to a significant extent to develop the vision of the future (→ אחרית *'acharîth*), which illustrates the fundamentally restorational and historical attitude of OT eschatology.[76] Once again, cosmic-mythological, physical, and (meta)historical features coalesce in the mountain imagery of the future.[77]

(a) The OT speaks of the mountains of Canaan as being well watered. Since they are close to the heavens, the peaks get the first benefit of rain (Ps. 104:13; etc.). At the same time, brooks and springs flow from and between the mountains (Ps. 104:10f.; Dt. 8:7). These facts are reflected in the description of the last days, when "upon every lofty mountain and every high hill there will be brooks running with water" (Isa. 30:25). Jerusalem, the Mount of Olives, and the temple mountain are the focal points of eschatological scenes: "A fountain shall come forth from the house of Yahweh" (Joel 4:18[3:18]); "On that day living waters shall flow out from Jerusalem, half of them to the eastern sea [i.e., the Dead Sea] and half of them to the western sea [i.e., the Mediterranean]; it shall continue in summer as in winter" (Zec. 14:8), so that the drought of summer is miraculously overcome. The abundance of water will produce a luxuriant growth of fruit trees (Ezk. 36:8). "The mountains shall drip sweet wine, and the hills shall flow with milk" (Joel 4:18[3:18]; cf. Am. 9:13: "all the hills will be fertile"). This symbolizes the future restoration of Israel's ancient fortunes (Am. 9:14f.). The mountain (Zion) will once more be the pride of the Davidic ruler, whom Yahweh "will plant on the mountain height of Israel" (Ezk. 17:22f.).

(b) Restoration of Israel's political fortunes is associated with the day of judgment. On the mountains of Israel the final battle against Gog will be fought (Ezk. 38f.). Then—as in the past—Yahweh will defeat the nations upon the Mount of Olives. "Then Yahweh will go forth and fight against those nations as when he fights on a day of battle. On that day his feet shall stand on the Mount of Olives which lies before Jerusalem on the east" (Zec. 14:3ff.; cf. Joel 4:1-17[3:1-17]). In these battle scenes, where the wrath of God is turned against the nations, "the mountains shall flow with their blood" (Isa. 34:2ff.), an antithesis to the ancient image of the "hills that flow with milk." On this canvas of the eschatological events is portrayed as well the great banquet that God will prepare upon his mountain for all nations, "a feast of wine on the lees, of fat things full of marrow" (Isa. 25:6-8; Ezk. 39:17-20). In these themes we catch an echo of the banquets on Mt. Zaphon given by El[78] and by Baal[79] after his victory over his enemies, or after building his temple.[80] From a mountaintop the liberation of Israel is proclaimed (Isa. 25:9ff.; 40:9ff.; 52:7ff.). All this prepares the way for the final

---

[76] Talmon, 574, 578f.
[77] Gressmann; Von Rad, *OT Theol,* II (trans. 1965), 112ff.
[78] *CTA,* 4 [II AB], IV, 30-38.
[79] *CTA,* 3 [V AB], I, 1-22.
[80] *CTA,* 4 [II AB], V, 106-110; VI, 38-59.

reconciliation, which in cosmic dimensions has as its focal point the temple mountain of Israel's God, the biblical "holy mountain" par excellence (Isa. 2:1-4 [=Mic. 4:1-4]; Isa. 11:6-9 [=65:25]; Jer. 31:6; Zec. 14:16).

Talmon

הָרַג *hāragh;* הֶרֶג *heregh;* הֲרֵגָה *hᵃrēghāh*

I. Etymology. II. Extrabiblical Parallels: 1. Old South Arabic; 2. Canaanite. III. Old Testament: 1. General Survey; 2. Killing Enemies in Battle; 3. Killing Political Opponents; 4. Killing Personal Rivals; 5. *hrg* as a Crime; 6. *hrg* as a Punishment; 7. Yahweh as Subject.

I. Etymology. The root *hrg* is attested in only a few of the Semitic languages. Heb. *hrg* probably corresponds to OSA *hrg*, "kill"; [1] cf. Arab. *haraǧa*, "slaughter" [2] or "hunt." [3] It is also related to Moabite *hrg*, [4] which is attested as a Canaanite loanword [5] in Ya'udic and Old Aramaic texts. [6] There may also be some connection with Egyp. *ḥrṭ*, "kill (enemies)," [7] but this is uncertain. It is linguistically significant that the root *hrg* is not found in Akkadian, Ugaritic, or Aramaic, but only in Hebrew/Moabite and Old South Arabic.

II. Extrabiblical Parallels.

1. *Old South Arabic.* In Old South Arabic, the basic meaning of *hrg* is "kill enemies." In their war with the Ḥabashites, 'Ilsharaḥ Yaḥḍub and his brother

---

hāragh. D. Daube, "Rechtsgedanken in den Erzählungen des Pentateuch," *Von Ugarit nach Qumran. Festschrift O. Eissfeldt. BZAW,* 77 (²1961), 32-41; R. Heinze, *Das Objekt der unerlaubten Tötung in Israel* (diss., Giessen, 1928); A. Jamme, *Sabaean Inscriptions from Maḥram Bilqîs (Marîb)* (1962); K. Koch, "Gibt es ein Vergeltungsdogma im AT?" *ZThK,* 52 (1955), 1-42; *idem,* "Der Spruch 'Sein Blut bleibe auf seinem Haupt'," *VT,* 12 (1962), 396-416; *idem,* ed., *Um das Prinzip der Vergeltung in Religion und Recht des AT. Wege der Forschung,* 125 (1972); H. McKeating, "The Development of the Law on Homicide in Ancient Israel," *VT,* 25 (1975), 46-68; E. Merz, *Die Blutrache bei den Israeliten. BWAT,* 20 (1916); H. Graf Reventlow, "'Sein Blut komme über sein Haupt,'" *VT,* 10 (1960), 311-327; H. Schüngel-Straumann, *Tod und Leben in der Gesetzesliteratur des Pentateuch* (diss., Bonn, 1969).

Additional bibliography: → מות *mûth;* → נכה *nkh;* → רצח *rṣḥ.*

[1] Jamme, 434.
[2] Beeston.
[3] Ingrams in *RES,* 4909, line 2; cf. E. Littmann in *ZDMG,* 101 (1951), 377.
[4] *KAI,* 181.11, 16; *DISO,* 69.
[5] J. Friedrich, *Phönizisch-punische Grammatik. AnOr,* 32 (1951), 153-163; C. Brockelmann, *OLZ,* 48 (1953), 257.
[6] *KAI,* 214.26,33f.; 215.3,5,7; 222 A.24; *DISO,* 69.
[7] *WbÄS,* III, 331; cf. Tigrē *ḥärädä,* "slaughter, cut the throat, kill," and Tigr. *härädä* (*TigrWb,* 70).

Ya'zil Bayyin, the kings of Saba' and Raydân, kill their enemies by cutting them to pieces (ḥsm), killing them (ḥrg), and destroying them (sḥt).[8] In their battle against the Nagrân, they kill 924 soldiers.[9] Two high military officials thank 'Ilumquh for protecting them from violence and humiliation and killing (ḥrg) at the hands of their enemies.[10] Ẓabîum Yarzaḥ gives thanks for a successful expedition in which he was able to kill 27 enemy pillagers.[11] An officer of Nasha'karib Yu'min Yuharḥib succeeds in killing two enemy messengers.[12] Qaṭbân 'Aukân gives thanks to 'Ilumquh for his mighty assistance "in killing (ḥrg) and cutting (ḥsm) and crushing and destroying (sḥt)" the enemy Ḥaba-shites.[13] Yada''il, the king of Ḥaḍramaut, kills 2000 enemy soldiers in a battle— and so on. In these texts, then, ḥrg means the killing of enemies, sometimes along with their women and children, in military engagements; probably the term includes all kinds of violence.

The word has a special use in the idiom wyhrgw mhrg(t)m ḏ'sm or ḏ' qdm.[14] This is obviously a fixed formula, which frequently concludes accounts of battles; it points in the direction of holy war terminology. Jamme translates: "they de-prived them of a war trophy, which was desired" or "according to their oath."[15] In these passages, ḥrg means "kill on account of a sworn obligation." Such an oath is sworn before battle in the presence of one's personal deity; it involves "all the chiefs and freemen"[16] of the captured city, or all the officers and soldiers together with their wives and children.[17]

In some texts, ḥrg is used in a weakened sense: "take possession of enemies or their property," hence "plunder." For example, 'Abkarib reports how they came back from battle "with animals and captives and riches and booty and horses which they took away (ḥrg) and which they captured alive."[18] And 'Aus'il Yaḍi' gives thanks to 'Ilumquh for booty (ḥrg) and profit in battle,[19] "and they took away (ḥrg) from them all their horses and their beasts of burden... and they killed (ḥrg) all those soldiers."[20] It is therefore hardly necessary to follow Jamme[21] in postulating a second root ḥrg with the meaning "take away, deprive."

2. *Canaanite*. A Moabite inscription also uses ḥrg as a term from the vocab-ulary of the holy war, with the meaning "kill on account of a sworn obligation or

---

8 Ja 575, 5-7.
9 Ja 577, 14.
10 Ja 578, 9-11.
11 Ja 586, 18.
12 Ja 612, 12.
13 Ja 631, 4f.
14 Ja 575, 7; 576, 5,9; 577, 1,12.
15 Jamme, 81.
16 Ja 577, 12.
17 Ja 575, 5f.; etc.
18 Ja 635, 30f.
19 Ja 644, 19.
20 Ja 644, 20-23.
21 Jamme, 434.

in performance of the ban." Mesha of Moab recounts: "... The king of Israel had built Aṭarot for himself. I attacked the city and took it. And I killed (*hrg*) all the people of the city as an offering (*ryt*[22]) for Chemosh and for Moab."[23] A little later we read: "I took it [Nebo] and killed (*hrg*) all ..., for I had dedicated it [by ban] to Ashtar-Chemosh."[24]

The inscription of Panammu II of Sam'al[25] recounts internal political conflicts, rebellion and revolution. A son rebels against his father Barṣur, and kills him and 70 of his kinsmen.[26] A brother escapes and takes refuge with the king of Assyria, "and he made him king over the house of his father and killed (*hrg*) the stone of destruction [presumably the instigator of the rebellion] from the house of his father"[27]—an interesting parallel to the story of Abimelech in Jgs. 9.

A totally different meaning of *hrg* is attested in the inscription of Panammu I carved on a statue of Hadad.[28] Unfortunately the text is damaged, so that it is no longer possible to draw firm conclusions. So much seems clear: lines 25ff. contain instructions for the one who will "sit on my throne and rule."[29] After a gap, we read: "He shall not kill (*hrg*) ... be killed (*mt*)."[30] Here *hrg* obviously refers to a criminal act punishable by death. The death penalty is here indicated by *mt*, but it can also be expressed by *hrg*, as line 33 suggests: "... you shall kill him in ... (or) in anger...."

In the text of a treaty between Barga'yah, king of KTK, and Mati'ilu, king of Arpad,[31] *hrg* occurs in the usual series of curses that take effect if the treaty is broken; we read: "And seven hens shall go in search of food and nevertheless kill nothing."[32] The meaning of this curse is not entirely clear. J. N. Epstein therefore proposes a different translation: "Seven women weavers shall go to spread their yarn and nevertheless be unsuccessful,"[33] thus evading the difficulty of the text.

III. Old Testament.

1. *General Survey.* There are 165 occurrences of *hrg* in the OT.[34] Qal: Gen., 4; Ex., 11; Lev., 2; Nu., 11; Dt., 2; Josh., 4; Jgs., 16; 1 S., 5; 2 S., 8; 1 K., 10; 2 K., 5; Isa., 8 (3 of which are in the Apocalypse: Isa. 26:21; 27:1,7); Jer., 4; Ezk., 8; Hos., 2; Am., 4; Hab. 1:17; Zec. 11:5; Pss., 8; Prov., 2; Eccl.

---

[22] Cf. the note in *KAI, in loc.*
[23] *KAI,* 181.10-12.
[24] *KAI,* 181.15-17.
[25] *KAI,* 215.
[26] *KAI,* 215.3.
[27] *KAI,* 215.7.
[28] *KAI,* 214.
[29] *KAI,* 214.25.
[30] *KAI,* 214.26.
[31] *KAI,* 222.
[32] *KAI,* 222 A.24.
[33] *Kedem,* 1 (1942), 39.
[34] According to *THAT,* I, 895, there are 167 occurrences (but see below on Dt. 13:10[9]).

3:3; Lam., 3; Est., 9; Neh., 4; 1 Ch., 3; 2 Ch., 12. Niphal: Ezk. 26:6,15; Lam. 2:20. Pual: Isa. 27:7; Ps. 44:23 (22). Two nouns are derived from the root: *heregh*, "killing," found in Isa. 27:7; Ezk. 26:15; Prov. 24:11; Est. 9:5; and *hᵃrēghāh*, "slaughter," found in Jer. 7:32; 12:3; 19:6; Zec. 11:4,7.

The occurrences are distributed rather evenly throughout the entire OT, beginning with the earliest texts (the Blessing of Jacob, Gen. 49:6, or the Song of Lamech, Gen. 4:23) and reaching into the latest strata (Esther, the Chronicler's history). The word is likewise evenly distributed among the various genres: it is found in narrative texts and the prophetic literature, in legal texts and in the songs and proverbs of Wisdom Literature. Nevertheless, the majority of the occurrences (108 out of 165) are in narrative texts, especially in the earlier sources of the Pentateuch J and E (41); here we clearly have the core of the various usages of *hrg*. Next comes the prophetic literature with 31 occurrences and proverbial and poetic wisdom with 19. The word occurs only 7 (or 5) times in legal texts: Ex. 21:14; 22:23(24); 23:7 (Covenant Code); Lev. 20:15f. (Holiness Code). The two occurrences in Dt. 13:10(9) are usually considered errors, following Budde. [35]

The subjects used with the verb are normally persons. They may be individuals, like Cain (Gen. 4:8), Lamech (Gen. 4:23); Israelites such as Moses (Ex. 2:14), Joshua (Josh. 9:26), Gideon (Jgs. 8:17), Saul (1 S. 16:2), or David (1 S. 24:11 [10]); and foreigners such as the pharaoh (Ex. 2:15), Balaam (Nu. 22:29), or Hazael (2 K. 8:12). They may also be groups: foreigners like the inhabitants of Gerar (Gen. 20:11), the servants of the pharaoh (Ex. 5:21), Assyrians (Ezk. 23:10), or men of Gath (1 Ch. 7:21); and Israelites like Simeon and Levi (Gen. 34:25; 49:6), Joseph's brothers (Gen. 37:20), Levites (Ex. 32:27), judges of Israel (Nu. 25:5), Israelites in general (Nu. 31:7ff.), the whole nation (1 K. 12:27), or Jews (Est. 8:11, etc.). Finally, the subject may be a particular group: the wicked (Ps. 10:8; 94:6), the impious (2 S. 4:11), enemies (Neh. 4:5[11]), and opponents (Neh. 6:10). There are a few exceptions: lions sent by Yahweh (2 K. 17:25); the vexation of a fool (Job 5:2); a viper's tongue (Job 20:16); apostasy from Yahweh (Prov. 1:32); here *hrg* is used metaphorically. Finally, special mention must be made of the passages where the subject of *hrg* is the angel of Yahweh (Nu. 22:33) or Yahweh himself (Ex. 4:23; 13:15; 22:23[24]; 32:12; Nu. 11:15; Isa. 14:30; 27:1; Hos. 6:5; Am. 2:3; 4:10; 9:1,4; Ps. 59:12[11]; 78:31,34, 47; 135:10; 136:18; Lam. 2:4,21; 3:43).

The objects, too, are normally persons: individuals or groups, Israelites and foreigners. Sometimes the individual or group is specified more closely: a neighbor (Ex. 21:14), a brother, companion, or neighbor (Ex. 32:27), the innocent (Ps. 10:8), the widow and stranger (Ps. 94:6). Metaphorical terms can be used for Israel as a group: a remnant (Am. 9:1), a vine (Ps. 78:47), a feast for the eyes (Lam. 2:4), a flock doomed to slaughter (Zec. 11:5). The dragon in Isa. 27:1 is also a metaphor, presumably for Babylon. The ass in Nu. 22:29 is personified

---

[35] K. Budde, "Dtn 13 ₁₀ und was daran hängt," *ZAW*, 36 (1916), 187-197; for a contrary point of view, see R. P. Merendino, *Das deuteronomische Gesetz. BBB,* 31 (1969), 67f.

in the style of the fable. The only instance of *hrg* without a personal object is Isa. 22:13, "slaying oxen"; everywhere else *hrg* is always used of persons killing persons.

In the immediate and extended context of *hrg* we find various parallel or synonymous verbs: → נכה *nākhāh* hiphil (Gen. 4:14; Josh. 13:22; 2 S. 12:9; 14:7; 23:20,21; Isa. 27:7; Ps. 135:10; 2 Ch. 25:3); → מות *mûth* hiphil (Josh. 11:17; Jgs. 9:54; 2 S. 3:30; 14:7; Isa. 14:30; Job 5:2)—*môth yûmāth* (Lev. 20:15f.); → אבד *'ābhadh* piel (Est. 3:13; 8:11; 9:6); → דכא *dākhā'* (Ps. 94:5); → רצח *rātsach* (Ps. 94: 6); *pāgha'* (Jgs. 8:21; 1 K. 2:32); → כרת *kārath* hiphil (Am. 2:3); *kāra'* hiphil (Ps. 78:31); → שחת *shāchath* (Isa. 22:13); *ṭābhach* (Lam. 3:43). Of the various nouns used in the same context, the forms deriving from → חלל *ḥll* deserve special mention (Nu. 31:8,19; Ezk. 9:6; Prov. 7:26).

Compound idioms include: *hāragh bacherebh* (Ex. 22:23; Josh. 10:11; 13:22; 1 K. 2:32; 19:1; 2 K. 8:12; Ezk. 23:10; 26:8,11; Am. 4:10; 9:1; 2 Ch. 21:4) or *hāragh lᵉphî cherebh* (Gen. 34:26) and *hᵃrûghê môth* (Jer. 18:21).

The LXX uniformly renders *hāragh* as *apokteínō* except for a few uses of *phoneúō* (Jgs. 16:2; 20:5; Neh. 4:5[11]; 6:10; Est. 9:12; Prov. 1:32; 7:26; Lam. 2:21).

2. *Killing Enemies in Battle.* The verb *hrg* with the meaning "kill enemies in battle or to carry out the ban" is found in one of the earliest texts of the OT, the so-called Blessing of Jacob (Gen. 49:2-27), a heterogeneous collection of tribal oracles. The oracle concerning Simeon and Levi (vv. 5-7) [36] states that they have slain (*hrg*) men in anger and hamstrung oxen (v. 6.). This refers presumably to the raid at Shechem (cf. Gen. 34), in the course of which they killed all the males (Gen. 34:25) and carried off the women and children as booty (34:29). But both tribes were soon annihilated in the vicinity of Shechem (Gen. 34:30 may have preserved a reminiscence of this catastrophe [37]), so that only scattered remnants of them are found dispersed throughout Israel (49:7).

Josh. 8 recounts the capture of Ai. In the present version, it is described as an undertaking of all Israel under the leadership of Joshua, more specifically as a Yahweh war. [38] The Israelites carry out the ban against the inhabitants of Ai by slaying (*hrg*) the men and women "with the edge of the sword," while keeping the cattle and other spoil for their own use (Josh. 8:26f.; cf. Dt. 2:34f.; 3:6; according to Dt. 20:10ff.; 7:22ff.; 13:16[15], however, the cattle must be killed as well). Further occurrences of *hrg* in this sense from the period of the occupation and the judges include Josh. 10:11 (Joshua carries out the ban against the coalition of five Canaanite city kings), Jgs. 7:25 (the Israelites kill Oreb and Zeeb in

---

[36] Cf. B. Vawter, "The Canaanite Background of Gen 49," *CBQ,* 17 (1955), 1-18; C. M. Carmichael, "Some Sayings in Genesis 49," *JBL,* 88 (1969), 435-444.

[37] For a contrary view, see L. Wächter, "Die Bedeutung Sichems bei der Landnahme der Israeliten," *WZ* Rostock, 17 (1968), 411-19.

[38] Cf. the critical comments in M. Weippert, "Heiliger Krieg in Israel und Assyrien," *ZAW,* 84 (1972), 460-493; and F. Stolz, *Jahwes und Israels Kriege. AThANT,* 60 (1972).

a battle against the Midianites), and finally Jgs. 8:21 (Gideon kills the captured Midianite princes Zebah and Zalmunna; 8:18f. might suggest blood vengeance). In his war with the Ammonites David slays the men of 700 chariots and 40,000 horsemen (2 S. 10:18, par. 1 Ch. 19:18); this may be the incident behind the brief phrase inserted in 1 K. 11:24: baharōgh dāvidh 'ôthām (= 'rm?). Finally, 1 K. 9:16 recounts an incident from the period of Solomon during one of the pharaoh's campaigns against Gezer, when he burned the city and killed all its inhabitants.

These examples show clearly that the *Sitz im Leben* of hrg is primarily the holy war; it refers to the killing of enemies to carry out the ban.

3. *Killing Political Opponents.* In a later stage, hrg comes to be used to refer to the killing of domestic political opponents in cases of rebellion and revolution, when a new king takes the throne in order to remove unpopular claimants, in disputes with the prophets, or in case of refusal to obey orders.

Gideon, for example, destroys Penuel and kills all the men of the city when it refuses to give him aid and support in his battle with the Midianites (Jgs. 8:17). The prophets' advocacy of pure Yahwism brought them into frequent conflict with the policies of the kings, who had them persecuted and killed as domestic enemies and conspirators. Samuel is afraid that Saul will kill him if he, acting at Yahweh's command, anoints one of Jesse's sons as the new king (1 S. 16:2). Saul has Ahimelech and all the priests of Nob slain for aiding David and supposedly abetting a conspiracy (1 S. 22:17, *mûth* hiphil; 22:21, *hrg*). Ahab's wife Jezebel kills all the prophets of Yahweh (1 K. 18:13). Zechariah, calling Israel to repentance during the reign of Joash, is stoned by the people on the king's orders (2 Ch. 24:22, *hrg*). Elijah laments to Yahweh that "The people of Israel have forsaken thy covenant, thrown down thy altars, and slain thy prophets with the sword" (1 K. 19:10). A later reflex of these killings is found in the so-called national confession in Neh. 9:6-37: [39] "They cast thy law behind their back and killed thy prophets, who had warned them in order to turn them back to thee" (9:26). Rebellion and revolution, the extermination of entire royal families upon the accession of a new king, are reported in such passages as Jgs. 9:5, where Abimelech kills his 70 brothers (cf. 2 K. 11:1). He bloodily suppresses a rebellion led by Gaal, destroys Shechem, and kills all the inhabitants of the city (Jgs. 9:45). Athaliah exterminates her entire family; she herself is killed in a rebellion under Joash, and with her Mattan, a priest of Baal (2 K. 11:16,18 par. 2 Ch. 23:17). Jehu kills Joram and exterminates the entire line of Ahab; according to 2 Ch. 22:8, he also kills the high officials of Judah and the sons of Ahaziah's brothers. Joash in turn falls victim to a conspiracy among his servants (2 Ch. 24:25). His son Amaziah kills (*hrg*) the conspirators who slew (*nkh*) his father, but does not put their children to death (*mûth* hiphil), an act of restraint that is mentioned with approval (2 Ch. 25:3f.). In the book of Esther, the festival

---

[39] W. S. Towner, "Retributional Theology in the Apocalyptic Setting," *Union Seminary Quarterly Review,* 26 (1971); 203-214; L. J. Liebreich, "The Impact of Nehemiah 9:5-37 on the Liturgy of the Synagogue," *HUCA,* 32 (1961), 227-237.

legend of Purim, *hrg* occurs with striking frequency, especially in conjunction with *šmd* hiphil and *'bd* piel (3:13; 7:4; 8:11; 9:6), attested only here.

4. *Killing Personal Rivals.* Applied to the private sphere, *hrg* is used neutrally for the killing of personal enemies or rivals. In Gen. 4:23f. (J/L) Lamech boasts that he has killed everyone who approached him too closely in any way and avenged every attack on his person, as well as every slight to his honor, "seventy-sevenfold" (v. 24).

This song has been variously interpreted. [40] Originally it was probably the boast of a mighty man before his wives, expressing an unbridled sense of power and pride in it, [41] oblivious to anything beyond self-assertion. [42] In the light of Arabic parallels, Montgomery takes it as a boast in the presence of enemies for the purpose of scaring them off; but v. 23 probably does not admit this interpretation.

We also encounter *hrg* in the narratives depicting the various dangers to which the wives of the patriarchs are exposed. Isaac is afraid that the people of Gerar might kill him on account of his wife Rebecca, and therefore claims that she is his sister (Gen. 26:7 [J/L]); cf. the parallel tradition of Abraham and Sarah at Gerar (Gen. 20 [E]) and the earlier version of Abram and Sarai in Egypt (Gen. 12:10-20 [J]). The word plays an important role in the story of Joseph and in the story of Esau and Jacob, in the context of conflicts between the brothers. Esau, not only cheated of his birthright but now of his blessing as well, seeks to take vengeance on his brother and kill him (Gen. 27:41). The preference of Israel/Jacob for his son Joseph over Joseph's older brothers arouses their envy and hatred, and they conceive a plan to kill him (Gen. 37:20). Fraternal conflict as a primary human phenomenon is the theme developed in the conflict between Cain and Abel, which finally ends in fratricide (*hrg*) (Gen. 4:1-16).

Scholars have ventured various interpretations of the Cain and Abel story. These interpretations fall into two essentially distinct categories: the first is individualistic and speaks in terms of primal history; the second is collective and speaks in terms of tribal or national history. [43] Most recently, W. Beltz has proposed an interpretation from a strongly religio-historical perspective; [44] for him, "the fraternal conflict between Cain and Abel" represents "...the biblical memorial, religio-historical in nature, of the transition from matriarchy to patriarchy." [45] But this interpretation raises problems. The collective interpretation can claim in its support that the stories of the patriarchs take their major figures as ancestors of tribes or nations, so that these texts are to be interpreted in the first instance

---

[40] For a survey of the cultural, tribal, and individual interpretations, see C. Westermann, *BK*, I/1 (1974), 455f.

[41] Gunkel, Gevirtz.

[42] Westermann.

[43] For a survey, see Westermann, *BK*, I/1, 385-88, with bibliography; *idem*, "Genesis 1–11," *Erträge der Forschung*, 7 (1972), 40-51.

[44] W. Beltz, "Religionsgeschichtliche Anmerkungen zu Gen 4," *ZAW*, 86 (1974), 83-86.

[45] *Ibid.*, 84.

as the deposit of the historical reminiscences associated with various tribes, in other words, ethnologically and etiologically. [46] From this perspective, Cain has been understood as the eponymous hero of the Kenites, and the story of Cain and Abel has been interpreted as an ethnological etiology. But this interpretation remains highly problematic, since it does not take sufficient account of the (present?) character of the narrative. Gen. 4 is a parallel narrative corresponding to Gen. 3, as can be observed even on the structural level. This means that Gen. 4 (at least in the narrative context of J) is a protohistorical narrative, standing in conjunction with the story of how the first human couple was created and banished. In other words, the primal relationship between brothers stands alongside the primal relationship between man and wife. Here, then, lie the roots of rivalry and enmity, which can lead to fratricide (*hrg*).

With the development of advancing civilization, new abilities and possibilities are opened to men; but these possibilities include a greater capacity for mutual destruction (*hrg*); thus the Yahwist interprets the Song of Lamech. [47] In other words, the term *hrg*, which refers to the permitted killing of enemies and opponents, or is at least neutral in connotation, takes on markedly negative overtones in J.

5. *hrg as a Crime.* Thus *hrg* can be used for a criminal act. That this aspect of its usage is fundamentally atypical can be seen in that views as to when *hrg* is to be considered criminal diverge widely, especially in earlier texts, and depend in part on the viewpoint of the parties involved. The divergence is also due to varying legal interpretations of Israel's being in a state of war, of the king's unlimited power over life and death as well as of his obligation to suppress hostile cults, and of the exaction of blood vengeance. [48] When Moses, for example, kills the Egyptian, he does so to avenge a tribal brother. Pharaoh looks upon this act as a crime to be punished by death (Ex. 2:14f.). Jgs. 8:18 has already been mentioned. [49] The problems involved become quite evident in the story of Joab and Abner: in pursuit of blood vengeance, Joab and Abishai kill Abner, who had killed their brother Asahel in the battle at Gibeon (2 S. 3:30). This act is termed a crime in 1 K. 2:5, on the grounds that Jacob had spilled "in time of peace blood which had been shed in war," etc. Among earlier texts, there is no dispute concerning the events described in Jgs. 10–21; likewise undisputed is David's killing of Uriah: "You have smitten (*nkh*) Uriah the Hittite with the sword, and have taken his wife to be your wife, and have slain (*hrg*) him with the sword of the Ammonites.... Because by this deed you have utterly scorned Yahweh, the child that is born to you shall die" (2 S. 12:9,14).

In legal texts *hrg* is used occasionally to refer to a crime. In the participially formulated series of capital offenses (Ex. 21:12-17), there appears a casuistically formulated interpolation (vv. 13-14), containing regulations governing asylum,

---

[46] G. von Rad.
[47] Cf. Westermann, *BK,* I/1, 457.
[48] Heinze, 18.
[49] See section 2 above.

which should be considered a later addition to the absolute statement in v. 12. [50] According to this interpolation, a homicide may be granted asylum (v. 13), but not a murderer (v. 14). In this passage, *hrg* refers to premeditated murder (*hāragh be'ormāh*). Nevertheless, Schüngel's observation is important: the emphasis is not on *hrg*, but on *be'ormāh*, "treacherously." The word *hrg* is used here "not as a technical term but as a common expression used to help describe an act." [51] Judicial murder is treated in the code for judges (Ex. 23:1-3,6-9); v. 7 states: "Do not slay (*hrg*) the innocent and righteous"—Gerstenberger translates: "Do not pronounce the guilty righteous." [52] The Psalms also use *hrg* in this sense. In Ps. 10:8, for example, we read that the wicked man "sits in ambush in the villages and secretly (*bemistārîm*) murders (*hrg*) the innocent." The wicked and evildoers crush (*dk'*) Yahweh's people, slay (*hrg*) widows and sojourners, and murder (*rṣḥ*) the fatherless (Ps. 94:5f.).

6. *hrg as a Punishment*. Finally, *hrg* can refer to the punishment for a crime: apostasy from Yahweh (Ex. 32:27; Nu. 25:5 [cf. 31:7-19]; Dt. 13:10[9]), killing the king, who is Yahweh's anointed (2 S. 4:10-12; cf. 1 S. 24:7[6]), fratricide (blood vengeance) (Gen. 4:14f., where, however, it is reserved to Yahweh; Ex. 21:14; Jgs. 8:21; 9:56; 2 S. 14:7; 1 K. 2:32), and bestiality (Lev. 20:15f. [H], albeit we are dealing here with redactional additions to an ancient *môth-yûmāth* series [53]).

In all these cases—in contrast, say, to the cultic declaration that some act deserves death—*hrg* refers to actual killing, as one would expect from its origin in the terminology of war. The verb does not imply any specific method of execution.

7. *Yahweh as Subject*. The varied spectrum of meanings of *hrg* is reflected in the passages where Yahweh appears as the subject: he punishes misdeeds; he is a military hero destroying enemies foreign and domestic; he kills personal opponents.

It is in this latter sense that one should perhaps understand the strange encounter of Balaam with the angel of Yahweh in Nu. 22:21-35. The angel of Yahweh, his sword menacingly drawn, blocks Balaam's way to prevent him from cursing Israel as Balak wishes him to. [54] The pharaoh's refusal to let Israel go is answered by Yahweh with the killing of his firstborn son (Ex. 4:23; cf. 13:15, where the punishment is extended to all the firstborn).

That Yahweh is a mighty warrior who destroys his enemies and punishes the wickedness of the nations with a mighty (or outstretched) arm is a notion en-

---

[50] M. Noth, *Exodus. OTL* (trans. 1962), 180.

[51] Schüngel-Straumann, 80.

[52] E. Gerstenberger, *Wesen und Herkunft des "apodiktischen Rechts." WMANT*, 20 (1965), 84; cf. also E. Auerbach, "Das Zehngebot," *VT*, 16 (1966), 263; J. W. McKay, "Exodus 23:1-3, 6-8," *VT*, 21 (1971), 311-325.

[53] Cf. K. Elliger, *HAT*, 4 (1966), 267; R. Kilian, *Literarkritische und formgeschichtliche Untersuchung des Heiligkeitsgesetzes. BBB*, 19 (1963), 73; Schüngel-Straumann, 86f.

[54] Cf. W. Gross, *Bileam. StANT*, 38 (1974).

countered in many forms in the early narrative traditions. [55] It leaves its deposit in the oracles against the nations, especially those of Amos and Isaiah. In Isaiah's oracle against the Philistines (Isa. 14:28-32), Yahweh announces: "I will kill (*mûth* hiphil) your root with famine, and your remnant I will slay (*hrg*)" (v. 30). In Isa. 14:4-21 we have a taunt song which the verses constituting the framework apply to the king of Babylon; it threatens him with destruction on account of an outrage: "because you have slain your people" (v. 20). Whether in its present form it derives from Isaiah is uncertain. [56] In Amos' oracle against Moab (Am. 2:1-3), Yahweh threatens the king of Edom on account of an outrage: "I will cut off (*krt* hiphil) the ruler from its midst, and will slay (*hrg*) all its princes with him" (v. 3). "Once again the threat envisions Yahweh's war of annihilation." [57] In Ezekiel's oracles against Tyre it is not Yahweh's direct intervention that produces destruction; he makes use instead of the Assyrians (Ezk. 26:8,11) or "the most terrible of the nations" (28:7ff.), who will slay with the sword (*hrg bhrb*, 26:8, 11) and wound (*hll*, 28:9). In a late passage from the Apocalypse of Isaiah (Isa. 27:1), this notion is combined with mythological motifs from the battle with chaos: with the sword Yahweh will punish (*pqd bhrb*) Leviathan and slay (*hrg*) the dragon that is in the sea. Finally, the Psalms hymn Yahweh's glorious deeds in battle, and give thanks that he "smote (*nkh*) many nations and slew (*hrg*) mighty kings" (Ps. 135:10; 136:17f.).

Not only does Yahweh take the field in battle against hostile nations; he also addresses himself to domestic enemies and brings war upon his own people, whose constant disobedience and apostasy make them Yahweh's enemies. The series of oracles against the nations in Amos culminates characteristically in an oracle against Israel. The account of Amos' vision in Amos 9:1-4 [58] announces the final destruction of Israel. With earthquake and sword Yahweh will slay them all. Even in captivity his sword will find them and kill them. "His eye, which once caused fatal confusion among the Egyptians (Ex. 14:24), now turns its devastating gaze upon his own people. Yahweh the warrior has performed a *volte-face*." [59] "There can be no thought of any remnant." [60] In Hosea the prophets are the special "units" of Yahweh in his battle with his people; they proclaim his words, and these words are deadly weapons (Hos. 6:5; cf. Am. 7:10; Jer. 5:14; 23:29). In contrast to Amos, however, for Hosea Yahweh's killing does not spell the end for Israel; Yahweh's purpose is rather to clear the way for the way of life he establishes (*mishpāt*) (Hos. 6:5). From v. 4 and the precept in v. 6

---

[55] Cf. H. Fredriksson, *Jahwe als Krieger* (1945).

[56] Botterweck.

[57] H. W. Wolff, *BK*, XIV/2 (1969), *in loc.;* cf. Fredriksson, 93f.

[58] Wolff, *BK*, XIV/2, 387; for the contrary view, see H. Graf Reventlow, *Das Amt des Propheten bei Amos. FRLANT*, 80 (1962), 49; G. Fohrer, "Die Gattung der Berichte über symbolische Handlungen der Propheten," *ZAW*, 64 (1952), 115 = *Studien zur alttestamentlichen Prophetie. BZAW*, 99 (1967), 107.

[59] Wolff, *ibid.*, 392; cf. J. A. Soggin, "Der prophetische Gedanke über den heiligen Krieg, als Gericht gegen Israel," *VT*, 10 (1960), 79-83; H.-M. Lutz, *Jahwe, Jerusalem und die Völker. WMANT*, 27 (1968), 190-200.

[60] Wolff, *ibid.*, 391.

we can see clearly that "the intention of the prophet's sermon of judgment, in accordance with Yahweh's present struggle with Israel, is to save Israel by a revitalization of Yahweh's מִשְׁפָּט." [61] But in Jeremiah's lament for Israel (Jer. 14:17–15:4) there is no longer any trace of this positive turn in favor of the people; this text should probably be assigned to the period of the military disaster in 598/97, just before the first deportation. The prophet's lament over the destruction of his people, presented in the style of a dirge (vv. 17f.), is followed by the people's renewed plea for relief from their plight, couched in the style of a lament (vv. 19-22); God's response, however, is a blunt rejection of their plea (15:1-4), as Yahweh tells Jeremiah that all intercession is fruitless. The notion of Yahweh's war against his people is taken up by Ezekiel and combined with other motifs. In his great ecstatic vision (Ezk. 8–11), [62] six or seven destroyers go about through the city with their weapons of destruction, killing and destroying without pity "old men and young men, maidens, little children, and women" (9:6), except for those with a mark upon their foreheads (9:4,6); here—as frequently in Ezekiel—the motif of the remnant appears. In the allegorical discourse concerning the two sisters (23:1-49), Israel's transgressions are subsumed under the image of "harlotry" (zānāh) and "doting" ('āghabh): Israel is handed over to her Assyrian lovers, who slay her sons and daughters and Israel herself with the sword (23:10; cf. also 23:47, a late addition). [63] Finally, the theme of "Yahweh's war against his people" finds a place in the Psalms; it is developed at length in Ps. 78, a late historical psalm influenced by Wisdom Literature [64] (vv. 31,34,37). It likewise has a secure place in Lamentations, which, after the catastrophe, became part of the regular penitential liturgies of the exilic and post-exilic community (Lam. 2:4,21; 3:43).

Fuhs

---

[61] Wolff, *Hosea* (trans. 1974), 120.
[62] Cf. W. Zimmerli, *BK*, XIII/1 (1969), 187-253.
[63] *Ibid.*, 528-555.
[64] Kraus calls it "didactic history" (H.-J. Kraus, *BK*, XV/2 [⁴1972], 539).

הָרָה hārāh; הָרֶה hāreh; הֵרָיוֹן hērāyôn; הֵרוֹן hērōn

I. Etymology; Ugaritic. II. OT Occurrences. III. Valuation of Pregnancy. IV. Announcement of Pregnancy.

I. Etymology; Ugaritic.

The root *hry*, "be pregnant, conceive," is attested in Hebrew (including Qumran and Middle Hebrew), Ugaritic,[1] Aramaic,[2] and Akkadian.[3] The Akkadian word *erû* is sometimes intransitive, "be pregnant" (used of humans and animals), sometimes transitive, "conceive." The Š-stem *šurû* means "impregnate" (used with humans and animals as object). Most of the Ugaritic passages combine the verb *hry* with *yld*, "bear";[4] we also find the word *hr*, "conception":[5] *bm nšq whr bhbq whmhmtm tqtnṣn wtldn*, "Through kissing and conception, through embracing and desiring, they are afflicted with pain and give birth" (on *hmhmt*, cf. *yhm* in Gen. 30:38f.,41).

II. OT Occurrences.

The technical terms for begetting, pregnancy, and birth are → בּוֹא *bô'*, *hārāh*, and → ילד *yāladh* (Gen. 16:4ff.; 19:31ff.; 30:4f.,16f.; 38:2f., 18ff.; 1 Ch. 7:23; Ruth 4:13). Other words besides *bô'* can be used for intercourse: → שׁכב *shākhabh* (2 S. 11:4; 12:24), → קרב *qārabh* (Isa. 8:3), and → ידע *yādhaʿ* (Gen. 4:1,17; 1 S. 1:19). The beginning of pregnancy is always expressed by the impf. cons. *vattahar*.

The verb occurs only once with a feminine subject in the sense "conceive" (1 Ch. 4:17). The expression is most likely equivalent to "be the mother of." It is used in a metaphorical sense in the words of Moses in Nu. 11:12: "Did I conceive all this people? Did I bring them forth (*yāladh*)?" It is against his will that Moses undertakes the duties of a mother when the people complain incessantly that they do not have enough to eat and drink. In at least one instance the fem. ptcp. *hôrāh* is synonymous with "mother": "Their mother (*'ēm*) has played the harlot, their *hôrāh* has acted shamefully" (Hos. 2:7[5]). In Gen. 49:26, too, the form *hôrai* may be a participle ("progenitors"); it is usually altered to *hārê*, "mountains," following Dt. 33:16; Hab. 3:6.

The adj. **hāreh*, "pregnant," is usually intransitive in meaning and is con-

---

hārāh. E. Hammershaimb, "The Immanuel Sign," *StTh*, 3 (1949), 124-142; P. Humbert, "Der biblische Verkündigungsstil und seine vermutliche Herkunft," *AfO*, 10 (1935), 77-80; M. Rehm, *Der königliche Messias im Licht der Immanuel-Weissagungen des Buches Jesaja* (1968); G. Widengren, "Hieros gamos och underjordsvistelse," *RoB*, 7 (1948), 17-46; *idem*, "Quelques remarques sur l'émasculation rituelle chez les peuples sémitiques," *Studia Orientalia J. Pedersen* (1953), 377-384.

[1] *WUS*, No. 859.
[2] *DISO*, 69; 1QGenAp 2:1: *hry't*, "conception."
[3] *erû/arû*; *AHw*, 72, 247; *CAD*, I/2, 312-16; IV, 325f.
[4] *CTA*, 5 [I* AB], V, 22; 11 [IV AB], III, 5.
[5] *CTA*, 23 [SS II], 17, 22.

structed with *le-*: *hārāh leʾîsh*, "with child by a man" (Gen. 38:25); *liznûnîm*, "by harlotry" (Gen. 38:24). (The verb is constructed with *le-*, Gen. 38:18, or *min*, Gen. 19:36.) In the figurative sense the adjective can also have transitive meaning, e.g., in Ps. 7:15(14): "Behold, the wicked man conceives evil (*yechabbel-ʾāven*), and is pregnant with mischief (*ʿāmāl*), and brings forth (*yāladh*) lies." Similar are Isa. 26:18 ("We were with child, we writhed, we have as it were brought forth wind"); [6] 33:11 ("You conceive chaff, you bring forth stubble"); 59:4 ("They conceive mischief and bring forth iniquity"); Job 15:35 ("They conceive mischief and bring forth evil"). The pual form means "be conceived": Job 3:3, "a man-child is conceived"; Isa. 59:13 (*hōrô vehōghô*) is obscure. The noun *hērōn* occurs in Gen. 3:16, the form *hērāyôn* twice: Ruth 4:13; Hos. 9:11.

III. Valuation of Pregnancy. In the story of the Fall, pregnancy is viewed as part of the punishment inflicted on the woman: *ʿitstsebhônēkh vehērōnēkh*, probably "your painful pregnancy" (Gen. 3:16f.). [7] Elsewhere the pain of childbirth is usually referred to; it even becomes proverbial (Isa. 13:8; 21:3; Jer. 6:24; 22:23; 50:43; Ps. 48:7[6]; etc.; → צִיר *tsîr*, חִיל *chîl*). When a woman gives birth, she writhes (*chîl*), cries out in her pangs (*chabhālîm*, Isa. 26:17; → חֶבֶל *hbl*), and gives birth in pain (*beʿētsebh*, 1 Ch. 4:9).

Pregnancy always occasions an emotional response in its vicinity. A pregnant woman is envied by her companions (Gen. 30:1); a barren woman is looked on with contempt (Gen. 16:4; 1 S. 1:6f.). There is no practical advice given for pregnant women; the only exception is the admonition to Manoah's wife not to drink wine or eat any unclean thing (Jgs. 3:14), but this prohibition is connected with the special future status of the expected child. Neither is there any mention of the magical practices common among the neighboring peoples. The only exception may be Gen. 30:14ff., where the mandrakes (*dûdhāʾîm*) clearly cause pregnancy, or at least facilitate it. There are no laws protecting the pregnant woman, only regulations governing her purification (Lev. 12). Ex. 21:22 is concerned only with the fetus: if someone strikes a pregnant woman so that she miscarries, he shall be fined an amount determined by the assessment (*biphlîlîm*) of the woman's husband. [8] Clearly no distinction is made between a male and a female fetus. At the future restoration of Israel, Yahweh will take special care of the weak; these include the blind and the lame, as well as pregnant women and women in labor (Jer. 31:8).

During wartime pregnant women were in particular danger. There are several mentions of the gruesome practice of ripping open pregnant women, obviously to keep the enemy from multiplying (Am. 1:13; Hos. 14:1[13:16]; 2 K. 8:12; 15:16). Widengren [9] conjectures that the purpose was ritual emasculation of the

---

[6] Cf. CT 27, 14, 23: "She is pregnant with wind and brings forth wind."

[7] For a discussion of the passage, cf. C. Rabin, "Egyptological Miscellanea," *ScrHier*, 8 (1961), 390. Rabin prefers to understand *hērōn* as "sexual desire" or "whining."

[8] See E. A. Speiser, "The Stem 'pll' in Hebrew," *JBL*, 82 (1963), 302f., where he cites a Hittite parallel from J. Friedrich, *Die hethitischen Gesetze* (1959), 20f.

[9] "Émasculation," 342f.

male fetus, a common practice among other Semitic peoples in their treatment of the enemy dead.

In general, when a marriage is childless the woman is blamed. If her husband is old, the opposite can be suggested (2 K. 4:14). The verb *'āqar,* "be barren," occurs once with a male subject (Dt. 7:14, in a quite general context).

When Job and Jeremiah curse the day of their birth, they are expressing vexation primarily over the fertility of their mothers (Job 3:10; Jer. 20:17). Both wish they had been allowed to die in their mothers' wombs; Jeremiah adds: "and that her womb had remained forever pregnant (*hᵃrath 'ôlām*)."

Pregnancy and birth were thought of as being determined by Yahweh (Ps. 139:13; Ruth 4:13; Jer. 1:5; cf. Jer. 20:17). But he can also "withhold the fruit of the womb" (Gen. 30:2) and "close the womb" (Gen. 16:2; 20:18; 1 S. 1:5f.). A barren woman considered herself as good as dead (Gen. 30:1). But she can pray to Yahweh for children and her prayer can be answered (1 S. 1:9ff.). This can be seen also from the explanations of the names given Jacob's sons (Gen. 29:31–30:24). Isaac prayed to Yahweh on behalf of Rebecca (Gen. 25:21), as did Abraham on behalf of Abimelech and his wives (Gen. 20:17).

One prays primarily for male offspring. The birth of a boy is greeted with rejoicing (Jer. 20:15; 1 S. 4:20f.). Pregnancy and birth are rarely mentioned in connection with daughters (1 S. 2:21; Hos. 1:6). Since Yahweh is the bestower of fertility, it is felt to be natural to consider the child as his property (Ex. 34:19); this is particularly true of the first-born (Ex. 13:2, etc.; → בכור *bᵉkhôr*).

IV. Announcement of Pregnancy. The barren woman frequently appears as the favorite wife of her husband. Her barrenness is dramatized, her husband tries to comfort her, and Yahweh's intervention is described with the expressions "open the womb" (Gen. 29:31; 30:22) or "visit" (→ פקד *pāqadh,* Gen. 21:1f.; 1 S. 2:21).

In the case of Sarah, which involves extraordinary divine intervention, Widengren conjectures [10] an echo of the ancient notion that a royal child comes from a union between the god and the queen, since at least in Middle Hebrew *pāqadh* can also mean "visit" in the sense of "sleep with." It is true that there is no mention of sexual intercourse between Abraham and Sarah, but the same is true for Leah and Rachel. It is therefore more likely that here, as in 1 S. 2:21, *pāqadh* merely refers to special divine intervention (cf. *zākhar* in 1 S. 1:19). A similar situation is presupposed in the case of the Shunammite woman (2 K. 4:17).

The divine intervention is provided with a solemn setting by an announcement formula that remains almost constant:

Gen. 16:11: *hinnākh hārāh vᵉyōladht bēn vᵉqārā'th shᵉmô...*
Gen. 17:19: *'ᵃbhāl śārāh 'ishtᵉkhā yōledheth lᵉkhā bēn vᵉqārā'thā 'eth shᵉmô...*
Jgs. 13:5: *kî hinnākh hārāh vᵉyōladht bēn*
Isa. 7:14: *hinnēh hā'almāh hārāh vᵉyōledheth bēn vᵉqārā'th shᵉmô...*
A similar formula occurs in the Ugaritic Nikkal text: *hl ġlmt tld bn.* [11]

---

[10] "Hieros gamos," 32.
[11] *CTA,* 24 [NK], 7.

Whether we are dealing here with a birth oracle composed in the ancient sacral style[12] or with a form of expression drawn from everyday speech[13] may remain undecided. In all instances the announcement concerns the birth of a boy with special qualifications. The birth is announced in Gen. 16:11 and Jgs. 13:5 by the angel of Yahweh, in Isa. 7:14 by the prophet, and in Gen. 17:19 by Yahweh himself. In the last two texts the men are addressed, in the others the women. Hagar is already pregnant; in the other texts the pregnancy lies in the future (Isa. 7:14 is uncertain). The last two texts refer to events of extraordinary importance. On Gen. 17:19 depend the fulfilment of the promise and the existence of the future people of God, on Isa. 7:14 undoubtedly the continued existence of the Davidic dynasty. A dynastic crisis is involved, since Isa. 7:6 speaks of Tabeel's son as a pretender to the throne. However hā'almāh (→ עלמה 'almāh) is to be understood, it can refer to the queen, who may have been barren.[14] Seen in the light of the idea that pregnancy and birth are determined by Yahweh, there is nothing especially striking about Isa. 7:14. Isaiah and his contemporaries were well acquainted with this view. His oracle was pronounced in the old traditional style; the allusion to the Davidic dynasty lends it special weight.

Ottosson

---

[12] Humbert, Widengren.
[13] Rehm.
[14] → את 'ēth, *TDOT*, I, 461f.

הָרַס hāras; הֶרֶס heres; הֲרִיסוּת *hªrîsûth;*
הֲרִיסָה *hªrîsāh*

I. The Root: 1. Etymology; 2. Occurrences; 3. Meaning. II. Theological Use: 1. Yahweh as Destroyer; 2. The End of Israel's *Heilsgeschichte?*

I. The Root.

1. *Etymology.* The root (written *hrś*) appears in Old South Arabic in the sense "attack, tear down"[1] or "penetrate, advance."[2] Its single occurrence in Moabite refers to the "destruction" of a city.[3] Also cognate are Arab. *harasa,* "pulverize, destroy," and Tigré *harša,* "break to pieces."[4]

---

hāras. R. Bach, "Bauen und Pflanzen," *Studien zur Theologie der alttestamentlichen Überlieferungen. Festschrift G. von Rad* (1961), 7-32; J. M. Berridge, *Prophet, People, and the Word of Yahweh. Basel Studies of Theology,* 4 (1970); S. Herrmann, *Die prophetischen Heilserwartungen im AT. BWANT,* 85 (1965); W. Thiel, *Die deuteronomistische Redaktion von Jeremia 1–25. WMANT,* 41 (1973).

[1] *KBL³,* 246.
[2] W. W. Müller, "Altsüdarabische Beiträge zur hebräischen Lexikon," *ZAW,* 75 (1963), 308.
[3] *DISO,* 69; *KAI,* 181.27.
[4] *TigrWb,* 10.

2. *Occurrences.* The verb occurs 42 times in the OT: 30 times in the qal, 10 in the niphal, and 2 in the piel. Its derivatives are *heres, hªrîsûth,* "destruction," and *hªrîsāh,* "ruins."

3. *Meaning.* The verb is used for the "tearing down" or "destroying" of cities (2 S. 11:25; 2 K. 3:25; Isa. 14:17; Jer. 31:40; Ezk. 36:35; Prov. 11:11; 1 Ch. 20:1), walls (Jer. 50:15; Ezk. 13:14; 26:4,12; Prov. 24:31), strongholds (Mic. 5:10[11]; Lam. 2:2), and a house (Prov. 14:1), as well as altars and cultic sites (Jgs. 6:25; 1 K. 18:30; 19:10,14; Ezk. 16:39). God can even throw down mountains (Ezk. 38:20), and he breaks the teeth in the mouth of the wicked (Ps. 58:7[6]).

The verb can be used metaphorically for the "ruin" of a land (Prov. 29:4) or its foundations (Ezk. 30:4), or for the "destruction" of the existing order (Ps. 11:3). Finally, the verb can refer to the humiliation or destruction of human beings (Ex. 15:7; Isa. 22:19; 49:17; Ps. 28:5). It can also be used without an object. [5]

The meaning "tear down, destroy," is supported by several occurrences in which *hāras* is used as the opposite of → בנה *bānāh* (Ezk. 36:36; Mal. 1:4; Ps. 28:5; Prov. 14:1; Job 12:14). In Ex. 19:21,24, the verb is to be understood as meaning "break into a restricted area." Joel 1:17 should probably be interpreted to mean that the granaries have been "broken into"; a single crop failure is no reason for the destruction of the granaries. [6] Or this might refer to blatant evidence of a total crop failure: no one bothered to keep the granaries in repair, so they fell to ruin. [7]

II. Theological Use.

1. *Yahweh as Destroyer.* The verb *hāras* becomes a term for Yahweh's act of judgment. When Israel's foes are finally destroyed, the walls of their cities are thrown down (Jer. 50:15; cf. Ezk. 26:4,12) and their foundations torn down (Ezk. 30:4); even the natural world can be affected (38:20).

The catastrophe of the southern kingdom was also understood as the work of Yahweh: he broke down the strongholds of Judah (Lam. 2:2), destroying the land and the people without pity (2:17). But while God's judgment upon the nations is final, the OT looks forward to a reconstruction of Jerusalem, which will never again be overthrown (Jer. 31:40). It is actually characteristic of Yahweh to rebuild what has been destroyed (Ezk. 36:35f.). The enemies who have destroyed Israel will take to their heels (Isa. 49:17).

Songs of lamentation and thanksgiving speak of Yahweh as overthrowing his enemies (Ex.15:7), or, more generally, the wicked (Ps. 28:5). Wisdom summarizes its experience of God's action in an aphorism: if he tears down, none can rebuild (Job 12:14; cf. Mal. 1:4).

---

[5] Cf. II.2.

[6] W. Rudolph, *KAT,* XIII/2 (1971), 40; *idem,* "Ein Beitrag zum hebr. Lexicon aus dem Joelbuch," *Hebräische Wortforschung. Festschrift W. Baumgartner. SVT,* 16 (1967), 247.

[7] H. W. Wolff, *BK,* XIV/2 (1969), 40.

2. *The End of Israel's Heilsgeschichte?* In the book of Jeremiah, *hāras* appears as part of a series of verbs that speak of Yahweh's building and planting, his tearing down and plucking up. The terms "building" and "planting" remain constant, while the others change. In the first instance, the series signals the end of *Heilsgeschichte,* God's historical involvement with his people: "What I have built I am breaking down, and what I have planted I am plucking up" (45:4). It can also mark a new beginning after judgment: I will build you up and not pull you down (42:10; 24:6; 31:28; cf. 31:40). In the narrative of Jeremiah's call, the individual elements stand side by side on the same footing: Jeremiah is charged "to pluck up and to break down, to destroy and to overthrow, to build and to plant" (1:10; in 18:7,9 *hāras* does not appear). In this context the individual terms have lost their original concrete meaning. *hāras* no longer refers to destruction of cities and countryside, but to "annihilation" pure and simple, the end of *Heilsgeschichte.* [8] The series reflects on the connection between the salvation and the disaster that proceed from God. If the constant elements of "building" and "planting" were part of the original terminology of *Heilsgeschichte,* it would mean that Jeremiah had added the terms referring to destruction within the framework of his message of disaster, thus announcing the end of *Heilsgeschichte.* [9] But it is only within the framework of this series that "building" and "planting" were joined together as a pair of terms with particular reference to *Heilsgeschichte,* [10] while the catastrophe of the southern kingdom was understood very early as the result of Yahweh's destruction (Lam. 2:2,17). In other words, *hāras* is used to designate Yahweh's act of judgment independently of its association with the verbs "build" and "plant." Israel's theological reflections on history therefore probably took contemporary destructions as their point of departure, and set them in contrast to the hope for Yahweh's future "building" and "planting," and thus the continuance of *Heilsgeschichte.* The series is therefore the product of exilic reflection on the history of Israel. [11] Exilic origin in Deuteronomistic circles is also suggested by linguistic observations: [12] (1) The series occurs only in prose passages, which (2) exhibit the characteristics of Deuteronomistic language. Finally, the expression (3) speaks in general and programmatic terms.

Otherwise, only relatively late texts speak abstractly of "building" and "tearing down" on the part of Yahweh (Ezk. 36:36; Mal. 1:4; Ps. 28:5; Job 12:14). All of them are probably dependent on the reflections of the book of Jeremiah.

Münderlein

---

[8] Bach, 28f.; U. Mauser, *Gottesbild und Menschwerdung. BHTh,* 43 (1971), 87.

[9] Bach, 29.

[10] Bach, 15.

[11] For a different view, see W. L. Holladay, "Prototype and Copies," *JBL,* 79 (1960), 363f.

[12] Herrmann, 165; Thiel, 51f.; cf. G. Wanke, *Untersuchungen zur sog. Baruchschrift. BZAW,* 122 (1971), 133ff.